BET WITH THE
BEST
2
LONGSHOTS

Beyer	Litfin
Brohamer	Quinn
Crist	Shuback
Davidowitz	Stich
Free	Watchmaker

Racing Daily Form

Published by
Daily Racing Form Press
100 Broadway, 7th Floor
New York, NY 10005

ISBN: 978–1-932910–81–0

Library of Congress Control Number: 2007943388

Cover and jacket designed by Chris Donofry
Text design by Neuwirth and Associates
Printed in the United States of America

TABLE of CONTENTS

BEYER
ON NEW HANDICAPPING TOOLS
By Andrew Beyer

1

EVERY HORSEPLAYER SAVORS the experience and relishes the memory of cashing a bet on a longshot. I remember the details of a $2 wager on a horse named M. J.'s Boy, who paid $298.50 to win four decades ago, more vividly than big bets I won or lost last week.

While longshots have always offered gratification, finding them has become especially important in some aspects of the modern game.

In the pick six and the pick four, bettors will usually identify a race or two as a "spread race"—meaning that the object is to use several contenders in the hope that one of them will pay a big price. Picking the right live longshot in such a situation can produce a score that makes a horseplayer's entire year a success—or even alters his life. Longshots, too, are the key to playing handicapping contests. The people who take home big checks from these events are usually the ones who have found an angle to support picking a long-priced winner.

Although I recognize the importance of ferreting out horses at big prices, and I will read with keen interest the advice of my fellow contributors to this volume, I do not think of myself as a "longshot player." Perhaps I am too much of a traditionalist, since my approach to the game was forged in the era before pick sixes and handicapping contests. In everyday gambling, I believe that exactas and trifectas yield more realistic opportunities of making a big score than longshot winners do. It is unremarkable to handicap a race and conclude, with some confidence, that the most likely outcome is an exacta returning $20 or $30. In fact, those payoffs seem so mundane that your fellow horseplayers will barely congratulate you for doping out such an obvious result. But how often will a handicapper find a horse he thinks is a genuine standout and collect a $20 or $30 win price? A few times a year, if he's very lucky.

Analyzing a race with the mindset "I'm going to find a longshot" turns the handicapping process upside down. I approach every race by studying what I consider to be the fundamentals—speed figures, trips, trainers, and track biases—and come to my conclusions. Sometimes I will then look at the tote board and see that a logical horse, with merits grounded in these fundamentals, is 10–1 or 20–1. I don't want to search for longshots by forcing the issue; I want opportunities to present themselves to me.

Finding horses with solid merits and high odds has never been more difficult, because the American betting public has never been more sophisticated. So how does a horseplayer find an edge in the contemporary game? That question has preoccupied me in recent years, forcing me to reexamine and alter my approach to handicapping.

I undertook this reevaluation after enduring an unproductive two years during which I felt I had lost my edge as a horseplayer. At first I couldn't understand why. I was well aware that I was not going to obtain an edge, or collect big prices, on horses with outstanding Beyer Speed Figures. Since their inclusion in the past performances, first in *The Racing Times* in 1991 and then in *Daily Racing Form* beginning in 1992, the betting public has embraced them and wagered on horses with standout figures to the extent that they rarely offer value. Figures are still the starting point for my analysis of any race, but I have long known that I must find other ways of picking horses that the public overlooks.

I have done this by watching races carefully and observing the nuances of horses' trips. No component of a horse's trip is more important than the effect of a track bias on his performance. If a racing surface has a strong bias, it can yield a multitude of betting opportunities. When front-runners on the rail are dominating at a track, a handicapper can pick winners simply by identifying the horse who will get to the rail; he can find future bets by noting horses who raced against the bias, trying to rally on the outside. For decades I was able to make a profit from this factor alone, because there were so many opportunities to be found—the legendary rail bias at Pimlico, the dead rail at Belmont, the insuperable speed-on-the-rail bias at Keeneland. My chapter in the original *Bet with the Best* outlined an approach based almost solely on spotting horses who had been hindered by a track bias. And then, slowly, nearly imperceptibly, strong biases became scarcer and scarcer in U.S. racing. Track superintendents, who were once oblivious to biases, learned to identify them and correct them. If a bias existed for a day or two, it would suddenly disappear. The introduction of synthetic racing surfaces has eliminated biases at many tracks (although Polytrack did create a strong closers' bias when it was installed at Keeneland in 2006). Biases ceased to be a regular source of longshot winners.

With this key part of my handicapping arsenal less effective, and my performance at the racetrack suffering, I knew I had to revamp my approach to the game. As I contemplated the possibilities, I had a revelation.

Like most horseplayers, I regularly fret about the negative aspects of modern racing—the tough parimutuel competition, the high takeout, the prevalence of drugs that distort horses' form, etc. But in recent years horseplayers have been blessed by an extremely important, positive development. Advances in computer technology have given us access to information that was once unimaginable. For much of my life as a horseplayer, the toughest part of the handicapping process was obtaining the information necessary to make informed judgments. I kept thousands of back issues of the *Daily Racing Form* stacked in my house because, in the precomputer era, leafing through those yellowed newspapers was often the only way to find certain data. Trip handicapping was hard because video replays of races were often difficult or impossible to see.

Yet now a horseplayer has almost every important type of information within easy reach. He can obtain an overwhelming amount of data about horses, trainers, jockeys, and bloodlines. (Even foreign horses are no longer a source of mystery; it is easy to find data—and, in some cases, race replays—for invaders from other continents.)

Of all the many technological developments relating to the sport, two have been so profound that they have revolutionized the handicapping process. One is the availability, from a variety of sources, of on-line video replays of past races. The other is the development of *Daily Racing Form*'s software known as Formulator. These tools now form the basis of my day-to-day approach to the game.

FORMULATOR

In the early 1990s, I received a phone call from a racing fan/computer programmer named David Ward, who told me about some of his ideas for using computers to marshal horse-racing data. One day, with a notebook computer under his arm, he showed up on the doorstep of my house in Washington and announced, "This is the *Racing Form* of the twenty-first century." Not only did the past performances appear on the computer screen—something I had never seen before—but the user could also click on parts of the data—the trainer's name, for example—and open a detailed statistical report. Ward's creation seemed fantastic back then, but by the time it became Formulator 4.1 it was a treasure trove of information. When I spoke about Formulator at the *Daily Racing Form*'s Handicapping Expo 2007, I apologized if I sounded like a shill for the company that sponsored the event and also publishes the Beyer Speed Figures. I must now add that I hesitate to sound as if I am shilling for the publisher of *Bet with the Best*. But I consider Formulator an absolutely indispensable tool. Horseplayers who aren't using it aren't really serious about the game.

Formulator has several distinct functions. It contains the equivalent of stacks of thousands of *Racing Forms*, enabling the user to summon charts of past races and past performances of individual horses. It lets a horseplayer enter his own notes about races or specific horses, saving those comments and embedding them in the past performances when the horses run again. It enables users to analyze five years of data to uncover the strengths and weaknesses of any trainer.

Evaluating Trainers

The identity and skill of the trainer has always been part of the handicapping equation, but this factor has never been so important as it is in contemporary American racing. In many situations, the trainer is as important as the ability of his horse. At racetracks from coast to coast, so-called supertrainers dominate the game; they operate large stables and possess the ability to get horses to deliver performances that sometimes defy conventional handicapping logic. Horses trained by men such as Todd Pletcher, Bobby Frankel, Steve Asmussen, Rick Dutrow, Scott Lake, Jeff Mullins, and Doug O'Neill almost always attract plenty of wagering support. Practically all horseplayers know who the best trainers are, and most handicappers know the ones who possess special skills. In the past, the name of a trainer who excelled with first-time starters, with recent claims, or with first-time turf runners constituted a precious nugget of information. But since the *Daily Racing Form* put a line of trainer statistics at the bottom of each horse's past performances, any reader can see at a glance that California's Art Sherman wins 31 percent of the time off the claim or that Christophe Clement wins with 22 percent of his turf starters. Most of these horses are bet accordingly, too. If a horseplayer hopes to have an edge in dealing with the trainer factor, he needs to spot situations that are less obvious, involving trainers who are not quite so well known. Because the trainer factor is so important, horseplayers should be willing to dig a little in order to unearth such nuggets.

Formulator allows users to specify numerous criteria by which they can assess a trainer's performance—the class of the race, turf or dirt, days since the last race, first race after a claim, blinkers on, first-time Lasix, etc. If you want to know how trainer Wesley Ward has performed over the last five years with 2-year-old first-time starters who go off as the favorite, it takes only a few seconds to set the criteria and for Formulator to display the results:

HORSES	WINS	WIN%	$2 ROI
27	14	52%	$2.64

More than half of the horses in the sample won, and betting them all would have produced an average return of $2.64 for each $2 bet—a 32 percent profit. In short, when the money shows for a Ward firster, watch out!

Such trainer statistics are a fertile source of longshot plays, and bettors can find an abundance of them in Dean Keppler's *Trainer Angles,* which explains the use of Formulator in depth. Here are a few that he cites:

- Jimmy Jerkens wins 32 percent of the time moving horses from dirt to turf, with a $2 ROI of $3.16.
- Rick Violette wins 21 percent of the time, with an ROI of $2.30, when dropping horses from maiden special weight to maiden-claiming company in their second career start.
- When John Alecci runs a horse for the second time after a claim, in a dirt sprint, he wins at a 35 percent rate with a $5.04 ROI.

The possibilities are endless, and longshot players—particularly contest players—may want to maintain a catalog of productive and hidden trainer angles.

When I handicap a race, I want to know if any trainer in the field has a particular strength or weakness that may be especially relevant to the outcome. Sometimes this information will be apparent from the data at the bottom line of the *Daily Racing Form* past performances, but sometimes it won't. Often a handicapper must dig into Formulator to get an accurate reading of a trainer's record under conditions similar to today's race. Keppler cites the case of trainer Ben Perkins Jr., who is well known for his skill with young horses. At Monmouth Park and other tracks in the Mid-Atlantic region, the Perkins name guarantees that a first-time starter will get betting support. His statistics show a solid win percentage. But over a five-year period, Perkins's record with 3-year-old first-time starters was a mediocre 3 for 35. Perkins was 0 for 14 with first-time starters in maiden-claiming races. His strength is strictly with 2-year-old firsters in maiden-special-weight company—a category in which he wins at a 24 percent clip. Making such distinctions is important in any situation where a trainer's skill is potentially an important factor.

If a horse has good recent form and has been running in races under conditions similar to today's, I don't pay much attention to the trainer's record. If I like a horse sufficiently, and the trainer is 0 for 100, I'll take a deep gulp and bet anyway. The trainer becomes relevant, and often becomes a central factor, when a horse is trying to do something he has never done before (e.g., running an unfamiliar distance or making his debut on turf) or is doing something that requires special skill on the trainer's part (e.g., making his career debut or coming back after a significant layoff). And, of course, the trainer is critical factor when a horse changes hands as a result of a claim or a private purchase.

One of the great virtues of Formulator is that it allows a handicapper to look at the past performances of all the horses a trainer has started in the previous five years. Looking at the PPs of horses who fit certain criteria will usually demonstrate a trainer's strengths or weaknesses much more clearly than his statistics alone. A trainer may have a good winning percentage with horses he has just claimed, but if most of those horses are coming off excellent races, the statistic may not be particularly meaningful. But if horses seem transformed after being claimed—if they improve their Beyer Speed Figures sharply—the trainer is probably a wise guy who needs to be watched closely.

In 2006 I planned to spend three weeks enjoying the turf and surf at Del Mar, and so I decided to focus on California all summer, beginning at Hollywood Park. I had not played the races in the West recently, and so I wasn't closely attuned to the methods of the trainers there. Formulator helped me immeasurably.

On June 21 I saw an interesting possibility in a maiden-claiming race at Hollywood. It was a very ordinary field; the four horses with the best recent form had last-race

Beyer Speed Figures of 54, 54, 53, and 52. Nobody in the lineup had run better than a 54 in 2006. I was intrigued by an animal named Mayor of Del Mar.

4 Mayor of Del Mar
Own: Harris Farms, Inc., Michael P. Orlando F — $25,000
Green and white diamonds, green
Bisono A (00 0 1 1 .00) 2006:(100 16 .00)
Gr/ro g. 4 (Apr)
Sire: Cee's Tizzy (Relaunch) $7,500
Dam: Jumberca (Carson City)
Br: Harris Farms Inc.(Cal)
Tr: Gaines Carla (34 7 4 4 .29) 2006:(75 21 .28)
L 124
Life 2 M 0 0 $800 49 | D.Fst 2 0 0 0 $800 49
2005 2 M 0 0 $800 49 | Wet (446) 0 0 0 0 $0 -
2004 0 M 0 0 $0 - | Turf (218) 0 0 0 0 $0 -
Hol 0 0 0 0 $0 | Dirt (287) 1 0 0 0 $400 47

7Aug05-1Dmr fst 6½f :214 :4511:11 1:172 3+ Md 25000(25-22.5) **49** 8 4 63¾ 52¼ 43 7 10¼ Enriquez I D LB120 14.60 77-10 *SccssflSkng* 1204¼ *JkthChf* 1202 PrdLT115no 4wd turn,weakened 12
25Jly05-8Dmr fst 5½f :213 :442 :5711:034 3+ [S]Md 40000(40-35) **47** 9 9 74¾ 76½ 99¼ 11 11½ Enriquez I D LB120b 30.70 86-09 Clmbn124½ *BlndHrr* 120½ AnnsIrshKng1223 Off rail,no response 12
WORKS: Jun14 SA 6f fst 1:151 H *9/13* Jun7 SA 6f fst 1:142 H *5/14* May31 SA 5f fst 1:013 H *15/35* May24 SA 5f fst 1:01 H *24/54* May17 SA 4f fst :491 H *21/32* May11 SA 4f fst :483 H *7/16*
TRAINER: +180Days (14 .14 $2.07) Dirt (122 .20 $1.90) Sprint (109 .14 $1.05) MdnClm (52 .21 $2.23) J/T 2005-06 HOL (4 .50 $3.45) J/T 2005-06 (14 .50 $7.10)

Mayor of Del Mar had shown nothing in his two previous starts, and hadn't raced since August 2005. Yet his speed figures of 49 and 47 weren't far behind his competition. I estimate that horses' figures improve about a point a month as they mature, until they reach the age of 4, and adding a few points to the gelding's numbers would give him a narrow edge. But in such a situation the trainer is the key factor: Would Carla Gaines have Mayor of Del Mar ready after a layoff of nearly ten months? I didn't know much about Gaines, though her statistics looked solid—she was 7 for 24 at the Hollywood meet. And she had won with horses off layoffs of more than 180 days. When I asked Formulator for the PPs of individual horses she trained, I was even more confident.

My Moonbeam
Own: B. Wayne Hughes
Orange and purple quarters, orange
Ch. f. 4 (Mar) OBSMAR05 $80,000
Sire: Malibu Moon (A.P. Indy) $30,000
Dam: Bickerstaff (Five Star Flight)
Br: Cathy T. Denelsbeck(NJ)
Tr: Gaines Carla
Life 3 2 0 0 $31,600 50 | D.Fst 3 2 0 0 $31,600 50
2006 3 2 0 0 $31,600 50 | Wet (340) 0 0 0 0 $0 -
2005 0 M 0 0 $0 - | Turf (205) 0 0 0 0 $0 -

6Apr06-2SA fst 1 :223 :4621:1141:394 ⒻClm 25000(25-22.5) **57** 1 1hd 1½ 1hd 2hd 1½ Gomez G K LB119fb 2.10 69-24 MMnbm119½ Srh'sHrt1123 PrvtHll1192¼ Fought back,gamely 5
16Mar06-8SA fst 1 :223 :4711:1311:411 ⒻMd 32000(32-28) **50** 3 31½ 3½ 1hd 13 2hd Gomez G K LB121fb 5.70 62-30 [D]*BlntPrft* 121hd *MMnb* 1215½ IdSlppr121¼ 4wd, bid, clear,caught 10
Placed first through disqualification.
13Jan06-4SA fst 6f :213 :453 :5831:12 ⒻMd 100000(100-85) **38** 1 7 42 73¾ 88¼ 9 11¼ Valdivia J Jr LB121b 43.30 68-16 RnyCn121no Ntrlt1211¾ *LtsLmns* 1211 Saved ground, weakened 11
WORKS: Mar30 SA 4f fst :513 H *41/43* Mar5 SA 6f fst 1:16 H *38/40* Feb23 SA 5f fst 1:002 H *6/56* Feb17 SA 4f fst :493 H *20/38* Feb4 SA 7f fst 1:291 H *3/3* Jan29 SA 4f fst :512 H *42/44*

My Moonbeam showed little in her first start, was laid off for two months, ran a much-improved race, and won on a disqualification. After her maiden loss at 43–1 odds, she went off at 5–1; this was a well-meant horse.

Make Mine Vodka
Own: Jacobson Richard
B. g. 5 (May)
Sire: Polish Numbers (Danzig) $20,000
Dam: Royal Reserves (Forty Niner)
Br: J.M.J. Stables Corporation (Ky)
Tr: West Ted H(13 7 1 0 .54) 2006:(142 35 .25)
Life 6 2 0 0 $22,380 86 | D.Fst 3 2 0 0 $21,180 86
2006 4 2 0 0 $21,580 86 | Wet(394) 1 0 0 0 $400 -
| Synth 0 0 0 0 $0 -
2005 2 M 0 0 $800 70 | Turf(314) 2 0 0 0 $800 70
Hol 1 0 0 0 $1,980 86 | Dst(340) 2 1 0 0 $11,580 86

3Jun06-9Hol fst 1 1/16 :232 :464 1:11 1:432 4+ Clm 32000(32-28) **86** 8 2½ 2hd 3nk 42¾ 43½ Bisono A LB119 14.00 80-14 RunsintheFmily121nk GoodGold1192¾ Cronnbold119½ 3wd,btwn,weakened 9
15Apr06-1SA wf 1⅛ ⊗ :4631:111 1:3741:512 4+ Alw 25000s **-** 5 - - - - - Bisono A LB118 6.10 - 19 DerAli113¾ RoyalClassic118hd FreedomsKey11815¼ Stumbld strt,lost jock 6
18Mar06-7SA fst 1 1/16 :23 :462 1:11 1:442 4+ Clm c-10000 **82** 8 4¾ 2½ 2hd 14 15½ Bisono A LB120 *2.00 78-19 MkMnVodk1205½ NtrlPhnmnn1201¾ WWIIPrvl1201½ 4wd, cleared, ridn out 11
Claimed from Williamson Warren B. for $10,000, Gaines Carla Trainer 2005: (139 16 27 13 0.12)
8Feb06-1SA fst 7f :223 :453 1:1041:24 4+ Md 25000(25-22.5) **83** 2 6 1hd 11 12½ 15½ Emigh C A LB122 *1.30 80-17 *MakeMineVodka* 1225½ *HesaTriehr* 1227¼ SwissStar1221¾ Inside,clear,driving 9
15May05-4Hol fm 1 1/16 Ⓣ :231 :463 1:1011:412 3+ Md Sp Wt 50k **70** 4 33½ 44½ 67½ 78 611 Martinez F F LB124 17.50 74-19 *MnstrBlr* 1245 JohnnyRdKrr124no HndsmMchlK112no Angled in,weakened 12
8Apr05-4SA fm *6½f Ⓣ :221 :442 1:07 1:131 4+ Md Sp Wt 46k **68** 10 2 85¾ 87¼ 912 98½ Espinoza V LB123 10.80 80-11 Remo1232½ *Minister Blair* 123nk Yankelevitz1231 4 wide, no rally 10

After two poor races, Make Mine Vodka was laid off for nearly nine months, dropped in class, and bet down to 6–5. He won by more than five lengths, demonstrating that Gaines can get them ready after a long layoff.

The record of other Gaines horses I saw on Formulator indicated that she is a sharp trainer. When Mayor of Del Mar received solid betting action despite his nondescript record, I felt even more confident.

EIGHTH RACE
Hollywood
JUNE 21, 2006

5½ FURLONGS. MAIDEN CLAIMING . Purse $15,000 (plus $2,900 Other Sources) FOR MAIDENS, THREE YEAR OLDS AND UPWARD. Three Year Olds, 117 lbs.; Older, 124 lbs. Claiming Price $25,000, if for $22,500, allowed 2 lbs.

Value of Race: $17,900 Winner $9,000; second $3,000; third $1,800; fourth $900; fifth $400; sixth $400; seventh $400; eighth $400; ninth $400; tenth $400; eleventh $400; twelfth $400. Mutuel Pool $216,229.00 Exacta Pool $170,579.00 Quinella Pool $10,560.00 Trifecta Pool $168,248.00 Superfecta Pool $135,723.00

Last Raced	Horse	M/Eqt. A. Wt	PP	St	¼	⅜	Str	Fin	Jockey	Cl'g Pr	Odds $1
27Aug05 1Dmr7	Mayor of Del Mar	LB 4 124	4	6	5$1\frac{1}{2}$	3$1\frac{1}{2}$	3$1\frac{1}{2}$	12$\frac{1}{4}$	Bisono A	25000	7.90
2Jun06 2Hol4	Engineer	LB b 3 117	3	5	1hd	11$\frac{1}{2}$	12$\frac{1}{2}$	2$\frac{3}{4}$	Valdivia J Jr	25000	3.20
21May06 7TuP7	Anozira	LB b 3 117	12	1	22	24	21$\frac{1}{2}$	3$\frac{3}{4}$	Baze T C	25000	14.20
2Jun06 8Hol4	Too Much George	LB b 3 116	7	7	6hd	6$\frac{1}{2}$	51$\frac{1}{2}$	4$\frac{1}{2}$	Potts C L	22500	7.30
2Jun06 2Hol3	Swift Winds	LB 3 112	1	11	4hd	51	4$\frac{1}{2}$	53$\frac{1}{2}$	Arias S5	25000	5.60
2Jun06 8Hol3	Olympian Medal	LB b 4 122	11	2	8$\frac{1}{2}$	71$\frac{1}{2}$	72	61	Cedeno O A	22500	9.40
12Aug05 1Dmr6	Dreamwood	LB 3 119	9	9	102	82$\frac{1}{2}$	6$\frac{1}{2}$	7$\frac{1}{2}$	Valenzuela P A	25000	4.90
	Styledtocarryon	B f 3 117	2	10	91$\frac{1}{2}$	93	8$\frac{1}{2}$	84$\frac{1}{2}$	Torres R V	25000	34.30
2Jun06 8Hol11	Sharp Witted	LB b 3 117	6	4	31	4hd	93	92$\frac{1}{2}$	Figueroa O	25000	55.70
24May06 2Hol5	De Straight Man	LB b 3 112	5	8	1110	118	105	1010	Garcia M5	25000	11.60
	J J Noble	B 3 117	8	12	12	12	12	11$\frac{3}{4}$	Baze M C	25000	32.30
8Oct05 2OSA7	Touch the Wood	LB b 3 117	10	3	7hd	101$\frac{1}{2}$	111	12	Enriquez I D	25000	11.80

OFF AT 4:54 Start Good. Won driving. Track fast.

TIME :22, :44⁴, :57⁴, 1:04³ (:22.07, :44.90, :57.94, 1:04.66)

$2 Mutuel Prices:

4 – MAYOR OF DEL MAR	17.80	9.20	6.20
3 – ENGINEER		5.40	4.00
12 – ANOZIRA			11.00

$1 EXACTA 4–3 PAID $42.70 $2 QUINELLA 3–4 PAID $41.80
$1 TRIFECTA 4–3–12 PAID $785.00 $1 SUPERFECTA 4–3–12–7 PAID $6,564.30

Gr/ro. g, (Apr), by Cee's Tizzy – Jumberca , by Carson City . Trainer Gaines Carla. Bred by Harris Farms Inc (Cal).

MAYOR OF DEL MAR chased outside a rival then off the rail on the turn, came out in the stretch and rallied under some left handed urging to gain the lead in deep stretch and won clear. ENGINEER had good early speed and dueled inside, kicked clear on the turn, came a bit off the rail into the stretch and held second. ANOZIRA angled in and dueled outside the runner-up, stalked off the rail on the turn, angled out some in the stretch and was coming back at the runner-up late. TOO MUCH GEORGE stalked between foes then outside, went three deep on the turn and outside a rival into the stretch, came out and put in a late bid at a minor award. SWIFT WINDS saved ground stalking the pace, remained inside throughout and lacked the needed rally. OLYMPIAN MEDAL wide between horses early, chased outside then five wide on the backstretch and four wide on the turn and was not a threat. DREAMWOOD between horses early, chased outside, split horses on the turn and did not rally. STYLEDTOCARRYON between foes early, saved ground off the pace and failed to menace. SHARP WITTED close up stalking the pace off the rail, came three deep into the stretch and weakened. DE STRAIGHT MAN allowed to settle off the rail, angled in on the turn and was not a factor. J J NOBLE broke inward, dropped back off the rail when a bit green, angled to the inside in the stretch and was outrun. TOUCH THE WOOD chased outside, dropped back on the turn, continued wide into the stretch and gave way.

Owners– 1, Harris Farms Inc Michael P Orlando Family Trust Parker Gary et al; 2, Triple AAA Ranch; 3, Bennett Don S and Vennett; 4, Huston Racing Stable Schwary George and Young Matt; 5, Burk Jack D; 6, Rancho Nueva Vida Inc; 7, Arbitrage Stables Hale Richard Roncelli Family Trust et al; 8, Cruz Sylvia and Ferrer Marie C; 9, Huey Gilbert; 10, Southern Comfort Stable and BG Stable; 11, Nutter Arnold G; 12, Costello John London Richard Raffel Stanley et al

Trainers– 1, Gaines Carla; 2, Owens R Kory; 3, McFarlane Dan L; 4, Abrams Barry; 5, Garcia Juan; 6, Alcala Jorge L; 7, Hess R B Jr; 8, Hunter Thomas W; 9, Dunham Daniel; 10, Palma Hector O; 11, Gonzalez Felix L; 12, Nunez Jesus

Mayor of Del Mar won, paying $17.80, and I launched a profitable season in California—an experience that was almost without precedent for me. The key to it was the access to information that Formulator gave me. I might have made a good guess about Mayor of Del Mar based on his figures and Gaines's statistics, but when I saw the PPs of her other starters, I knew I had a live horse with a live trainer.

Judging Class in Turf Races

Of all the ways in which Formulator has changed and helped my handicapping, none has been so important as its usefulness in analyzing turf races. For most of my gambling life, grass has been my Achilles' heel. I never handicapped turf races well; I didn't understand them; I tried to ignore them and concentrate on dirt. This became increasingly difficult as turf races proliferated and intruded on pick fours and pick sixes that I wanted to play.

My weakness on turf was partly a result of my philosophical commitment to speed figures. I wrote in *Picking Winners* that speed figures are "the way, the truth and the light." I believe that a horse's ability is largely defined by how fast he runs. But speed figures don't define horses as definitively on turf as they do on dirt.

In most dirt races, horses have delivered their maximum effort as they reach the finish line. If the early pace is slow, they run faster late. But there are many turf races in which the pace is so slow that horses can't accelerate enough to run the final time of which they are capable. In such cases, speed figures can't be a true measure of the horses' ability.

On the day of the 2007 Kentucky Oaks, Churchill Downs carded a pair of 1 1/16-mile stakes races, the Edgewood for 3-year-old fillies and the Crown Royal American Turf for 3-year-old colts. The field of colts was much superior by any measurement; it included four graded stakes winners and several horses who ran figures in the low 90s. Among the fillies there were no graded stakes winners, and none had ever earned a figure better than 86. These were the fractional times of the two events:

Edgewood   23.82 48.70 1:11.26 1:37.85 1:43.99
Crown Royal 24.70 50.09 1:14.98 1:38.06 1:44.03

The pace set by the males in the Crown Royal was so dawdling that they were 3.72 seconds slower than the fillies at the six-furlong mark. Then the colts showed their ability with a powerful late acceleration, but they still finished 4/100 of a second slower than the fillies. With the responsibility for making the Churchill numbers, I had no choice but to give the winner of each race the same figure—93. But any rational handicapper who looked at the past performances of the respective groups would have little doubt that the colts were a superior bunch.

Given the difficulties involved in calculating speed figures on the turf, I am often surprised that they perform as well as they do; top-figure grass horses win a solid percentage of races. Nevertheless, when I handicap a grass race, I also employ traditional class handicapping, by looking at the fields against which horses have competed. While this is an old-fashioned approach, Formulator lets handicappers do their homework with speed and efficiency instead of leafing through stacks of *Daily Racing Forms*. Click on the date of a horse's recent race and you summon the chart of that race; click on any name in the chart and you summon that horse's past performances. Often the information will reveal relative strengths and weaknesses of horses that could not be gleaned from a study of the past performances alone. This was the case in the 2006 The Very One Handicap at Gulfstream Park. These were the three top contenders.

1 Dynamite Lass
Own: Alfred Corrado
Green, Blue Blocks, Blue Sleeves, Blue
Bejarano R (286 44 45 43 .15) 2006:(1346 264 .20)

Dk. b or br f. 4 (Apr)
Sire: Dynaformer (Roberto) $100,000
Dam: Lismore Lass (Vigors)
Br: Alfred G. Corrado(Ky)
Tr: McLaughlin Kiaran P (23 4 2 3 .17) 2006:(424 60 .14)

L 114

Life	12	3	4	1	$170,108	95	D.Fst	0	0	0	0	$0	-
2006	1	0	0	0	$4,500	92	Wet (346)	0	0	0	0	$0	-
2005	9	1	4	1	$132,608	95	Turf (336)	12	3	4	1	$170,108	95
GP [T]	3	0	2	0	$36,500	92	Dist (340)	0	0	0	0	$0	-

14Jan06-9GP	fm 1 1/16 [T] :22⁴ :46³1:10¹1:40²	3↑[F]MrshsRiver75k	92	9	64½	55	54	54½	42¼	Bejarano R	L	4.50	*MyLordshp* 124¹ OnthBs118¹¼ NtlBch118no	3 wide, late gain	12
														Little spd–nobody closed	
21Oct05-9Kee BRT	yl 1 1/16 [T] :24 :48¹1:13²1:45	[F]VllyView-G3	95	2	810	99	85¾	42½	2no	Bejarano R	L	10.60	AsSpr120no DntLss116¹¾ VctrLp120½	fin well vs ace closer	9
24Sep05-9Lrl	fm 1 1/16 [T] :24 :48⁴1:12⁴1:41³	[F]MWashtonBC150k	89	1	77	76¼	63¾	43½	3²	Castellano A Jr	L	8.00	*Sweet Talker* 122¹¼ Lucrezia116¾ Dynamite Lass116¾	Rallied	7
17Aug05-6Sar	fm 1 3/16 [T] :50¹1:14⁴1:39³1:58	3↑[F]Alw 50000N2X	87	2	1½	1½	1½	1hd	1hd	Coa E M	L	6.40	DynmiteLss116hd SgittR121hd *MingCov* 121nk	led r vs lil spd	6
														Little spd, spd 1–2	
3Jly05-6Bel	fm 1 1/16 [T] :25 :48⁴1:12¹1:41²	3↑[F]Alw 48000N2X	74	4	35	3²	3²	3⁴	47½	Coa E M	L	3.00	Plenty122nk *BndLittl* 122²¾ MissCorondo122⁴½	No response	6
														Lone f wins	
5Jun05-8Bel	fm 1⅛ [T] :48¹1:12¹1:36 1:47²	[F]SandsPnt-G3	81	6	43	5³	54½	68½	57¼	Migliore R	L	8.00	MlhorAnd123²¾ *Lrfn* 115¹½ *MyTyphn* 121²¾	Wide, no response	7
6May05-5CD	fm 1 1/16 [T] :23⁴ :47³1:11³1:41⁴	[F]Edgewood112k	81	1	62	62¾	73¾	87¾	57	Velazquez J R	L	2.80	*SwtTlkr* 122¾ *RichinSpirit* 122² InsnMl117²½	Lack room3/16s	8
19Mar05-10GP	fm 1⅛ [T] :49⁴1:13⁴1:36²1:48	[F]Hcmbride-G3	87	3	72¾	61¾	73¼	53½	2¾	Coa E M	L	4.00	CpHp119¾ DntLss117² DnsttLht121hd	Stdy early, gaining	8
20Feb05-10GP	fm 1 1/16 [T] :22⁴ :46¹1:09³1:39	[F]GailyGaily60k	86	4	33½	41½	3¹	1hd	2²	Coa E M	L	3.80	*CpHp* 117² DynmtLss117¹¾ Pdd'sDs121²	4 wide, outfinished	9
1Jan05-10Crc	gd 1 1/16 [T] :22¹ :47¹1:11²1:42	[F]TrPOaks100k	82	8	73¾	62½	42½	3²	2nk	Coa E M	L	2.60	DnsttLght118nk DnmtLss116nk SlrSt116no	3 wide, gaining	11

WORKS: Feb22 PmM [T] 4f fm :50 B (d) *4/11* Jan7 PmM 4f fst :48³ H *9/50* Dec31 PmM 4f fst :48⁴ H *27/81*

TRAINER: 31-60Days (164 .16 $2.00) Turf (131 .11 $1.30) Routes (293 .15 $1.44) GrdStk (45 .02 $0.40)

3 Noble Stella (Ger)
Own: Gary A. Tanaka
Emerald Green, Gold Trim on White Sash,
Castro E (250 21 36 27 .08) 2006:(1634 329 .20)

Dk. b or br m. 5 (Jan)
Sire: Monsun*Ger (Konigsstuhl*Ger) $21,000
Dam: Noble Pearl*Ger (Dashing Blade)
Br: Gestut Etzean(Ger)
Tr: Attfield Roger L (8 0 0 2 .00) 2006:(278 33 .12)

L 116

Life	19	5	2	3	$354,394	97	D.Fst	0	0	0	0	$0	-
2005	9	2	1	1	$267,225	97	Wet (280*)	0	0	0	0	$0	-
2004	6	2	1	1	$53,828	83	Turf (272)	19	5	2	3	$354,394	97
GP [T]	1	0	0	0	$0	88	Dist (309)	0	0	0	0	$0	-

17Dec05-8Crc	fm 1½ [T] :50⁴1:15⁴2:03⁴2:27³	3↑[F]LaPvyteH-G2	93	1	31½	41¼	41¼	2hd	33¾	Castro E	L	4.40	FlmMkr119³½ KtWnslt115nk NoblStll114²¾	Steadied early	12
														Fig lower?	
23Oct05-6WO	yl 1¼ [T] :51 1:15⁴1:41³2:06³	3↑[F]EPTaylor-G1	91	1	72¼	124¼	102	72¾	6³	Ramsammy E	L	21.00	HnRdr123½ Ltc123hd AmbtsCt123no	Rail,lost whip str,hng	12
25Sep05-6WO	gd 1½ [T] :47⁴1:12¹2:03 2:27	3↑[F]FlaminPage110k	97	7	57½	51¾	1⁴	1⁵	19¼	Ramsammy E	L	*.85	NblStll119¾ Nstbtt117²¾ SrEctt118¹¹	Sharp move to lead,drv	9
18Sep05-6WO	sf *1⅛ [T] :48¹ 1:47	3↑[F]BellCdnH-G2	89	4	63¼	62¼	63¼	84¾	43½	Ramsammy E	L	9.65	ClsscStp116¹¼ AbtsCt117¾ MnRs114¹½	Hung briefly,dug in	9
7Aug05-11Mth	fm 1⅛ [T] :50¹1:14³1:38²1:50	3↑[F]Matchmkr-G3	85	9	96½	94¾	83¼	106¾	103¾	Ramsammy E	L	10.10	LMtch116¹ CtAlrt118½ EmrldErrngs116no	Outside,no rally	10
16Jly05-8WO	fm 1⅛ [T] :48³1:13 1:37 1:49⁴	3↑[F]DNCSmrtH-G3	96	7	62¼	6³	2½	1hd	1¹	Ramsammy E	L	10.00	NblStll113¹ ClsscStp118¹½ JltsKss109¾	Sharp move 4wd bid,drv	7
4Jun05-8WO	fm 1 1/16 [T] :23³ :47 1:11³1:41⁴	3↑[F]Nassau-G2	87	6	61¾	82¾	113½	68½	64¾	Olguin G L	L	27.85	QPntl115½ AmbtosCt115½ MonRos119hd	Checked,all out	12
9Apr05-5Kee	fm*1½ [T] :50³1:15⁴2:05 2:29	4↑[F]Alw 59760N3X	88	4	11	1²	1hd	1½	21¾	Stevens G L	L	2.70	CpTnLss118¹¾ NblStll118⁶¼ *Krsny* 118nk	Pace,no match late	7
6Mar05-8GP	fm 1⅜ [T] :47³1:12²1:36 2:11³	3↑[F]VeryOneH-G3	88	7	55½	43½	6³	84¾	95½	Santos J A		27.80	*Honey Ryder* 114nk Briviesca114¹¾ Vous113¹½	Faltered	10
6Nov04-8Aqu	gd 1½ [T] :50¹1:16 2:05³2:31²	3↑[F]LngIlndH-G2	83	7	42	6³	7⁹	7⁸	5⁹	Velasquez C		1.65e	Eleusis115²¼ Literacy114½ *Arvd* 117¹¾	Between foes, no rally	7

WORKS: Feb26 Pay 5f fst 1:05² B *4/5* Feb17 Pay 5f fst 1:03² B *2/7* Feb10 Pay [T] 4f fm :50 B *2/3* ● Jan24 Pay [T] 4f fm :48 B *1/5* ● Jan6 Pay [T] 5f fm 1:01² B *1/6* Dec10 Pay 4f fst :49 B *2/22*

TRAINER: 61-180Days (33 .06 $1.33) Turf (158 .13 $1.71) Routes (170 .12 $2.00) GrdStk (20 .15 $5.76)

6 Olaya
Own: Faisal Salman
Forest Green, Gold Belt, Forest Green
Prado E S (199 33 28 28 .16) 2006:(1460 299 .20)

B. f. 4 (Mar)
Sire: Theatrical*Ire (Nureyev) $40,000
Dam: Solaia (Miswaki)
Br: Belgrave Bloodstock(Ky)
Tr: Motion H Graham (39 4 1 9 .10) 2006:(551 100 .18)

L 118

Life	10	4	2	1	$184,452	92	D.Fst	0 0 0 0	$0	-
2006	1	1	0	0	$23,400	91	Wet (352)	0 0 0 0	$0	-
2005	6	2	1	0	$137,115	92	Turf (366)	10 4 2 1	$184,452	92
GP Ⓣ	1	1	0	0	$23,400	91	Dist (370)	0 0 0 0	$0	-

6Feb06-8GP fm 1 1/16 Ⓣ :25 :484 1:402 4+ⒻOC 100k/N4X-N **91** 4 2 1½ 3 1½ 3 1 2½ 1¾ Prado E S L *1.00 Oly119¾ Redy'sGl1193 CpeHope11911 rbts caught loose spd 4
5Nov05-9Aqu fm 1½ Ⓣ :5041:1622:06 2:30 3+ⒻLngIlndH-G2 **92** 4 6 2½ 6 2½ 5 4 4 1¾ 1nk Prado E S L 3.70 *Oly* 114nk Spotlight1161 KteWinslet115hd Along late inside 7
Previously trained by Jean-Claude Rouget
23Aug05♦Deauville(Fr) sf *1 7/8 ⓉRH 2:503 ⒻPrix Minerve-G3 514 Mendizabal I 8.50 Oiseau Rare1216 Allexina1211½ Without A Trace1212½ 6
Timeform Rating: 92 Stk 91700 *Towards rear throughout.Law of Chance 6th*
19Jun05♦Toulouse(Fr) gd*1½ ⓉRH 2:274 Derby du Languedoc(Listed) 1¾ Mendizabal I 5.40 Olaya124¾ Windya1242 Grand Bahama128hd 6
Timeform Rating: 100 Stk 57700 *Tracked in 3rd,led 100y out*
28May05♦Marseille-Borelsf *1¼ ⓉRH 2:03 ⒻLa Coupe des Pouliches(Listed) 46½ Dubosc J-R .00 Ozone Bere123½ Wild Winner1234 Back The Winner1232 8
Timeform Rating: 86 Stk 59100 *Tracked in 3rd,weakened 1f out.River Bride 5th*
3May05♦Toulouse(Fr) gs*1¼ ⓉRH 2:062 ⒻPrix Caravelle (Listed) 65¾ Langlois A 17.00 DHLake Toya1231½ DHTivadare1231½ *Law of Chance* 1232½ 10
Timeform Rating: 88 Stk 60400 *Towards rear,evenly late.RiverBride4th,TooMarvelous10th*
10Apr05♦Le Bouscat(Fr)hy*1 3/16 ⓉRH 2:092 ⒻPrix Achille Fould 21 Langlois A .00 Chavela1231 Olaya123hd Too Marvelous1231 4
Timeform Rating: 92 Alw 28500 *Rated in last,gained 2nd near line*
13Oct04♦Le Bouscat(Fr)sf *1 ⓉRH 1:41 Grand Criterium de Bordeaux(Lstd) 35 Mendizabal I *2.50 Witten1202 Medigating1233 Olaya1201 8
Timeform Rating: 92 Stk 55600 *Unhurried in 4th,gained 3rd 100y out.River Bride 4th*
9Sep04♦Longchamp(Fr)gd*1 ⓉRH 1:393 ⒻPrix de la Masseliere-EBF 21½ Mendizabal I 5.00 Mirabilis1221½ Olaya124hd Kerasha124¾ 6
Timeform Rating: 97 Alw 31000 *Rated in 5th,wide bid,just up for 2nd*
14Aug04♦La Teste de Bucgs*1r) ⓉRH ⒻPrix des Sirenes-EBF 12½ Mendizabal I *.70 Olaya1232½ Reactivite1232 Yola Bella1234 6
Md Sp Wt 13k *Tracked leader,led 2f out,soon clear.Time not taken*

WORKS: Feb24 PmM Ⓣ 5f fm 1:03 B (d) *8/17* Jan27 PmM Ⓣ 5f fm :59 H *2/12* Jan18 PmM Ⓣ 5f fm 1:021 B (d) *9/14* Jan11 PmM Ⓣ 5f fm 1:053 B (d) *7/10* Jan4 PmM Ⓣ 5f fm 1:043 B (d) *9/13* Dec21 PmM Ⓣ 4f fm :50 B (d) *2/1.*
TRAINER: 2Off45-180 (63 .11 $0.98) WonLastStart (102 .18 $1.67) Turf (271 .17 $1.72) Routes (425 .18 $1.68) GrdStk (35 .23 $2.92)

Olaya was the 6–5 favorite in the $100,000 stakes on the strength of her victory, at a similar distance, in Aqueduct's Grade 2 Long Island Handicap. Only one of her Gulfstream rivals had won a graded stakes—Noble Stella had taken a Grade 3—and by conventional measurements Olaya was the class of the field. But was she, really? A handicapper using Formulator could summon the chart of the Long Island Handicap and then display the past performances of the rivals Olaya beat—second-place finisher Spotlight and third-place Kate Winslet.

Spotlight (GB)
Own: Green Hills Farm
Green & Blue Halves, Blue Sleeves,

Ch. f. 6 (Apr)
Sire: Dr Fong (Kris S.) $30,696
Dam: Dust Dancer*GB (Suave Dancer)
Br: Hesmonds Stud Ltd(GB)
Tr: Clement Christophe

Life	17	5	4	2	$313,632	100	D.Fst	0 0 0 0	$0	-
2005	6	1	1	1	$91,839	92	Wet (340*)	0 0 0 0	$0	-
2004	7	2	2	0	$187,058	100	Turf (326)	17 5 4 2	$313,632	100

17Dec05-8Crc fm 1½Ⓣ:5041:1542:0342:273 3+ⒻLaPvyteH-G2 **75** 3 21 1hd 1hd 52¼ 11 13¾ Blanc B L116 6.40 72-09 Film Maker1193½ KateWinslet115nk NobleStella1142¾ Used up 12
5Nov05-9Aqufm 1½Ⓣ:5041:1622:06 2:301 3+ⒻLngIlndH-G2 **92** 6 2½ 2½ 1hd 11½ 2nk Dominguez R A L116 4.00 106-09 Olaya114nk Spotlight1161 KteWinslet115hd With pace, gamely 7
3Oct05-8Del fm 1⅛Ⓣ:4911:1341:38 1:492 3+ⒻCicada60k **83** 1 53 42 31 2hd 11 Dominguez R A L117 2.30 90-08 Spotlight1171 WithAffction119½ Ltic123½ Good energy inside 8
18Sep05-6WO sf *1⅛Ⓣ:481 1:471 3+ⒻBellCdnH-G2 **87** 5 31½ 31 41½ 32 64½ Velazquez J R L116 3.50 73-27 ClsscStmp1161¼ AmbtosCt117¾ MnRs1141½ Failed bid top str 9
7Aug05-11Mthfm 1⅛Ⓣ:5011:1431:3821:501 3+ⒻMatchmkr-G3 **90** 4 53½ 52¾ 62 52¾ 41½ Bailey J D L116 *1.00 78-15 LMtch1161 CtAlrt118½ ErldErrns116no Btwn foes,some gain 10
3Jly05-9Mthsf 1 1/16Ⓣ:253 :51 1:1631:461 3+ⒻEatntwnH-G3 **89** 5 63½ 62¾ 52 42 3nk Bravo J L118 *1.60 68-32 SmrtNClssy115no Lntl116nk Sptlght118½ Btwn stretch,gamely 7
23Oct04-7Crc gd 1⅛Ⓣ:4941:1411:39 1:512 ⒻCalderOaks200k **86** 9 76 65½ 41 41 44 Bailey J D L121f *.40 68-28 *HplsslyDvtd* 1212¾ Vs118¾ SkpCmmnd116½ Steadied early, 4 wide 12
18Sep04-9AP fm 1⅛Ⓣ:4741:1211:3641:483 ⒻPuckerUp-G3 **87** 10 97 97¾ 63½ 53½ 22¾ Douglas R R L122 1.30 93-05 *TckrTp* 1222¾ Sptlght122hd SstrSwnk116½ 4-5 wide, second best 11
23Aug04-8Sar gd 1⅛Ⓣ:50 1:1411:3811:502 ⒻLakPlcdH-G2 **100** 5 32 21 2½ 1½ 13½ Bailey J D L116 *1.55 78-31 Spotlght1163½ MmbSlw120¾ *FrtntDmsl* 1163 When roused, clear 7
23Jly04-8Bel sf 1⅛Ⓣ:4931:1441:4031:531 3+ⒻAlw 48000N2X **91** 4 42½ 1½ 12 13½ 12 Bailey J D L115 *1.15 64-40 *Spotlight* 1152 Finery1213 Pattiano1213¼ Took over after a half 7
WORKS: Dec11 Pay 4f fst :52 B *4/11* ●Dec4 Pay 4f fst :51 B *1/10* Nov28 Pay 4f fst :52 B *8/8* Nov19 Pay 4f fst :512 B *7/15* Oct27 Bel 4f fst :482 B *10/25* Oct18 Bel 4f fst :494 B *20/43*

Kate Winslet
Own: Team Valor Stables LLC

B. m. 5 (Apr)
Sire: Signal Tap (Fappiano) $2,500
Dam: Frances Synatra (Eastern Echo)
Br: John Franks (NY)
Tr: Violette R A Jr(34 5 6 6 .15) 2006:(344 62 .18)

Life 23 5 2 2 $249,054 94 | D.Fst 0 0 0 0 $0 -
2006 1 0 0 0 $0 52 | Wet(268) 0 0 0 0 $0 -
| Synth 0 0 0 0 $0 -
2005 7 1 1 1 $119,495 94 | Turf(247) 23 5 2 2 $249,054 94
Gp Ⓣ 2 0 0 0 $460 75 | DstⓉ(340) 4 0 1 1 $60,397 94

1Apr06-8GP fm 1½ Ⓣ :48 1:113 1:593 2:23 3↑ⒻOrchidH-G3 52 8 32½ 31½ 76 715 729 Castellano J J L116 b 11.80 85 - *Honey Ryder*1204 Olaya1182 *Noble Stella*1161½ Faded, eased 8
17Dec05-8Crc fm 1½ Ⓣ :504 1:154 2:034 2:273 3↑ⒻLaPvyteH-G2 94 11 52½ 72¾ 52¼ 31½ 23½ Bridgmohan S X L115 b 23.20 82-09 *Film Maker*1193½ Kate Winslet115nk Noble Stella1142¾ Traffic, rallied 12
5Nov05-9Aqu fm 1½ Ⓣ :504 1:162 2:06 2:301 3↑ⒻLngIlndH-G2 90 1 31 41½ 31½ 21½ 31¼ Velasquez C L115 b 11.10 105-09 *Olaya*114nk Spotlight1161 Kate Winslet115hd Stayed on gamely 7
17Aug05-9Sar fm 1⅛ T :492 1:131 1:371 1:49 3↑ⒻⓈYaddoH83k 86 6 22 2½ 2hd 13 12¾ Migliore R L117 b 6.40 92-05 KteWinslt1172¾ RhysAppl1141 ThLmpIsLit117nk Drew clear when roused 9
Run in divisions
16Jly05-9Del yl 1⅜ Ⓣ :512 1:164 1:414 2:202 3↑ⒻRGDickBCH296k 84 9 42 52 31 21½ 57½ Lumpkins J L117 b 18.50 65-27 *HoneyRyder*1205¼ SweetScience1141½ NtliBch117no Close up 4w, gave way 10
19Jun05-6Bel fm 1⅛ T :50 1:133 1:37 1:49 3↑ⒻⓈMtVernonH84k 82 7 1½ 1½ 1½ 2½ 42¼ Migliore R L117 b 6.20 80-18 Lady Bi Bi117nk Little Buttercup117no *Sabellina*1182 Set pace, tired 7
Run in divisions
22May05-8Bel fm 1⅜ Ⓣ :503 1:15 1:392 2:153 3↑ⒻShpshdBH-G2 86 2 77 87¾ 86¾ 74 74½ Migliore R L116 b 40.25 80-20 Sauvage115½ Angara118nk Barancella116½ Mild rally outside 8
10Apr05-8GP fm 1 1/16 Ⓣ :234 :472 1:112 1:401 4↑ⒻAlw 46000NC 75 7 74½ 64¾ 52 67 67¼ Maragh R5 L112 b 3.70 - - Fast Cookie1151½ Brunilda115½ Sniffles1154¼ 4 wide, faltered 7
23Oct04-9Bel gd 1⅛ T :491 1:133 1:38 1:50 3↑ⒻⓈTicndrogaH150k 76 10 1010 98¾ 94¼ 88 68 Santos J A 116 5.90 72-17 On the Bus1182 Sabellina1161 Little Buttercup116¾ Bumped start, wide 12
WORKS: Mar27 PmM 4f fst :482 H *4/25* Mar22 PmM 6f fst 1:144 B *1/1* Mar16 PmM 4f fst :50 B *13/29* Mar10 PmM 4f fst :502 B *18/28* ●Feb28 PmM 3f fst :362 B *1/17* Feb19 PmM 4f fst :50 B *30/49*
TRAINER: +180Days(27 .22 $2.15) Turf(150 .11 $1.23) Routes(307 .18 $1.69) Stakes(80 .12 $1.08)

Defeating Spotlight was certainly no great achievement. The filly's only win in a year had come in a minor stakes at Delaware Park; after her second-place finish to Olaya, she had been trounced in a Calder stakes. Kate Winslet, who was 1¼ lengths behind Olaya, had beaten New York-breds for her only victory in the previous 17 months. Olaya may have been credited with winning a Grade 2 stakes, but this was not a bona fide Grade 2 field.

Noble Stella's stakes credentials were decent, but hardly imposing. She had finished a neck behind the aforementioned Kate Winslet in her most recent start, and her last win had come against weak competition at Woodbine.

On the surface, Dynamite Lass appeared overmatched against these rivals. Her last win had come in a moderate allowance race, and she had lost three stakes in a row. But—click! click! click!—a look at the winners of those races put her form into a different perspective.

Three races back, Dynamite Lass had lost by two lengths to Sweet Talker in an ungraded stakes at Laurel, a performance that looked a lot better after a glance at Sweet Talker's record.

Sweet Talker
Own: Adam Donald A

Dk. b or b. f. 4 (Apr) FTKNOV02 $50,000
Sire: Stormin Fever (Storm Cat) $15,000
Dam: Another Vegetarian (Stalwart)
Br: Brereton C. Jones (Ky)
Tr: Motion H. G(27 10 4 2 .37) 2006:(519 90 .17)

Life 14 8 2 1 $718,723 98 | D.Fst 4 2 1 0 $54,922 81
2006 1 1 0 0 $36,000 92 | Wet(341) 2 0 0 0 $12,000 68
| Synth 0 0 0 0 $0 -
2005 8 4 1 1 $582,963 98 | Turf(273) 8 6 1 1 $651,801 98
Lrl Ⓣ 2 2 0 0 $126,000 93 | DstⓉ(337) 2 1 0 1 $47,280 92

15Apr06-9Lrl fm 1 Ⓣ :23 :471 1:11 1:34 3↑ⒻDahlia60k 92 5 33½ 42 2½ 12½ 11½ Dominguez R A L118 *.80 101-03 *Sweet Talker*1181½ Smart NClassy118½ Humoristic118nk 2wd move, driving 12
Previously trained by Pitts Helen 2005(as of 10/15): (60 11 7 9 0.18)
15Oct05-9Kee fm 1⅛ Ⓣ :504 1:152 1:392 1:511 ⒻQEIICup-G1 98 7 41½ 31½ 42 1½ 1no Bejarano R L121 18.70 79-16 *Sweet Talker*121no Karen's Caper121hd Gorella121½ 5w,gamely,all out 7
24Sep05-9Lrl fm 1 1/16 Ⓣ :24 :484 1:124 1:413 ⒻMWashtonBC150k 93 2 55 33½ 31½ 2½ 11¼ Fogelsonger R L122 2.20 96 - *Sweet Talker*1221¼ Lucrezia116¾ Dynamite Lass116¾ Swung wide, driving 7
Previously trained by McPeek Kenneth G 2005(as of 6/18): (159 14 23 18 0.09)
18Jun05-8CD fm 1⅛ Ⓣ :494 1:142 1:381 1:493 ⒻRegret-G3 89 5 1hd 1hd 1hd 11 21¼ Blanc B L120 3.10 84-11 Rich in Spirit1201¼ *Sweet Talker*1202¼ RoyalBean116no Duel,inside,2ndbest 8
27May05-9CD fm 1 1/16 Ⓣ :24 :473 1:124 1:432 ⒻAlw 70510NC 89 1 33½ 34½ 42½ 1hd 1½ Blanc B L122 *.40 88-14 Sweet Talker122½ Royal Bean1181½ Godsend1201½ Bmp start,4-5w,drvg 6
6May05-5CD fm 1 1/16 Ⓣ :234 :473 1:113 1:414 ⒻEdgewood112k 96 4 31 31 3nk 14 1¾ Blanc B L122 7.40 96-04 *Sweet Talker*122¾ *Rich in Spirit*1222 Insan Mala1172½ Inside,driving,lasted 8
WORKS: Apr10 PmM 6f sly 1:143 H *1/2* Mar31 PmM Ⓣ 6f fm 1:16 B(d) *1/2* Mar25 PmM Ⓣ 5f fm 1:04 B(d) *4/10* Mar17 PmM Ⓣ 4f fm :491 B *5/14* Mar10 PmM Ⓣ 4f fm :503 B *16/18* Feb10 PmM Ⓣ 4f fm :48 H *3/11*
TRAINER: +180Days(64 .23 $2.59) Turf(492 .19 $1.91) Routes(733 .21 $2.04) Stakes(177 .15 $1.76)

Sweet Talker came out of the Laurel race and beat one of the world's best female turf runners, Gorella, in the Grade 1 Queen Elizabeth Cup at Keeneland.

Dynamite Lass's nose loss at Keeneland was equally impressive. The filly who beat her, Asi Siempre, was a highly regarded European import who had finished second in a Grade 1 stakes in New York, earning a speed figure of 101.

Asi Siempre
Own: Schwartz Martin S

Gr/ro. f. 4 (Mar)
Sire: El Prado*Ire (Sadler's Wells) $125,000
Dam: Siempre Asi (Silver Hawk)
Br: Almagro de Actividades Commerciales (Ky)
Tr: Biancone Patrick L(31 6 6 5 .19) 2006:(311 66 .21)

Life	10	4	3	1	$257,066	101	D.Fst	0	0	0	0	$0	-
2006	1	0	1	0	$40,000	95	Wet(316)	0	0	0	0	$0	-
							Synth	0	0	0	0	$0	-
2005	9	4	2	1	$217,066	101	Turf(341)	10	4	3	1	$257,066	101
Kee Ⓣ	3	2	1	0	$145,958	95	DstⓉ(343)	2	1	1	0	$117,500	95

15Apr06–7Kee fm 1 1/16 Ⓣ :24 :48 1:114 1:411 4↑ⒻJenyWily-G2 **95** 5 75 74½ 62¼ 41 21½ Leparoux J R L117 b 3.70 94–06 Wend1171½ Asi Siempre1171 *Mirabilis*118hd Reared start 8
21Oct05–9Kee yl 1 1/16 Ⓣ :24 :481 1:132 1:451 ⒻVllyView-G3 **95** 1 910 78 63 31½ 1no Stevens G L L120 b *.40 81–25 AsiSiempre120no DynamiteLss1161¾ VictoryLp120½ Drift start,9w,driving 9
7Oct05–10Kee fm 1 3/16 Ⓣ :502 1:161 1:423 2:014 3↑ⒻAlw 48735n2x **95** 6 610 57 53½ 21½ 11¼ Stevens G L L119 b *.20 70–31 *AsiSiempre*1191¼ SunnyDisposition1211 *YesBth*117¾ Hop start,hand urging 9
10Sep05–8Bel fm 1⅛ Ⓣ :472 1:101 1:34 1:453 ⒻGrdnCyBC-G1 **101** 1 48½ 47 45½ 31½ 21½ Stevens G L 116 b 3.20 97–07 Luas Line1161½ *Asi Siempre*1163¼ My Typhoon1165 Game finish outside 4
Previously trained by Carlos Laffon-Parias
18Jly05 Vichy (Fr) gs *1¼ Ⓣ RH 2:052 ⒻPrix Mme Jean Couturie (Listed) Stk 56600 1nk Blancpain M 128 3.90 Asi Siempre128nk *Hideaway*1231 *Oiseau Rare*123no 9
Unruly in gate,tracked in 3rd,led 1f out,held well
26Jun05 Saint-Cloud (Fr) gs *1½ Ⓣ LH 2:351 ⒻPrix de Malleret-G2 Stk 145000 53¼ Blancpain M 121 12.00 Royal Highness121hd Fraloga1211½ Grand Opening121nk 6
Racing Post Rating: 103
Tracked in 3rd,4th 2-1/2f out,outfinished
4Jun05 Chantilly (Fr) gd *1½ Ⓣ RH 2:33 ⒻPrix de Royaumont-G3 Stk 91700 32½ Blancpain M 126 7.70 *Shawanda*1262½ *Royal Highness*126no Asi Siempre1262½ 5
Racing Post Rating: 107
Trailed slow pace,4th 4f out,2nd 2f out,lost 2nd on line
15May05 Longchamp (Fr) sf *1⅜ Ⓣ RH 2:213 ⒻPrix de la Seine (Listed) Stk 59300 21½ Blancpain M 123 b 14.00 *Shawanda*1231½ Asi Siempre123½ *Grand Opening*123½ 6
Led for 2-1/2f ,tracked winner,brief bid 2f out,saved 2nd
15Apr05 Longchamp (Fr) hy *1⅛ Ⓣ RH 2:11 ⒻPrix Finlande (Listed) Stk 60200 89¼ Blancpain M 123 13.00 Viane Rose123hd Vassileva1231½ Fading Light1232½ 10
Rated at rear on rail,never a factor
14Mar05 Compiegne (Fr) hy *1⅛ Ⓣ LH 1:59 ⒻPrix de la Michelette-EBF Maiden (FT) 24200 11 Blancpain M 126 *2.80 Asi Siempre1261 Shatabdi1263 Fontanella1261½ 15
Led to halfway,led again 3f out,held well

WORKS: Apr12 TP ◈4f fst :501 B *11/18* Apr5 TP ◈1 fst 1:403 Bg *1/3* Mar30 TP ◈5f fst 1:004 B *3/10* Mar24 TP ◈5f fst 1:013 B *3/21* ●Mar17 TP ◈4f fst :463 B *1/23* Mar11 TP ◈4f fst :492 B *3/30*
TRAINER: 61-180Days(93 .32 $2.36) Dirt/Turf(24 .25 $2.57) Turf(231 .22 $1.70) Routes(365 .21 $1.69) Stakes(227 .16 $1.39)

The competition in Dynamite Lass's most recent race had been solid, too, even though it was a mere $75,000 stakes. The winner, My Lordship, had come out of the race to defeat a strong stakes field at Tampa Bay Downs, earning a figure of 100.

This was one of the cases where speed figures in a turf race did not properly reflect the relative ability of the horses. Dynamite Lass, who had been running in relatively slow-paced races, had earned figures roughly equal to those of her main rivals. But an examination of horses she had been competing against suggested strongly that she was the best in the Gulfstream field. She had run solid races against legitimate Grade 1 rivals—something Olaya and Noble Stella could not claim. Under the circumstances, the payoff was extraordinary:

NINTH RACE
Gulfstream
MARCH 4, 2006

1 1/16 MILES. (Turf) (2.17^{3}) 18TH RUNNING OF THE VERY ONE HANDICAP. Grade III. Purse $100,000 FOR FILLIES AND MARES, THREE YEAR OLDS AND UPWARD. By subscription of $200 each, which shall accompany the nomination, $1,000 to pass the entry box and $1,000 additional to start, with $100,000 guaranteed. The owner of the winner to receive $60,000, $20,000 to second, $11,000 to third, $6,000 to fourth and $3,000 to fifth. Trophy to winning Owner. In the event this stake is taken off the turf, it may be subject to downgrading upon review by the Graded Stakes Committee. Closed Wednesday February 22, 2006 with 22 nominations. (Rail at 60 feet).

Value of Race: $100,000 Winner $60,000; second $20,000; third $11,000; fourth $6,000; fifth $3,000. Mutuel Pool $736,778.00 Exacta Pool $522,281.00 Trifecta Pool $388,263.00 Superfecta Pool $138,646.00

Last Raced	Horse	M/Eqt	A	Wt	PP	1/4	1/2	1	1 1/4	Str	Fin	Jockey	Odds $1
14Jan06 9GP4	Dynamite Lass	L	4	114	1	6½	6hd	92½	91	4hd	1¾	Bejarano R	6.30
6Feb06 8GP1	Olaya	L	4	118	6	10	5hd	4hd	31	31½	2no	Prado E S	1.30
17Dec05 8Crc3	Noble Stella-Ger	L	5	116	3	7½	71½	61	41	53	31½	Castro E	3.10
18Feb06 5GP4	Potra Clasica-Arg	L	5	116	9	12	13	11	11	2½	4hd	Douglas R R	58.30
29Jan06 7GP2	AlmostInnocent-Ire	L	4	116	4	3hd	31	31	2hd	1hd	53¾	Velasquez C	11.80
19Nov05 7Lrl3	Moon Dazzle	L	5	113	7	8½	92	8hd	6hd	62	65	Castellano J J	9.60
4Feb06 7GP4	Cotopaxi	L b	5	113	2	91	8½	7hd	72	75	75½	Bridgmohan S X	15.60
10Feb06 8GP5	Mona Rose	L	6	115	8	41	41	5hd	8hd	81	82½	Velazquez J R	8.70
29Jan06 7GP9	Seanachai	L b	4	116	5	5½	10	10	10	10	92¾	Landry R C	79.30
14Feb06 9Tam1	Mama I'm Home	L b	4	113	10	2hd	2hd	2½	5hd	91	10	Sutherland C	101.40

OFF AT 4:58 Start Good. Won driving. Course firm.

TIME :24^{2}, :48^{3}, 1:13^{3}, 1:37^{2}, 2:01^{1}, 2:18^{4} (:24.41, :48.65, 1:13.78, 1:37.54, 2:01.37, 2:18.81)

$2 Mutuel Prices:

1 – DYNAMITE LASS	14.60	5.20	3.20
6 – OLAYA		3.20	2.40
3 – NOBLE STELLA-GER			2.80

$1 EXACTA 1-6 PAID $20.70 $1 TRIFECTA 1-6-3 PAID $56.30
$1 SUPERFECTA 1-6-3-10 PAID $1,094.50

Dk. b or br. f, (Apr), by Dynaformer – Lismore Lass, by Vigors. Trainer McLaughlin Kiaran P. Bred by Alfred G Corrado (Ky).

DYNAMITE LASS reserved off the pace, saved ground around the final turn, angled outside the leaders for room in the stretch and rallied to be up late. OLAYA stalked the pace, angled out three wide on the final turn, rallied to gain a slim lead inside the eighth pole but couldn't resist the winner in the closing strides while just saving the place. NOBLE STELLA (GER) rated off the pace, raced four wide on the final turn and finished willingly to just miss the place. POTRA CLASICA (ARG) set the pace along the rail into the stretch and gave way. ALMOST INNOCENT (IRE) stalked the pace, moved to gain a slim lead in the stretch, then weakened. MOON DAZZLE unhurried early, raced four wide on the final turn and had no response when asked. COTOPAXI steadied in traffic on the first turn and failed to menace. MONA ROSE raced in striking position for more than a mile, then faltered. SEANACHAI was not a factor. MAMA I'M HOME chased the pace into the final turn and faded.

Owners– 1, Corrado Alfred; 2, Salman Prince F; 3, Tanaka Gary A; 4, M-2 Stable LLC; 5, Swettenham Stud; 6, Kantor Bernard; 7, Gunther John and Holmes Anthony; 8, O'Brien P and F; 9, Chiefswood Stable; 10, Long Katherine

Trainers– 1, McLaughlin Kiaran P; 2, Motion H Graham; 3, Attfield Roger L; 4, Wolfson Martin D; 5, Mott William I; 6, Clement Christophe; 7, Stewart Dallas; 8, Walder Peter R; 9, Coatrieux Eric; 10, Stewart Cecil

Scratched– Asti (IRE) (18Feb06 9GP 2)

$1 Pick Three (11-4-1) Paid $785.50 ; Pick Three Pool $112,925 .

I recommend that a handicapper do this kind of basic research on every grass race. Look at the competition that horses have been facing in their prior turf races. The effort can be laborious (it would be intolerable without Formulator) and sometimes it can be unproductive; in many cases no horse will have a clear edge. But sometimes the research will produce a $14.60 standout like Dynamite Lass. And once in a while it will reveal a superior horse whose virtues are even more hidden. Three weeks before the Dynamite Lass race, I uncovered a horse at Gulfstream whom I consider the best single pick I have made in this millennium. I still remember that five-furlong sprint on February 11, 2006, in vivid detail—and I am haunted by the memory.

8 Gulfstream Park

Alw 33000N1X

5 Furlongs. **(Turf) (:53³) ALLOWANCE. Purse $33,000 FOR FOUR YEAR OLDS AND UPWARD WHICH HAVE NEVER WON A RACE OTHER THAN MAIDEN, CLAIMING OR STARTER OR WHICH HAVE NEVER WON TWO RACES. Weight, 124 lbs. Non-winners of a race other than Claiming since January 12 Allowed 2 lbs. Such a race since December 13 Allowed 4 lbs. (Condition Eligibility). (If deemed inadvisable to run this race over the Turf course, it will be run on the main track at Five and One Half Fulongs) (Rail at 48 feet).**

Exacta / Trifecta / Superfecta / Bet 3 (8–9–10) & Pick 4 (8–9–10–11)

~~Entered For Main Track Only~~

1 Southern Missile

Own: Rafael Celis
White, Royal Blue Stripes, Red Stars on
Alvarado R Jr (40 1 3 2 .02) 2005:(766 163 .21)

Ch. g. 4 (May) KEESEP03 $32,000
Sire: Devil His Due (Devil's Bag) $15,000
Dam: Miss Mercedes (Mercedes Won)
Br: Dr. J. David Richardson & D. Britton Richardson(K
Tr: Lake Scott A (21 4 2 3 .19) 2005:(1812 421 .23)

L 120

Life	8	2	1	1	$26,080	90	D.Fst	8 2 1 1	$26,080	90
2006	2	1	0	0	$9,120	90	Wet (348)	0 0 0 0	$0	–
2005	6	1	1	1	$16,960	80	Turf (270)	0 0 0 0	$0	–
GP	2	1	0	0	$9,120	90	Dist (323)	1 1 0 0	$9,600	78

26Jan06-9GP	N	fst 7f	:22 :443 1:091 1:212	4↑ Alw 33000N1X	88/96	67	5 4	1hd 1hd 33½ 413	Alvarado R Jr	L	4.20	Bucharest1203½ War Plan1209½ Senza Aglio120nk	r bat 3 bats die	10
11Jan06-6GP	N	fst 6f	:22 :444 :57 1:093	4↑ Clm 30000(30-25)N2L	98/90	90p	1 7	1½ 11 15 16¾	~~Alvarado R Jr~~	L	*1.70	StrMssl1246¾ MdFcs1242 ItsBlsT1241½	loose quick r drew off	9
Previously trained by Cioffi Antonio														
18Dec05-7Crc	N	fst 6½f	:224 :463 1:12 1:182	3↑ Alw 20000N2L	69/88	67	5 1	53 54 67½ 59¼	Olivero C A	L f	6.60	THrs1203¾ InfntyBl1205 *CsNts* 120nk	rb sdy (2L), again rt 2s	7
26Nov05-9Crc		fst 6f	:214 :451 :583 1:123	3↑ Alw 24000N1X		74	9 11	115½ 87 65 52	Olivero C A	L	3.30	DnlsFst117½ Knckt'sImg120½ KpprKlgr117¾	Belated rally	11
19Nov05-11Crc		fst 6f	:22 :454 :583 1:12	3↑ OC 16k/N1X-N		80	6 7	62¼ 3nk 1hd 22	Olivero C A	L	4.50	FlrdEprss1152 StrMssl1174¼ CprOHl120½	Dueled, 2nd best	7
8Oct05-12Crc		fst 7f	:223 :461 1:12 1:251	3↑ Alw 23000N2L		76	2 6	63½ 41½ 32½ 32¾	Olivero C A	L	2.80	*RnrdBlu* 1231¾ HonstTrdr1181 SothrnMssl1188¼	Broke in air	6
30May05-5Crc		fst 6½f	:214 :444 1:12 1:193	3↑ Alw 26000N2L		72	7 7	74½ 67 56½ 54½	Olivero C A		12.20	Qrll1181 BlPpsLodg118hd ClsscWn1231	Off slowly, 4 wide	9
9May05-6Crc		fst 5½f	:221 :461 :591 1:061	3↑ Md 32000		78	9 6	56¼ 54 34 11¼	Olivero C A		8.80	SthrMssl1181¼ FtblCt123nk *HrldsHl* 1188¼	Off slowly, up late	9

TRAINER: Dirt (1922 .24 $1.58) Sprint (1535 .25 $1.73) Alw (368 .23 $1.69)

2 Nacascolo

Own: Nacascolo Stud
Red and Blue Stripes, Blue Diamonds on
Leyva J C (56 2 4 4 .03) 2005:(350 25 .07)

B. g. 5 (Mar)
Sire: Rahy (Blushing Groom*Fr) $75,000
Dam: Baby Feels So Good (Baldski)
Br: Nacascolo Stud, Inc.(Fla)
Tr: Azpurua Manuel J (23 0 3 3 .00) 2005:(303 27 .09)

L 120

Life	17	1	2	6	$33,165	79	D.Fst	12 0 1 4	$16,685	67
2005	11	1	1	2	$18,740	79	Wet (324)	3 1 1 1	$13,650	62
2004	6	M	1	4	$14,425	65	Turf (345)	2 0 0 1	$2,830	79
GP Ⓣ	2	0	0	1	$2,830	79	Dist (345)	2 0 0 1	$2,830	79

8Aug05-8Crc		fst 6½f	:214 :451 1:114 1:184	3↑ Clm 16000N2L		49	6 2	58¾ 510 67 514¾	Sanchez J7	L b	12.50	*Csy'sBsct* 1183¼ *VgrsGy* 1134½ *WndrflMmSns* 1231½	Saved ground	6
4Jly05-7Crc		fst 6½f	:22 :454 1:121 1:192	3↑ Clm 25000N2L		–0	8 9	63½ 76 1019 1045	Sanchez J7	b	22.70	HrdStr118no DDpt1232 WdrflMSs1161½	Bobbled st, eased	10
26Jun05-10Crc		fst 5½f	:214 :46 :59 1:06	3↑ Alw 23000N1X		42	6 4	43½ 44½ 77¾ 613½	Sanchez J7	b	34.80	AsmAlln1201 Em1204 Chncnlftm118½	Hit rail, checked str	7
10Jun05-3Crc		sly 5½f	:221 :464 1:002 1:074	3↑ Md 20000		60	4 2	1hd 1hd 14 18	Sanchez J7	b	1.90	Ncscolo1168 AnthrSnst1131½ *AmrcnJ* 118¾	Vied well off rail	8
9May05-6Crc		fst 5½f	:221 :461 :591 1:061	3↑ Md 32000		50	2 2	2hd 2½ 45 510¼	Castro E	b	3.80	**SothrnMssl**1181¼ FontnblCt123nk *Hrold'sHlo* 1188¼	Rail, tired	9
29Apr05-9Crc		fst 5½f	:223 :463 :593 1:064	3↑ Md Sp Wt 25k		45	4 1	32 22 47½ 811¼	Toribio A Jr	b	8.30	HotZm1183½ TorofthTgr1182¾ JhnsHnr1183	Chased, faded	8
14Apr05-7GP		fm 5f Ⓣ	:21 :44 :551	4↑ Alw 33000N1X		62	1 7	66 79½ 65 66¼	Sanchez J10	fb	3.90	IrishGato118no Hrpoon1183¼ LindenLne118½	Saved ground	8
1Apr05-3GP		fm 5f Ⓣ	:22 :441 :56	4↑ Clm 50000(50-40)		79	3 1	21½ 24½ 31½ 34	Lopez J E	b	33.60	SothrnCl1203 LvThtMn1201 Ncscl120nk	Chased, gave way	8
18Mar05-2GP		gd 6f	:231 :471 :593 1:122	Md 32000(32-30)		62	4 1	2½ 2hd 2hd 2no	Lopez J E	b	3.00	BrsJrd122no Ncscl122nk StpllBrr1226¼	Brushed str, failed	5
9Feb05-8GP	GRS	fst 7f	:221 :451 1:101 1:224	Md Sp Wt 32k	79/88	52	1 6	61¾ 53½ 79 719	Lopez J E	b	22.10	Anew1228 *Smart Growth* 1221¼ *Unbridledwood* 1221¾	Faltered	11

WORKS: Feb8 Crc 3f fst :37 B *8/22* Feb4 Crc 3f sly :391 B *11/11* Jan21 Crc 3f fst :373 B *10/30*

TRAINER: +180Days (3 .00 $0.00) Dirt/Turf (19 .05 $0.97) Turf (31 .03 $0.59) Sprint (230 .09 $1.05) Alw (39 .03 $0.11)

3 Lox and Kippers

Own: Robert Bakerman
Blue, White Circled RB, Blue Sleeves,
Cruz M R (45 4 5 3 .08) 2005:(1678 322 .19)

B. c. 4 (Jan)
Sire: Kipper Kelly (Valid Appeal) $2,000
Dam: My Own True Love (Regal and Royal)
Br: Robert Bakerman(Fla)
Tr: Wolfendale Ross B (9 0 0 1 .00) 2005:(182 24 .13)

L 120

Life	12	2	2	0	$35,700	80	D.Fst	10 2 2 0	$35,280	80
2005	10	2	1	0	$30,410	80	Wet (342)	1 0 0 0	$220	–
2004	2	M	1	0	$5,290	64	Turf (220)	1 0 0 0	$200	40
GP Ⓣ	0	0	0	0	$0	–	Dist (357)	0 0 0 0	$0	–

28Dec05-3Crc	S-	fst 5½f	:223 :461 :591 1:06	3↑ Clm 16000B	77/79	43	6 1	1½ 1hd 42¾ 713¼	Bridgmohan S X	L b	5.70	**So Savvy**1203¾ My Friend Deke1232 *Dilistar* 1231	led r duel	7
14Dec05-9Crc	N	fst 6f	:22 :46 :591 1:123	3↑ Clm 16000B	75/73	58	8 2	12 1½ 2½ 66	Garcia J A	L b	5.20	HrldsHl1201 GtWld120nk ClsscW123no	loose vs mod spd 3pe	8
13Nov05-5Crc		fm 1¹⁄₁₆ Ⓣ	:23 :48 1:122 1:424	3↑ Alw 20000N1X		40	3 2hd	21½ 21½ 1011 1019¼	Aguilar M	L b	11.70	ChrstcRb1201¾ RchthKd117¾ *OthBrdl* 117¾	Prompted, faded	10
23Oct05-10Crc		fst 5½f	:221 :461 :583 1:051	3↑ Clm 16000N2L		80	1 2	11½ 1½ 12½ 16¼	Cruz M R	L b	*.90	LndKpprs1206¼ SncrMn1203 QcStrd1132½	Inside, drew off	7
30Sep05-4Crc		fst 5f ⊗	:22 :46 :59	Clm 25000		70	3 2	31½ 43 34 47	Cruz M R	L b	13.00	*RbyDo* 1195¼ Obsdn119nk AgntWn1191½	Bumped early, tired	7
27Aug05-8Crc		gd 1 ⊗	:244 :49 1:134 1:40	3↑ Clm 40000N2L		—	9 6	6¼ 55½ 810 1026 —	Cruz M R	L b	8.10e	FrtT12313 WrfrtRss1182¼ VlccFrc1111	Bore out 1st tn, eased	10
6Aug05-12Crc		fst 6f	:22 :454 :583 1:123	Alw 26000N1X		41	5 1	41¾ 41 65¼ 614¾	Castro E	L b	6.10	BlndRvrFx1121½ RbyD1193¾ SwftMrcds114nk	3 wide, faded	7
26Jun05-10Crc		fst 5½f	:214 :46 :59 1:06	3↑ Alw 23000N1X		51	5 5	66½ 67½ 56½ 510¼	Castro E	L b	5.20	AsmAlln1201 E1204 Chncnlft118½	Hit gate, bmpd hard st	7
7Jun05-1Crc		fst 5f	:221 :461 :594	3↑ Md Sp Wt 25k		74	4 3	1½ 11 11½ 1nk	Cruz M R	L b	*.60	LoxndKpprs118nk Strk1183 SChst1181½	Prevailed, driving	6
15May05-7Crc		fst 5½f	:221 :463 :593 1:062	3↑ Md Sp Wt 25k		75	1 6	22 22 22 21¾	Cruz M R	L b	3.90	MrStrhtn1181¾ *LndKpprs* 1181¼ JhsHr118½	Off rail, 2nd best	10

WORKS: Jan28 Crc 4f fst :52 B *55/64*

TRAINER: Dirt/Turf (14 .14 $4.14) 31-60Days (38 .18 $1.11) Turf (39 .10 $1.86) Sprint (168 .15 $1.59) Alw (21 .10 $0.37)

4 City Academy

Own: Augustin Stable
White & Green Halves, White Sleeves,
Castellano J J (138 20 16 20 .14) 2005:(1158 206 .18)

B. g. 6 (Mar)
Sire: Royal Academy (Nijinsky II) $15,000
Dam: Central City*GB (Midyan)
Br: George Strawbridge Jr.(Pa)
Tr: Sheppard Jonathan E (12 1 2 2 .08) 2005:(449 68 .15)

L 120

Life	16	2	4	1	$61,161	84	D.Fst	2	0	0	0	$1,612	55
2006	1	0	0	0	$330	63	Wet (328)	0	0	0	0	$0	-
2005	8	1	3	1	$27,420	78	Turf (335)	14	2	4	1	$59,549	84
GP Ⓣ	3	1	0	0	$8,870	78	Dist (311)	7	1	2	1	$22,960	78

20Jan06-8GP fm 1 1/16 Ⓣ :22 :45 4 1:09 1 1:38 4+Alw 33000N1X 63 2 3 3 1/2 34 5 1 3/4 3 4 1/2 8 16 1/4 Rose J L 32.00 Congleve120 5 3/4 Pitchnicholas119 2 3/4 Gigger120 2 1/2 rbt 11
Lone f doms
27Nov05-7Lrl gd 5f Ⓣ :24 :47 :59 3+Alw 28000N1X 70 6 9 63 6 5 1/2 6 4 3/4 4 3 1/2 Pino M G L 1.90 NotAcclm122 3/4 SfFromHrm120 2 Ngttr120 1/2 Steadied 1/16 11
10Nov05-7Lrl fm 5f Ⓣ :21 :44 3 :56 4 3+Alw 28000N1X 68 12 12 9 7 3/4 6 4 3/4 4 1 1/2 2 1/2 Napravnik A R5 L *2.10 TthDctr122 1/2 CtyAcdmy115 1 1/2 Jzzng115 1/2 Rail,blocked 1/8 13
22Sep05-7Lrl fm 1 1/16 Ⓣ :23 3 :47 1 1:11 4 1:41 4 3+Alw 28000N1X 73 5 1hd 1 1/2 1 1 1/2 1hd 2 1 3/4 VanHassel C L 14.10 *RmorHslt* 120 1 3/4 CtyAcdmy120 3/4 Rshm113 1/2 Rail, pace, gamely 13
23Jly05-9Pha fm 5f Ⓣ :22 4 :45 4 :57 1 3+ⓈRWCamacMem50k 65 5 7 74 5 3 1/2 6 4 3/4 6 7 3/4 Flores J L L 8.10 ShdsfSnny117 3/4 Nmqst117 1 1/2 MdAnthny117 1/2 Showed little 8
16Jly05-3Cnl gd 5 1/2f Ⓣ :22 1 :45 :57 1 1:04 3+Clm 25000(25-20)N3L 68 5 7 4 4 1/2 4 6 1/2 5 7 1/2 2 4 1/4 Karamanos H A L *1.50 ThBstGsOn122 4 1/4 CtAcdm120 1/2 Fng118 3/4 Steadied, blocked 7
18Jun05-8Cnl fm 5f Ⓣ :22 :45 3 :57 4 3+Clm 25000(25-20)N3L 65 3 4 4 1 1/2 2 1 1/2 1hd 3 2 1/4 VanHassel C L *1.70 RprdrlI120 1 Crssldr120 1 1/4 CtAcd120 1 1/4 Rated bck,ins bid,fade 7
16Apr05-3GP fm 5f Ⓣ :22 :44 1 :55 3 4+Clm 30000(30-25)N2L 78 1 5 2hd 12 13 11 Trujillo E L 3.30 CtyAcdmy122 1 QtRcks122hd Sbbtcl122nk Rail, held sway 7
21Mar05-10GP fm 1 1/16 Ⓣ :23 3 :46 1:09 1:40 2 4+Clm 30000(30-25)N2L 30 12 6 5 5 11 6 13 11 15 11 12 4 1/4 Santos J A L 18.00 Double Shotgun122 1 Arteur122 3 *Sicilian Boy* 122 3 1/2 Faded 12
19Sep04-8Del fst 5f ⊗ :22 :45 1 :57 4 3+Alw 36600N1X 42 5 7 7 7 1/2 5 7 1/2 48 6 10 3/4 Pino M G L 17.70 Curb117 2 1/2 *ChifNgotitor* 117nk *Anf* 116 5 Erratic action stretch 7

WORKS: Feb8 GP 3f fst :37 B *5/7*

TRAINER: 2Off45-180 (79 .15 $1.10) Route/Sprint (31 .10 $0.71) Turf (218 .15 $1.58) Sprint (150 .10 $1.34) Alw (145 .19 $1.23)

5 Eddie C.

Own: Bruce Levy
Royal Blue, White 445, Red Sleeves,
Bejarano R (187 27 30 33 .14) 2005:(1346 264 .20)

B. c. 4 (Feb)
Sire: Flying Chevron (Carson City) $2,500
Dam: Jim's Alley Dancer (I'ma Hell Raiser)
Br: Bruce Levy(Ky)
Tr: Weaver George (15 1 3 1 .06) 2005:(254 44 .17)

L 120

Life	5	1	0	0	$21,694	88	D.Fst	1	0	0	0	$330	40
2006	2	0	0	0	$1,980	80	Wet (331)	0	0	0	0	$0	-
2005	3	1	0	0	$19,714	88	Turf (247)	4	1	0	0	$21,364	88
GP Ⓣ	3	1	0	0	$21,180	88	Dist (348)	1	0	0	0	$1,650	80

22Jan06-7GP fm 5f Ⓣ :21 :43 1 :54 3 4+Alw 33000N1X 80 7 7 87 76 32 43 Rose J Lfb 5.60 Saffir120 2 **So Savvy**120no Outer Marker120 1 rts 9
Good speed
12Jan06-9GP S- fst 1 :23 :45 3 1:10 3 1:35 2 4+Alw 33000N1X 92/95 40 6 3nk 5 2 1/2 7 6 1/2 716 729 Rose J Lfb 28.60 MonrchLne120 6 1/2 TimeOut120 5 1/2 SilverVist120 2 **3b brief bat** 7
20May05-6Bel fm 1 1/16 Ⓣ :23 :46 1 1:10 2 1:42 3+Alw 46000N1X 71 4 4 9 1/2 511 5 2 3/4 9 6 3/4 9 9 1/4 Luzzi M J L 3.95 ChfCdr111 1 1/4 CrdsDlt118no *GtWrcr* 116 2 1/4 3 wide, no response 10
24Apr05-6GP fm 1 1/16 Ⓣ :23 4 :47 1 1:10 2 1:40 3 Alw 33000N1X 68 5 2 1 1/2 21 2 1/2 3 1 1/2 6 7 1/4 Coa E M Lb *.80 HlthHd118 2 1/4 WrthS118no Tpp118 2 1/4 Bid far turn, faltered 7
20Mar05-11GP fm 1 Ⓣ :23 4 :47 1 1:10 3 1:34 2 Md Sp Wt 32k 88 11 2 1 1/2 21 2hd 1 1 1/2 1 2 1/4 Castellano J J Lb 25.80 EddieC.122 2 1/4 *ReelLegend* 122 3/4 *Kristli* 122 1/2 Drew clear, driving 12

WORKS: Feb3 PBD 4f gd :51 B *1/2* Jan7 PBD 5f gd 1:03 B *2/3* Jan1 PBD 5f gd 1:03 2 B *1/1* Dec27 PBD 5f gd 1:04 B *1/3* Dec20 PBD 5f gd 1:03 B *1/2* ●Dec13 PBD 4f gd :50 B *1/4*

TRAINER: Turf (136 .13 $1.93) Sprint (94 .13 $1.67) Alw (84 .18 $1.70)

6 So Savvy

Own: Mary Ellen Coenen
Purple, Pink Palm Tree, Purple & Pink
Olivero C A (36 2 2 4 .05) 2005:(862 97 .11)

Dk. b or br g. 4 (Feb) OBSAUG03 $29,000
Sire: Commitisize (Explodent) $2,000
Dam: Just Say Whoa (Secretariat)
Br: Christine K. Jones(Fla)
Tr: Posada Laura (19 0 1 2 .00) 2005:(263 27 .10)

L 120

Life	9	3	1	1	$35,960	83	D.Fst	7	3	0	1	$29,160	79
2006	1	0	1	0	$6,600	83	Wet (281)	0	0	0	0	$0	-
2005	8	3	0	1	$29,360	79	Turf (320)	2	0	1	0	$6,800	83
GP Ⓣ	1	0	1	0	$6,600	83	Dist (323)	1	0	1	0	$6,600	83

22Jan06-7GP fm 5f Ⓣ :21 :43 1 :54 3 4+Alw 33000N1X 83 2 2 1 1/2 11 1 1 1/2 22 Olivero C A L 22.20 Saffir120 2 So Savvy120no Outer Marker120 1 **led r vs gd spd** 9
Good speed
28Dec05-3Crc S- fst 5 1/2f :22 3 :46 1 :59 1 1:06 3+Clm 16000B 77/79 79 7 2 2 1/2 2hd 1 2 1/2 1 3 3/4 Ferrer J C L 7.30 SoSvvy120 3 3/4 MyFrindDk123 2 *Dilistr* 123 1 **2b duel inherit rs** 7
1Dec05-7Crc gd 1 Ⓣ :23 1 :47 1 1:11 1 1:34 4 Alw 20000N1X 65 5 1 1/2 1 1 1/2 1 1 1/2 3nk 6 11 1/4 Ferrer J C L 15.00 Minister'sJoy119 5 1/4 LegendryPcer119 2 3/4 *RichithKid* 119 1/2 **led r** 8
Fast sprinter dies
13Oct05-7Crc fst 6f :22 :46 :58 4 1:12 3 3+Clm 16000N2L 70 1 6 11 11 12 1 2 3/4 Toribio A Jr L 10.20 SSvvy120 2 3/4 SncrMn120 4 1/2 NtWhtn120nk Inside, drew clear 8
16Sep05-9Crc fst 6f :22 :46 :59 4 1:12 3 3+Clm 16000N2L 47 7 2 34 33 44 6 10 1/2 Cruz M R L *1.80 SlrBl123no CRDncngF111 5 1/2 QcStrd111 1 3/4 Bumped st, tired 8
30Aug05-5Crc fst 5f :23 :47 1 1:00 1 3+Md 25000 71 3 1 3 1 1/2 4 1 1/2 22 1hd Cruz M R L 1.90 SoSvvy118hd SqrPhlp118 5 1/2 WlltDnc118 1/2 Prevailed, all out 7
7Aug05-4Crc fst 6f :22 4 :47 :59 3 1:13 1 3+Md 25000 57 1 7 1 1/2 1hd 2hd 44 Cruz M R L 2.90 Sm'sPrime123 3/4 *MchGlt* 118 1 1/4 *Drivingthln* 123 2 Rail, weakened 11
16Jly05-6Crc fst 6 1/2f :22 :46 1 1:13 1 1:20 3 3+Md 25000 63 8 2 1hd 1 1/2 1 2 1/2 3 1/2 Cruz M R L 17.60 PnNsr118no Drvngthln123 1/2 SSvv118 1 Inside, gave way late 12
25Jun05-8Crc fst 6f :22 :45 4 :58 4 1:12 1 3+Md Sp Wt 25k 46 7 4 5 3 1/2 8 7 1/2 811 7 13 1/4 Cruz M R L 18.50 JstLvttM118hd GldSccss118 4 *TrfthTgr* 118 1 1/4 3 wide, faltered 8

WORKS: Nov19 Crc 4f gd :50 B *5/47*

TRAINER: Turf (66 .06 $1.16) Sprint (143 .10 $1.69) Alw (42 .05 $0.44)

7 Ultimate

Own: William J. Condren & Michael H Sherman
Gold, White Sash, White Bars on Gold
Castro E (143 8 17 14 .05) 2005:(1634 329 .20)

Ch. c. 4 (Feb) OBSAPR04 $675,000
Sire: Double Honor (Gone West) $3,500
Dam: Camptown Miss (Carr de Naskra)
Br: Farnsworth Farms(Fla)
Tr: Zito Nicholas P (44 6 7 7 .13) 2005:(462 86 .19)

L 120

Life	7	1	1	2	$46,358	91	D.Fst	6	1	0	2	$37,498	91
2005	7	1	1	2	$46,358	91	Wet (370)	1	0	1	0	$8,860	81
2004	0	M	0	0	$0	-	Turf (233)	0	0	0	0	$0	-
GP Ⓣ	0	0	0	0	$0	-	Dist (389)	0	0	0	0	$0	-

25Nov05-4CD N fst 6f :21 4 :45 4 :57 3 1:10 3 3+Alw 48955N1X 73/82 78 9 4 3 1/2 5 3/4 4 3 1/2 4 2 1/2 Bejarano R Lf 3.40 SmkWrnng118 1 1/2 JW.118nk NHvnHrbr118 3/4 5w,no final gain 9
13Oct05-7Kee GRS fst 6f :21 4 :45 4 :58 3 1:12 3 3+Alw 52000N2L 00/80 31 9 7 8 4 1/2 912 710 8 19 1/2 Bejarano R L *1.90 Jos120 1 1/2 RnwyJwl118hd AppontVctory122 2 3/4 6w, no threat 10
Duellers 1-2
30Apr05-11CD fst 1 :22 1 :45 1:10 2 1:36 DerbyTrial113k 56 4 1hd 2 1/2 22 49 5 22 1/2 Bejarano R L 7.00 Don'tGetMd116 7 Gllrdo116 3/4 Vicrg116 12 Ck start,duel,tired 7
13Apr05-5Kee my 7f :21 3 :44 4 1:11 1 1:24 2 Alw 52060N2L 81 8 8 21 1 1 1/2 2hd 26 Bejarano R L *1.40 AsmTst121 6 Ultmt121 6 3/4 Dvlmnt119 4 Forced,led,no match 9
5Mar05-10TP fst 1 1/16 :23 :46 4 1:12 1:43 4 JBttgliaMm100k 81 8 1 1/2 1 1 1/2 1hd 21 3 5 1/2 Prescott R L *1.40 MgnGrdut114 3 3/4 Pvo118 1 1/2 Ultimt114 1/2 Drifted in after start 9
7Feb05-6GP fst 7 1/2f :22 4 :46 1 1:11 1:29 4 Md Sp Wt 32k 91 10 4 1hd 11 14 18 Castellano J J L *2.80 Ultmt122 8 Rmsprn122no *Strlnprspctr* 122 1 3/4 Kept to pressure 12
6Jan05-4GP S-? fst 6f :22 :45 :56 4 1:09 1 Md Sp Wt 32k 85/93 84 12 10 54 4 1 1/2 3 2 1/2 3 3 1/2 Castellano J J L 11.70 *ArdthCp* 122 2 Prpls122 1 1/2 *Ultt* 122 6 3/4 **3t made run no punch late** 12

WORKS: Feb3 PmM 4f fst :50 B *18/34* Jan27 PmM 4f fst :48 3 H *4/35* Dec10 PmM 4f fst :51 3 B *42/50* Nov19 TTC 4f fst :49 4 B *15/35*

TRAINER: 61-180Days (58 .17 $0.88) 1stTurf (17 .00 $0.00) Dirt/Turf (21 .00 $0.00) Turf (38 .03 $0.25) Sprint (218 .16 $1.45) Alw (150 .24 $1.88)

8 Michaelistheone
Own: Long Shot Stables LLC
White, Royal Blue Braces & Half Moon,
Prado E S (111 14 21 8 .12) 2005:(1460 299 .20)

B. g. 4 (Apr) OBSJUN04 $20,000
Sire: Eltish (Cox's Ridge) $3,500
Dam: Fortune's Smile (Track Barron)
Br: Susan Seper & Kathryn Wilbanks(Fla)
Tr: Sheppard Jonathan E (12 1 2 2 .08) 2005:(449 68 .15)

Blinkers OFF L 120

Life	15	1	3	0	$36,680	80	D.Fst	7	1	0	0	$16,520 79
2006	1	0	0	0	$330	62	Wet (303)	2	0	1	0	$5,160 80
2005	11	0	3	0	$25,150	80	Turf (180)	6	0	2	0	$15,000 80
GP ⓣ	2	0	1	0	$6,930	80	Dist (347)	4	0	2	0	$13,410 80

20Jan06-6GP fm 1 1/16 ⓣ :231 :4641:102 1:394 4↑ Alw 33000N1X 62 3 43 63½ 72¾ 64 108¼ Rose J Lb 21.30 RectoryHill1222 DevilAtSe120hd TkthBluff1202½ 2t tight 2e 10
13Nov05-7Del fst 6f :22 :451 :581 1:112 3↑ Alw 42900N1X 70 8 6 66 66¾ 55½ 55¾ Pino M G Lb 9.60 FtherWeist1212½ Hrdtobthbst119½ CnrMdly119nk Evenly 8
29Oct05-8Del fst 6f :22 :451 :574 1:101 3↑ Alw 42600N1X 79 3 7 73¾ 73¾ 54½ 55 Lumpkins J Lb 14.30 Rmsprn1181 RffndRd1203½ FllEnd119nk Failed to threaten 7
12Oct05-8Del fst 6f :22 :451 :574 1:102 3↑ Alw 42900N1X 76 4 5 52 53 54¾ 45½ Castillo H Jr Lb 9.80 CtyWknd120½ Upscld1173½ Tdsc1191¾ Lacked needed rally 8
12Sep05-8Del hd 1 1/16 ⓣ :23 :4641:104 1:414 3↑ Alw 42900N1X 73 7 97½ 95¾ 64½ 45½ 57¾ Pino M G Lb 3.60 Rmtt119nk OhMyCyt1231½ R C Ind115¾ Needed closing bid 11
29Aug05-5Sar gd 5½f ⓣ :211 :441 :561 1:024 Clm 75000(100-75) 73 3 6 68¾ 611 44 54½ Prado E S Lb 3.15 TrrfcCll1192¾ NAllc1201½ Upscld120nk Inside trip, no rally 6
1Aug05-5Cnl fm 5f ⓣ :214 :443 :564 3↑ Alw 27430N1X 73 2 7 65 75½ 67¾ 24½ Napravnik A R7 Lb 4.40 EithrOrr1204½ Michlisthon1091½ Swyin1241 Swung 6wd 1/4 9
4Jly05-6Cnl fm 5f ⓣ :213 :441 :564 3↑ Alw 33410N1X 51 11 10 87¾ 87¾ 713 99½ Napravnik A R10 Lb 3.40 BrnnRmb1202¾ CrlnsPnch120nk SndbrJns120hd No factor 13
7Apr05-4GP fm 5f ⓣ :21 :431 :551 Alw 33000N1X 80 1 6 2hd 1hd 2hd 2nk Coa E M Lb 4.90 T.D.Vnc118nk Mchlsthn1182¾ SrPyy118¾ Rail duel, gamely 9
18Mar05-8GP gd 5½f ⊗ :22 :453 :58 1:043 Alw 33000N1X 65 4 6 78½ 77 76 66¾ Martin C W Lb 12.60 *MyBuddyRichie* 118nk DanIsFast1185½ HaloLad118½ Hit gate 7

WORKS: ●Feb9 GP 4f fst :47 H *1/12* Feb7 GP 4f fst :483 B *8/25*

TRAINER: 2Off45-180 (79 .15 $1.10) BlinkOff (8 .25 $0.00) Route/Sprint (31 .10 $0.71) Turf (218 .15 $1.58) Sprint (150 .10 $1.34) Alw (145 .19 $1.23)

9 Conquistador's Cat
Own: Scarlet Stable
Scarlet, Black Cross Sashes, Scarlet
King E L Jr (75 8 7 8 .10) 2005:(736 66 .09)

B. g. 5 (Mar)
Sire: Forest Wildcat (Storm Cat) $35,000
Dam: Conquista (Conquistador Cielo)
Br: Gail A. Curtsinger & Michael G. Marenchic MD(Ky)
Tr: Guciardo Kathy (1 0 0 0 .00) 2005:(70 6 .09)

L 120

Life	18	4	3	3	$53,208	82	D.Fst	17	4	3	3	$52,878 82
2006	1	0	0	0	$330	67	Wet (350)	0	0	0	0	$0 -
2005	13	2	3	3	$36,438	82	Turf (284)	1	0	0	0	$330 67
GP ⓣ	1	0	0	0	$330	67	Dist (373)	1	0	0	0	$330 67

22Jan06-7GP fm 5f ⓣ :21 :431 :543 4↑ Alw 33000N1X 67 3 3 2½ 21 53½ 66¾ Bridgmohan S X Lb 8.60 Saffir1202 So Savvy120no Outer Marker1201 2b press gd spd 9
Previously trained by Brueggemann Roger Good speed
16Dec05-7Haw N fst 6f :211 :45 :574 1:104 3↑ Alw 28000N1X 43 8 1 2hd 2½ 41¾ 616½ Meier R Lb 4.70 Scottie1227¾ MgicJde122no Rivrson120nk Off rail, gave way 10
26Nov05-7Haw N fst 6½f :221 :4541:113 1:183 3↑ Alw 28000N1X 77 3 1 13 12 11½ 2nk Meier R Lb 4.80 QcdCrft122nk CstdrsCt122½ *Wcts* 122¾ Broke sharply, caught 11
5Nov05-8Haw fst 6f :211 :451 :581 1:113 3↑ Alw 30000N1X 80 8 1 1hd 1½ 12 3½ Baird E T Lb *2.80 Frnchbrg122nk RhnChsr122nk Cnstdr'sCt1222 Held on well 11
15Oct05-8Haw fst 6½f :214 :4411:11 1:174 3↑ Alw 30000N1X 80 2 1 1hd 12 11½ 52½ Baird E T Lb 15.80 OtsRd119¾ HtsIsHt122¾ ShsprnStr122½ Off rail, weakened 12
24Sep05-3Haw fst 6f :214 :454 :581 1:11 3↑ Alw 30000N1X 72 2 1 14 13 2hd 34 Baird E T Lb 5.90 RtsHp122no DdAcct1224 CstdrsCt1222½ Inside, couldn't last 9
Previously trained by Guciardo John
4Sep05-9Mnr fst 6f :211 :441 :57 1:101 3↑ Clm 15000(15-13)N4L 82 4 1 12 13 13 14 Pereira O M Lb 6.00 CnstdrsCt1154 Trl1152½ CrsnCtStr115¾ All pace, held firm 8
6Aug05-9CT fst 4½f :213 :461 :523 3↑ Alw 26000N1X 67 1 6 42 64 42¾ Mawing M A Lb 3.60 Voryias1161 Ulloa1161 JcobndJulin116¾ Lacked closing bid 8
1Jly05-6Mnr fst 5½f :22 :461 :583 1:051 3↑ Clm 8000(10-8)N4L 82 4 1 11 11 12 2½ Pereira O M Lb *1.70 ElsDlt118½ CnstdrsCt1174½ QcL115nk Hard pace, run down 7
7Jun05-10Mnr fst 6f :214 :451 :581 1:121 3↑ Clm 5000N3L 69 10 2 1½ 15 16 13½ Pereira O M Lb *1.90 CstdrsCt1153½ AsstsfLc115no *Gtl* 1151¾ Rushed off, held safe 10

WORKS: Jan12 Tam 3f fst :381 B *8/9*

TRAINER: Turf (21 .00 $0.00) Sprint (58 .10 $1.50) Alw (15 .00 $0.00)

10 Heza Storm
Own: Star Search Stable, Inc.
Red, Black Star, Red Stars on Black
Maragh R (103 8 9 11 .07) 2005:(1086 146 .13)

Ch. c. 4 (Mar) KEESEP03 $30,000
Sire: Storm Boot (Storm Cat) $15,000
Dam: Sheza Rahy (Rahy)
Br: Mt. Joy Stables, Dan Dressel & Dan Burns(Ky)
Tr: Lee Gary (-) 2005:(1 0 .00)

L 120

Life	3	1	0	0	$22,225	75	D.Fst	2	1	0	0	$20,025 75
2005	1	0	0	0	$2,200	58	Wet (338)	1	0	0	0	$2,200 58
2004	2	1	0	0	$20,025	75	Turf (315)	0	0	0	0	$0 -
GP ⓣ	0	0	0	0	$0	-	Dist (360)	0	0	0	0	$0 -

Previously trained by Iwinski Allen
9Jan05-8Aqu gd 1 ⊡ :24 :4811:132 1:383 Alw 44000N1X 58 1 2½ 2½ 31 411 414½ Arroyo N Jr L 17.00 DndWldct1201½ *Bnsj* 1201¾ Intrln12011 Prompted pace, tired 6
20Nov04-3Aqu fst 6f :221 :46 :581 1:114 Md 75000(75-65) 75 3 1 2½ 2hd 2hd 1¾ Chavez J F L 10.20 HzStrm120¾ Brtl1165½ MttDddy1204½ Vied outside, prevail 7
11Oct04-4Bel GR- fst 6f :22 :453 :574 1:103 Md Sp Wt 45k 87/86 39 7 7 66½ 65 915 918½ Fragoso P L 58.50 Mr. Cold Call1192 Space Hero1191¾ Daddy Joe1192½ 1 slo 4t 9

WORKS: Jan26 GP 6f fst 1:154 B *3/3* Jan16 GP 5f fst 1:024 B *15/17* Jan6 GP 5f fst 1:012 B *3/9* Dec24 GP 5f fst 1:021 Bg *34/48* Dec13 Cru 5f gd 1:06 B *1/2* Dec3 Cru 5f fst 1:06 B *2/4*

TRAINER: 1stW/Trn (1 .00 $0.00) +180Days (1 .00 $0.00) Sprint (1 .00 $0.00)

11 Uncontested
Own: Carolyn M. Chapman
White & Green Blocks, White Sleeves,
Chapman K L (37 0 0 5 .00) 2005:(278 24 .09)

B. g. 6 (Feb)
Sire: Valid Wager (Valid Appeal) $5,000
Dam: Unchained Princess (Clever Trick)
Br: Richard P. Arnold(Fla)
Tr: Chapman James R (14 0 0 4 .00) 2005:(139 13 .09)

L 120

Life	7	1	1	2	$29,970	73	D.Fst	4	1	1	1	$24,270 73
2006	1	0	0	1	$990	54	Wet (366)	3	0	0	1	$5,700 73
2004	4	1	1	1	$25,560	73	Turf (330)	0	0	0	0	$0 -
GP ⓣ	0	0	0	0	$0	-	Dist (369)	0	0	0	0	$0 -

21Jan06-4GP N fst 6f :214 :443 :574 1:112 4↑ Clm 16000(16-14)N2L96/65 54 3 5 32 32½ 33½ 34½ Chapman K L Lb 4.20 BdD1172 MrStrt1222½ Uctstd124hd 2bv urge beh duel 3eoutfin 7
Previously trained by Scott Kelly Lynn Good spd; hard duellers wkn
23Jly04-10CT my 4½f :211 :444 :511 3↑ Alw 29000N1X 65 4 6 22½ 25 37 Cornwell R M Lfb 5.70 FstSlr1163¾ VrClr1163½ Uctstd116nk Well placed, no rally 10
12Jun04-7CT fst 4½f :22 :46 :523 3↑ Alw 33000N3L 69 2 6 2½ 1hd 2nk Cortez A C Lfb 8.80 PostPttrn116nk Uncontstd118¾ Stkmn1211½ Lost head bob 9
21Apr04-1CT fst 4½f :22 :463 :531 3↑ Md Sp Wt 26k 73 7 3 1½ 13½ 16½ Luzzi J B Jr Lb 5.50 Uctstd1216½ TPch121¾ Bblr121nk Moderate strtch urging 10
Previously trained by Estvanko Richard
1Apr04-6TP my 6f :22 :444 :564 1:093 3↑ Md Sp Wt 32k 54 1 4 32 42½ 48 510¾ Ouzts P W Lb 5.10 SrrCrssn1152 *Inlmnt* 1227¾ CnthnsSn122no Off inside, tired 11
Previously trained by Chapman James K
22Nov03-3Hol fst 6f :22 :451 :58 1:101 3↑ Md Sp Wt 39k 73 4 4 21½ 23½ 43½ 56½ Pedroza M A LBb 22.70 GdGld121nk *EtrMch* 1214½ BrtshBl1211 3wd into lane,wkened 7
3May03-6Hol wf 6f :214 :434 :561 1:084 3↑ Md Sp Wt 44k 73 7 6 65 66½ 65¾ 46¾ Berrio O A LB 12.40 BrhmBll117¾ *SmrtAgn* 1171 ErlySn1175 Off bit slow,outside 7

WORKS: Feb6 PmM ⓣ 4f gd :524 B (d) *4/20* Jan2 PmM 3f fst :37 B *1/3* Dec21 PmM 5f fst 1:02 B *3/10* Dec11 PmM 4f fst :48 H *3/44*

TRAINER: 2OffOver180 (5 .00 $0.00) 1stTurf (6 .00 $0.00) Dirt/Turf (24 .04 $0.81) Turf (52 .04 $0.84) Sprint (84 .12 $1.41) Alw (51 .10 $0.87)

The logical contenders in this bottom-level allowance race were an ordinary bunch. So Savvy, the favorite, had finished second against similar company in his last start but had been a $16,000 claimer before that. So I looked to find either a promising turf pedigree among the runners who hadn't previously started on the grass, or else a glimmer of talent in the other horses with turf experience. I made some exciting discoveries when I examined the race that Nacascolo had run on April 1, 2005. The event was a $50,000 claiming race at five furlongs on the grass, but the winner, Southern Cal—whom Nacascolo had chased before finishing third—was much more than a claimer. The speedster subsequently led all the way to win the $100,000 Calder Turf Sprint Handicap, and he won another stakes as well.

Southern Cal
Own: David S. Romanik
Red, Blue Hoops, Red Sleeves, Red Cap

B. g. 6 (Mar) OBSJUN03 $17,000
Sire: Halo's Image (Halo) $10,000
Dam: Biotech (Caltech)
Br: David Romanik(Fla)
Tr: Spatz Ronald B

Life	14	7	2	1	$201,290	101	D.Fst	2	0	0	0	$1,620	58
2005	7	4	0	1	$138,570	101	Wet (325)	1	1	0	0	$17,800	73
2004	7	3	2	0	$62,720	90	Turf (250)	11	6	2	1	$181,870	101

5Sep05-7Crc	yl	1	Ⓣ:223 :46 1:11 1:38	3↑ MiaMIBCH-G3	94 7 13 14 13 16 31½	Nunez E O	L119fb	*1.40	78-23	BbsPrdMt115nk DcMstr1131¼ StrCl1195¼	Shortened stride late 9
31Jly05-6Crc	gd	1	Ⓣ:223 :453 1:094 1:353	3↑ TheVid40k	98 4 12½ 13½ 14 14 1¾	Nunez E O	L118fb	*2.70	92-12	SthrCl118¾ BbsPrdMt1182 FlPrpc1232½	Shortened stride late 12
10Jly05-10Crc	yl	5f	Ⓣ:213 :444 :58	3↑ CrcTurfSpH100k	101 2 4 1½ 12 13½ 12¾	Baze R A	L117fb	9.40	83-17	*SthrnCl* 1172¾ GnRChp114hd TrLsScrt115nk	Hedge, drew clear 11
6May05-2Crc	gd	1	Ⓣ:223 :454 1:104 1:361	3↑ OC 40k/N3X -N	98 5 15 110 17 16 12¼	Nunez E O	L120fb	*1.50	89-22	*SothrnCl* 1202¼ BgLck1204 SovrgnHonor1202¾	Inside, held sway 7
9Apr05-9GP	fm	5f	Ⓣ:204 :422 :533	3↑ YankeeAffr50k	85 1 6 42 33½ 47 57½	Clemente A V	L116fb	17.60	— —	Prcrt1165¼ TrL'sScrt118½ ShthBn1161¾	Angled out, gave way 9
1Apr05-3GP	fm	5f	Ⓣ:22 :441 :56	4↑ Clm 50000(50-40)	92 2 3 11½ 14½ 11½ 13	Coa E M	L120fb	3.40	— —	SothrnCl1203 LvThtMn1201 Ncscl120nk	Bore out top stretch 8
12Feb05-6GP	fm	1	Ⓣ:222 :443 1:084 1:324	4↑ Alw 37000N3X	26 3 13½ 13 32½ 1017 1032¼	Nunez E O	L118fb	29.40	— —	BigBooster120½ Hckl118nk MorBourb1182½	Rail, used on lead 10
17Aug04-5Crc	gd	1 1/16	Ⓣ:23 :473 1:12 1:44	3↑ Alw 29000N2X	90 7 12 11 1½ 11½ 1½	Nunez E O	L117fb	4.40	79-21	SothrnCl117½ WththIrsh115hd *SvrgnHnr* 116¾	Drifted str, lasted 10
25Jly04-5Crc	sly	1 1/16	⊗:224 :47 1:131 1:493	3↑ Alw 27000N1X	73 1 14 15 12½ 11 1½	Nunez E O	L117fb	2.80	64-32	*SouthrnCl* 117½ PokyPn1147½ HloGoodby1124	Off rail, prevailed 6
4Jly04-9Crc	gd	1 1/16	Ⓣ:222 :461 1:102 1:414	Alw 27000N1X	82 5 2hd 1hd 12½ 13½ 2hd	Nunez E O	L122fb	*1.60	90-12	DsrtBordr119hd *SouthrnCl* 1221¼ GoldWyWst119nk	Just failed 9
19Jun04-4Crc	fm	1	Ⓣ:23 :463 1:104 1:353	3↑ Md Sp Wt 25k	81 3 1hd 12 12 14 14¼	Nunez E O	L117fb	*1.50	90-10	SouthernCl1174¼ Redon1222¼ *TexsRed* 117hd	Hedge, drew away 12
7May04-2Crc	fm	1 1/16	Ⓣ:224 :483 1:123 1:424	3↑ Md Sp Wt 25k	76 8 16 12 11½ 12½ 2nk	Nunez E O	L117fb	15.30	85-18	Postnuptial117nk *Southern Cal* 1171¼ Slant1172¼	Rail, just failed 10
16Apr04-7GP	fst	1 1/16	:224 :464 1:12 1:45	Md Sp Wt 32k	39 1 22½ 21½ 21½ 811 1025¾	Boulanger G	L122fb	13.80	58-17	OprBox1222¾ *SmmrBook* 1223½ *Pm'sWldct* 122nk	Chased, stopped 12
17Mar04-2GP	fst	6f	:222 :461 :584 1:114	Md 75000(80-75)	58 4 6 87¼ 63¾ 54½ 58	Boulanger G	L120fb	32.10	75-20	CourgousKing1221¾ Ortn1223¼ *Runnntothltr* 1221	Taken up late 8

Placed 4th through disqualification.

WORKS: Aug29 Crc 4f fst :512 B *61/71* ● Aug16 Crc 4f fst :48 H *1/28* Jly24 Crc 4f fst :49 B *2/25* Jly3 Crc 4f fst :503 B *25/34* Jun25 Crc 3f gd :382 B *39/52* Apr30 Crc 4f fst :50 B *22/68*

Even more revealing were the past performances of the veteran who had finished fourth in that claiming race.

True Love's Secret
Own: Feliciano Laura, Coniglio, Frank and

B. g. 9 (Feb)
Sire: Desert Secret*Ire (Sadler's Wells)
Dam: My Own True Love (Regal and Royal)
Br: Robert Bakerman (Fla)
Tr: Wolfendale Ross B(3 0 0 0 .00) 2005:(0 0 .00)

Life	67	18	7	9	$467,995	101	D.Fst	6	1	1	0	$36,796	94
2006	2	1	0	0	$16,168	85	Wet(286)	4	0	0	2	$5,751	80
							Synth	0	0	0	0	$0	-
2005	12	0	4	1	$44,180	94	Turf(289)	57	17	6	7	$425,448	101
Tam Ⓣ	1	0	0	0	$168	74	DstⓉ(280)	35	13	5	6	$328,436	101

16Feb06-10Tam	fm	5f	Ⓣ :211 :442 :561	4↑ OC 40k/N3x	74 4 6 54½ 54½ 65¾ 96	Lezcano J	L118 b	5.20	92-02	MrleysRevenge120nk *ChoticAchiever*1182 TioLup118no	Well placed, empty 10
2Jan06-6Crc	fm	5f	Ⓣ :214 :441 :56	4↑ OC 16k/N1x	85 9 1 53 22 21 12	Velasquez C	L120 b	2.50	93-09	TrueLovesSecret1202 Pth1203½ *DetourExpress*120½	Saved grnd, drew clear 10
19Dec05-5Crc	fm	5f	Ⓣ :214 :443 :56	3↑ OC 16k/N1x	79 8 2 65¼ 45 44 42	Cruz M R	L120 b	4.00	91-07	Placido120¾ Ptah120nk Sami's Majic1201	Wide late move 9
13Nov05-8Crc	fm	1	Ⓣ :232 :471 1:102 1:343	3↑ OC 25k/N2x	60 5 32 31 42 87½ 914½	Garcia J A	L120 b	4.40	82-10	FrenchCharmer1203¾ ThunderMb120¾ LoveYourWhit120¾	3 wide, faltered 10
8Oct05-5Crc	gd	5f	⊗ :221 :452 :58	3↑ HootngStar40k	80 3 5 65 65¼ 66¾ 57	Garcia J A	L118 b	7.30	91-15	Scrubs1231 Gregson123½ Bow Out1183¾	Failed to menace 7
5Sep05-10Crc	yl	7½f	Ⓣ :232 :464 1:123 1:322	3↑ OC 25k/N2x	73 11 9 2hd 1hd 1hd 76½	Garcia J A	L120 b	*1.70	68-25	Cut Back120½ Noah A.1201½ Halo Heaven1131½	Vied, gave way 11
16Aug05-3Crc	fm	1	Ⓣ :234 :481 1:12 1:354	3↑ Clm 40000	88 5 1½ 2hd 2hd 1hd 2¾	Garcia J A	L120 b	3.30	90-11	HndsomSmil123¾ TruLovsScrt120nk Cllthshrff1201	Couldn't resist winner 10
31Jly05-6Crc	gd	1	Ⓣ :223 :453 1:094 1:353	3↑ TheVid40k	86 5 35½ 36½ 34 24 45¼	Garcia J A	L118 b	15.70	87-12	SouthernCl118¾ BobsProudMomnt1182 FinlProphcy1232½	Hedge, no rally 12
10Jly05-10Crc	yl	5f	Ⓣ :213 :444 :58	3↑ CrcTurfSpH100k	92 8 7 83¼ 55 57 32¾	Velasquez C	L115 b	12.40	80-17	*SouthrnCl*1172¾ GnRummyChmp114hd TrLovsScrt115nk	Finished willingly 11
14May05-10Crc	fm	5f	Ⓣ :211 :434 :553	3↑ Reappeal40k	94 7 3 31½ 31½ 21½ 2hd	Cruz M R	L119 b	5.20	95-05	Placido119hd True Love's Secret119nk Simmer119½	Just missed 10
21Apr05-5GP	fm	5f	Ⓣ :214 :434 :55	4↑ Clm 40000(50-40)	87 6 3 2hd 1hd 1½ 2½	Cruz M R	L118 b	2.40	- -	OurWildct120½ TrueLovesSecret118½ LittlRdRockt120½	Vied, yielded late 8
9Apr05-9GP	fm	5f	Ⓣ :204 :422 :533	3↑ YankeeAffr50k	92 6 4 53½ 55½ 35 25¼	Cruz M R	L118 b	25.50	- -	Procreate1165¼ TrueLovesSecret118½ ShketheBnk1161¾	3 wide, no match 9
1Apr05-3GP	fm	5f	Ⓣ :22 :441 :56	4↑ Clm 40000(50-40)	78 4 7 77½ 610 44 44¼	Castro E	L118 b	2.30e	- -	Southern Cal1203 Love That Moon1201 Nacascolo120nk	Stumbled start 8
19Mar05-8GP	fm	5f	Ⓣ :211 :433 :544	4↑ Alw 46000NC	76 6 3 3½ 4¾ 63½ 55¾	Castro E	L122 b	11.70	- -	DH Tacirring118 DH Choose1203¼ Placido1201	3 wide, tired 8
10Jly04-7Crc	fm	5f	Ⓣ :213 :433 :552	3↑ CrcTurfSpH100k	81 10 1 41¾ 31½ 62 84½	Velasquez C	L118 b	19.60	93-04	Whenthedoveflies114hd SwiftRplic114¾ *BishopCourtHill*113½	Chased, tired 11
16May04-5Crc	gd	5f	Ⓣ :213 :434 :554	3↑ Trippi40k	85 7 2 2½ 2hd 21 34½	Garcia J A	L119 b	*1.60	90-05	Clltheshriff116½ Simmer1154 TrueLovesSecret119hd	3 wide, outfinished 8
11Apr04-9GP	fm	5f	Ⓣ :223 :444 :56	3↑ YankeeAffr50k	99 3 2 2hd 1hd 2hd 1nk	Garcia J A	L120 b	11.50	95-05	TrLovsScrt120nk TkAchncOnM1201 GhostlyNmbrs124½	Dueled, prevailed 7
24Mar04-9GP	fm	*5f	Ⓣ :22 :46 :572	4↑ Clm 40000(50-40)	86 8 1 1hd 11½ 12 1nk	Velasquez C	L118 b	*1.20	92-08	*True Love's Secret*118nk Grangeville1201¼ *Simmer*118nk	Inside, lasted 8
24Feb04-10Tam	sly	5f	⊗ :223 :452 :59	4↑ Alw 18000NC	74 1 6 2½ 21 2½ 35½	Arango L E	L119 b	8.40	85-16	MlkyWyGuy1214¼ OntoRchmond1191¼ *TrLovsScrt*119½	Got thru,bid,wknd 10

27Jan04-10Tam gd 5f ⊗ :23 :463 :584 4↑OC 40k/N3x 70 6 3 2hd 22 32 34¾ Arango L E L118 b *2.00 87- 16 HndsomHunk1181 BogHntr1183¾ TrLovsScrt118¾ Pressed pace, gave way 7
2Jan04- 5Crc fm 5f Ⓣ :213 :44 :552 4↑OC 57k/c 83 3 3 52 72 84¾ 54 Garcia J A L115 b 3.30e 93- 03 *Var*1191½ Tacirring1172 Callthesheriff117nk Steadied turn 11
20Dec03- 5Crc fm 5f Ⓣ :221 :443 :554 3↑OC 25k/N2x 94 9 4 41½ 21 22 11½ Velasquez C L119 b *1.30 95- 01 TrueLovesSecret1191½ Pegylation119¾ SpecilJudge116½ Edged away late 10
18Oct03- 5Crc gd 1⅛ Ⓣ :47 1:112 1:361 1:481 3↑FlyngPdgnH100k 65 11 22 1hd 2hd 1111 1115 Arango L E L113 b 49.60 75- 21 FrenchChrmer1201¼ LostAppl112nk DrinkTost1121 Stumbled start, faded 12
22Sep03- 5Crc fm 5f Ⓣ :21 :44 :554 3↑OC 40k/N3x 97 2 5 41¾ 21 1hd 14 Arango L E L117 b 2.10 95- 05 TrueLovesSecret1174 StrTier114hd *SwepingAnlysis*1101¼ Strong hand ride 8
1Sep03- 3Crc gd 6f :21 :441 :572 1:11 3↑NotSurpsng41k 69 5 3 78¼ 77¾ 59½ 512 Arango L E L115 b 4.90e 77- 19 *Love That Moon*1151½ Showmeitall1151½ Swift Replica1196½ Outrun 7
10Aug03- 4Crc gd 5f Ⓣ :213 :453 :58 3↑OC 25k/N2x 96 1 3 1hd 1½ 11 12 Arango L E L119 b *.70 84- 16 TrueLovesSecret1192 StrTir1173¼ KingofThivs119hd Edged clear, driving 8
25Jly03- 5Crc gd 7½f Ⓣ :23 :453 1:092 1:274 3↑NijskyScrt39k 97 5 1 11½ 2hd 11 4½ Arango L E L115 b 23.30 99 - MrLvngston115hd StormyRmn115nk CllrsMrlt115nk Gave way grudgingly 11
12Jly03- 8Crc fm 5f Ⓣ :213 :441 :553 3↑CrcTurfSpH100k 89 12 2 63¼ 62¼ 72 64½ Luzzi M J L113 b 43.60 91- 04 *Joe's Son Joey*1141¼ Callthesheriff113¾ Abderian115½ 4 wide, weakened 12
14Jun03- 3Crc fm 5f Ⓣ :221 :45 :564 3↑Linear42k 88 4 4 51¾ 52¾ 43 53¾ Cruz M R L115 b 2.70 86- 10 SwiftReplic115½ SmsConcord117¾ TourofthCt1222½ Bumped start, 3 wide 6
4May03- 9Crc fst 6f :221 :451 :573 1:104 3↑ThtsOurBck41k 74 1 1 1hd 42½ 57 613½ Castanon J L L115 b 10.40 76- 09 Danaher Steve115no Hana Highway1194½ *Built Up*1222½ Vied inside, faded 6
12Apr03- 9GP fm 5f Ⓣ :212 :433 :55 3↑YankeeAffr75k 101 11 1 31 2hd 32½ 41 Garcia J A L124 b 7.40 102 - Bop124¾ *Take Achance On Me*124hd Jeb's Wild124nk Outmoved, willingly 11
28Jly02-10Crc fm 5f Ⓣ :214 :443 :563 3↑ElGrnFrndH44k 99 1 5 32½ 32½ 21½ 12¾ Velasquez C L118 b 1.90 92- 08 TrLovsScrt1182¾ SnnyApprvl115¾ RysRcks113nk Stumbled st, drew away 10
13Jly02- 4Crc fst 5f :221 :451 :573 3↑Comet50k 94 7 3 44 41 25 25¾ Garcia J A L119 b 5.60 95- 07 GroomstckStcks1155¾ *TrLvsScrt*1192¼ HndsmSml1171¼ 4 wide, gained 2nd 7
18Jun02- 9Crc fst 6f :22 :451 :573 1:10 3↑ExclsvPlnH43k 89 5 1 42¼ 41¾ 43 45 Berrios H L113 b 9.40 89- 09 Tour oftheCat119no BuiltUp1143¾ UncleRocco1141¼ Stumbled start, tired 7
1Jun02- 1Crc fst 5f ⊗ :22 :452 :58 3↑LinearH38k 94 6 4 31 3nk 31 1no Berrios H L112 b 4.60 99- 10 TrueLovesSecrt112no UnclRocco115hd HndsomSmil118½ 3 wide, prevailed 8
13Apr02- 9GP fm 5f Ⓣ :213 :441 :553 3↑YankeeAffr75k 95 4 6 65¾ 43 42 32 Berrios H L124 b *.70e 99- 01 TexsGlitter124hd *JoesSonJoey*1182 *TrueLovsScrt*1241¾ Stdy turn, up for 3rd 6
27Mar02- 8GP fm *5f Ⓣ :224 :454 :571 4↑Alw 46000NC 96 6 3 2½ 12 11 1¾ Berrios H L116 b 3.10 93- 07 TrueLovesSecret116¾ WithAnticiption122½ UnclRocco118½ All out, lasted 6
27Feb02- 6GP fm *1 Ⓣ :251 :504 1:154 1:401 4↑Alw 38000N3x 90 5 11½ 11 1½ 1hd 51¾ Homeister R B Jr L118 b 33.00 70- 26 Megantic118¾ Whitton Court118½ Officer's Sword122½ On rail, gave way 8
11Jan02- 7GP fm *1 1/16 Ⓣ :232 :483 1:133 1:454 4↑Alw 38000N3x 62 2 1½ 2½ 22 64 915¾ Garcia J A L118 b 17.00 57- 29 *Boastful*118¾ Star Over the Bay1183¾ Junior Deputy118nk On rail, gave way 10
23Dec01-10Crc fm 5f Ⓣ :211 :433 :551 3↑GoToWillH38k 96 7 6 33 23½ 23½ 23 Garcia J A L113 b *.70e 95- 02 Kipperscope1213 TrueLovesScrt1132 FirfightrRob115nk Chased, 2nd best 10
11Nov01- 7Crc fm 5f Ⓣ :213 :442 :561 3↑Alw 32000NC 86 1 5 54½ 64¼ 44 56 Homeister R B Jr L119 b *.80e 87- 07 *Kipperscope*1193¼ UnclRocco1151¾ SjmsMdnss122½ On hedge, no response 8
14Oct01- 8Crc fm 5f Ⓣ :212 :442 :561 3↑BillORghtH38k 94 4 7 54 55 32½ 31 Homeister R B Jr L113 b 4.30 92- 12 *SejmsMdness*118½ UncleRocco115½ TrueLovsScrt113½ On hedge, slow gain 8
24Sep01- 7Crc fm 5f Ⓣ :211 :442 :56 3↑OC 25k/N2x 90 10 1 31½ 2hd 11½ 1½ Homeister R B Jr L122 b *1.60 94- 06 True Love'sSecret122½ NouGraha1151¼ AwolHoney122no 3 wide, prevailed 10
1Sep01- 2Crc fm 5f Ⓣ :211 :44 :56 3↑OC 25k/N2x 91 4 3 31½ 32½ 2hd 11½ Homeister R B Jr L122 b *.90e 94- 06 *TrueLove'sSecret*1221½ BorntoPic119hd AwolHoney1223¼ Forced wide turn 7
18Aug01- 1Crc fm 5f Ⓣ :222 :451 :563 3↑OC 25k/N2x 76 4 3 5¾ 63¾ 44½ 43 Homeister R B Jr L122 b *.60 88- 09 AwolHony1192 CrownDmond119¾ [D]VldFlght115nk Checked bkstr, stdy tn 7
Placed third through disqualification
30Jly01-10Crc fm 5f Ⓣ :221 :45 :57 3↑OC 25k/N2x 94 8 4 42¾ 32 1hd 13¼ Homeister R B Jr L122 b *1.60 89- 11 True Love's Secret1223¼ *Awol Honey*119½ *BlueGrey*119no 3 wide, drew clear 9
2Jly01- 5Crc gd 5f Ⓣ :212 :444 :571 3↑OC 25k/N2x 87 2 3 52¾ 31 1½ 11 Homeister R B Jr L122 b 2.70 88- 12 *True Love's Secret*1221 Blue Grey1192¾ *Winterfield*117½ 3 wide, drew clear 9
17Jun01- 2Crc gd 5f Ⓣ :22 :443 :564 3↑Clm 25000(25-22.5) 86 2 7 66 64¾ 22½ 11 Castellano A Jr5 L112 b 3.50 90- 10 *True Love'sSecret*1121 Roy'sRuckus117¾ AwolHoney119nk Hit gate, up late 7

WORKS: **Feb9 Crc 4f fst :503 B** *11/16* **Jan29 Crc 3f fst :38 B** *4/5* **Dec12 GP 4f fst :53 B** *34/35*

TRAINER: 61-180Days(4 .00 $0.00) Turf(27 .11 $3.91) Sprint(71 .08 $2.28) Stakes(2 .00 $0.00)

True Love's Secret was a remarkable five-furlong turf specialist; he had won a dozen races, including some modest stakes, at the distance. He did have an excuse in the April 1 race but, even so, the fact that Nacascolo finished a neck ahead of him was a notable achievement. Nacascolo's form had been considerably darkened since then. He had lost his one other try on the turf with a 10-pound apprentice aboard. Then he had raced several times on the dirt, with mostly dismal results. Now he had been absent from the races for six months. Trainer Manny Azpurua's statistics looked dismal too, but he is a better trainer than those numbers suggest and the full Formulator stats did show him with one win after a 180+ day layoff. I thought it was a positive sign that he had entered Nacascolo in an allowance race instead of a cheap claiming event. Obviously, I had to take a few things about Nacascolo on faith, but based on the form of his race against Southern Cal and True Love's Secret, I was completely confident that he was the best horse in the field.

On the morning of the race, I telephoned a few friends with whom I share opinions and said, "I know this horse looks ridiculous, but . . ." My conviction didn't waver when I looked at the tote board and saw that Nacascolo was 65–1. This, I thought, is what a longshot play is supposed to be—not a stab at a price, but a horse with solid credentials that the public is overlooking completely.

EIGHTH RACE
Gulfstream
FEBRUARY 11, 2006

5 FURLONGS. (Turf) (.53³) ALLOWANCE . Purse $33,000 FOR FOUR YEAR OLDS AND UPWARD WHICH HAVE NEVER WON A RACE OTHER THAN MAIDEN, CLAIMING OR STARTER OR WHICH HAVE NEVER WON TWO RACES. Weight, 124 lbs. Non-winners of a race other than Claiming since January 12 Allowed 2 lbs. Such a race since December 13 Allowed 4 lbs. (Condition Eligibility). (If deemed inadvisable to run this race over the Turf course, it will be run on the main track at Five and One Half Fulongs) (Rail at 48 feet).

Value of Race: $33,000 Winner $19,800; second $6,600; third $3,300; fourth $1,320; fifth $330; sixth $330; seventh $330; eighth $330; ninth $330; tenth $330. Mutuel Pool $318,021.00 Exacta Pool $215,280.00 Trifecta Pool $148,934.00 Superfecta Pool $44,351.00

Last Raced	Horse	M/Eqt. A. Wt	PP	St	$\frac{3}{16}$	$\frac{3}{8}$	Str	Fin	Jockey	Odds $1
28Dec05 3Crc⁷	Lox and Kippers	L b 4 120	2	3	1 1	1hd	12½	1nk	Cruz M R	45.20
8Aug05 8Crc⁵	Nacascolo	L b 5 120	1	4	41	4hd	41½	2¾	Leyva J C	65.10
22Jan06 7GP⁴	Eddie C.	L b 4 120	4	6	71½	7hd	6hd	31	Bejarano R	2.50
21Jan06 4GP³	Uncontested	L b 6 120	10	2	32½	21	2½	4½	Chapman K L	31.40
20Jan06 8GP⁸	City Academy	L 6 120	3	9	8hd	10	51	5¾	Castellano J J	4.60
22Jan06 7GP⁶	Conquistador's Cat	L b 5 120	8	1	2hd	33	31½	6hd	King E L Jr	20.50
22Jan06 7GP²	So Savvy	L 4 120	5	5	5½	5hd	71½	72	Olivero C A	3.70
25Nov05 4CD⁴	Ultimate	L 4 120	6	10	9½	9½	82	8¾	Castro E	3.70
20Jan06 6GP¹⁰	Michaelistheone	L 4 120	7	8	10	8hd	9hd	9¾	Prado E S	5.80
9Jan05 8Aqu⁴	Heza Storm	L 4 120	9	7	6½	61	10	10	Maragh R	23.70

OFF AT 4:21 Start Good For All But ULTIMATE. Won driving. Course firm.

TIME :43¹, :55¹ (:43.29, :55.35)

$2 Mutuel Prices:	3 – LOX AND KIPPERS	92.40	37.20	13.60
	2 – NACASCOLO		61.00	19.00
	5 – EDDIE C.			3.40

$1 EXACTA 3-2 PAID $587.70 $1 TRIFECTA 3-2-5 PAID $4,654.10
$1 SUPERFECTA 3-2-5-11 PAID $33,263.20

B. c, (Jan), by Kipper Kelly – My Own True Love , by Regal and Royal . Trainer Wolfendale Ross B. Bred by Robert Bakerman (Fla).

LOX AND KIPPERS showed speed along the rail, drew clear in the stretch, then was fully extended to last over NACASCOLO. The latter, chased the pace along the inside, eased out in the stretch and rallied to just miss. EDDIE C. reserved off the pace, angled outside the leaders for the stretch run and closed well for the show. UNCONTESTED chased the pace three wide, made a run at the winner on the turn, then gave way. CITY ACADEMY unhurried after breaking slowly, saved ground and finished willingly. CONQUISTADOR'S CAT chased the winner around the turn and weakened. SO SAVVY failed to menace. ULTIMATE was never a threat after breaking poorly. MICHAELISTHEONE raced four wide and was not a factor. HEZA STORM raced three wide and tired.

Owners– 1, Bakerman Robert; 2, Nacascolo Stud; 3, Levy Bruce; 4, Chapman Carolyn M; 5, Augustin Stable; 6, Scarlet Stable; 7, Coenen Mary E; 8, Condren William J and Sherman Michael H; 9, Long Shot Stables LLC; 10, Star Search Stable Inc

Trainers– 1, Wolfendale Ross B; 2, Azpurua Manuel J; 3, Weaver George; 4, Chapman James R; 5, Sheppard Jonathan E; 6, Guciardo Kathy; 7, Posada Laura; 8, Zito Nicholas P; 9, Sheppard Jonathan E; 10, Lee Garry F

Scratched– Southern Missile (26Jan06 9GP 4)

$1 Pick Three (2-9-3) Paid $2,196.80 ; Pick Three Pool $63,160 .

As soon as the gate opened, I knew I had been right about Nacascolo. He broke sharply, got into contention immediately, saved ground around the turn, and then took aim at the leader, the 45–1 Lox and Kippers. The pacesetter was tiring and Nacascolo was surging—but he surged too late and fell short by a neck. I didn't have the exacta and I certainly didn't have the $61 place payoff. I got nothing for my brilliant piece of handicapping—nothing but pain. As I reviewed the race and looked again at the form of Lox and Kippers, I realized I had been guilty of a terrible oversight. I had cursorily dismissed Lox and Kippers because he'd been trounced in his lone turf race and his sire, Kipper Kelly, isn't a successful sire of turf horses. But that one grass defeat had been at 1 1/16 miles, a distance too far for the speedster under any conditions. When I looked again at the name of the colt's dam, I saw my mistake. My Own True Love, dam of Lox and Kippers, was also the dam of True Love's Secret, the 12-time turf winner I had seen in Nacascolo's past performances. With a notable turf pedigree on the female side, combined with his good speed on the dirt, Lox and Kippers was the horse I should have been afraid of. I could have crushed the exacta. Although I pride myself for the ability to shake off any defeat, no matter how costly, I was rattled by this one for days and I still haven't forgotten it. The performance of Nacascolo had certainly vindicated my judgment and underscored the importance of digging deep into a turf horse's past performances, but that was small consolation.

Digging into Dirt Form

I use Formulator more extensively for grass races than for dirt, because the Beyer Speed Figures in dirt races tell me most of what I need to know about the quality of a horse's performance and his competition. If a horse has earned a speed figure of 80, or 90, or 100, I understand his level of ability, and there is usually no need to make a painstaking study of the horses he has been facing.

Of course, Formulator offers many other tools for analyzing both dirt and turf races—by putting result charts at the user's fingertips. When I encounter a horse in a dirt race with whom I am not familiar, the first thing I want to know is whether he raced over a track with a bias that could have affected his performance. With Formulator I can easily look at the charts from all the races on the day a horse ran, read the footnotes, and judge if the track was speed-favoring, rail-favoring, etc. If a bias did appear to exist, I will assess the horse's performance accordingly.

Reading the chart of a horse's previous race will also yield vital information about the way the pace of the race may have affected his performance. Many handicappers use the term "race shape" to describe the way a race unfolded. If the leaders ran 1–2 all the way around the track, the pace may have favored speed horses and hindered closers. Conversely, if the top finishers all rallied from far behind, the pace of the race probably helped them and hurt the speed horses in the field. Those speedsters should be upgraded the next time they run.

When I am evaluating a speed horse, I glance through the charts of his previous races to see how his early fractions compare with other races on the card. If he was going head-and-head for the lead, I use Formulator to call up the past performances of the rival or rivals with whom he was battling. If a horse has been in a destructive speed duel with another very fast front-runner—the type who gets the early lead in almost all of his starts—he may be an excellent bet in a field with a less competitive pace. On the other hand, if a horse made the lead in a recent race without encountering much pace pressure, I'll downgrade him.

The recent versions of Formulator also offer a feature that enables users to do something that has never been practical before: to examine the Beyer Speed Figures and judge whether the number is a solid reflection of a horse's ability or whether it may be ambiguous.

Although I would like to declare that every one of our numbers has the authority of Holy Writ, there are situations when the fig-makers are uncertain about their own numbers. The last two races on a card appear very slow: Did both fields run poorly or did the track itself change? A horse runs a race so fast that his figure seems utterly implausible: Is the big figure legitimate or the result of some aberration? In such cases, we will make notes that the figure is questionable and we will monitor the subsequent performances of horses coming out of the race. Sometimes we will conclude that we need to adjust the original number. In the meantime, handicappers may be basing decisions on a number that is too high or too low.

Even people who aren't figure-oriented handicappers need to examine horses with a toweringly superior speed figure. If, say, a horse improved sharply to earn a figure of 106 in his last start, and his rivals have never run a number better than the mid-90s, that top-figure horse is going to be a solid favorite. The key to the race is knowing whether that 106 is legitimate.

Although we regularly make adjustments of published figures that attract little attention, a high-profile case arose in the 3-year-old prep races for the 2007 Kentucky Derby. The previously unheralded colt Summer Doldrums ran a smashing race to win the Whirlaway Stakes at Aqueduct by more than five lengths. If his fast time was taken at face value, he would earn a Beyer Speed Figure of 106, making him one of the top contenders for the Derby. This is the way the speed figures of the top four finishers in the Whirlaway compared with their previous starts.

WHIRLAWAY	3 PREVIOUS RACES		
Summer Doldrums 106	90	65	87
Sir Whimsey 97	77	74	83
Sports Town 95	75	84	81
Brass Run 87	79	47	34

Was the 106 plausible? Could four horses all have improved sharply to run the best races of their lives at the same time? My partner Mark Hopkins, who is responsible for our New York figures, was dubious, but he also knew that 3-year-olds often do improve suddenly and unexpectedly early in the season. Hesitantly, he credited Summer Doldrums with his 106, the fastest figure of the year by a 3-year-old. (Other speed-figure services also gave the race a high rating; Summer Doldrums earned a 2 ¾ on the Ragozin Sheets.)

Summer Doldrums next ran in the Gotham Stakes on March 10. Sir Whimsey, the runner-up in the Whirlaway, was in the field, too. Because of the big figure, Summer Doldrums was the 1.15–1 favorite. These were the past performances of the colt and his main rival:

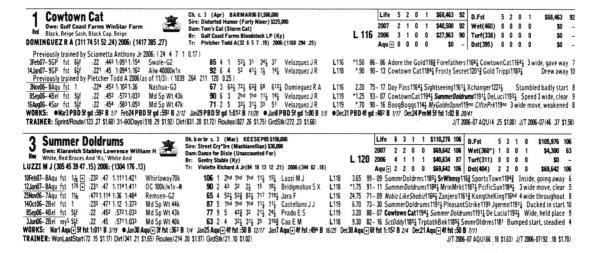

Cowtown Cat won the Gotham comfortably, even though he earned a modest Beyer Speed Figure of 98. Summer Doldrums was third, with a figure of 84, and Sir Whimsey was farther behind. On the basis of these results, Mark sharply reduced the figure of the Whirlaway. We'll never know the reason, but the fast time of the Whirlaway was phony.

For most of the years that the Beyer Speed Figures have been published, readers have not had a convenient way to examine a race as I did the Whirlaway Stakes—by comparing the numbers in a race with those that the horses earned before and after. Formulator 4.1 incorporates a feature that enables users to do just that—and lets them probe more deeply into figures that appear questionable. On June 2, 2007, handicappers studying the Aristides Stakes at Churchill Downs might have been skeptical of the big figures belonging to an invader from Mountaineer Park.

```
5 Fabulous Strike                               Dk. b or br g. 4 (Apr)                                      Life  11 7 1 0  $278,250 119 D.Fst      7 5 0 0  $196,525 118
  Own: Tea Party Stable, Inc.                   Sire: Smart Strike (Mr. Prospector) $75,000                 2007   1 1 0 0   $48,750 118 Wet (393)  3 2 1 0   $81,125 119
5-2 Brown and white quarters, green dots on     Dam:  Fabulous Find (Lost Code)                      L 120  2006   9 6 1 0  $229,345 119 Turf (347) 1 0 0 0     $600  83
Dominguez R A (2 0 0 0 .00) 2007:(500 133 .27)  Br:   Tea Party Stable, Inc.(Pa)                            CD     0 0 0 0        $0   - Dist (383) 6 4 1 0  $166,450 119
                                                Tr:   Beattie Todd M (-) 2007:(167 52 .31)

5May07-9Mnrfst 5f    :221 :45      :57  3↑PanhandleH75k  118 3 1  1hd 11½ 15 16½ Whitney D G  L126f *.30 95-20 FblsStrk1266½ SmMntn1181 BrnBl1178  Never asked,much best 4
26Dec06-8Mnrmy 6f    :214 :451 :571 1:101 3↑Christmas75k  119 7 2  1½ 12 17 111 Whitney D G  L122f *.10 93-23 FblsStrk12211 Yctn1241¾ CbHrdr1212½  Much best, under wraps 7
21Nov06-9Mnrfst 6f   :221 :451 :57 1:093 SophSprChm75k    115 1 1  11 11 15 18¾ Whitney D G  L122f *.40 96-29 FblsStr1228¾ TlntSrch1152¼ McSnst1175½  In charge, won easily 8
7Oct06-7Phawf 6f     :213 :433 :552 1:082 GallntBobH97k    104 1 2  11 2hd 21 22½ Vega H  L119f *.40 95-14 Dblcl1182½ FblsStrk1199 WlddDrmr1131¾  Set pace, outfinished 4
21Sep06 7Mthgd 6f Ⓣ :204 :434      :564 RstoratioN60k    83 3 6  12½ 11½ 11¼ 57½ Vega H  L121f 2.00 83 04 SmrtEnh121nk InStn121hd WldR121?  Bumped start, inside 6
7Jly06-8Bel fst 6f   :222 :444 :561 1:083 ZiggysBoy65k     108 3 2  1½ 1½ 15½ 13¼ Vega H  L123f *.95 95-13 FblsStr1233¼ Lmbrg116nk SntDmn1184¼  Set pace, drew away 5
10Jun06-8Bel fst 7f  :221 :444 1:084 1:212 WStphnBC-G2     97 4 3  11½ 1½ 1hd 42¾ Vega H  L119f 7.70 91-08 Sngstr1232 TMchBlng123¾ Nnmr115no  Between foes, weakened 7
10May06-3Bel fst 6½f :22 :443 1:082 1:144 RomGuc65k        102 5 2  1hd 1½ 13½ 11¾ Vega H  L116f 3.30 98-12 FblsStr1161¾ Dntfrthrpr1161 SntDmn1166½  Vied outside, clear 5
8Apr06-9Phasly 6f    :214 :452 :572 1:092 Alw24150N1X      95 6 2  11 11½ 14 16¼ Vega H  L118f *.80 93-16 FblsStr1186¼ CrlK1167¼ Strcldsthr1165¾  Ridden out to draw off 9
23Feb06-2Penfst 5½f  :22 :452 :571 1:031 Md Sp Wt 16k     85 3 2  21 21 1hd 15¾ Perez E R  L122 *1.50 100-13 Fabulous Strike1225¾ Galano1225¾ Shifty Five1221¼  2 wide, driving 8
   Previously trained by Downing William 2005(as of 12/27):(87 19 12 12 0.22)
27Dec05-5Tamfst 6f   :222 :46 :584 1:12  Md Sp Wt 18k     51 11 4  127½ 96½ 75½ 58 Castillo O O  120f 40.70 82-14 MrdOr1201¾ AtltcP1201¼ FlrdJcPt1203¾  Passed tiring rivals 12
WORKS: May26 CD 5f fst :593 B 2/24  Apr29 Pen 5f fst :593 H 1/2  Apr21 Pen 5f fst 1:004 B 6/30  Apr7 Pen 4f fst :484 H 3/37  Mar31 Pen 4f fst :493 B 7/15
TRAINER: 20ff45-180 (75 .37 $1.87) WonLastStart (146 .30 $2.04) Dirt (522 .33 $2.18) Sprint (452 .33 $2.21) GrdStk (1 .00 $0.00)    J/T 2006-07(6 .50 $2.53)
```

Fabulous Strike had earned a figure of 118 in his first start of the year, after running a pair of blockbuster numbers the previous season. If the 118 was accurate, he would trounce his stakes rivals at Churchill. Could a horse from the boondocks really be this good? Formulator users could answer this question quickly, by opening the chart of Fabulous Strike's last race and then clicking on "Beyer Figures" from a dropdown menu. This action produces a version of the chart that shows the figure a horse earned in the current race, the figures he earned in his previous 10 starts, and the figure he earned in his subsequent start, if available. The report for the Panhandle Stakes at Mountaineer looked like this:

Ninth Race
Mountaineer
May 5,2007

5 Furlongs. PANHANDLEH75K. Purse $75,000 FOR THREE YEAR OLDS AND UPWARD. Money to be divided: $45,000 to Winner; $15,000 to Second; $7,500 to Third; $3,750 to Fourth; $1,875 to Fifth; $1,125 to Sixth and $375 for Seventh and Eighth. TROPHY TO THE WINNING OWNER.

Value of Race: $75,000 Winner $48,750; second $15,000; third $7,500; fourth $3,750. Mutuel Pool $750,000

LastRaced	Horse	Next	Chart	1 Bk	2 Bk	3 Bk	4 Bk	5 Bk	6 Bk	7 Bk	8 Bk	9 Bk	10 Bk	Odds $1
26Dec06 8MNR 1	**Fabulous Strike**		118	119	115	104	83	108	97	102	95	85	51	.30
24Mar07 9FG 3	*Smoke Mountain*	NA	98	99	88	100	101	98	62	73	72	67	56	2.50
10Mar07 10TAM 4	Bernie Blue	NA	94	76	87	70	94	88	93	92	90	100	96	7.30
06Oct06 8TDN 1	I Cant Refuse		69	86	79	84	89	87	86	82	81	81	77	15.20

OFF AT 10:32 Start Good, Won Handily. Track Fast.
TIME :221, :45, :57 (:22.35, :45.10, :57.18)

$2 Mutuel Prices:				
	4--FABULOUS STRIKE	2.60	.00	.00
	3--SMOKE MOUNTAIN		.00	.00
	2--BERNIE BLUE			.00

Gelding Dark Bay or Brown; 2003; Smart Strike-Fabulous Find (Lost Code) Bred By:Tea Party Stable, Inc. (Pennsylvania)
FABULOUS STRIKE broke alertly, raced off the rail setting the pace while in hand, began to widen in upper stretch, was never asked for best and won being geared down in the final sixteenth. SMOKE MOUNTAIN was outrun to top of the stretch, came wide for the stretch drive, gave a belated rally to get up for the place position but was no threat to the winner. BERNIE BLUE hustled, pressed FABULOUS STRIKE to mid turn, chased under a drive from the quarter pole, was no match and got out finished late, settled for the show position. I CANT REFUSE raced up close to mid turn, could not keep up leaving the quarter pole, gave way in upper stretch.

Owners—1, Tea Party Stable Inc; 2, Fletcher Charles W; 3, Pyrite Stables; 4, Bosley Arthur M
Trainers—1, Beattie Todd M; 2, Autrey Cody; 3, Feliciano Miguel A; 4, Bosley Arthur M
Scratched—Kelp(04Apr07 6LRL 1),Wild Geese(21Apr07 3GP 3),Gregson(29Mar07 2GP 3)

As Fabulous Strike earned his figure of 118 in a runaway, second-place Smoke Mountain received a figure of 98 in defeat. Smoke Mountain had run figures between 98 and 101 in four of his five previous starts, so the big number for the race was perfectly plausible. Fabulous Strike's giant figures in 2006 were similarly confirmed by the horses behind him. When Fabulous Strike was entered in the Aristides, DRF reporter Marty McGee interviewed me about the figures, and I told him, "We put these figures under a microscope and they're solid as a rock." Indeed they were: Fabulous Strike narrowly missed breaking the six-furlong track record as he won at Churchill.

When a handicapper sees an eye-catching figure like Fabulous Strike's, we have probably put them under a microscope already, and we hope in most cases they are solid as a rock. But by using Formulator, a handicapper can identify big figures that haven't been confirmed, and should perhaps be viewed with skepticism—as was the case with Summer Doldrums.

Recording Notes

Many horseplayers first embraced Formulator because it lets them store their personal notes about a horse and imbed them in his past performances. In the past I wrote my notes for a race on each day's program; before handicapping a card, I spread out all my old programs and laboriously transcribed the notes onto the past performances in the *Daily Racing Form.* Now I enter everything into Formulator: my notations about track bias; my rudimentary pace figures; overall comments about a race or the quality of the field; and, most important, my trip notes—comments on the way a horse ran his race. The information is preserved forever, long after a horseplayer with imperfect memory might have forgotten it.

The notes are incorporated into Formulator underneath the regular comment line in the past performances:

My comment on Stylish Joe's last race begins R-Speed 1-2-3—with *R* signifying a trip note for the entire race (adding an *N* would mean a normal, unbiased race-track) and *Speed 1-2-3* indicating that three speed horses dominated the race. "R duel drop back to stlk 3t just up" suggests that Stylish Joe had a relatively easy trip. He eased back to sit behind the two other speedsters and barely wore them down. In his previous race he had a tough trip: He was battling for the lead five-wide and a closer rallied to beat all the speed horses. The power to save and store so much information so conveniently marks a major change in the mechanics of handicapping. Of course, acquiring this information and building up a storehouse of trip data requires scrutinizing a lot of races. This is a process that has been affected by another great revolution in the game.

STREAMING VIDEO

Sometimes great changes occur so gradually that we barely notice them, until one day we wake up and see that a revolution has occurred before our eyes. Such is the case with one of the most important developments in handicapping: the availability of horse races (and, in particular, race replays) on the computer screen.

When Youbet.com was in its infancy, and put horse races on-line for the first time, I gave the product a scathing review in my *Washington Post* column. The videos looked like a herky-jerky Charlie Chaplin movie. Sometimes the horses would be heading to the finish line and the video would come to a complete stop. When I expressed my disappointment, Youbet officials told me, "Just wait." The necessary technology didn't exist yet, but it was coming. When streaming video got past the herky-jerky stage, it wasn't good enough for a trip handicapper to see the important nuances of the action in a horse race. But the technology kept getting better—bandwidth increased and a vital piece of software known as the codec improved. In early 2006 I was watching races on a new laptop computer and realized that I could see the action almost as sharply as I could on a videotape.

Ever since the mid-1970s, when I decided to learn about trip handicapping and started watching races intently, seeing the races was never easy. At first the only place to see them was at the racetrack—one live view and one replay. When some tracks put a replay show on television, and many of those shows were available on DirecTV, handicappers could tape them—but they didn't have access to the vital head-on camera shots. Now, at Youbet.com, Racereplays.com, and some individual tracks' websites, a handicapper can watch the replays for almost any race he wants.

There is no source of racing information more important than replays—particularly for handicappers who want to identify longshots with solid merit. The vast majority of modern-day bettors rely on published data. Some of the biggest players bet strictly with computerized systems that allow for no subjective observations. In the age of simulcasting, most bettors don't have time to make notes on dozens of races per day. Fewer horseplayers are trying to make assessments of horses through visual observations. So the player willing to pore over race videos can come up with nuggets of information that give him an edge over the crowd.

Watching races intelligently and critically is a demanding and time-consuming undertaking. Realistically, a horseplayer won't have the time to watch a film of every horse in every race on a card he is handicapping. But there are certain circumstances where review of the films is apt to be most important:

1. When the comment line in the past performances indicates some trouble. The chart callers who write the footnotes to the official charts are individuals who may see races differently and whose comments may understate or overstate trouble that befell a horse during a race. One chart caller may use the term "steadied" to describe an inconsequential, momentary hesitation by the jockey. Another "steadied" may denote an event serious enough to cost a horse the race.

How should a handicapper interpret "Bmp start, empty late," the comment on Looky Yonder's racing debut?

7 **Looky Yonder**	Dk. b or br. f. 3 (May) KEESEP05 $25,000		Life	1 M 0 0	$2,400 72	**D.Fst**	1 0 0 0	$2,400 72
Own: Lansdon B. Robbins, III	Sire: **Johannesburg** (Hennessy) $65,000		2006	1 M 0 0	$2,400 72	**Wet (328)**	0 0 0 0	$0 –
3–1 White, Maroon & Blue Emblem, Maroon	Dam: **Victorian Angel** (Vice Regent)		2005	0 M 0 0	$0 –	**Turf (278)**	0 0 0 0	$0 –
Cruz M R (123 10 11 9 .08) 2006:(1617 323 .20)	Br: James Millar & Janice Millar(Ky)	L 121	GP	0 0 0 0	$0 –	**Dist (280)**	1 0 0 0	$2,400 72
	Tr: McPeek Kenneth G (24 3 3 1 .12) 2006:(144 25 .17)							

25Nov06–6CD fst 7f :23 :46² 1:11¹ 1:24 ℗ Md Sp Wt 46k 72 4 12 3 2½ 6 1½ 3nk 4 1 Castro E L120 12.20 81–15 MssBrwHH120hd EllBrd120¾ Quot120no Bmp start, empty late 12
*R–N

WORKS: Feb10 PmM 5f fst 1:01³ H 5/19 ● Jan31 PmM 4f fst :47³ H 1/15 Jan25 PmM 4f fst :48 H 4/19 ● Jan19 PmM 5f fst 1:00³ H 1/13 Jan12 PmM 4f fst :48¹ H 2/37

TRAINER: 61–180Days (16 .06 $0.33) 2ndStart (26 .23 $3.21) Dirt (121 .14 $2.13) Sprint (61 .15 $1.81) MdnSpWt (70 .21 $3.10) J/T 2006–07 GP (8 .00 $0.00) J/T 2006–07(8 .00 $0.00)

The comment sounds innocuous, but the replay of the race conveys another impression. Looky Yonder was bumped and knocked back to last place, three lengths behind the field. She rushed along the rail and almost got up to second place when she found herself in a bit of traffic. After angling out for running room in the stretch, she battled between horses before succumbing in the final yards. This was a performance that stamped the maiden as a potential stakes horse. A handicapper had to see it to appreciate it. Looky Yonder won her next start comfortably at Gulfstream as the 2–1 favorite.

2. When a maiden has run only one or two previous races. If a horse encounters trouble or otherwise has a difficult trip in his racing debut, he might possess talent that is totally concealed from the vast majority of handicappers. If he was never in contention, the chart callers might overlook the horse entirely. If he was far back in the field, he might not even be visible in the standard pan shot with which tracks televise their races. When dealing with maiden races, bettors should make the effort to watch the head-on films that may reveal longshots with well-hidden virtues—horses such as M J in the Garden.

7	**M J in the Garden**		Ch. g. 3 (Apr) OBSWIN05 $17,000		Life	1 M 0 0	$81	24	D.Fst	1 0 0 0	$81	24
	Own: Narciso Ubide		Sire: Impeachment (Deputy Minister) $1,500		2007	1 M 0 0	$81	24	Wet (367)	0 0 0 0	$0	–
15–1	Blue, Orange Chevrons, Yellow Sleeves	$8,000	Dam: Mrs. Kensington (Citidancer)	120	2006	0 M 0 0	$0	–	Turf (325)	0 0 0 0	$0	–
	Iturrez A (4 0 1 0 .00) 2006:(7 0 .00)		Br: Lawrence D. Shaffer DVM(Fla)		Tam	1 0 0 0	$81	24	Dist (313)	1 0 0 0	$81	24
			Tr: Rodriquez Julie C (1 0 0 0 .00) (–)									

4 Jan07 10 Tam fst 6f :23 :47 :59³ 1:12⁴ Md 8000(8–7)   24 712 118½ 76¾ 77¾ 6 15½ Iturrez A   120   61.50 68–15 LnEro120⁵½ *TodoTrrno* 120⁶½ SprPrtnr 120¹½   Passed tiring rivals 12

WORKS: Nov25 OTC 4f fst :49⁴ B *3/11* ● Nov18 OTC 5f fst 1:04² B *1/5*   Nov11 OTC 5f fst 1:05¹ B *4/7*

TRAINER: Dirt (1 .00 $0.00)   Sprint (1 .00 $0.00)   MdnClm (1 .00 $0.00)   J/T 2006–07 TAM (1 .00 $0.00) J/T 2006–07 (1 .00 $0.00)

In January 2007, I was studying a cheap maiden-claiming race at Tampa Bay Downs because it was part of a twin trifecta—my favorite wager—with a small carryover. The field could hardly have been more dismal; nobody had ever earned a Beyer Speed Figure higher than 33. I knew I wasn't going to find the next Secretariat in this bunch, but I hoped to find in the films a horse who showed even a glimmer of ability. And I did.

The pan shot of his racing debut revealed almost nothing about M J in the Garden. But the head-on shot showed the first-time starter going left and right while his jockey held on, evidently trying to figure out what the green youngster was going to do next. When he turned into the stretch, though, M J in the Garden got his act together and passed a few of the stragglers in the field to finish sixth. He had shown enough to make me think that he was capable of improving his figure by 10 points or so—which might be good enough to win. In fact, he improved even more, running a figure of 44 that enabled him to trounce the field and produce a $52.20 win payoff.

3. **When a race is part of a pick six or other wager with a carryover.** Studying the films of races is hard, time-consuming work. It is impractical to watch every relevant past race of every horse in a field. Inevitably, even the most disciplined and energetic handicapper is going to fail to watch a race and realize, after the fact, that he missed seeing a trip that produced, say, a $52.20 winner. But when big money is at stake in a pick six, handicappers should leave no stone unturned. Nobody wants to look back and realize that an oversight cost him a $100,000 payoff.

Watching races skillfully is an art. It requires diligent study, experience, and an eye capable of seeing nuances that other race-watchers might miss. I devoted an entire book, *The Winning Horseplayer,* to the subject of trip handicapping, and it is not a subject that can be covered meaningfully in a few paragraphs or pages. But for people who want to improve their race-watching skills, I can offer a few precepts.

Pay special attention to the start of a race

More meaningful trouble occurs at the starting gate than at any other point of Thoroughbred races. Horses routinely bump each other in the first few strides. In almost every race, one or two horses will break a step slow—or sometimes several lengths slow. Sometimes these incidents are inconsequential, but when they happen to a horse with natural early speed they can ruin his performance. The aforementioned Looky Yonder was a perfect example: Horses who have early trouble, and then try to make a fast sustained run to get back into contention, usually fail—and often make good bets when they race again.

5 **Image of Mom**		Ch. f. 3 (Jan)	Blinkers ON	Life	1 M	0	0	$380	44	D.Fst	1	0	0	0	$380	44
Own: Alters Racing Stable Inc		Sire: Halo's Image (Halo) $7,500		2007	1 M	0	0	$380	44	Wet(331)	0	0	0	0	$0	–
Green Gold, Brown Boxing Gloves, Brown Braces		Dam: Withmom'sapproval (With Approval)	L 121	2006	0 M	0	0	$0	–	Synth	0	0	0	0	$0	–
		Br: Happy Alter (Fla)								Turf(271)	0	0	0	0	$0	–
VELASQUEZ C (438 67 52 53 .15) 2006: (1519 237 .16)		Tr: Spatz Ronald B(38 3 3 2 .08) 2006:(197 28 .14)		GP ⊕	0 0	0	0	$0	–	Dst⊕(355)	0	0	0	0	$0	–

25Feb07–6GP   fst   6f   :21³ :44¹ :57 1:10³   ⊕Md Sp Wt 38k   **44** 4 12 88½ 7¹³ 6¹⁰ 7¹²½ Velasquez C   L121f   9.20   76– 13 LdyMrlboro121½ *PrincssJn*121¹½ DniTomBoy121³½   Poor st, bumped bkstr 12
WORKS: Mar19 Crc 4f fst :50¹ B *8/20*   Mar12 Crc 4f fst :50⁴ Bg *12/27*   ●Feb16 Crc 5f gd 1:00 H *1/6*   Feb7 Crc 4f fst :48¹ H *3/18*   Jan31 Crc 4f fst :52³ B *39/43*   Jan13 Crc 5f fst 1:04 B *26/37*
TRAINER: 2ndStart(14 .07 $5.29)   1stTurf(14 .14 $5.96)   1stBlink(10 .00 $0.00)   Dirt/Turf(30 .17 $4.55)   BlinkOn(14 .07 $0.29)   31-60Days(61 .15 $0.93)   J/T 2006-07 GP(10 .30 $3.62)   J/T 2006-07(10 .30 $3.62)

The most intriguing single trip I saw at the 2007 Gulfstream meeting was one delivered by a first-time starter named Image of Mom. I watched the replay of her maiden race half a dozen times to appreciate everything that happened to the 3-year-old. My notes read, "2 slo, rush, bumped hard t—has big speed." The filly broke two lengths behind the field and then accelerated sharply to race into contention—and she did it in a fast-paced race, with the leader going the first quarter-mile in 21.75 seconds. She got into traffic on the turn and weakened thereafter. But the quickness she displayed after her bad break suggested that she would be a formidable front-runner if she got out of the gate cleanly. Image of Mom made her next start at five furlongs on the turf and led all the way, paying $11.80.

Watch for horses being "shuffled"

Even casual race-watchers pay attention to the dramatic instances of bad luck that can befall a horse during the running of a race. He gets badly blocked; he clips another horse's heels; he is caught in traffic, forcing the jockey to grab the reins and drop back sharply. But trip handicappers learn from experience that the most eye-catching instances of trouble are frequently the least productive. When everybody at the track sees the same event, and everybody puts the same name on a "horses to watch" list, the horse with the troubled trip is often absurdly overbet when he runs again.

There is one form of serious trouble, however, that fans as well as chart callers regularly overlook. It most often happens when a horse is racing on the rail, in the middle of the pack. One of the leaders starts to fade, and he forces the horse behind him to drop back. The jockey doesn't stand up or snatch the reins, but he essentially puts his mount into a neutral gear and drops back. Sometimes he loses many lengths. Yet because the rider doesn't overreact, the trouble goes unnoticed. Shuffling is one of the most productive types of trouble.

5 **Ballado's Thunder**	B. f. 3 (Feb) KEESEP04 $270,000		Life	2 M 0 0	$800	64	D.Fst	1 0 0 0	$400	54
Own: Stan E. Fulton	Sire: Saint Ballado (Halo) $125,000		2006	2 M 0 0	$800	64	Wet (373)	0 0 0 0	$0	–
5–1 Lime green, white 'F' on blue ball,	Dam: Instinct (Thunder Gulch)	L 120	2005	0 M 0 0	$0	–	Turf (299)	1 0 0 0	$400	64
Baze T C (116 10 11 12 .08) 2006:(713 75 .11)	Br: Robert B. Raphaelson & Richard & Michell e Simo		Dmr	1 0 0 0	$400	54	Dist (381)	0 0 0 0	$0	–
	Tr: Becerra Rafael (14 2 1 5 .14) 2006:(112 16 .14)									

28 Jly06–5 Dmr fst 6f   :21⁴ :44⁴ :57² 1:10¹ 3↑ⒻMd Sp Wt 54k   54 1 7   73½ 87½ 8¹² 6¹² Baze T C   LB 119   15.90 76–17 DelMrCt119¼ Tizzy'sTune119⁴½ SilkQun1145   Bit tight 3/8,no bid   9
                                                                                                                              *R–N 86/85 *T–urge g tight rb shuf to last(5L+) 4s some gain

10 Jun06–8 Hol fm 5½f①:21² :44   :56 1:02² 3↑ⒻMd Sp Wt 46k   64 1 6   4³ 5⁴ 77¾ 95½ Baze T C   LB117f   17.40 86–09 StylishWldct 112¹½ TllyPht124½ QltyStff 117½   Rail trip, weakened   9

WORKS: Aug18 Dmr 5f fst :59² H 7/45   Aug12 Dmr 5f fst 1:00¹ H 28/70   Aug6 Dmr 4f fst :46¹ H 3/58   Jly22 Dmr 5f fst 1:00 H 10/73   Jly14 SA 5f fst 1:01² H 48/76   ● Jly8 SA 5f fst :59³ H 1/41

TRAINER: 2Off45–180 (25 .24 $3.12)   Sprint/Route (36 .14 $0.82)   Dirt (243 .16 $1.47)   Routes (126 .15 $1.50)   MdnSpWt (53 .08 $0.72)   J/T 2005–06 DMR (7 .00 $0.00) J/T 2005–06 (32 .06 $0.62)

My comment read: "urge g tight rb shuf to last (5L+) 4s some gain." The jockey was hustling Ballado's Thunder out of the gate until his mount ran into traffic. Then, as another horse backed into her face, the filly was shuffled to the rear of the field. I estimated that she had lost more than five lengths because of this trouble—a much more serious assessment than the "Bit tight" comment in the official footnote. Despite these misadventures, the filly was gaining some ground four-wide at the finish. Few trip notes will be as pregnant with meaning as this one, and few will be as productive: Ballado's Thunder came back against many of the same rivals in her next start and won, paying $38.80.

Understand the special nature of turf races

Most trip handicappers concentrate their attention on turf races, because the dynamics that affect all Thoroughbred races are magnified on the grass. Pace is certainly important on dirt, but on turf it frequently determines the outcome of a race. Many grass races are characterized by an extremely slow pace that hinders the chances of horses who prefer to rally from far behind. Conversely, fast-paced grass races regularly allow the closers to dominate while the speed horses collapse. Every performance on grass needs to be viewed in the context of the race's pace dynamics.

Losing ground on turns is especially significant on turf. The rough rule of thumb is that a horse travels an extra length for each horse-width by which he is removed from the rail on a turn. (In others words, if four horses are abreast around a turn, the widest horse is said to be in the "four path," and he is three widths removed from the rail. He has traveled three extra lengths.) I believe that this calculation overstates the impact of wide trips on dirt, but every foot of lost ground matters on grass. That is why top jockeys always try to secure a position on or near the rail in the early stages of turf races. And that is why trip handicappers always note horses' positions on the turns.

11 Einstein (Brz)
Own: Midnight Cry Stable
Black and Blue Diagonal Quarters, Black
Albarado R J (343 78 57 49 .22) 2006:(1069 175 .16)

Dk. b or br h. 5 (Oct)
Sire: Spend a Buck (Buckaroo) $5,000
Dam: Gay Charm (Ghadeer*Fr)
Br: Fazenda Mondesir(Brz)
Tr: Pitts Helen (–) 2006:(210 34 .16)

L 119

Life	10	4	0	1	$213,472	105	D.Fst	0	0	0	0	$0	–
2007	2	0	0	1	$24,225	103	Wet (312)	3	2	0	0	$46,765	94
2006	5	3	0	0	$161,407	105	Turf (298)	7	2	0	1	$166,707	105
FG Ⓣ	0	0	0	0	$0	–	Dist (336)	2	1	0	0	$41,407	105

24Feb07-9GP fm 1⅜ Ⓣ:48¹1:13²1:37²2:12¹ 4+ GPBC-G1 103 10 5³ 5³ 4¹½ 2hd 3¾ Bejarano R L123 3.60 92-16 Jmbly123nk HonyRydr118½ Einstin1231¼ Led late, outfinished 11
*T-3ft 4ct 4t wkn late
31Jan07-7GP fm 1 Ⓣ:23¹ :46¹1:10¹1:33⁴ 4+ OC 100k/N4X -N 93 1 4²½ 4² 6²¼ 4¹½ 4³½ Bejarano R L120 *1.40 84-20 Tgnll1201½ ElctrcLght122½ Prdss1201½ Lacked room far turn 8
*T-2bv 2e no punch
6May06-9CD fm 1⅛ Ⓣ:48¹1:12 1:35²1:47 3+ TurfClsc-G1 105 5 2¹½ 2²½ 2hd 3² 4¹¼ Bejarano R L126 15.80 97-04 EnglshChnnl122½ Ccq122¾ MlkItMck126no 4w,no final account 10
1Apr06 10GP fm 1¼ Ⓣ:48²1:12¹2:01²2:24¹ 3+ PanAmerH-G2 80 8 6⁵ 7³½ 6⁴¼ 6⁵ 4⁷¼ Bejarano R L110 3.60 106 SilvrWhistl115nk Rmautti112? CoDputy118hd Best stride late 8
25Feb06-10GP yl 1 1/16 Ⓣ:51²1:18 1:42³2:23⁴ 3+ GPBC-G1 99 4 1½ 1½ 1hd 1¹½ 1nk Bejarano R L123 7.20 — — Einstein123nk GoDputy123³ GunSlut1232½ Game duel,held on 8
4Feb06-11GP sly^S 1⅛ ⊗:47²1:12¹1:37 1:49¹ 4+ Alw 35000N2X 94 3 1½ 1hd 1½ 1³ 1⁷ Bejarano R L124 *1.60 96-04 *Einstein* 124⁷ CtchMe1201¼ Ministr'sJoy1202¼ Drew off, driving 9
7Jan06-10GP fm 1⅛ Ⓣ:46⁴1:10⁴1:34²1:45⁴ 4+ Alw 33000N1X 93 12 10⁵ 8⁵¼ 6³ 2¹½ 1½ Bejarano R L120 5.30 94-12 *Einstein* 120½ Merger1201¼ Cat's On a Prowl122¹ 4 wide, up late 12
25Nov05-7CD fm 1 1/16 Ⓣ:23³ :48 1:13¹1:43² 3+ Alw 50145N1X 87 1 9⁶¾ 9⁷¾ 9⁶¼ 6⁴½ 4¹½ Bejarano R L121 9.90 86-15 *TrrfcStr* 120nk CtsOnPrl121¾ BrdIdl117½ Circle 9w lane,gaining 12
6Nov05-4CD my^S 1 ⊗:23 :46 1:11¹1:36⁴ 3+ Md Sp Wt 40k 87 9 7⁸½ 6⁷¾ 5⁴¼ 3²½ 1⁵¾ Bejarano R L121 *2.40 86-14 Einstin1215¾ McShn'sHlo121hd Dyngold1218¼ Inside run turn 9
22Oct05-10Kee gd *7f :22² :45³1:12¹1:28 3+ Md Sp Wt 50k 51 11 9 7³½ 6³¾ 4⁷½ 5¹⁶ Bejarano R L118 4.70 69-13 Rdtzky1187¾ DrlingTrick1183¼ PhlthBrt1184½ 5-6w,empty late 11

WORKS: ●Feb18 GP 5f fst 1:00 B *1/25* Feb10 GP 5f fst 1:01 B *4/21* ●Jan18 GP 6f fst 1:12 H *1/6* ●Jan12 GP 5f fst 1:00 B *1/15* Jan6 GP 5f fst 1:00¹ B *10/44* Dec31 GP 5f fst 1:01 B *6/28*
TRAINER: Turf (79 .10 $0.93) Routes (169 .15 $1.26) GrdStk (19 .11 $2.91) J/T 2006-07(2.00 $0.00)

Einstein's last race at Gulfstream Park had been run at 1⅜ miles, around three turns. My notes said he was three-wide at the first turn, four-wide at the second (clubhouse) turn, and four-wide as he turned into the stretch. No dramatic trouble befell him in the Grade 1 stakes; he wasn't blocked or bumped at any stage. But in turf races, routine events can become very significant, and losing ground on all three turns in a three-turn race constitutes an extremely difficult trip. Einstein's narrow loss under the circumstances was an admirable effort. He went to the Fair Grounds for his next race and won a $500,000 stakes with one of the most impressive turf performances of the year.

Recognize perfect trips

Handicappers study race videos in the search for horses who have troubled, difficult trips that may conceal their ability and produce a big payoff in the future. But it is equally important, and potentially rewarding, to identify horses who have run well with the benefit of perfect trips. One of the best ways to cash a bet on a longshot is to spot a favorite who isn't as good as he looks on paper.

Bettors should always be skeptical of a horse who has been aided by some form of perfect trip: He takes advantage of a track bias. He gets an uncontested lead at a slow pace. He sits in perfect stalking position behind two dueling leaders. He rallies after three or more horses have collapsed from a fast-paced battle for the lead. He saves ground throughout a turf race while all his rivals are going wide.

When horses acquire lofty reputations after a perfect-trip performance, betting against them is almost mandatory. Fusaichi Pegasus was being hailed as the second coming of Secretariat after he won the 2000 Kentucky Derby, but even a neophyte trip handicapper should have recognized that he was the beneficiary of an ideal set-up. The leaders in the Derby set a fast pace—six furlongs in 1:09.99—and collapsed, enabling the top three finishers to rally from far behind. Of the ralliers, Fusaichi Pegasus had the easiest trip, saving ground on the turns. He never deserved the accolades he received—and he was a loser in his big challenges after the Derby, notably the Preakness and the Breeders' Cup. Taking a position against a hyped horse such as Fusaichi Pegasus requires a contrarian outlook on life, but a horseplayer needs to be a contrarian if he hopes to pick longshots and beat the game.

Most of all, he needs to have the willingness to study hard. Scrutinizing race videos to observe the nuances of horses' trips is a time-consuming, painstaking process. So, too, is extracting crucial information from the mass of data contained in Formulator. But the existence of these new technologies has given unprecedented opportunities to handicappers who can exploit them.

BROHAMER

ON THE TURN-BACK PLAY

By Tom Brohamer

THE THEME OF THIS book is longshots, but I expect that many of us have slightly different opinions as to what constitutes a price horse. The concept of a longshot varies directly with field size. Weekday cards at even the finest venues are littered with small fields and limited choices for play. In this era of five- and six-horse fields, a longshot may well be a nonfavorite at a price as small as 4–1. Many of these races feature a pair of 7–5 shots with the public forcing its play into that narrow betting slot. I think the rational bettor is well served by considering 4–1 or better as a legitimate longshot in a field of this size.

As field size increases, so does the possibility of finding decent-odds horses. In a 12-horse field I consider 6–1 or better to be a price worth catching. The patient bettor usually waits for these larger fields, but most of us do not have that patience. We want to play those races we feel are within our capabilities as handicappers. We just need a method of play that produces the occasional price horse as well as a steady stream of nonfavorites. The play I'll discuss in this chapter addresses both of these points. It is easily my favorite day-to-day play, and will produce more than a fair share of profits.

At *Daily Racing Form*'s 2007 Horseplayers Expo at the Wynn Las Vegas hotel, I was asked by a group of attendees to offer more than theory within my presentation. My response was to discuss the "turn-back" play, or horses shortening in distance off their last race. If the horse meets the basic race pars and certain other criteria and is not a confirmed router, this particular approach regularly produces winners throughout the odds spectrum. It has been part of my game since my days with the Sartin Methodology. That was in the 1980s, and the approach has remained a staple of my play to this day. With the current trend toward more computer data influencing the handicapping procedure, the ability to find *fast* horses turning back in distance has maintained a stable source of winners at fair-to-long odds.

The reason the odds have remained fair is twofold. Much of the early handicapping literature cautioned against the "dulling" effect route races may have on sprinter speed. That is not bad information and was probably true when written. But things change. Year-round racing has taken its toll on the horse population, and old-line traditional advice must be adjusted to the current state of racing. Horses that were throwouts twenty years ago are often the way to go today.

THE 1980s AND THE SARTIN METHODOLOGY

I first became a fan of the turn-back play while working with the Sartin Methodology in the 1980s. A key part of the method was to select a pace line that was indicative of a horse's abilities and his recent form. Then, as now, that was always a tricky proposition. Basing a horse's chances to win on a single race is probably not the best way to go. However, with enough skill and experience, the task was doable. Selecting a key race for a router entered in a sprint was trickier yet.

The Sartin method produced a series of ratings that illustrated abilities to run early and late as well as an overall average pace. Using a route pace line skewed the ratings, with the route race producing ratings that promoted late pace and minimized early pace ability. That just doesn't cut it in a sprint. Much research produced better, yet still flawed, ratings. The Sartin players adjusted by deducting two lengths from the first and second route calls. The logic behind the adjustment was to account for the fact that the runners simply weren't running "all-out" during the early fractions of the route race. While absolutely true, the ratings were still unbalanced toward the more sustained ratings. But the good news was that the routers with early or pressing speed won more than their fair share, usually at square-to-long odds. That was enough for me to become enamored of the turn-back-in-distance play. Before long I was simply looking for routers that turned back while possessing a six-furlong figure that met or exceeded par for the race at hand. If the horse matched or exceeded the capabilities of the other contenders, had a pressing or early pace style, and the odds warranted it, he usually became a play.

More good news was that the whole idea transferred nicely to turf route turn-backs and switches from turf to dirt. It was, and still is, a remarkable and consistent method for both everyday play and as a longshot-getter. Check out Refusal, who was turning back from a turf route to a dirt sprint.

On March 17, 2007, Refusal set and forced fractions of 22⅘, 46⅕, and 1:10⅕ while running over the Santa Anita turf course. He was on the pace through that very fast half-mile while fading a bit by the six-furlong mark. The splits of the race and his performance are attention-getting when you consider the pars for that turf course. The six-furlong par for the race class level is 1:11⅖, or six lengths slower than the race at hand. The race was also six lengths faster than par at the four-furlong mark. In light of the $25,000 crew he was facing on May 5, those fractions were practically from another planet. This was a weak field for the level, his easiest chance in more than a year. He made the most of the opportunity at 5.70–1 in a seven-horse field.

FIFTH RACE

Hollywood

MAY 5, 2007

6½ FURLONGS. (1.13³) CLAIMING . Purse $27,000 (plus $800 Other Sources) FOR FOUR YEAR OLDS AND UPWARD. Weight, 123 lbs. Non–winners of two races in 2007 Allowed 2 lbs. A race in 2007 Allowed 4 lbs. Claiming Price $25,000, if for $22,500, allowed 1 lb. (Maiden and Claiming races for $20,000 or less not considered).

Value of Race: $27,800 Winner $16,200; second $5,400; third $3,240; fourth $1,620; fifth $540; sixth $400; seventh $400. Mutuel Pool $524,915.00 Exacta Pool $270,595.00 Quinella Pool $15,515.00 Trifecta Pool $251,242.00 Superfecta Pool $117,530.00

Last Raced	Horse	M/Eqt. A. Wt	PP	St	¼	½	Str	Fin	Jockey	Cl'g Pr	Odds $1
17Mar07 8SA7	Refusal	LB b 6 119	2	5	43½	31	1½	11¼	Court J K	25000	5.70
2Jly06 7Hol6	Oceanus–Brz	LB f 8 119	7	7	7	7	62	22½	Berrio O A	25000	4.30
19Apr07 6SA4	Moon Mission	LB f 7 119	1	6	54	54	41½	31¾	Potts C L	25000	31.40
11Apr07 3SA4	Echezeaux	LB b 4 119	4	7	61½	61½	5hd	42¾	Antongrgi III W	25000	10.20
18Mar07 2SA2	John Hennessy	LB bf 4 119	5	3	1½	1hd	32	52	Valdivia J Jr	25000	2.40
22Apr07 5SA10	Manyouk	LB 4 119	6	1	23	22	2hd	64½	Pedroza M A	25000	4.70
8Apr07 6SA2	Clan Chief	LB b 4 119	3	4	3½	41	7	7	Migliore R	25000	2.80

OFF AT 2:18 Start Good. Won driving. Track fast.

TIME :21⁴, :44³, 1:09³, 1:16¹ (:21.81, :44.64, 1:09.77, 1:16.32)

$2 Mutuel Prices:				
2 – REFUSAL	13.40	6.40	4.40
8 – OCEANUS–BRZ		5.80	3.80
1 – MOON MISSION			7.80

$1 EXACTA 2–8 PAID $39.70 $2 QUINELLA 2–8 PAID $35.20
$1 TRIFECTA 2–8–1 PAID $361.00 $1 SUPERFECTA 2–8–1–4 PAID $1,902.70

Ch. g, (May), by Dusty Screen – Rose Ice , by Icecapade . Trainer Meairs John M. Bred by Hume Wornall (Ky).

REFUSAL stalked the pace inside, came out leaving the turn and three deep into the stretch, gained the lead outside foes in upper stretch and won clear under urging. OCEANUS (BRZ) unhurried off the rail on the backstretch and turn, came out into the stretch and gained the place. MOON MISSION chased a bit off the rail then inside on the turn, came out in upper stretch and bested the others. ECHEZEAUX a bit slow to begin, saved ground off the pace, remained inside in the stretch and lacked the needed rally. JOHN HENNESSY angled in and dueled inside, fought back a bit off the rail in the stretch but weakened in the final furlong. MANYOUK also angled in early, dueled outside a foe, put a head in front into the stretch, was between horses in midstretch and also weakened. CLAN CHIEF chased outside a rival, dropped back in the stretch and gave way.

Owners– 1, Niederrad Stables; 2, L-Bo Racing Paseta Baldo M and Pyle Monte; 3, Okuda Schmidt and Yaghlegian; 4, Heintschel Mike and O'Neill Doug; 5, E-RacingCom; 6, Lo Charles; 7, Dubb Michael

Trainers– 1, Meairs John M; 2, Avila A C; 3, Schmidt Heidi; 4, O'Neill Doug; 5, Koriner Brian; 6, Peery Chuck; 7, Dutrow Richard E Jr

Scratched– I'magambler (07Jul06 7Hol3)

$2 Daily Double (1–2) Paid $81.00 ; Daily Double Pool $24,126 .
$1 Pick Three (3–1–2) Paid $87.60 ; Pick Three Pool $61,099 .

A MORE DEFINITIVE LOOK

What may seem obvious at first blush may not hold together with deeper analysis. Fast times and fast fractions at the longer distances must be tempered with the overall characteristics of the racetrack over which the times were recorded. For example, on a fast racetrack, route fractions do not have the same significance as those recorded over a slower venue such as the newly retooled Hollywood Park. Turf Paradise routes for decent horses are very likely to feature extremely fast fractions, and playing horses shortening up in distance is a less reliable play than at other tracks. At Hollywood Park's Cushion Track, a 1:11 fraction at 1¹⁄₁₆ miles is actually very fast, and horses running that fast are dangerous on the turn-back. The key here is a decent set of pars for the track.

Pars, of course, are the average winner's times separated by class and distance—for example, the $20,000 claiming level at Hollywood Park's new Cushion Track:

Six furlongs:　　45⅗　　1:11

1¹⁄₁₆ miles:　　1:12.0　　1:44⅗

Even without actual pace and speed figures (the ultimate look at the turn-back play), we are still capable of shopping for longshots based on raw times alone. We just need a little "fat" built into the recorded times. Simply put, a horse running 1:12 theoretically earns a figure comparable to a 1:11 sprinter. Unadjusted Quirin-style figures would have both pace numbers at 103. With actual adjusted pace figures, that may well be true, but we need a greater cushion when using raw times for our play.

From long experience with this approach, I need the router to run within a length or two of the sprint par for the level. That could be the ultimate look at any given race. The route fractions, or "splits," may be enough to make the play. The faster the better. With the router exceeding par, and fair-to-long odds, the bet is usually warranted. The odds of the router will dictate. During Expo 2007, St Wager was shortening up from a route to a sprint.

The raw-time par for a $25,000 sprint at six furlongs for 3-year-old fillies at Santa Anita in March is 1:11⅕. With the exception of one suspicious class dropper, not a single sprinter in the fifth race on March 1, 2007, had the current ability to match that number. Enter St Wager at 5.50–1 odds. The filly was turning back from a very fast mile in which she chased hard against a pace of 1:10⅘, and was within three lengths at the six-furlong mark. That should be enough information by itself to draw our attention to this filly. But it gets better.

The fractional par for a mile race for this level in March is 1:12, or six lengths slower than the race from which St Wager exits. The filly's own time would be 1:10⅘ plus three lengths, or 1:11⅖. That's four lengths faster than the route fractional par and within one length of the sprint par for the level. Since nothing else in the field of eight had the form or capability, wouldn't St Wager kind of stand out here? She did, and she won comfortably at an overlaid price; and guess what? The final time for the win was 1:11⅕, the exact par for the class level and distance.

USING PARS TO TIGHTEN THE TURN-BACK PLAY

As with virtually any figure play, the bottom line will be whether the horse is fast enough to win today's race. Not all fields are created equal, and a solid understanding as to what time/figure *usually* wins races at this level and field strength is absolutely essential. For a figure player, there is no more definitive approach than the use of fractional and final-time pars to determine playable contenders. This is a big part of the classes I host each year at Santa Anita with Jim Quinn. And for good reason. The approach has reliably produced the winner in the final handicapping mix year after year, meeting after meeting. Horses turning back in distance are generally great plays, but only when the runners are fast enough to handle the speed and pace requirements of the race at hand. I highly recommend the use of par times in establishing the basic win contention and to sort out possible winners among horses turning back in distance.

USING PAR TIMES TO DETERMINE THE BASIC WIN CONTENTION

Horses incapable of matching the winning par of the race represent the poorest possible plays and the most significant drain on the player's bankroll. It never ceases to amaze me that favorites and near favorites unable to match par capture significant amounts of the betting pools. Word of mouth, appearance, jockeys, or barns can be meaningful factors, but they are secondary to the overall ability of the horse. Backing the fastest horses is what we are about, so why not give it our best shot? The following approach is pretty lenient, yet will include the winner at least 85 percent of the time.

Except under unusual circumstances, I will not back any runner that is unable to run within two lengths of the race par, period. I've been at this long enough to agree with a supposed Pittsburgh Phil observation that the race is not always won by the swiftest horse, but that's the way to bet. True statement or not, I say amen to that. Horses unable to run within two lengths of the race par simply don't win many races. That should not be earth-shattering, but too many players fail to grasp the importance of the concept. Don't you be one of them. Before betting a race, give yourself the opportunity to fire your best shot. And why within two lengths of par? The answer lies in the nature of par times themselves.

THE MAKEUP OF PAR TIMES

Par times represent the bulk of winning times of races at each class and distance at a given track. As I wrote this, Hollywood Park's new Cushion Track, for example, had just enough races over that surface to give us a strong clue as to what running times are now necessary (unadjusted by variants) to win at each distance and class level. The new $10,000 par I'm using for six furlongs is 1:11, a change from the old par of 1:10⅖. That time looked pretty solid after a fall and summer meeting had been conducted over the course. There seemed to be enough data to support that conclusion. Now, why two lengths of par for our possible contenders?

Consider the following:

Given 20 races at the $10,000 class level, let's use 10 races with winning times of 1:11⅖ and 10 more with winning times of 1:10⅗. The $10,000 par for Hollywood would be an average of those times, thus making the par 1:11 flat for the class. This is an oversimplification, but the procedure is spot-on. To complete a usable par chart you need a readily obtainable class hierarchy for Hollywood Park and you are in business. With $10,000 at 1:11 we can fill in some blanks.

$10,000 1:11
$12,500 1:10⅘
$16,000 1:10⅗
$20,000 1:10⅖

The allowance levels vary with the class of the track, but at a major track the first-level allowance condition is usually five lengths, or five class levels above the $10,000 par. So let's add to the pars. The key example in this chapter will utilize that par so we'll deal with it now.

$10,000 1:11
$12,500 1:10⅘
$16,000 1:10⅗
$20,000 1:10⅖
NW1 Alw. 1:10

Most of us do not have the time to make the pars and class hierarchy for the tracks we play but, fortunately, that data is readily available from a number of commercial sources. Our task is simply to creatively apply the data available. Now consider the makeup of the $10,000 par for Hollywood's Cushion Track. The simplified example averages 10 races at 1:10⅗ and 10 races at 1:11⅖ to determine a par of 1:11. Pars are uniformly made this way, and by allowing two lengths of "wiggle room" we manage to keep all 20 winners in the mix. Enforcing an exact par number of 1:11 at Hollywood Park serves only to quickly eliminate exactly half of our $10,000 winners. That we cannot afford. Within two lengths of par works just fine, thank you. You will have included the winner in the handicapping mix a solid 80 to 85 percent of the time.

For a runner to be a serious contender, barring other factors to be considered a bit later:

1. The horse must show at least two races where he managed to run within two lengths of the par of today's race.
2. The races must be at the same approximate distance as today's race and over the same surface.
3. Lightly raced horses need only show a single race with that par.
4. Beware the "giraffe." A runner with a single race that exceeds today's par without having followed that race with a similar effort is one of the poorer plays we can make. That one race will stand out versus the competition and bettors will chase that race until someone finally cries "Enough already!" Don't be that person.

A SIMPLE YET HIGHLY RELIABLE CONTENDER SOURCE: BEYER SPEED FIGURES

I have for many years made my own figures, variants, and par times; yet I use the readily available Beyer Speed Figures for establishing the basic contention in every race I handicap. The reason is quite simple: They just flat work. They are a perfect vehicle for determining the basic contention in nearly every race I handicap. They are made by knowledgeable and conscientious players and I trust them nearly as much as I do my own numbers. So why not use them? Given an understanding of the class hierarchy of the track we're handicapping, the Beyers are simple and quickly applied. First, a quick review of the numbers themselves.

The Beyer figures value a length in basically two increments: 2 Beyer points per length in races at distances from seven furlongs and beyond, and 2.5 points per length in sprint races. At a major track, the average winning figure for the $10,000 claiming level (older males) is around 83. From that number we can build a useable par chart:

	Sprints	Routes
$10,000	83	83
$12,500	85.5	85
$16,000	88	87

Maiden races at a major track are usually two lengths better than the $10,000 claimers and equivalent to the $16,000 claiming level. First-level allowances or N1X are about five lengths superior to the $10,000s. The contender selection chart now looks like this:

	Sprints	Routes
$10,000	83	83
$12,500	85.5	85
$16,000	88	87
MdSpWt	88	87
N1X	95.5	93

(The N1X sprints are 2.5 x 5 = 12.5; 83 + 12.5 = 95.5. The routes are calculated using 2 points per length.)

When handicapping a N1X allowance race we will insist that our contenders be capable of recording at least two figures within two lengths of the 95.5 par. Any horse, unless lightly raced, will normally be a throwout unless he has demonstrated the ability to run at least a 90 Beyer. Females and younger horses are held to a lesser standard, and those adjustments have been recorded in numerous other works including readily obtained par-time charts.

The third race on opening day at Santa Anita's 2007 Oak Tree meeting was for N1X allowance horses at six furlongs. It was a field of eight, with several lightly raced runners. The average winning Beyer figure for the level is 95, and two lengths off that figure is 90 on the Beyer scale. We will insist that our contenders have a demonstrated ability to run that figure at least twice in their past performances.

3 **Santa Anita** *6 Furlongs* **Alw 45000N1X** Purse $45,000 (plus $13,500 CBOIF – California Bred Owner Fund) For Three Year Olds And Upward Which Have Never Won $7,500 Other Than Maiden, Claiming Or Starter Or Which Have Never Won Two Races. Three Year Olds, 121 lbs.; Older, 124 lbs. Non–winners of a race other than Maiden, Claiming or Starter Allowed 2 lbs. A race other than Claiming, or Starter Allowed 4 lbs.

2 A Stare and Me
Own: Everest Stables Inc
White Black, Red Mountain Emblem On Back, Red
COURT J K (—) 2007: (653 60 .09)

B. c. 3 (Feb)
Sire: Petionville (Seeking the Gold) $15,000
Dam: Out of Step (Affirmed)
Br: Everest Stables Inc (Ky)
Tr: Polanco Marcelo(—) 2007:(113 12 .11)

L 117

Life	2	1	0	0	$14,200	70	D.Fst	0	0	0	0	$0	-
2007	1	0	0	0	$400	-	Wet(313)	0	0	0	0	$0	-
2006	1	1	0	0	$13,800	70	Synth	1	1	0	0	$13,800	70
							Turf(257)	1	0	0	0	$400	-
SA	0	0	0	0	$0	-	Dst(342)	0	0	0	0	$0	-

29Aug07-2Dmr fm 5f ⓣ :211 :433 :553 3+OC 40k/n1x-N – 7 2 78¾ - - - Espinoza V LB118 10.90 - 05 MyCitybytheBay122½ Grrison124½ MrChing124nk Pulled up lame,vanned 7
29Nov06-6Hol fst 7f ◈ :22 :442 1:093 1:23 Md 50000(50-45) 70 7 6 108½ 98½ 74¾ 1no Court J K LB120 58.50 - - AStrndM120no HrryHomWrrn120½ OnSckWndr120hd 3wd into str,up wire 10
WORKS: Sep17 SA ◈5f fst 1:033 H 36/40 Sep14 SA ◈5f fst 1:03 H 41/42 Sep8 SA ◈3f fst :362 H 5/7 Aug25 Dmr ◈3f fst :36 H 7/27 Aug19 Dmr ◈6f fst 1:144 H 11/12 Aug11 Dmr ◈5f fst 1:043 H 70/72
TRAINER: 2OffOver180(8 .00 $0.00) Synth(53 .13 $4.05) Turf/Synth(10 .30 $2.88) Sprint(171 .09 $1.97) Alw(24 .12 $5.08) J/T 2006-07 SA(34 .09 $1.09) J/T 2006-07(77 .16 $3.72)

3 Pick Vic
Own: K K Sangara
Blue Navy Blue, Silver 'Kk' On Front, Silver
ESPINOZA V (—) 2007: (871 150 .17)

Dk. b or br c. 3 (Mar)
Sire: Vicar (Wild Again)
Dam: Phone Signal (Pick Up the Phone)
Br: Herman Heinlein (Ky)
Tr: Becerra Rafael(—) 2007:(182 39 .21)

L 117

Life	9	1	3	2	$59,815	93	D.Fst	4	1	2	0	$33,915	93
2007	8	1	2	2	$56,560	93	Wet(357)	0	0	0	0	$0	-
2006	1	M	1	0	$3,255	71	Synth	4	0	1	2	$25,500	86
							Turf(245)	1	0	0	0	$400	79
SA	3	1	1	0	$30,660	93	Dst(358)	4	1	2	0	$42,540	93

18Aug07-7Dmr fst 7f ◈ :224 :461 1:114 1:253 3+Alw 61000n1x 74 1 9 87¼ 66½ 33½ 36½ Espinoza V LB118 5.00 - - BarbecueEddie1204¼ SilverSquall1182¼ PickVic1181 4wd into str,best rest 10
22Jly07-5Dmr fst 6f ◈ :224 :463 :591 1:114 Clm c-(50-45) 86 7 4 85¼ 84¾ 4nk 21¾ Espinoza V LB120 *2.40 - - Grits1201¾ Pick Vic120¾ ⒹAreutrue120hd Swung 6wd into lane 10
Claimed from C R K Stable for $50,000, Sadler John W Trainer 2007(as of 7/22): (339 57 58 50 0.17)
7Jly07-8Hol fm 1 ⓣ :233 :464 1:11 1:343 3+Alw 69310n1x 79 5 24 45 74 74 65¼ Talamo J5 LB110 11.00 86- 10 Kendargent120no StrightRun1221 HetedRebel124hd Inside to lane,wkened 7
17Jun07-7Hol fst 7f ◈ :214 :443 1:101 1:233 Alw 51294n1x 86 9 1 52¾ 62¼ 2hd 32¼ Baze T C LB118 17.40 86- 17 Taxi Fleet1151¼ Abalanche1201 Pick Vic1181 3wd bid,led,held 3rd 10
23May07-7Hol fst 6f ◈ :221 :451 :572 1:101 Alw 60384n1x 77 1 6 63 43 43 45¼ Chavez J F LB118 6.90 82- 16 Idiot Proof1222¾ ScatThief1201½ SomethingSonic1221 Broke out bit,inside 7
8Apr07-4SA fst 6f :212 :441 :562 1:092 Md 100000(100-85) 93 6 1 62¾ 43 21 1nk Gomez G K LB121 *1.00 92- 12 Pick Vic121nk Squires Wingman1211¾ Carman1214½ Chased 3wd,rallied 7
9Mar07-2SA fst 6f :212 :444 :57 1:10 Md 80000(80-70) 89 4 1 42¾ 31½ 21½ 21¼ Gomez G K LB121 *1.90 88- 17 Con Juan1211¼ Pick Vic1216 Icanmakeitrain1193¼ 3wd into str,2nd best 6
15Feb07-5SA fst 6½f :211 :441 1:101 1:164 Md c-(62.5-55) 76 6 6 77¾ 67¼ 35 53¼ Gomez G K LB121 4.20 82- 13 AmericnOfficr1212¾ HddforHom121½ Oshinsky121nk Btwn lane,no late bid 14
Claimed from La Canada Stable LLC for $62,500, Carava Jack Trainer 2006: (292 38 57 42 0.13) Previously trained by Pinchin Jose 2006(as of 12/4): (172 19 32 18 0.11)
4Dec06-5Crc fst 7f :232 :47 1:121 1:254 Md 40000 71 4 3 31½ 31½ 1hd 21¼ Cruz M R L118 10.60 83- 19 VoorhesBlld1131½ PickVic1181¼ AShorThing1186¼ Greenly under pressure 7
WORKS: Sep20 SA ◈5f fst :591 H 10/54 Sep13 SA ◈5f fst 1:001 H 14/39 Sep3 Dmr ◈4f fst :483 H 12/55 Aug11 Dmr ◈5f fst 1:002 H 27/72 Aug4 Dmr ◈4f fst :48 H 3/69 Jly17 Dmr ◈4f fst :491 H 20/62
TRAINER: Synth(96 .17 $1.57) 31-60Days(125 .14 $1.09) Sprint(223 .19 $1.84) Alw(81 .19 $1.85) J/T 2006-07 SA(8 .25 $1.82) J/T 2006-07(18 .17 $1.06)

4 Six Pack Abs
Own: Desert Sun Stables
Yellow Black, Turquoise And Gold Emblem, Gold
JARA F (—) 2007: (397 35 .09)

B. g. 3 (Apr) KEESEP05 $50,000
Sire: Forest Wildcat (Storm Cat) $35,000
Dam: Warren's Whistle (Wolf Power*SAf)
Br: William A Carl (Ky)
Tr: Peery Chuck(—) 2007:(80 10 .12)

L 117

Life	8	2	0	2	$36,720	82	D.Fst	4	1	0	0	$13,280	81
2007	6	2	0	2	$35,520	82	Wet(357)	2	0	0	2	$5,400	82
2006	2	M	0	0	$1,200	64	Synth	2	1	0	0	$18,040	77
							Turf(306)	0	0	0	0	$0	-
SA	0	0	0	0	$0	-	Dst(363)	3	1	0	1	$15,520	82

15Aug07-5Dmr fst 6½f ◈ :223 :463 1:13 1:194 3+Clm c-(25-22.5)n2L 77 7 1 63¼ 52¼ 2½ 13¼ Talamo J LB120 b 3.30 - - Six Pack Abs1203¼ Tranquilo1231¼ Dennybuck1202¼ 3wd,4wd,led past 1/8 11
Claimed from Mullikin Kevin R. for $25,000, Autrey Cody Trainer 2007(as of 8/15): (350 85 67 56 0.24)
18Jly07-8Dmr fst 6f ◈ :223 :462 :591 1:123 3+Alw 40000s 74 9 3 32½ 42 34 44¼ Talamo J5 LB113 b *2.30 - - Icnmkeitrin1201¾ MellowCmmi1201½ WrrnsPp1201¼ 3wd,4wd,drift out 1/16 9
Disqualified and placed 5th
5Jly07-5CD sly 6f :212 :442 :564 1:101 Clm 50000 82 5 8 88½ 86¼ 65 31¼ Lanerie C J L118 b 8.90 85- 16 Classic Robbery120nk Jack Grant1181 Six Pack Abs1182¾ Closed well 8
29Apr07-5CD fst 6f :214 :452 :572 1:093 3+Md c-(30-25) 81 9 3 42½ 3nk 2hd 2nk Leparoux J R L118 b *2.30 89- 12 ⒹMyPalAlex118nk SixPackAbs1189 Mybellemn1241¼ '4w,bmp in lane,p 1st 11
Claimed from Homewrecker Stable LLC for $30,000, Kenneally Eddie Trainer 2007(as of 4/29): (76 19 12 14 0.25) Placed first through disqualification
22Mar07-2GP slyS 1 :231 :453 1:112 1:382 Md 50000(50-45) 62 3 31 21½ 12 11½ 34¼ Velasquez C L122 b 2.10 74- 17 Value Player1224 Nosybody122nk Six Pack Abs1228¼ Gave way 8
23Feb07-7GP fst 6½f :222 :452 1:10 1:162 Md 80000(80-75) 56 4 9 2½ 42 46½ 613¾ Prado E S L122 4.40 76- 13 FtTksHnd1208½ TxsBllyBy122nk ScttshDmnd1223¼ Bumped early, faltered 11
2Jly06-10CD fst 5½f :221 :453 :571 1:032 Md Sp Wt 50k 64 2 2 51½ 64 65½ 56¼ Leparoux J R5 L115 5.90 94- 06 War Wolf1204¾ First Degree1201½ Bold Start120½ 3w lane,empty 9
11Jun06-5CD fst 5½f :223 :461 :581 1:043 Md Sp Wt 50k 44 11 12 1210 1213 118½ 117½ Leparoux J R5 L114 *2.60 88- 14 Shermanesque1192¼ Shipmte119½ Wnnbeinclued119hd Broke in air,outrun 12
WORKS: ●Sep14 SA ◈5f fst :563 H 1/42 Sep8 SA tr.t 4f fst :503 H 2/2 Aug31 Dmr ◈3f fst :36 H 2/12 Aug10 Dmr ◈4f fst :50 H 43/65 Aug3 Dmr ◈4f fst :502 H 41/49
TRAINER: 1stClaim(24 .12 $0.97) Synth(33 .03 $0.16) 31-60Days(43 .07 $0.98) Sprint(137 .12 $1.94) Alw(25 .08 $1.14)

5 Street Boss
Own: Bluegate Corp Headley & Naify
Green Royal Blue And White Stripes, Blue Cuffs
SOLIS A (—) 2007: (471 61 .13)

Ch. c. 3 (Mar) KEESEP05 $300,000
Sire: Street Cry*Ire (Machiavellian) $30,000
Dam: Blushing Ogygian (Ogygian)
Br: Brilliant Stable Inc (Ky)
Tr: Headley Bruce(—) 2007:(106 13 .12)

L 119

Life	1	1	0	0	$31,800	86	D.Fst	0	0	0	0	$0	-
2007	1	1	0	0	$31,800	86	Wet(375)	0	0	0	0	$0	-
2006	0	M	0	0	$0	-	Synth	1	1	0	0	$31,800	86
							Turf(308)	0	0	0	0	$0	-
SA	0	0	0	0	$0	-	Dst(420)	1	1	0	0	$31,800	86

2Sep07-6Dmr fst 6f ◈ :222 :462 :592 1:123 3+Md Sp Wt 55k 86 6 11 911 910 66¾ 11½ Solis A LB120 *2.20e - - StreetBoss1201½ OrinttlSlw1203½ CvlryChrg123no Off slow,bumped,4w bid 11
WORKS: Sep23 SA ◈3f fst :362 H 2/16 Sep15 SA ◈5f fst :582 H 3/39 Aug26 Dmr ◈4f fst :461 Hg 2/75 Aug18 Dmr ◈5f fst :591 Hg 3/60 Aug11 Dmr ◈6f fst 1:114 H 3/24 Aug4 Dmr ◈5f fst 1:004 H 8/70
TRAINER: 2ndStart(25 .20 $0.99) Synth(58 .09 $0.72) WonLastStart(35 .23 $1.18) Sprint(185 .17 $1.28) Alw(42 .19 $1.37) J/T 2006-07 SA(83 .30 $1.93) J/T 2006-07(162 .21 $1.36)

6 Enforcement
Own: The Robert & Beverly Lewis Trust
Black Green, Yellow Hoops And Sleeves, Yellow
BAZE T C (—) 2007: (634 75 .12)

B. c. 4 (Feb) BARMAR05 $350,000
Sire: Tiznow (Cee's Tizzy) $25,000
Dam: Golden Tiy (Dixieland Band)
Br: William A Carl (Ky)
Tr: Baffert Bob(—) 2007:(326 55 .17)

L 122

Life	2	1	1	0	$42,600	88	D.Fst	2	1	1	0	$42,600	88
2005	2	1	1	0	$42,600	88	Wet(432)	0	0	0	0	$0	-
2004	0	M	0	0	$0	-	Synth	0	0	0	0	$0	-
							Turf(278)	0	0	0	0	$0	-
SA	0	0	0	0	$0	-	Dst(376)	2	1	1	0	$42,600	88

24Jly05-5Dmr fst 6f :22 :451 :573 1:10 Md Sp Wt 53k 88 8 1 51¾ 21½ 2hd 14 Espinoza V LB120 *.70 89- 10 Enforcement1204 ElSenorHlo1206 OldThunder120¾ 3wd,strong hand ride 10
3Jly05-5Hol fst 6f :214 :451 :58 1:11 Md Sp Wt 74k 69 2 9 53¾ 41¾ 21½ 22 Bailey J D LB120 *.80 80- 09 Dark Nose1202 Enforcement1201½ Yodelen Dan1203 Off bit slow,3wd lane 9
WORKS: Sep21 SA ◈5f fst :583 H 4/55 ●Sep15 SA ◈6f fst 1:112 Hg 1/22 Sep9 SA ◈5f fst :593 H 9/35 Sep3 Hol ◈5f fst 1:011 H 7/20 Aug27 Hol ◈5f fst 1:003 H 2/16 Aug20 Hol ◈5f fst 1:002 H 4/34
TRAINER: +180Days(40 .22 $2.49) Synth(140 .13 $1.30) WonLastStart(144 .24 $1.19) Sprint(434 .22 $1.57) Alw(171 .22 $1.76) J/T 2006-07 SA(4 .25 $0.85) J/T 2006-07(26 .19 $2.13)

7 Snow Fighter Gr/ro. c. 4 (Apr) CALAUG04 $20,000

Own: George Krikorian — Sire: Siberian Summer (Siberian Express) $5,000

Orange Magenta, Black And Silver 'K' Emblems — Dam: Oasis (Water Bank)

Br: Dawn Lucas (Cal)

TALAMO J (—) 2007: (1214 211 .17) — Tr: Sherman Art(—) 2007:(639 153 .24)

L 124

Life	7	2	0	2	$79,220	100	D.Fst	3	0	0	1	$7,160	76
2007	4	2	0	1	$72,060	100	Wet(319)	0	0	0	0	$0	-
2006	3	M	0	1	$7,160	76	Synth	3	2	0	1	$68,520	100
							Turf(294)	1	0	0	0	$3,540	75
SA	0	0	0	0	$0	-	Dst(330)	3	1	0	1	$41,320	93

25Aug07-9Dmr fst 6f ◈ :223 :46 :581 1:111 3↑[S]OC 25k/n1x-N 93 7 4 1½ 1½ 1½ 1¾ Talamo J LB124 *1.60 - - SnowFightr124¾ DkotPdr120no PocosinsGmBoy1242½ Dueled,held gamely 11

19Jly07-6Dmr fm 5f ⓣ :221 :444 :561 3↑[S]OC 25k/n1x-N 75 1 5 1hd 1½ 2hd 43 Court J K LB124 2.70 89-08 BllisticHet124no IndinAshton1201 SpoilsofExcss1202 Inside,weakened late 7

22Jun07-6Hol fst 6½f ◈ :221 :45 1:093 1:16 3↑[S]Md Sp Wt 48k 100 3 5 2½ 1hd 11½ 12½ Court J K LB124 7.70 93-15 SnowFighter1242½ AttackJack1186 BuckBsolo113nk Rail,strong handling 10

2Jun07-6Hol fst 6f ◈ :214 :452 :573 1:104 3↑[S]Md Sp Wt 49k 76 13 3 2½ 2hd 1½ 3¾ Court J K LB124 13.00 83-18 **Johnny Eves**118½ AttackJack118nk SnowFighter1241¼ Dueled btwn,held 3rd 14

26Aug06-3Dmr fst 6f :22 :453 :584 1:113 3↑[S]Md Sp Wt 54k 45 3 5 1hd 1hd 1½ 610 Flores D R LB120 b *1.80 71-14 LnsLon1203 SrChCh120¾ MrSmoothOprtr120no Dueled btwn,vanned off 8

22Jly06-3Dmr fst 6½f :213 :443 1:104 1:181 3↑[S]Md Sp Wt 54k 76 5 4 21 2½ 2hd 3nk Flores D R LB119 b 5.30 82-12 So Bewarned119hd Father Sky119hd SnowFighter1191¼ Lost 2nd btwn late 8

2Jly06-11Hol fst 6½f :212 :441 1:102 1:171 3↑[S]Md Sp Wt 62k 62 11 1 2½ 31½ 31½ 66 Baze R A LB118 4.00 78-09 Discuss1181½ Marquis Form118½ My FirstBigKiss1181¼ 4wd,3wd,weakened 11

WORKS: Sep23 Hol ◈3f fst :354 H 4/31 Sep16 Hol ◈5f fst :592 H 2/45 Sep8 Hol ◈4f fst :49 H 7/33 Aug16 Dmr ◈5f fst :594 H 4/54 Aug9 Dmr ◈5f fst 1:00 H 4/50 ●Aug2 Dmr ◈4f fst :464 H 1/49

TRAINER: Synth(136 .16 $3.38) 31-60Days(432 .26 $1.82) WonLastStart(313 .24 $1.53) Sprint(958 .25 $1.95) Alw(143 .22 $2.71) J/T 2006-07 SA(1 .00 $0.00) J/T 2006-07(19 .21 $1.79)

8 Can This Be True B. c. 3 (Apr) BARMAY06 $70,000

Own: Class Racing or Grumke or Muratore Et — Sire: Yes It's True (Is It True) $35,000

Pink Navy And Silver Stripes, White Sleeves — Dam: Color Unlimited (Houston)

Br: Milan Kosanovich (Fla)

BAZE M C (—) 2007: (985 172 .17) — Tr: Hofmans David(—) 2007:(140 15 .11)

L 119

Life	5	1	0	1	$34,400	91	D.Fst	4	1	0	1	$34,000	91
2007	4	1	0	1	$34,000	91	Wet(321)	0	0	0	0	$0	-
2006	1	M	0	0	$400	65	Synth	1	0	0	0	$400	65
							Turf(211)	0	0	0	0	$0	-
SA	3	1	0	1	$34,000	91	Dst(378)	4	1	0	1	$34,000	91

Previously trained by Stute Glen 2006: (22 3 6 4 0.14)

7Mar07-7SA fst 6½f :214 :443 1:092 1:16 Alw 50800n1x 63 3 4 32½ 54 710 713¼ Baze T C LB118 14.10 77-14 LesGrndsTrois1181 AbInche1201¼ BlckSvntn1181 Stalked pace, weakened 7

14Feb07-2SA fst 6f :214 :444 :563 1:09 Alw 53000n1x 80 2 2 11½ 2hd 31½ 36½ Baze T C LB120 *1.20 87-14 CobltBlue1181 StretLights1185½ CnThisBTru120¾ Speed inside, weakened 5

27Jan07-7GP fst 6f :212 :434 :563 1:101 [R]SunMilDash250k 46 3 7 2hd 42 810 1119 Guidry M L120 20.60 72-09 Storm inMay1201¼ IdiotProof1201½ TexasVoyager1201½ Vied on rail, faded 14

1Jan07-5SA fst 6f :212 :443 :564 1:094 Md Sp Wt 48k 91 8 1 1½ 11 11½ 1nk Baze T C LB121 13.60 90-11 CnThisBeTrue121nk PintdShdow1214¼ ChoctwChif1211 Dueled,clear,held 10

9Dec06-5Hol fst 6f ◈ :214 :441 :563 1:094 Md Sp Wt 42k 65 2 5 3nk 1hd 2½ 85 Espinoza V LB120 5.50 - - Taxi Fleet120½ Tenfold120¾ Cool Hand Lucca1202 Inside duel,weakened 12

WORKS: Sep22 SA ◈5f fst 1:00 H 6/24 Sep16 SA ◈7f fst 1:274 H 5/5 Sep7 SA ◈6f fst 1:132 H 2/3 Aug30 Hol ◈6f fst 1:142 H 8/11 Aug23 Hol ◈6f fst 1:143 H 6/11 ●Aug17 Hol ◈5f fst :593 H 1/16

TRAINER: 1stW/Trn(13 .23 $3.02) +180Days(21 .19 $2.01) Synth(73 .10 $1.07) Sprint(140 .14 $1.24) Alw(47 .21 $1.34) J/T 2006-07(8 .13 $0.42)

1. Johnny Eves has two consecutive races at par or better. He is a strong contender.
2. A Stare and Me is not even close to the necessary figure.
3. Pick Vic is not in great form but has two solid numbers earlier in the year. He's in a top barn now and the figures make him a consideration.
4. Six Pack Abs is an absolute throwout. He hasn't a single number near par.
5. Street Boss has only a single and troubled start in which he won impressively. This lightly raced colt is another strong contender.
6. Enforcement is very lightly raced and has a near-par number from July at Del Mar.
7. Snow Fighter has two races that match or exceed par.
8. Can This Be True has a single par number from five races. Beware the giraffe number and eliminate this one for now. Chasing that 91 Beyer from last January is generally an amateur's mistake and not one we want to be making.

From this eight-horse field, in about a two-minute effort, we wind up with the following live contenders for further consideration: (1) Johnny Eves; (3) Pick Vic; (5) Street Boss; (6) Enforcement; and (7) Snow Fighter.

THIRD RACE

Oak Tree at SA

SEPTEMBER 26, 2007

6 FURLONGS. (1.07¹) ALLOWANCE . Purse $45,000 (plus $13,500 CBOIF – California Bred Owner Fund) FOR THREE YEAR OLDS AND UPWARD WHICH HAVE NEVER WON $7,500 OTHER THAN MAIDEN, CLAIMING OR STARTER OR WHICH HAVE NEVER WON TWO RACES. Three Year Olds, 121 lbs.; Older, 124 lbs. Non–winners of a race other than Maiden, Claiming or Starter Allowed 2 lbs. A race other than Claiming, or Starter Allowed 4 lbs.

Value of Race: $54,300 Winner $35,100; second $9,000; third $5,400; fourth $2,700; fifth $900; sixth $400; seventh $400; eighth $400. Mutuel Pool $279,855.00 Exacta Pool $166,035.00 Trifecta Pool $151,888.00 Superfecta Pool $80,205.00

Last Raced	Horse	M/Eqt.	A.	Wt	PP	St	¼	½	Str	Fin	Jockey	Odds $1
1Sep07 ⁸Dmr²	Johnny Eves	LB	3	121	1	4	1¹	1¹	1³	1¹¼	Flores D R	2.00
2Sep07 ⁶Dmr¹	Street Boss	LB	3	119	5	7	7⁷	6²	2½	2²½	Solis A	2.30
15Aug07 ⁵Dmr¹	Six Pack Abs	LB b	3	117	4	6	6¹½	5ʰᵈ	5½	3²½	Jara F	13.10
24Jly05 ⁵Dmr¹	Enforcement	LB b	4	122	6	3	3²	4²	3ʰᵈ	4²	Baze T C	6.20
18Aug07 ⁷Dmr³	Pick Vic	LB	3	117	3	5	5½	3ʰᵈ	4ʰᵈ	5¹¾	Espinoza V	6.90
25Aug07 ⁹Dmr¹	Snow Fighter	LB	4	124	7	2	2½	2¹½	6⁴	6³	Talamo J	5.70
7Mar07 ⁷SA⁷	Can This Be True	LB	3	119	8	1	4ʰᵈ	7⁸	7⁸	7⁶	Baze M C	16.60
29Aug07 ²Dmr⁷	A Stare and Me	LB	3	117	2	8	8	8	8	8	Court J K	55.40

OFF AT 2:04 Start Good. Won ridden out. Track fast.

TIME :21², :44, :55³, 1:08 (:21.57, :44.02, :55.78, 1:08.05)

$2 Mutuel Prices:				
	1 – JOHNNY EVES.....................	6.00	3.00	2.60
	5 – STREET BOSS.....................		3.20	2.60
	4 – SIX PACK ABS.....................			5.00

$1 EXACTA 1–5 PAID $8.70 $1 TRIFECTA 1–5–4 PAID $77.50
$1 SUPERFECTA 1–5–4–6 PAID $298.00

B. g, (Feb), by Skimming – Capote's Halo , by Capote . Trainer Robbins Jay M. Bred by Mooncoin LCC (Cal).

JOHNNY EVES sped to the early lead, set the pace inside, came a bit off the rail into the stretch, continued inside, was ridden along some to open up and and held while in hand late. STREET BOSS chased three deep then off the rail, angled in on the second turn, came out into the stretch, split rivals nearing midstretch and was second best. SIX PACK ABS chased between horses then outside a rival, came out into the stretch and picked up the show. ENFORCEMENT stalked a bit off the rail then inside on the turn and into the stretch and weakened. PICK VIC chased inside, came out leaving the turn and four wide into the stretch and lacked the needed rally. SNOW FIGHTER stalked outside a rival then off the rail on the turn and weakened in the stretch. CAN THIS BE TRUE stalked three deep, dropped back off the rail on the turn and had little left for the stretch. A STARE AND ME dropped back inside then settled a bit off the rail, came out into the stretch and was outrun.

Owners– 1, Mooncoin LLC; 2, Bluegate Corp Headley and Naify; 3, Desert Sun Stables; 4, Robert and Beverly Lewis Trust; 5, Sangara K K; 6, Krikorian George; 7, Class Racing Stable Grumke James Muratore John et al; 8, Everest Stables Inc

Trainers– 1, Robbins Jay M; 2, Headley Bruce; 3, Peery Chuck; 4, Baffert Bob; 5, Becerra Rafael; 6, Sherman Art; 7, Hofmans David; 8, Polanco Marcelo

$2 Daily Double (9–1) Paid $23.40 ; Daily Double Pool $24,147 .
$1 Pick Three (4–9–1) Paid $95.70 ; Pick Three Pool $60,625 .

Johnny Eves won smartly while earning a 100+ Beyer (based on my figures) and Street Boss ran a big second, improving his figure to a high-90s Beyer.

7 Santa Anita 6½ Furlongs Clm 20000(20–18)

Purse $20,000 For Three Year Olds And Upward. Three Year Olds, 121 lbs.; Older, 124 lbs. Non–winners Of A Race Allowed 2 lbs. Claiming Price $20,000, For Each $1,000 To $18,000 1 lb.

START / 6½ FURLONGS / FINISH

1 Double Parked

Red
Own: Beachamp or Smith or Whitney
White, Royal Blue Wave Hoop, Fuchsia Dot — $18,000
MIGLIORE R (—) 2007: (717 99 .14)

B. c. 4 (Mar) KEESEP04 $4,000
Sire: Ecton Park (Forty Niner) $12,500
Dam: Flying Nellie (Ogygian)
Br: Walter B Mills (Ky)
Tr: Spawr Bill(—) 2007:(174 29 .17)

L 120

Life	12	4	3	2	$87,990	84	D.Fst	12	4	3	2	$87,990	84
2006	7	3	2	1	$65,180	84	Wet(367)	0	0	0	0	$0	–
2005	5	1	1	1	$22,810	63	Synth	0	0	0	0	$0	–
							Turf(183)	0	0	0	0	$0	–
SA	2	0	0	1	$5,820	59	Dst(317)	1	0	0	1	$5,280	81

9Aug06–1Dmr fst 6½f :22 :451 1:101 1:17 Clm 40000(40–35) 81 4 2 3½ 2½ 2hd 32 Espinoza V LB120 fb 2.40 86– 15 Manyouk120¾ NtionlHonor1201¼ DoublePrked120¾ Dueled 3wd,outkicked 5
20Jly06–1Dmr fst 6f :22 :45 :57 1:10 Clm c-(32-28) 84 7 1 31 31½ 11 14½ Garcia M5 LB115 fb 3.20 87– 12 DoubleParked1154½ Evnston1201½ HotOffTheBench120½ 3wd into lane,clear 7
Claimed from O'Neill and Wood for $28,000, O'Neill Doug Trainer 2006(as of 7/26): (534 86 74 66 0.16)
21Jun06–6Hol fst 6f :214 :45 :574 1:111 Clm 28000(32–28) 77 1 5 1hd 1hd 2hd 15 Garcia M5 LB113 fb 3.80 81– 15 DH DblPrkd113 DH WlbrsMrEd1215 Hpngndwshng1231¾ Inside duel,gamely 7
3Jun06–1Hol fst 6f :22 :453 :574 1:11 Clm c-(20–18) 78 4 4 41½ 41½ 32 2hd Garcia M5 LB114 fb 2.00 82– 13 Fightinthect119hd DoublPrkd114hd PhillyBulldog1214½ Came out,3wd wire 6
Claimed from Aizenstadt, Foltz, Michelet, et al for $20,000, Dominguez Caesar F Trainer 2006(as of 6/3): (34 6 2 2 0.18)
15May06–1Hol fst 6f :222 :451 :571 1:102 Clm 25000(25–22.5) 70 5 1 21 21½ 23½ 23¾ Garcia M5 LB114 fb 2.10 81– 13 ThMissilCm1193¾ DoublPrkd1147¼ Hlmsmstr1194¼ Pressed pace, 2nd best 5
29Apr06–9Hol fst 6f :214 :444 :571 1:102 Clm 16000(16–14) 80 8 1 2½ 2hd 21½ 1hd Espinoza V LB119 fb 3.30 85– 13 DoublPrkd119hd PhllyBulldog1213 Sddnlyglttr1192½ Vied btwn,came back 9
9Apr06–7SA fst 5½f :213 :443 :571 1:04 Clm 20000(20–18) 59 9 1 52½ 56 36½ 46 Arias S7 LB111 fb 5.20 83– 14 ThMissilCm1212½ BLsCooCooCody1183 TopOn118½ 4wd into str,missed 3d 11
16Jly05–3Hol fst 6f :214 :442 :562 1:092 HolJuvCh-G3 59 2 3 53½ 57½ 58½ 512¾ Solis A LB117 b 29.10 77– 11 WhtSong117nk Bshert1171 StevieWondrboy1159½ Saved ground, weakened 5
9Jun05–8Hol fst 5½f :214 :46 :584 1:052 Md 40000(40–35) 63 2 3 31½ 2hd 13½ 12½ Espinoza V LB120 b *3.00 81– 18 DoublePrked1202½ YodelenDn1206 BriteMneuvers1202 Led into lane,clear 9
25May05–1Hol fst 5f :221 :462 :593 Md 40000(40–35) 50 2 1 1hd 1hd 2hd 22 Cohen D5 LB115 b 2.60 81– 18 StrikinoutNMim1202 DoublPrkd115½ StrtYodlng1206 Dueled,lost whip 1/16 8
14May05–3Hol fst 4½f :212 :453 :514 Md Sp Wt 57k 38 7 5 54¼ 77¾ 711¼ Nakatani C S LB120 8.40 84– 10 Brother Derek120½ Swiss Sonata1201 Bashert120¾ 4wd into str,wkened 7
31Mar05–1SA fst 2f :111 :213 Md Sp Wt 38k – 2 2 3nk 31½ Baze M C B118 *1.60 95– 09 Good News118nk Dorval Special1221¼ DoubleParked118no Off rail,held 3rd 9

WORKS: Sep19 SA ◈5f fst 1:02 H 48/58 Sep6 Dmr ◈5f fst 1:044 H 21/22 Aug30 Dmr ◈7f fst 1:28 H 2/2 Aug24 Dmr ◈7f fst 1:274 H 3/7 Aug18 Dmr ◈6f fst 1:143 H 21/31 Aug11 Dmr ◈6f fst 1:152 H 22/24
TRAINER: +180Days(13 .08 $2.35) Synth(100 .16 $1.44) Sprint(225 .12 $1.29) Claim(200 .14 $1.30) J/T 2006-07 SA(33 .21 $3.39) J/T 2006-07(86 .17 $2.14)

2 Celtic Sword (Arg)

White
Own: Naify & Woodside Farms LLC
Royal Blue And White Stripes, Blue Cuffs — $20,000
PEDROZA M A (—) 2007: (682 102 .15)

Gr/ro. g. 8 (Jul)
Sire: Hidden Prize (Mr. Prospector)
Dam: Cessna*Arg (Ringaro)
Br: Orilla Del Monte (Arg)
Tr: Canani Julio C(—) 2007:(174 29 .17)

L 122

Life	18	4	3	3	$111,326	100	D.Fst	2	1	0	1	$2,692	–
2007	7	0	2	1	$23,220	85	Wet(329*)	0	0	0	0	$0	–
2006	2	0	0	0	$1,860	84	Synth	3	0	1	1	$10,040	79
							Turf(220)	13	3	2	1	$98,594	100
SA	0	0	0	0	$0	–	Dst(293)	0	0	0	0	$0	–

3Sep07–6Dmr fst 6f ◈ :224 :464 1:00 1:132 4↑Clm 20000(20–18) 73 7 9 1114 1110 77½ 43½ Pedroza M A LB120 b 11.00 – – CaptainSacto120no IndianWeaver1201¼ Queen'sImage1222¼ Rail rally lane 11
6Aug07–5Dmr fst 6f ◈ :23 :47 1:00 1:123 4↑Clm 20000(20–18) 76 3 5 45 46 44 25¼ Nakatani C S LB120 b 2.50 – – Wheaton Hall1205¼ Celtic Sword1201¾ Zayed120½ Split foes,2nd best 5
6Jly07–1Hol fst 6f ◈ :23 :454 :573 1:094 4↑Clm 20000(20–18) 79 1 5 53 54½ 44½ 34½ Chavez J F LB119 b 5.00 84– 11 Semi Lost1194 Kaianagandaia119½ Celtic Sword1193¾ Off bit slow,inside 5
9May07–6Hol fm 6f Ⓣ :222 :443 :562 1:082 4↑Clm 40000(40–35) 82 9 1 99 99½ 97½ 53¼ Pedroza M A LB119 b 4.70 96– 01 Bills Paid1181½ Blue Torpedo1201 Leo Getz119¾ Inside,btwn wire 9
7Apr07–4SA fm *6½f Ⓣ :214 :44 1:072 1:133 4↑Clm 28000(32–28) 85 6 10 109¾ 98¼ 96½ 2hd Migliore R LB118 b 4.30 87– 14 Bills Paid118hd Celtic Sword118no Witness This120nk Rallied,4wd on wire 10
11Mar07–8SA fm *6½f Ⓣ :204 :431 1:061 1:123 4↑Clm 35000(40–35) 83 6 11 1113 1012 75 42¼ Pedroza M A LB118 b 6.90 90– 08 LimitedCrol120¾ StrwbrryLk118nk WitnssThis1201¼ Off bit slow,willingly 11
13Jan07–4SA fm *6½f Ⓣ :212 :43 1:064 1:124 4↑Clm 35000(40–35) 69 5 12 912 812 78½ 88 Pedroza M A LB118 b 5.40 83– 09 WitnessThis1201½ DebonairJoe1201¼ YesMster1201¾ Off bit slow,angled in 12
24Nov06–5Hol fm 6f Ⓣ :224 :452 :572 1:092 3↑Clm 40000(40–35) 84 4 8 87¾ 87¼ 74¾ 42¼ Pedroza M A LB120 b *2.90 – – AmericanAllStar1221½ FiddlersCt120nk WitnessThis124½ Late bid outside 9
10Oct06–8OSA fm *6½f Ⓣ :221 :434 1:054 1:114 3↑ⓇBlueJayWay60k 66 7 6 75 88¾ 811 812½ Pedroza M A LB118 b 15.10 84– 06 Osidy118hd Deputy Kris120¾ Railroad1241¼ Angled in hill,no bid 8
28Oct05–7OSA fm 1 Ⓣ :241 :482 1:113 1:35 3↑Alw 54000c 88 1 32½ 42¾ 55¾ 54½ 54¾ Pedroza M A LB120 b 1.90 83– 16 SaintBuddy1201¼ Terroplane120no TobeSuve120½ Saved ground, weakened 5
1Oct05–3OSA fm *6½f Ⓣ :211 :431 1:054 1:114 3↑ⓇBlueJayWay71k 100 9 1 810 99¼ 64½ 41¾ Pedroza M A LB120 b 3.70 94– 04 Siren Lure124hd Geronimo118¾ Crystal Castle1181 Came out str,rallied 10
8Aug05–6Dmr fm 5f Ⓣ :211 :433 :551 3↑OC 62k/n2x-N 100 2 8 86¾ 87¾ 63¼ 12¼ Pedroza M A LB122 b *2.10 99– 01 CelticSword1222¼ OutoftheBluSlw120no Crosscut122no Off bit slow,inside 8

WORKS: ●Sep14 SA ◈3f fst :343 B 1/5 Aug29 Dmr ◈4f fst :474 H 7/57 Aug22 Dmr ◈5f fst 1:02 H 34/66 Aug15 Dmr ◈3f fst :372 H 12/22 Jly28 Dmr ◈5f fst 1:021 H 42/78 Jly22 Dmr ◈5f fst 1:014 H 48/89
TRAINER: Synth(55 .16 $2.68) Sprint(169 .18 $2.04) Claim(45 .29 $2.46) J/T 2006-07 SA(53 .17 $2.08) J/T 2006-07(134 .16 $1.67)

3 B L's Danzig

Blue
Own: Holly & David Wilson
Orange And White Checks, Orange And — $20,000
GARCIA M (—) 2007: (685 83 .12)

B. g. 4 (Mar)
Sire: B L's Appeal (Valid Appeal) $2,500
Dam: Northern Danzig (Sejm)
Br: John S Scott (Fla)
Tr: Cerin Vladimir(—) 2007:(186 37 .20)

L 122

Life	7	2	0	1	$45,070	91	D.Fst	5	2	0	0	$42,570	91
2006	1	0	0	0	$2,600	63	Wet(414)	1	0	0	0	$0	40
2005	6	2	0	1	$42,470	91	Synth	0	0	0	0	$0	–
							Turf(305)	1	0	0	1	$2,500	67
SA	0	0	0	0	$0	–	Dst(369)	1	0	0	0	$2,600	63

8Sep06–12Fpx fst 6½f :22 :453 1:093 1:162 Foothill61k 63 5 4 59¼ 510 511 516½ Garcia M S LB118 7.60 76– 17 SilorsSunset12211¼ KnightsLstStr120¾ HySlick122½ 3wd into str,no threat 5
Previously trained by Pilotti Larry 2005(as of 10/3): (214 35 21 19 0.16)
30Oct05–4Crc fst 5f ⊗ :221 :46 :584 Alw 30000n1x 91 3 1 1hd 1½ 11½ 13 Cruz M R L117 4.30 94– 16 B L's Danzig1173 El Quixote117¾ Thanks Dubya1171 Inside, drew clear 7
24Sep05–4Crc fst 6f :22 :461 :583 1:121 Alw 30000n1x 56 9 3 31½ 21½ 44½ 69½ Toribio A R L117 10.40 77– 17 GinRummyKing1171¼ Prayersndsong120½ UniverslStory1175 Chased, tired 9
3Sep05–9Crc slyS 5f ⊗ :223 :462 :584 FsgTptnDsh50k 40 9 2 41¾ 86¾ 47½ 719½ Cruz M R L121 14.00 74– 16 Forest Danz11812 Connoisseur118¾ Golden Flame116½ Bumped st, faded 10
15Aug05–6Crc fm 5f Ⓣ :213 :443 :563 Alw 30000n1x 67 3 5 21½ 22½ 23½ 34¼ Cruz M R L115 7.90 86– 10 Mr. Silver1183¾ Gin Rummy King118½ B L's Danzig1151 Chased, weakened 10
7May05–8Crc fst 5f :223 :471 1:01 Md Sp Wt 28k 54 2 3 1hd 2hd 12½ 1nk Castro E L118 4.60 83– 17 B L's Danzig118nk Rehoboth1181¾ El Quixote118nk Inside, lasted 9
25Apr05–3Crc fst 4½f :231 :474 :543 Md Sp Wt 23k 34 5 2 710 69 45¾ Morales P7 L111 6.00 81– 19 TizzysNoSnt1182¾ GrndMgcn1182½ Hlothndychmp118½ Improved position 10

WORKS: Sep21 SA ◈4f fst :481 H 18/33 Sep8 SA ◈5f fst 1:004 H 12/21 Aug30 Dmr ◈5f fst 1:011 H 14/35 Aug24 Dmr ◈5f fst 1:022 H 43/58 Aug12 Dmr ◈5f fst 1:01 H 23/67 Jly31 Dmr ◈4f fst :502 H 30/46
TRAINER: +180Days(31 .16 $1.20) Synth(102 .25 $3.05) Sprint(288 .18 $1.91) Claim(145 .21 $1.85) J/T 2006-07 SA(14 .21 $1.09) J/T 2006-07(83 .20 $1.91)

4 Chips Are Down
Own: The Robert & Beverly Lewis Trust
Yellow   Green, Yellow Hoops and Sleeves, Yellow $20,000
ESPINOZA V (—) 2007: (871 150 .17)

Dk. b or br h. 5 (Mar)
Sire: Distorted Humor (Forty Niner) $225,000
Dam: Tly Buster (Housebuster)
Br: Charles Nuckols Jr & Sons (Ky)
Tr: Baffert Bob(—) 2007:(326 55 .17)

L 122

	Life	17	3	3	0	$167,535	93		D.Fst	14	3	3	0	$163,255	93
	2007	4	0	0	0	$8,060	89		Wet(435)	0	0	0	0	$0	—
	2006	2	0	0	0	$1,560	72		Synth	3	0	0	0	$4,280	78
									Turf(304)	0	0	0	0	$0	—
	SA	5	1	1	0	$55,425	89		Dst(352)	2	1	0	0	$23,800	79

5 McNasty
Own: Crevier & Plumb Crazy Racing Stable
Green   Turquoise, Yellow Diamond Stripe On $20,000
QUINONEZ A (—) 2007: (947 133 .14)

Dk. b or br g. 6 (Apr)
Sire: Bertrando (Skywalker) $12,500
Dam: Tiny Kristin (Steelinctive*GB)
Br: Arnold Family Trust (Cal)
Tr: Yakteen Tim(—) 2007:(100 12 .12)

L 117⁵

	Life	19	4	3	2	$139,654	100		D.Fst	12	2	3	1	$101,489	100
	2007	7	2	0	1	$41,080	85		Wet(384)	1	1	0	0	$22,165	82
	2006	7	2	0	1	$74,294	94		Synth	5	1	0	1	$15,600	85
									Turf(312)	1	0	0	0	$400	76
	SA	3	0	1	0	$8,832	75		Dst(304)	2	1	0	0	$70,832	100

6 Wild Nekia
Own: B G Stable or Royalty Stable
Black   Navy Blue, Red Bg On Back, Red Collar $18,000
ROSARIO J (—) 2007: (813 133 .16)

B. g. 4 (Feb) KEEJAN04 $26,000
Sire: Wild Rush (Wild Again)
Dam: Mary Margaret (Mane Minister)
Br: Clover IV Stables LLC (Ky)
Tr: Palma Hector O(—) 2007:(82 6 .07)

L 120

	Life	27	7	4	6	$82,275	85		D.Fst	20	6	3	5	$67,090	85
	2007	9	3	1	4	$36,570	85		Wet(361)	3	1	1	0	$10,525	79
	2006	15	4	3	2	$44,205	79		Synth	2	0	0	1	$3,160	82
									Turf(252)	2	0	0	0	$1,500	68
	SA	4	1	1	2	$18,280	79		Dst(359)	2	1	0	0	$10,200	85

7 Oliver Twisted
Own: James A Wilson
Orange   Forest Green, Red Bar On Yellow Sleeves $20,000
DELGADILLO A (—) 2007: (445 46 .10)

Ch. g. 4 (Mar)
Sire: Theatrical*Ire (Nureyev) $40,000
Dam: Avani (Gulch)
Br: Madeleine A Paulson & Ernest Moody (Ky)
Tr: Becerra Rafael(—) 2007:(182 39 .21)

L 122

	Life	10	2	2	0	$40,980	88		D.Fst	3	1	1	0	$17,400	88
	2007	9	2	2	0	$40,580	88		Wet(358)	0	0	0	0	$0	—
	2006	1	0	0	0	$400	25		Synth	4	1	1	0	$22,380	78
									Turf(252)	3	0	0	0	$1,200	60
	SA	3	1	1	0	$17,400	88		Dst(332)	2	0	1	0	$6,980	79

8 Polo Bender Own: George R Dill — Pink — Royal Blue, Blue 'Mg' On White Diamond — $20,000
BAZE T C (—) 2007: (634 75 .12)
Dk. b or br g. 6 (Apr)
Sire: Cahill Road (Fappiano) $4,000
Dam: Force Within (Cool Halo)
Br: George Dill (Wash)
Tr: Glatt Mark(—) 2007:(147 16 .11)
Blinkers ON — L 122

Life	9	3	2	0	$45,465	89	D.Fst	5	2	1	0	$22,043	80
2007	1	0	0	0	$400	55	Wet(345)	3	1	1	0	$23,022	89
2005	6	3	0	0	$40,335	89	Synth	1	0	0	0	$400	55
							Turf(287)	0	0	0	0	$0	–
SA	0	0	0	0	$0	–	Dst(345)	2	1	0	0	$8,745	80

5Aug07–5Dmr fst 6f ◈ :223 :463 :594 1:13 4↑Clm 32000(32-28) 55 5 7 84¼ 73¾ 85¾ 814 Rosario J LB120 14.00 - - CountOrnge120¼ WitnessThis120¾ PtsGreyEgl120¼ Tight 4-1/2,no rally 12
Previously trained by Penney Jim 2005(as of 10/15): (213 50 31 25 0.23)
15Oct05–3EmD slys 6f :213 :44 :561 1:09 3↑OC 25k/N$Y-N 54 4 4 42 42½ 67 612¾ Gutierrez J M LB123 f *1.40 80– 14 Packy1191 Gold RushBanker1171½ PrizeWeaver1193¾ Chased 4 w, stopped 6
2Oct05–8EmD slys 6f :211 :431 :552 1:083 3↑[S]ChinokPass40k 89 2 3 2hd 1½ 14 14½ Gutierrez J M LB121 f 13.30 95– 10 Polo Bender1214½ Wasserman1171¼ *Starbird Road*119½ Dueled, drew clear 6
17Sep05–8EmD fst 6f :221 :442 :562 1:091 3↑OC 25k/N$Y 77 7 3 2½ 2½ 11½ 1nk Gutierrez J M LB119 f 10.80 92– 13 *PoloBender*119nk Packy118hd BestGmeinTown1201¾ Long drive 4 w, lasted 8
27Aug05–8EmD fst 6½f :214 :44 1:084 1:153 3↑OC 25k/N$Y-N 54 1 4 42 53½ 810 812¼ Mitchell G V LB119 f 5.80 78– 17 NturlToch119¾ *AshbyHl*118¾ BstGmnTown1191½ Saved ground,weakened 9
6Aug05–9EmD fst 6f :211 :44 :554 1:083 3↑OC 25k/N$Y-N 73 1 3 2hd 3½ 2½ 62 Mitchell G V LB119 f 3.70 93– 11 On the Ave1191 Tamper119no Call Columbo121½ Bobbled break, bump 8
23Jly05–2EmD fst 6½f :22 :444 1:102 1:172 3↑Moc 30000N 80 7 1 11 1½ 13 15 Mitchell G V LB124 f 2.40 81– 21 Polo Bender1245 *Escalante*1216½ Booker Time1201 Met bid 1/2, handily 7
21May04–4EmD fst 6f :22 :443 :564 1:09 Md Sp Wt 13k 76 6 1 2hd 1½ 11½ 2nk Mitchell G V LB121 4.10 93– 12 *MilitrySinger*121nk *PoloBendr*1214¾ DvilishFct1214¾ Duel2w,clear1/4,caught 9
8May04–7EmD sly 6f :213 :443 :57 1:094 3↑Md 25000(25-20) 59 3 7 53 22½ 22½ 25¾ Mitchell G V LB117 4.70 83– 16 Eecheero1185¾ Polo Bender1171 Lovefromafar119½ Off slow, bid 3 w,hung 7
WORKS: Sep16 Hol ◈6f fst 1:15 H *15/20* Sep9 Hol ◈5f fst 1:011 H *8/38* Sep2 Hol ◈4f fst :491 H *11/22* ●Jly27 Dmr ◈5f fst :581 Hg *1/68* ●Jly8 Hol ◈6f fst 1:121 H *1/21* ●Jly1 Hol ◈5f fst :59 H *1/72*
TRAINER: 1stBlink(12 .08 $0.82) Synth(59 .14 $1.11) BlinkOn(15 .07 $0.65) 31-60Days(81 .04 $0.47) Sprint(251 .09 $1.66) Claim(164 .08 $0.98) J/T 2006-07 SA(13 .00 $0.00) J/T 2006-07(24 .00 $0.00)

9 Megabyte Own: Robert D Bone — Turqse — Black, Gold Crown Emblem On Back, Gold — $20,000
BAZE M C (—) 2007: (985 172 .17)
B. g. 5 (Mar)
Sire: Chief Seattle (Seattle Slew) $5,000
Dam: Bright Royal (Cure the Blues)
Br: C F Newman (Ark)
Tr: Mitchell Mike(—) 2007:(226 50 .22)
L 122

Life	32	7	5	6	$230,997	96	D.Fst	24	6	4	5	$188,752	96
2007	8	3	1	1	$76,277	95	Wet(435)	2	0	0	1	$7,725	92
2006	12	3	2	2	$84,300	92	Synth	3	1	1	0	$32,800	95
							Turf(259)	3	0	0	0	$1,720	80
SA	4	1	1	1	$42,140	91	Dst(329)	1	0	1	0	$9,800	81

10Sep07–8Fpx fst 6f :221 :46 :583 1:11 3↑Clm 25000(25-22.5) 85 2 5 67½ 67½ 45 31½ Baze M C LB122 b *1.30 86– 17 All Pro120hd Yes Master1201½ Megabyte1222½ Lagged,5w,willingly 7
2Sep07–1Dmr fst 7f ◈ :222 :452 1:112 1:25 4↑Clm 32000(32-28) 95 8 2 610 613 33 11¼ Baze M C LB120 b *1.80 - - Megabyte1201¼ Oceanus1221¾ Ghosttrapper1202½ 3wd into lane,rallied 8
18Aug07–9Dmr fst 1116 ◈ :25 :50 1:152 1:484 4↑Clm 32000(32-28) 82 8 21 31½ 41¼ 1hd 2no Baze M C LB120 b 9.50 - - Desert Sea120no *Megabyte*1201½ RaisetheHeat1202¾ 3wd bid,led,outgamed 11
27Jun07–6Hol fst 1116 ◈ :232 :47 1:112 1:442 4↑Clm 40000(40-35) 74 7 21 41¼ 43 56 68¾ Talamo J5 LB118 b 6.80 77– 15 **Datticus**119no Lazio119nk Zappa1193 Stalked rail,weakened 8
Previously trained by Diaz A L 2007(as of 4/15): (56 11 8 8 0.20)
15Apr07–3BM fst 1 :213 :45 1:094 1:363 4↑Clm 40000(40-35) 79 2 22 25 26 34½ 56½ Rosario J LB121 b 1.70 80– 19 Yougottawann1193¼ MeMyMine1213 TheFourteenth119hd Chased, empty 5
16Mar07–7BM fst 1116 :232 :463 1:11 1:433 4↑Clm 50000(50-40) 86 4 2½ 2½ 1hd 11 1no Ochoa J LB121 fb 3.20 82– 27 Megabyte121no Attack Force1195 Youhadyourchance1194 Dug in late rail 4
14Feb07–7BM fst 1 :222 :453 1:103 1:361 4↑Clm c-(40-35) 82 1 1½ 1hd 1½ 2½ 43½ Carr D LB123 fb 2.70 84– 14 Me My Mine121¾ Attack Force119½ *Franklin's Tower*1192¼ Gave way rail 7
Claimed from Hollendorfer, Jerry, Todaro, George and Turner, John F. for $40,000, Hollendorfer Jerry Trainer 2006: (908 234 172 132 0.26)
7Jan07–8GG fst 1 :221 :452 1:101 1:361 4↑OC 50k/N2x 91 1 21 1hd 1½ 13½ 13 Baze R A LB123 b *1.60 88– 21 Megabyte1233 Yougottawanna1236 Zappa123nk Pace factor, driving 6
2Dec06–3BM fst 1 :224 :464 1:101 1:352 3↑Clm c-(40-35) 87 2 11 1½ 1½ 13 1¾ Ochoa J LB119 b *.90 94– 16 *Megabyte*119¾ Logician1192 Donnybrook Pride1192 Set pace, driving 5
Claimed from Bone Robert D. for $40,000, Bennett Keith Trainer 2006(as of 12/2): (229 56 47 27 0.24)
17Nov06–7BM fst 1 :223 :461 1:101 1:361 3↑OC 62k/N2x 88 3 23½ 23 22 22 2no Ochoa J LB119 b 3.40 90– 10 Bobby Dazzler121no *Megabyte*1193¾ Six Numbers1192¼ 2w trip, led, tagged 5
21Oct06–10SA fst 7f :22 :441 1:091 1:231 3↑Clm 40000(40-35) 86 3 4 42½ 32 42½ 41¼ Gryder A T LB122 b 7.20 82– 15 Hello Fame122¾ *SundayTimes*122hd Rushin'toAltar122¾ Willingly btwn late 7
9Oct06–3GG fst 1 :222 :452 1:092 1:354 3↑OC 50k/N2x 89 2 21½ 21 2hd 2½ 22 Ochoa J LB123 b 4.10 88– 12 Dr. Einstein1202 Megabyte1233 Prince of Gold1232 Prssd winnr 2w, wknd 4
WORKS: Aug13 Dmr ◈5f fst 1:042 B *56/57* Aug1 Dmr ◈5f fst 1:033 H *53/58* Jly24 Dmr ◈5f fst 1:013 H *26/54* Jly17 Dmr ◈4f fst :503 H *45/62* Jly7 Hol ◈4f fst :501 H *39/48*
TRAINER: Synth(139 .25 $2.78) Sprint(269 .20 $1.75) Claim(282 .21 $1.86) J/T 2006-07 SA(7 .29 $3.37) J/T 2006-07(101 .23 $1.91)

10 Datticus Own: Southern Equine Stable LLC — Purple — White, Blue And Yellow Em Squares — $20,000
ARTIEDA P J (—) 2007: (86 1 .01)
Dk. b or br g. 7 (Apr)
Sire: Atticus (Nureyev) $5,000
Dam: Devil's Banner (Devil's Bag)
Br: Whisper Hill Farm (Ky)
Tr: Guillot Eric(—) 2007:(129 18 .14)
L 122

Life	9	3	1	1	$116,200	99	D.Fst	6	2	1	1	$89,620	99
2007	5	1	0	0	$34,320	89	Wet(332)	0	0	0	0	$0	–
2005	3	2	1	0	$76,000	99	Synth	3	1	0	0	$26,580	89
							Turf(315)	0	0	0	0	$0	–
SA	2	0	0	0	$7,740	89	Dst(358)	1	1	0	0	$27,000	99

Entered 24Sep07- 8 FPX
1Aug07–5Dmr fst 1 ◈ :232 :474 1:13 1:403 4↑Clm c-(40-35) 73 3 14 11½ 1hd 22½ 45½ Talamo J LB122 f 2.70 - - *Gddngbot*1131½ [DH]SnstonlScor120 [DH]PrncfGld1204 Speed,inside,wkened 8
Claimed from Jay Em Ess Stable for $40,000, Ellis Ronald W Trainer 2007(as of 8/1): (114 25 17 13 0.22)
27Jun07–6Hol fst 1116 ◈ :232 :47 1:112 1:442 4↑Clm 40000(40-35) 89 8 11 11 11½ 12 1no Valdivia J Jr LB119 f *2.40 86– 15 Datticus119no Lazio119nk Zappa1193 Inside,clear,just held 8
25May07–6Hol fst 6f ◈ :214 :441 :561 1:091 4↑Clm 50000(50-45) 84 5 4 21 22 32 44 Valdivia J Jr LB119 f 2.80 88– 11 Wind Water119½ Brooker1193½ Wheaton Hall119no Angled in,lost 3rd 7
3Mar07–2SA fst 1 :222 :453 1:10 1:364 4↑OC 62k/N2x-N 83 6 2½ 2½ 2hd 41¾ 45¾ Valdivia J Jr LB119 f 6.30 78– 15 Rcketr1211½ SinistrMinistr119½ GrndPoint1213¾ Pressed pace, weakened 7
9Feb07–5SA fst 6f :212 :442 :562 1:091 4↑OC 62k/N2x-N 89 6 6 53¼ 31½ 32 45½ Valdivia J Jr LB119 f 3.20 87– 14 Jack'sKid1193¾ GrindingItOut119½ WindWater1191¼ Off rail,btwn,wkened 7
20Aug05–5Dmr fst 1 :221 :453 1:101 1:362 3↑OC 62k/N2x-N 92 4 21½ 21½ 21 1½ 2¾ Espinoza V LB122 *.80 91– 08 Victory Light120¾ Datticus1221½ El Elogiado1202½ Bid,led,worn down 7
29Jly05–6Dmr fst 1 :221 :453 1:094 1:354 3↑Alw 62280N1x 97 2 1½ 1½ 11 13½ 15½ Espinoza V LB122 *1.30 95– 11 Datticus1225½ Pao Com Ovo1221 Gold Bridle117¾ Rid out,in hand late 8
11Jun05–3Hol fst 6½f :22 :442 1:09 1:144 3↑Md Sp Wt 45k 99 4 3 1hd 1½ 11 11½ Espinoza V LB124 f *1.60 97– 06 *Datticus*1241½ Wing Kai1187 Poker Rules1241½ Inside, ridden out 6
1Aug04–9Dmr fst 6f :213 :442 :564 1:094 3↑Md Sp Wt 51k 78 7 9 88¾ 56 45½ 35 Baze T C LB123 15.50 85– 12 GoldenSouvenir1194 WhtSoldier1191 *Dtticus*1231½ 4wd,3wd turn,best rest 10
WORKS: Sep16 SA ◈4f fst :48 H *12/37* Aug24 Dmr ◈4f fst :484 H *11/47* ●Aug19 Dmr ◈4f fst :461 H *1/50* Jly26 Hol ◈4f fst :493 H *19/37* Jly18 Hol ◈7f fst 1:291 B *2/2* Jly11 Hol ◈4f fst :48 H *4/50*
TRAINER: 1stClaim(31 .13 $1.48) Synth(37 .16 $1.89) Route/Sprint(24 .21 $1.47) 31-60Days(53 .15 $3.87) Sprint(164 .13 $2.47) Claim(74 .05 $1.07)

11 Blue Eyed Blond Own: Wind River Stables Berta Lyons Et Al — Gray — Black, Black Jb On White Diamond — $20,000
GRYDER A T (—) 2007: (685 82 .12)
Ch. h. 5 (Mar)
Sire: Northern Afleet (Afleet) $15,000
Dam: Rusty's Best Girl (Avatar)
Br: James Hatchett (Fla)
Tr: Koriner Brian(—) 2007:(259 53 .20)
L 122

Life	12	2	2	1	$54,600	87	D.Fst	9	2	2	1	$53,500	87
2007	6	1	1	0	$27,890	87	Wet(322)	0	0	0	0	$0	–
2005	3	0	1	1	$11,600	82	Synth	2	0	0	0	$800	73
							Turf(299)	1	0	0	0	$300	74
SA	0	0	0	0	$0	–	Dst(326)	2	0	0	0	$800	73

23Aug07–5Dmr fst 6½f ◈ :224 :462 1:12 1:182 4↑Clm 25000(25-22.5) 73 7 2 21½ 2½ 21½ 65¾ Gryder A T LB120 b 16.70 - - SwitzerInd1201½ PtsGreyEgle120½ DrivnbyExcss1201½ Bid turn,weakened 9
5Aug07–5Dmr fst 6f ◈ :223 :463 :594 1:13 4↑Clm 32000(32-28) 45 4 10 73¼ 119 119¾ 1118½ Potts C L LB120 b 16.80 - - CountOrnge120¼ WitnessThis120¾ PtsGreyEgl120¼ Shuffled back 4-1/2 12
4Jly07–5Pln fst 6f :223 :443 :563 1:09 3↑OC 50k/N2x-N 60 2 4 32 35 410 413 Schvaneveldt C P LB122 b 4.00 82– 11 Fete1224½ Crosscut1224 Sweet Roberto1224½ Some speed,no kick 6
28Apr07–2GG fm 1 ⓣ :232 :47 1:113 1:36 3↑OC 50k/N2x-N 74 5 2hd 1hd 2hd 65 66¾ Baze R A LB123 b 3.70 84– 09 Chadlington1231½ MeMyMine123hd ShiningDay123hd Dueled 2w, gave way 7
8Apr07–3BM fst 6f :221 :443 :562 1:084 4↑OC 62k/N2x-N 87 4 1 21 21 2hd 2½ Baze R A LB121 b 4.00 92– 18 Brber119½ BlueEyedBlond1211½ ColonlCourtny1193½ 2w,loomed,outfnshd 5
3Mar07–8BM fst 6f :221 :444 :57 1:10 4↑Alw 33625N1x 87 2 2 21½ 1hd 11 11¼ Schvaneveldt C P LB122 b 6.10 87– 14 BlueEydBlond1221¼ StlthAttck115no MomIsRdy122¾ Stlkd 2w, held drvng 6
3Nov05–7GG fst 6f :212 :434 :561 1:093 3↑OC 25k/N1x-N 82 5 1 32 22 22½ 32 Schvaneveldt C P LB121 fb 3.30 87– 15 Barron H1231 Marsh Creek1211 *Blue Eyed Blond*121hd Stlkd 3w, even late 8
7Oct05–6BM fst 6f :22 :443 :57 1:094 3↑Alw 38840N1x 82 1 5 31½ 32 21½ 2½ Silva C I LB120 b 10.10 87– 15 BoltdHrt123½ BlEydBlond120½ [DH]*LnAndthLmb*123 Angled 3w, just missed 7
23Sep05–11Fpx fst 6½f :212 :443 1:09 1:16 Alw 43276N1x 73 6 2 3½ 32 34 78 Silva C I LB121 b 15.10 89– 09 ThingsHappen1201½ YesMster120½ GretAction1202½ Btwn, 2wide, wkened 7
14Oct04–4BM fst 1 :224 :464 1:12 1:372 Md Sp Wt 27k 75 2 1hd 1hd 1hd 12 14½ Warren R J Jr LB118 b 3.50 83– 20 BlueEyedBlond1184½ ShrpWritr118¾ CllingHom1181¼ Responded, driving 7
26Sep04–6BM fst 6f :22 :45 :572 1:11 Md Sp Wt 29k 45 10 5 53½ 45 59 710½ Warren R J Jr LB118 b 4.70 73– 16 Mazelman1182½ Southern Rule1181¼ Irish Immigrant118¾ 3w turn, no rally 11
7Aug04–10SR fst 5½f :22 :452 :58 1:042 Md Sp Wt 32k 38 9 4 54 53½ 42¼ 77¾ Warren R J Jr LB118 b 4.00 82– 09 Danny Dingle1181¼ Irish Dodger118¾ Hot Tizzy1182 Blckd 3/16s,weakened 10
WORKS: Sep18 Hol ◈4f fst :491 H *20/38* Sep11 Hol ◈5f fst 1:001 H *3/34* Sep4 Hol ◈4f fst :514 H *28/30* Aug16 Dmr ◈6f fst 1:141 H *5/23* Jly25 Dmr ◈5f fst 1:011 H *35/67* Jly18 Hol ◈4f fst :492 H *14/26*
TRAINER: Synth(75 .20 $1.17) 31-60Days(181 .22 $1.54) Sprint(466 .26 $1.93) Claim(240 .25 $1.57) J/T 2006-07 SA(45 .24 $1.68) J/T 2006-07(122 .22 $1.79)

12 Ridingwiththeking Own: Moran or Sobel — Lime — Black, White Martini Glass Emblem On — $20,000
ENRIQUEZ I D (—) 2007: (389 40 .10)
B. g. 5 (Apr)
Sire: Comic Strip (Red Ransom) $5,000
Dam: Perfect Sense (Tabasco Cat)
Br: Jack Hatch & Barb Hatch (Cal)
Tr: Sherman Art(—) 2007:(639 153 .24)
L 122

Life	10	3	1	2	$54,800	91	D.Fst	2	1	0	1	$15,840	81
2007	5	2	0	0	$31,200	91	Wet(338)	0	0	0	0	$0	–
2006	5	1	1	2	$23,600	85	Synth	6	2	1	1	$38,160	91
							Turf(280)	2	0	0	0	$800	66
SA	0	0	0	0	$0	–	Dst(270)	1	1	0	0	$16,200	91

Previously trained by West Ted H 2007(as of 8/25): (113 13 25 11 0.12)
25Aug07–9Dmr fst 6f ◈ :223 :46 :581 1:111 3↑[S]OC 25k/N1x-N 73 8 10 1014 98¼ 77¼ 77¾ Pedroza M A LB122 10.70 - - SnowFighter124¾ *DkotPdre*120no PocosinsGmeBoy1242½ Off rail,no threat 11
21Jly07–8Dmr fst 5½f ◈ :221 :46 :583 1:044 3↑[S]OC 25k/N1x-N 67 2 8 914 915 910 78¼ Enriquez I D LB121 3.70 - - GloblHet1211¼ MyCitybytheBy121¾ Bestdrssd1173¾ Off bit slow,no threat 9
15Jun07–6Hol fst 6½f ◈ :22 :45 1:102 1:163 4↑Clm c-(25-22.5) 91 3 10 1116 1110 52¼ 14¼ Enriquez I D LB121 4.10 90– 16 Rdngwththkng1214¼ QtProd121no NtrlPhnmnn1211½ 5wd into lane,rallied 11
Claimed from Chandler, Bruce and Matlow, Richard for $25,000, Matlow Richard P Trainer 2007(as of 6/15): (37 7 4 4 0.19)
5May07–7Hol fst 6f ◈ :213 :444 :571 1:103 3↑Clm 25000(25-22.5)N2L 89 5 12 1116 1110 46½ 11¼ Enriquez I D LB122 8.40 85– 12 *Ridingwiththeking*1221¼ Prssthpc1241¾ PpgoRod1241½ 5wd into lane,rallied 12
15Jan07–9SA fm *6½f ⓣ :22 :442 1:07 1:131 4↑Alw 40000s 66 8 11 119¾ 1110 1011 86¾ Enriquez I D LB119 11.90 82– 11 BeyondLoded1222½ *FrnchSouvnir*119½ *VictoryStyl*119½ 3wd into lane,no bid 12
15Dec06–6Hol fm 6f ⓣ :224 :451 :571 1:09 3↑Alw 40000s 62 3 10 98½ 910 99 88½ Flores D R LB124 *1.80 - - IslndLunch1241 FrnchSovnr121½ DrvnbyExcss1214½ Came out str,no rally 10
25Nov06–5Hol fst 7f ◈ :221 :441 1:091 1:223 3↑Alw 40000s 79 2 10 77¾ 67½ 31½ 31¼ Enriquez I D LB124 3.30 - - PowrShift121½ CtofFftySvn124¾ Rdngwththkng124hd Off bit slow,gamely 10
4Nov06–4Hol fst 6f ◈ :22 :443 :564 1:10 3↑Alw 40000s 85 3 7 86½ 810 47 22 Enriquez I D LB124 2.90 - - Save1242 Ridingwiththeking124½ Smart Hit121¾ 3wd into str,late 2nd 8
19Aug06–4Dmr fst 6f :213 :444 :571 1:103 3↑Alw 40000s 81 4 7 75½ 66½ 45 3½ Enriquez I D LB124 4.80 85– 13 HsTrihr122hd IndinChnt116½ Ridingwiththking1242½ 3wd into lane,late bid 8
23Jly06–3Dmr fst 6f :22 :451 :58 1:103 3↑Md 25000(25-22.5) 80 11 2 55 53½ 21 11 Enriquez I D LB124 19.00 86– 11 Ridingwiththeking1241 SylvanHill1191½ Fanaticl1172 4wd into lane,rallied 12
WORKS: Sep23 Hol ◈3f fst :372 H *20/31* Sep16 Hol ◈4f fst :512 H *30/37* Aug20 Dmr ◈5f fst 1:022 H *43/69* Aug15 Dmr ◈3f fst :373 H *14/22* Jly16 Dmr ◈4f fst :493 H *15/43* Jun30 SA 5f fst 1:041 H *34/37*
TRAINER: 1stW/Trn(214 .31 $1.89) Synth(136 .16 $3.38) 31-60Days(432 .26 $1.82) Sprint(958 .25 $1.95) Claim(658 .25 $1.62) J/T 2006-07(2 .00 $0.00)

The seventh race on opening day was for $20,000 older males with a par of 90. We'll accept anything within two lengths and look for the ability to record an 85 Beyer.

1. Double Parked has only one race at that Beyer level and is not a contender. That's also a pretty early class drop off that $28,000 claim.
2. Celtic Sword has no recent races that qualify, and all his best efforts have been in turf sprints. That's apples and oranges as far as today's situation is concerned.
3. B L's Danzig has a single giraffe effort at Calder and it was at the odd five-furlong distance.
4. Chips Are Down has multiple races that qualify him for this class level.
5. McNasty has 11 consecutive races while threatening the par only once. He's not close to what he was.
6. Wild Nekia has only a single effort that would win a truly run $20,000 claimer.
7. Oliver Twisted has a single 88—a giraffe race—and nothing to support that number. He's a noncontender.
8. Polo Bender is much like Oliver Twisted—a single effort in this Beyer ballpark. That race was at Emerald Downs on a sloppy track.
9. Megabyte is a strong contender and has the benefit of previous route stamina. An indirect "turn-back" play.
10. Datticus has several qualifying races and has to be considered. That drop off the claim from $40,000 should tell us they're not happy with the new purchase.
11. Blue Eyed Blond has two races at Bay Meadows that qualify as a contending possibility, but most bettors will require a significant edge when backing horses from lesser tracks.
12. Ridingwiththeking fits on figures but looks dull in terms of current condition.

The contenders for this 12-horse field are: (4) Chips Are Down; (9) Megabyte; (10) Datticus; (11) Blue Eyed Blond; and (12) Ridingwiththeking.

SEVENTH RACE 6½ FURLONGS. (1.14) CLAIMING . Purse $20,000 (plus $2,800 Other Sources) FOR THREE YEAR
OLDS AND UPWARD. Three Year Olds, 121 lbs.; Older, 124 lbs. Non–winners Of A Race Since August
10th Allowed 2 lbs. Claiming Price $20,000, For Each $1,000 To $18,000 1 lb. (Maiden And Claiming Races
For $16,000 Or Less Not Considered.)

Oak Tree at SA
SEPTEMBER 26, 2007

Value of Race: $22,800 Winner $12,000; second $4,000; third $2,400; fourth $1,200; fifth $400; sixth $400; seventh $400; eighth $400; ninth $400; tenth $400; eleventh $400; twelfth $400. Mutuel Pool $303,274.00 Exacta Pool $177,371.00 Trifecta Pool $146,363.00 Superfecta Pool $103,736.00

Last Raced	Horse	M/Eqt.	A.	Wt	PP	St	¼	½	Str	Fin	Jockey	Cl'g Pr	Odds $1
10Sep07 8Fpx3	Megabyte	LB h	5	124	9	4	6¹	8¹½	4¹½	1¹	Baze M C	20000	1.30
26Aug07 8Dmr9	Chips Are Down	LB b	5	122	4	7	9hd	5hd	1hd	2¾	Espinoza V	20000	8.70
8Sep06 12Fpx5	B L's Danzig	LB	4	122	3	6	4hd	3¹½	3¹½	3nk	Garcia M	20000	49.70
19Sep07 10Fpx3	Wild Nekia	LB bf	4	120	6	9	7¹½	6hd	5²	4²	Rosario J	18000	14.20
3Sep07 6Dmr4	Celtic Sword–Arg	LB b	8	122	2	12	10¹	9²	6²½	5½	Pedroza M A	20000	6.90
5Sep07 1Dmr9	Oliver Twisted	LB b	4	122	7	11	11⁴½	11²½	7hd	6hd	Jara F	20000	12.00
1Aug07 5Dmr4	Datticus	LB f	7	122	10	1	2¹	1½	2hd	7⁴½	Artieda P J	20000	12.90
25Aug07 9Dmr7	Ridingwiththeking	LB	5	122	12	3	12	12	10½	8¹¾	Enriquez I D	20000	6.60
25Aug07 9Dmr11	McNasty	LB b	6	117	5	8	8hd	10¹	9hd	9¹¾	Quinonez A5	20000	28.40
23Aug07 5Dmr6	Blue Eyed Blond	LB b	5	122	11	2	3¹	4¹	8¹	10⁴½	Gryder A T	20000	28.70
9Aug06 1Dmr3	Double Parked	LB bf	4	120	1	10	5¹½	7¹	11²½	11²	Migliore R	18000	18.70
5Aug07 5Dmr8	Polo Bender	LB b	6	122	8	5	1½	2¹	12	12	Baze T C	20000	25.40

OFF AT 4:09 Start Good. Won driving. Track fast.
TIME :21⁴, :45, 1:10, 1:16² (:21.83, :45.02, 1:10.07, 1:16.57)

$2 Mutuel Prices:	9 – MEGABYTE..................... 4.60	3.00	2.60
	4 – CHIPS ARE DOWN..................	7.00	4.80
	3 – B L'S DANZIG......................		14.80

$1 EXACTA 9–4 PAID $17.60 $1 TRIFECTA 9–4–3 PAID $488.10
$1 SUPERFECTA 9–4–3–6 PAID $4,777.30

B. g, (Mar), by Chief Seattle – Bright Royal, by Cure the Blues. Trainer Mitchell Mike. Bred by C F Newman (Ark).

MEGABYTE chased off the rail then outside, went three deep on the turn and into the stretch, rallied to the lead outside foes in deep stretch under some urging and proved best. CHIPS ARE DOWN steadied in tight early, chased outside a rival then three deep into and on the turn and into the stretch, gained a short lead nearing midstretch and held second. B L'S DANZIG stalked a bit off the rail then between foes, bid between rivals in the stretch and just held third. WILD NEKIA bobbled a bit at the start, chased just off the rail then between foes on the turn and just missed the show. CELTIC SWORD (ARG) broke a bit slowly, settled inside, came out leaving the turn and three deep into the stretch and bested the others. OLIVER TWISTED settled off the rail, went outside leaving the turn and three wide into the stretch and was not a threat. DATTICUS between foes early, dueled outside a rival, put a head in front on the turn, fought back inside in the stretch and weakened in the final furlong. RIDINGWITHTHEKING dropped back off the rail, angled in some for the turn, came out four wide into the stretch and did not rally. MCNASTY chased between foes then a bit off the rail and did not rally. BLUE EYED BLOND close up stalking the pace outside then three deep on the turn and into the stretch, weakened. DOUBLE PARKED went up inside to stalk the pace, came out into the stretch and also weakened. POLO BENDER had speed between foes then dueled inside, fought back on the turn but had little left for the stretch.

Owners– 1, Bone Robert D; 2, Robert and Beverly Lewis Trust; 3, Wilson David W and Holly F; 4, B G Stable and Royalty Stable; 5, Naify Marsha and Woodside Farms LLC; 6, Wilson James A; 7, Southern Equine Stable LLC; 8, Moran Michael and Sobel Steve; 9, Crevier and Plum Crazy Racing Stable; 10, Wind River Stables Berta Julie Koriner Brian et al; 11, Beauchamp Smith and Whitney; 12, Dill George R

Trainers– 1, Mitchell Mike; 2, Baffert Bob; 3, Cerin Vladimir; 4, Palma Hector O; 5, Canani Julio C; 6, Becerra Rafael; 7, Guillot Eric; 8, Sherman Art; 9, Yakteen Tim; 10, Koriner Brian; 11, Spawr Bill; 12, Glatt Mark

$2 Daily Double (1–9) Paid $91.60 ; Daily Double Pool $23,867 .
$1 Pick Three (3–1–9) Paid $219.90 ; Pick Three Pool $62,643 .

Megabyte won this as the favorite, but Chips Are Down came home second at 8–1 and produced a juicy $35.20 exacta for $2. The contender-selection process took about two minutes and I promise you that the results will be similar over time. Jim Quinn and I have taught this little technique for years with great success. The only difficult part of the task will be to set reasonable pars for these races. With a set of par times and some experience, this procedure will be a snap. It will also be a sweet surprise to see how many price horses are included in the mix. Good hunting.

PACE AND THE SYNTHETIC SURFACES

When Sinister Minister blew away his field in the 2006 Bluegrass Stakes, few of us knew that a dramatic change in the application of pace as a major handicapping factor was about to occur. Sinister Minister gained the lead early and was never challenged in the 1⅛-mile Kentucky Derby prep. He won as the rider pleased, recording pace and speed figures far superior to any other 3-year-old on the Derby trail, including eventual winner Barbaro. He became an instant "steam" horse, gaining far more support than was warranted. In truth, the race was bogus. The early-speed bias at Keeneland had propelled the winner to figures he would not achieve in any subsequent race. The prevailing early-pace bias was at its absolute zenith. Horses won on or very near the lead, race after race, season after season. Through mid-season 2007, Sinister Minister had not won another race. Things have changed at Keeneland.

The pre-Polytrack Keeneland was a pace handicapper's paradise. Horseplayers with a decent set of speed figures were assured a big chance at seasonal profits. There were only two negatives: first, that the Keeneland meetings were so short—another month or so would have been welcomed by every pace handicapper, me included—and second, that lots of players were tuned in to the ongoing bias, and the prices reflected that knowledge. But there were still plenty of winners to go around. The installation of Polytrack, however, changed everything.

Whether it's Polytrack, Cushion Track, Tapeta, or anything else that may soon come along, the impact of synthetic tracks on pace handicapping has been enormous. And the changes were instantaneous. The 2007 version of the Bluegrass was the ultimate example. The race was laboriously slow and draining at every call and was won in a multihorse blanket finish. It was downright ugly, and the pace and speed figures were dreadful for that class of 3-year-old colts. The eventual Kentucky Derby winner, Street Sense, labored all the way to the wire without really looking the part of a classics contender. What many of us missed was the effect of a synthetic track on overall stamina. Not exactly a turn-back play, but it was essentially the same. When he subsequently won the Derby it was more than simply a return to his favorite racetrack; it also affirmed the stamina-building effects of running on synthetic surfaces. The entire 2007 Keeneland spring meeting surprised most of us. The changes in the track profile were dramatic, and not entirely unwelcome.

TRACK PROFILES: MORE IMPORTANT THAN EVER

In the original *Modern Pace Handicapping,* I offered an argument on the creation and uses of a track profile. That was in 1989, and the concept certainly caught on with handicappers, especially pace handicappers. Knowing where the bulk of winners were best positioned in a race was, and is, of immense importance. In today's market the data is readily available through a number of websites and is absolutely indispensable as an aid to catching that one extra winner that puts the player into the black. With the onslaught of synthetic surfaces, the concept has become even more vital to successful play.

Prior to the synthetics, early speed had long been recognized as the universal bias. Especially in California, virtually every profile I ever created placed the bulk of winners in the top third of the field early and positioned just a few lengths off the lead. Early speed is still, and will probably remain, a key factor in the selection of winners. But the bloom is a bit off this rose as stamina becomes more a part of main-track racing in the United States. With the advent of Polytrack, Cushion Track, and Tapeta, more winners are coming from deeper in the field of runners. Deliciously, many more will come from horses turning back in distance, which is what we're all about in this chapter. The stamina gained by these runners will provide a greater edge than ever before, and that fits my personal play to a T. A useable track profile should provide a solid edge to finding many of those winners. A quick review of the procedure, and we'll return to the main point of the chapter.

The object of the profile is simply to identify winning running styles and the ideal position throughout the running of the race. An easily updated worksheet should be well within the daily time constraints of even the most casual player, and the results are invaluable. Something similar to the following should do the trick:

Dist	Ent.	Post	1Call	2Call	Style	Dist	Ent.	Post	1Call	2Call	Style

Working from the results charts, the entries are pretty self-explanatory.

1. Dist: The distance of the race, with separate profiles for each distance. The profiles can differ greatly between even the most minor shifts in distance: 6½ furlongs will often be significantly different from the six-furlong category at the same track.
2. Ent: The number of entries in the recorded race. The significance of fourth position early in a 12-horse race is far greater than the same position in a six-horse field. The former may be a pace presser while the latter is almost certainly a closer.
3. Post: Why not track for possible post-position bias while we have the results charts right in front of us?
4. 1Call: Position and beaten lengths of the race winner at the first call (four furlongs in a route and two furlongs in a sprint).
5. 2Call: Position and beaten lengths of the race winner at the second call of the race (six furlongs in a route and four furlongs in a sprint).
6. Style: The perceived running style of the winner. I consider position more important than beaten lengths in determining the winner's running style.

Be sure and date the entries and frequently summarize the data. With a reliable track profile, even the most inexperienced handicappers have a fighting chance against the knowledgeable players on the circuit. The data from the profile is indispensable, and the chapter's main thrust, the turn-back play, will be tightened through the use of the profile.

POWER SPRINTERS

In the late 1980s, Jim Quinn and I became close friends and handicapping partners in seminar activities. The friendship has lasted, as have certain insights gained from each other. A topic of conversation each season has been one of my favorite races of the year, the Breeders' Cup Sprint. My previous approach was to apply the Sartin Methodology to the race, and that did produce moderate success. Jim had a different approach, one I use to this day.

Traditional handicapping had always cautioned against betting horses shortening to a sprint distance after one or two routes. The logic was solid and still is, but there was a basic flaw in that logic. What about the runners demonstrating the speed and ability to win against top company at either distance category? The Sprint features the very best sprinters in the country, each giving every ounce of available energy at every step of the six-furlong distance. It takes a gritty, classy horse to withstand the pressure cooker that is the Sprint. Few can handle that pressure, and some of the best sprinters in the country have failed the test. The turn-back play has provided the winner often enough to show a nice profit and a number of live runners.

Quinn referred to these sprinters as power sprinters, and his ideas snugly fit my own and others using the Sartin Methodology. Unlike the staple turn-back, however, there are some other conditions that must be met beyond the ability to exceed the fractional pars in their routes. First, a few examples:

1. The ultimate power sprinter remains the 1985 Sprint winner, Precisionist. This Fred Hooper runner had won Grade 1 races up to 1¼ miles against the absolute best horses of his generation. He simply oozed class, and brought both stamina and blazing speed to the Breeders' Cup party. The traditional thinkers assumed the distance would be too short for this guy and let him go as a low-priced overlay. He powered his way to one of the most impressive wins in Sprint history. His speed and Grade 1 ability at middle distances set him apart from his field, and the price was more than fair for the effort.

2. Using this approach to graded sprint races, I tackled the 1994 Sprint for a popular racing magazine and landed on Cherokee Run. This one had just lost the Grade 1 Vosburgh (a blessing at the time), but was consistently one of the fastest sprinters in the country. He had more than sprint ability, however; Cherokee Run had also shown that speed coupled with a competitive desire to win against graded company at middle distances. He won as another low-priced overlay.

3. The best recent version of the prototypical power sprinter came in the 2005 renewal of the Sprint at Belmont Park. In a race typically loaded with very strong sprinters, Silver Train fit the mold as the power sprinter to watch. He was coming off a win in the Grade 2 Jerome Handicap at a mile over the same track, so at 11–1 he was absolutely the play and was my top call at a Breeders' Cup Day seminar at Santa Anita. He returned $25.80 and made the day for many of us.

These examples of the power sprinter are not freakish occurrences. The play remains a staple in my own betting and is a valuable extension of the turn-back. Here is what we're looking for:

1. The ability to handle both sprints and middle distances against top company. In the Breeders' Cup Sprint, that means Grade 1 company.
2. A horse that has earned figures that match or exceed the class level at both distance categories. The top sprints and middle-distance races in this country usually exceed 110 on the Beyer figure scale and our contender must match or exceed that number sprinting *and* routing.
3. The horse must clearly be in top form and should have a recent middle-distance race in his past performances.

Keying on power sprinters in graded sprint stakes has long been my method of choice for these events. I doubt the reader could go far astray by adopting a similar approach to these highly contentious races.

A PERFECT TURN-BACK PLAY: THE SENATOR KEN MADDY STAKES

The traditional opening-day feature at the Oak Tree at Santa Anita meeting is the Grade 3 Senator Ken Maddy Stakes. It is run on Santa Anita's unique hillside turf course and features some of the best fillies and mares on the local circuit. The 2007 version was a perfect example of this chapter's theme.

8 **Santa Anita** ***About 6½ Furlongs*** **(Turf). (1:11) ⒻSKMaddyH-G3 39th Running of THE SENATOR KEN MADDY HANDICAP. Grade III. Purse $100,000 Downhill Turf For Fillies And Mares, Three Years Old And Upward. By subscription of $100 each if made on or before Thursday, September 20, 2007 or by supplementary nomination of $2,000 by 10 AM, Saturday, September 22. All horses to pay $1,000 to startwith $100,000 added. The added money and all fees to be divided 60% to the winner, 20% to second, 12% to third, 6% to fourth and 2% to fifth. Weights: Saturday, September 22. Starters to be named through the entry box by the usual time of closing. Three Year Olds allowed 3 lbs. on scale. Closed with 20 nominations.**

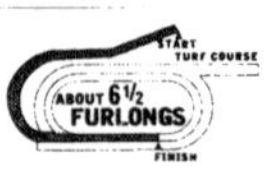

1 Super Freaky Red
Own: Suarez Racing Inc or Venneri Racing I
Royal Blue, White 'Reme' On Blue And
COURT J K (—) 2007: (653 60 .09)

Dk. b or br f. 3 (Jan) KEESEP05 $140,000
Sire: Smart Strike (Mr. Prospector) $75,000
Dam: Elrose (Deputy Minister)
Br: Starlight Stables (Fla)
Tr: O'Neill Doug(—) 2007:(787 123 .16)

L 115

Life	12	3	3	2	$313,070	94	D.Fst	2	0	0	1	$25,400	74
2007	8	2	3	1	$276,470	94	Wet(407)	0	0	0	0	$0	–
							Synth	1	0	0	0	$0	68
2006	4	1	0	1	$36,600	74	Turf(339)	9	3	3	1	$287,670	94
SAⓉ	4	3	1	0	$170,800	94	DstⓉ(393)	2	1	1	0	$78,040	89

18Aug07-8Dmr	fm	1⅛	Ⓣ	:462 1:102 1:35 1:463	ⒻDMrOaks-G1	84	4	41¾	41½	41¼	11	36½	Espinoza V	LB122	8.80	83-10	Rutherienne1222 Valbenny1224½ SuperFreaky122nk	3wd into lane,held 3rd	10
28Jly07-9Dmr	fm	1	Ⓣ	:213 :462 1:102 1:34	ⒻSnClmntH-G2	78	6	64½	64¼	63¼	55	54¾	Court J K	LB120	*1.30	86-08	Passified119½ Fleet Caroline1141 Spenditallbaby118½	3wd,4wd,no rally	10
9Jun07-5Hol	fm	1⅛	Ⓣ	:484 1:123 1:362 1:48	+ⒻHnymnBCH-G2	91	6	2½	1hd	2hd	1hd	21¾	Court J K	LB120	3.20	79-09	Valbenny1231¾ Super Freaky120hd Mystic Soul1171¾	Pulled,vied,held 2nd	7
12May07-7Hol	fm	1	Ⓣ	:232 :471 1:104 1:342	ⒻSenorita-G3	91	3	43	31½	3½	3nk	21¾	Court J K	LB121	2.80	90-16	*Valbenny*1211¾ Super Freaky1211¼ Passified121½	Bid 3wd,led,held 2nd	8
7Apr07-7SA	fm	1	Ⓣ	:231 :471 1:112 1:352	ⒻPrvdncia-G3	94	3	32½	33½	32	2hd	1¾	Court J K	LB117	8.90	87-12	Super Freaky117¾ Passified119¾ Gotta Have Her1151¼	3wd bid,led,gamely	11
4Mar07-8SA	fm	*6½f	Ⓣ	:204 :423 1:061 1:123	ⒻLaHabra113k	89	1	5	24½	23½	13½	11¼	Court J K	LB116	6.70	92-09	*Super Freaky*1161¼ [D]**Macadamia**116½ Pay Wright122no	Led dirt,clear,held	11
27Jan07-2SA	fst	6f		:211 :443 :571 1:102	Ⓕ[R]SunMilOaks250k	74	8	7	63¼	75¼	55	45¼	Court J K	LB120	12.30	82-09	*MisticalPln*120no TizElementl1203½ *DoubleMjor*1201¾	4wd into str,best rest	12
15Jan07-6SA	fm	*6½f	Ⓣ	:213 :433 1:07 1:132	ⒻOC 80k/n1x-N	76	10	2	31	2½	31½	22	Nakatani C S	LB118	*1.60	86-11	*Passified*1182 Super Freaky118¾ **Macadamia**1121	Bid,vied,edged foe 2nd	10
17Dec06-9Hol	fst	1 1/16	◈	:222 :452 1:101 1:423	ⒻHolStrlt-G1	68	3	23½	22	11	22	99¾	Garcia M	LB120 b	28.00	- -	RomanceIsDine1201 QuickLittleMiss120½ Down1202½	Rail bid,led,wkened	12
25Nov06-9Hol	fm	1	Ⓣ	:242 :491 1:131 1:362	ⒻMiesque-G3	73	4	43	32	31	2hd	41½	Valenzuela P A	LB117 b	8.50	80-14	*Valbenny*117¾ Mystic Soul115nk **Spenditallbaby**119½	Pulled,bid,btwn late	12
27Oct06-5OSA	fm	1	Ⓣ	:232 :472 1:112 1:352	ⒻMd Sp Wt 44k	74	4	21	2½	21½	21	1¾	Gomez G K	LB120 b	3.30	86-14	SuperFreaky120¾ Moujane1201¼ PinkPolkadots120½	Re-bid lane,led,game	11
15Jun06-6Hol	fst	5f		:212 :45 :574	ⒻMd Sp Wt 46k	71	4	6	32½	33½	33	37½	Valenzuela P A	LB120 b	3.40	84-13	Thru n'Thru1201 CocoBelle1156½ *SuperFreaky*1202½	Came out str,best rest	9

WORKS: Sep19 **Hol ◈5f fst 1:02 H** *20/36* Sep12 **Hol ◈4f fst :484 H** *11/28* Aug11 **Dmr ◈5f fst 1:01 H** *36/72* Jly21 **Dmr ◈5f fst 1:002 H** *6/81* Jly19 **Dmr ◈3f fst :364 H** *11/33* Jly14 **Hol ◈5f fst 1:021 H** *26/52*
TRAINER: Route/Sprint(153 .16 $1.77) 31-60Days(507 .18 $1.80) Turf(419 .14 $1.34) Sprint(1095 .17 $1.57) GrdStk(151 .17 $1.74) J/T 2006-07 SA(57 .18 $1.42) J/T 2006-07(125 .17 $1.21)

2 Itsawonderfullife (Ire) | B. f. 3 (Apr) | Life 3 1 1 1 $34,591 81 | D.Fst 0 0 0 0 $0 –

White Own: Fab Oak Stable & Lakin | Sire: Danehill Dancer*Ire (Danehill) | 2007 2 1 1 0 $32,308 81 | Wet(268*) 0 0 0 0 $0 –

Green, Yellow 'Kj' In Red Diamond Frame | Dam: Cahermee Queen (King of Kings*Ire) | L 109 | 2006 1 M 0 1 $2,283 – | Synth 0 0 0 0 $0 –

QUINONEZ A (—) 2007: (947 133 .14) | Br: Lynn Lodge Stud (Ire) | SAⓉ 0 0 0 0 $0 – | Turf(348) 3 1 1 1 $34,591 81

Tr: Biancone Patrick L(—) 2007:(250 47 .19) | DstⓉ(254) 0 0 0 0 $0 –

28Jun07-4CD fm 1 Ⓣ :234 :473 1:12 1:372 3↑ⒻMd Sp Wt 42k 81 7 64½ 73¾ 52½ 13 15½ Leparoux J R L117 *.60 83-17 Itswondrfullif1175½ QuitAlc1172¼ BrdgtOFlynn117nk Awk start,ridden out 9

2Jun07-4CD fm 1 Ⓣ :233 :472 1:121 1:363 3↑ⒻMd Sp Wt 45k 75 1 1011 107¼ 106¾ 56 23 Leparoux J R L118 1.60 84-11 *LdyAttck*1183 *Itswonderfullife*1181¼ FlyingDggers1183¾ Broke slowly in air 12

Previously trained by David Wachman

14Jun06 Leopardstwn (Ire) gf 7f Ⓣ LH 1:304 ⒻIrish Stallion Farms EBF Maiden 34¼ Lordan W M 126 6.50 Miss Beatrix1263½ Evening Rushour126¾ Itsawonderfullife126¼ 10

Racing Post Rating: 64 Maiden 25100 *Rated in 5th,3rd 170y out,stayed on*

WORKS: ●Sep22 SA ◇4f fst :45 H *1/30* Sep4 Kee ◇5f fst 1:003 B *4/7* Jly30 Sar tr.tⓉ 5f fm 1:003 H *11/26* ●Jly15 Kee ◇5f fst 1:00 B *1/7*

TRAINER: 61-180Days(90 .32 $2.37) Route/Sprint(31 .19 $1.43) WonLastStart(108 .19 $1.20) Turf(229 .22 $1.72) Sprint(200 .18 $1.35) GrdStk(156 .15 $1.47)

3 Runway Rosie | Gr/ro. f. 3 (Feb) KEESEP05 $30,000 | Life 9 2 1 1 $145,700 90 | D.Fst 5 0 1 1 $61,700 90

Blue Own: Class Racing Rosenblum & Rosenblum | Sire: Include (Broad Brush) $25,000 | 2007 4 0 1 1 $57,640 90 | Wet(235) 0 0 0 0 $0 –

Yellow, White R On Blue Lightning | Dam: Kids Today (Siphon*Brz) | L 111 | 2006 5 2 0 0 $88,060 74 | Synth 3 1 0 0 $60,000 74

BAZE M C (—) 2007: (985 172 .17) | Br: Equus Farm (Ky) | SAⓉ 1 1 0 0 $24,000 65 | Turf(230) 1 1 0 0 $24,000 65

Tr: Hofmans David(—) 2007:(140 15 .11) | DstⓉ(331) 1 1 0 0 $24,000 65

2Sep07-7Dmr fst 1 ◇ :241 :484 1:144 1:41 ⒻTorryPines140k 66 9 99¾ 813 67½ 1112 1115¼ Talamo J LB123 15.80 - - SesideAffir1194¾ RomnceIsDine123½ SilverSwllow1171½ 3 wide, weakened 11

11Mar07-9SA fst 1¹⁄₁₆ :231 :47 1:113 1:424 ⒻSAOaks-G1 57 1 42½ 51¾ 53 511 522¼ Migliore R LB122 15.40 64-12 *RagstoRiches*1225½ SilverSwllow1221 CshIncluded1222½ Chased, gave way 5

10Feb07-9SA fst 1 :231 :472 1:114 1:374 ⒻLsVrgnes-G1 88 3 44 53 41½ 21½ 32¾ Migliore R LB120 11.10 76-26 *RgstoRiches*116¾ BronessThtcher1202 RunwyRosi1201¾ Inside,bested rest 8

6Jan07-7SA fst 1¹⁄₁₆ :231 :472 1:114 1:441 ⒻSntYsabl-G3 90 3 44½ 42½ 41½ 41½ 2½ Migliore R LB122 6.40 78-21 BronessThtcher114½ RunwyRosi1225½ *MisticlPln*1192½ Waited 1/4,willingly 7

17Dec06-9Hol fst 1¹⁄₁₆ ◇ :222 :452 1:101 1:423 ⒻHolStrlt-G1 65 10 1115 1116 118½ 117½ 1011¼ Gomez G K LB120 6.50 - - Romance Is Diane1201 QuickLittleMiss120½ Down1202½ Angled in, no rally 12

5Nov06-8Hol fst 1¹⁄₁₆ ◇ :244 :484 1:131 1:452 ⒻSharpCat100k 74 1 53 52 51½ 3½ 1½ Gomez G K LB117 5.00 - - RunwyRosie117½ **Spenditllbby**119¾ BckintheShde1172 Bid 3wd 1/8,led,held 6

14Oct06-4OSA fm *6½f Ⓣ :221 :444 1:08 1:134 ⒻMd Sp Wt 41k 65 2 6 52½ 64½ 31 1hd Arroyo N Jr LB120 4.80 86-10 *Runway Rosie*120hd *Lavender Sky*1201 *Angel Eyed*1151 3wd into lane,rallied 9

20Aug06-5Dmr fst 6f :22 :452 :581 1:113 ⒻMd Sp Wt 72k 61 9 3 42 64½ 53¾ 55¾ Gryder A T LB120 14.40 75-12 Berriestoheven120¾ Moujne1202½ SolidBrssCt120hd Stalked pace, no rally 11

16Jly06-8Hol fst 6f :214 :444 :58 1:111 ⒻMd Sp Wt 47k 57 9 2 51½ 44 45 46¾ Garcia M5 LB115 6.60 74-14 CompanySecret1151½ *Berriestoheaven*1203½ Moujne1152½ 3wd turn,no rally 10

WORKS: Sep23 SA ◇4f fst :502 H *24/35* ●Sep17 Hol ◇6f fst 1:124 H *1/17* ●Aug24 Dmr ◇7f fst 1:272 H *1/7* Aug18 Dmr ◇6f fst 1:141 H *15/31* Aug11 Dmr ◇5f fst 1:021 H *51/72* Aug5 Dmr ◇4f fst :511 H *53/58*

TRAINER: 2Off45-180(25 .24 $1.43) Synth/Turf(6 .00 $0.00) Route/Sprint(24 .08 $0.96) Turf(80 .15 $1.38) Sprint(140 .14 $1.24) GrdStk(37 .19 $1.19) J/T 2006-07(8 .13 $0.42)

4 Dancing Edie | B. m. 5 (Jan) | Life 19 3 7 2 $713,595 101 | D.Fst 6 0 1 1 $26,680 67

Yellow Own: Basin Fast Lane Farms Reddam Et Al | Sire: Moscow Ballet (Nijinsky II) $3,000 | 2007 3 0 2 0 $100,015 96 | Wet(347) 0 0 0 0 $0 –

White, Purple Hoop, White Bar On Purple | Dam: Duchess of Ack (Slewpy) | L 122 | 2006 8 2 3 0 $513,400 101 | Synth 0 0 0 0 $0 –

NAKATANI C S (—) 2007: (553 89 .16) | Br: Fast Lane Farms & Donald Reiker (Cal) | SAⓉ 2 1 1 0 $114,800 101 | Turf(303) 13 3 6 1 $686,915 101

Tr: Dollase Craig(—) 2007:(167 33 .20) | DstⓉ(341) 0 0 0 0 $0 –

4Aug07-9Dmr fm 1⅛ Ⓣ :464 1:102 1:342 1:461 3↑ⒻJCMabeeH-G1 96 1 12 11 11½ 21½ 21½ Nakatani C S LB119 3.20 90-09 *PreciousKitten*1191½ DncingEdie119no Memorett115½ Speed,held 2nd btwn 5

6Jly07-5Hol fm 1 Ⓣ :224 :46 1:093 1:332 3↑ⒻCshCllMl-G2 87 4 41½ 52¼ 95¾ 85¼ 88 Nakatani C S LB123 10.90 89-08 LadyofVenice1191¼ *PreciousKitten*121hd PriceTag1231½ Steadied into lane 9

9Jun07-8Hol fm 1 Ⓣ :24 :474 1:112 1:343 3↑Ⓕ[R]RedondoBch95k 94 1 1½ 1½ 1hd 2hd 2hd Nakatani C S LB121 2.80 91-09 *Somthinboutlur*121hd DncingEd121nk ArmCndy119¾ Fought back rail,game 8

4Nov06-5CD fm 1⅜ Ⓣ :493 1:144 1:384 2:142 3↑ⒻBCFMTrf-G1 86 1 1½ 1½ 2½ 810 812¼ Nakatani C S L123 36.50 86 - OuijaBoard1232¼ FilmMker123nk HoneyRyder1231¾ Inside pace,weakened 10

30Sep06-4OSA fm 1¼ Ⓣ :481 1:124 1:362 1:592 3↑ⒻYlwRibbn-G1 101 7 1½ 11 1hd 22½ 24½ Nakatani C S LB123 14.00 87-12 WitWhile1204½ DncingEdie123nk ThreeDegres1231¼ Pulled,inside,held 2nd 8

22Jly06-6Dmr fm 1⅛ Ⓣ :49 1:131 1:363 1:481 3↑ⒻJCMabeeH-G1 93 1 11½ 11½ 1½ 1hd 1no Nakatani C S LB119 4.00 88-10 DncngEd119no MoscwBrnng119nk IslndFshn116hd Drifted bit,game btwn 7

1Jly06-6Hol fm 1 Ⓣ :23 :461 1:094 1:331 3↑ⒻCashCall-G3 95 4 43 32 42½ 43 42½ Valenzuela P A LB119 14.00 95-08 DnceintheMood1231¾ SweetTlker123½ LusLine123nk Stdied 7/8,missed 3rd 8

29May06-6Hol fm 1⅛ Ⓣ :483 1:114 1:351 1:464+3↑ⒻGamelyBC-G1 89 6 11½ 11½ 1hd 2hd 21¾ Baze T C LB116 10.90 95-01 ShiningEnergy1181¾ DancingEdie116hd Argentin116½ Inside,game for 2nd 7

30Apr06-3Hol fm 1¹⁄₁₆ Ⓣ :224 :453 1:091 1:392 4↑Ⓕ[S]FrnsValntn150k 88 5 2½ 11 11½ 12½ 2nk Gomez G K LB116 2.50 95 - Memorette116nk DncingEdi116¾ MoscowBurning1242½ Inside,caught late 7

2Apr06-9SA fm 1⅛ Ⓣ :482 1:124 1:37 1:49 4↑Ⓕ[S]OC 32k/n1x-N 88 7 11½ 11½ 11½ 12½ 14 Gomez G K LB118 *1.30 84-17 DncingEdie1184 SipOneforMom1183 *ChelceesHop*118hd Inside, ridden out 8

10Mar06-7SA fst 1 :224 :463 1:121 1:391 4↑Ⓕ[S]OC 32k/n1x-N 60 6 11 1hd 31½ 45 410½ Nakatani C S LB119 *1.40 61-26 DanceoftheYear119nk OlRazzleDazzle119¾ LChol1211½ Dueled, weakened 7

10Sep05-7Bel fst 1⅛ :463 1:104 1:361 1:493 ⒻGazelle-G1 – 1 53 511 522 - - Nakatani C S L118 10.00 - 18 IntheGold1172¼ LeveMeAlone1191 YolndBToo1153¼ Stumbled badly start 5

WORKS: Sep19 Hol ◇6f fst 1:14 H *9/12* Sep12 Hol ◇5f fst 1:003 H *8/41* Sep6 Hol ◇4f fst :492 H *11/35* Jly29 DmrⓉ 6f fm 1:143 H(d) *3/5* Jly23 Dmr ◇5f fst 1:02 H *41/69* Jun30 Hol ◇6f fst 1:154 H *9/12*

TRAINER: Route/Sprint(21 .14 $1.02) 31-60Days(108 .20 $1.85) Turf(138 .17 $1.98) Sprint(136 .21 $1.77) GrdStk(50 .06 $1.19) J/T 2006-07 SA(25 .16 $1.71) J/T 2006-07(62 .19 $1.75)

5 Lady Gamer | B. f. 4 (Jan) | Life 9 4 2 1 $186,610 99 | D.Fst 3 1 1 0 $44,400 85

Green Own: Clark & Janine Hansen | Sire: Game Plan (Danzig) $3,500 | 2007 2 1 0 1 $69,870 99 | Wet(377) 0 0 0 0 $0 –

White, Gold Circle Rose Wreath H, Gold | Dam: Mariah Reyna (Far North) | L 115 | 2006 7 3 2 0 $116,740 85 | Synth 4 3 0 1 $129,210 99

FLORES D R (—) 2007: (674 119 .18) | Br: Clark A Hansen & Janine Rae Hansen (Cal) | SAⓉ 1 0 0 0 $400 75 | Turf(296) 2 0 1 0 $13,000 79

Tr: Sadler John W(—) 2007:(443 76 .17) | DstⓉ(318) 0 0 0 0 $0 –

17Aug07-7Dmr fst 6½f ◇ :223 :46 1:111 1:174 3↑ⒻRchBrdoH-G3 87 2 3 11 1½ 31½ 35¼ Flores D R LB116 3.80 - - RiversPrayer121½ **StrongFaith**1154¾ LadyGamer1161¾ Btwn,inside,held 3rd 5

24Jun07-3Hol fst 6f ◇ :222 :451 :572 1:094 3↑Ⓕ[S]Valkyr76k 99 2 3 11 12 12½ 12¼ Flores D R LB117 7.50 89-16 LadyGmer1172¼ GetbckTime1213 VcCityFlyer1174½ Rail,strong hand ride 5

10Dec06-8Hol fst 6½f ◇ :222 :452 1:101 1:163 3↑ⒻAlw 53514n1x 81 8 1 41½ 72¼ 32 11½ Gomez G K LB122 *1.80 - - *Lady Gamer*1221½ True Xena122hd *Smart Crowd*1241½ 4wd,3wd,rallied 10

5Nov06-6Hol fst 6½f ◇ :221 :452 1:102 1:164 3↑Ⓕ[S]Alw 44200n1x 85 5 3 51½ 62¼ 1½ 12 Gomez G K LB122 3.20 - - *LdyGmer*1222 QurterlyReport117nk MonkeyFce1223½ Bit tight3-1/2,rallied 8

8Oct06-7OSA fm 1 Ⓣ :222 :461 1:10 1:342 3↑Ⓕ[S]OC 25k/n1x-N 75 4 11 1½ 1hd 42½ 94½ Nakatani C S LB119 *2.70 87-11 YerlyAttitude120½ SilkKerchief1201 *BchelorettOn*116¾ Lugged out,wkened 11

31Aug06-2Dmr fm 5f Ⓣ :212 :442 :561 3↑Ⓕ[S]OC 25k/n1x-N 79 3 3 1hd 1hd 11½ 2hd Nakatani C S LB121 *1.30 94-06 VelvetySmooth124hd LdyGmer1211½ MmsllAris1211½ Dueled,clear,caught 7

4Aug06-6Dmr fst 6f :214 :451 :58 1:111 3↑Ⓕ[S]Md Sp Wt 55k 79 2 6 2hd 1hd 1½ 1½ Nakatani C S LB119 2.90 83-20 LdyGmer119½ *Forthewrongreson*1191¾ Rspctd1194¼ Shifted out 1/8,gamely 12

1Jly06-2Hol fst 6½f :214 :444 1:102 1:17 3↑Ⓕ[S]Md Sp Wt 62k 59 1 11 72¼ 75¼ 66½ 47¼ Garcia M5 LB114 *1.00 79-11 MmselleAries119¾ RushtoJustice119¾ ProudCecy1195¾ Broke in,stumbled 11

14May06-3Hol fst 6f :213 :443 :572 1:102 3↑Ⓕ[S]Md Sp Wt 45k 85 1 6 52¾ 53¼ 31 2no Garcia M5 LB112 12.70 85-14 Tiz a Gem117no Lady Gamer112¾ Neutrality1176½ 4wd,drift in,out lane 6

WORKS: Sep20 SA ◇6f fst 1:122 H *14/29* ●Sep14 SA ◇6f fst 1:123 H *1/8* Sep8 SA ◇5f fst :59 H *6/21* Sep2 Dmr ◇4f fst :502 H *30/40* Aug13 Dmr ◇4f fst :474 H *5/66* Aug6 Dmr ◇5f fst 1:003 H *6/56*

TRAINER: 2Off45-180(118 .18 $1.33) Synth/Turf(24 .08 $0.59) 31-60Days(330 .20 $1.50) Turf(309 .16 $1.61) Sprint(584 .18 $1.51) GrdStk(46 .20 $1.60) J/T 2006-07 SA(27 .26 $1.46) J/T 2006-07(54 .24 $1.62)

6 Fantastic Spring

Own: Magenta Racing Inc

Black Magenta, Gold Collar And Cuffs, Magenta

TALAMO J (—) 2007: (1214 211 .17)

B. f. 4 (Apr) KEESEP04 $400,000
Sire: Fantastic Light (Rahy)
Dam: Spring Pitch (Storm Cat)
Br: Robert S Evans (Ky)
Tr: Miller Peter(—) 2007:(184 29 .16)

L 115

Life	6	3	1	0	$116,040	94	D.Fst	0	0	0	0	$0	–
2007	5	3	1	0	$113,400	94	Wet(352*)	0	0	0	0	$0	–
2006	1	M	0	0	$2,640	63	Synth	0	0	0	0	$0	–
SAⓉ	3	1	1	0	$39,440	84	Turf(421)	6	3	1	0	$116,040	94
							DstⓉ(284)	3	1	1	0	$39,440	84

16Aug07-4Dmr fm 5f Ⓣ :212 :432 :551 3↑ⒻOC 62k/n2x-N 94 6 2 12 1½ 11½ 12 Talamo J LB122 fb *1.90 97- 03 FantsticSpring1222 CocoBelle1163 IntoRelity118hd Speed,angled in,clear 8

2Aug07-7Dmr fm 5f Ⓣ :212 :433 :55 3↑ⒻOC 40k/n1x-N 86 2 4 1hd 11 12½ 11¾ Nakatani C S LB124 fb 3.10 98- 02 *FantasticSpring*1241¾ StrletofSettle1241¾ LdyMtild124¾ Inside, ridden out 7

5May07-9Hol fm 1 1/16 Ⓣ :24 :482 1:12 1:411 4↑ⒻAlw 54836n1x 44 6 21 21 2½ 55½ 1019¾ Espinoza V LB118 fb 2.80 67- 15 BrncComoNv1181½ AnglCrft1152½ RocktKtty1232 Bid btwn foes,gave way 10

13Apr07-1SA fm *6½f Ⓣ :221 :441 1:07 1:13 4↑ⒻMd Sp Wt 49k 84 3 2 1hd 1hd 11½ 14¾ Espinoza V LB122 fb *.40 90- 10 FntstcSprng1224¾ SdnsScrt1221¾ IslndLghtnn1223½ Vied,clear,ridden out 7

14Mar07-3SA fm *6½f Ⓣ :214 :433 1:053 1:114 4↑ⒻMd Sp Wt 47k 82 2 2 21 22 21½ 23 Espinoza V LB122 fb 10.40 93- 04 RunRosi1223 *FntsticSpring*122nk *ThvrythoughtofU*122hd Held 2nd btwn late 8

Previously trained by Baffert Bob 2005: (467 94 67 62 0.20)

8Jan06-4SA fm *6½f Ⓣ :223 :453 1:084 1:144 ⒻMd Sp Wt 48k 63 5 6 63¼ 85 52¾ 43¾ Ochoa J7 LB114 b 9.00 77- 19 FrostyMomnts1212¼ ChrmingLgcy121hd JoliClur1211½ Steadied into lane 12

WORKS: Sep20 SLR 5f fst 1:021 H *3/4* Sep14 SLR 4f fst :501 H *5/10* Jly23 Dmr ◈5f fst 1:004 H *14/69* Jly17 Dmr ◈4f fst :493 H *25/62* Jly11 SLR 4f fst :49 H *3/3* Jly5 SLR 3f fst :382 H *1/1*

TRAINER: 31-60Days(58 .19 $2.97) WonLastStart(56 .29 $2.82) Turf(103 .18 $2.22) Sprint(220 .20 $2.12) GrdStk(19 .11 $2.01) J/T 2006-07 SA(1 .00 $0.00) J/T 2006-07(12 .17 $0.97)

7 Strong Faith

Own: Sahud Sahud & Saleby

Orange Coffee, Cream Yoke, Chocolate Dots On

BLANC B (—) 2007: (425 44 .10)

Dk. b or br m. 6 (Feb)
Sire: Pioneering (Mr. Prospector) $5,000
Dam: Let's Eat Out (Banquet Table)
Br: Rose Hill Farm Inc (Ky)
Tr: Mullins Jeff(—) 2007:(397 92 .23)

L 115

Life	46	8	11	8	$326,312	98	D.Fst	16	1	3	4	$34,273	73
2007	8	0	4	1	$103,484	98	Wet(369)	7	3	2	1	$74,780	92
2006	10	4	0	0	$114,975	93	Synth	3	0	2	0	$73,000	98
SAⓉ	5	0	1	1	$25,234	93	Turf(318)	20	4	4	3	$144,259	93
							DstⓉ(350)	2	0	0	1	$13,044	93

17Aug07-7Dmr fst 6½f ◈ :223 :46 1:111 1:174 3↑ⒻRchBrdoH-G3 98 5 2 43½ 33 21½ 2½ Garcia M LB115 3.90 - - RiversPrayer121½ StrongFaith1154¾ **LadyGamer**1161¾ 3wd into lane,rallied 5

6Jly07-7Hol fst 7f ◈ :222 :45 1:092 1:214 3↑ⒻAGleamH-G2 97 3 3 1½ 2hd 11 2¾ Garcia M LB114 51.80 96- 11 Somthnbtlr122¾ StrngFth1141¼ *ThvrythghtfU*1123 Inched away,worn down 10

9Jun07-8Hol fm 1 Ⓣ :24 :474 1:112 1:343 3↑ⒻⓇRedondoBch95k 86 6 86¼ 62¾ 53¼ 74 73¾ Garcia M LB119 4.80 87- 09 *Somethinaboutlur*121hd **DncingEdie**121nk ArmCndy119¾ Stdied 7/8,4wd lane 8

Previously trained by Martin John F 2007(as of 4/15): (75 14 18 10 0.19)

15Apr07-7SA fm *6½f Ⓣ :214 :441 1:063 1:124 4↑ⒻLsCngasH-G3 93 5 3 67 65½ 64½ 3½ Garcia M LB113 11.30 90- 11 *River's Prayer*117½ *Indian Flare*118hd StrongFaith1131¾ 4wd into lane,rallied 7

24Mar07-8BM gd 1 1/16 Ⓣ :244 :502 1:143 1:453 4↑ⒻHillsboroH54k 93 3 52½ 54½ 31½ 2hd 2hd Gonzalez R M LB115 6.30 79- 28 *CharmtheGint*117hd StrongFith115¾ *Somethinboutlur*1262 3-4w trip, gamely 6

24Feb07-3BM fst 1 :222 :453 1:092 1:344 4↑ⒻFosterCtyH60k 72 7 56½ 57 55½ 611 511¼ Gonzalez R M LB117 5.20 84- 12 Somethinboutlur1234¼ GinsMjesty1192 MkPss1154 No speed,3-4w,empty 7

Previously trained by Vienna Darrell 2006: (133 17 16 17 0.13)

4Feb07-3SA fm 1⅛ Ⓣ :492 1:14 1:373 1:494 4↑ⒻSprBwlPtyH45k 86 5 43½ 44 53 42½ 2¾ Gomez G K LB123 *1.00 78- 18 Christmas Stocking119¾ Strong Faith1231 Brag118no Steadied into lane 6

7Jan07-8SA fm 1⅛ Ⓣ :473 1:102 1:34 1:464 4↑ⒻSnGrgnoH-G2 70 4 21 2½ 21 77¾ 613½ Garcia M LB112 42.20 80- 12 *Citronnade*1153 Rahys'Appeal115¾ ThreeDegrees117hd Stalked,bid,wkened 7

18Dec06-9Hol fm 1 1/16 Ⓣ :232 :473 1:111 1:404 3↑ⒻDahliaH-G2 93 1 55½ 64¾ 53½ 42 54 Garcia M LB113 53.80 84- 16 GrndeMelody114no NissnceRoyl1202¼ *Singlong*1141 Waited 1/8,stdied 1/16 10

3Dec06-8Hol fst 1 1/16 ◈ :221 :443 1:092 1:414 3↑ⒻBayakoaH-G2 84 3 1014 918 79¾ 84¾ 53½ Garcia M LB115 18.60 - - Foxysox118nk Round Heels1151¼ DonaAmelia116no 3wd into str,outkicked 12

29Oct06-9OSA fm 1 Ⓣ :224 :454 1:092 1:331 3↑ⒻLsPlmasH-G2 90 6 79 811 86½ 74¼ 52¾ Arroyo N Jr LB115 29.70 94- 03 Beautyandthebeast119hd **Clinet**116½ Quemar1141¾ Came out str,btwn late 8

27Sep06-8OSA fm *6½f Ⓣ :212 :431 1:06 1:12 3↑ⒻSKMaddyH-G3 86 5 9 107½ 108¾ 95¾ 65 Arroyo N Jr LB116 47.70 90- 05 Cambiocorsa1222½ Sandra's Rose116¾ Bettarun Fast115¾ Drifted out dirt 11

WORKS: Sep18 Hol ◈5f fst 1:023 H *26/33* Sep11 Hol ◈5f fst 1:041 H *33/34* Sep4 Hol ◈5f fst 1:014 H *14/37* Aug28 Dmr ◈4f fst :484 H *13/35* Aug10 Dmr ◈5f fst 1:02 H *28/56* Aug3 Dmr ◈5f fst 1:05 H *62/63*

TRAINER: Synth/Turf(20 .20 $1.56) 31-60Days(283 .24 $2.00) Turf(231 .16 $1.50) Sprint(629 .24 $1.91) GrdStk(25 .00 $0.00) J/T 2006-07(3 .00 $0.00)

8 Sophie's Trophy

Own: Budget Stable

Pink Orange, Blue 'B' On Back, Blue Sleeves

JARA F (—) 2007: (397 35 .09)

Ch. f. 4 (Feb) BARMAR05 $62,000
Sire: Valid Wager (Valid Appeal) $5,000
Dam: No Trouble Tweenus (Deputed Testamony)
Br: Mr & Mrs Martin J Wygod (Cal)
Tr: Walsh Kathy(—) 2007:(60 8 .13)

L 113

Life	11	3	2	2	$107,967	86	D.Fst	8	2	2	1	$81,683	85
2007	3	0	0	1	$15,390	86	Wet(388)	2	1	0	0	$12,019	70
2006	8	3	2	1	$92,577	85	Synth	1	0	0	1	$14,265	86
SAⓉ	0	0	0	0	$0	–	Turf(286)	0	0	0	0	$0	–
							DstⓉ(353)	0	0	0	0	$0	–

5Sep07-7Dmr fst 6f ◈ :231 :473 :593 1:113 3↑ⒻⓇCERFH97k 86 8 12 128 126½ 75¼ 32¾ Gomez G K LB114 b 30.70 - - ThvrythghtfU1161 SndyWthnS1151¾ SphsTrph1141½ Came out str,late 3rd 13

Previously trained by Armstrong Janet 2007(as of 6/10): (25 3 3 2 0.12)

10Jun07-7EmD fst 6½f :212 :434 1:09 1:154 3↑ⒻWaLgslatrH45k 68 10 7 78 68 65¾ 64 Mawing L A LB116 10.80 82- 16 ShsAllSlk1171¾ *SddnDprtr*116¾ Kssnthboysgoodby120¾ 3w-turn, no threat 11

20May07-9EmD sly 6f :22 :444 :564 1:092 3↑ⒻHstingsPkH45k 70 3 8 79½ 77½ 75¾ 56 Mawing L A LB118 5.60 84- 20 DnnrAtArlns1172¾ Kssnthbysgdb1201 GldnPn119nk 4w-turn,some late run 9

14Oct06-8Hst fst 1⅛ :472 1:131 1:384 1:524 3↑ⒻBlrinaBC-G3 65 5 1113 96¼ 62¼ 86½ 85¾ Valdez F S L121 12.95 74- 23 Gins Majesty124¾ Slewpast124hd Starlite Strike121no Failed to menace 12

23Sep06-9Hst fst 1⅛ :46 1:103 1:361 1:502 ⒻBCBCOaks-G3 71 1 915 812 611 78 75 Valdez F S L121 2.45 87- 15 Real Candy121no Hurry an Notis1212 Langara Lass121½ Failed to respond 9

2Sep06-7Hst fst 1 1/16 :231 :463 1:112 1:44 ⒻHKJockClbH53k 84 2 613 69 47 22½ 23¾ Walker M K L118 2.90 88- 17 Excited Miss1213¾ Sophie's Trophy1184 *Real Candy*1141 Second best 7

19Aug06-9EmD fst 1⅛ :462 1:102 1:362 1:502 ⒻWashBCOaks97k 71 5 43 44 36½ 35½ 34¾ Krigger K LB119 b 1.60 76- 25 *ShsAllSlk*119hd ChstntLdy1194¾ SophsTrophy1198 Bump start, 3w2ndturn 6

16Jly06-9Hst fst 1 1/16 :241 :483 1:13 1:442 ⒻEmrldDwnsH54k 77 1 44 31½ 33 33½ 24 Wilson D H L122 b *.60 86- 21 *Excited Miss*1194 Sophie's Trophy1221¾ No Ka Oi1163¼ Second best 5

25Jun06-5EmD fst 1 :223 :462 1:11 1:362 ⒻIrishDayH40k 82 4 811 87¼ 75¾ 22½ 1nk Krigger K LB119 b *1.80 83- 21 SphsTrphy119nk *ChstntLdy*1161¾ LngrLss1171 Broke awkward&bump-5w 10

20May06-3Hst fst 6½f :222 :452 1:102 1:17 ⒻLangleyH50k 85 1 5 55 37 2hd 12¾ Wilson D H L116 b 4.35 91- 16 *Sophie's Trophy*1162¾ Bond Queen1192 *ExcitedMiss*1163 Drew clear, driving 5

29Apr06-5Hst slyS 6½f :223 :47 1:122 1:184 ⒻMd Sp Wt 21k 61 10 7 74½ 74½ 3½ 13½ Wilson D H L122 b 4.25 82- 17 *SophsTrophy*1223½ ChrokFrdom117½ Dncwthstrngrs118½ 4 wide, drew clear 10

WORKS: Sep20 SA ◈4f fst :492 H *16/28* Sep1 Dmr ◈4f fst :471 H *2/60* Aug25 Dmr ◈6f fst 1:12 H *2/19* Aug17 Dmr ◈5f fst 1:00 B *5/48* ●Aug10 Dmr ◈4f fst :46 H *1/65* Jly15 EmD 4f fst :54 B *56/56*

TRAINER: 2Off45-180(20 .25 $2.50) 1stTurf(7 .00 $0.00) Synth/Turf(6 .17 $0.70) Turf(43 .07 $0.35) Sprint(87 .11 $2.51) GrdStk(5 .20 $2.72)

9 Attima (GB)

Own: Fanticola & Scardino

Turqse Fuchsia And Purple Diamonds, Purple

ESPINOZA V (—) 2007: (871 150 .17)

B. f. 4 (Mar)
Sire: Zafonic (Gone West) $29,862
Dam: Guarded*GB (Eagle Eyed)
Br: Chantilly Bloodstock Agency (GB)
Tr: Canani Julio C(—) 2007:(174 29 .17)

L 121

Life	13	5	2	1	$327,336	95	D.Fst	0	0	0	0	$0	–
2007	2	1	0	1	$66,660	95	Wet(298)	0	0	0	0	$0	–
2006	6	3	0	0	$210,890	93	Synth	0	0	0	0	$0	–
SAⓉ	2	1	0	1	$66,660	95	Turf(308)	13	5	2	1	$327,336	95
							DstⓉ(274)	1	1	0	0	$48,660	95

19Feb07-9SA gd 1 Ⓣ :23 :463 1:104 1:353 4↑ⒻBnaVstaH-G2 95 7 22 23½ 21½ 1hd 31 Espinoza V LB120 2.60 85- 14 Conveyor's Angel114hd Singalong1151 Attima120½ Pulled,bid,led,held 3d 8

28Jan07-6SA fm *6½f Ⓣ :214 :434 1:063 1:123 4↑ⒻWishinWelH81k 95 2 7 31½ 31½ 11 11¾ Espinoza V LB120 *2.30 92- 12 Attima1201¾ Somethinaboutbetty118½ WildStorm1191 4wd into lane,clear 10

26Nov06-8Hol fm 1 Ⓣ :232 :462 1:103 1:343 3↑ⒻMatriarc-G1 92 1 89½ 89½ 83¾ 85¼ 93 Espinoza V LB120 12.00 88- 08 *PriceTg*120½ ThreeDegrees123hd PommesFrits123hd Saved ground to lane 14

19Aug06-8Dmr fm 1⅛ Ⓣ :48 1:123 1:362 1:48 ⒻDMrOaks-G1 93 9 33 33 31 1hd 52½ Espinoza V LB122 *2.60 87- 13 Arravale1221½ ⒹTake the Ribbon122hd Foxysox122¾ Bid 3wd,led,wkened 10

29Jly06-5Dmr fm 1 Ⓣ :222 :47 1:11 1:343 ⒻSnClmntH-G2 92 7 1½ 1½ 11 11 11¼ Espinoza V LB120 *1.10 88- 11 Attima1201¼ Sol Mi Fa116hd Soothsay119no Pulled,inside,gamely 8

2Jly06-8Hol fm 1¼ Ⓣ :474 1:12 1:36 1:591 ⒻAmrcnOks-G1 79 5 11 1½ 21 57½ 814¼ Flores D R LB121 2.60 85- 07 *Wait a While*1214½ Asahi Rising121½ *Arravale*1216 Bumped 1/4,wkened 8

4Jun06-8Hol fm 1⅛ Ⓣ :474 1:114 1:354 1:471 + ⒻHnymnBCH-G2 86 2 11½ 12 12 1½ 11¼ Espinoza V LB118 *.80 95- 04 Attima1181¼ Foxysox1221¾ Proxenia1164¼ Rail,steady handling 7

10May06-7Hol fm 1 Ⓣ :224 :453 1:093 1:341 ⒻAlw 52200n1x 79 3 22½ 22½ 22 11½ 13½ Espinoza V LB120 *.70 93- 11 *Attima*1203½ Proxenia1222 Musical High120½ Bid,clear,handily 8

Previously trained by Pascal Bary

2Oct05 Longchamp (Fr) gs *1 Ⓣ RH 1:371 ⒻPrix Marcel Boussac-G1 117¾ Lemaire C-P 123 29.00 Rumplestiltskin1231 *Quiet Royal*1231½ Deveron1232 15
Racing Post Rating: 97 Stk 360000 *Towards rear on rail,never threatened*

8Sep05 Longchamp (Fr) gd *7f Ⓣ RH 1:234 Prix La Rochette-G3 32 Lemaire C-P 120 8.00 ⒹYasoodd123½ *Multiplex*1231½ Attima120nk 5
Racing Post Rating: 97 Stk 93100 *Led,outpaced and last 2f out,came again,up for 3rd*

Placed second through disqualification

WORKS: ●Sep18 SA ◈5f fst :57 H *1/49* ●Sep11 SA ◈5f fst :573 H *1/27* Sep5 Dmr Ⓣ 5f fm 1:034 H(d) *3/3* Aug29 Dmr Ⓣ 5f fm 1:01 H(d) *1/3* Aug22 Dmr Ⓣ 4f fm :483 H(d) *1/1* Aug16 Dmr Ⓣ 3f fm :363 H(d) *1/2*

TRAINER: +180Days(23 .17 $0.97) Route/Sprint(34 .18 $2.85) Turf(183 .17 $1.38) Sprint(169 .18 $2.04) GrdStk(56 .11 $0.92) J/T 2006-07 SA(8 .38 $2.38) J/T 2006-07(38 .37 $2.35)

11 Macadamia
Gray
Own: Janavar Thoroughbreds LLC
White, Blue Janavar On Back, Red, Blue
BAZE T C (—) 2007: (634 75 .12)

Dk. b or br f. 3 (Mar) KEESEP05 $18,000
Sire: Artax (Marquetry)
Dam: Unique Creek (Tricky Creek)
Br: Hardy Thoroughbreds (Ky)
Tr: Lobo Paulo H(—) 2007:(97 12 .12)

L 111

Life	13	1	1	5	$69,395	87	D.Fst	5	1	0	1	$27,261	64
2007	7	0	1	3	$37,484	87	Wet(342)	0	0	0	0	$0	-
							Synth	0	0	0	0	$0	-
2006	6	1	0	2	$31,911	64	Turf(268)	8	0	1	4	$42,134	87
SA[T]	3	0	0	1	$8,252	87	Dst[T](320)	2	0	0	1	$6,000	86

3Sep07-8BM fm 7½f [T] :233 :482 1:113 1:312 [F]PaloAltoH75k 80 8 5 2½ 2½ 3½ 2½ Ochoa J LB123 6.40 86-09 Rockella1234½ Macadamia123¾ Forest Huntress123no Prssd 2w, wknd 8
15Jly07-5Hol fm 6f [T] :224 :451 :572 1:092 3↑[F]Alw 49400n1x 75 5 1 1½ 1½ 1½ 3¾ Talamo J5 LB111 2.30 92-01 Delicate Cat120½ Lady Matilda1241¼ Macadamia111¾ Btwn,clear,caught 6
13Jun07-4Hol fm 1 1/16 [T] :234 :48 1:12 1:414 [F]OC 80k/n1x-N 80 1 31 3½ 31 3½ 3¾ Talamo J5 LB113 *.90 82-11 *NootkaIsland*118no DivasSeastar122¾ Macadmi113½ Came out str,willingly 8
12May07-7Hol fm 1 [T] :232 :471 1:104 1:342 [F]Senorita-G3 84 2 32½ 41½ 42 51¾ 55 Blanc B LB116 16.70 87-16 *Valbenny*1211¾ **Super Freaky**1211¼ Passified121½ Stalked rail,no rally 8
7Apr07-7SA fm 1 [T] :231 :471 1:112 1:352 [F]Prvdncia-G3 87 8 63¾ 65½ 76 95½ 53¼ Blanc B LB115 27.50 84-12 **SuperFreaky**117¾ Passified119¾ GottaHveHer1151¼ 4wd into str,outkicked 11
4Mar07-8SA fm *6½f [T] :204 :423 1:061 1:123 [F]LaHabra113k 86 4 6 36½ 310 33½ 21¼ Blanc B LB116 52.40 91-09 *SuperFreaky*1161¼ [D]Macadamia116½ PyWright122no Shifted out,bump 1/16 11
Disqualified and placed 6th
15Jan07-6SA fm *6½f [T] :213 :433 1:07 1:132 [F]OC 80k/n1x-N 74 1 7 21 42½ 43½ 32¾ Antongrgi III W7 LB112 62.40 85-11 *Passified*1182 **Super Freaky**118¾ Macadamia1121 Came out str,up 3rd 10
22Nov06-3BM fst 6f :213 :443 :57 1:10 [F]Alw 31532n1x 53 3 6 56¼ 54½ 45½ 48¼ Ochoa J LB120 23.10 79-10 QuiteaRush1202¼ [D]SegoLily1201 FilliebytheBy1205 Bmpd strt,3w,no rally 6
Placed third through disqualification
21Oct06-3OSA fst 6f :212 :442 :571 1:111 [F]Anoakia74k 49 2 6 67¼ 65¾ 67 510 Arias S LB116 17.20 73-15 Berriestoheaven1181¾ Tizthen118hd Sego Lily1187 Angled in turn,no bid 6
9Sep06-1GG fm 1 [T] :233 :484 1:14 1:381 [F]Alw 36338n1x 55 3 32 21 22 42½ 36½ Alvarado F T LB119 11.30 78-12 **Spenditallbaby**1192 ShesGotSkills1194½ Macadmi119½ Pulled early, empty 5
16Aug06-1Dmr fst 5½f :22 :452 :583 1:051 [F]Md 55000(62.5-55) 64 4 3 22½ 22½ 1hd 11¾ Arias S5 LB113 22.30 85-14 Macadmi1131¾ KissinPrty1202¾ KimmyPotter1201¼ Stalked,led,clear,held 7
15Jun06-8Hol fst 5f :214 :454 :584 [F]Md 40000(40-32) 42 1 6 41¼ 33½ 36½ 511½ Garcia M5 LB115 6.10 75-13 ShortSentence1207¼ SalsaCaliente1202¾ Kldy120nk Sent inside, weakened 10
WORKS: Aug30 Hol ◇4f fst :511 H *25/27* Aug25 Hol ◇6f fst 1:152 H *6/9* Aug18 Hol ◇4f fst :491 H *17/36* Jly8 Hol ◇4f fst :493 H *29/62*
TRAINER: 2Off45-180(31 .06 $0.97) Turf(96 .09 $1.28) Sprint(113 .13 $2.53) GrdStk(18 .11 $1.10) J/T 2006-07 SA(1 .00 $0.00) J/T 2006-07(5 .00 $0.00)

14 Clinet (Ire)
Maroon
Own: Wood Hall Stud
Royal Blue, White Woodhall Stud And
SOLIS A (—) 2007: (471 61 .13)

B. m. 5 (Apr)
Sire: Docksider (Diesis*GB)
Dam: Oiche Mhaith*GB (Night Shift)
Br: Mrs J Costelloe (Ire)
Tr: Gallagher Patrick(—) 2007:(360 40 .11)

L 116

Life	29	5	5	5	$318,052	98	D.Fst	0	0	0	0	$0	-
2007	4	0	1	0	$36,720	98	Wet(219*)	0	0	0	0	$0	-
							Synth	4	1	0	0	$10,371	77
2006	5	2	1	0	$199,000	96	Turf(311*)	25	4	5	5	$307,681	98
SA[T]	2	0	2	0	$53,220	98	Dst[T](222)	1	0	1	0	$23,220	98

1Sep07-9Dmr fm 1 1/16 [T] :234 :471 1:11 1:402 3↑[F]PalomarH-G2 88 2 810 914 87¼ 76¼ 44 Solis A LB116 11.70 92-10 Precious Kitten122¾ Black Mamba1121 Kris' Sis1152¼ Pulled,inside to 1/4 9
17Aug07-2Dmr fm 1 [T] :241 :482 1:113 1:344 3↑[F]OC 100k/c-N 86 5 54½ 43 4¾ 42½ 42½ Solis A LB120 2.10 84-13 SwtBll1221 [D]PrivtBnkng120hd DoublTroubl1241½ 4wd 2nd turn,outkicked 5
6Jly07-7Hol fst 7f ◇ :222 :45 1:092 1:214 3↑[F]AGleamH-G2 77 7 8 74¼ 63¼ 65 810 Solis A LB116 9.80 87-11 Somthnbotlr122¾ **StrongFth**1141¼ *ThvrythghtfU*1123 Pulled early,3wd turn 10
1Jan07-8SA fm *6½f [T] :212 :431 1:061 1:124 4↑[F]MnroviaH-G3 98 10 3 67¾ 65¼ 34 21 Solis A LB117 5.70 90-10 Society Hostess1191 Clinet1171 Kitty Hawk113nk Came out str,led late 12
Previously trained by Hills John 2006(as of 11/26): (5 1 2 0 0.20)
26Nov06-8Hol fm 1 [T] :232 :462 1:103 1:343 3↑[F]Matriarc-G1 90 6 1012 1011 105¾ 139¼ 114¼ Valdivia J Jr LB123 10.40 87-08 *PriceTg*120½ ThreeDegrees123hd PommesFrites123hd 5wd into lane,no bid 14
29Oct06-9OSA fm 1 [T] :224 :454 1:092 1:331 3↑[F]LsPlmasH-G2 96 8 810 711 76 63¼ 2hd Solis A LB116 2.70 97-03 Beautyandthebeast119hd Clinet116½ Quemar1141¾ 4wd into lane,rallied 8
2Mar06 Nad Al Sheba (UAE) gf *1⅛ [T] LH 1:52 3↑ Jebel Hatta-G2 1016¼ Ahern E 126 - Touch of Land1301¼ Lord Admiral1301¾ *Seihali*130½ 10
Racing Post Rating: 80 Stk 250000 *6th on rail,weakened over 2f out. Valixir 7th,Layman 8th*
9Feb06 Nad Al Sheba (UAE) gf *1 [T] LH 1:372 3↑[F]Cape Verdi Stakes (Listed) 12¼ Ahern E 129 - Clinet1292¼ Brindisi1293¼ Shersha1291 9
Racing Post Rating: 106 Stk 150000 *Wide at rear,8th 2-1/2f out,rallied to lead 1f out*
19Jan06 Nad Al Sheba (UAE) gf *7½f [T] LH 1:322 3↑[F]Shadwell Farm Handicap 1nk Ahern E 121 - *Clinet*121nk Satwa Queen132½ Rock Opera118nk 11
Racing Post Rating: 100 Hcp 110000 *Rated in 6th,angled out 2f out,led final strides.Brindisi(116)4th*
25Sep05 Newmarket (GB) gd 7f [T] Str 1:241 3↑[F]October Stakes (Listed) 31½ Ahern E 120 7.00 *Echelon*123¾ Attune123¾ *Clinet*120½ 14
Racing Post Rating: 95 Stk 53300 *Twrds rear,progress 2f out,drifted left,gamely.Roodeye 6th*
WORKS: Sep20 SA ◇5f fst :592 H *16/54* Sep13 SA ◇3f fst :361 H *2/11* Aug28 Dmr ◇5f fst 1:001 H *17/48* Aug11 Dmr [T] 7f fm 1:311 H(d) *1/1* Aug2 Dmr [T] 7f fm 1:26 H(d) *1/1* Jly26 Dmr [T] 7f fm 1:29 H(d) *1/1*
TRAINER: Route/Sprint(73 .14 $1.87) Turf(396 .13 $1.15) Sprint(319 .13 $1.71) GrdStk(53 .06 $0.58) J/T 2006-07 SA(71 .18 $1.50) J/T 2006-07(206 .17 $1.53)

For our contender selection, the Beyer par for this level is approximately 100, so we'll accept a 95 as a possible contender.

1. Super Freaky likes the course, but the 3-year-old hasn't quite earned the figures necessary to win at this level.
2. Itsawonderfullife hails from a good barn and has super works, but her figures don't put her in the picture with these.
3. Runway Rosie is another sophomore without the figures to support her at this level.
4. Dancing Edie is a legitimate Grade 1 contender with figures that would win this race. Note the turn-back in distance for this race.
5. Lady Gamer has just one figure that would get the job done with these. She's much improved, but beware the giraffe number.
6. Fantastic Spring has but a single figure that would contend, and that was at five furlongs. She's a noncontender.
7. Strong Faith has multiple races that could win this and is in top form.

8. Sophie's Trophy just doesn't fit with these.

9. Attima has several contending races but hasn't been on the track in seven months. She's a possibility but would be a weak play unless she's overlaid in the betting.

10. Stylish Wildcat was scratched.

11. Macadamia is an inconsistent sort and is weak on figures.

12. Spenditallbaby was scratched.

13. True And True was also scratched.

14. Clinet looks in soft form but she has the figures to win here. She's a contender.

The contenders are (4) Dancing Edie; (7) Strong Faith; (9) Attima; and (14) Clinet, with Dancing Edie standing out versus the others. She's the ideal turn-back play and also has a solid class edge over all but Attima, who may need a race. Dancing Edie fits the Beyer pars for the race and shortens up from a huge pace effort over the Del Mar turf course finishing second in a Grade 1 race. How strong was that effort? A quick look at the Del Mar turf pace pars for her level will answer the question emphatically:

8 F	1:11
8½ F	1:11$\frac{2}{5}$
9 F	1:11$\frac{4}{5}$

The pace of the race was seven lengths fast for the level, making her an ideal candidate for the bet in this event. As to her actual pace figure? A quick refresher on the Quirin-style pace and speed figures will provide us with a quantitative measurement tool.

My personal figures are based on the Quirin-style numbers where 100, rather than the Beyer 83, equals the $10,000 par. The advantage to those figures is that we have a pace figure as well as a final number. The $10,000 par is expressed as 100–100, giving both a pace and final number. An approximate scale for this track would look like this:

$10,000	100–100
$12,500	101–101
$16,000	102–102
NW1	105–105
Maddy Stk	107–107

The par figure for the Del Mar race was 109–109, and today's par is 107. And Dancing Edie's pace figure? The raw pace figure came back at *121*, which even on a faster-than-par surface leaves a lot of wiggle room for comparing that race with today's par.

EIGHTH RACE
Oak Tree at SA
SEPTEMBER 26, 2007

ABOUT 6½ FURLONGS. (Turf) (1.11) 39TH RUNNING OF THE SENATOR KEN MADDY HANDICAP. Grade III. Purse $100,000 DOWNHILL TURF FOR FILLIES AND MARES, THREE YEARS OLD AND UPWARD. By subscription of $100 each if made on or before Thursday, September 20, 2007 or by supplementary nomination of $2,000 by 10 AM, Saturday, September 22. All horses to pay $1,000 to start with $100,000 added. The added money and all fees to be divided 60% to the winner, 20% to second, 12% to third, 6% to fourth and 2% to fifth. Weights: Saturday, September 22. Starters to be named through the entry box by the usual time of closing. Three Year Olds allowed 3 lbs. on scale. Closed with 20 nominations. (Rail at 15 feet).

Value of Race: $114,900 Winner $68,940; second $22,980; third $13,788; fourth $6,894; fifth $2,298. Mutuel Pool $387,225.00 Exacta Pool $214,739.00 Trifecta Pool $176,282.00 Superfecta Pool $128,243.00

Last Raced	Horse	M/Eqt.	A.	Wt	PP	St	¼	½	Str	Fin	Jockey	Odds $1
4Aug07 9Dmr2	Dancing Edie	LB	5	122	4	6	5hd	6½	3½	1½	Nakatani C S	5.00
17Aug07 7Dmr3	Lady Gamer	LB	4	116	5	8	41	41½	41	2nk	Flores D R	22.80
17Aug07 7Dmr2	Strong Faith	LB	6	116	7	10	10½	102	82	3no	Blanc B	6.30
3Sep07 8BM2	Macadamia	LB	3	112	10	1	8hd	82	6½	4¾	Baze T C	63.70
1Sep07 9Dmr4	Clinet-Ire	LB	5	116	11	2	9½	71	5hd	5½	Solis A	6.20
5Sep07 7Dmr3	Sophie's Trophy	LB b	4	114	8	9	11	11	102	6¾	Jara F	51.00
2Sep07 7Dmr11	Runway Rosie	LB	3	111	3	7	71	9½	7hd	7¾	Baze M C	41.10
28Jun07 4CD1	Itswonderfullife-Ire	LB	3	111	2	11	2hd	32½	1hd	8½	Quinonez A	21.50
18Aug07 8Dmr3	Super Freaky	LB	3	115	1	5	3½	2hd	2hd	9¼	Court J K	6.60
19Feb07 9SA3	Attima-GB	LB	4	121	9	4	61	5hd	9hd	108½	Espinoza V	1.70
16Aug07 4Dmr1	Fantastic Spring	LB bf	4	115	6	3	1½	1hd	11	11	Talamo J	8.70

OFF AT 4:39 Start Good. Won driving. Course firm.
TIME :22¹, :44, 1:07, 1:13¹ (:22.26, :44.03, 1:07.15, 1:13.30)

$2 Mutuel Prices:

4 – DANCING EDIE	12.00	5.60	4.60
5 – LADY GAMER		23.00	10.80
7 – STRONG FAITH			4.40

$1 EXACTA 4–5 PAID $117.80 $1 TRIFECTA 4–5–7 PAID $700.00
$1 SUPERFECTA 4–5–7–11 PAID $10,802.90

B. m, (Jan), by Moscow Ballet – Duchess of Ack , by Slewpy . Trainer Dollase Craig. Bred by Fast Lane Farms & Donald Reiker (Cal).

DANCING EDIE chased between foes then inside, bid along the rail in the stretch, gained a short lead in deep stretch and held gamely under urging. LADY GAMER stalked between foes then off the rail, came four wide into the stretch, bid outside and drifted in some in the lane and continued willingly to the wire. STRONG FAITH hopped slightly at the start, settled off the rail, came three deep into the stretch and finished well. MACADAMIA dropped back outside then settled off the rail, came a bit wide into the stretch and also finished with interest. CLINET (IRE) chased off the rail then between foes, was in tight in upper stretch, drifted out a bit and steadied behind the runner-up in midstretch and was outfinished. SOPHIE'S TROPHY unhurried off the rail, came out in the stretch and improved position. RUNWAY ROSIE between foes early, chased inside to the stretch and did not rally. ITSAWONDERFULLIFE (IRE) pulled her way along inside to duel for the lead, fought back into the stretch, was between foes in midstretch and weakened in the final furlong. SUPER FREAKY stalked inside then bid between foes and dueled for the lead, fought back into the stretch and also weakened in the final furlong. ATTIMA (GB) chased outside, came five wide into the stretch and weakened, then returned bleeding from the nostrils. FANTASTIC SPRING sped to the early lead off the rail, dueled three deep to the stretch and weakened. A claim of foul by the rider of CLINET against the runner-up for alleged interference in the stretch was not allowed by the stewards, who ruled both runners contributed to the incident. Rail on hill at zero.

Owners– 1, Basin Julian Fast Lane Farms Reddam J Paul; 2, Hansen Clark and Janine; 3, Sahud Mervyn and Jacqueline and Saleby Mark; 4, Janavar Thoroughbreds LLC; 5, Wood Hall Stud Ltd; 6, Budget Stable; 7, Class Racing Stable and Rosenblum Leslie and Allen; 8, Fab Oak Stable and Lakin Lewis G; 9, Suarez Racing Inc and Venneri Alex A; 10, Fanticola Anthony and Scardino Joseph; 11, Magenta Racing Inc

Trainers– 1, Dollase Craig; 2, Sadler John W; 3, Mullins Jeff; 4, Lobo Paulo H; 5, Gallagher Patrick; 6, Walsh Kathy; 7, Hofmans David; 8, Biancone Patrick L; 9, O'Neill Doug; 10, Canani Julio C; 11, Miller Peter

Scratched– Stylish Wildcat (26Jul07 7Dmr2) , Spenditallbaby (25Aug07 8Dmr2) , True and True (05Sep07 7Dmr10)

$2 Daily Double (9–4) Paid $31.20 ; Daily Double Pool $29,202 .
$1 Pick Three (1–9–4) Paid $230.60 ; Pick Three Pool $56,949 .

Dancing Edie asserted her class late to win this as the ideal turn-back play, and at a juicy 5–1. Also note the positions of our main contenders based on no more than determining overall ability using the Beyer figures. The second-place finisher, Lady Gamer at 22–1, also had a recent race that would have put her strongly in the mix. The giraffe figure from her second race back turned out to be legitimate. Dancing Edie's pace figure from Del Mar also turned out to be legitimate. Give this method of contender selection a serious look; it's simple and it works big-time.

A FINAL EXAMPLE: A MIX OF THE TURN-BACK PLAY AND A HUGE PRICE

The final illustrative race was my favorite play in 2007. At first glance I threw out the eventual winner based on competitive figures. Only the final race analysis saved what would have been a serious mistake, especially for someone utilizing pace figures.

8 **Hollywood Park** *6 Furlongs* (1:073) [S]Alw 49000N1X **Purse $49,000 For California Bred Three Year Olds And Upward Which Have Never Won $7,500 Other Than Maiden, Claiming, Or Starter Or Which Have Never Won Two Races. Three Year Olds, 119 lbs.; Older, 124 lbs. Non-winners of a race other than Maiden, Claiming, or Starter Allowed 2 lbs. A race other than Claiming, or Starter Allowed 4 lbs.**

START · 6 FURLONGS · FINISH

1 Moonlit Habit — Red
Own: B Wayne Hughes
Orange And Purple Quarters, Orange
BAZE M C (107 22 9 15 .21) 2007: (397 66 .17)

B. g. 4 (Mar)
Sire: Malibu Moon (A.P. Indy) $40,000
Dam: Lady Habit (My Habitony)
Br: Annabelle Stute (Cal)
Tr: Mandella Richard(12 0 4 0 .00) 2007:(72 11 .15)

L 122

Life	4	1	2	1	$67,400	92	D.Fst	4	1	2	1	$67,400	92
2006	4	1	2	1	$67,400	92	Wet(382)	0	0	0	0	$0	-
2005	0	M	0	0	$0	-	Synth	0	0	0	0	$0	-
							Turf(218)	0	0	0	0	$0	-
Hol	2	0	1	1	$18,200	92	Dst(346)	0	0	0	0	$0	-

20Jly06-6Dmr fst 1 1/16 :23 :463 1:112 1:432 3↑[S]OC 25k/N1x-N 91 6 2hd 3½ 3½ 11 2nk Espinoza V LB119 *1.60 92-13 *Robador*124nk Moonlit Habit1194½ Sixcess1192½ 4wd into str,led,edged 7
28May06-5Hol fst 7½f :232 :463 1:103 1:30 3↑[S]Alw 49800N1x 92 6 1 11 1½ 2hd 2hd Espinoza V LB117 2.00 85-18 FightingCtyHll115hd MoonltHbt1171¼ Boocfuss1221 Bumped,game inside 7
30Apr06-7Hol fst 7f :22 :444 1:091 1:222 3↑[S]Barretts70k 86 1 6 31 32 32½ 32 Espinoza V LB116 4.20 89-08 *SwissAddress*1221½ Ctouttthbg118½ MoonlitHbit116¾ 3wd into str,held 3rd 9
8Apr06-8SA fst 6½f :213 :443 1:102 1:171 3↑[S]Md Sp Wt 63k 84 5 9 21 2½ 2hd 11¼ Bejarano R LB118 7.80 84-16 MoonlitHbit1181¼ MidnightCbint1182½ *Boocfuss*124½ Squeezed start,game 12

WORKS: May16 Hol ◈3f fst :374 B *29/42* May10 Hol ◈6f fst 1:13 H *2/22* ●May3 Hol ◈6f fst 1:123 H *1/18* Apr26 Hol ◈5f fst 1:01 H *8/41* Apr19 Hol ◈5f fst 1:003 H *14/50* ●Apr12 Hol ◈4f fst :47 H *1/28*
TRAINER: +180Days(32 .12 $0.91) Synth(17 .06 $0.28) Route/Sprint(26 .08 $0.60) Sprint(139 .12 $0.83) Alw(96 .14 $1.02) J/T 2006-07 HOL(1 .00 $0.00) J/T 2006-07(1 .00 $0.00)

2 My City by the Bay — White
Own: Johnston Johnston & Johnston
Red, White Belt And Bar On Sleeves, Red
GARCIA M (70 6 10 9 .09) 2007: (334 37 .11)

Ch. g. 4 (Jan)
Sire: Perfect Mandate (Gone West) $5,000
Dam: Shes Enchantingtoo (Publicity)
Br: Mr & Mrs John J Cayer & Old English Rancho (Cal)
Tr: Warren Donald(7 3 0 1 .43) 2007:(34 8 .24)

L 120

Life	3	2	1	0	$35,600	80	D.Fst	2	1	1	0	$17,600	80
2007	3	2	1	0	$35,600	80	Wet(260)	0	0	0	0	$0	-
2006	0	M	0	0	$0	-	Synth	1	1	0	0	$18,000	79
							Turf(263)	0	0	0	0	$0	-
Hol	1	1	0	0	$18,000	79	Dst(347)	1	1	0	0	$13,200	80

28Apr07-7Hol fst 6½f ◈ :214 :443 1:103 1:174 3↑ Alw 40000s 79 2 7 41½ 44 21 1¾ Talamo J5 LB119 7.30 84-17 MyCitybytheBy119¾ OliverTwisted1242¼ BlzeIt1222½ Came out str,gamely 10
12Apr07-4SA fst 6f :212 :443 :57 1:102 4↑[S]Md 40000 80 6 2 3nk 1½ 11½ 13 Garcia M LB122 2.80 87-16 *MyCitybytheBy*1223 HerbieLove122¾ AwsomGrf1175½ Dueled,clear,driving 6
23Feb07-3SA fst 6½f :223 :47 1:12 1:183 4↑[S]Md 40000 64 3 5 1hd 2hd 2hd 21¾ Garcia M LB122 5.00 75-18 WivLibility1221¾ *MyCitybythBy*1226¼ BigMnOC122no Btwn,inside,2nd best 8

WORKS: May15 Hol ◈4f fst :481 H *11/53* May9 Hol ◈4f fst :513 H *53/57* Apr25 Hol ◈3f fst :371 H *16/31* Apr6 SA 5f fst :591 Hg *3/38* Mar30 SA 6f fst 1:122 H *3/12* Mar24 SA 5f fst 1:01 H *10/31*
TRAINER: Synth(13 .23 $2.75) WonLastStart(14 .21 $3.37) Sprint(123 .14 $1.54) Alw(5 .00 $0.00) J/T 2006-07 HOL(2 .50 $2.10) J/T 2006-07(21 .29 $2.10)

3 Cayambe — Blue
Own: Filouette Enterprises
Yellow, Red Cross Sashes, Red Bars On
COURT J K (75 5 9 7 .07) 2007: (393 35 .09)

Ch. g. 3 (Jan)
Sire: Helmsman (El Gran Senor) $4,000
Dam: Pacaya (Restless Con)
Br: Geri Forrester (Cal)
Tr: Sherman Art(18 3 1 1 .17) 2007:(309 76 .25)

L 117

Life	7	1	1	2	$45,176	75	D.Fst	3	1	0	1	$28,470	75
2007	4	1	0	2	$33,476	75	Wet(357)	2	0	1	0	$10,725	66
2006	3	M	1	0	$11,700	66	Synth	0	0	0	0	$0	-
							Turf(256)	2	0	0	1	$5,981	75
Hol	0	0	0	0	$0	-	Dst(362)	1	0	0	0	$2,925	61

28Apr07-5Hol fm 1 ⓣ :224 :453 1:10 1:341 Alw 55660N1x 60 5 2hd 1hd 2hd 65 812¾ Court J K LB120 b 22.50 80-06 Silent Soul120¾ Teeman1183¼ Bernasconi1131 Steadied 1/8,wkened 9
28Mar07-3BM gd 1 1/16 ⓣ :233 :49 1:14 1:444 OC 40k/N1x-N 75 1 2hd 1½ 1hd 3nk 33 ↓Kaenel K LB120 b 5.60 80-19 Boxelder120½ *Amazin Blue*1202½ [DH]Taxi Fleet120 Dueled, weakened 6
15Feb07-4BM fst 1 :221 :453 1:111 1:364 OC 40k/N1x-N 75 2 1hd 1hd 1hd 2hd 33 Kaenel K LB120 b 13.60 82-16 Brave Sun120no Sorta Gold1203 Cayambe1202 Lost whip stretch,wknd 7
19Jan07-4GG fst 1 :223 :46 1:114 1:39 Md Sp Wt 35k 72 5 22 22 31½ 1½ 1½ Kaenel K LB120 *1.50 74-29 Cayambe120½ Domoron Again1202 Gustavo1201¼ Stlkd 2-3w, dug in 5
Previously trained by Jenda Charles J 2006(as of 12/10): (262 38 39 50 0.15)
10Dec06-5BM slyS 6f :22 :452 :572 1:102 Md Sp Wt 37k 61 2 5 52½ 41½ 48 411 Lopez D G LB121 13.70 74-13 AcquiretheFire1203¼ *MysticWood*1206½ PowrBlnd1201¼ Tracked 2w, faded 8
6Oct06-1GG wf 1 ⊗ :224 :461 1:112 1:391 Md Sp Wt 33k 66 8 12 12 15 12 21½ Kaenel K LB119 19.40 71-25 Regal Times1191½ Cayambe1192 Ticketsandtomatoes1191 Set pace, tired 9
20Sep06-3GG fst 5½f :204 :44 :57 1:033 Md Sp Wt 32k 61 7 6 75½ 57 54 54 Kaenel K LB119 23.80 87-13 *Candy's Bro*1191½ Gold Label1191½ *Thegame'sonus*119¾ 3w turn, rallied 7

WORKS: May12 Hol ◈4f fst :52 H *73/75* Apr21 Hol ◈4f fst :491 H *31/69* Apr10 BM 4f fst :483 H *3/9* Mar15 BM 5f fst 1:024 H *10/17* Mar8 BM 5f fst 1:01 H *4/18* Mar1 BM 4f gd :48 H *3/17*
TRAINER: Synth(50 .14 $4.35) Turf/Synth(7 .14 $0.51) Route/Sprint(55 .31 $3.13) Sprint(737 .25 $1.81) Alw(109 .20 $1.67) J/T 2006-07 HOL(9 .33 $5.22) J/T 2006-07(29 .24 $3.16)

4 Sir Toasty
Own: Lisa Cox
Yellow Turquoise, Gold Horse In Gold Circle
RODRIGUEZ A C (3 0 0 0 .00) 2007: (138 9 .07)

Ch. g. 5 (Apr)
Sire: Benchmark (Alydar) $10,000
Dam: Naskrananie (Shananie)
Br: Charlotte M Wrather (Cal)
Tr: Martin Frank Jr(3 0 0 0 .00) 2007:(18 0 .00)

L 120

Life	25	4	4	6	$112,535	88	D.Fst	8	2	2	0	$37,222 85
2006	12	1	4	2	$48,242	88	Wet(410)	6	1	1	2	$22,198 88
2005	12	3	0	4	$63,993	82	Synth	0	0	0	0	$0 -
Hol	0	0	0	0	$0	-	Turf(280)	11	1	1	4	$53,115 82
							Dst(362)	2	1	0	1	$8,775 66

10Dec06-3Hol gd 1 1/16 (T) :224 :464 1:111 1:421 3↑[S]Alw 46800N1x 62 6 710 79 610 611 611½ Court J K LB120 fb 3.80 69-24 Dr. Seacliff1214 *Milltown Road*1202¼ Hot Grip1203 Off rail, no factor 7
3Nov06-4BM wf 1 1/16 ⊗ :222 :453 1:103 1:421 3↑Clm c-(12.5-10.5) 88 6 87¾ 86½ 52¾ 13 16½ Baze R A LB119 fb *1.70 89-18 SirTosty1196½ TruckWrror118no Prscrptonndd11910 Explosive bid 2d turn 8
Claimed from Hollendorfer, Jerry and Todaro, George for $12,500, Hollendorfer Jerry Trainer 2006(as of 11/3): (756 191 147 111 0.25)
27Sep06-1GG fst 1 :23 :462 1:102 1:35 3↑Clm 20000(20-18) 85 2 42½ 53 32 33 24½ Schvaneveldt C P LB119 fb 11.20 89-20 *Zappa*1214½ *Sir Toasty*1191 Datzig1193 2w,no threat,up for 2d 6
26Aug06-5GG fm 1 1/16 (T) :224 :471 1:103 1:433+3↑Clm 25000(25-22.5) 76 5 77¼ 78¾ 77 33 35 Baze R A LB119 fb 5.50 85-12 Skyros1212 Tonco1193 Sir Toasty1193 Angled 4w, flttnd out 8
29Jly06-7SR fm 1 1/16 (T) :241 :492 1:131 1:43 3↑Clm 25000(25-22.5) 78 1 21 22 32½ 33½ 33 Martinez C LB120 fb *1.20e 93-02 *MotelStaff*1193 Klamathfllssleep119hd SirTosty1201 3w,lacked needed bid 6
28Jun06-8Pln fst 170 :23 :462 1:10 1:39 3↑OC 25k/N1x-N 69 10 52¼ 33½ 33 37 611 Castro J M LB122 fb 25.80 84-15 Swen1220 Panama Lane122nk *Gold Bankers Gold*1222¼ 4w early, no rally 10
10Jun06-6BM fm 1 (T) :23 :464 1:11 1:364 3↑Alw 34427N1x 77 4 56 98½ 74¼ 95¾ 73¾ Martinez C LB123 fb 14.50 87-14 Sky Wolf123¾ *Salty Humor*1231¼ Red Wagon123no Fanned 4w, mild gain 11
20May06-7BM fm 1 1/16 (T) :232 :463 1:103 1:442 3↑Alw 35058N1x 82 2 88 910 78 55 22½ Baze M C LB123 fb 13.20 82-16 Daggernought1172½ SirToasty123¾ SndsofTime123no Rallied btwn horses 10
16Apr06-8GG wf 1 ⊗ :23 :46 1:101 1:362 4↑Alw 40502N1x 70 3 46½ 57½ 711 69½ 67 Baze R A LB119 fb *.90e 80-13 BlckHorseMony119¾ HppyZon119¾ ChrokChrli1192 Saved ground, empty 8
26Mar06-8GG fst 1⅛ ⊗ :47 1:112 1:374 1:514 4↑Alw 35087N1x 82 6 66 67¼ 54 33½ 2½ ♦Baze R A LB119 fb *1.90 85-21 Datzig119½ [DH]Happy Zone119 [DH]Sir Toasty1193¼ Bid 3w, too late 7
5Mar06-7GG slyS 1 ⊗ :23 :454 1:094 1:361 4↑Alw 35785N1x 71 3 45½ 48 36½ 23 29 Baze R A LB119 fb 4.30 79-20 PrinceofGold1199 SirTosty119nk CherokeeChrli1121 2w 2nd trn, bid, hung 7
13Jan06-7BM fst 1 ⊗ :232 :47 1:103 1:36 4↑Alw 33840N1x 63 2 43½ 43½ 44½ 37 413 Baze R A LB122 fb 3.20 78-16 Megabyte12210 Rare Request123¾ Native Approval1232¼ Failed to rally 4

WORKS: May9 Fpx 4f fst :503 Hg *4/4* Apr29 Hol ◈5f fst 1:042 H *63/65* ●Apr22 Fpx 4f fst :484 Hg *1/12* Apr14 Fpx 4f fst :49 Hg *3/9* Apr1 Fpx 4f fst :501 H *11/15*
TRAINER: 61-180Days(7 .14 $3.00) Synth(4 .00 $0.00) Route/Sprint(5 .00 $0.00) Sprint(67 .04 $0.57) Alw(1 .00 $0.00) J/T 2006-07 HOL(3 .00 $0.00) J/T 2006-07(4 .00 $0.00)

5 One On the House
Own: James R Vreeland
Green White, Green Circle V On Back, Green
TALAMO J (66 14 13 9 .21) 2007: (616 118 .19)

Dk. b or br g. 4 (Feb) BAROCT04 $35,000
Sire: Free House (Smokester) $15,000
Dam: To B. Super (To B. Or Not)
Br: Vessels Stallion Farm LLC (Cal)
Tr: Walsh Kathy(4 0 2 0 .00) 2007:(23 3 .13)

L 117[5]

Life	10	1	3	2	$78,840	93	D.Fst	7	1	2	2	$61,440 88
2007	3	0	1	0	$17,400	93	Wet(307)	0	0	0	0	$0 -
2006	6	1	2	2	$61,040	88	Synth	1	0	1	0	$14,000 93
Hol	3	0	2	1	$29,680	93	Turf(265)	2	0	0	0	$3,400 85
							Dst(309)	2	0	1	0	$10,200 88

29Apr07-7Hol fst 7f ◈ :213 :442 1:103 1:234 3↑[S]Barretts72k 93 2 9 52¼ 52 41¼ 2½ Espinoza V LB122 f 5.50 86-11 Social Climber116½ OneOntheHouse1221 Sixcess1221 Waited into str,rally 12
30Mar07-7SA fm *6½f (T) :211 :432 1:061 1:121 3↑[S]Alw 52000N1x 75 1 9 73¾ 85 64½ 64 Valdivia J Jr LB121 f 4.20 90-06 *Iza General*124¾ Global Heat119nk Rock'n U S A121nk Inside,no late bid 10
2Mar07-7SA fm *6½f (T) :214 :44 1:064 1:13 4↑[S]OC 32k/N1x-N 85 12 9 118½ 1010 64¾ 41¼ Valdivia J Jr LB119 f 8.40 89-12 BckTddyBck119no ByndLdd1211¼ AmrcnAllStr119no Broke thru gate,rally 12
15Jun06-7Hol fst 6½f :212 :44 1:094 1:17 3↑[S]Alw 50200N1x 87 6 5 55½ 45½ 33½ 3¾ Valdivia J Jr LB118 f 3.90 85-13 Red State119nk Shootist118½ One On the House118¾ Came out str,rallied 8
19May06-7Hol fst 6f :213 :441 :561 1:09 3↑[S]Alw 49800N1x 88 4 5 46 44½ 33 22¾ Valdivia J Jr LB118 f 10.60 89-16 Plagirist1182¾ OneOntheHouse1181¼ QuitenBoy1151¾ Angled in,up for 2nd 7
6Apr06-6SA fst 1 :213 :443 1:094 1:37 3↑[S]Alw 58400N1x 77 1 13½ 13½ 1½ 22½ 34½ Valdivia J Jr LB116 fb 3.90 78-24 AnzynsSng1221¾ TchdwnUSC1222¾ OnOnthHs1161½ Speed,inside,held 3rd 6
1Mar06-5SA fst 1 ⊗ :221 :46 1:101 1:372 [S]Md Sp Wt 49k 80 5 11 12½ 110 17 16¼ Valdivia J Jr LB120 fb 2.40 81-13 OneOntheHouse1206¼ LinisLion1201½ RisDncr12018¾ Speed,inside,driving 9
12Feb06-1SA fst 1 :223 :461 1:112 1:382 [S]Md Sp Wt 46k 56 4 31½ 31 31 22 28¼ Valdivia J Jr LB121 fb 5.40 68-15 Beautifier1218¼ *OneOntheHouse*1215¼ JoeMrket1213½ 3wd into str,2nd best 6
28Jan06-8SA fst 6f :213 :444 :573 1:11 [S]Md Sp Wt 46k 55 8 3 53 21½ 44 69 Valdivia J Jr LB121 fb 9.20 75-13 VlintEffort1211¾ ArtisticMomnt1213 MokBowl1212½ Angled in, weakened 10
7Aug05-6Dmr fst 5½f :223 :453 :573 1:034 [S]Md Sp Wt 52k 49 1 8 54 63¾ 56¼ 614¼ Gomez G K LB120 b 16.90 83-08 DaStoops1208¼ Thelaststrfighter115¾ Beutifier120hd Hopped,off bit slow 8

WORKS: May13 Hol ◈5f fst :593 H *5/47* Apr22 Hol ◈6f fst 1:122 H *4/31* ●Apr13 Hol ◈6f fst 1:122 H *1/19* Mar24 Hol ◈5f fst 1:014 H *47/67* ●Mar17 Hol ◈6f fst 1:122 H *1/20* ●Feb25 Hol ◈5f fst :584 H *1/61*
TRAINER: Synth(11 .27 $1.96) Sprint(59 .12 $3.09) Alw(23 .09 $4.71)

6 Lit'sgoodlookngray
Own: John E Pinner
Black Pink And Turquoise Halves, Pink And
VALDIVIA J JR (55 7 7 7 .13) 2007: (244 27 .11)

Gr/ro. c. 3 (Feb) BARJAN06 $23,000
Sire: Lit de Justice (El Gran Senor) $6,000
Dam: Color Collection (Souvenir Copy)
Br: Pablo A Suarez & Michelle Suarez (Cal)
Tr: Velasquez Danny(2 0 0 0 .00) 2007:(13 0 .00)

L 117

Life	8	1	1	2	$49,792	68	D.Fst	8	1	1	2	$49,792 68
2006	8	1	1	2	$49,792	68	Wet(371)	0	0	0	0	$0 -
2005	0	M	0	0	$0	-	Synth	0	0	0	0	$0 -
Hol	2	0	0	1	$8,100	64	Turf(313)	0	0	0	0	$0 -
							Dst(381)	2	0	1	0	$5,400 52

17Sep06-12Fpx fst 6½f :213 :453 1:112 1:182 [R]BrrettsJuv131k 68 2 6 63¼ 31½ 22½ 33½ Gryder A T LB116 b 24.00 79-14 RomnCommndr116½ ChfsMgc1183 Ltsgodlkngry116½ Chased, inside rally 9
9Sep06-10Fpx fst 6½f :214 :46 1:12 1:192 [S]Md Sp Wt 34k 66 7 6 31½ 2hd 13 14 Gryder A T LB119 b 5.40 78-18 Litsgoodlookngray1194 SidepocketCt1191 Siberzr119no Rail bid,led,clear 9
21Aug06-5Dmr fst 6f :221 :454 :584 1:122 [S]Md 40000(40-35) 52 1 9 2½ 1hd 1hd 22 Cohen D LB120 b 2.20 75-20 Inxcssbu1202 *Litsgoodlookngry*1202¾ CryMNoRivr1153¾ Off bit slow,inside 10
6Aug06-6Dmr fst 6f :22 :453 :58 1:111 [S]Md Sp Wt 55k 43 3 5 2hd 31 89¾ 1014¾ Garcia M5 LB115 b 7.60 68-13 LuckyThirteen1203 PalladinGenerl1205 DrJJ120no Dueled btwn,weakened 11
19Jly06-3Dmr fst 5½f :212 :44 :57 1:04 [S]Md Sp Wt 54k 41 8 5 63¾ 66¼ 711 814½ Atkinson P LB120 28.70 76-09 Indian Ashton120¾ Flip the Penny1152¾ Belknap1201 No rally outside 8
18Jun06-9Hol fst 5f :22 :451 :574 [S]Md Sp Wt 46k 64 3 7 42½ 44½ 35 36 Atkinson P LB120 10.90 86-13 TwnFn1151¼ FlpthPnny1154¾ Ltsgoodlokngry1204¾ Came out str,best rest 9
18May06-4BM fst 4½f :221 :461 :523 Md Sp Wt 32k 26 6 5 42½ 45½ 68¼ Lopez D G LB119 3.20 83-13 Boxelder1191 Starcast114no Bwana Bull119nk 4wide, gave out 7
5May06-3Hol fst 4½f :22 :453 :514 [S]Md Sp Wt 46k 49 4 7 55 56 48 Ochoa J5 LB115 5.50 87-11 PutItinWriting1202¾ FlipthePenny1204¾ WrrnRod120½ Off rail,missed 3rd 8

WORKS: May12 Hol ◈5f fst :59 H *2/68* May7 SA 4f fst :491 H *20/26* ●May1 SA 6f fst 1:111 H *1/9* Apr25 SA 6f fst 1:141 H *4/12* Apr17 SA 5f fst :592 H *2/16* Apr11 SA 5f fst :594 H *2/35*
TRAINER: Synth(6 .00 $0.00) Sprint(55 .13 $2.40) J/T 2006-07(4 .00 $0.00)

7 Unusual Suspect
Own: Barry or David or Dyan Abrams
Orange Purple And Green Halves, Green 'Da' On
SMITH M E (27 2 2 7 .07) 2007: (174 20 .11)

Dk. b or br c. 3 (Apr)
Sire: Unusual Heat (Nureyev) $12,500
Dam: Penpont*NZ (Crested Wave)
Br: David Abrams (Cal)
Tr: Abrams Barry(15 1 2 4 .07) 2007:(95 5 .05)

L 117

Life	8	1	2	2	$102,600	89	D.Fst	1	0	0	0	$400 55
2007	1	0	0	1	$7,644	73	Wet(288)	0	0	0	0	$0 -
2006	7	1	2	1	$94,956	89	Synth	2	0	1	0	$20,000 89
Hol	2	0	1	0	$20,000	89	Turf(323)	5	1	1	2	$82,200 74
							Dst(328)	1	0	0	0	$400 55

6May07-2Hol fm 6f (T) :241 :472 :584 1:101 Alw 51458N1x 73 5 6 64 52¾ 42 3¾ Smith M E LB120 2.20 89-06 Gweebarra115¾ Rummada118hd UnusulSuspect1202¼ Came out str,rallied 6
30Dec06-7SA fm 1 (T) :24 :493 1:131 1:372 EddieLogan82k 72 6 73½ 63½ 74¾ 64¼ 42 Cohen D LB119 3.50 74-18 Kolo118nk Mystery Island118no *Law Breaker*1181¾ Steadied past 1/4 10
16Dec06-9Hol fst 1 1/16 ◈ :232 :473 1:113 1:42 HolFut-G1 89 3 78½ 76 42 42¼ 72¾ Cohen D LB121 46.60 - - Stormello121nk Liquidity1211¼ RomnCommndr121no Rail,btwn,no late bid 10
24Nov06-3Hol fm 1 (T) :243 :49 1:124 1:362 Generous-G3 71 1 64 64 64½ 51¾ 22¼ Cohen D LB118 5.80 80-13 WrningZon1192¼ UnusulSuspct118½ [D]PrivtWind118¾ Inside,bit tight 1/16 8
Run in divisions
4Nov06-8Hol fst 1 1/16 ◈ :241 :481 1:123 1:443 RealQuiet100k 76 5 61¾ 61½ 31 2hd 2¾ Potts C L LB117 3.20 - - RomnCommndr121¾ UnusulSuspct1171¾ Lqdty1171 Bit tight5-1/2,held 2d 6
26Oct06-7OSA fm 1 (T) :24 :484 1:123 1:354 [R]Pinjara65k 74 4 66 52¼ 41¼ 62¼ 42 Potts C L LB118 4.00 82-15 *Whtsthescript*118½ *WrningZone*119hd [D]Edwrdin1181½ 4wd bid,lugged in 1/8 8
Placed third through disqualification
24Aug06-6Dmr fm 1 (T) :222 :462 1:104 1:354 Md Sp Wt 68k 69 2 77¼ 68 63¾ 21 1¾ Potts C L LB119 6.30 82-15 UnusulSuspect119¾ FrnktheBrbr1191½ Entourg119nk 4wd into lane,rallied 10
6Aug06-6Dmr fst 6f :22 :453 :58 1:111 [S]Md Sp Wt 55k 55 4 11 811 109¼ 1010 710 Arias S5 LB115 67.60 73-13 Lucky Thirteen1203 Palladian General1205 Dr. J J120no Off bit slow,inside 11

WORKS: May15 Hol ◈4f fst :491 H *26/53* May2 Hol ◈4f fst :473 H *7/49* Apr26 Hol ◈6f fst 1:133 H *4/19* Apr21 SA 5f gd 1:03 H *2/2* Apr14 SA 5f fst 1:021 H *24/30* Apr8 SA 4f fst :474 H *13/47*
TRAINER: 2Off45-180(16 .06 $1.56) Synth(28 .04 $1.24) Turf/Synth(13 .00 $0.00) Sprint(161 .06 $1.60) Alw(63 .05 $0.53) J/T 2006-07 HOL(2 .00 $0.00) J/T 2006-07(2 .00 $0.00)

8 Swift Demand
Own: C R K Stable
Pink White, Burgundy Diamond Frame On Back
NAKATANI C S (12 2 2 1 .17) 2007: (267 39 .15)
B. c. 3 (Jan) BAROCT05 $290,000
Sire: High Demand (Danzig) $5,000
Dam: Cover Letter (Kingmambo)
Br: Betty L Mabee & Larry Mabee (Cal)
Tr: Sadler John W(37 5 7 1 .14) 2007:(220 41 .19)
L 117

Life	3	1	0	0	$32,300	87	
2007	3	1	0	0	$32,300	87	
2006	0	M	0	0	$0	-	
Hol	1	0	0	0	$1,400	87	
D.Fst	2	1	0	0	$30,900	85	
Wet(389*)	0	0	0	0	$0	-	
Synth	1	0	0	0	$1,400	87	
Turf(372*)	0	0	0	0	$0	-	
Dst(403*)	0	0	0	0	$0	-	

29Apr07–7Hol fst 7f ◈ :213 :442 1:103 1:234 3↑ⓈBarretts72k 87 6 10 106 93¾ 72¾ 53¼ Flores D R LB116 8.20 84– 11 Social Climber116½ **One OntheHouse**1221 Sixcess1221 Swung 3wd into lane 12
30Mar07–3SA fst 1 :221 :452 1:11 1:374 3↑ⓈAlw 55000n1x 66 2 42½ 41½ 44½ 46½ 413½ Talamo J5 LB107 *1.30 65– 23 Like New Money1203½ *Leesider*1168¼ Valid Star1151¾ In tight 3/8,no rally 5
15Feb07–3SA fst 6½f :212 :441 1:10 1:164 ⓈMd Sp Wt 48k 85 11 11 1116 89 33½ 1hd Gomez G K LB121 10.50 86– 13 SwiftDemand121hd VictoryJoe1211½ StormyGrnt1211¾ Hesitated,off slow 11
WORKS: May14 Hol ◈5f fst :592 H *2/54* ●Apr21 Hol ◈6f fst 1:11 H *1/32* Apr15 Hol ◈5f fst :594 H *8/47* Apr8 Hol ◈4f fst :472 H *5/41* Mar26 Hol ◈4f fst :481 H *8/38* Mar20 Hol ◈7f fst 1:262 H *1/1*
TRAINER: Synth(69 .30 $2.46) Sprint(438 .19 $1.60) Alw(138 .20 $2.35) J/T 2006-07 HOL(11 .55 $3.49) J/T 2006-07(35 .49 $2.62)

9 Voracious
Own: La Canada Stables LLC or Sahadi
Turqse Red, Black Crest Emblem On White Hoop On
GRYDER A T (4 0 1 0 .00) 2007: (340 44 .13)
Dk. b or br g. 4 (Feb)
Sire: Souvenir Copy (Mr. Prospector) $7,500
Dam: Hasty and Happy (Seattle Slew)
Br: Fred N Sahadi (Cal)
Tr: Carava Jack(12 4 0 0 .33) 2007:(122 22 .18)
L 120

Life	8	2	1	3	$42,200	92	
2007	3	2	1	0	$30,100	92	
2006	4	M	0	3	$9,780	69	
Hol	1	0	0	1	$2,040	69	
D.Fst	7	2	1	2	$40,240	92	
Wet(402)	0	0	0	0	$0	-	
Synth	1	0	0	1	$2,040	69	
Turf(287)	0	0	0	0	$0	-	
Dst(391)	4	0	0	2	$10,140	68	

10Mar07–5SA fst 6½f :211 :441 1:093 1:164 3↑ Alw 40000s 84 11 2 11 11½ 12½ 11 Gryder A T LB124 b *3.00 86– 14 Voracious1241 *Threeatonce*1211½ Duty Roster114½ Speed,inside,held 11
16Feb07–6SA fst 5½f :211 :441 :562 1:031 4↑ Md 25000(25-22.5) 92 5 6 11 12 14 17¼ Flores D R LB122 b *1.20 93– 16 *Voracious*1227¼ Sabio1221½ Fuseout1201½ Drew off, easily 11
24Jan07–8SA fst 6½f :212 :441 1:09 1:154 4↑ Md 25000(25-22.5) 87 11 4 13 12 2hd 23½ Flores D R LB122 b 4.00 87– 14 Tony Montana1223½ *Voracious*122½ Highly Gallant1226½ Angled in,held 2nd 14
12Nov06–2Hol fst 6½f ◈ :212 :441 1:094 1:162 3↑ Md 32000(32-28) 69 6 4 2hd 1hd 21½ 35 Flores D R LB122 b 4.20 - - Black Spot122¾ Lead Stealer1224¼ Voracious1224¾ Inside duel,held 3rd 8
20Oct06–6OSA fst 6f :213 :451 :573 1:10 3↑ Md 32000(32-28) 68 7 5 2hd 1hd 2½ 39 Flores D R LB121 b 5.60 80– 16 Twin Turbo1248¼ Golden Smoke121¾ Voracious1212 Dueled,held 3rd 10
5Oct06–5OSA fst 6f :21 :442 :574 1:113 3↑ⓈMd 40000 55 5 9 74¼ 63¼ 62¾ 33¾ Flores D R LB121 b *2.00 77– 16 Smart Hit121¾ *Souvenir Evening*1213 Voracious121hd 4wd into lane,late 3rd 13
26Aug06–3Dmr fst 6f :22 :453 :584 1:113 3↑ⓈMd Sp Wt 54k 58 2 8 3nk 2hd 2½ 44¾ Potts C L LB120 7.20 76– 14 LnsLon1203 SrChCh1201¾ MrSmoothOprtr120no Lugged out late,wkened 8
10Oct05–10SA fst 6f :213 :444 :564 1:094 ⓈMd Sp Wt 40k 61 2 6 31 31½ 34 48½ Gomez G K LB120 *.80 80– 14 Ctouttthebg1207 StephenBruce120½ LordClenSweep1201 Off slow,pulled 6
WORKS: May1 SA 5f fst 1:003 H *11/25* Apr24 SA 5f fst 1:01 H *13/34* Apr16 SA 4f fst :473 H *7/38* Apr2 SA 4f fst :474 H *9/22* Mar24 SA 4f fst :482 H *8/36* Mar2 SA 4f fst :47 H *2/39*
TRAINER: 61-180Days(10 .10 $1.16) Synth(34 .26 $2.78) WonLastStart(55 .22 $1.86) Sprint(286 .14 $1.58) Alw(22 .00 $0.00) J/T 2006-07(3 .33 $2.67)

10 Warrensgildedtime
Own: Benjamin C Warren
Purple White, Black 'W' On Back, Black Bars On
FLORES D R (45 6 10 5 .13) 2007: (344 57 .17)
Ch. c. 3 (Jan)
Sire: Gilded Time (Timeless Moment) $10,000
Dam: Salish Slew (Slewdledo)
Br: Benjamin C Warren (Cal)
Tr: Sise Clifford Jr(17 0 6 4 .00) 2007:(103 12 .12)
L 115

Life	6	2	2	0	$49,300	85	
2007	4	1	2	0	$37,500	85	
2006	2	1	0	0	$11,800	75	
Hol	2	1	0	0	$11,800	75	
D.Fst	3	1	2	0	$37,100	85	
Wet(382)	0	0	0	0	$0	-	
Synth	2	1	0	0	$11,800	75	
Turf(286)	1	0	0	0	$400	67	
Dst(400)	3	1	1	0	$26,900	85	

11Apr07–4SA fm *6½f ⓣ :211 :432 1:064 1:13 OC 80k/n1x 67 12 1 54¾ 57½ 98¾ 1011½ Flores D R LB118 12.30 78– 11 Yario1181 *Hurry Home Warren*1153½ *Luis's Especial*118½ 3wd,4wd,weakened 12
16Mar07–3SA fst 6f :212 :443 :564 1:093 ⓈOC 62k/n1x-N 85 2 5 51¾ 21 22 22¼ Sorenson D LB118 12.20 89– 10 IdiotProof1182¼ Wrrnsgilddtim1181 CptSprrow1194 Stalked rail,held 2nd 6
17Feb07–2SA fst 6½f :211 :44 1:093 1:164 ⓈAlw 53400n1x 77 4 3 21½ 22 21½ 21½ Sorenson D LB118 3.00 84– 10 SomthngSonc1181½ Wrrnsglddtm1182¼ ByNw120no Stalked pace,2nd best 6
14Jan07–1SA fst 6f :213 :451 :573 1:11 Alw 40000s 79 6 2 2hd 2hd 1½ 15 Sorenson D LB122 4.30 84– 20 Wrrnsglddtm1225 TylorsRout122nk CurosCody1191½ Dueled,clear,driving 7
15Dec06–4Hol fst 5½f ◈ :222 :452 :573 1:034 ⓈMd 40000(40-35) 75 2 5 1hd 1½ 11½ 13 Sorenson D LB120 3.40 - - *Wrrensgildedtim*1203 BrhmsFshion1203½ DsrtRin120¾ Bumped early,inside 11
30Nov06–4Hol fst 6f ◈ :22 :443 :561 1:084 Md 80000(80-70) 58 1 10 63¼ 65 78 99¾ Sorenson D LB120 43.10 - - Gregorian Bay120hd Carman120½ Luis's Especial120hd Off bit slow,inside 11
WORKS: May9 Hol ◈4f fst :494 H *41/57* May2 Hol ◈5f fst 1:033 H *41/46* Apr25 Hol ◈4f fst :51 H *44/51* Apr4 Hol ◈4f fst :521 H *33/34* Mar9 Hol ◈5f fst 1:043 H *39/41* Mar3 Hol ◈4f fst :50 H *34/48*
TRAINER: Synth(33 .21 $4.09) Turf/Synth(7 .14 $2.57) 31-60Days(119 .15 $1.28) Sprint(295 .16 $1.49) Alw(66 .11 $0.79) J/T 2006-07 HOL(3 .00 $0.00) J/T 2006-07(20 .20 $2.02)

11 Spoils of Excess
Own: Acker Lapera Hurrin Hoosiers Horses L
Gray Turquoise, Pink Diamond Frame 'Ala' On
MIGLIORE R (84 12 14 5 .14) 2007: (406 59 .15)
Dk. b or br g. 3 (Apr) BAROCT05 $49,000
Sire: In Excess*Ire (Siberian Express)
Dam: Cosmetic Lift (Miswaki)
Br: Foothills Farm (Cal)
Tr: Spawr Bill(8 2 1 0 .25) 2007:(77 15 .19)
L 117

Life	2	1	1	0	$36,800	91	
2007	2	1	1	0	$36,800	91	
2006	0	M	0	0	$0	-	
Hol	0	0	0	0	$0	-	
D.Fst	2	1	1	0	$36,800	91	
Wet(399)	0	0	0	0	$0	-	
Synth	0	0	0	0	$0	-	
Turf(341)	0	0	0	0	$0	-	
Dst(397)	1	1	0	0	$27,600	91	

4Apr07–2SA fst 6f :214 :444 :564 1:093 3↑ⓈMd Sp Wt 46k 91 6 2 2½ 2hd 1½ 13 Espinoza V LB117 *.90 91– 11 SpoilsofExcess1173 SocilStir1244½ HndsomBill1171¾ Dueled,clear,driving 6
20Jan07–6SA fst 5½f :214 :45 :572 1:04 ⓈMd Sp Wt 48k 83 7 10 73¼ 54½ 54 2no Espinoza V LB121 13.90 89– 11 Comoros121no *Spoils of Excess*121no Victory Joe1211¼ Hopped,off bit slow 11
WORKS: ●May12 Hol ◈6f fst 1:12 H *1/17* May6 Hol ◈5f fst 1:034 H *50/51* Apr30 Hol ◈4f fst :511 H *57/62* Apr24 Hol ◈4f fst :524 H *47/47* Apr17 SA 4f fst :514 H *11/12* Apr1 SA 3f fst :344 H *3/20*
TRAINER: 2Off45-180(53 .21 $3.03) Synth(30 .17 $1.17) 31-60Days(88 .16 $1.26) WonLastStart(44 .23 $1.90) Sprint(170 .12 $1.24) Alw(29 .17 $1.65) J/T 2006-07 HOL(7 .14 $1.31) J/T 2006-07(41 .22 $3.02)

This six-furlong race for was for N1X allowance California-breds. Par for the race is one less than the open N1X race, making the Beyer par 93 rather than the 95 we used for the Johnny Eves race at Oak Tree. We'll accept 88 as a contending number.

1. Moonlit Habit has two races that qualify, but he hasn't been out in 10 months. He's suspect at anything less than an overlaid price, something you seldom get from this barn.
2. My City by the Bay hasn't a race that would put him in the picture.
3. Cayambe is a 3-year-old, something I usually prefer against these older N1Xs. However, he hasn't a figure that puts him in the mix.
4. Sir Toasty has had 25 chances without a single race that fits the par.
5. One On the House qualifies from several good races at the level. He looks to be a "hanger," but he does fit on numbers.

6. Lit'sgoodlookngray may look good to his owners, but he's not much of a racehorse.

7. Unusual Suspect has a single figure at a route that fits the par, but he looks more comfortable on the turf.

8. Swift Demand's Beyers are just marginally off the target par and I would not hesitate to consider this 3-year-old in this spot.

9. Voracious has a pair of races that qualify him as a contender. This is a big step up in class, but the numbers say okay.

10. Warrensgildedtime tries hard but doesn't have the 88 Beyer we're looking for.

11. Spoils of Excess is lightly raced, and the figure from his maiden victory could win here.

Based on qualifying par numbers, our contenders are (1) Moonlit Habit; (5) One On the House; (8) Swift Demand; (9) Voracious; and (11) Spoils of Excess. This sprint shapes up as a contentious N1X with several ways to go in the betting. Only on further inspection did this race become really interesting. Let's take another look at Cayambe.

Art Sherman brought this nondescript 3-year-old to Hollywood Park and promptly sent him two turns over a non-speed-favoring turf course. Only in the final analysis of today's race did I catch the significance of that effort. The fractions he pressed past the six-furlong mark were absolutely incredible for a turf race: 22⅘, 45⅗, and 1:10 through the second call. How good was that effort? Let's look at the par for that N1X allowance race:

8F   1:11⅖   1:35

All Cayambe did was duel through a 114 (Quirin figures) pace figure (graded-stakes-level) and fought every step of the way before the stretch call. Today's Quirin par is 104 and the acceptable Beyer par 88.

There are some differences of opinion as to how much adjustment must be made to the pace figures to translate that number to a sprint figure. The adjustments range from two points to five, with the latter being my call in the argument. My reasoning is again the idea of wiggle room; the more the better. If the figure stands strong after a five-point adjustment, the bet should be rock-solid. In the case of Cayambe, the 114 pace figure adjusts to a *109* Quirin figure. Par for this race is 104 (Beyer 88), so a 109 looms large if the horse sprints to that figure. Is Cayambe worth a gamble? At 60–1 you be the judge.

EIGHTH RACE
Hollywood
MAY 19, 2007

6 FURLONGS. (1.07³) ALLOWANCE . Purse $49,000 (plus $2,000 Other Sources) FOR CALIFORNIA BRED THREE YEAR OLDS AND UPWARD WHICH HAVE NEVER WON $7,500 OTHER THAN MAIDEN, CLAIMING, OR STARTER OR WHICH HAVE NEVER WON TWO RACES. Three Year Olds, 119 lbs.; Older, 124 lbs. Non–winners of a race other than Maiden, Claiming, or Starter Allowed 2 lbs. A race other than Claiming, or Starter Allowed 4 lbs.

Value of Race: $51,000 Winner $29,400; second $9,800; third $5,880; fourth $2,940; fifth $980; sixth $400; seventh $400; eighth $400; ninth $400; tenth $400. Mutuel Pool $494,844.00 Exacta Pool $246,344.00 Quinella Pool $17,408.00 Trifecta Pool $217,875.00 Superfecta Pool $137,026.00

Last Raced	Horse	M/Eqt.	A.	Wt	PP	St	¼	½	Str	Fin	Jockey	Odds $1
28Apr07 5Hol8	Cayambe	LB b	3	117	3	4	1½	1¹	1²	1⁴	Court J K	60.60
28Apr07 7Hol1	My City by the Bay	LB	4	120	2	6	3hd	2¹½	2²½	2½	Garcia M	18.60
29Apr07 7Hol2	One On the House	LB f	4	117	5	5	7²½	7¹	4¹	3¹¼	Talamo J5	2.40
11Apr07 4SA10	Warrensgildedtime	LB	3	115	9	1	4hd	5¹½	3hd	4nk	Flores D R	13.60
29Apr07 7Hol5	Swift Demand	LB	3	119	7	9	9⁴	8²	7²	5¹	Nakatani C S	5.60
17Sep06 12Fpx3	Lit'sgoodlookngray	LB	3	117	6	10	10¹	10	8¹½	6¹½	Valdivia J Jr	60.10
4Apr07 2SA1	Spoils of Excess	LB f	3	117	10	2	5¹½	4hd	6hd	7no	Migliore R	2.10
20Jly06 6Dmr2	Moonlit Habit	LB	4	122	1	7	6¹	6hd	5hd	8⁴	Baze M C	4.40
10Dec06 3Hol6	Sir Toasty	LB b	5	122	4	8	8¹½	9²	9²½	9⁷¼	Rodriguez A C	125.00
10Mar07 5SA1	Voracious	LB b	4	120	8	3	2¹½	3hd	10	10	Gryder A T	10.20

OFF AT 5:23 Start Good. Won driving. Track fast.
TIME :21⁴, :45¹, :57¹, 1:09⁴ (:21.92, :45.28, :57.39, 1:09.93)

$2 Mutuel Prices:

3 – CAYAMBE	123.20	37.60	21.60
2 – MY CITY BY THE BAY		18.40	7.40
5 – ONE ON THE HOUSE			3.40

$1 EXACTA 3–2 PAID $536.50 $2 QUINELLA 2–3 PAID $351.20
$1 TRIFECTA 3–2–5 PAID $2,414.00 $1 SUPERFECTA 3–2–5–10 PAID $17,502.00

Ch. g, (Jan), by Helmsman – Pacaya , by Restless Con . Trainer Sherman Art. Bred by Geri Forrester (Cal).

CAYAMBE had speed between horses then dueled a bit off the rail, inched away and angled in on the turn and drew clear under urging. MY CITY BY THE BAY close up stalking the pace inside, came out into the stretch and held second. ONE ON THE HOUSE chased alongside a rival then outside on the turn, came our five wide into the stretch and was edged for the place. WARRENSGILDEDTIME had speed outside then stalked three deep, came four wide into the stretch and lacked the needed response. SWIFT DEMAND settled off the rail, went outside on the turn and three deep into the stretch and could not offer the necessary late kick. LIT'SGOODLOOKNGRAY broke a bit slowly, settled just off the rail, came out into the stretch and was not a threat. SPOILS OF EXCESS wide early, angled in and stalked between horses, came three deep into the stretch and weakened. MOONLIT HABIT was in a good position stalking the pace inside to the stretch and also weakened. SIR TOASTY bobbled slightly at the start, angled in and chased inside to the stretch and did not rally. VORACIOUS fractious in the gate, had speed outside then forced the pace outside the winner, dropped back between foes leaving the turn and gave way.

Owners– 1, Filouette Enterprises; 2, Johnston E W and Judy and Johnston Lessee E W ; 3, Vreeland James R ; 4, Warren Benjamin C ; 5, C R K Stable; 6, Pinner John E ; 7, Acker Lapera Hurrin Hoosiers Horses LLC et al; 8, Hughes B Wayne; 9, Cox Lisa; 10, La Canada Stable LLC and Sahadi Fred

Trainers– 1, Sherman Art; 2, Warren Donald; 3, Walsh Kathy; 4, Sise Clifford Jr; 5, Sadler John W; 6, Velasquez Danny; 7, Spawr Bill; 8, Mandella Richard; 9, Martin Frank Jr; 10, Carava Jack

Scratched– Unusual Suspect (06May07 2Hol3)

$2 Daily Double (2–3) Paid $337.00 ; Daily Double Pool $38,351 .
$1 Pick Three (1–2–3) Paid $2,415.20 ; Pick Three Pool $100,549 .

CRIST
ON EXOTICS AND VALUE
by Steven Crist

THE ENTIRE ISSUE OF betting longshots has been turned on its head by the ascendance of exotic betting in American racing over the last 30 years, raising entirely new and complex concepts and possibilities.

In simpler times, when straight win-place-show betting accounted for over 90 percent of the handle, the primary way to get a return of 10–1 or better on a racetrack wager was to find a horse offering that high a price to win, and the only questions were whether he had a reasonable chance and if it made any sense to back him to place or show as well as in the win pool. Today, nearly 70 percent of the annual $15 billion handle on American racing is on multiple-horse wagers where a 10–1 return is at the very low end of the scale, widely considered the equivalent of a chalky $3.40 payoff of yesteryear.

The core concept of making winning bets at favorable prices is the same, but both the landscape and the methodologies have changed. The overview herein will approach the issues under three broad headings.

First, when is a longshot a "value bet," and do those at the higher or lower end of the double-digit range provide the best risk/reward ratio? Second, how do multihorse wagers create longshot opportunities in the absence of true longshots? Finally, what is the role and optimal use of traditional longshots in the new wagers that now rule the game?

LONGSHOTS AND VALUE BETTING

The thesis of my chapter on "Value" in the original *Bet with the Best* could (if necessary) be boiled down to five words: price times probability equals value. A horse with a 50 percent chance of winning offers positive value at 6–5 or higher and negative value at 4–5 or lower. My suggestion was that rather than wedding themselves to ego-driven selections of appealing horses regardless of their price, successful players need to be flexible enough to embrace value wherever they find it.

As a practical matter, this equation works best with horses at shorter rather than longer prices, simply because the discrepancies are more glaring and quantifiable. When Smarty Jones was 2–5 to win the 2004 Belmont Stakes, something that nine consecutive Derby-Preakness winners had failed to do, he obviously was a horrendous underlay and an automatic bet-against. A gross overlay might occur in a situation where the crowd is making two horses 2–1 co-favorites but one of them is clearly superior to the other and offers outstanding value at 2–1 if he is closer to 50 than 33 percent to win the race.

Those disparities, however, become both harder to find, and more difficult to calibrate, when considering horses whose true chances of victory are much smaller. On rare occasions you will find a horse at 8–1 who you truly believe has a 30 percent chance of winning, and of course you should unload on such a proposition if you are confident in your assessment. More often, though, you are on shakier ground at high odds.

In the case of a 12–1 shot you think should be 8–1, it might at first seem you have found a highly promising situation: Getting a $26 win mutuel on overlaid horses who win 11 percent of the time translates to around a 44 percent profit—a $26 return for $18 (nine $2 bets) invested. But how confident can you really be that the horse's true chances of victory are 11 percent as opposed to 7 percent? At the latter strike rate, you're now losing 9 percent rather than making 44 percent, a massive swing on a relatively small difference. Do you really want to base your profitability on being able to say whether a horse has a 7 vs. 11 percent chance of winning a race?

It is especially hard to make that determination amid the psychological factors surrounding the selection of a relatively unpopular horse. All thoughtful horseplayers are by nature contrarian, believing that they at least occasionally have a better opinion than the collective wisdom of the crowd. Finding an "error" on the tote board produces an adrenaline rush of discovery, fueled by ego. It is almost irresistible to attempt to monetize that supposedly superior opinion, but one must resist if the fundamentals of the price/probability equation are not there.

Consider a six-horse field where the odds are 2–1, 2–1, 4–1, 8–1, 12–1, and 20–1. Let's say you agree with the crowd that the two favorites are absolutely the likeliest winners and have roughly equal merits, but your third choice is the 8–1 shot, not the 4–1 shot. In fact, you despise the latter, a horse you think has virtually no chance of winning. Those backing him are insane for making him half the price of the horse you prefer. You feel you must punish them for their mistake and reward yourself for preferring an 8–1 to a 4–1.

So you bet to win at 8–1 and maybe take your horse back and forth with the two favorites in big exactas and even throw in a dollar front- and back-wheel in the exactas because you sure don't want to get nothing if he runs second to that 20–1 shot. Then you watch him finish a distant third to the two favorites and you get nothing but the empty victory of beating the despised 4–1 shot.

This is a classic longshot trap. You were right about liking the 8–1 better than the 4–1, but that did not make him a good bet at 8–1. *Longshots often outrun their relative odds within a race without outrunning their absolute odds of winning.* Perhaps in this example, the "correct" odds were 4–5, 6–5, 20–1, 15–1, 50–1, and 50–1. While the crowd may have made an incorrect third choice in the race, you were still taking 8–1 on a horse who was legitimately 15–1.

As we'll see shortly, there may have been a way to capitalize on your opinion by playing intrarace exotic wagers, because horses who are good bets to outrun their relative odds or ordinal positions in the betting can be profitably used on the bottom of trifecta and superfecta tickets. But by playing such a horse to win (or using him to win in multirace wagers), you were actually taking a severely underlaid price.

One way to avoid such situations is to concentrate on finding spots where, rather than merely seeking a pricier alternative to clearly superior horses who will probably have to misfire to lose, you aggressively attack races in which you believe the favorites are both underlaid and highly vulnerable to defeat in an absolute sense. False favorites, like rising tides, lift all boats: In a race where you detest the chances of a 3–2 shot, you are eliminating a third of the win pool, and are virtually guaranteed an overlaid price on every other starter.

When this is the case, you now are getting some real value in preferring the fourth choice to the third choice. You're getting an overlaid price to begin with thanks to the hopeless favorite, and a further advantage because of the crowd error on the third choice. You've got two things going for you instead of merely the illusion of one, giving you both a square straight price and an opportunity for even greater value in the exotics.

LONG AND LONGER

Before leaving the topic of straight-price value on longshots, we should make a distinction between the contentious and the truly hopeless. While the crowd does make mistakes, and good horseplayers know how to recognize and take advantage of them, one must never forget that the crowd as a whole is consistently a better handicapper than any individual player. Not only do the horses the crowd makes 2–1 win more often than the horses it makes 3–1, but over any meaningful sample its 2.10–1 choices win slightly more often than its 2.20–1 shots, which win more often than its 2.30–1 selections, and so on down the line.

While the crowd makes the occasional gross error and frequent minor ones, it simply does not let too many legitimate contenders go off at 20–1 or better. If you blindly bet every odds-on choice, you will lose money but beat the takeout, recouping roughly 90 percent of your investment. That return goes down with each higher odds increment, falling below 60 percent at 20–1 or better.

Yet plenty of racing commentators and bettors continue to fall for the idea that a high-priced horse from a leading stable or trainer is always a good bet. The reasoning seems to be that if an outfit wins at a 20 percent rate, 20–1 is by definition an overlay on any of its starters. In fact, these are some of the worst propositions in racing.

Consider the records of the following top trainers with horses at different odds ranges. For each I used *Daily Racing Form*'s Formulator 4.1 software to look at all of their starters in a five-year stretch from mid-2002 to mid-2007. The first two examples are Todd Pletcher and Jerry Hollendorfer. Pletcher, the Eclipse Award winner as the nation's leading trainer in 2004, 2005, and 2006, runs a vast nationwide stable focused on expensive young horses and older stakes winners; Hollendorfer is the leading trainer in Northern California, with a stable of bread-and-butter claiming and allowance horses and the occasional stakes runner.

Todd Pletcher	WINS	STARTS	%	RETURN ON $2
2–1 or lower	719	1,807	40%	$1.67
2–1 to 5–1	402	1,919	21%	$1.71
5–1 to 10–1	122	969	13%	$1.94
10–1 or higher	21	496	4%	$1.36
Total	1,254	5,191	24%	$1.70

Jerry Hollendorfer	WINS	STARTS	%	RETURN ON $2
2–1 or lower	866	2,273	38%	$1.61
2–1 to 5–1	376	1,979	19%	$1.57
5–1 to 10–1	82	829	10%	$1.62
10–1 or higher	28	562	5%	$1.52
Total	1,352	5,640	24%	$1.59

In both cases, these 24 percent trainers become less than 5 percent trainers with starters who go off at 10–1 or more, and those longshot starters provide the worst return on investment at any odds tier. Yet it's even money that if you listen to television and simulcast hosts, you will be told that no horse sent out by either should ever be such a big price and is automatically a "live longshot."

The drop-off is even more dramatic if we separate the longshots into those who go off at higher and lower than 20–1. Hollendorfer, for example, is 25 for 426 (6 percent with a $1.63 ROI) on horses between 10–1 and 20–1, and 3 for 136 (2 percent with a $1.31 ROI) at 20–1 or higher. Pletcher is a similarly dismal 3 for 132 (2 percent with a $1.50 ROI) at 20–1 and up.

The difference in performance between these two types of longshots is consistent among most of racing's leading outfits. Bettors clearly find the idea of getting 20–1 or better on top trainers such as Bobby Frankel and Christophe Clement simply irresistible, despite the clear results:

Bobby Frankel	Wins	Starts	%	Return on $2
All starters	642	2,617	25%	$1.70
10–1 to 20–1	13	192	7%	$1.72
20–1 or higher	0	49	0%	$0.00

Christophe Clement	Wins	Starts	%	Return on $2
All starters	391	1,871	21%	$1.54
10–1 to 20–1	12	183	7%	$1.79
20–1 or higher	2	72	3%	$1.32

Even Rick Dutrow, who has some of the game's best numbers with starters at double-digit odds, shows a severe drop-off at 20–1 or higher:

Rick Dutrow	Wins	Starts	%	Return on $2
All starters	767	3,066	25%	$1.78
10–1 to 20–1	17	212	8%	$2.25
20–1 or higher	2	50	4%	$1.75

The revelation here isn't that 10–1 to 20–1 shots win more often than even bigger longshots, but that the return is so low in the latter group.

Pletcher, Hollendorfer, Frankel, Clement, and Dutrow are all high-percentage trainers who run a lot of favorites. What about so-called longshot trainers, who win less frequently and with lesser stock? I canvassed some fellow New York horseplayers to nominate trainers they thought were especially good at big prices, and three names that kept coming up were Del Carroll II, Pat Kelly, and Ramon "Mike" Hernandez. Here were their results from the same five-year period:

Del Carroll II	Wins	Starts	%	Return on $2
All starters	73	775	9%	$1.57
10–1 to 20–1	13	197	7%	$2.04
20–1 or higher	4	234	2%	$0.89

Mike Hernandez	Wins	Starts	%	Return on $2
All starters	58	551	11%	$1.59
10–1 to 20–1	12	129	9%	$2.70
20–1 or higher	1	152	1%	$0.61

Pat Kelly	Wins	Starts	%	Return on $2
All starters	97	1,211	8%	$1.43
10–1 to 20–1	21	295	7%	$1.79
20–1 or higher	6	427	1%	$0.90

Clearly, Carroll, Hernandez, and Kelly are indeed "good with longshots," in the 10–1 to 20–1 range, showing a profit or beating the takeout in that category. But taking this a greedy step further, and thinking they're even better at higher odds, is clearly a trap. All three start even more horses at 20–1 than in the 10–1 to 20–1 range, and these runners win barely 1 in 100 starts while producing a loss of over 50 percent.

COUNTING THE COMBINATIONS

A large percentage of current horseplayers, especially those over the age of 40, came of age as bettors in the midst of the exotics revolution of the last few decades. They were schooled or mentored by an even older generation, most of whom were initially wary of the exotics as "gimmicks." Starting out with limited bankrolls, as almost all new players do, they saw the exotics as a way to get a more exciting return than $7.60, $3.80, and $2.40 across the board. Compared to those mutuels, a $32 exacta sounded pretty good. "I had the exacta!" a player might pronounce proudly after hitting one of those, as if he had picked a 15–1 shot and bet him on the nose.

The problem is that this same generation of players was taught, through allegedly helpful charts in track programs and from unsophisticated comrades, that "boxing" and "wheeling" exactas was the best way to hit one of those supposedly juicy payoffs. In an eight-horse field, front- and back-wheeling one horse in $2 exactas costs $28, making that $32 winner the equivalent of a $2.30 show payoff. Players came to realize that having a few exactas in the $30 to $50 range on a card was not such a great achievement or a road to profit if they were spending $24 or $28 a race on four-horse boxes or up-and-down wheels. Many probably began including unlikely longshots in their boxes or keying on such horses in their wheels in an attempt to be getting a bigger exacta when they proclaimed "I had it!"

Lost in the search for ever-higher payoffs is the fact that there are two ways to collect more: (1) You can try to hit an unlikelier combination at higher odds, or (2) you can increase profits by making fewer combinations. That $32 exacta really is a longshot if it's the only combination you buy, and even if you buy two combinations to hit for $32, it's every bit as clever and rewarding as betting a $16 winner straight.

Consider that staple of many bettors, the three-horse exacta box, a $12 investment on a $2 base bet that buys you the six possible exacta permutations. To get the equivalent of a 3–1 return, your winning combination has to pay $48. You might feel as if you've done something daring and special to be cashing a ticket that paid off at 23–1, but by making six bets you've cut yourself down to 3–1. This can be especially frustrating if the horse you liked the best won, and at better than 3–1.

The point of playing exotics is to improve on win prices, not to decrease them, and when this is done successfully, a smart player can turn a non-longshot winner into the equivalent of a longshot through one or more good additional opinions on the race.

At their best, exotics can turn otherwise unplayable races into longshot opportunities. A frequent case is the short-field event in which a favorite seems perfectly solid—he looks 50–50 to win the race and his odds are dancing between 4–5 and even money. Such a horse presents no value as a win proposition.

Suppose, however, that you really don't like the 2–1 second choice in the race, preferring a 4–1 shot as the most likely runner-up if the favorite wins. The favorite/your-horse exacta might be paying $18, which at first may strike you as a very unsexy payoff. If you think of it as a potential cold punch, however, it's just like backing an 8–1 shot, and may in fact be a bigger overlay than many 8–1 shots. If you believe the favorite is 50 percent to win and your horse is 40 percent to beat the rest, then there is a 20 percent chance of the race's finishing that way, but at $18 you're getting paid as if there's only an 11 percent chance.

This exact thinking can be extended to more complex bets. A race that ends with a trifecta payoff of "only" $102 for $2 is mediocre news at best for many trifecta players, who might have boxed four or five horses or purchased a series of lengthy part-wheels in order to "have it" for a dollar. But if you bought just two or even eight combinations rather than dozens to get there, you've hit yourself a longshot.

Obviously, some races call for casting a wide net and trying simply to "have" a dime or a dollar of a large payoff. This may well be the right approach for a very contentious race in which you believe there are vulnerable favorites or a scenario for chaos. Identifying such opportunities is a key to successful wagering, but such an approach is wasteful and self-defeating in races where your handicapping leads you to a limited number of likely outcomes.

Suppose there's a nine-horse field where you have a clear first and second preference, three second-tier possibilities, and four throwouts. Many trifecta players will simply box their five open horses for $1, a $60 investment, and hope for the highest-odds 1-2-3 finish among that quintet, even if that means rooting against the two strongest horses.

Instead of that five-horse box, consider taking a more aggressive stance. Demand that your top choice wins and that your second choice runs second or third. There are a few different ways you could spend that $60:

$10 tri 1/2/3,4,5 = $30
$10 tri 1/3,4,5/2 = $30

Or you could press your opinion a bit more one way, collecting an extra $2 worth if you're precisely right:

$12 tri 1/2/3,4,5 = $36
$ 8 tri 1/3,4,5/2 = $24

If you're really going to lose sleep if your second choice wins, or he's a decent price, you could go:

$10 tri 1/2/3,4,5 = $30
$ 6 tri 1/3,4,5/2 = $18
$ 4 tri 2/1/3,4,5 = $12

In all of these cases, you now would have the winning combination from 4 to 10 times stronger than you would with a simple box. Instead of moaning about putting in $60 and getting back $51, you could be getting nearly 10–1 on your highly logical proposition. You've created an effective longshot in the absence of a conventional one.

LONGSHOTS IN THE EXOTICS

There are many intricacies to the use and value of longshots in the various kinds of exotic wagers, but there are two common themes that recur across bet types: the diminishing value of longshots on the "bottom" of intrarace wagers such as trifectas and superfectas, and the importance of a horse's rank in the betting order, rather than his absolute odds, in multirace wagers.

A common source of disappointment for many horseplayers comes when they have successfully included a horse at 12–1 or better in the third slot of a trifecta or the fourth position in a superfecta. Suppose an even-money shot wins, the 4–1 third choice runs second, and that clever 15–1 shot you smoked out runs third. What should the trifecta pay? If you think it computes out to a $4 win mutuel, multiplied by 5 (4–1) and then by 16 (15–1) for a $320 return, you're going to be crestfallen when it instead comes back in the neighborhood of $75, which is what it will pay.

There are two forces at work here. The first is the fallacy of multiplying odds within a race that only apply to each horse's chance of finishing first, and which change drastically for each succeeding position once someone else has won the race.

Think of it as three separate races. In the race for actual victory, the winner had 42 percent of the pool bet on him. With that race over, there's now a separate race for second place in which the winner is no longer involved. The runner-up, who commanded only 17 percent of the betting in race 1, now has 30 rather than 17 percent of the betting in race 2. He's not 4–1 anymore—he's more like 9–5.

In the race for third, you now have to subtract both the winner's original 42 percent and the runner-up's original 17 percent. That 15–1 shot, who started out with just 6.5 percent of the pool, is now up to 16 percent of what's left. With the even-money and 4–1 shot out of the race for third, the 15–1 shot is now only a little better than 4–1 to beat the others.

The same thing would happen if the first two finishers had been scratched at the gate. Everyone's odds would plummet and the horse who would have originally paid $32 now will pay only $10.40. When you look at it that way, it's clear why that trifecta should pay more like $75 than $320, and why getting a 15–1 shot to run third is not quite the heroic achievement it may have first seemed.

This diminishing value is compounded by the fact that 15–1 shots are probably overbet in precisely the third position in trifectas because of the similar way that so many people structure their tickets. Two very common trifecta part-wheel templates are the widening part-wheel (2 x 4 x 6) or the key-horse gamble (1 x 4 x all), both plays in which a 15–1 shot will be bet more heavily for third-only than his raw price would suggest.

The same thing happens in superfectas, especially now that widespread 10-cent minimums have made hitting the "all" button for fourth affordable to many more players. A fourth-place finish by a 30–1 shot in your winning super is no guarantee of a juicy payoff. In addition to his being as low as 10–1 to finish fourth unless two or three other bombs have finished in front of him, the widespread use of "all" in the bottom slot may make him a lot closer in price—in that particular position—to the actual 10–1 shots in the race.

This is related to the phenomenon of ordinal rank in multirace wagers because in both cases the public is overbetting certain combinations due to bankroll restraints and realities, and to similar ticket-structuring.

In multirace wagers such as the pick four and pick six, players of modest means are forced to narrow their selections to keep their investments affordable. Bettors with only $24 or $36 to invest in a multirace sequence should probably be playing daily doubles or pick threes rather than the pick four, but tempted by high payouts, they forge ahead with limited-coverage part-wheels, such as a 2 x 2 x 2 x 3 or a 2 x 3 x 2 x 3.

At a $1 minimum, a pick four limits the many players in this range to going only two- or three-deep in these races. The effect is that those two or three favorites get overbet in the pick-four pools. When this overbetting occurs four times in a row, it leads to a severe depression of the prices on the extremely common duplicative tickets combining these favorites.

This doesn't occur solely with the two or three favorites in each race. There are many pick-four sequences in which there is clearly one standout favorite and one messy race where everyone will go deepest. In those instances, a 1 x 2 x 3 x 6 play may be as over-bet as a 2 x 3 x 2 x 3 if most people have the same single and the same six-horse spread.

In all these cases, a horse's ordinal rank in the betting is as important as his absolute odds. The difference between a 9–5 second choice and a 4–1 second choice is not as great as it might seem, and a 7–1 fifth choice can be far less valuable in a race where "everyone" is spreading than in a race with two strong favorites.

The latter effect is even clearer in the pick six, where even well-heeled players are generally spread thin due to the geometrically more expensive investment required by having two additional races to get through. If there's been a tough winner or two earlier in the sequence, by the time you get to the last leg, you will often see a set of will-pays that are a major distortion of the actual odds for each horse. Here's an example from a one-day carryover pool at Aqueduct in the fall of 2007:

PICK-SIX WILL-PAYS:
1, 3, 7, 9, 10: $102,629 (1 ticket each)
2, 5: $2,703 (38 tickets each)
4: $6,758 (15 tickets)
8: $2,079 (50 tickets)

Of the 146 live tickets, 126 of them (86 percent) are alive to only three horses—the 2, 5, and 8—and 141 of the 146 (96 percent) are alive to just five of them. It's as if there were a win pool of $146 with only $1 bet to win on each of the five outsiders, making them around 120–1 apiece (after takeout). In the actual betting on the race, those horses ranged in price from only 16–1 to 41–1, but if you made it that far you were getting over 100–1 on each—not because those were their true odds, or their market odds in a meaningful pool, but because affordability factors had forced them to be severely underbet.

On a smaller scale, the same thing happens every day in multirace bets. Due to bankroll limitations and crude betting strategies, second and third choices are less valuable than their win odds suggest, while a fifth or sixth choice in the betting may be effectively triple his legitimate odds. It's far more likely that betting inefficiencies will make a 30–1 shot out of a 10–1 shot than that the crowd will make so severe an error in the win pool.

The good news is that these inefficiencies present an extraordinary opportunity for those who can recognize them.

DAVIDOWITZ
ON TRAINER AND
TRACK-SPECIFIC ANGLES

By Steve Davidowitz

FOR NEARLY THREE DECADES, my typical play focused predominantly on "prime win bets"—wagers that concentrated on the single best horse in a given race at a price significantly higher than my private estimate: a solid 7–5 shot, for example, going off at 2–1, as Greg's Gold did when he won the 2007 Pat O'Brien Handicap at Del Mar as the second betting choice.

Yet despite such occasional prime bets, the bulk of my action since the mid-1990s has been in various exotic pools where live longshots are the jewels in my multirace wagers, but do not necessarily have to win to make a positive impact on exacta and trifecta payoffs.

While every successful horseplayer needs an arsenal of angles that will ferret out fit and ready horses not otherwise singled out via straightforward handicapping methods, a little digging and some personal research is required. Different methods can be applied, but the key to spotting playable longshot contenders can be summarized in one word: "change."

The great horses Cigar and John Henry had a lot in common. Both exemplified the radical difference that can occur in horse performance with a simple switch from one racing surface to another.

As a son of the world-class turf horse Palace Music, Cigar seemed bred in the purple to be a major-league grass horse, yet he began his career on the dirt. After winning a maiden race, he was switched to turf for his next 11 starts, and although he had some moderate success, he was completely transformed when Hall of Fame trainer Bill Mott put him back on the dirt at Aqueduct in the fall of his 4-year-old season.

The date was October 28, 1994, and the poor horses that were entered in that allowance race at one mile did not know what whizzed by them. Cigar won by eight lengths under a hand ride by Mike Smith, earning a Beyer Speed Figure of 104—a career best to that point. As it would turn out, that 104 would be the lowest Beyer fig Cigar would earn through the rest of his spectacular career. The victory was in fact the first of Cigar's 16 straight wins, including the 1995 Breeders' Cup Classic and the $4 million Dubai World Cup in 1996 that would be centerpieces of two consecutive Horse of the Year campaigns.

In contrast to Cigar, John Henry was hardly bred to be anything at all, unless you believe that his sire, Ole Bob Bowers, had some special potency for sprints at Evangeline Downs and/or $25,000 claiming races at the Fair Grounds and Aqueduct.

Through John Henry's first 17 races under the care of trainer Phil Marino and one additional race for trainer Harold Snowden Jr., there were no expectations that he would develop into a graded-stakes performer. Although he had won the six-furlong Lafayette Futurity in his seventh career start in 1977, he descended to the claiming ranks through May of his 3-year-old season. It was on June 1, 1978, that John Henry's low-profile new trainer, Bob Donato, decided to put the gelding on the turf in a $35,000 claiming race at $1\frac{1}{16}$ miles at Belmont Park.

The result was just as dramatic for John Henry as it had been in reverse for Cigar: John Henry cruised to an effortless 14-length triumph, the first of many victories on the grass for this legendary horse who would develop into a four-time turf champion (1980, 1981, 1983, and 1984) as well as a two-time Horse of the Year in 1981 and

1984, the latter accomplishment occurring when John Henry was nine years old!

The parallel that is expressed by the switch over from turf to dirt for Cigar and from dirt to turf for John Henry is not really airtight, but it is noteworthy.

For one thing, John Henry later became almost as good on dirt as he was on turf, but trainer Ron McAnally, who handled the great gelding during his championship seasons, says that "it was the confidence John Henry gained from winning important turf stakes" that helped him when he was matched against top-flight company on dirt later in his career.

For the record, John Henry's greatest triumphs on dirt were in the 1981 Jockey Club Gold Cup at Belmont Park, the 1981 Santa Anita Handicap under top weight of 128 pounds, and the 1982 Santa Anita Handicap under 130 (following the disqualification of Perrault for interfering with John Henry in deep stretch). All that said, the key point is that the change in surfaces was the perfect maneuver for these two historic champions.

There are important handicapping lessons to be gleaned from the stories of both horses, lessons that play out every day at every racetrack in America. Not only is "change" worth some attention when you are looking for potential longshot winners, but also, sometimes the change that helped produce a good result last time out is the reason why the horse you are looking at today should be regarded as "brand new."

KEY CHANGES THAT OFTEN LEAD TO IMPROVED PERFORMANCE

A variety of changes can influence horse performance in ways that may be either subtle or dramatic. *To dismiss any significant change is to ignore one of the best clues to a possible breakthrough performance.*

Moreover, it is from shifts in distance, surface, equipment, and the like that players gain access to the mind of the trainer. Sometimes the clue will be relatively straightforward; sometimes the intended impact will only occur when one change is implemented in tandem with another, or in various combinations. Here are some to consider.

Dirt to Turf

Obviously, when a horse is bred for grass racing and is in the hands of a trainer with positive statistics with turf horses—see Bill Mott, Bobby Frankel, Graham Motion, Ron McAnally, Neil Drysdale, Angel Penna Jr., Christophe Clement, Julio Canani, Tom Amoss, Martin Wolfson, Barclay Tagg, Ronny Werner, Tom Voss, etc.—the switch from dirt to turf commands attention all by itself. But the longshot power of this angle comes from low-profile trainers who have some turf success and/or horses that seem as if their only chance to be successful will be on the new surface. Coupled with a change to a jockey that does well on the grass, and/or some added distance, any horse bred for the lawn that is moving from dirt to turf deserves a closer look. If the price is right, such a horse would be worth including in any exotics play as long as the trainer historically has a clue. In other words, you sometimes will get undeserved high parimutuel prices on the acknowledged masters of the turf, but you will gain longshot power by watching for trainers whose win percentage with turf horses—especially first-time turf horses—is substantially higher than their overall win rate.

Turf to Dirt

Turf to dirt is much trickier to deal with. Generally speaking, a longtime turf horse will not turn himself into a major winner on any level, much less replicate Bill Mott's success with Cigar. But a versatile horse with decent performances on turf and dirt should be examined very carefully for signs that the most recent turf race might have been a useful prep for today's task on dirt.

There is price-getting value when a horse shows speed going long in a turf route and cuts back to a seven-furlong sprint. (See "Longshot Distance-Switch Angles" later in this chapter for more on the topic.)

There is also a speed-sharpening value in placing a horse in a grass sprint, then stretching him out to a dirt route.

Either of these maneuvers can be the key to a longshot play when the horse is going back to a previous pattern that might not be apparent in the printed past performances. That is one reason why it will pay players to use *Daily Racing Form*'s Formulator software. With Formulator, the player can look beyond the published past performances of a given horse in a given race to see if and when this horse or this trainer previously used this maneuver. If you do nothing more with the tips provided in this book than experiment with Formulator's instant-research capability, you will have advanced your game sharply.

Blinkers On

This common equipment change is most effective with lightly raced horses that may have stopped abruptly after losing the lead and/or failed to break alertly from the starting gate. The addition of blinkers is much less effective when the change applies to an older horse. It is virtually meaningless when a veteran horse gets blinkers again after having had them with minimal effect when he was younger.

First-Time Lasix

Not too many years ago, the mere addition of Lasix to a young horse was a "go" signal. Nowadays the vast majority of Thoroughbreds get Lasix as a precautionary measure to prevent bleeding in the lungs, which can occur under the stress of racing. Yet, it still has potency as a key to potential longshots in a few specific situations, as indicated below.

Foreign Horses, First-Time Lasix

Lasix is not permitted in most countries other than the United States. Therefore, today's horseplayer should take special notice when Lasix is being given to a horse racing in the U.S. for the first time. In many cases, European trainers know that the administration of Lasix will provide a boost in performance to the import. Lasix is technically a diuretic, which means that it reduces the amount of fluid in the body, thereby also reducing pressure on the capillaries in the lungs. Its effect on racing performance is not fully understood; regardless, first-time Lasix use is a notable factor in the performances of foreign horses in this country.

Blinkers On and First-Time Lasix

The combination of Lasix and blinkers, along with other possible changes, still has potency—especially for a young horse that showed some speed and faded in his career debut or did the same in his second start without either Lasix or blinkers. The fade may have been due to a variety of factors: a bleeding incident and/or the horse's reticence in dealing with competition for the lead, or its attention span. Obviously, the dual change can be especially powerful in the hands of a trainer with a winning history with such changes, but that also can hurt the price.

The Drop-Down Angle

There is no one single drop-down angle. But there are numerous variations that frequently point out horses ready for a vastly improved performance.

Among the most effective drop-down angles that produce longshot winners are:

1. A drop from any level to any lower level, combined with one or more of the positive distance-switching or surface-switching angles cited earlier.
2. A drop from an open claiming race with many multiple winners to an allowance race for nonwinners of two races lifetime, or even for nonwinners of three lifetime. Stipulation: There can be no standout maiden graduates with high Beyer Speed Figures in the field.

3. A drop from open allowance company into an allowance race restricted to state-breds, where the competition is inherently weaker. Stipulation: For price-getting value, the drop-down usually has to show only a hint of early speed, rather than a solid previous race.

4. The best-known and still most effective drop-down is the classic drop from maiden special weight races to maiden claiming. Quite simply, this is regarded as the most potent drop in the game. Surprisingly, it still has price potential, especially when a low-profile trainer is involved.

The following example did not produce a blockbuster mutuel, but the horse in question wasn't the betting favorite, either. Ski Alexis Ski merely embodies a multitude of positive changes that led to a runaway victory at 3.95–1 and anchored the daily double as well as a winning start to the pick four at Aqueduct on January 31, 2007.

Not only did Ski Alexis Ski drop from maiden special weight to maiden claiming, he also added Lasix and turned back in distance after racing within two lengths of the pace for more than half the 1 1/16-mile race on January 13. The jockey switch also made sense: Alan Garcia, an aggressive young rider, replaced Jose Santos, who would retire during the summer of 2007, a week before his induction into racing's Hall of Fame. Santos was mostly effective with midpack closers and rarely allowed his mounts to run to daylight from the gate.

While I rarely play horses trained by extremely low-percentage trainers, some are much better than their records indicate. This is where your personal knowledge of the trainer and/or the racing circuit must come into play. Some trainers may have been more successful a few years back or have had horses finish second and/or third with a particular angle that does not show up in their current statistical profiles at the bottom of the past-performance records. If you spot a maiden-to-maiden-claimer drop-down from one of these trainers, the rewards can be staggering if you include them in your exotic play.

TRAINER-SPECIFIC LONGSHOT ANGLES

It would be impossible to list all the good trainer-specific angles in this chapter, but here are just a few, with obvious implications for all interested players to do some personal research.

Absentees Conditioned over Deeper Training Tracks

Bill Mott is an acknowledged expert with grass horses and a most versatile horseman who wins a fair share of races in every other category, even scoring with a surprising number of first-time starters. Even so, Mott has a profit profile with absentee horses he has trained at the pastoral Payson Park facility about 75 miles north of Gulfstream Park.

During the winter Gulfstream meet, Mott's absentees that have been galloping and working out over the deeper training track at Payson consistently outperform both their odds and all his other horses stabled at Gulfstream. During the warm-weather months, when Mott is based primarily at Belmont Park, he uses the Saratoga training track 170 miles away to similar effect.

Christophe Clement, another expert with absentees and long-distance runners on the turf, also trains horses at Payson during the winter and the deeper Saratoga training track during the spring and summer. Fact is, Clement's absentees are among the most reliable in the game, and he gets much better prices than he deserves with the best horses in his barn, which he ships away from Florida and/or New York for stakes engagements.

Just as horses trained at Tampa Bay Downs and Calder generally do well wherever they ship, it pays to take a closer look at any horse that has been legged up at a training center such as Payson Park, or the Saratoga training track, or the specialty training tracks at Fair Hill in Maryland, and/or the private Bonita and Tapeta Farm tracks in that state. This is especially true for horses that ship away from their home base.

Skipping a Condition, or Two

Conceptually, it is a most aggressive indication of confidence when a trainer takes a sharp $20,000 claimer and moves him up past the $25,000 level to run for $30,000, or perhaps even enters him against moderate-level allowance company. So many good trainers use this maneuver that you will surely find them in your casual research of any track in the country. At the same time, there are trainers on each circuit who are expert in spotting runners trained by other horsemen that deserve to be moved up in the near future. These trainers can be found through the past-performance statistics that reveal a positive return on investment (ROI) with recent claims and newly acquired horses. While some of these trainers have done this so often that their price value is limited (for example, Jack Carava, Jeff Mullins, and Mike Mitchell in Southern California; Bruce Levine and Rick Dutrow in New York; Tom Amoss and Wayne Catalano in the Midwest), a minimum amount of research will unveil several on your home circuit.

On a whole other level, notoriety is not an automatic price-getting depressant. For instance, Hall of Famer Bobby Frankel is a high-percentage trainer in virtually every major category of performance. But his most prolific longshot-friendly tendency is to move a fit and improving horse sharply up in class—for instance, an allowance-race winner is entered in a graded stakes, or a recent winner at one track ships a significant distance to step up in class.

Frankel is deadly with this aggressive class-change maneuver, and surprisingly, he is just as effective from a win-percentage standpoint with his drop-downs into allowance company—to help a specific horse get its confidence. As I said, the best way to acquire a strong arsenal of winning angles is to do your own trainer research.

Please note: The strategy of raising a few levels in class may seem to include moving a juvenile maiden-race winner sharply up in class to run in a stakes. In today's game, however, juvenile maiden winners rarely are entered in the next logical step—an allowance race—when a stakes for more money and prestige is on the schedule. Why run for a $40,000 to $60,000 purse when $100,000 or more is available against other lightly raced horses with similar maiden-race credentials?

At the bottom line, I should repeat a point made earlier: Horses that are getting equipment changes coupled with class drops and/or surface and/or distance changes should be studied carefully. It is from this group of changes that the best prices usually emerge.

It is somewhat curious, but important to note, that many trainers who are strong with turf horses tend to produce positive ROIs in a variety of categories. It is more than a guess to suggest that training for the turf requires more than a jog and a gallop plus a four-furlong workout every week. Quality horsemanship is involved.

Trainers who win with recent claims, with absentees, and with first-time starters or newly acquired imports are similarly worth noting whenever they enter a horse that conforms to their positive specialties. There also are low-profile, esoteric trainers on selected circuits who are price-getters every season:

- Nick "Sarge" Hines is one such trainer who scores with claimers on the lower levels of Southern California racing.

- Michael Trombetta, based in Delaware and Maryland, has an uncanny strike rate with first-time starters, including those he sends to New York. One of Trombetta's pet moves is to set his young horses up for a sharp maiden debut via a seven-furlong workout. Usually the target race is a shorter distance.
- Dove Houghton, also based in Maryland, is equally deadly with second-time starters and has been getting terrific prices when hooked up with jockey Mario Pino.
- Peter Walder's horses at Gulfstream Park tend to get bet down. Nevertheless, Walder has hit with longshots in several consecutive seasons.
- Phillip Thomas Jr., a relatively obscure, talented horseman based in Kentucky who handles any type of horse, has a long history of longshot scores with seemingly overmatched claimers. Many require handicapping legwork over a period of months and must be followed through more than one race to get the ultimate longshot payoff.
- Moon Han, another obscure horseman—based in California—can be very streaky, but his best longshot work over the past decade has been with absentee cheapies and/or maiden claimers in Northern and Southern California, including the county fairs.

Beyond the low-profile longshot trainers cited above, here are some higher-profile horsemen who have provided unusually good payoffs with underrated horses in specific situations.

- Wayne Catalano, a high-percentage trainer in all categories, has outperformed his overall success with newly claimed horses stepping up in class in Chicago and New Orleans.
- John Sadler, a perennial force in SoCal, is vastly underrated as a trainer of turf horses. Just as important, Sadler tends to get unusually good prices with dirt horses he moves to grass for the first time.
- William P. White is nearly as deadly with second-time starters in Florida, especially when White adds blinkers and/or stretches a horse out in distance.
- Wesley Ward, like Catalano, a former jockey, has maintained a high strike rate and a high ROI with horses on either coast that have been absent longer than three months.

- Larry Pilotti, well known in Florida, is at his best with first-time starters during the summer and fall at Calder.
- Michael Matz in Florida, Delaware, Maryland, and New York is one of the best trainers in America with horses stretching out in distance and stepping up in class. Matz won the 2006 Kentucky Derby with Barbaro at generous 6–1 odds while employing methods that many labeled unorthodox. Some said that Matz failed to prepare his horse for the grueling 1¼-mile test when he elected to run the unbeaten colt off a five-week rest, rather than the traditional three or four weeks. So, if you saw the ease with which Barbaro handled the Derby distance and thoroughly outclassed a seemingly good field of 3-year-olds, you can appreciate Matz's outstanding talent for training long-distance runners. Of equal importance, he still gets prices with his best work.
- Have I mentioned Allen Jerkens in graded stakes? At Belmont or Saratoga during the warm-weather months and Gulfstream Park during the winter, it is never wise to discount anything Jerkens enters in a major stakes race. Still going strong after more than 50 years as one of the great trainers in history, "the Giant Killer" scored longshot graded-stakes victories in 2007 with Political Force and Miss Shop. These, of course, were added to a long list of historic triumphs that could fill the next full page. Included among the Hall of Fame trainer's roster of longshot winners were three upset victories by Beau Purple over five-time Horse of the Year Kelso in the early 1960s and separate victories over Secretariat by Onion and Prove Out in 1973. While difficult to pin down, and admittedly weak when shipping out of town, Jerkens horses seem to run strongest when they rank third or fourth best in the race.

There are many more trainers with high win percentages and high ROIs with specific types of horses under clearly defined circumstances. It is your job as a horseplayer to find them and take your best shots with their best shots.

TRACK-SPECIFIC LONGSHOT ANGLES
Tampa Bay Downs Shippers

I always take a very close look at horses shipping to a Midwestern or Eastern track after having raced and/or trained at Tampa Bay Downs on the west coast of Florida. Through the years, I have seen Tampa Bay shippers outperform their previous class levels and Beyer Speed Figures in their first and second starts at Turfway Park, Churchill Downs, Ellis Park, Canterbury Park, Great Lakes Downs, Finger Lakes, Suffolk Downs, and occasionally the premier Northeastern tracks.

Tampa's racing surface is deeper and yet kinder to horses, perhaps to the same extent or better than the supposed benefit gained from synthetic track surfaces. It helps build stamina in the horses who race and train over it. This gives many horses that ship from there a hidden edge in conditioning. Sometimes this will translate to a horse ready to step up a notch or two in class while meeting winter (over)raced horses and horses that have been dealing with infirmities and minor ailments, horses ready to be challenged by a fitter animal.

Calder Shippers

Calder has good turf racing and a deep, well-developed program for Florida-bred 2-year-olds that culminates in rich stakes on dirt and turf at all distances up to 1$\frac{1}{16}$ miles. A few of the best Calder-based 2-year-olds invariably deserve close inspection in Breeders' Cup Juvenile events, but the key value to me as a horseplayer is to be alert to Calder's claimers and maiden claimers that ship elsewhere, including to the West Coast.

Just as Tampa Bay Downs helps "leg up" horses that race over its kind but deeper surface, Calder has a similar positive effect on the dozens of claiming horses who seem to be more sensitive to hard track conditions due to lingering physical issues. It contributes to the healing process and to overall conditioning. That is perhaps why so many Calder claimers do so well when shipped to faster racing surfaces. Often, the new trainer at the new track does not have to do a thing other than gallop the recent acquisition before slipping the horse's name in the entry box. Interestingly, even maiden claimers who ship out of Calder to tracks with noticeably harder and faster racing surfaces seem to outperform their odds more often than mere coincidence.

Keeneland Polytrack Angles

Playing front-runners and pace-pressing horses in Keeneland routes on the new synthetic Polytrack surface is a great way to throw money away. Looking at this another way, stretch-runners and horses with clear-cut signs of stamina are much preferred in Keeneland's two-turn races.

Reason: During the fall meet in 2006, when Keeneland introduced its version of the British-made synthetic Polytrack, very few front-runners and pace-pressers were able to hang on to win or secure second-place finishing positions. The track surface was tiring beyond anything previously seen at Keeneland, where the dirt track had posed a dominant inside-speed-favoring bias for many years.

During the spring meet in 2007, the stretch-running tendency of the new Polytrack surface was muted only marginally as jockeys made adjustments to the overly-cautious waiting approach they had employed during the initial Polytrack meet the previous fall. Yet from all indications, the anti-early-speed bias that apparently was built into the surface remained a provocative way to downgrade and/or eliminate speed horses in the vast majority of two-turn races. While I personally expect this trend to stabilize somewhat while Keeneland officials tinker with the surface, most synthetic tracks in America have accented stamina while minimizing front-running speed, especially in route races around two turns.

For instance, at Del Mar, which introduced Polytrack in the summer of 2007, front-runners in two-turn races won about half as often as they did over the dirt surface in 2006.

In one-mile races on the Polytrack, horses with the lead after the quarter-mile call won about 15 percent in 2007 compared to 27 percent in 2006.

In 1 1/16-mile races, the wire-to-wire win rate was a substandard 7 percent compared to 12 percent the previous year.

An even more dramatic statistic: In more than 60 percent of the two-turn races at Del Mar in 2007, the horse running at the rear of the pack at the first quarter-mile call finished in front of the horse leading at that call.

Monmouth Park and Other Speed Biases

Few tracks in modern American racing have as many days when early speed—and inside early speed—dominates race results. If you are playing at Monmouth during the summer months, virtually all handicapping has to take this powerful track bias into account. Ironically, the speed-favoring trend was not altered by the new dirt racing surface Monmouth installed for the 2007 season.

For a sample peek at the bias, which can be compared to an unbalanced roulette wheel, consider the following statistics taken from a typical five-day racing week: Wednesday, August 15, 2007, through Sunday, August 19.

There were 40 dirt races at Monmouth during that five-day period.

Nine were won by horses that were fourth or worse at the first quarter-mile call. Thirty-one were won by horses in the first three running positions at that call. Of the 31 pace-pressing or front-running winners, 11 went wire to wire and six were within a length of the leader at the first call.

Of the nine that rallied from fourth or farther back, only three were more than three lengths behind the leader. These statistics applied to all distances at Monmouth, not just to sprints.

Since the mid-1960s, Monmouth's dirt surface has been kind to early speed. But during the summer the surface becomes even faster and more one-dimensional. While most experienced players at Monmouth seem to grasp the bias concept as it applies to picking logical horses in today's races, *the price-getting value of a speed bias lies more with identifying horses that struggle against it.*

When Monmouth horses show up at another track that I play more often—perhaps Belmont Park, or a track that has many days when stretch-runners dominate, such as Philadelphia Park—my casual bias notes help me upgrade or downgrade a good or bad Monmouth performance.

A fourth-place finisher who ran evenly through the stretch will deserve extra points when shipped to a track without a speed bias. Conversely, a runaway front-running Monmouth winner probably will face much tougher sledding at the new track.

Given the power of this angle, I can only suggest strongly to all readers that they take note of any track when a powerful bias takes over the game for a day, or a week, or even longer. "Track bias," a term I coined in the mid-1960s, helped me gain a serious edge in my first years of playing the game. While the concept has become overused and frequently misinterpreted, the appreciation of a true track bias remains one of the most potent interpretive tools in the game. It is also a key to many longshot winners and useful exotic partners.

Here are some suggestions to help identify a true track bias:

- It pays to know in advance of today's races which horses are the likely front-runners. If you know how many front-runners there are and approximately how fast they will be running during the early stages, you can evaluate *after the race* if it was easy or hard for the speed horse, or horses, to fold or wilt on their own. When multiple speed horses get involved in a hot pace duel, you would expect the race to set up for a closer. But when the dueling front-runners stay the trip, it is possible that you have just been given an early clue that a speed bias is in play. One or two more races should tell the story.

- When you encounter a pronounced bias of any kind, you do not need three days of results to verify it. What you need is a good evaluation of the pace scenarios that are taking place in front of you and how the race most logically should have played out. When you get much different results than anticipated, you should explore the possibility of a bias at work.

End-of-the-Meet Specials

There are only a few times each year when this powerful angle applies, but the logic behind it is so crystal-clear that its potency for snaring longshots still amazes me. The situation, however, does not fit all race meets coming to an end. It fits only when the end of the meet corresponds to a switch to another track in the same circuit that is not within a short cab ride. It is not a system—no longshot angle is a system—but it does have important and logical guidelines.

The first and most important one is that the horse must have worked out recently at the track that is the next stop on the region's racing calendar. Other than stakes and specialty races that cannot be run at any other track or turf course, the only other stipulation is that the horse is entered to race on the final weekend or final racing day of the current meet.

At Saratoga: The end of the meet includes the final weekend of races, as in the Saturday, Sunday, and Monday of the Labor Day Weekend. The next stop on the racing calendar is Belmont, but because Aqueduct is so close to Belmont and both tracks are about 170 miles from Saratoga, the angle horse would be one that is entered on the final weekend at Saratoga and has recent published workouts at Aqueduct or Belmont Park.

Because Saratoga offers many turf sprints at the 5½-furlong distance and Belmont's turf sprints are only carded at six or seven furlongs, I do not use this angle for Belmont and/or Aqueduct shippers entered in the Spa's shorter turf sprints on the final weekend, unless the horse in question has won at the 5½-furlong distance and lost his previous races at six or seven furlongs on the Belmont turf. Obviously, the intent to compete in a shorter sprint is linked to the reason why the horse is at Saratoga. But the true power of this angle is linked to another line of logic.

What I am looking for is a horse *that does not have to ship north to run in a specific race.* He could be kept downstate to await the next logical spot, probably in less than a week. Thus his presence in a run-of-the-mill race at Saratoga is a stronger sign of immediate fitness, a stronger hint that a top effort is forthcoming.

Occasionally, just as I might play a horse shipping to Saratoga to run in an abbreviated turf sprint, I will use this angle on the final weekend at Belmont in mid-July when a turf sprinter ships from Saratoga to run in a six- or seven-furlong turf sprint at Belmont. In this case, the horse is being sent downstate to compete at a distance the trainer believes would be much better than the 5½-furlong races he is going to get in abundance during the Saratoga meet.

In most years I can remember, I have caught numerous longshots by using qualified end-of-the-meet shippers for straight win bets and as exacta or trifecta keys. In rare situations where more than one of my "angle horses" fit the guidelines, I do not try to split hairs. I use them as co-win keys in exacta or trifecta spreads.

A very lucrative example of this angle occurred at Saratoga on September 1, 2007, while I was preparing this chapter during the final days of the Saratoga and Del Mar meets.

There were three horses in the seventh race at Saratoga that qualified, which is two more than I usually find in the same race. No matter. I used number 9, Bethpage Black; number 2, Chasing the Crown; and number 4, Good Going Darl, as three-headed co-win keys in a trifecta spread that added the two wagering favorites to the second and third levels at a total cost of $36 for each $1 invested.

Bethpage Black had been away for almost 14 months, but had a strong Aqueduct workout line for trainer Gary Contessa. Hall of Famer Kent Desormeaux took the mount. The 40–1 odds were way out of line based on the simple logic of this angle: Why would any trainer ship a horse up to Saratoga for a race he would surely get the opportunity to compete in downstate within the next week? Why would a top jockey in a tight competition for the meet championship take a ride on a 14-month absentee unless the horse was close to ready or dead fit? (Through no fault of Bethpage Black, Desormeaux would lose the 2007 Saratoga jockey title to Cornelio Velasquez by one win on closing day.)

While a somewhat less convincing case could have been made for Good Going Darl (Velasquez was the listed jockey), he did finish in a dead heat for fourth at 11–1, just a length and two necks behind the winner. As for the other end-of-the-meet special, Chasing the Crown finished dead last at 3–1 odds under John Velazquez.

The trifecta connected and paid $1,282 for each dollar invested. My only regret was a common horseplayer's lament: "I wish I had bet more."

At Del Mar: The angle applies to horses training at Santa Anita or Hollywood Park who ship down to Del Mar for its final weekend, but there is a logical twist to consider. Because there will be no racing at either Santa Anita and/or Hollywood until the intermediary Fairplex meet runs its course in late September, this angle's potency is limited to relatively cheap horses that could run at Fairplex but instead are being sent down to Del Mar for many of the same reasons cited previously.

In Northern California: The only applicable meets to consider are the county-fair meets, and the horse must be trained at the next county-fair meet to qualify as an angle play on the last weekend of racing at the current county-fair meet.

In Texas: The angle applies to any horse that has been training at the next stop on the Texas racing schedule and has been shipped to race as the current meet is winding down.

In Maryland: The angle does not apply because horses ship back and forth to and from Laurel and Pimlico without significance.

In other states and regions there are some meets that may present similar angle plays, but refinements will be needed to conform to specific circumstances.

LONGSHOT DISTANCE-SWITCH ANGLES
Short to Long

Speed types that stretch out in distance are often good plays when they project to be the controlling speed in a race filled with closers and midpack stalkers. This type of horse does not need a pronounced speed bias to be effective. But for me, the price-getting quotient of this basic handicapping angle has a neat little twist that continues to produce outrageous results under the right set of circumstances.

I am not talking about obvious short-to-long contenders that are likely to get the lead and the rail from an inside post—or at least a post inside other speed types. While that sometimes produces above-average prices—especially in fields loaded with deep closers—the longshot power attached to a stretch-out sprinter in a two-turn route comes most often when there is a speed type that can outbreak the field from an *outside post.* Yes, I said an outside post!

Think of it this way: At any track where there is a short run to the first turn, most players will not expect any horse to get to the front from post 9, 10, 11, or 12. Admittedly, not many speed horses can do that without wasting a lot of their energy in the process. But when you do have such a horse, the apparent degree of difficulty is precisely why he may be ignored in the mutuels even though he possesses all the speed he will need to clear the field.

When a speed horse with some distance breeding is involved, when a speed horse is handled by a trainer with good stretch-out performance statistics, or when the horse is being ridden by an aggressive jockey—one that has talent with front-running types—the power of this angle is magnified. From my experience, I know of no track in America—with the exception of the Polytracks that have nullified early speed in route races—where this angle does not snag a few logical longshot winners every year.

Consider the trifecta power presented by 29–1 shot Highly Spoken, who served as a terrific win-and-place key in a situation that unfolded to near perfection in the 10th race at Belmont Park on September 8, 2007.

In this race, Highly Spoken actually was ridden by Channing Hill, who replaced injured Joe Bravo for aggressive trainer David Jacobson. Certainly Jacobson had Highly Spoken in a good position to fire his best after a speed-sharpening 5½-furlong Saratoga sprint. Clearly the game plan was to attempt a front-running try from the outside post in this nine-furlong turf race.

Sent immediately to the lead and crossing over in front of the field to take control of the pace, Highly Spoken was a difficult target to catch. Eventually, though, he was caught in the final jump by the 2.90–1 betting favorite, My Man Lars, with second betting choice Keen Irish finishing a close third.

While a monster trifecta payoff was thwarted by the favorite's winning rally, the trifecta still paid $518.50 for each $1 unit.

To underscore the importance of logical twists that lead to longshot winners, consider this key point that should explain why a slightly off-key approach to sound logic can be so effective.

In many instances, longshot angles go against the grain of common assumptions, or perceived realities. In the case of the speed horse from an outside post in a route race cited above, the angle singles out a horse that might be facing a difficult assignment.

Yet there may well be strong clues to suggest that his predicament is a mere illusion. This "angle horse" is not going to be hurt by his post position, if he has the speed to clear the field and a jockey not afraid to send.

The post-position predicament may bother many horseplayers, but a well-meant, well-placed horse in the right situation, who is going against the grain of common handicapping assumptions, is a horse that may be capable of outperforming expectations while delivering an outrageous mutuel.

Long to Short

Whenever I am handicapping 6½- and seven-furlong races, I pay special attention to horses that have narrowly set or actively pressed the pace for six furlongs or longer in a recent two-turn route race. The potency of this angle is in the extra conditioning such horses get from the longer race.

In many cases, the extra distance tires these horses out, leaves them short of breath with weary legs and hearts pounding all the way past the finish line to the unsaddling area. But as any athlete will tell you, getting tired is a fundamental part of a good conditioning program. Getting tired, extending the lung capacity, strengthening leg power—those are precursors to positive physical benefits for a healthy horse.

If he is indeed a healthy specimen, if he is not injured, he will recover from the weight loss, recover from the burning sensation in the lungs to gallop and train stronger for the next assignment.

If the trainer recognizes that this horse will now fit into a typical 6 ½- or seven-furlong race in which his added stamina can be most effective, there often will be a generous payoff.

Please note: When you encounter a racetrack where stretch-runners and midpack closers are dominant, the stamina gained during a route race can positively impact horses turning back to sprints.

The previously mentioned Philadelphia Park track periodically provides a forum for stamina types and stretch-runners at sprint distances. The same seems true for many of the synthetic tracks currently in play. This need for stamina even creates a positive forum for turn-backs going from a race beyond one mile to straightforward six-furlong sprints.

To cite just one of many similar cases, consider that the $5,000 claimer Lune's Legend was a sharp stretch-running second at 60–1 in the six-furlong second race at Philadelphia Park on June 23, 2007. This improved performance at outrageous odds occurred after Lune's Legend had shown mild speed while finishing third and fourth in consecutive route races at the same claiming level over similar nonwinners of two lifetime over the same racetrack. While the price was way beyond normal parameters, the improvement under such circumstances was not.

Frankly, it is astonishing how many juicy-priced winners are generated by this simple angle each and every year. For some reason, the turn-back from a speedy try in a route race to a 6½- or seven-furlong sprint never has made it into the unofficial "Hall of Fame for Longshot Selections."

Forgive me for sincerely hoping that the trend continues despite so many experienced players knowing about it.

USING LONGSHOTS IN EXOTIC PLAYS

The value of longshots goes way beyond finding worthwhile horses at inflated prices for win-pool bets. Today's game includes dozens of exotic-wagering options, and to be perfectly blunt about it, skilled players must learn how to play these pools to have any realistic chance of beating the game. A steady diet of win bets just won't cut it.

Finding exacta and/or trifecta keys is somewhat akin to finding winners at good prices, but there are sufficient differences to suggest a separate set of criteria.

In the first place, I am looking for horses that I may use in the win *and/or* place position and sometimes I am looking for two win keys, to be used in tandem on the top level of a trifecta spread. My selection criteria always include positive odds value, but I am more inclined to accept a high-profile contender as a win key if I have isolated several realistic longshots for the second and third levels. I also will be willing to use a high-profile contender as a trifecta win key if I can find a realistic longshot to accompany the high-profile contender as a co-win key.

The topic of using longshots in exotic wagers is covered elsewhere in this book, in the chapter by Steven Crist.

As described earlier in this chapter, my search for longshots for pick threes, pick fours, and pick sixes leads me to fairly liberal standards, rather than the detailed, finite handicapping approaches that are necessary to pick the best horse, or the most likely winner.

It is important to keep in mind that longshot-angle horses rarely deserve to be the betting favorite; they are merely being overlooked, or underrated in a competitive contest. Once in a blue moon you will see a 10–1 longshot that really should be favored, but most often you are trying to find horses that have a respectable winning chance based on the historical perspective of so many prior good outcomes under similar circumstances. These circumstances go beyond the individual races a horse has run and/or its proven worth. The key is in the prospect for improvement, or a return to the horse's best possible performance while the public is looking the other way.

Worthwhile angle horses do win, thank heaven; but mostly they outperform their odds, which is good enough in the long run to boost profits.

FREE
ON USING FUNDAMENTAL
HANDICAPPING
By Brad Free

SOME PEOPLE ARE BORN geniuses. The rest of us

have to wait until we get to the racetrack.

I became a genius at Santa Anita in 1977, a

few months after graduating from nearby Arcadia

High School. With more free time than common

sense, I spent my teenage afternoons in the

upper rows of the Santa Anita grandstand, usu-

ally in section M, adjacent to the eighth pole.

The winter-spring meet at Santa Anita was in

full swing when a 6-year-old gelding named

Mouret entered a $40,000 claiming sprint on

the twisting downhill turf course, race 5 on the January 27 program. Just two weeks before, Mouret had set a fast pace in a two-turn allowance, led until inside the eighth pole, then tired to third.

It was a good comeback, the ideal prep race for Mouret. Now he was shortening from a route to a sprint, and figured to run his best race second start back at odds of 9.80–1. I was privy to inside information. The trainer of Mouret was R. N. Free, otherwise known as my uncle Bob.

The circumstances were ideal: Uncle Bob said Mouret was doing well, and everybody bet—friends, family, and hangers-on. The gates opened and Mouret was quickly outrun under jockey Tony Noguez. That was good, because the pace was swift.

Mouret was eighth early, and then sixth at the quarter pole. The field entered the turf-course straightaway, and Mouret took off. He still had four horses in front of him at the eighth pole, but he was flying. Mouret shot clear in deep stretch, won by a length and a half, and paid $21.60.

We were so smart. Or maybe, we just got lucky. But I still remember how the past performances of Mouret looked, and how some live longshots still look—they are "new" horses trying something different. They are first-time starters, comebackers, and shippers. Mouret also was "new," running for the second time after a layoff, and going route to sprint.

For a long time after Mouret, I searched for upset winners just like him—turf sprinters shortening up, second start back. Finding them was hard, and so was maintaining my reputation as a teenage longshot picker. When you tout your friends on a $21.60 winner, you can only brag for so long before you have to come up with another.

I did not know how to find them. It seemed my standing as expert youth handicapper might not last beyond my first year of college.

Looking back, I was not particularly clever the day that Mouret won. Few of us ever are as smart as we think, even on those too-seldom occasions when we do stumble onto a winning horse at a high price. The challenge is finding them. And this much is certain—rather than look for specific types of horses, horseplayers should look for specific types of situations.

The recipe is fairly simple. Find a vulnerable favorite in a big field, identify a "new shooter" with attributes, and the chances increase that parimutuel fireworks will ensue.

To win with a longshot, you have to beat the favorite. Gee, no kidding. Of course, that means being able to find the favorite. Horseplayers unable to recognize the favorite have no idea what they are up against.

Anyone can throw darts at high-odds horses, and occasionally get lucky. But even when betting longshots, horseplayers can increase their win percentage if they first consider the pros and cons of the "most likely winner." This must be the first step. When the favorite is solid, longshots are up against it. It is such a basic idea, yet many otherwise intelligent horseplayers bang their heads against the wall daily, trying to beat good horses because their odds are low.

Sometimes, a horseplayer must accept the inevitable. Sometimes, the best horse is likely to win, regardless of price. It doesn't mean you have to bet on, or against, that horse. There is nothing wrong with passing a race.

But find a vulnerable favorite, and opportunity knocks. It happened at Belmont Park on June 14, 2007. The card was modest; the crowd was small. But at simulcast venues and on computer screens across the country, hundreds of bettors sifted through the Belmont card looking for two things—a suspect favorite to wager against, and a high-odds contender to wager on. It takes both to position oneself for a score.

Race 3 was a seven-furlong, $25,000 claiming event for fillies and mares. There were only six starters, not the type of full field that generally leads to overlay payoffs. But something was amiss with the chalk.

Short Fuse Tara
Own: Ourbestpal Stable

B. f. 4 (Apr) OBSAUG04 $16,000
Sire: Pentelicus (Fappiano) $5,000
Dam: I'm a Trooper (You and I)
Br: Brylynn Farm, Inc. (Fla)
Tr: Barbara Robert(45 3 4 7 .07) 2007:(162 14 .09)

Life	22	5	4	5	$135,750	83	D.Fst	19	5	4	5	$133,950	83
2007	7	3	2	2	$87,100	83	Wet(362)	1	0	0	0	$1,140	49
							Synth	0	0	0	0	$0	–
2006	12	0	2	2	$24,250	72	Turf(259)	2	0	0	0	$660	60
Bel	2	0	0	1	$4,800	73	Dst(320)	2	0	0	1	$4,940	62

18May07–1Bel fst 6f :223 :453 :574 1:104 4↑ⒻClm 50000(50–40) **73** 4 4 33 34 36 37¾ Garcia Alan L122 b 2.20 76– 24 JustStarting1222 *GoldLikeU*1205¾ ShortFuseTar1224¼ Chased 3 wide, tired 4
20Apr07–8Aqu fst 6f :214 :45 :572 1:102 4↑ⒻAlw 45000N1X **83** 6 1 42½ 21½ 1hd 13¼ Garcia Alan L118 b *1.75 90– 14 Short Fuse Tara1183¼ LadyJove118½ BabyGray1182¼ 3 wide rally, drew off 8
22Mar07–7Aqu fst 6f ⊡ :231 :46 :574 1:102 4↑ⒻHcp 25000s **79** 5 1 2½ 21½ 23 23½ Morales P L118 b 5.30 88– 12 *JustStarting*1213½ *ShortFuseTr*1181¾ ChunkofLove1213¼ Chased, held place 6
11Mar07–8Aqu fst 6f ⊡ :224 :464 :591 1:114 4↑ⒻOC 75k/N1X **70** 6 1 54¼ 44½ 44 34½ Morales P L118 b 2.45 80– 17 ExpirationDay1181¼ Spenny1183¼ ShortFuseTar118no 3 wide trip, no rally 6
23Feb07–7Aqu fst 6f ⊡ :23 :47 :592 1:114 ⒻClm 50000(50–40) **82** 1 6 74 53¼ 2½ 14½ Morales P L119 b *1.30e 85– 21 Short Fuse Tara1194½ Ballymist1121¾ *Expiration Day*1192¾ Going away late 8
21Jan07–5Aqu fst 6f ⊡ :234 :474 1:002 1:121 4↑ⒻClm c-(30–25)N3L **72** 6 1 2½ 1½ 11½ 13¼ Dominguez R A L120 b *2.05 83– 17 *ShortFuseTr*1203¼ *LightClssic*1202½ JrsFredom1201 Drew clear when asked 7
Claimed from Vires, George and Panzera, Salvatore for $30,000, Hills Timothy A Trainer 2006: (512 72 76 63 0.14)
7Jan07–5Aqu fst 6f ⊡ :223 :46 :581 1:11 4↑ⒻClm 30000(30–25)N3L **65** 8 1 51¾ 21½ 25½ 24¾ Bridgmohan S X L120 b 4.50 84– 10 Significant Other1204¾ *ShortFuseTara*1203 MissBaba120¾ Rallied for place 8

WORKS: May3 **Aqu 4f fst :491 B** *5/11* Apr7 **Aqu 5f fst 1:003 B** *4/36* Feb17 **Aqu⊡ 3f fst :362 B** *2/9*

TRAINER: 1stClaim(12 .33 $3.83) 2Off45-180(59 .07 $1.52) Dirt(243 .12 $1.53) Sprint(172 .13 $1.82) Stakes(33 .09 $1.82)

Short Fuse Tara had blossomed during the winter-spring meet at Aqueduct. She won for a $30,000 claiming tag, then $50,000 claiming, and then won again in first-level allowance. Short Fuse Tara had become a midlevel monster.

But when the circuit moved from Aqueduct to Belmont Park, something went awry with Short Fuse Tara. Entered in a $50,000 claiming race with only four starters, Short Fuse Tara merely went through the motions. She beat just one horse and finished nearly eight lengths behind the winner.

Every horse is entitled to a bad day. So which way will he or she go next time? The question sometimes is answered by the level at which the horse is placed. In the case of Short Fuse Tara, if her trainer brought her back in a similar $50,000 claimer, or dropped her just slightly, it might have indicated that he thought she remained in reasonable form.

Instead, he dropped her off the proverbial cliff. Two months after a blowout win in a first-level allowance, and not far removed from a $50,000 claiming win versus 4-year-old fillies, Short Fuse Tara was in for $25,000.

Short Fuse Tara was falling apart. Could she win anyway? Of course. But horses in declining form must always be treated with skepticism. Find a suspect favorite in declining form, and it is an invitation for chaos.

Short Fuse Tara was at the tail end of her form cycle. And when she started at odds-on, she was the best type of favorite to wager against. Short Fuse Tara started at 7–10, chased the pace, and finished a flat second.

When an odds-on favorite blows, crazy things happen. Mt Langfuhr was first off the claim (something new) and moving up in class against a favorite that was going down. Mt Langfuhr won clear and paid $38 in the six-horse field. Could a case have been made for the winner? Perhaps. That is not the point. Rather, in any race with a suspect favorite, skeptics often can find terrific overlays.

Yet horseplayers sometimes miss an opportunity by not reaching deep enough. The mistake is betting against a vulnerable favorite by backing merely the second- or third-best horse in the race. It's like skipping French fries, just to have bowl of ice cream for dessert. What's the point? When the favorite is vulnerable, other seemingly "logical" horses often are vulnerable, too.

I committed that blunder at Del Mar in 2007 when A. P. Xcellent started as the odds-on favorite in a minor turf stakes. It was a weekday card, and only a few weeks after A. P. Xcellent had given the venerable Lava Man all he could handle in the Grade 1, $750,000 Hollywood Gold Cup, missing by a nose.

The race seemed to stamp A. P. Xcellent as one of the top handicap horses in California, and a midsummer threat in the $1 million Pacific Classic at Del Mar. But when the circuit moved from Hollywood to Del Mar, a new racetrack was in place. The synthetic surface Polytrack was unique, and soon it was obvious that front-runners such as A. P. Xcellent were at a huge disadvantage over the anti-speed artificial surface.

A. P. Xcellent's trainer, John Shirreffs, also recognized the bias. And he called an audible. Rather than wait for the Pacific Classic on Polytrack, Shirreffs entered A. P. Xcellent on grass, in a restricted stakes race called the Cougar II. A. P. Xcellent was the right horse, but he was in the wrong spot. His turf races were not good.

Shortsighted bettors hammered A. P. Xcellent to odds-on anyway. The support, in the turf race, was based on races run on a main track. Wrong reasoning. Furthermore, like a suspicious claimer dropping in class due to declining form, A. P. Xcellent's placement in the $85,000 event, only weeks after a runner-up finish in a $750,000 race, was downright bizarre.

A. P. Xcellent might have won the stakes anyway. But at odds of 9–10, he had to be wagered against. My miscue was backing the so-called second-best horse in the race, a comebacker named Toasted. There were two problems: Toasted had not raced in three months, and at 2.80–1 odds, he offered negligible value. I did not dig deep enough.

Toasted ran well, but only finished second. The winner was back-class veteran Atlando, whose attributes were proven turf form including a graded stakes win, and a big price. Atlando also was making his second start following a layoff. Horses making their second start back certainly have a right to improve, and Atlando did. He got a dream trip saving ground, and sprang a $23.40 upset.

It was a missed opportunity. Thankfully, it was not the end of the world. Handicapping fundamentals never go out of style. They allow one to identify contenders, as well as vulnerable favorites. After that, all you need is imagination to find the longshot alternatives. Only a few simple guidelines are required to position oneself for a single-race score.

The first step is to know what it takes to win a particular race. A handicapper should be able to recognize suspect droppers such as Short Fuse Tara or a horse in the wrong spot, such as A. P. Xcellent. One must understand what an in-form horse looks like (good recent races against similar), and know the speed-figure requirements of a particular class level.

For example, in a $25,000 claiming sprint for fillies and mares at Belmont Park, the Beyer Speed Figure par is 74. Contenders will have recently earned a number within five points of par, against similar company.

Many handicappers do not even make it this far, which is too bad. Horseplayers without comprehension of the speed-figure requirements for a particular class will find it difficult to distinguish the difference between a favorite that is vulnerable, and one that is genuine.

Speed-figure pars remain one of the best tools to determine if a dirt race is weak. Beyer Speed Figure pars are published in *DRF Simulcast Weekly*, and are also available online at drf.com. When no horse in the field has recently run to par, the race might be ripe for an upset.

Beyond speed, handicappers should have an understanding of basic class requirements, and be able to identify other signs of potential vulnerability. It's basic stuff, and includes steep class drops, low-odds horses switching surfaces, or horses whose best recent races were achieved under advantageous conditions not likely to be repeated (such as lone speed).

The next step is to identify the contenders, and assess their strengths and weaknesses. Before backing a horse at high odds, a bettor must be able to at the very least recognize the favorites. How else does one know if they are vulnerable?

It is not enough to bet against a favorite "just because." There has to be a reason. Favorites win one out of three races overall. If the favorite is in acceptable condition, recently has been competitive against similar, has a running style that suits the pace, and has earned speed figures within par, maybe the race is not a good spot to shop for a price. Form, class, pace, and speed remain the building blocks of handicapping.

Finally, and only when the favorites are suspect, one can examine alternatives. Some so-called longshot bettors skip directly to this step. Good luck to them. It's not enough to find a horse that might outrun its odds. To reach the winner's circle, a longshot must beat the favorite. And it is a lot easier to do when the favorite is vulnerable.

By using fundamental guidelines, a horseplayer can identify situations that are more likely to lead to longshot winners. Do legitimate favorites get beat by longshots? Of course they do. Luck can play a factor. But there is nothing lucky about prerace preparation, and recognizing situations that have greater chances of producing a longshot result. You never know when they will happen.

I was in Las Vegas in early 2005 for the DRF/NTRA National Handicapping Championship at the Bally's Las Vegas race book, and was treated to a coast-to-coast wagering menu. This can be a good thing, even for a circuit-specific handicapper. Sometimes it is refreshing to step outside your comfort zone. And sometimes you find a nugget.

The winter racing season was hitting its full stride at Gulfstream Park, and horses were coming from everywhere for the January 21 card, which included a $25,000 maiden-claiming race with 12 starters.

You do not need to know the nuances of the East Coast maiden-claiming ranks to understand that the drop from maiden special weight to maiden claiming remains one of the biggest class drops in racing, anywhere. Maiden special weight races may include future stakes runners, or future claimers.

Any horse that has shown a semblance of ability in a special-weight race must be considered as a possible contender when he or she drops for the first time into a maiden-claiming race. The problem is, such droppers typically get hammered in the betting. Handicappers are clever. Well, most of the time.

The fifth race January 21 at Gulfstream had a full field of 12. Perfect. It was the type in which contenders sometimes get lost. And more important, the contenders all had a significant flaw. Every horse in the field had already lost a maiden-claiming race. They were all proven losers. All of them, that is, except one—Letterman's Humor.

Letterman's Humor
Own: Humphreys Jerry K

Dk. b or b. g. 3 (Mar) KEENOV02 $29,000
Sire: Distorted Humor (Forty Niner) $60,000
Dam: Richie (Olden Times)
Br: Thundering Home Farm & WinStar Farm LLC (Ky)
Tr: Voss R L III(21 2 3 3 .10) 2004:(0 0 .00)

Life	**4**	**M**	**0**	**0**	**$905**	**48**	**D.Fst**	**4**	**0**	**0**	**0**	**$905**	**48**
2004	**4**	**M**	**0**	**0**	**$905**	**48**	**Wet(403)**	**0**	**0**	**0**	**0**	**$0**	**-**
							Synth	**0**	**0**	**0**	**0**	**$0**	**-**
2003	**0**	**M**	**0**	**0**	**$0**	**-**	**Turf(299)**	**0**	**0**	**0**	**0**	**$0**	**-**
Gp	**0**	**0**	**0**	**0**	**$0**	**-**	**Dst(393)**	**1**	**0**	**0**	**0**	**$195**	**41**

26Dec04-8Crc	fst	7f	:23^{2}	:47	1:13	1:25^{3}	Md Sp Wt 20k	**46**	6	4	2$^{2\frac{1}{2}}$	5$^{4\frac{1}{2}}$	6$^{9\frac{1}{2}}$	6$^{18\frac{1}{2}}$	Sarmiento R	L118 fb	47.00	69-	17	Andromeda's Hero118^{7} Bond King118$^{2\frac{3}{4}}$ Shy Harbor118$^{3\frac{1}{4}}$	Faltered	8
11Dec04-10Crc	fst	7f	:23^{1}	:47^{3}	1:12^{4}	1:25^{4}	Md Sp Wt 20k	**48**	4	8	4^{2}	4^{3}	4^{8}	5$^{16\frac{1}{2}}$	Lopez J E	L118 fb	124.40	70-	16	Devil At Sea118$^{10\frac{1}{4}}$ *Bird of Paradise*118^{1} Line of Thought118^{3}	Inside, tired	11
13Nov04-4Crc	fst	6f	:22^{2}	:46	:58^{4}	1:12^{1}	Md Sp Wt 23k	**41**	7	4	9$^{7\frac{3}{4}}$	8$^{9\frac{1}{2}}$	7^{11}	7$^{14\frac{3}{4}}$	Diaz R	118 fb	54.90	73-	10	Dan Is Fast118$^{\frac{3}{4}}$ Mazaage118$^{2\frac{1}{2}}$ Honest Trader118^{hd}	No factor	9
26Oct04-7Del	fst	5½f	:22	:46	:59	1:05^{3}	Md Sp Wt 34k	–	1	8	8^{12}	8^{16}	-	-	Perez M L^{7}	113 fb	27.70	-	17	T. D. Vance120$^{1\frac{1}{2}}$ *Dj's Choice*120$^{2\frac{1}{2}}$ B Trick120$^{1\frac{1}{2}}$	Eased final furlong	8

WORKS: Jan8 **PmM 4f fst :50 B** *39/49* Dec22 **PmM 4f fst :50^{4} B** *15/22* Dec4 **PmM 4f fst :49^{3} B** *12/20* Nov27 **PmM 4f fst :50 B** *14/19*

TRAINER: 61-180Days(9 .00 $0.00) Dirt(113 .08 $1.22) Sprint(95 .09 $1.45)

At 10 minutes to post, Letterman's Humor was 30–1 and floating up. It was weird, because he was the only dropper in the field. He was trying something new, racing for a claiming tag.

Letterman's Humor had raced four times at Delaware and Calder, with negligible success, while facing special-weight maidens. But in his most recent start, he had shown brief speed before he was trounced by better horses including future graded stakes winner Andromeda's Hero. Letterman's Humor was now in a maiden claimer for the first time. And his odds were huge.

Letterman's Humor did not "have to" win. But all the favorites were proven losers. And it was a big field. Letterman's Humor fired.

Jockey Clinton Potts positioned him right behind the speed, he angled out four-wide, hit the front at the eighth pole, and drew away through the lane. Letterman's Humor paid $84.80.

Maiden-claiming droppers often are overbet. But in a big field, sometimes they slip through the cracks. You just have to stay on your toes, because you never know when a mistake will be made. And the thing that made Letterman's Humor so imminently "playable" is that every other horse in the field was a proven loser at the level. It was in the past performances.

It also happens in races for winners. The "nonwinners of two races lifetime" clause (N2L in past performances) is a popular tool for racing secretaries. It creates a lower class level, irrespective of claiming price, because it restricts multiple winners from entering. And just like spotting Letterman's Humor in the maiden-claiming race, sometimes a bettor can find an N2L that is filled with proven losers.

Gulfstream Park must be a haven for class-based longshots, because it happened February 29, 2004, in race 2. It was a sprint for 3-year-old fillies, $16,000 claiming, N2L. The favorite was Teeney Bubbles, a cheap speedball who needed eight starts before she won a maiden race, then finished second in her first try against winners at the same level. She was a proven loser. The second favorite was Wild Winner, with similar weak attributes. Her class was suspect, and she had not run well beyond five furlongs.

With two shaky favorites in the large field (10 starters), it was the perfect race for a possible upset. Only four of the 10 runners had not previously lost an N2L race, and two of them (Another Brianna, Passionate Girl) were so hopelessly slow that they could be easily eliminated.

Sweet Laural
Own: Shoot To Thrill Inc

B. f. 3 (Mar)
Sire: Outflanker (Danzig) $7,500
Dam: Mislaural (Blushing John)
Br: Robert C. Roffey Jr. (Fla)
Tr: Loveless Sandra L(0 0 0 0 .00) 2003:(0 0 .00)

Life	11	1	3	3	$13,800	59	D.Fst	10	1	3	3	$13,630 59
2004	3	0	0	2	$2,750	59	Wet(326)	1	0	0	0	$170 26
							Synth	0	0	0	0	$0 -
2003	8	1	3	1	$11,050	50	Turf(276)	0	0	0	0	$0 -
Gp	3	0	0	2	$2,750	59	Dst(348)	3	0	0	3	$4,135 59

16Feb04–1GP	fst	6f	:221 :46 :59 1:124	ⒻClm 10000(10-9)	49	2	1	56	55¾	56½	31¾	Diaz R7	L112 b	7.40	76–18	*Fiesty Jones*121no Callsports1141¾ *Sweet Laural*112hd	4 wide, up for 3rd	6
30Jan04–2GP	fst	7f	:23 :463 1:1211:253	ⒻClm c-(10-9)	38	1	3	1hd	1hd	53¼	510	Toscano P R	119 b	3.90	64–17	Missvalley1192¾ Birdies Secret1212¾ High On Luck119¾	Inside, faltered	8
Claimed from Roffey, Jr. Robert C. for $10,000, Muench David L Trainer 2003: (115 11 22 15 0.10)																		
11Jan04–2GP	fst	6f	:224 :464 :5911:121	ⒻClm 10000(10-9)	59	5	4	63¼	63¼	21	33	Toscano P R	119 b	25.80	78–12	*Fiesty Jones*1212½ Callsports114½ Sweet Laural1193¼	Couldn't sustain bid	10
22Dec03–9Crc	fst	6½f	:231 :471 1:1321:20	ⒻClm 10000(10-9)	42	7	1	3½	21	35	48½	Beckner D V	119 fb	5.60	70–18	Bailey's Reprized1162¼ Soup for Dinner1196¼ Callsports114hd	3 wide, tired	8
29Nov03–4Crc	fst	1	:241 :49 1:15 1:431	ⒻClm 12500(12.5-10.5)	25	8	54	77¼	712	814	821	Coa E M	119 b	4.00	44–34	GloriousRj116hd IveGottoWin11910½ CountryNtive1172	Through after 1/2	10
31Oct03–3Crc	fst	6f	:232 :473 1:0011:134	ⒻClm 16000(16-14)	50	3	1	3½	32	32	32½	Teator P A	116 b	13.70	72–17	SoupforDinner1161½ CutesnAngl1111 SwtLurl116hd	Lacked late response	7
16Oct03–9Crc	fst	5f	:231 :474	1:012 ⒻMd 12500	48	7	3	21½	22	21½	11¼	Teator P A	118 b	3.80	81–15	SweetLurl1181¼ TrustedRumor1182¼ PrettyHonore1181¼	Edged away late	10
22Sep03–9Crc	fst	5f	:23 :481	1:021 ⒻMd 12500	39	9	4	33	43	41½	21	Teator P A	118 b	2.10	76–18	DownRightCrfty1181 *SwtLurl*118½ MoonlightMlody1092	3 wide, up for 2nd	9
8Sep03–4Crc	fst	4½f	:231 :474	:542 ⒻMd 12500	42	3	2	3nk		1hd	22½	Teator P A	118 b	3.80	84–15	Formal Fanny1182½ SweetLaural118¾ Bailey'sWish1181¼	Vied, outfinished	6
29Aug03–8Crc	fst	4½f	:224 :473	:541 ⒻMd 12500	36	3	1	3½		33	24¾	Teator P A	118 b	14.00	83–17	Dinner Mint1184¾ Sweet Laural118¾ *Fortune Won*1111¾	Chased, no match	8
20Jly03–6Crc	sly	5f	:222 :462	1:003 ⒻMd 35000(40-35)	26	1	4	69	814	910	99½	Toscano P R	116	26.20	75–15	True Moments118nk Loveland1181¾ Stormin' Daina1162	Done early	9

WORKS: Jan22 GP 4f fst :53 B *23/24* Jan5 GP 4f fst :502 B *18/24* Dec19 Crc 3f fst :374 B *4/8* Dec13 Crc 4f fst :511 B *57/71* Nov21 Crc 4f fst :512 B *30/38*

TRAINER: +180Days(2 .00 $0.00) Dirt(17 .06 $0.92) Sprint(16 .06 $0.98)

Valid Skip
Own: O'Brien Maura C

Ch. f. 3 (Mar) OBSAUG02 $22,000
Sire: Skip Trial (Bailjumper) $5,000
Dam: Valid Coins (Valid Appeal)
Br: Harry Bono & Louise Bono (Fla)
Tr: O'Brien Maura C(0 0 0 0 .00) 2003:(0 0 .00)

Life	10	1	2	0	$17,335	71	D.Fst	10	1	2	0	$17,335 71
2004	2	0	0	0	$740	47	Wet(358)	0	0	0	0	$0 -
							Synth	0	0	0	0	$0 -
2003	8	1	2	0	$16,595	71	Turf(252)	0	0	0	0	$0 -
Gp	2	0	0	0	$740	47	Dst(379)	5	0	1	0	$4,635 71

Previously trained by Ciardullo Richard Jr 2003: (406 69 62 42 0.17)

30Jan04–2GP	fst	7f	:23 :463 1:1211:253	ⒻClm 10000(10-9)	46	6	2	51¾	3nk	21½	46¼	Lopez J E5	L114 fb	*2.20	68–17	Missvalley1192¾ Birdies Secret1212¾ High On Luck119¾	4 wide, bid, tired	8
3Jan04–3GP	fst	6f	:231 :464 :5841:111	ⒻClm 25000(25-20)	47	4	3	52¾	31½	65½	510¾	Lopez J E5	L114 b	4.40	75–10	*GrandPiano*1174¼ SteppinShoot1195¾ Slvester119nk	Chased,6wd,flattened	6
18Dec03–8Crc	fst	6f	:222 :462 :5911:123	ⒻClm 32000(32-30)	55	4	4	32½	54½	45	48¼	Lopez J E5	L111 b	3.00	73–18	*Foxie Bertie*1163¼ Heavenly Powder116nk Salvester1074¾	Tired	8
5Dec03–9Crc	fst	6f	:222 :462 :5921:13	ⒻClm 35000(40-35)	55	1	5	52¼	76	76¾	46¾	Lopez J E5	L109 b	*1.60	72–23	HighestHonoree119¾ MsBnker1165¼ MComePrtndi111¾	Failed to menace	7
2Nov03–5Crc	fst	6f	:22 :453 :5841:122	ⒻClm 25000(25-22.5)	71	8	2	55½	44	21½	21½	Lopez J E5	L111 b	4.40	80–17	Lissfriendlylover1161½ VlidSkip1117½ Actcentric1191¼	4 wide, no late gain	10
20Oct03–3Crc	fst	5½f	:222 :47 1:0011:071	ⒻMd 18000(20-18)	61	3	2	31	2hd	12	18½	Lopez J E5	L111 b	*1.20	85–16	Valid Skip1118½ *Lynn's Song*1184½ Drop Dead Red1181¾	3 wide, drew off	6
1Sep03–11Crc	fst	6f	:22 :46 :5921:134	ⒻMd c-(20-18)	42	6	4	32½	22	45	58	Penalba C	L118 b	*3.00	67–19	*Lissfrindlylovr*118¾ *BckByB*1182 Imgbylmplght1184¼	Bumped stretch, tired	11
Claimed from Alesso Al for $20,000, Wilensky Herman Trainer 2003(as of 9/1): (68 9 11 4 0.13)																		
15Aug03–8Crc	fst	7f	:213 :451 1:1141:253	ⒻMd 32000(32-30)	27	10	11	99¾	912	912	921½	Penalba C	L118 b	2.90	65–13	Malindi1133½ Maiden Tour1187 Atlantic Snow116nk	Hesitated start	11
3Aug03–12Crc	fst	5½f	:224 :47 :5941:062	ⒻMd 32000(32-30)	57	2	10	41¾	42	44½	25½	Penalba C	L118 b	3.80	83–16	Alarkandadove1115½ VlidSkip1183½ AmericnMiss118¾	Off slowly, 2nd best	10
8Jly03–6Crc	fst	4½f	:224 :473	:543 ⒻMd 32000(32-30)	43	6	6	52¾		42¾	41	Penalba C	L118 b	22.60	85–18	FloRosnNt118¾ MComPrtnd118nk FblosLokr118hd	Lugged in str, gaining	10

TRAINER: +180Days(1 .00 $0.00) Dirt(47 .09 $1.81) Sprint(45 .09 $1.90)

That left Sweet Laural and Valid Skip. They were "new faces" who had not previously lost under the N2L condition. Sweet Laural started at 12.60–1, and Valid Skip started at 5.80–1. They finished in that order to complete a $94.40 exacta (for $1). The formula was simple—big field, vulnerable favorites, and two new shooters.

Would you bet a horse without knowing its odds? Of course you would not. Likewise, it makes no sense to back a longshot in any race without recognizing the requirements of the race—what it takes to win—and knowing how the favorites stack up.

As the 2006–07 Santa Anita winter meet entered the final weekend, I was battling two other handicappers for the title of leading newspaper selector in Southern California. Going into the final two days of the 85-day meet, I was dead-even with syndicated handicapper Bob Ike and *Los Angeles Times* handicapper Bob Mieserski, based on number of winners. Bragging rights were at stake.

The 11th race at Santa Anita on April 21, 2007, was a $32,000 maiden-claiming sprint in which the main contenders were slow. The Beyer par for the class level is 66; an entrant would qualify on speed if he had run at least a 61. None of them had.

The favorite, Oh I Tripped, had finished a distant second in his debut, with a 56 Beyer; the second favorite was Tenvince, who improved third time out and earned a 60. Nobody else was remotely close to par. It was a race ripe for a new shooter, ripe for a longshot.

That covered the first two steps in finding a potential longshot. The field was big, and according to the speed-figure parameters, none of the contenders had run within five points of par.

Yes, this was a good spot to seek alternatives. Maybe there was a new face—a comebacker or a first-time starter.

Certain sires produce offspring that win first out more than random chance, or higher than 12 percent. One such stallion that was getting an inordinately high rate of debut winners was Trippi, sire of first-time starter Tribble.

A 3-year-old, Tribble was purchased at auction for $85,000 and was making his debut for about one-third that price. Strike one. His work pattern consisted of only four published works. Strike two. These are standard bet-againsts—horses that debut for considerably less than their sale price, and first-time starters with sporadic work patterns. Most firsters have at least six recorded workouts.

The knocks were obvious, and mainstream handicapping logic said to toss out Tribble. If you want mainstream, then you want the favorite. But the favorites were bad. Maybe this was a good race to pass. Nothing wrong with that. When the favorites are weak, and so are the alternatives, sometimes the best strategy is to sit it out.

But something kept bugging me about Tribble, trained by James Kasparoff and ridden by David Flores. That combination rang a bell. *Daily Racing Form* handicapping software Formulator showed why. Only three months earlier, Kasparoff put Flores on a similar longshot firster. Meritsndemerits did not win, but he ran well and finished second at odds of 8–1. Formulator indicated that the trainer and jockey had a positive history together.

Now it was Tribble's turn, and despite claim-price knocks and workout deficiency, Tribble was "live." So was I, and picked Tribble to win. After selecting five winners from the first 10 races on the 11-race Santa Anita card, I was positioned for the knockout blow. All I had to be was right.

Tribble broke running, sat third behind the speed while full of run, angled outside for the drive, and powered home to win by 3¼ lengths. He paid $18.20, was my sixth winner on the card, and gave me a two-win cushion in the race for the title of leading Southern California public handicapper. The next day, I clinched it.

ELEVENTH RACE **6 FURLONGS. MAIDEN CLAIMING . Purse $20,000 (plus $2,800 Other Sources) FOR MAIDENS, THREE YEAR OLDS. Weight, 121 lbs. Claiming Price $32,000.**

Santa Anita

APRIL 21, 2007

Value of Race: $22,800 Winner $12,000; second $4,000; third $2,400; fourth $1,200; fifth $400; sixth $400; seventh $400; eighth $400; ninth $400; tenth $400; eleventh $400; twelfth $400. Mutuel Pool $471,821.00 Exacta Pool $284,012.00 Trifecta Pool $281,059.00 Superfecta Pool $240,277.00

Last Raced	Horse	M/Eqt.	A.	Wt	PP	St	¼	½	Str	Fin	Jockey	Cl'g Pr	Odds $1
	Tribble	LB	f	3	121	4	9	4^{hd}	$3^{3\frac{1}{2}}$	1^{hd}	$1^{3\frac{1}{4}}$	Flores D R	32000	8.10
14Apr07 ^{10}SA^{4}	Rocky Joe	LB	b	3	121	8	12	$11^{\frac{1}{2}}$	$8^{1\frac{1}{2}}$	$6^{\frac{1}{2}}$	2no	Portillo D A	32000	21.70
31Mar07 ^{10}SA^{2}	Tenvince	B	f	3	121	1	8	1^{hd}	1^{hd}	2^{2}	$3^{\frac{1}{2}}$	Figueroa O	32000	2.50
8Mar07 ^{4}SA^{6}	Baranka	LB	b	3	121	6	7	$8^{1\frac{1}{2}}$	4^{1}	$4^{1\frac{1}{2}}$	4^{2}	Arias S	32000	9.90
	Heads UpGoodLuck	LB	bf	3	121	5	6	2^{hd}	2^{1}	$3^{1\frac{1}{2}}$	$5^{\frac{3}{4}}$	DeAlba C	32000	58.00
	Henry D.	LB	b	3	121	3	11	$10^{1\frac{1}{2}}$	6^{1}	7^{3}	6^{1}	Delgadillo A	32000	9.50
8Apr07 ^{9}SA^{6}	Jona's Prospector	LB	b	3	121	9	3	7^{hd}	$5^{1\frac{1}{2}}$	5^{1}	$7^{5\frac{1}{2}}$	Baze M C	32000	29.30
8Apr07 ^{9}SA^{3}	Brave Karol	LB	bf	3	121	11	1	$9^{2\frac{1}{2}}$	$9^{\frac{1}{2}}$	8^{1}	8^{2}	Garcia M	32000	6.70
8Mar07 ^{4}SA^{8}	Ziyanick	B	f	3	123	2	10	12	$10^{1\frac{1}{2}}$	9^{6}	$9^{12\frac{1}{2}}$	Segundo M A	32000	130.40
4Apr07 ^{8}SA^{2}	Oh I Tripped	LB	b	3	121	10	4	5^{hd}	$11^{\frac{1}{2}}$	10^{1}	$10^{3\frac{1}{4}}$	Migliore R	32000	2.10
4Apr07 ^{8}SA^{7}	Correinado	LB	f	3	121	7	5	3^{1}	7^{hd}	11^{5}	11	Potts C L	32000	44.70
8Apr07 ^{9}SA^{7}	Balance the Score	LB	b	3	121	12	2	$6^{1\frac{1}{2}}$	12	12	—	Bisono A	32000	28.60

OFF AT 5:40 Start Good. Won driving. Track fast.

TIME :21^{3}, :45, :58, 1:11^{1} (:21.76, :45.09, :58.06, 1:11.34)

$2 Mutuel Prices:			
4 – TRIBBLE	18.20	9.60	6.60
8 – ROCKY JOE		15.20	8.80
1 – TENVINCE			3.80

$1 EXACTA 4–8 PAID $170.40 $1 TRIFECTA 4–8–1 PAID $918.60

$1 SUPERFECTA 4–8–1–6 PAID $4,355.60

B. g, (Feb), by Trippi – Rachael's Rumba , by Pine Bluff . Trainer Kasparoff James M. Bred by Ginger Parker & Charles A Baldree Jr (Fla).

Anyone could have known the parameters of that maiden-claiming race, identified the favorites, and recognized their vulnerability. That can be the most important part of the battle. The second part, finding the potential upsetters, sometimes is easy.

The basics are as valid now as ever. Regardless of surface—man-made or dirt—horses still must be in condition. Pace is always a factor, though perhaps in reverse.

Early speed—once the most important asset in racing—has been turned on its head. At Del Mar in 2007, if you found a front-runner in a two-turn race, you bet against him. Handicappers are twisting the fundamentals inside out, and analyzing races from back to front.

That is how it works for me—by finding flaws in favorites, and looking for alternatives. It must be done in that order. Frequently, the alternatives are comebackers or first-time starters—new faces in weak races. The methodology can lead to a single-race jackpot, as it did one ordinary winter Saturday during the 2006–07 meet at Santa Anita.

Skeptics looked forward to January 6, because there were reasons to mistrust favorites in both two-turn stakes races. Mistical Plan, a sprinter, was 6–5 while trying to carry her speed in the Grade 3 Santa Ysabel Stakes for 3-year-old fillies. Declan's Moon, in dubious form, was 5–2 in the Grade 2 San Pasqual Handicap for older horses. The problem with the stakes races was that each race had only seven starters.

Field size is vital in finding longshot winners. Although overlays pop up occasionally in short fields, opportunities are more frequent in races with more starters. In the Santa Ysabel, only one of the seven runners started at 10–1 or higher; in the San Pasqual, only two of the seven runners started at 10–1 or higher.

But earlier on the card, a $32,000 maiden-claiming sprint for 3-year-old fillies drew 14 runners including 10 that started at double-digit odds. If nothing else, the race had a lot of longshots. Before considering if any of the outsiders could run, the logical contenders had to be evaluated. And the closer one looked at the maiden-claiming race, the uglier it got.

Lady in Love was favored first-off-the-claim by Bill Spawr, but her last start was a dreadful effort around two turns. One race back she earned a 61 Beyer Speed Figure, within five points of the 66 Beyer par for the level. However, Lady in Love was not quick, and she was stuck on the rail. She would need to rally from behind at 2.90–1. Not exactly a winning profile for the old dirt track at Santa Anita.

Fappiano's Legacy was second choice based on a 60 Beyer in a modest runner-up debut. The figure was six points less than par. (Speed handicappers use five points as the cutoff; the line must be drawn somewhere.) Her jockey was ice cold; her odds were 3.10–1.

Lady Yodeler was the third choice with sorry Beyers of 50 and 59. Syntillating was the fourth choice. She had speed, but no finish in either start. End result? The first four wagering choices were fundamentally flawed.

The trouble was that nine of the other 10 starters also had raced poorly, and the only first-time starter in the field had a series of slow works, a nondescript pedigree, and a trainer (Craig Lewis) not known for winning first time out.

Eye Candy Sandi *life a/pmT*

Own: Craig A & Larry D Lewis
R/b, Red Cal On Black Diamond On Back $32,000
GRYDER A T (27 3 3 5 .11) 2006: (1040 118 .11)

Dk. b or br f. 3 (May)
Sire: Larry the Legend (Local Talent) $2,500
Dam: Cut to Paris (Cutlass Reality)
Br: Robert Englekirk Craig A Lewis & Mira Loma TB Farm L (Cal)
Tr: Lewis Craig A (2 0 1 1 .00) 2006:(161 14 .09)

121

Life	0 M 0 0	$0	–	D.Fst	0 0 0 0	$0	–
2007	0 M 0 0	$0	–	Wet(394)	0 0 0 0	$0	–
2006	0 M 0 0	$0	–	Turf(216)	0 0 0 0	$0	–
SA	0 0 0 0	$0	–	Dst(325)	0 0 0 0	$0	–

WORKS: Dec29 SA 6f fst 1:14⁴ H 19/29 Dec19 SA 6f fst 1:14¹ H 4/9 Dec9 SA 6f fst 1:14⁴ H 7/11 Nov30 SA 6f fst 1:15³ H 3(/ Nov20 SA 5f fst 1:00³ Hg 8/26 Nov12 SA 6f fst 1:15² H 11/21
Nov5 SA 5f fst 1:01³ Hg 26/38 Oct27 SA 5f fst 1:02 H 15/24 Oct16 SA 5f fst 1:04 H 48/51 Oct5 SA 4f fst :49 H 7/27 Sep29 SA 4f fst :50 H 28/34 Sep23 SA 3f fst :37³ H 9/17
TRAINER: 1stStart(27 .11 $2.44) DebutMCL(25 .12 $2.64) Dirt(133 .10 $1.00) Sprint(106 .08 $1.01) MdnClm(91 .11 $1.14)

J/T 2006–07 SA (20 .05 $0.30) J/T 2006–07(38 .03 $0.16)

Longshots are not perfect. Maybe there was more to first-time starter Eye Candy Sandi. She was sired by the ordinary stallion Larry the Legend; trainer stats in the filly's past performances showed Lewis won first out at 11 percent. But closer inspection, again using Formulator software, revealed a more complete picture of Lewis, specifically the previous five years in the first month of the Santa Anita winter meet.

Formulator showed Lewis had started nine firsters in maiden-claiming sprints for fillies. Three of them had won, and all at prices ($17.60 Rubin's Rose on January 6, 2002; $60.40 Dee Dee's Spell on January 1, 2004; and $15.60 She's So Vain on January 11, 2006). Two of those were by Larry the Legend; he was the 1995 Santa Anita Derby winner that Lewis owned and trained.

Could the debut filly Eye Candy Sandi be another longshot debut winner trained by Lewis? She was 15–1 on the morning line, and when betting opened, Eye Candy Sandi sank to 6–1. It seemingly dashed hopes of a big payoff. But then conventional, old-school handicapping took over the betting market, as it usually does. The public gravitated toward "safe" selections. The odds crept higher and higher on Eye Candy Sandi, and by the time the field reached the starting gate, she was 13–1.

And as it turns out, she also had speed. Eye Candy Sandi broke running under jockey Aaron Gryder, made the rail, shook off a crazy longshot after a quarter-mile, maintained the lead to deep stretch, and inched clear by a length and a quarter. She paid $28.60.

The moral of the story: In a field of slow maiden claimers whose limited ability has been exposed, there can be overlay potential in a first-time starter, even one sired by the $2,500 stallion Larry the Legend. (A side note—three weeks after Eye Candy Sandi, Lewis sprang with another Larry the Legend first-time starter. Marry Me Larry paid $27.40 on January 28.)

Maybe if the favorites did not look so bad, Eye Candy Sandi would have been tougher to find. But that is the point—they *were* bad. That was a known factor. If you know something is bad, you can wager that the unknown might include something good.

The betting public finds comfort in the familiar. There is so much uncertainty surrounding first-time starters, imports, or layoff horses. Who really knows how fast they can run? You cannot know for sure. The only thing a handicapper can know is how fast, or slow, the familiar horses are. In situations where the chalk is bad, chances increase that a new shooter, or a horse trying something, will be in position to upset.

Most high-price winners occur in big fields. Sounds pretty simple. Field size and vulnerable favorites are the most important factors in finding high-odds winners. The bigger the field, the higher the odds, and the greater the possibility a contender will fall through the parimutuel cracks. In a big field, legitimate contenders sometimes are misanalyzed.

It happened at Del Mar on July 28, 2007, the second week of the summer meet. It was a Saturday, and the 10-race card included a second-level allowance sprint with 10 starters. The field was big enough.

Race 8 was smack in the middle of every possible horizontal wager—daily doubles, pick threes, pick four, pick six, and place pick all. And the race was a potential trap for horseplayers who thought they could handicap their way out of the mess. And what a mess it was.

Principle Secret was 7–5 coming off a bad race, and facing older for the first time. Sinister Minister had done absolutely nothing since his Blue Grass farce (116 Beyer) a year and a half earlier at Keeneland. Although he was cutting back to a sprint that might be more his preference, 3–1 odds were awfully short for a one-hit wonder.

The others were a jumbled mess of has-beens, wannabes, and claiming-caliber nobodies. If there ever was a race ready-made for an upset winner, this was it. It had the two most important ingredients—a big field, and shaky favorites.

The odds for the borderline contenders were at middle digits. They included sharp class-hiker Midwesterner (17–1); Grade 1-placed router Roman Commander (19–1), making his second start back from a layoff; and a new South American import, Fly Dorcego (32–1). If the favorites blew, any of those fringe contenders could win.

Somewhere in this scrambled two-other-than sprint, a mistake might be made. It would not be the first one in a big field. At very least, the large size of the field made it the type of race to attack.

Fly Dorcego (Brz)
Own: Brincaggiore Stable
Red, Green Bar And Cuffs On Sleeves
FLORES D R (20 2 7 2 .10) 2007: (496 87 .18)

B. h. 5 (Oct)
Sire: Choctaw Ridge (Mr. Prospector)
Dam: Flight to Rome (Storm Bird)
Br: Haras San Francesco (Brz)
Tr: Lobo Paulo H(1 0 0 0 .00) 2007:(75 12 .16)

122

Life	15	3	4	5	$40,663	-	
2006	7	1	1	2	$29,078	-	
2005	8	2	3	3	$11,585	-	
Dmr	0	0	0	0	$0	-	
D.Fst	0	0	0	0	$0	-	
Wet(341*)	6	1	2	3	$6,549	-	
Synth	0	0	0	0	$0	-	
Turf(254)	9	2	2	2	$34,114	-	
Dst(354)	1	1	0	0	$3,002	-	

Previously trained by C Cury

6Aug06	Gavea (Brz)	hy	*1	Ⓣ LH 1:35^{2}	3↑ GP Presidente da Republica-G1 Stk 67400	15^{18½}	Gulart A	130	21.70	Quick Gipsy115^{1½} Out of Control115^{1¼} Quick Hawk115^{nk}	19
9Jly06	Gavea (Brz)	gd	*1	Ⓣ LH 1:35^{4}	3↑ Grande Premio Gervasio Seabra-G2 Stk 33200	1^{1¼}	Gulart A	130	2.30	Fly Dorcego130^{1¼} Puro Dominio132^{nk} Future130^{1¾}	12
21May06	Ciudad Jardim (Brz)	gd	*1	Ⓣ LH 1:32^{2}	3↑ GP Pres da Republica-G1 Stk 61700	8^{5½}	Gulart A	128	5.20	Bandido Secreto128^{1¾} Serial Winner128^{1¼} Lucky Dance128^{1½}	17
15Apr06	Gavea (Brz)	gd	*1	Ⓣ LH 1:33^{2}	3↑ Classico Outono (Listed) Stk 11500	2^{2¼}	Gulart A	126	*1.50	Laurenciano132^{2¼} Fly Dorcego126^{nk} Sea Cruise126^{1}	12
19Mar06	Gavea (Brz)	gd	*1⅛	Ⓣ LH 1.58^{4}	GP F E de Paula Machado G1 Stk 16800	3^{1}	Leme J	123	19.00	*Heroi do Bafra*123^{hd} Northern Pan123^{1} Fly Dorcego123^{1¾}	18
19Feb06	Gavea (Brz)	gd	*1	Ⓣ LH 1:33^{4}	GP Estado do Rio de Janeiro-G1 Stk 46800	11^{6}	Mota A	123	4.10	O Dragao123^{2} London Eye123^{nk} Nicolalau123^{½}	17
15Jan06	Gavea (Brz)	gd	*1	Ⓣ LH 1:33^{3}	GP Jose Buarque de Macedo-G3 Stk 14800	3^{¾}	Gulart A	123	8.70	*O Dragao*123^{½} Atlas Mountain123^{nk} Fly Dorcego123^{2¼}	20
4Dec05	Gavea (Brz)	hy	*1	Ⓣ LH 1:34^{1}	GP Frederico Lundgren-G3 Stk 13400	2^{5}	Duarte L	123	3.10	Right Special123^{5} Fly Dorcego123^{½} Pueblo Bonito123^{2}	15
30Oct05	Gavea (Brz)	hy	*1	LH 1:38^{4}	3↑ Epsecial G Philadelpho Azevedo Alw 5700	2^{1}	Duarte L	119	6.00	Ze Americano117^{1} Fly Dorcego119^{¾} Padrino Dodge119^{5¼}	9
24Sep05	Gavea (Brz)	hy	*6½f	LH 1:20	Premio Sparkie Alw 5000	1^{3¼}	Correa I	123	3.80	Fly Dorcego123^{3¼} Black Lightning123^{4½} Inbusiness123^{2½}	6
13Aug05	Gavea (Brz)	gd	*5½f	LH 1:07^{1}	Premio Grumete Alw 4700	3^{4½}	Correa I	123	2.30	Hooks123^{nk} Don Chico123^{4¼} *Fly Dorcego*123^{1½}	5
24Jly05	Gavea (Brz)	gd	*5½f	LH 1:08	Premio Arlindo Manes Alw 4700	2^{5}	Correa I	123	5.00	Nos Trinques123^{5} Fly Dorcego123^{1} *Hooks*123^{½}	10

WORKS: Jly22 Hol ◈5f fst 1:01^{3} Hg *7/13* Jly15 Hol ◈6f fst 1:14^{1} H *6/18* Jly8 Hol ◈5f fst 1:01^{2} H *24/70* Jly1 Hol ◈5f fst 1:01^{3} H *42/72* Jun24 Hol ◈6f fst 1:14 H *7/22* Jun16 Hol ◈5f fst 1:00^{2} H *9/61*
TRAINER: 1stNA(9 .22 $6.87) 1stW/Tm(16 .12 $3.86) +180Days(18 .17 $4.62) Synth(41 .20 $2.60) Turf/Synth(5 .20 $1.24) Sprint(100 .14 $2.20) J/T 2006-07 DMR(1 .00 $0.00) J/T 2006-07(39 .10 $1.66)

Fly Dorcego was being sent out by Paulo Lobo, a native of Brazil who has successfully trained several South American shippers to win their U.S. debuts.

In fact, the South American-import angle had permeated Southern California. Shippers from the Southern Hemisphere once were bet-against prospects until they acclimated, but in 2007 they were increasingly live. At the spring meet at Hollywood, seven South American imports made their U.S. debuts. Three won—Right Special ($35.60) from Brazil, El Manuel ($31) from Chile, and Masterly ($35.20) from Argentina. Two others lost, and then won their second start (Double Trouble, Private Dreams).

In the Del Mar allowance, Fly Dorcego was 20–1 on the line, and nothing more than a shot at a price. If he turned out to be a stiff, so what? When you back high-odds runners, even for the right reasons, most of the time you will be wrong. As it turns out, Fly Dorcego was well meant, and in the right spot. Even facing vulnerable favorites, his odds were abnormally high.

Fly Dorcego was not even close to his 20–1 morning line. In the 10-horse field, Fly Dorcego started at 32–1. Under jockey David Flores, Fly Dorcego broke well, sat fifth behind the speed, looped the field into the lane, and blew them away. He won by four lengths, and returned $66.60.

EIGHTH RACE
Del Mar
JULY 28, 2007

6½ FURLONGS. (1.17³) ALLOWANCE OPTIONAL CLAIMING . Purse $64,000 (plus $19,200 CBOIF – California Bred Owner Fund) FOR THREE YEAR OLDS AND UPWARD WHICH HAVE NEVER WON $7,500 TWICE OTHER THAN MAIDEN, CLAIMING, OR STARTER OR WHICH HAVE NEVER WON THREE RACES OR CLAIMING PRICE $62,500. Three Year Olds, 120 lbs.; Older, 124 lbs. Non–winners of two races since April 28 Allowed 2 lbs. A race since then Allowed 4 lbs. (Maiden races and Claiming races for $50,000 or less not considered).

Value of Race: $69,840 Winner $38,400; second $16,640; third $7,680; fourth $3,840; fifth $1,280; sixth $400; seventh $400; eighth $400; ninth $400; tenth $400. Mutuel Pool $545,805.00 Exacta Pool $297,135.00 Quinella Pool $22,551.00 Trifecta Pool $256,071.00 Superfecta Pool $160,959.00

Last Raced	Horse	M/Eqt. A. Wt	PP	St	¼	½	Str	Fin	Jockey	Cl'g Pr	Odds $1
6Aug06 GVA15	Fly Dorcego-Brz	LB 5 120	8	4	5¹	4¹½	3²½	1⁴	Flores D R		32.30
6Oct06 7OSA4	Bro Lo	LB 4 120	10	1	1¹	1hd	2hd	2¾	Baze M C		9.30
6Jly07 8Hol1	Midwesterner	LB 4 120	9	2	2hd	2²	1½	3¹½	Smith M E	62500	17.40
8Jly07 8CD2	Forest Phantom	LB b 4 120	1	10	9²½	9⁴½	6hd	4¹¼	Gryder A T	62500	8.40
15Jun07 7Hol4	Sinister Minister	LB b 4 120	3	7	3½	3hd	4²	5hd	Espinoza V		3.30
7Jly07 5Hol2	Taxi Fleet	LB 3 118	7	3	8hd	6hd	5¹	6¹	Talamo J		7.80
28Apr07 2Hol4	Black Spot	LB b 4 120	2	9	6½	7hd	7¹½	7¹	Court J K		19.70
4Jly07 9Mth3	Principle Secret	LB 3 116	4	5	4¹½	5¹½	9³	8hd	Solis A		1.40
12Jly07 7Hol5	Roman Commander	LB f 3 111	6	8	10	10	10	9½	Quinonez A5		19.40
7Jly07 5Hol3	Swiss Address	LB f 5 120	5	6	7²½	8¹½	8hd	10	Garcia M		18.50

OFF AT 5:40 Start Good. Won ridden out. Track fast.
TIME :22³, :46, 1:12¹, 1:19 (:22.61, :46.12, 1:12.37, 1:19.15)

$2 Mutuel Prices:	8 – FLY DORCEGO–BRZ	66.60	27.60	14.80
	10 – BRO LO		10.00	6.40
	9 – MIDWESTERNER			10.20

$1 EXACTA 8–10 PAID $439.30 $2 QUINELLA 8–10 PAID $256.00
$1 TRIFECTA 8–10–9 PAID $3,413.10 $1 SUPERFECTA 8–10–9–1 PAID $43,958.80

B. h, (Oct), by Choctaw Ridge – Flight to Rome , by Storm Bird . Trainer Lobo Paulo H. Bred by Haras San Francesco (Brz).

FLY DORCEGO (BRZ) bobbled a bit at the start, settled outside chasing the pace, came three deep into the stretch, gained the advantage outside foes past the eighth pole and won clear under a brisk hand ride. BRO LO sped to the early lead off the rail, angled in and set the pace a bit off the rail, dueled inside on the turn, fought back in the stretch, could not match the winner but edged a rival for second. MIDWESTERNER stalked the pace three deep on the backstretch, bid alongside the runner-up on the turn, gained a short lead between horses in midstretch and held third. FOREST PHANTOM broke a bit slowly and drifted in, chased inside, came out into the stretch and bested the others. SINISTER MINISTER close up stalking the pace inside on the backstretch and turn, weakened in the stretch. TAXI FLEET chased outside then three deep on the turn and four wide into the stretch and lacked the needed rally. BLACK SPOT was in a good position inside chasing the pace to the stretch and could not summon the necessary response. PRINCIPLE SECRET chased between horses then a bit off the rail and weakened. ROMAN COMMANDER settled off the inside, angled in some on the turn, came out into the stretch and failed to menace. SWISS ADDRESS settled between foes chasing the pace, came out leaving the turn and four wide into the stretch and lacked a further response.

Owners– 1, Brincaggiore Stable; 2, Farr David C and Billie A; 3, Lanning Curt and Lila; 4, Browning Kent; 5, Lanni Family Trust Mercedes Stable LLC and Schiappa Bernard C; 6, Gregg R and Anderson Jr Robert G; 7, Bell John C Sommars Julie and Williams Peter; 8, Charles Cono LLC; 9, Mann Kendall; 10, Harrington Mike

Trainers– 1, Lobo Paulo H; 2, O'Neill Doug; 3, Moger Ed Jr; 4, Autrey Cody; 5, Baffert Bob; 6, Gallagher Patrick; 7, Bell Thomas R II; 8, Paasch Christopher S; 9, Stute Gary; 10, Harrington Mike

Forest Phantom was claimed by Carmel Carmel and Hazan; trainer, Puype Mike.

$2 Daily Double (10–8) Paid $384.00 ; Daily Double Pool $34,872 .
$1 Pick Three (5–10–8) Paid $563.20 ; Pick Three Pool $129,256 .

Combine a big field with potentially vulnerable favorites, and the result can be a boxcar payoff.

How important is field size? A study of the median $2 win payoffs during the long Santa Anita winter meet illustrated the effect of field size. "Median" means half the payoffs are higher, and half are lower.

Bettors probably don't think much about field size when they sit down to attack a card, but perhaps they should. These are the median payoffs, ranked by field size (wagering interests), during the 2006–07 Santa Anita winter meet.

FIELD SIZE	WIN PAYOFF MEDIAN
14 runners	$14.40
13 runners	$14.40
12 runners	$11.40
11 runners	$ 9.80
10 runners	$10.40
9 runners	$ 9.80
8 runners	$ 8.40
7 runners	$ 7.20
6 runners	$ 6.20
5 runners	$ 6.40
4 runners	$ 3.60

The bigger the field, the higher the payoffs. Bettors can aim accordingly. In fields with nine or more starters, half the winners paid $10 or more.

This does not mean that a bettor cannot back a "longshot" in a small field, but the definition of longshot will change. A "longshot" in a six-horse field might only pay $9.

A second chart below shows the effect of field size on the percentage of winners that returned $20 or higher. Bettors that shoot for the moon will necessarily have to aim in the direction of fields that produce higher payoffs.

The chart below shows percentage of winners that returned $20 or more during the 2006–07 Santa Anita winter meet, ranked by field size.

FIELD SIZE	$20 WINNERS, %	(WINS-RACES)
14 runners	30.7 %	(4–13)
13 runners	30.0 %	(6–20)
12 runners	23.6 %	(17–72)
11 runners	18.3 %	(11–60)

10 runners	22.0 %	(19–86)
9 runners	26.2 %	(26–99)
8 runners	15.7 %	(19–121)
7 runners	8.0 %	(9–112)
6 runners	2.1 %	(2–93)
5 runners	1.8 %	(1–53)
4 runners	0.0 %	(0–9)

To find a winner that pays $20 or more, it makes sense to focus on a field with 13 or 14 starters. In fields that big, the winner pays $20 or more roughly 30 percent of the time. In races with fields of 9 to 12 starters, the winner pays $20 or higher about 25 percent of the time. Fields with 8 or fewer starters typically do not produce such generous payoffs.

Small fields do not lend themselves to overlay potential. With just a handful of starters, the betting public usually "prices" the horses with uncanny precision. Mistakes are few—the favorite should be the favorite, the second choice should be the second choice, and on down the line. Yet even in a small field, bettors sometimes miscalculate.

This can happen when it is least expected, sometimes even in a five-horse field such as the one that lined up June 24, 2007, at Hollywood Park in a stakes race for California-bred fillies and mares.

Getback Time was a known commodity. She had won three straight while earning Beyers higher than any recent figure posted by her rivals. Getback Time was supposed to win the Valkyr Stakes, plain and simple, as the 2–5 favorite.

But sometimes the public underestimates the chances of the others. That would represent another type of potential longshot—a horse that is simply underpriced.

Vaca City Flyer, the 3–1 second choice, was a shell of her former self. Defeated at 5–2 or less her last three starts, her recent races suggested she had lost her speed. She was six years old, and possibly wearing down.

Likewise, stakes winner Gn. Group Meeting had regressed. Bettors priced her correctly at 10–1. Her speed figures were in decline, six furlongs was too short, and there was little reason to like her. She had been exposed.

Hey Hey Renee, 30–1 in the five-horse field, was impossible to like. She was too slow.

There was one other starter in the race. Lady Gamer had not raced since December, when she won her second straight start on Cushion Track. Her speed figures were inferior to Getback Time, but she was fresh and lightly raced. The question was, what was her current ability? It could not be quantified.

2 Lady Gamer
Own: Clark & Janine Hansen
White — White, Gold Circle Rose Wreath H, Gold
FLORES D R (124 25 19 17 .20) 2007: (432 76 .18)

B. f. 4 (Jan)
Sire: Game Plan (Danzig) $3,500
Dam: Mariah Reyna (Far North)
Br: Clark A Hansen & Janine Rae Hansen (Cal)
Tr: Sadler John W(97 13 14 10 .13) 2007:(289 51 .18)

L 117

Life	7	3	2	0	$116,740	85	D.Fst	3	1	1	0	$44,400	85
2006	7	3	2	0	$116,740	85	Wet(372)	0	0	0	0	$0	-
2005	0	M	0	0	$0	-	Synth	2	2	0	0	$59,340	85
Hol	4	2	1	0	$71,940	85	Turf(299)	2	0	1	0	$13,000	79
							Dst(361)	2	1	1	0	$40,800	85

10Dec06-8Hol	fst	6½f ◈	:22²	:45²	1:10¹	1:16³	3↑ⒻAlw 53514N1x	81	8	1	41½	72½	3²	11½	Gomez G K	LB122	*1.80	- -	Lady Gamer1221½ True Xena122hd *Smart Crowd*1241¼	4wd,3wd,rallied	10
5Nov06-6Hol	fst	6½f ◈	:22¹	:45²	1:10²	1:16⁴	3↑ⒻⓈAlw 44200N1x	85	5	3	51¼	62¼	1½	1²	Gomez G K	LB122	3.20	- -	*LdyGmer*122² QurterlyReport117nk MonkeyFce1223½	Bit tight3-1/2.rallied	8
8Oct06-7OSA	fm	1 Ⓣ	:22²	:46¹	1:10	1:34²	3↑ⒻⓈOC 25k/N1x-N	75	4	11	1½	1hd	42½	94¼	Nakatani C S	LB119	*2.70	87- 11	YerlyAttitude120½ SilkKerchief120¹ *BchelorettOn*116¾	Lugged out,wkened	11
31Aug06-2Dmr	fm	5f Ⓣ	:21²	:44²		:56¹	3↑ⒻⓈOC 25k/N1x-N	79	3	3	1hd	1hd	11½	2hd	Nakatani C S	LB121	*1.30	94- 06	VelvetySmooth124hd LdyGmer1211½ MmsIlAris1211½	Dueled,clear,caught	7
4Aug06-6Dmr	fst	6f	:21⁴	:45¹	:58	1:11¹	3↑ⒻⓈMd Sp Wt 55k	79	2	6	2hd	1hd	1½	1½	Nakatani C S	LB119	2.90	83- 20	LdyGmer119½ *Forthewrongreson*1191¾ Rspctd1194¼	Shifted out 1/8,gamely	12
1Jly06-2Hol	fst	6½f	:21⁴	:44⁴	1:10²	1:17	3↑ⒻⓈMd Sp Wt 62k	59	1	11	72¼	75¼	66½	47¼	Garcia M5	LB114	*1.00	79- 11	MmselleAries119¾ RushtoJustice119¾ ProudCecy1195¾	Broke in,stumbled	11
14May06-3Hol	fst	6f	:21³	:44³	:57²	1:10²	3↑ⒻⓈMd Sp Wt 45k	85	1	6	52¾	53¼	3¹	2no	Garcia M5	LB112	12.70	85- 14	Tiz a Gem117no Lady Gamer112¾ Neutrality1176½	4wd,drift in,out lane	6

WORKS: Jun16 Hol ◈6f fst 1:13¹ H *3/20* Jun9 Hol ◈6f fst 1:13 H *4/15* Jun2 Hol ◈6f fst 1:13 H *5/22* May26 Hol ◈5f fst :59⁴ H *2/61* May19 Hol ◈5f fst 1:02¹ H *32/66* May12 Hol ◈5f fst 1:01⁴ H *41/68*
TRAINER: +180Days(38 .13 $2.64) Synth(108 .21 $1.86) WonLastStart(127 .18 $1.71) Sprint(491 .19 $1.56) Stakes(85 .15 $1.12) J/T 2006-07 HOL(12 .17 $1.45) J/T 2006-07(42 .21 $1.35)

The unknown can be a good thing. Horseplayers prefer to wager on the known, such as horses that earn high figures, ones that win races, lone speeds, and droppers. The public likes to back horses they can rely on. Conversely, longshot bettors like to wager on the unreliable. Chaos, first-time starters, and comebackers are fun.

Six months had passed since 4-year-old Lady Gamer had raced. It was reasonable to believe the lightly raced (seven starts) filly had improved. Her workouts were sharp—three consecutive six-furlong works. Lady Gamer had a history of outrunning her odds when fresh. A year earlier in her career debut, she finished second by a nose as a 12–1 outsider.

No rational bettor would predict Lady Gamer would win. However, if Vaca City Flyer, the only other front-runner, had lost her speed, then Lady Gamer might be the one to catch. As the field of five loaded into the gate, Lady Gamer was 7–1 for trainer John Sadler, whose comebackers were typically ready to fire.

THIRD RACE
Hollywood
JUNE 24, 2007

6 FURLONGS. (1.07³) 23RD RUNNING OF THE VALKYR. Purse $75,000 (plus $22,500 CBOIF - California Bred Owner Fund) FOR FILLIES AND MARES THREE YEARS OLD AND UPWARD, BRED IN CALIFORNIA . By subscription of $75 each on or before Wednesday, June 13 or by supplementary nomination of $1,500 each by closing time of entries. $125 additional to start with $75,000 added, of which 60% to the winner, 20% to second, 12% to third, 6% to fourth and 2% to fifth. Weight: Three-year-olds 117 lbs.; older 123 lbs. Non-winners of $60,000 allowed 2 lbs.,non-winners of two races other than claiming or starter in 2007 allowed 4 lbs. Such arace in 2007 allowed 6 lbs. Starters to be named through the entry box by closing time of entries. A trophy will be presented to the winning owner. Closed with 11 nominations.

Value of Race: $76,450 Winner $45,870; second $15,290; third $9,174; fourth $4,587; fifth $1,529. Mutuel Pool $179,288.00 Exacta Pool $124,692.00 Quinella Pool $9,340.00

Last Raced	Horse	M/Eqt.	A.	Wt	PP	St	¼	½	Str	Fin	Jockey	Odds $1
10Dec06 8Hol1	Lady Gamer	LB	4	117	2	3	11	12	12½	12¼	Flores D R	7.50
29Apr07 3Hol2	Getback Time	LB b	4	121	5	2	31½	31½	34	23	Nakatani C S	0.40
21Apr07 8BM2	Vaca City Flyer	LB bf	6	117	4	1	2½	21	2hd	34½	Talamo J	3.00
29Apr07 3Hol5	Gn. Group Meeting	LB	5	123	3	5	5	5	5	44	Solis A	10.50
28Oct06 4OSA5	Hey Hey Renee	LB	4	117	1	4	45	43½	41½	5	Landeros C	30.30

OFF AT 2:20 Start Good. Won driving. Track fast.

TIME :22², :45¹, :57², 1:09⁴ (:22.40, :45.35, :57.40, 1:09.86)

$2 Mutuel Prices:

2 - LADY GAMER	17.00	4.40	2.40
5 - GETBACK TIME		2.20	2.10
4 - VACA CITY FLYER			2.20

$1 EXACTA 2-5 PAID $16.50 $2 QUINELLA 2-5 PAID $8.60

B. f, (Jan), by Game Plan - Mariah Reyna , by Far North . Trainer Sadler John W. Bred by Clark A Hansen & Janine Rae Hansen (Cal).

Lady Gamer popped the gate, made the lead through a comfortable opening quarter of 22⅖, and was strong for the drive. Getback Time ran her race, but Lady Gamer had in fact improved since she last raced. She was gone, gate to wire at $17.

A fresh horse, a vulnerable second choice, and two throw-outs in a five-horse field made Lady Gamer a reasonable alternative to the favorite. Had she started at 3–1 instead of higher, Lady Gamer would not have been worth a gamble. But her chances were miscalculated.

Lady Gamer was an unknown, facing only one identifiable contender. It did not make her a sure winner, but it did make her a reasonable wager. Know the parameters, identify the favorites, and assess their vulnerability. And if they are vulnerable, then find a longshot. It does sound easy.

The thing is, opportunities pop up unexpectedly. You never know when a horse will be mistakenly priced, even in the rain. Wet weather is usually a good time to find cover, literally and figuratively. Field sizes decrease, while opportunities narrow.

Once upon a time, horses trained by Doug O'Neill offered consistent value. That was before O'Neill became so recognizable, and a reasonable case often could be made for a marginal O'Neill-trained starter. It was cold and wet at Santa Anita on January 7, 2005. It was a Friday, and the card was forgettable.

With only two races left to run, many horseplayers had already begun turning their attention to the next day of racing. But as the eight-horse field for the feature race came onto the track, one thing was clear—bettors could only see one horse.

Frankelstein
Own: King Edward

Dk. b or b. g. 3 (Mar)
Sire: Bertrando (Skywalker) $12,500
Dam: Anachristina (Slewpy)
Br: Edward Nahem (Cal)
Tr: Jones Martin F(0 0 0 0 .00) 2004:(0 0 .00)

Life	3	1	0	2	$37,740	94	D.Fst	3	1	0	2	$37,740	94
2004	3	1	0	2	$37,740	94	Wet(407)	0	0	0	0	$0	–
							Synth	0	0	0	0	$0	–
2003	0	M	0	0	$0	–	Turf(340)	0	0	0	0	$0	–
Sa	1	0	0	1	$4,680	85	Dst(400)	1	1	0	0	$28,860	93

24Nov04–8Hol	fst	1 1/16	:23^1	:46^2	1:10^3	1:43^2	3↑ Md Sp Wt 44k	**93**	1	1½	1½	1^{hd}	2^{hd}	1^1	Smith M E	**LB**120	*1.30	84– 20	Frnkelstein120^1 KeepOnPunching120^7 Precis120½	Rail,headed,came back	7
3Nov04–4Hol	fst	6½f	:21^3	:43^4	1:07^4	1:14^1	3↑ [S]Md Sp Wt 36k	**94**	8	1	3^1	3^{1½}	3^{2½}	3^3	Smith M E	**LB**121	4.50	99– 08	*Greg's Gold*121½ *McNasty*121^{2½} *Frankelstein*121^6	Outside,best rest	8
30ct04–9SA	fst	6f	:21^3	:44^3	:56^3	1:09^2	3↑ [S]Md Sp Wt 41k	**85**	11	2	9^{5½}	8^{6½}	4^{3¾}	3^{5¾}	Smith M E	**LB**121	42.20	85– 16	*WatchOverMe*121^{1¼} *Greg'sGold*121^{4½} Frankelstein121^3	4wd,5wd,bested rest	12

WORKS: Dec17 **Hol 5f fst 1:02^3 H** *12/12* Dec11 **Hol 4f fst :48^4 H** *19/46* Nov17 **Hol 4f fst :49^3 H** *15/22* Oct31 **Hol 3f fst :36^4 H** *4/14* Oct23 **Hol 5f fst 1:00^3 H** *16/68* Oct15 **Hol 4f fst :50^2 H** *15/19*

TRAINER: +180Days(28 .25 $3.53) Turf/Dirt(34 .21 $1.76) Dirt(186 .12 $1.16) Routes(154 .13 $1.47) Stakes(39 .10 $1.24)

Frankelstein was favored at even money based on a last-start maiden win in which he earned a 93 Beyer, well within the Cal-bred N1X par. However, he was facing winners for the first time and racing over a "sloppy" track at Santa Anita after winning on "fast" at Hollywood Park. It is an old handicapping adage that still applies—be wary of low-odds runners switching surfaces. Be wary of horses like Frankelstein, the even-money favorite.

At Dawn
Own: La Canada Stable LLC

Dk. b or b. g. 4 (May)
Sire: Robannier (Batonnier) $2,000
Dam: Halo At Dawn (Halo)
Br: PTS Ranch (Cal)

Life	13	1	1	2	$59,884	84	**D.Fst**	4	0	0	1	$3,920	75
2004	3	0	0	1	$3,920	75	**Wet(362)**	0	0	0	0	$0	–
							Synth	0	0	0	0	$0	–
2003	10	1	1	1	$55,964	84	**Turf(314)**	9	1	1	1	$55,964	84
Sa	1	0	0	0	$400	72	**Dst(388)**	2	0	0	1	$3,520	75

19Dec04–7Hol fst 1 1/16 ⊗ :231 :462 1:103 1:423 3↑ Clm 32000(32–28) **75** 1 1hd 1hd 1hd 1hd 34½ Court J K **LB**119 b 15.40 83–10 *Juniper Kris*1191½ Malmaison1193 *At Dawn*1192 Inside duel,held 3rd 7
Previously trained by Bernstein David 2004(as of 10/6): (51 6 3 4 0.12)
6Oct04–7SA fst 1 1/16 :231 :47 1:111 1:442 3↑ [S]Alw 44800N1x **72** 5 76½ 77 76 76½ 77½ Figueroa O **LB**123 b 21.90 75–19 Overkill120¾ MsMintonsExcess118nk PoliticlRhetoric1212 Stumbled start 7
6Sep04–7Dmr fst 6f :213 :433 :56 1:083 3↑ Alw 56724N1x **69** 11 1 1114 1116 1110 1111¾ Puglisi I **LB**123 b 66.50 84–06 *LongRngMssl*1193 GoldnSouvnr119hd OutofthBlSlw1163 Angled in, outrun 11
Previously trained by Lage Armando 2003(as of 11/28): (730 132 133 104 0.18)
28Nov03 2GG gd 1 1/16 Ⓣ :24 :492 1:132 1:441 + 3↑ Alw 33000N1x **78** 7 63 62½ 41½ 4¾ 54¾ Baze R A **LB**118 b 4.70 83–19 ClubFortyOne11821½ CourtsinSession120nk Mirific1203 Fanned 4w, no rally 7
6Nov03–3GG fm 1 1/16 Ⓣ :233 :473 1:12 1:424 + OC 40k/N1x-N **67** 2 52½ 52½ 42 58½ 510¼ Duran F **LB**118 b *1.70 85–09 *ClubFortyOne*1188 GrandpaChn1182 ImSoccerBoy118nk 4wide throughout 6
9Oct03–2BM fm 1 1/16 Ⓣ :232 :471 1:112 1:43 OC 40k/N1x-N **84** 5 33½ 33 32 21 2no Duran F **LB**118 b 1.90 91–09 Obermeister118no At Dawn1182 *Club Forty One*1184 Bid 3w,rallied,missed 5
21Sep03–3BM fm 1 1/16 Ⓣ :214 :451 1:11 1:431 HalfMnBayH68k **81** 3 59 48 31 31½ 32¾ Duran F **LB**113 b 4.10 87–09 BlueBloodBoot1152½ WinningStrips117nk AtDwn1133 Came 3w, missed 2d 5
Previously trained by O'Neill Doug 2003(as of 8/29): (475 81 70 62 0.17)
29Aug03–4Dmr fm 1 1/16 Ⓣ :233 :472 1:112 1:412 Clm 62500(62.5–55) **80** 9 75½ 73¾ 83¾ 86 62¾ Martinez F F **LB**118 b 42.40 91–03 RoylPlc118hd SixNumbrs118nk DrmofDshng1181½ 4wd 2nd turn,outkicked 10
15Aug03–4Dmr fm 1 1/16 Ⓣ :231 :47 1:112 1:414 Clm 50000(50–45) **78** 8 95¾ 86¼ 34 34 45 Martinez F F **LB**118 b 8.80 87–07 *DsrtBoom*1181 TwoNghtStnd1183½ BstYorBbbl118½ 4wd,angled in,lost 3rd 10
25Jly03–2Dmr fm 1 1/16 Ⓣ :242 :484 1:121 1:42 Alw 58000N1x **74** 4 42 64½ 76 77½ 78 Baze T C **LB**119 b 24.90 83–08 Helms Deep119¾ *Ashoka*119nk Strength Within1171½ Rank,stdied 5-1/2 7
4Jly03–5Hol fm 1 1/16 Ⓣ :23 :46 1:101 1:41 3↑ [S]Alw 51000N1x **78** 1 77¾ 88¾ 85¾ 75¾ 66¼ Martinez F F **LB**115 b 9.80 85–08 Sharp Boi119nk *Tizawinner*1211 Roberto's Show1193 Washy,steadied 3/16 9
30May03–6Hol fm 1 1/16 Ⓣ :23 :464 1:112 1:431 3↑ [S]Md Sp Wt 51k **81** 3 53 52¾ 32 21½ 11 Martinez F F **LB**116 b 26.40 80–20 AtDwn1161 Excellentchrcter123no SkywlkerRd116½ Off slow,rallied,game 8
17May03–6Hol fst 6f :213 :44 :564 1:094 3↑ [S]Md Sp Wt 44k **52** 4 13 1320 1316 1313 1010¼ Martinez F F **LB**117 91.80 81–07 *JustParkin*1173 SlvjeMemo123½ *SunCityBrdley*117no Off slow,imp position 13
WORKS: Dec11 **Hol 6f fst 1:144 H** *12/23* Dec1 **SLR 6f fst 1:131 H** *1/1* Nov24 **SLR 5f fst 1:014 H** *5/9* Nov18 **SLR 4f fst :484 H** *2/8* Nov13 **SLR 3f fst :38 H** *8/9* Oct1 **SA 4f fst :484 H** *15/29*
TRAINER: +180Days(15 .13 $1.35) Dirt(278 .13 $1.33) Routes(182 .15 $1.67) Stakes(22 .23 $4.45)

Meanwhile, At Dawn was making his second start after a layoff, and his second start since he transferred to O'Neill. Three weeks earlier, At Dawn set a contested pace against $32,000 claimers, battled to midstretch, and finished third. It was a respectable effort that received a low figure. Perhaps the 75 Beyer that At Dawn earned was one reason he was being ignored.

At Dawn represented a timeless class "angle"—dropping in company after a competitive effort against tougher. Any horse that has been competitive against tougher must be considered as a possible contender when he faces easier.

At Dawn had faced open company, $32,000 claiming, in his comeback race. Now, in the sloppy-track race January 7, he was dropping to face California-breds, nonwinners of one race other than maiden, claiming, or starter.

His form was acceptable, he fit on class, and he had proven himself adaptable to difference pace scenarios. The only thing At Dawn did not have was a good recent speed figure. Longshots are not perfect, and as the field approached the starting gate of the 1 1/16-mile race, At Dawn's odds got higher and higher.

When the field broke from the gate, At Dawn was 33–1, and one furlong into the race it did not look good. At Dawn steadied on the inside while in tight quarters, and he dropped back to next to last. Jockey Felipe Martinez was in a bad spot with At Dawn.

Then a funny thing happened. Despite being shuffled out of contention early, At Dawn got into a rhythm. He was still buried inside, but he running into the bridle and into the mud. He loved it out there. At Dawn might not win, but he was not going to surrender, either. At the quarter pole, he had two horses beat. But he was still trying to run.

Martinez, a fearless rider who has since retired, stayed cool as At Dawn cut the corner into the lane. He was in contention, and by the time he reached the furlong marker he was less than a length and a half from the lead. But he was still trapped on the rail, and steadying.

In deep stretch, the pacesetter drifted out slightly, just enough for Martinez to push At Dawn up into a small opening between the front-runner and the rail. "Get through, Felipe!" I yelled, violating the no-cheering-in-the-press-box rule.

At Dawn dove through inside, made the lead in the shadow of the wire, and won by a length at $68.40.

SEVENTH RACE
Santa Anita
JANUARY 7, 2005

1 1/16 MILES. ALLOWANCE . Purse $52,000 (plus $1,200 Other Sources) FOR CALIFORNIA BRED FOUR YEAR OLDS AND UPWARD WHICH HAVE NEVER WON $7,500 ONCE OTHER THAN MAIDEN, CLAIMING OR STARTER OR WHICH HAVE NEVER WON TWO RACES. Weight, 122 lbs. Non-winners Of A Race Other Than Maiden, Claiming Or Starter At A Mile Or Over Allowed 3 lbs. A Race Other Than Claiming, Or Starter At A Mile Or Over Allowed 5 lbs.

Value of Race: $53,200 Winner $31,200; second $10,400; third $6,240; fourth $3,120; fifth $1,040; sixth $400; seventh $400; eighth $400.
Mutuel Pool $279,116.00 Exacta Pool $206,288.00 Trifecta Pool $220,086.00 Superfecta Pool $97,859.00 Quinella Pool $15,497.00

Last Raced	Horse	M/Eqt. A. Wt	PP	St	1/4	1/2	3/4	Str	Fin	Jockey	Odds $1
19Dec04 7Hol3	At Dawn	LB bf 5 119	2	3	74 1/2	74	61	41	11	Martinez F F	33.20
10Dec04 7Hol11	Cielo Blincoe	LB bf 4 117	4	4	41 1/2	3hd	22	1hd	22	Pedroza M A	21.70
24Nov04 8Hol1	Frankelstein	LB f 4 119	1	1	62 1/2	52 1/2	3hd	21	32	Smith M E	1.00
24Nov04 3Hol2	Ms Mintons Excess	LB b 4 117	6	8	8	8	8	66	41	Espinoza V	2.80
12Dec04 4Hol1	My Onomatopoeia	LB 4 118	3	2	31 1/2	41 1/2	42	5hd	52	Atkinson P	15.10
18Nov04 3Hol1	J J Jake	LB f 4 114	5	6	1hd	1hd	1hd	3hd	618 1/2	Cohen D7	7.60
14Nov04 3Hol1	Tangmalangaloo	LB 4 117	8	7	5 1/2	6 1/2	7 1/2	7	7	Flores D R	7.60
16Dec04 5Hol1	Budget Surplus	LB f 4 119	7	5	21	21 1/2	51	—	—	Baze T C	13.50

OFF AT 4:12 Start Good. Won driving. Track sloppy.

TIME :223, :463, 1:122, 1:394, 1:463 (:22.70, :46.73, 1:12.51, 1:39.85, 1:46.63)

$2 Mutuel Prices:

3 – AT DAWN	68.40	30.00	9.20
5 – CIELO BLINCOE		20.80	7.60
2 – FRANKELSTEIN			2.80

$1 EXACTA 3–5 PAID $313.40 $1 TRIFECTA 3–5–2 PAID $1,728.40
$1 SUPERFECTA 3–5–2–7 PAID $6,468.40 $2 QUINELLA 3–5 PAID $245.80

Dk. b or br. g, (May), by Robannier – Halo At Dawn , by Halo . Trainer O'Neill Doug. Bred by P T S Ranch (Cal).

AT DAWN settled off the rail then angled in on the backstretch, came out into the stretch, steadied when blocked off heels in midstretch, angled in and rallied gamely along the rail to prove best. CIELO BLINCOE between foes early, stalked outside a rival, bid three deep into the second turn, continued outside a foe, gained a short lead in the stretch but could not hold off the winner. FRANKELSTEIN chased inside then off the rail leaving the backstretch, advanced three deep on the second turn and into the stretch, reached even terms with the leader in the stretch but settled for the show. MS MINTONS EXCESS unhurried off the rail early, moved up four wide on the second turn and into the stretch and bested the others. MY ONOMATOPOEIA saved ground stalking the pace, came out a bit in the stretch, steadied off heels in midstretch, came out again and lacked the needed response. J J JAKE had good early speed and dueled a bit off the rail then inside, came just off the fence in the stretch and weakened. TANGMALANGALOO five wide early, chased three deep on the first turn then outside a rival, angled in on the second turn and gave way. BUDGET SURPLUS pulled his way along four wide early, pressed the pace outside a rival then between foes into the second turn, steadied early on that turn, drifted out into the stretch, was pulled up but walked off.

Owners– 1, P T S Ranch LLC; 2, Bell Richard A; 3, King Edward Racing Stable; 4, Vessels Stallion Farm LLC; 5, Higman Daniel and Jerome and Smith; 6, Young Stephen A; 7, Kelly J Garvan and Yearsley Nancy; 8, Harris Farms Inc

Trainers– 1, O'Neill Doug; 2, Blincoe Thomas H; 3, Jones Martin F; 4, Marlow Mike; 5, Hendricks Dan L; 6, Aguirre Paul G; 7, Headley Bruce; 8, Jones Martin F

Scratched– Black Horse Money (29Aug04 5Dmr2)

$2 Daily Double (5–3) Paid $143.60 ; Daily Double Pool $23,384 .
$1 Pick Three (9–3/5/6–3) Paid $1,665.60 ; Pick Three Pool $37,798 .

Few would have picked At Dawn as a likely winner prior to the January 7 card. But few expected him to start at 33–1, either. A class-dropper in good form, slipping through the parimutuel cracks because his figures were not fast enough, made January 2005 a memorable month just on one single race.

You just never know when opportunity will present itself.

All you really need is to apply the fundamentals—condition, class, speed, and pace—to a big field anywhere.

Before wagering on the unknown, a bettor must first acknowledge the known. This is where the nuts and bolts of handicapping apply. And the first question a bettor should ask is, which of the known runners are qualified to win? Basic stuff.

When the known element lacks sufficient ability (as measured by par), shippers have a better chance. This happened in the Grade 1 Bing Crosby Handicap in July 2007 at Del Mar.

The six-furlong Bing Crosby is often the toughest six-furlong sprint on the West Coast. But the 2007 field was a weak lot. The Beyer par for the Bing Crosby is 112. The contenders on speed would recently have earned a figure within five points, 107 or higher.

The favorites for the 2007 Bing Crosby were suspect. E Z Warrior was a 3-year-old facing older, making his first start in six months with a lifetime best Beyer of 97. Battle Won, Greg's Gold, and Bordonaro were back-class sprinters whose recent figures were below par.

None of the "logical contenders" fit the parameters, the favorites were the same old bunch, and they were vulnerable.

The Bing Crosby was begging to be won by a new shooter. In Summation, shipping to California for high-percentage trainer Christophe Clement, supplied the knockout blow, winning by a nose at $18.

It was a prime opportunity, a race with vulnerable favorites and an "unknown" shipper. Only three weeks later, the same thing happened in the $1 million Pacific Classic. Lava Man, whose up-front running style placed him at a severe disadvantage racing on the closer-friendly Polytrack, started as the 6–5 favorite.

The winner? A ship-in longshot named Student Council ($48.80). He was a new face in a weak race.

Winning on a longshot means backing the unknown. Because who really knows if a first-time starter will be up to the challenge? Who knows if an import has sufficient ability?

You don't, and that is why they sometimes start at high prices. But if you can know that the familiar faces cannot run, and that they are slow and vulnerable, that is when you can put yourself in the driver's seat.

Know what it takes to win a race. Identify the contenders. Assess their vulnerability. And if they are suspect, go shopping for a price.

You never know what you might find, or when you might find it. You never know when you can become a genius again.

LITFIN

ON FINDING VULNERABLE FAVORITES

Dave Litfin

6

YOU CAN'T HAVE A meaningful discussion about longshots without talking about favorites. Speaking as a public handicapper who mass-produces winners for a living, there is nothing like a good run of chalk to make me feel like a relevant and contributing member of society.

For years, "How many winners?" was the standard greeting from my kids when I got home from work. (I'm often told I don't go to "work," I go to the racetrack, but that's beside the point.) Before too long, the little tykes understood that three winners was about average. If I said "six" they squealed with delight, happily oblivious to the fact that my biggest price might've been $5.20. When the number was "one" they groaned and went right back to whatever they were doing. Those days usually made me feel like groaning too, but every so often that solitary winner paid more than a handful of favorites and I felt pretty good about showing a flat-bet profit for the card. But the kids didn't quite grasp this aspect of the parimutuel game: "Pick more winners tomorrow," they would say, and that was that.

Here is one thing about racetrack life I've never been able to figure out: Everyone I know swears they have never in their lives bet a horse that was under 4–1, so who the heck is betting all this money on the favorites?

It must be the silent majority. The fact remains that no one does a better job of picking winners than the general public. Take it from someone who's been in the trenches for nearly two decades: It's impossible to outpick John Q. Punter. In the eight-year period from 1999 through 2006, my annual performance in terms of winner selection ranged from a high of 32.6 percent to a low of 28.8 percent, and the most common result (four times) was slightly above 30 percent. Picking every race on the card two days in advance is a tough way to make an easy living.

Favorites annually do better than I did in my best year, winning at a "universal average" of approximately 33 percent—or so horseplayers have been told for generations. But as I watched a never-ending parade of short-priced winners in New York the past few years (at Saratoga, the so-called Graveyard of Favorites, the chalk won anywhere from 38 percent to 41 percent of the time from 2003 through 2005), I sensed they were winning at more than 33 percent.

A little research courtesy of *Daily Racing Form*'s information-technology whiz Duane Burke and a massive database showed that to be true. From 491,327 races run in North America from 2000 through 2006, favorites won 168,474, a rate of 34.3 percent. On the New York circuit (Aqueduct, Belmont Park, and Saratoga) they won 5,929 of 17,194 races, or 34.5 percent.

A categorical breakdown of favorites overall and in New York during the same period has significant ramifications:

Dirt—all tracks:	34.5%
Dirt—New York:	35.5%
Turf—all tracks:	31.6%
Turf—New York:	30.2%

No real surprise. Turf races attract larger, more competitive fields.

Dirt sprint—all tracks:	34.7%
Dirt sprint—New York:	35.5%
Dirt route—all tracks:	33.6%
Dirt route—New York:	35.2%

Favorites in sprints win a bit more often than favorites in routes, a phenomenon likely due to the fact that routes are more susceptible to false paces.

Turf sprint—all tracks:	32.6%
Turf sprint—New York:	30.1%

New York began carding turf sprints regularly in 2005, so the sample there was only 176 races. Preliminary data suggests bettors in New York are still getting used to them.

Graded stakes—all tracks:	34.8%
Graded stakes—New York:	37.2%

The 37.2 percent for graded stakes in New York is the single highest win rate I came across, and simply a combination of the top-grade horses running in small fields.

Allowance—all tracks:	36%
Allowance—New York:	36.5%

Like stakes races, allowances draw better-quality horses and not that many of them in an average field. (Open allowance races have become more difficult to fill in New York.)

Maiden special weight—all tracks:	36.9%
Maiden special weight—New York:	36.2%

Nationally, nonclaiming maiden favorites are among the most reliable in the game, and New York's maidens aren't far behind.

Maiden claiming—all tracks:	34.9%
Maiden claiming—New York:	33.9%

I thought the maiden claimers would win at a lower rate than this, but evidently the crowd has a good handle on them. Another contributing factor could be a large number of hopeless throw-outs in a typical field.

Older claiming—all tracks:	32.1%
Older claiming—New York:	29.5%

Older claiming favorites are slightly below average nationwide, but they have been well below average in New York, where form reversals coinciding with trainer changes occur on a regular basis.

Three-year-old claiming—all tracks:	32.2%
Three-year-old claiming—New York:	28.4%

The sophomore claimers in New York were the single most unreliable favorites in this study, often making for good "spread" situations in multirace exotics.

Males—all tracks:	34.2%
Males—New York:	33.8%
Females—all tracks:	34.5%
Females—New York:	35.4%

I've often heard people say they don't bet on fillies and mares because they're less reliable, but they are in fact just as reliable as the boys, and more so in New York.

Two-year-olds—all tracks:	36.3%
Two-year-olds—New York:	35.8%

A common perception is that 2-year-old races are a crapshoot, but the data shows that is hardly the case.

Overall, in terms of return on investment (ROI), nonclaiming maidens were the only group to top $1.70, producing a return of $1.72 for each $2 invested; nonclaiming maidens in New York produced the highest ROI in the study at $1.76.

The ROI totals were generally clustered around $1.65. The lowest totals occurred in 3-year-old claiming races, where the overall ROI was $1.60, and New York's was $1.48, by far the lowest ROI of all categories.

Facts are facts: Favorites win more often than they used to. Moreover, data from

Equibase Company shows that the national average $2 win payoff has fallen from $12.65 in 1996 to $12.18 in 2006.

The reasons for more winning favorites and lower average win payoff are fairly straightforward:

- Average field size is down. In 1985, an average of 9.03 horses started in 75,687 races. In 2006, the average field was down to 8.14 horses in 56,902 races.
- There is an ever-deepening sea of information available, including expanded past performances, ground-breaking literature, speed figures, and computer-generated statistics and handicapping programs.
- The fan base of casual horseplayers has been steadily eroded by competition from casinos, racinos, lotteries, and myriad entertainment/gambling options such as on-line poker.

With all the advantages enjoyed by the modern horseplayer, one would think the favorite would win far more often than it did back in the day. Happily, a portion of what goes on between the rails is random and unexplainable; there are limits to what is knowable beforehand, and sometimes even in hindsight all we can do is shrug our shoulders and move on to the next race. There are no absolutes, only probabilities—and no man or machine can figure out exactly what those probabilities are.

More frequently than we would like, perfectly logical horses slip through the cracks due to our fallible powers of collective perception. Consider the case of War Emblem in the 2002 Kentucky Derby:

Going into the Derby, War Emblem was the "top fig" off his most recent effort. He had run such a huge race in the Illinois Derby that he was purchased for a seven-figure sum and given over to Bob Baffert, who had scored Derby wins with Silver Charm and Real Quiet in 1997 and 1998. But it was difficult to imagine War Emblem getting loose on the lead again, because the image of the previous year's Derby winner was still fresh in the minds of handicappers.

Monarchos had settled far behind some of the fastest fractions in Derby history, and had blown by in the stretch to win going away. The image of this race was still fresh in the minds of the jockeys, too, so no one went with War Emblem as he loped along setting a measured pace, and the rest is history.

It's been my experience that four main avenues lead to the promised land of winners who pay big balloons:

1. You make a case for the horse for whatever reason(s).
2. You can make a case against the favorite.
3. In a competitive race, the odds make the decision for you.
4. The race contains lightly raced horses who might improve.

Combinations of any or all of the above factors occur regularly. Examples of the first two situations occurred at Gulfstream Park in the 2007 Sunshine Millions about an hour apart:

1. YOU MAKE A CASE FOR THE HORSE FOR WHATEVER REASON(S)

Shaggy Mane seemed like a filly you could really build a solid case for in the Filly and Mare Sprint. After winning a California-bred $8,000 maiden claimer in her second lifetime start, she had been claimed out of a win for $12,500 and had risen meteorically through the ranks in Northern California to win two allowance conditions and a $90,000 stakes with blazing early speed.

Shaggy Mane's five-race win streak came to a screeching halt as the 2–1 favorite in the Cat's Cradle, a long sprint at 7 ½ furlongs in which she led through typically fast fractions and weakened late. Not only did the distance of the Cat's Cradle work against her, but the race was run during the inaugural Cushion Track meet at Hollywood Park, and the synthetic surface was proving to be much more conducive to stalkers and stretch-runners than most conventional dirt tracks.

Freshened since the Cat's Cradle, but training all the while over the stamina-building Cushion Track at her Hollywood base, Shaggy Mane projected as the main speed over a conventional dirt track at Gulfstream that was often a conveyor belt to the winner's circle for such types, and the result was a lengthy score with a new top Beyer Speed Figure at better than 8–1.

When handicapping sprints on conventional dirt tracks, a good starting-off point involves trying to identify the probable pacesetter. When speedballs like Shaggy Mane come off subpar performances in unfavorable circumstances but things look more favorable today, the result is often a return to top form.

2. YOU CAN MAKE A CASE AGAINST THE FAVORITE

In the Sunshine Millions Classic two races later, few handicappers could have zeroed in on McCann's Mojave and bet him to win at nearly 34–1, but for multirace exotic purposes the vulnerability of the first two betting choices signaled it might be a good spot to cast as wide a net as possible:

McCann's Mojave
Own: Willman Mike

B. h. 7 (Feb)
Sire: Memo*Chi (Mocito Guapo*Arg) $6,000
Dam: Joni U. Bar (Nordic Prince)
Br: Alix Nikki Hunt & Mike Willman (Cal)
Tr: Specht Steven(1 1 0 0 1.00) 2006:(243 41 .17)

Life	24	10	2	0	$1,174,955	108	D.Fst	14	7	1	0	$990,730	106
2007	1	1	0	0	$550,000	103	Wet(363)	4	2	1	0	$111,570	108
							Synth	0	0	0	0	$0	-
2006	7	2	0	0	$69,575	99	Turf(247)	6	1	0	0	$72,655	105
Gp	1	1	0	0	$550,000	103	Dst(327)	4	2	0	0	$700,000	104

27Jan07-10GP fst 1⅛ :464 1:104 1:362 1:494 4↑ⓇSunMilClsc1000k 103 8 21 2½ 2hd 12 1¾ Alvarado F T L122 33.90 89-15 McCann's Mojave122¾ SummerBook122½ *SilverWagon*122nk All out, lasted 12
26Dec06-8GG slyS 1$\frac{1}{16}$:231 :462 1:094 1:422 3↑UnionSqr60k 98 6 21½ 21½ 21 1½ 12 Alvarado F T LB117 2.00 91-17 *McCann's Mojave*1172 *Dr. Einstein*115no My Creed118½ Prssd outside, drvng 6
10Dec06-3BM slyS 1 :221 :451 1:092 1:35 3↑OC 80k/N$Y-N 99 2 32½ 22 21½ 2hd 1no Alvarado F T LB119 2.70 96-18 *McCnnsMojve*119no DrEinstein1182 RisethBluff1205½ Stlkd 2w,battled,nod 5
24Nov06-7BM gd 1 Ⓣ :234 :484 1:13 1:38 3↑JohnHenryH57k 79 5 54 53 63¾ 87¾ 78 Frazier R L LB117 16.50 77-20 Railroad1152 Clipperdown1171¼ Capitano116nk 2w into lane, no rally 11
Previously trained by Gallagher Patrick 2006(as of 10/28): (347 54 43 54 0.16)
28Oct06-8OSA fm 1 Ⓣ :232 :473 1:11 1:343 3↑ⓈCalCpMileH175k 89 1 1½ 1½ 1hd 21 63 Valdivia J Jr LB118 4.90 87-10 EpicPower119hd RunningFre116no SuprStrut119no Inside duel,weakened 9
1Oct06-8OSA fm *6½f Ⓣ :221 :434 1:054 1:114 3↑ⓇBlueJayWay60k 92 5 2 31½ 3½ 3½ 42 Valdivia J Jr LB118 5.50 94-06 Osidy118hd Deputy Kris120¾ Railroad1241¼ Bid,dueled,wkened late 8
19Mar06-8SA fm 1 Ⓣ :23 :464 1:104 1:35 4↑ⓈCrystlWtrH113k 86 11 2hd 2hd 2½ 41½ 63 Desormeaux K J LB119 3.60 85-12 SuperStrut119no *MrWolverine*116no UncleDnny1182 Pressed, 2wd, wkened 11
28Jan06-6SA fst 1⅛ :444 1:083 1:354 1:494 4↑ⓇSunMilClsc1000k 87 12 3½ 32½ 33 33½ 67 Valdivia J Jr LB122 15.70 80-20 *Lava Man*1222¼ Whos Crying Now1221½ Texcess1202 3wd,off rail,wkened 12
10Dec05-8Hol fst 1⅛ :46 1:102 1:36 1:494 3↑NtvDivrH-G3 86 6 43 54¼ 62¾ 65¼ 87½ Valdivia J Jr LB118 3.50 78-14 Trotamondo117½ Bully Hayes116½ Spellbinder1161¼ 4 wide, weakened 10
6Nov05-9OSA fst 1⅛ :462 1:094 1:344 1:481 3↑ⓈCalCpClscH250k 104 2 11 11 11 1hd 11 Valdivia J Jr LB118 3.30 93-13 McCnnsMojve1181 DesertBoom1221 Cheroot1132½ Drifted out bit,gamely 8
8Oct05-6OSA fst 6f :21 :431 :554 1:084 3↑AncTtlBC-G1 95 3 3 2hd 2½ 21 52½ Gomez G K LB124 b 3.10 91-10 CaptainSquire124½ Znzibr124no IndinCountry1241 Dueled btwn,weakened 7
21Aug05-4Dmr fst 7f :214 :44 1:09 1:213 3↑OBrinBCH-G2 76 4 3 4¾ 52½ 76 711½ Valdivia J Jr LB117 6.30 85-07 Imprlsm117¾ Gotghostofchnc1142½ *TstofPrds*115¾ Btwn,angled in,wkened 8
3Jly05-9Hol fst 7f :214 :434 1:074 1:204 3↑TrplBndH-G1 106 11 2 31½ 51¾ 21½ 22 ♦Valdivia J Jr LB117 5.70 97-09 UnfrlthFlg1172 DHBrnthWds112 DHMcCnnsMj1172 Stalked 3wd,held 2nd 13
11Jun05-8Hol fst 7½f :22 :442 1:08 1:271 3↑AckAckH91k 105 2 2 2hd 2hd 1½ 11½ Valdivia J Jr LB116 8.80 99-06 McCann's Mojave1161½ Congrats1212½ St Averil1152 Dueled,led,gamely 8
WORKS: Jan18 GG 1 fst 1:372 H *1/1* Jan9 GG 5f fst 1:024 H *11/14* Jan3 GG 4f fst :492 H *9/38* ●Dec20 GG 5f fst :573 H *1/37* ●Dec5 GG 5f fst :591 H *1/7* Nov16 GG 6f fst 1:133 H *2/4*
TRAINER: 31-60Days(87 .22 $3.29) Dirt(329 .17 $2.07) Routes(142 .21 $2.85) Stakes(14 .29 $6.14)

Sweetnorthernsaint
Own: Balsamo Joseph J. and Theos, Ted

Dk. b or b. g. 4 (Mar)
Sire: Sweetsouthernsaint (Saint Ballado) $3,500
Dam: Ice Beauty (Waquoit)
Br: Eduardo Azpurua (Fla)
Tr: Trombetta Michael J(26 7 3 3 .27) 2006:(312 78 .25)

Life	12	5	1	2	$692,300	109	D.Fst	10	4	1	2	$662,300	109
2007	2	0	0	1	$61,000	102	Wet(321)	1	1	0	0	$30,000	104
							Synth	0	0	0	0	$0	-
2006	8	5	1	1	$630,100	109	Turf(249)	1	0	0	0	$0	12
Gp	2	0	0	1	$61,000	102	Dst(369)	2	1	0	0	$350,000	109

27Jan07-10GP fst 1⅛ :464 1:104 1:362 1:494 4↑ⓇSunMilClsc1000k 97 12 31½ 31 1hd 22 53½ Dominguez R A L120 fb *1.90 85-15 McCannsMojave122¾ SummerBook122½ *SilverWagon*122nk Vied, gave way 12
6Jan07-9GP fst 1 :232 :454 1:084 1:334 4↑HalHopeH-G3 102 3 21 21 2hd 2hd 31 Dominguez R A L120 fb *1.20 100-04 Chtin115hd SirGreeley1181 Sweetnorthrnsint1204 Led into str, weakened 10
11Nov06-8Del fst 1$\frac{1}{16}$:233 :464 1:103 1:43 Odessa51k 104 3 2½ 2hd 2hd 1½ 18¼ Dominguez R A L122 b *.20 98-18 Swtnorthrnsnt1228¼ MstrfDsstr12219¼ Brrytm116 Ridden out to draw off 3
19Oct06-8Lrl fst 7f :232 :471 1:113 1:233 3↑OC 32k/N3x-N 85 3 2 1½ 11½ 12½ 14½ Dominguez R A L117 b *.05 92-13 *Swtnorthrnsnt*1174½ TrrfcTom12066¼ Itsllbotyolo120 Bobbled st,3wd,easily 3
20May06-12Pim fst 1$\frac{3}{16}$:463 1:101 1:353 1:543 Preaknes-G1 105 7 2½ 31 2½ 23½ 25¼ Desormeaux K J L126 b 8.40 97-06 *Bernrdini*1265¼ *Swetnorthrnsint*1266 HmingwysKy1264 2-3w,led 1/4,shied in 9
6May06-10CD fst 1¼ :46 1:104 1:37 2:011 KyDerby-G1 92 11 118¾ 53½ 44 46 713 Desormeaux K J L126 b *5.50 86-04 Barbaro1266½ BluegrassCt1262 Steppenwolfer1261 Bmp strt,steadied,tire 20
8Apr06-7Haw fst 1⅛ :48 1:13 1:373 1:494 IllDerby-G2 109 10 21 21 2½ 12 19¼ Desormeaux K J L122 b *1.30 96-27 Swtnorthrnsint1229¼ MistrTristr1221 CustoBlv1221½ Challenged, drew off 10
18Mar06-9Aqu fst 1$\frac{1}{16}$ ⊡ :231 :473 1:121 1:43 Gotham-G3 104 10 34½ 32 31½ 33½ 3¾ Desormeaux K J L116 b 4.30 94-11 LikeNow116nk KeyedEntry120½ *Sweetnorthernsint*116½ 3 wide trip, gamely 10
4Feb06-9Lrl slyS 1 :233 :48 1:14 1:383 MiraclWood57k 104 1 1½ 12½ 14 13½ 110 Pino M G L116 b *.30 90-21 Swetnorthrnsint11610 VgsPly1183 SirrQuorum116¾ Stp slw,drivng off ins 10
7Jan06-6Aqu fst 6f ⊡ :223 :453 :571 1:09 Md Sp Wt 43k 102 3 2 11½ 12½ 15½ 17¾ Dominguez R A L120 b 2.25 94-14 *Sweetnorthrnsint*1207¾ ThirHGos1155¼ ClrthWy120hd Drew off when ready 9
21Dec05-1Lrl fst 6f :231 :472 :593 1:112 Md 40000(40-35) 81 6 2 13½ 15 17 116 Karamanos H A L122 b 1.70 85-22 Ⓓ*Swtnorthrnsnt*12216 MdwJmpr1224 Sknmrnk1224½ Bore in start,rddn out 7
Disqualified and placed 4th Previously trained by Azpurua Leo Sr 2005(as of 8/1): (19 2 3 1 0.11)
1Aug05-1Cnl fm 1 Ⓣ :223 :462 1:122 1:382 Md Sp Wt 26k 12 12 1332 1431 1431 1428 1224 VanHassel C L122 25.70 63-08 Vegas Play122no King County122¾ Perfect Cruise1222 Fractious prerace 14
WORKS: Jan21 GP 4f fst :49 B *10/29* ●Dec31 GP 4f fst :464 B *1/33* ●Dec23 GP 5f fst :583 H *1/15* ●Dec12 Lrl 5f fst 1:012 B *1/9* Dec5 Lrl 4f fst :502 B *6/8* ●Nov1 Lrl 5f fst 1:002 B *1/15*
TRAINER: 61-180Days(25 .20 $1.64) Dirt(418 .28 $2.15) Routes(141 .23 $1.55) Stakes(93 .27 $1.80)

When Sweetnorthernsaint drew post 12, it should have been readily apparent he would not be marching into the winner's circle. Gulfstream's main track, reconfigured in 2005, is now 1⅛ miles around, and races at that distance feature a very short run to the clubhouse turn. Not a single horse at the meet had won a route race farther out than post 7, and Sweetnorthernsaint had exactly the sort of pace-pressing style that assured a wide trip to oblivion. At odds of less than 2–1, and coming off a loss at 6–5 in the Hal's Hope in which he wore front bandages for the first time, Sweetnorthernsaint was the type of horse longshot bettors should have been salivating to bet against.

Silver Wagon had made his reputation as a deep-closing sprinter who was at his absolute best going seven furlongs. His lifetime top Beyer Speed Figure of 111 had come about under perfect circumstances in the Sport Page, when he inhaled a suicidal pace duel on a track strongly biased to outside closers. The lure of an inflated $1 million purse induced Rick Dutrow Jr. to try and stretch the 6-year-old out to 1⅛ miles, and the gray ran admirably to finish third. Even so, when a horse is up against it in terms of such a basic handicapping factor as distance, it is not much of a bargain at 3–1 in a full field of 12.

The benefit of 20–20 hindsight shows that as 33–1 shots go, McCann's Mojave was anything but a hopeless case, with nine wins from 23 starts going into the Sunshine Millions, including a front-running score in the 2005 edition of the $250,000 Cal Cup Classic and two straight wins in the slop to close out 2006 in Northern California.

After putting away Sweetnorthernsaint, who had to be used early just to get to the first turn three-wide, McCann's Mojave held off a last-ditch bid from Summer Book, who was an even bigger price at 42–1.

No one's saying that coming up with this exacta was easy (it paid $1,168 for $1), but anyone willing to poke holes in the first two choices at least was starting out on the right track because the race had bust-out potential.

A best-case scenario occurs when you can make a case for an overlooked horse *and* make a case against the favorite, as happened on Belmont Stakes Day 2007 in the $200,000, Grade 2 True North Handicap:

6 **Belmont Park** *6 Furlongs* (1:07³) **TruNrthH–G2** 29th Running of THE TRUE NORTH HANDICAP. Grade II. Purse $200,000 A Handicap For Three Year Olds And Upward. By subscription of $200 each, which should accompany the nomination; $1,000 to pass the entry box; $1,000 to start. The purse to be divided 60% to the winner, 20% to second, 10% to third, 5% to fourth, 3% to fifth and 2% divided equally among remaining finishers. Closed Saturday, May 26, 2007 with 21 Nominations.

Coupled – Dashboard Drummer and Suave Jazz

[Past performance chart for Council Member and Dashboard Drummer]

3 Keyed Entry
Own: Starlight St&Saylor P&Lucarelli D
Blue — Blue, Yellow Circle And 'Jl,' Yellow
VELAZQUEZ J R (102 22 17 14 .22) 2007: (456 104 .23)

Dk. b or br c. 4 (Mar) FTKJUL04 $145,000
Sire: Honour and Glory (Relaunch) $12,500
Dam: Ava Knowsthecode (Cryptoclearance)
Br: Oakbrook Farm (Ky)
Tr: Pletcher Todd A(38 13 5 9 .34) 2007:(450 125 .28)

L 116

Life	9	4	1	1	$319,000	110	D.Fst	7	3	1	0	$154,000	105
2007	2	1	0	0	$69,000	105	Wet(358)	2	1	0	1	$165,000	110
2006	6	2	1	1	$227,800	110	Synth	0	0	0	0	$0	–
							Turf(246)	0	0	0	0	$0	–
Bel	1	0	0	0	$3,000	50	Dst(344)	1	1	0	0	$19,800	96

7Apr07–9Aqu fst 7f :213 :441 1:09 1:212 3↑CarterH-G1 84 6 2 2hd 2½ 53¼ 511¾ Velazquez J R L116 *2.00 82–09 Silver Wagon1181¼ *Diabolical*117¾ Ah Day115¾ Vied 3 wide, tired 6
Previously trained by Sciametta Anthony Jr 2006: (24 4 7 1 0.17)
3Feb07–3GP fst 6½f :221 :442 1:09 1:153 4↑DpMnstrH-G3 105 1 2 11 1½ 12½ 15 Velazquez J R L113 1.90 94–06 Keyed Entry1135 Sir Greeley1171¾ Nar113nk Inside, drew off 5
Previously trained by Pletcher Todd A 2006(as of 7/4): (617 179 127 71 0.29)
4Jly06–9Bel fst 1$\frac{1}{16}$:231 :462 1:1141:451 Dwyer-G2 50 1 11 11 45 525 634¾ Velazquez J R L119 *1.80 39–26 StrongContender1157¾ DocChny1155¾ DStoops115¾ Ducked in start, tired 6
6May06–10CD fst 1¼ :46 1:104 1:37 2:011 KyDerby-G1 51 3 12 11½ 137½ 1818 2040¾ Valenzuela P A L126 28.80 58–04 Barbaro1266½ BluegrssCt1262 Steppenwolfer1261 Duck in bmp strt,faded 20
8Apr06–8Aqu sly^s 1⅛ :4611:11 1:3721:512 WoodMem-G1 96 3 11½ 11½ 1½ 2hd 32 Prado E S L123 f *.95 76–23 Bob and John1231½ Jazil123½ Keyed Entry1236 Weakened inside late 9
18Mar06–9Aqu fst 1$\frac{1}{16}$ ⊡ :231 :473 1:1211:43 Gotham-G3 105 7 23 21½ 21 21½ 2nk Prado E S L120 1.65 95–11 LikeNow116nk KeyedEntry120½ *Sweetnorthrnsint*116½ Game finish outside 10
4Feb06–8GP sly^s 7½f :22 :44 1:0731:27 Hutchesn-G2 110 1 7 11 11 11½ 11¼ Velazquez J R L116 2.70 107–04 KeyedEntry1161¼ *FirstSamuri*12216 ExpressNews118½ Step slow st, 4 wide 7
7Jan06–3GP fst 6f :222 :452 :5711:092 Alw 33000N1x 96 9 2 1hd 1½ 12 15½ Velazquez J R L118 6.00 97–05 *KeyedEntry*1185½ MinersLamp118½ FormalAppeal1206¼ Off rail, drew away 10
10Jly05–1Mth fst 5f :222 :462 :583 Md Sp Wt 37k 61 7 6 2hd 2hd 2hd 1¾ Decarlo C P L119 6.80 88–10 *Keyed Entry*119¾ *Awfully Smart*119hd Wilentz1193¼ Pressed,proved best 7

WORKS: Jun3 Bel 4f fst :481 B *2/57* May21 Bel 4f fst :472 B *9/69* ●May5 Bel 4f fst :471 H *1/45* Apr19 Bel 4f fst :482 H *14/36* ●Mar24 PBD 5f gd :59 B *1/11* ●Mar17 PBD 4f gd :48 B *1/5*
TRAINER: 61-180Days(174 .22 $1.48) Dirt(978 .28 $1.72) Sprint(550 .23 $1.54) GrdStk(347 .24 $1.63) J/T 2006-07 BEL(103 .28 $1.58) J/T 2006-07(571 .29 $1.82)

4 Will He Shine
Own: Pugliese Savario Wexler Marc
Yellow — Blue, White Stars, Red And White
PRADO E S (126 22 30 19 .17) 2007: (594 117 .20)

Ch. h. 5 (Mar)
Sire: Silver Deputy (Deputy Minister) $30,000
Dam: Christmas Star (Star de Naskra)
Br: Verne H Winchell (Ky)
Tr: Romans Dale(11 0 2 1 .00) 2007:(235 35 .15)

L 116

Life	11	4	2	3	$189,241	106	D.Fst	7	4	1	1	$147,375	106
2007	4	0	0	2	$51,066	103	Wet(370)	2	0	1	1	$36,297	93
2006	4	2	1	1	$77,460	106	Synth	1	0	0	1	$5,000	86
							Turf(260)	1	0	0	0	$569	85
Bel	1	1	0	0	$28,200	98	Dst(378)	4	3	0	1	$91,755	106

27May07–8Bel fm 6f Ⓣ :213 :441 :5541:073 3↑Jaipur-G3 85 5 8 712 75¾ 85¼ 96¾ Prado E S L118 4.10 90–07 Ecclesiastic1182¾ SlutetheCount120no Weigeli1201½ Bumped start, inside 9
5May07–5CD gd^s 7f :23 :453 1:0921:221 4↑CD-G2 93 1 5 4¾ 42 34½ 34½ Desormeaux K J L118 3.70 86–09 Saint Anddan1202 Ah Day1182½ Will He Shine118¾ Angled 4w,no kick late 6
19Feb07–9Lrl fst 7f :231 :461 1:1021:23 3↑GnGrgBCH-G2 103 7 6 73½ 31½ 22½ 43 Desormeaux K J L116 3.90 94–19 *Silver Wagon*1201¼ Ah Day1171½ *Ryan's for Real*114nk Shuffled back start 9
27Jan07–11TP fst 6½f ◈ :221 :453 1:164 4↑Forego50k 86 2 7 61¾ 44 22 23 Mena M L120 1.40 89–18 BddyGtEvn1163 ⒹWllHShn120¼ Otrgslyfnny116¾ Steadied, hit opponent 8
Disqualified and placed third
17Dec06–8Aqu fst 6f ⊡ :22 :442 :5621:091 3↑GravesdH-G3 98 4 4 21 21½ 22 31 Dominguez R A L115 *1.70 92–13 *BshopCortHll*1171 SntnStrngs115hd WllHShn1154¼ Stalked outside,gamely 9
27Oct06–3Aqu fst 6f :223 :452 :57 1:09 3↑OC 75k/N3x-N 106 1 4 1hd 1½ 13 13¾ Desormeaux K J L122 2.40 93–28 Will He Shine1223¾ *First Word*119hd Callmetony119hd Speed inside, clear 5
5Oct06–3Bel fst 6½f :223 :451 1:0921:154 3↑Alw 46060N2x 98 5 5 32½ 2hd 13½ 13½ Desormeaux K J L119 3.60 93–18 *Will HeShine*1193½ Tuffertiger1191¾ *RiverCityRebel*1122¼ 3 wide move, clear 5
5Sep06–7Del sly^s 5½f :22 :46 :5831:05 3↑Alw 44300N2x 84 6 6 65 53½ 41½ 2¾ Rose J L119 *2.30 91–13 PowerbyLeigh116¾ *WillHShin*1192 Mtorologist116½ Angled out 5w, gaining 6
Previously trained by Pletcher Todd A 2005(as of 10/30): (883 206 147 119 0.23)
30Oct05–7CD fst 6f :213 :444 :5641:092 3↑Alw 49400N1x 93 6 6 52¼ 1hd 12½ 11½ Bejarano R L121 *2.50 94–12 WllHShn1211½ CrftyBrutus1172½ Outrgouslyfunny1191¾ Bmp start,driving 12
30Sep05–1Med fst 6f :22 :441 :5611:084 3↑Md Sp Wt 34k 88 4 5 31½ 41½ 3½ 1nk Velazquez J R L119 *1.50 96–05 *Will He Shine*119nk *My True*119hd *Eslan*1221¾ Split rivals, driving 7
Previously trained by Walden W Elliott 2005(as of 5/21): (69 13 14 8 0.19)
21May05–10CD fst 5½f :223 :46 :5741:04 3↑Md Sp Wt 46k 71 4 6 54½ 55 34½ 25¾ Day P L118 *1.40 89–12 ColonelMtt1185¾ *WillHeShine*1182¼ Friendsturnedfos124nk Hit rail 1/2pole 8

WORKS: Apr20 CD 4f fst :483 B *10/51* Apr1 CD 4f fst :494 B *5/7* ●Mar22 CD 4f fst :483 B *1/5*
TRAINER: Turf/Dirt(54 .11 $1.01) Dirt(520 .18 $1.61) Sprint(486 .17 $1.67) GrdStk(65 .09 $1.12) J/T 2006-07 BEL(13 .23 $2.62) J/T 2006-07(32 .19 $2.32)

5 Bordonaro
Own: Carrillo Fred W&Cassella Daniel A
Green — White, Blue And Green Hoop, Blue And
MIGLIORE R (—) 2007: (467 68 .15)

Ch. g. 6 (Apr)
Sire: Memo*Chi (Mocito Guapo*Arg) $6,000
Dam: Miss Excitement (Rajab)
Br: Fred Carrillo & Daniel A Cassella (Cal)
Tr: Spawr Bill(—) 2007:(92 16 .17)

L 122

Life	15	10	1	1	$876,794	119	D.Fst	14	9	1	1	$830,774	119
2007	2	1	0	1	$126,000	102	Wet(392)	0	0	0	0	$0	–
2006	5	3	1	0	$543,630	119	Synth	0	0	0	0	$0	–
							Turf(261)	1	1	0	0	$46,020	95
Bel	0	0	0	0	$0	–	Dst(388)	13	8	1	1	$819,374	119

13Apr07–10OP fst 6f :22 :451 :57 1:09 4↑CtFltSpH-G3 102 5 1 1½ 1hd 11 1½ Migliore R L121 *.40 98–14 Bordonaro121½ Semaphore Man1151½ Off Duty116no Pace, resilient late 6
27Jan07–4SA fst 6f :212 :44 :5521:08 4↑ⓇSunMilSprn300k 100 6 3 22½ 2hd 21 34¾ Migliore R LB122 *1.10 94–09 *SmokeyStover*1213¼ ProudTowrToo1221½ *Bordonro*1224 Bid btwn,best rest 8
4Nov06–6CD fst 6f :212 :442 :5611:084 3↑BCSprint-G1 104 6 3 2hd 3nk 21½ 44¼ Valenzuela P A L126 4.10 88–09 *Thor'sEcho*1264 *FriendlyIsland*126½ NightmareAffair126hd Dueled rail, tired 14
7Oct06–9OSA fst 6f :212 :434 :5521:074 3↑AncTtlBC-G1 119 6 1 11 1½ 11½ 11 Valenzuela P A LB124 *.40 100–14 Bordonaro1241 *ThorsEcho*1245¾ JunglePrince1241¾ Angled in, held gamely 6
30Jly06–8Dmr fst 6f :213 :44 :56 1:083 3↑BCrosbyH-G1 104 5 3 31 3nk 2½ 2½ Solis A LB120 *.80 95–13 Pure as Gold113½ *Bordonaro*120hd Battle Won1148¾ Hit w/ foe's whip 1/8 6
13Apr06–10OP fst 6f :213 :441 :5611:083 3↑CtFltSpH-G3 115 6 1 1hd 2hd 1½ 11¼ Valenzuela P A L122 *.40 100–14 Bordonaro1221¼ *FriendlyIslnd*1155 SemphoreMn1151¼ Edged away off rail 7
28Jan06–6GP fst 6f :212 :433 :5521:082 4↑ⓇSunMilSprn300k 106 6 3 3½ 2hd 11 1¾ Valenzuela P A L122 *1.50 102–02 *Bordonaro*122¾ Tacirring1221½ Bushwacker121no All out, prevailed 13
3Dec05–3Hol fst 6f :213 :434 :5521:08 3↑VOUndrwd-G3 115 3 1 11½ 12½ 13½ 13 Valenzuela P A LB120 2.20 97–10 *Bordonaro*1203 Turnbolt1201¾ Captain Squire1249¼ Speed,angled in,clear 4
6Nov05–11OSA fst 6f :212 :44 :5531:08 3↑ⓈCalCpStSpH50k 111 3 5 11 11½ 13 12½ Gomez G K LB120 *1.00 98–03 *Bordonaro*1202½ Hello Fame118no Stalking Tiger1154¼ Speed,clear,driving 9
7Sep05–3Dmr fst 6f :212 :44 :5611:084 3↑ⓇPirtsBntyH87k 93 5 4 3½ 3½ 2hd 42 Gomez G K LB115 2.50 93–05 IndinCountry115¾ Aryoutlkintom1191¼ Smoochr116no 3 wide, lost 3rd late 8
24Aug05–5Dmr fm 5f Ⓣ :212 :434 :553 3↑OC 40k/N1x-N 95 3 7 2hd 2½ 1hd 1¾ Gomez G K LB124 *1.70 97–03 Bordonaro124¾ Trail Mix124hd Zayed124½ Hopped bit start,game 8
30Jly05–9Dmr fst 6f :213 :441 :5541:081 3↑ⓈOC 25k/N1x-N 103 10 3 3nk 1hd 11½ 1¾ Gomez G K LB122 *3.10 98–12 *Bordonaro*122¾ ExcessTempttions1202 Scottsbluff1203½ Dueled,clear,held 11

WORKS: Jun1 Hol ◈5f fst 1:00 H *3/37* May26 Hol ◈5f fst 1:001 H *5/61* May18 Hol ◈3f fst :363 H *5/18* Apr30 Hol ◈4f fst :484 H *22/62* Apr6 SA 4f fst :503 B *21/27* Apr1 SA 6f fst 1:12 B *2/25*
TRAINER: 31-60Days(93 .15 $1.20) WonLastStart(46 .24 $2.00) Dirt(213 .14 $1.32) Sprint(178 .12 $1.23) GrdStk(5 .60 $1.68) J/T 2006-07(47 .19 $2.63)

6 Sir Five Star
Own: King H Gus
Black — White, Red Yoke And Star, Blue Sleeves
LUZZI M J (103 11 9 11 .11) 2007: (470 71 .15)

Ch. c. 3 (Apr) KEESEP05 $40,000
Sire: Five Star Day (Carson City) $20,000
Dam: Sir Harriett (Sir Harry Lewis)
Br: Robert W Sanford (Ky)
Tr: Sanders Jamie(—) 2007:(115 2 .02)

L 110

Life	15	5	4	3	$223,446	90	D.Fst	12	3	4	3	$175,620	85
2007	5	1	1	2	$53,576	90	Wet(423)	2	2	0	0	$45,000	90
2006	10	4	3	1	$169,870	81	Synth	1	0	0	0	$2,826	75
							Turf(217)	0	0	0	0	$0	–
Bel	0	0	0	0	$0	–	Dst(410)	7	2	1	2	$83,526	90

Previously trained by Asmussen Steven M 2007(as of 5/4): (701 147 133 99 0.21)
4May07–5AP fst 6f ◈ :24 :471 :5841:104 ShckyGreen47k 75 3 4 2½ 32 21½ 41¾ Emigh C A L122 *2.40 – – PirateSaint1161½ FrontCourt116nk *Thtslottbull*116hd Second flight, evenly 7
21Apr07–8PrM fst 6f :22 :444 :5641:092 GoldnCrcle53k 85 3 5 55 53½ 2hd 31¾ Doocy T T LB122 *1.00 90–11 BigliSmllworld1191½ *CrimsonKingCt*119nk SirFvStr1226¼ 3 wide rally, hung 6
31Mar07–11Sun fst 6f :222 :451 :5711:093 DyLghtSprt50k 81 7 1 62¾ 41¼ 1½ 2nk Murphy B G L122 *.10 93–15 Folsum122nk Sir Five Star1222 Game of Skill1161 Gained lead, denied 9
24Feb07–9OP gd 6f :211 :451 :5741:113 MntnValley50k 90 5 3 41¼ 4nk 13½ 18½ Shepherd J L122 12.50 85–19 SirFiveStar1228½ IrishDreamer1191¾ TheHitmn1171 4-w, kicked well clear 6
19Jan07–8OP fst 5½f :22 :46 :58 1:042 Dixieland50k 79 10 1 73¼ 63½ 22½ 34 Shepherd J L122 10.80 92–15 Irish Dreamer1153¼ *First Regent*115¾ *Sir Five Star*122½ 4-w 1/4, evenly late 11
Previously trained by Blasi Scott 2006(as of 12/31): (998 198 171 158 0.20)
31Dec06–10Sun fst 6½f :214 :451 1:1041:173 RAllisonFu136k 76 9 1 2½ 1½ 13 1nk Murphy B G L120 *1.60 83–16 SirFiveStr120nk SongofNvrone1203½ TheZipstr120¾ Vied 2w,clear,held on 9
16Dec06–6Sun fst 6½f :232 :454 1:12 1:172 Alw 8500NC 77 7 1 3½ 2hd 2½ 2½ Murphy B G L120 *.50 83–15 The Zipster120½ *Sir Five Star*1204¼ Folsum1201¾ Vied,4wd turn,2nd best 7
25Nov06–8Hou fst 6f :213 :44 :5641:103 BntflHrvst45k 63 6 4 41½ 31 2hd 34½ Jacinto J L122 *1.20 89–13 Jack Grant119no Tytus1174¼ Sir Five Star1221 Fixed shoe, 4w, empty 6
3Nov06–8DeD fst 1 :231 :48 1:1311:383 JeanLafitt144k 80 2 21 22 32 34½ 310 Meche D J L118 3.10 88–09 ⒹGoPoppaFooze1189 *TortugaStraits*1151 SirFiveStr1186¾ Finished evenly 6
Awarded second purse money
4Sep06–8RP fst 6f :213 :442 :5631:093 ClevrTrevr50k 80 7 2 21 2½ 1hd 11 Murphy B G L119 4.00 96–08 Sir Five Star1191 *Hadacure*1213 *Proud Leader*116¾ Kept to task 9
12Aug06–6RP fst 5½f :22 :454 :5731:034 OC 75k/N1x-N 81 6 1 1hd 2½ 12 17 Murphy B G L116 *1.20 98–12 *Sir Five Star*1167 Command Cat1161 Catit1151½ Drew off 8
23Jly06–9LS fst 6f :212 :441 :5721:11 MddlgrndBC60k 67 2 7 63 62¼ 62 63 Murphy B G L121 3.70 81–15 *DrmofAngls*121nk Spoonrism121nk AxlPgsus1211 Lacked needed response 9

WORKS: ●Jun1 Kee ◈4f fst :462 H *1/43* May25 Kee ◈6f fst 1:123 H *1/3* May18 Kee ◈5f fst 1:004 B *16/27* Apr15 CD 4f my :511 B *6/6* Mar27 Sun 4f fst :49 B *26/47* Mar19 OP 5f fst 1:031 B *22/40*
TRAINER: 1stW/Tm(16 .00 $0.00) 31-60Days(55 .04 $2.61) Dirt(163 .04 $1.22) Sprint(163 .05 $0.84) GrdStk(23 .00 $0.00)

1a Suave Jazz Own: Dubb M&Grant S&Joscelyn R
Red Yellow, Pink Circle And Rose, Pink Cuffs
DOMINGUEZ R A (—) 2007: (530 142 .27)

B. g. 4 (Apr)
Sire: Suave Prospect (Fortunate Prospect) $6,500
Dam: Cavite Starlet (Jazzing Around)
Br: Farnsworth Farms (Fla)
Tr: Houghton Dove P(4 0 0 1 .00) 2007:(67 17 .25)

L 114

Life 23 9 5 3 $265,986 108 | D.Fst 22 9 5 3 $264,486 108
2007 4 3 1 0 $89,876 108 | Wet(369) 1 0 0 0 $1,500 49
2006 11 4 3 3 $142,100 86 | Synth 0 0 0 0 $0 -
Bel 2 1 1 0 $35,000 86 | Turf(207) 0 0 0 0 $0 -
Dst(371) 15 8 4 3 $237,706 108

Previously trained by Dutrow Anthony W 2007(as of 5/19): (226 62 40 36 0.27)
19May07-4Pim fst 6f :231 :462 :5821:104 3+OC 32k/n3x-N 93 6 6 5¾ 5¼ 2hd 1½ Pino M G L120 b *.80 93-05 SvJzz120½ KnownBckHom1221½ CopprtonKd120nk Ratd,angld 4-5w,drvng 9
28Apr07-7Del fst 6f :22 :44 :5611:082 3+OC 50k/n3x-N 108 3 2 2½ 21 2½ 2¾ Pino M G L121 b 1.90 96-11 Fleet Valid119¾ *SuaveJazz*1216½ WarTempo1212¾ Jumped shadow,2nd best 5
24Mar07-6Aqu fst 6f ⊡ :224 :46 :5741:10 4+OC 75k/n1x 93 3 5 41 41½ 1hd 11 Dominguez R A L123 b *1.65 94-09 SuaveJazz1231 TrilingTwelve1231¾ RockyBlue118nk Came wide, clear late 7
27Jan07-7Aqu fst 6f ⊡ :22 :443 :57 1:10 4+OC 75k/n1x 90 8 3 45 43½ 42½ 11¼ Pino M G L123 b *2.50 94-06 *Suave Jazz*1231¼ Bold Mon118½ *Coppertone Kid*118no Came wide, clear late 10
30Dec06-1Aqu fst 6f ⊡ :221 :45 :5711:102 3+OC 75k/n1x 86 3 4 41½ 42¼ 1hd 1½ Dominguez R A L119 b *1.50e 87-16 *Suave Jazz*119½ Lord Snowdon1191 Coppertone Kid119hd Rallied 3 wide 7
19Sep06-7Del fst 6f :224 :462 :5831:111 3+OC 35k/n2x-N 85 6 3 21½ 2½ 2½ 12 Rose J L120 b 2.50 85-17 *Suave Jazz*1202 Fabled116¾ Dancehall Fever118¾ Long drive, shook free 6
26Aug06-6Del fst 6f :223 :461 :5841:111 3+Alw 42900n1x 85 3 4 41¼ 3½ 1hd 1nk Rose J L117 b *1.30 85-16 *Suave Jazz*117nk Colonial Silver1233½ The Boiler1193½ Traffic turn, driving 8
3Aug06-7Sar fst 6½f :22 :451 1:1111:181 Clm 87500(100-75) 65 4 5 3nk 42 48 411 Velazquez J R L119 b 3.05 72-17 Gribldi1151¾ *TmtoGrowUp*1194½ Glttrnmporrdg1204¾ Stumbled badly start 6
9Jly06-3Bel fst 6f :224 :46 :5741:101 3+Alw 50000s 86 6 4 32½ 21 21½ 1½ Velazquez J R L116 b 2.85 87-14 Suave Jazz116½ Time to Grow Up117¾ *Bold Mon*1161½ 3 wide move, in time 7
25Jun06-6Mth fst 6f :221 :442 :5621:091 3+Alw 35000s 86 3 4 41¼ 42 32 2½ Lopez C C L117 b 1.70 93-13 Prince Tutta117½ *Suave Jazz*117hd *Podgy*1174 Chased,dueled for 2nd 5
13May06-7Bel fst 6f :214 :444 :57 1:094 3+Alw 50000s 84 1 5 63¾ 43 22½ 22 Prado E S L116 *2.35 87-10 *It'saPerfectDay*1222 SuaveJazz1162½ Propulsion122hd Inside move, gamely 8
26Apr06-1Aqu fst 6f :223 :453 :5741:11 Alw 45000s 76 2 4 53 56 56½ 31½ Santos J A L118 2.20 81-18 Florida Thunder118no Bold Mon1181½ Suave Jazz1181½ Going well late 7

WORKS: Apr7 Aqu 5f fst 1:021 B *24/36* ●Mar20 Aqu ⊡ 3f fst :364 B *1/5* ●Mar12 Aqu ⊡ 4f fst :484 B *1/6*
TRAINER: 1stW/Trn(46 .20 $1.68) Dirt(199 .21 $2.03) Sprint(157 .21 $2.44) J/T 2006-07(11 .27 $1.62)

7 Joey P. Own: Petrini John
Orange Brown, Yellow Circle And 'Jp,' Yellow
BRAVO J (14 3 3 3 .21) 2007: (338 52 .15)

Dk. b or br g. 5 (Mar)
Sire: Close Up (Capote) $3,000
Dam: Luckey Lipco (Luckey Jin Beau)
Br: John Petrini (NJ)
Tr: Perkins Ben W Jr(2 0 1 1 .00) 2007:(59 8 .14)

L 116

Life 17 10 0 1 $458,599 108 | D.Fst 16 10 0 1 $455,799 108
2007 2 1 0 0 $38,800 102 | Wet(213) 1 0 0 0 $2,800 89
2006 5 2 0 0 $95,050 104 | Synth 0 0 0 0 $0 -
Bel 1 0 0 0 $1,408 77 | Turf(244*) 0 0 0 0 $0 -
Dst(266) 11 7 0 0 $340,070 108

12May07-9Mth fst 5½f :213 :441 :5541:014 3+Decathlon60k 102 4 2 32 31 11 12 Bravo J L117 *1.40 105-06 Joey P.1172 Slam Bammy1172 Who's the Cowboy117¾ Stalked three wide 5
5Apr07-8Aqu gd 6f :22 :443 :5611:083 4+OC 100k/c-N 89 1 5 41¾ 42 41¾ 41¾ Garcia Alan L119 3.55 97-12 Pavo1171¼ Yes Yes Yes117no Kazoo114½ Steadied inside turn 5
4Sep06-9Mth fst 6f :214 :441 :5611:09 3+Icecapade140k 74 7 1 1hd 2hd 55½ 711¼ Garcia Alan L123 4.00 84-11 *WhostheCowboy*1231 *Weigelia*1191¼ *GoldandRoses*1232¼ Vied for lead, wknd 7
6Aug06-10Mth fst 6f :221 :443 :5631:084 3+TeddyDrone115k 89 1 6 31 2hd 2hd 45½ Bravo J L122 *2.40 90-09 *WhostheCowboy*1221¼ Kazoo1202¾ MaddysLion1201½ Drifted out,gave way 7
15Jly06-11Crc fst 6f :213 :441 :5641:102 3+SmlSprtH-G2 93 3 5 11 1hd 2hd 65½ Bravo J L115 9.80 88-08 Nightmare Affair1152 *Pomeroy*1161¼ Weigelia1151 Inside, gave way 13
18Jun06-7Mth fst 5½f :22 :444 :5631:031 3+Longfellow70k 104 1 5 11½ 11½ 13 12¼ Bravo J L121 1.40 99-13 Joey P.1212¼ Slam Bammy1214 Kazoo1213¾ Off inside,coasted 5
27May06-3Mth fst 6f :22 :451 :5721:104 3+ⓈJJReillyH60k 84 4 2 2hd 1½ 11½ 1½ Bravo J L123 *.60 86-16 *JoeyP*123½ *QuietDespertion*1141 KrkorumTuxdo1132¾ Btwn early,clear,drvg 5
Previously trained by Costa Frank 2005(as of 11/12): (131 14 10 11 0.11)
12Nov05-8Med fst 6f :213 :433 :5531:081 3+Rutgers70k 104 4 5 3½ 31½ 21 14½ Bravo J L121 *1.10e 99-10 *JoeyP*1214½ *SlmBmmy*1191 TwoDownAutomtic123nk 3wd bid,up 1/8,drw off 9
29Oct05-1Bel fst 7f :222 :443 1:0931:23 3+SportPgH-G3 77 3 8 89¾ 810 86¾ 710¼ Bravo J L113 5.90 75-10 Gotghostofchnc118½ CptinSquir121nk WildTl1161 Bumped start, steadied 9
17Sep05-5Mth fst 6f :221 :443 :5611:082 3+ⓈFrndlyLvrH100k 108 6 2 31½ 21 21 11¼ Bravo J L119 1.30 98-12 JoeyP1191¼ WrsProspect1223 SecondCollection113½ Stalked 3 wide, clear 6
7Aug05-12Mth fst 1⅛ :4731:113 1:3631:494 HsklInvH-G1 72 6 31 21 2½ 58 721¾ Gryder A T L116 13.60 67-16 RomnRuler1191¼ *SunKing*1192 PrkAvenuBll1181 3deep,aim btwn,weakend 7
22Jly05-5Mth fst 1 :232 :47 1:1111:363 3+OC 75k/n1m-N 91 3 11½ 1½ 1hd 1½ 3¾ Chavez J F L118 *.50 92-16 Ricardo A118¾ Play Bingo118no Joey P.118½ Saved ground, yielded 4

WORKS: Jun3 Mth 4f fst :504 B *35/48* ●May26 Mth 5f fst :59 H *1/30* ●May5 Mth 4f fst :46 H *1/62* Apr14 Bel tr.t 5f fst 1:01 B *7/59* Mar30 Bel tr.t 5f fst 1:011 B *10/21* ●Mar24 Bel tr.t 5f fst :594 H *1/19*
TRAINER: WonLastStart(38 .24 $1.86) Dirt(196 .17 $1.66) Sprint(170 .18 $1.77) GrdStk(7 .29 $3.06) J/T 2006-07(22 .32 $1.66)

The even-money favorite was Bordonaro, whose best races from the previous year would have absolutely buried this field. But Bordonaro was now six years old, and had not run a Bordonaro-like figure since wiring the Ancient Title eight months earlier. He had won Oaklawn's Count Fleet with a Beyer of 115 at 2–5 in 2006, but at the same price a year later he had been hard-pressed to hang on with a figure of only 102—which was also his average from the past three starts.

Be that as it may, a Bordonaro operating at 80 percent efficiency might still be good enough to beat this less than stellar group. Also, he had drawn a favorable position to stalk Keyed Entry, whose best sprints had been at Gulfstream when he was able to shake loose.

An intriguing horse at a price, however, was Will He Shine, who had received a freshening after the General George, a Grade 2 sprint that was probably a bit longer than he prefers. He had been shuffled back at the start that day and raced wide behind Silver Wagon, who had come back to win the Grade 1 Carter Handicap at Aqueduct. His form cycle had begun in May on a sealed drying-out track at Churchill Downs on Kentucky Derby Day, and in a turf sprint three weeks later, both of which were excusable. He had run figures of 106 and 103 in the third start of his two previous form cycles, and a similar effort today gave him a decent chance to knock off Bordonaro.

Had I known Bordonaro would come onto the track wearing front bandages for the first time, thus confirming my suspicions that his best races were behind him, Will He Shine would've been my top selection. But there's no way to know that beforehand.

Instead of getting a clean stalking trip just off Keyed Entry, Bordonaro was carried out to the parking lot when Keyed Entry bore out on the turn, which allowed Will He Shine to come through a big opening on the inside.

SIXTH RACE
Belmont
JUNE 9, 2007

6 FURLONGS. (1.07³) 29TH RUNNING OF THE TRUE NORTH HANDICAP. Grade II. Purse $200,000 A HANDICAP FOR THREE YEAR OLDS AND UPWARD. By subscription of $200 each, which should accompany the nomination; $1,000 to pass the entry box; $1,000 to start. The purse to be divided 60% to the winner, 20% to second, 10% to third, 5% to fourth, 3% to fifth and 2% divided equally among remaining finishers. A trophy will be presented to the winning owner. Closed Saturday, May 26, 2007 with 21 Nominations.

Value of Race: $200,000 Winner $120,000; second $40,000; third $20,000; fourth $10,000; fifth $6,000; sixth $1,334; seventh $1,334; eighth $1,332. Mutuel Pool $1,387,841.00 Exacta Pool $1,068,147.00 Trifecta Pool $809,237.00

Last Raced	Horse	M/Eqt.	A.	Wt	PP	St	¼	½	Str	Fin	Jockey	Odds $1
27May07 8Bel⁹	Will He Shine	L	5	116	4	6	3½	1²	1⁵	1¹¾	Prado E S	10.40
19May07 4Pim¹	Suave Jazz	L b	4	115	7	8	7hd	7½	6hd	2½	Dominguez R A	a- 7.70
12May07 8Bel²	DashboardDrummer	L f	6	116	2	1	5½	51½	5hd	3nk	Velasquez C	a- 7.70
10May07 8Bel¹	Council Member	L	5	116	1	4	8	6½	7⁵	4¾	Gomez G K	4.30
4May07 5AP⁴	Sir Five Star	L	3	114	6	7	61½	4³	41½	51¾	Luzzi M J	44.75
12May07 9Mth¹	Joey P.	L	5	116	8	5	4²	2hd	2½	6³	Bravo J	10.70
13Apr07 10OP¹	Bordonaro	L f	6	122	5	3	2½	32½	3¹	7⁸	Migliore R	1.00
7Apr07 9Aqu⁵	Keyed Entry	L	4	116	3	2	1½	8	8	8	Velazquez J R	4.30

a–Coupled: Suave Jazz and Dashboard Drummer.

OFF AT 3:09 Start Good. Won driving. Track fast.
TIME :22, :44¹, :56, 1:08³ (:22.07, :44.38, :56.16, 1:08.70)

$2 Mutuel Prices:

4 – WILL HE SHINE	22.80	9.50	6.10
1A– SUAVE JAZZ(a–entry)		7.10	6.70
1 – DASHBOARD DRUMMER(a–entry)		7.10	6.70

$2 EXACTA 4-1 PAID $135.00 $2 TRIFECTA 4-1-2 PAID $577.00

Ch. h, (Mar), by Silver Deputy – Christmas Star , by Star de Naskra . Trainer Romans Dale. Bred by Verne H Winchell (Ky).

WILL HE SHINE showed good speed along the inside, enjoyed a clear journey on the rail, drew away when roused in upper stretch and was kept to the task to remain clear to the finish. SUAVE JAZZ was outrun early, came wide into the stretch and finished well outside to earn the place. DASHBOARD DRUMMER was outrun early, raced inside and finished well while between rivals in the stretch. COUNCIL MEMBER was in hand while outrun early, raced inside and finished well on the rail. SIR FIVE STAR was outrun early, came wide into the stretch and offered a mild rally outside. JOEY P. was carried out into the turn, angled in on the turn, chased the pace and tired in the stretch. BORDONARO showed good speed outside, was carried wide on the turn and tired in the stretch. KEYED ENTRY flashed good speed from the start, bore out on the turn then bore out badly in the stretch.

Owners– 1, Pugliese Savario and Wexler Marc; 2, Dubb Michael Grant Stuart and Joscelyn Robert; 3, Dubb Michael Goldfarb Sanford J Joscelyn Robert and Brafman Larry N; 4, Godolphin Racing LLC; 5, King H Gus; 6, Petrini John; 7, Carrillo Fred and Cassella Daniel A; 8, Starlight Stable LLC Saylor Paul H and Lucarelli Donald J

Trainers– 1, Romans Dale; 2, Houghton Dove P; 3, Houghton Dove P; 4, bin Suroor Saeed; 5, Sanders Jamie; 6, Perkins Ben W Jr; 7, Spawr Bill; 8, Pletcher Todd A

$2 Pick Three (3-7-4) Paid $332.00 ; Pick Three Pool $266,731.

Handicappers should always be on the lookout for what writer Dick Jerardi has dubbed Reputation Induced Phenomena horses—or "RIP" horses. These are horses that have received a lot of attention in the media, and they are usually overbet regardless of whether they're still in top form or entered in a particularly good spot.

On closing day of Keeneland's 2007 spring meet, value-oriented bettors had a special interest in the Elkhorn Stakes, because the three-turn marathon marked the turf debut of 2006 Belmont Stakes winner Jazil.

8 Ascertain (Ire) — Pink
Own: Mrs S K Johnston Jr Gene Voss and Pau
Orange, Brown 'J', Brown Sleeves, Orange
THERIOT H J II (36 2 3 6 .06) 2007: (336 44 .13)

Ch. g. 6 (Apr)
Sire: Intikhab (Red Ransom)
Dam: Self Assured*Ire (Ahonoora*GB)
Br: Darley (Ire)
Tr: O'Callaghan Niall M(8 1 1 1 .12) 2007:(51 6 .12)

L 118

Life	22	6	3	1	$250,232	103	D.Fst	9	1	0	0	$98,375 95
2007	2	1	0	0	$38,080	103	Wet(276*)	1	0	0	0	$0 90
2006	4	1	2	1	$71,380	101	Synth	5	3	1	0	$41,677 88
							Turf(297)	7	2	2	1	$110,180 103
Kee Ⓣ	1	1	0	0	$36,580	103	DstⓉ(310)	1	0	0	1	$22,000 96

7Apr07-7Kee	fm	1⅛ Ⓣ	:50 1:141 1:373 1:493	4↑ Alw 61800c	103	9	2½	2½	1hd	11½	12	Theriot H J II	L118 f	5.50e	87-16	Ascertain1182 Minister's Joy118nk Brilliant1233	Tracked pace,drvg 10
17Mar07-11TP	fst	1⅛ ◈	:452 1:103 1:371 1:50	4↑ TejanoRun50k	88	2	511	418	49½	21	54¾	Mena M	L115 f	*1.20e	86-23	Jade's Revenge1151¾ Sidcup1212 Dynareign115½	4 wide run 2nd turn 11
2Jly06-8AP	fm	1½ Ⓣ	:514 1:163 2:061 2:294	3↑ StrStBCH-G3	96	4	11	2½	2½	3nk	3nk	Hernandez B J Jr	L115	4.90	92-10	Major Rhythm116hd Come On Jazz112nk Ascertain1151¼	No winning bid 8
27May06-9CD	fm	1⅛ Ⓣ	:482 1:12 1:36 1:481	3↑ OC 80k/N$Y-N	98	8	64½	75	74¼	42½	11¾	Hernandez B J Jr	L120	5.00	92-05	Ascertain1201¾ Brickell1201¾ *Ole Faunty*120nk	5w,edged clear late 11
6May06-4CD	fm	1 1/16 Ⓣ	:243 :481 1:121 1:412	3↑ OC 80k/N$Y-N	101	7	3½	32½	31½	2½	2hd	Albarado R J	L120	4.00	99-04	*Rush Bay*120hd *Ascertain*1201¾ Everything to Gain1244	Couldn't get up,4w 8
26Mar06-8GP	fm	1⅛ Ⓣ	:47 1:104 1:344 1:46	4↑ Alw 46000c	98	1	42	43	42½	1hd	2nk	Smith M E	L118	42.10	93-11	Request for Parole118nk Ascertain1182½ Megantic1181½	Just failed 9
11Dec05-12WO	fst	1¾	1:153 1:414 3:014	3↑ ValdictryH140k	73	7	32	32½	69	617	624½	Landry R C	L116	26.60	67-18	*Seattlespectculr*12010¾ **LstAnswer**1181¾ VegsVenture1121¼	Tired final turn 9
4Oct05-9Mnr	fst	1⅛	:473 1:111 1:353 1:481	3↑ Fall75k	55	1	21	22	69	719	731	Melancon L	L118	9.00	59-22	Discreet Hero1246 *Silver Axe*12112 Azucar1092¾	Close for1/2,stop3/8 7
30Jly05-6PrM	fst	1⅛	:50 1:133 1:374 1:50	3↑ PrairiMedH76k	83	2	53½	64	64	65¾	68	Essman D W	LB115	6.70	75-15	*Silver Axe*1191½ Azucar116hd Tricky Mocha115hd	No factor 6
8Jly05-9CD	fst	1 1/16	:24 :471 1:112 1:42	3↑ OC 100k/N$Y-N	72	5	35	47½	55	59½	617¼	Albarado R J	L124	13.10	83-08	Wiggins1203¼ Stockholder1203½ *M B Sea*1241½	4-5w,tired in lane 7
25May05-9CD	fst	1 1/16	:234 :474 1:124 1:434	3↑ OC 80k/N$Y-N	95	1	32½	33	1hd	12½	11½	Albarado R J	L120	7.50	91-12	Ascrtin1201½ LostChrok120hd RivrMountinRd1204¾	Swerved,drift late,drv 7
15Apr05-8Kee	fst	1 1/16	:231 :47 1:12 1:451	4↑ Alw 61440N3X	88	1	78	79½	75¾	54¼	56	Melancon L	L118	20.00	80-25	Go Now118hd Confirmed1201¼ *Big Will*1184½	Empty in drive 10

WORKS: Apr21 Kee ◈ 5f fst 1:002 B *24/33* Apr4 Kee ◈ 4f fst :491 B *22/35* Mar15 Hpt 3f fst :371 B *1/1*
TRAINER: WonLastStart(18 .11 $1.33) Turf(44 .16 $3.35) Routes(110 .10 $1.65) GrdStk(15 .07 $4.77)
J/T 2006-07 KEE(1 1.00 $13.00) J/T 2006-07(1 1.00 $13.00)

12 Jazil — Lime
Own: Shadwell Stable
Blue, White Epaulets, Blue Cap
JARA F (28 1 2 1 .04) 2007: (201 19 .09)

B. c. 4 (Feb) KEESEP04 $725,000
Sire: Seeking the Gold (Mr. Prospector) $125,000
Dam: Better Than Honour (Deputy Minister)
Br: Skara Glen Stables (Ky)
Tr: McLaughlin Kiaran P(19 3 4 1 .16) 2007:(178 45 .25)

L 118

Life	10	2	5	0	$890,532	102	D.Fst	7	2	3	0	$730,645 102
2007	2	0	2	0	$18,315	94	Wet(411)	3	0	2	0	$159,887 97
2006	5	1	2	0	$836,930	102	Synth	0	0	0	0	$0 -
							Turf(281)	0	0	0	0	$0 -
Kee Ⓣ	0	0	0	0	$0	-	DstⓉ(298)	0	0	0	0	$0 -

8Feb07-7GP	fst	1⅛	:473 1:113 1:352 1:48	4↑ OC 60k/N2X-N	90	6	66½	63½	2½	25	29½	Jara F	L120	*.80	88-08	*Corinthian*1209½ Jazil1204 Too Good122½	Bid, no match 7
5Jan07-8Aqu	gd	1 1/16 ⊡	:234 :473 1:121 1:443	4↑ OC 40k/N2X-N	94	6	68½	611	56½	25½	22¼	Jara F	L118	*.45	85-26	*Take the Bluff*1182¼ Jazil1185¾ Admiral's Arch1185¾	Good finish outside 6
10Jun06-11Bel	fst	1½	:471 1:12 2:023 2:274	Belmont-G1	102	8	1210	72¼	1hd	1½	11¼	Jara F	L126	6.20	98-11	Jazil1261¼ *Bluegrass Cat*1262¼ Sunriver1261¼	Hit gate, 6 wide run 12
6May06-10CD	fst	1¼	:46 1:104 1:37 2:011	KyDerby-G1	97	1	2017	1911	178¾	67	49½	•Jara F	L126	24.20	89-04	Barbaro1266½ BluegrassCt1262 Steppenwolfer1261	Swerve in start,empty 20
8Apr06-8Aqu	slyS	1⅛	:461 1:11 1:372 1:512	WoodMem-G1	97	1	813	920	918	37	21½	Jara F	L123	15.70	76-23	Bob and John1231½ Jazil123½ Keyed Entry1236	Coming fast outside 9
4Mar06-10GP	fst	1⅛	:481 1:121 1:36 1:49	FntnOYth-G2	84	4	93¾	85¾	95¾	89	77¼	Velasquez C	L116	24.50	90-02	DCorinthian1161 First Samurai120nk Flashy Bull116½	Failed to menace 10
2Feb06-6GP	fst	1⅛	:482 1:122 1:371 1:493	Alw 33000N1X	86	3	52½	52½	42	2hd	2¾	Velasquez C	L120	7.10	93-06	Corinthian118¾ Jazil1203½ High Blues1184¾	Led into str, outgamed 8
7Dec05-6Aqu	fst	1 1/16 ⊗	:232 :474 1:134 1:472	Md Sp Wt 44k	78	6	66	59	53	36½	1hd	Jara F	L120	*.55e	73-29	Jazil120hd Tasteyville1204 Scots Pine1203¼	Fast finish outside 6
12Nov05-4Aqu	fst	7f	:221 :452 1:104 1:242	Md Sp Wt 43k	77	7	8	1018	1116	63½	2no	Jara F	L120	12.50e	79-19	Steppenwolfer120no *Jazil*1201 Don't Park Now1201½	Fast finish outside 11
23Oct05-4Bel	gd	5½f	:231 :463 :58 1:034	Md Sp Wt 43k	53	5	7	713	814	718	615¾	Jara F	L119	16.00	76-18	*Noonmark*11910¼ Book Bishop1192¼ *Armament*1191¾	Steadied after start 8

WORKS: Apr20 Kee ◈ 5f fst :592 H *6/36* Apr14 Kee ◈ 4f fst :52 B *35/35* Apr6 Kee ◈ 4f fst :48 B *21/69* Mar30 PmM 5f fst 1:013 H *6/18* Mar22 PmM 4f fst :50 B *20/25* Mar9 PmM Ⓣ 4f fm :50 B(d) *7/22*
TRAINER: 61-180Days(68 .26 $3.19) 1stTurf(31 .13 $5.32) Dirt/Turf(44 .16 $5.37) Turf(136 .15 $2.77) Routes(298 .19 $2.41) GrdStk(57 .21 $2.87)
J/T 2006-07 KEE(8 .00 $0.00) J/T 2006-07(164 .19 $2.67)

Jazil had still been eligible for his first-level allowance condition when he came from far back to win a watered-down renewal of the Belmont Stakes that did not include Kentucky Derby winner Barbaro or Preakness winner and eventual 3-year-old champion Bernardini. Nevertheless, Jazil had won "the Test of the Champion," and so whenever he was subsequently in the news he was always referred to as "Belmont Stakes winner Jazil."

Of course, winning a weak running of the Belmont more than 10 months earlier had very little impact on how he might fare in the Elkhorn, but by this point Jazil had become one of those RIP horses that savvy bettors should always try to beat.

Following two comeback starts during the winter in which he had finished a well-beaten second, Jazil had been back to the drawing board again, and was now running in a 12-furlong race first time out in 11 weeks, and running on an unfamiliar surface. To make matters worse, Jazil was drawn on the far outside in a race that featured a short run to the first turn.

Despite it all, Jazil was co-favored through most of the betting with Cloudy's Knight, before eventually going off as the 3–1 second choice.

Meanwhile, Ascertain had recorded the best turf figure in the field, and had done it winning a high-quality allowance from an outside post over the Keeneland turf course during the first week of the meet. That had been Ascertain's first start on turf since the Grade 3 Stars and Stripes Breeders' Cup Handicap at Arlington Park nine months earlier—a performance that indicated the Elkhorn distance was within his scope.

Where the modern-day Thoroughbred is concerned, handicappers are right to be leery about horses coming back in three weeks following a career-top Beyer figure. But it is worth reviewing the fact that turf routers are less susceptible to a regression than dirt sprinters, particularly horses like Ascertain, who have marginally exceeded their previous top figure.

The determining factor is price. At better than 7–1, bettors can live with the fact that horses such as Ascertain might occasionally regress.

NINTH RACE
Keeneland
APRIL 27, 2007

1½ MILES. (Turf) (2.27²) 22ND RUNNING OF THE FIFTH THIRD ELKHORN. Grade III. Purse $200,000 FOR FOUR YEAR OLDS AND UPWARD.

Value of Race: $200,000 Winner $124,000; second $40,000; third $20,000; fourth $10,000; fifth $6,000. Mutuel Pool $570,322.00 Exacta Pool $353,463.00 Trifecta Pool $275,144.00 Superfecta Pool $161,767.00

Last Raced	Horse	M/Eqt.	A.	Wt	PP	¼	½	1	1¼	Str	Fin	Jockey	Odds $1
7Apr07 7Kee¹	Ascertain-Ire	L f	6	118	8	2½	21½	2¹	2²	1½	1ⁿᵏ	Theriot H J II	7.60
6Oct06 8Kee³	Always First-GB	L b	6	118	4	81½	8³	82½	7²	41½	2¾	Gomez G K	6.00
15Apr07 5Kee³	Drilling for Oil	L b	4	118	2	3½	4½	4½	3ʰᵈ	3²	3½	Albarado R J	20.00
10Mar07 7FG⁴	Transduction Gold	L	4	118	7	1¹	1²	1¹	1ʰᵈ	2¹½	4ⁿᵏ	Desormeaux K J	16.00
10Mar07 7FG²	Cloudy's Knight	L	7	118	3	11¹	10¹	10¹	9¹	6¹	5⁶	Leparoux J R	2.80
31Mar07 9GP⁴	Ramazutti	L	5	120	6	5½	5½	5½	5ʰᵈ	7²	6ⁿᵒ	Velazquez J R	9.00
7Apr07 7Kee⁶	Pellegrino-Brz	L	8	118	11	4½	3½	3½	4²	5ʰᵈ	71¾	Bridgmohan S X	48.90
19Mar07 7GP²	Hard Deck		4	118	5	91½	9½	11ʰᵈ	111½	9²	82¾	Castellano J J	43.40
7Apr07 7Kee⁸	Spider Power-Ire	L	4	118	10	12	11ʰᵈ	9ʰᵈ	8ʰᵈ	10²	9¾	Bejarano R	20.80
28Jan07 9GP¹²	Bee Charmer-Ire	L	5	118	1	6½	7¹	7ʰᵈ	6ʰᵈ	8¹	10²	Prado E S	8.70
10Dec06 9WO⁵	Last Answer	L f	7	118	9	7¹	6½	6¹	10ʰᵈ	112½	112¼	Ramsammy E	22.00
8Feb07 7GP²	Jazil	L	4	118	12	10ʰᵈ	12	12	12	12	12	Jara F	3.20

OFF AT 5:17 Start Good. Won driving. Course good.

TIME :26, :51¹, 1:16², 1:41³, 2:06, 2:30² (:26.18, :51.36, 1:16.52, 1:41.66, 2:06.13, 2:30.40)

	8 – ASCERTAIN–IRE.	17.20	9.00	6.20
$2 Mutuel Prices:	4 – ALWAYS FIRST–GB.		7.60	5.60
	2 – DRILLING FOR OIL.			10.00

$2 EXACTA 8–4 PAID $126.60 $2 TRIFECTA 8–4–2 PAID $1,921.60
$2 SUPERFECTA 8–4–2–7 PAID $24,802.80

Ch. g, (Apr), by Intikhab – Self Assured-Ire , by Ahonoora-GB . Trainer O'Callaghan Niall M. Bred by Darley (Ire).

ASCERTAIN (IRE) rated while racing closest to the pace, challenged when ready approaching the stretch, drifted out when taking over in mid stretch then lasted late. ALWAYS FIRST (GB) unhurried for a mile while off the inside, moved between rivals thereafter, angled out for the drive when rallying and closed fast to miss. DRILLING FOR OIL close up along the inside while patiently ridden, angled off the rail for the drive and finished willingly. TRANSDUCTION GOLD sprinted clear and angled in, set a comfortable pace, responded willingly when challenged approaching the stretch but weakened late. CLOUDY'S KNIGHT outrun for a mile while in hand, worked his way out in upper stretch and finished fast on the outside. RAMAZUTTI within striking distance off the inside, held on well to the stretch and tired. PELLEGRINO (BRZ) close up three wide, stayed on well for ten furlongs and tired. HARD DECK unhurried early, saved ground after a mild and could not menace. SPIDER POWER (IRE) outrun for a half, made a good four wide move to the quarter mile marker but could not sustain the bid. BEE CHARMER (IRE) well placed from the start, stayed forwardly placed to the stretch and faded. LAST ANSWER could not menace. JAZIL was outrun.

3. IN A COMPETITIVE RACE, THE ODDS MAKE THE DECISION FOR YOU

The Breeders' Cup Sprint invariably comes up an ultracompetitive race. In a 14-horse field containing the fastest sprinters on the planet, one false move and your goose is cooked. For horseplayers who are intent on selecting the horse "most likely to win," the race is a handicapping nightmare; but for those who recognize the Sprint's inherent volatility and arrive at a wagering decision accordingly, it annually provides huge overlays in the win pool.

Past performance charts for Thor's Echo (1), Friendly Island (2), and Henny Hughes (4).

6 Bordonaro
Black
Own: Fred Carrillo & Daniel A Cassella
White, Turquoise C, Blue And Turquoise
VALENZUELA P A (—) 2006: (791 150 .19)

Ch. g. 5 (Apr)
Sire: Memo*Chi (Mocito Guapo*Arg) $6,000
Dam: Miss Excitement (Rajab)
Br: Fred Carrillo & Daniel A Cassella (Cal)
Tr: Spawr Bill(—) 2006:(175 20 .11)

L 126

Life	12	9	1	0	$642,164	119	**D.Fst**	11	8	1	0	$596,144	119
2006	4	3	1	0	$435,000	119	**Wet(397)**	0	0	0	0	$0	-
2005	8	6	0	0	$207,164	115	**Turf(251)**	1	1	0	0	$46,020	95
CD	0	0	0	0	$0	-	**Dst(398)**	10	7	1	0	$584,744	119

7Oct06-9OSA	fst	6f		:212 :434 :552 1:074	3↑AncTtlBC-G1	**119**	6	1	11	1½	11½	11	Valenzuela P A	LB124	*.40	100-14	Bordonro1241 **ThorsEcho**1245¾ JunglePrince1241¾	Angled in, held gamely	6
30Jly06-8Dmr	fst	6f		:213 :44 :56 1:083	3↑BCrosbyH-G1	**104**	5	3	31	3nk	2½	2½	Solis A	LB120	*.80	95-13	Pure as Gold113½ *Bordonaro*120hd Battle Won1148¾	Hit w/ foe's whip 1/8	6
13Apr06-10OP	fst	6f		:213 :441 :561 1:083	3↑CtFltSpH-G3	**115**	6	1	1hd	2hd	1½	11¼	Valenzuela P A	L122	*.40	100-14	Bordonaro1221¼ ***FriendlyIsland***1155 SemphoreMn1151¼	Edged away off rail	7
28Jan06-6GP	fst	6f		:212 :433 :552 1:082	4↑[R]SunMilSprn300k	**106**	6	3	3½	2hd	11	1¾	Valenzuela P A	L122	*1.50	102-02	*Bordonaro*122¾ Tacirring1221½ Bushwacker121no	All out, prevailed	13
3Dec05-3Hol	fst	6f		:213 :434 :552 1:08	3↑VOUndrwd-G3	**115**	3	1	11½	12½	13½	13	Valenzuela P A	LB120	2.20	97-10	*Bordonaro*1203 Turnbolt1201¾ Captain Squire1249¼	Speed,angled in,clear	4
6Nov05-11OSA	fst	6f		:212 :44 :553 1:08	3↑[S]CalCpStSpH50k	**111**	3	5	11	11½	13	12½	Gomez G K	LB120	*1.00	98-03	*Bordonaro*1202½ Hello Fame118no Stalking Tiger1154¼	Speed,clear,driving	9
7Sep05-3Dmr	fst	6f		:212 :44 :561 1:084	3↑[R]PirtsBntyH87k	**93**	5	4	3½	3½	2hd	42	Gomez G K	LB115	2.50	93-05	IndinCountry115¾ **Areyoutlkintom**1191¼ Smoochr116no	3 wide, lost 3rd late	8
24Aug05-5Dmr	fm	5f	Ⓣ	:212 :434 :553	3↑OC 40k/N1X-N	**95**	3	7	2hd	2½	1hd	1¾	Gomez G K	LB124	*1.70	97-03	Bordonaro124¾ Trail Mix124hd Zayed124½	Hopped bit start,game	8
30Jly05-9Dmr	fst	6f		:213 :441 :554 1:081	3↑[S]OC 25k/N1X-N	**103**	10	3	3nk	1hd	11½	1¾	Gomez G K	LB122	*3.10	98-12	*Bordonaro*122¾ ExcessTempttions1202 Scottsbluff1203½	Dueled,clear,held	11
30Apr05-7Hol	fst	6f		:213 :441 :562 1:092	3↑Alw 40000s	**94**	12	4	2hd	1hd	13	12½	Gomez G K	LB124	*1.40	90-10	*Bordonaro*1242½ Quality Armor1242 Sonriente1222	4wd early,vied,clear	13
1Apr05-3SA	fst	5½f		:211 :441 :56 1:021	4↑Md 32000(32-28)	**96**	5	5	1½	11	12½	15	Smith M E	LB122	3.70	100-07	*Bordonaro*1225 *Snapped Up*1229½ Joys Last One1232	Off rail, ridden out	8
2Feb05-1SA	fst	6f		:213 :442 :564 1:101	4↑[S]Md Sp Wt 44k	**51**	5	3	31	56½	610	613¼	Douglas R R	LB122	6.10	74-13	*Viento Fuerte*1225½ *Saint of the City*122½ *TizAfire*122nk	Lugged in turn,green	7

WORKS: Oct29**CD** 4f fst :482 B *7/71* Oct22**SA** 4f fst :483 B *12/29* Oct2**SA** 4f fst :463 H *2/28* Sep27**SA** 6f fst 1:134 H *15/28* Sep21**SA** 6f fst 1:12 H *2/15* Sep14**SA** 5f fst 1:003 H *12/40*
TRAINER: 2Off45-180(79 .19 $1.38) WonLastStart(82 .20 $1.25) Dirt(380 .18 $1.35) Sprint(269 .17 $1.29) GrdStk(5 .60 $2.40) J/T 2005-06(49 .20 $1.15)

On the eve of the 2006 Sprint, the media buzz on the East-West rivalry centered on Henny Hughes, the brilliant winner of the King's Bishop and Vosburgh, and our friend Bordonaro, who had won three of four starts during the year and had earned a Beyer of 119 while wiring the Ancient Title four weeks earlier.

Henny Hughes and Bordonaro were among the four horses with the best last-out Beyer Speed Figures, listed here along with their odds:

Horse	**Beyer Figure**	**Odds**
Bordonaro	119	4–1
Thor's Echo	116	15–1
Henny Hughes	113	8–5
Siren Lure	110	6–1

With a top Beyer of 113, the 3-year-old Henny Hughes had no edge over older rivals Bordonaro and Thor's Echo, but had been in the headlines regularly and was bet like a clear-cut favorite. Bordonaro looked like the speed of the speed, so he seemed like a fair price. But if 4–1 was fair on Bordonaro, odds nearly four times as great on Thor's Echo, beaten a length by Bordonaro in the Ancient Title, were extraordinarily generous.

Thor's Echo had lost all five of his starts during the year, and indeed had not won since winning a stakes restricted to California-breds nearly 15 months earlier. But as longshot bettors have come to know, 15–1 shots by definition do not come gift-wrapped in a perfect set of past performances. On the plus side, though, Thor's Echo had beaten 13 other sprinters to finish a close second in the $2 million Golden Shaheen back in March, and appeared fully recovered from the long trip to Dubai, judging from a sharp try in the Ancient Title.

Thor's Echo might have been considered a "bounce" candidate off a new top figure of 116, but the same possibility existed for Bordonaro and Henny Hughes as well.

The rail post can be treacherous in a race like the Sprint, but as the card unfolded it looked to be a potential plus for Thor's Echo because the inside lane had been golden: Dreaming of Anna had wired the Juvenile Fillies from post 1, and Street Sense had slipped through on the rail turning for home to win the Juvenile by 10 lengths at 15–1.

Thor's Echo worked out a perfect trip from the live rail and stalked a duel between Bordonaro and Attila's Storm, while Henny Hughes was eliminated after stumbling and getting caught in traffic early.

The eventual runner-up was Friendly Island, a 58–1 bomb who attained good early position and had a solid finishing kick coming off two longer races on dirt and turf. Those willing to go five races back on Friendly Island might have given him a chance based on a second to Bordonaro, with a 112 Beyer, in the Count Fleet in April.

There is a lot of educated guesswork involved in trying to foresee who might or might not bounce off a new top figure, and who might be the beneficiary or victim of racing luck. In competitive full fields, handicappers might not necessarily "love" horses like Thor's Echo, but when they go off at 15–1 they offer a comfortable, and necessary, margin for error.

4. THE RACE CONTAINS LIGHTLY RACED HORSES WHO MIGHT IMPROVE

Races that contain lightly raced horses are fertile ground for longshots. The crowd likes to bet on the status quo, but has a tougher time anticipating change, or at least betting on change. There is an old adage that says, "Never bet a horse as the favorite to do something it's never done before." But opportunities abound when horses are trying something new at worthwhile odds.

On the May 12, 2007, card at Belmont Park there were two instructive maiden special weight races, one on dirt and the other on turf:

The fourth race was a 1¹⁄₁₆-mile route out of the chute, and the fairly obvious favorite at 7–5 was Hedge Fund, a homebred from the legendary Phipps Stable.

Hedge Fund was a "double fig," with two Beyers faster than anything else in the field, but aside from his exposed form there were two problems: (a) Hedge Fund was a 4-year-old, and in maiden races for 3-year-olds and up, it's prudent to prefer the younger horses; and (b) Hedge Fund was stretching out from sprints. There is nothing inherently wrong about playing horses stretching out—you just can't take 7–5 on them.

When confronted with short-priced older maidens like Hedge Fund, it often pays to cultivate a prejudice in favor of second-time starters who look as though they might improve. A horse's first start is often the least definitive start of his career (see Secretariat's fourth-place finish at Belmont on July 4, 1972), and the second start is often where he shows major improvement.

The second-time starters in this field, Uncle Indy and Daaher, both looked as though they might move forward.

Uncle Indy had already been the distance on Polytrack at Keeneland, where he raced through a snow squall and finished a respectable sixth in a full field of 12. He had worked four times in the ensuing five weeks, including a five-furlong move first time over Belmont's main track that was second-fastest of 14 at the distance, and as the 2–1 second choice he seemed the most likely alternative to Hedge Fund.

Daaher had also begun his career at Keeneland's spring meet, and with a Beyer of 48 for that effort he was technically the "slowest" horse in the race. But aside from the fact that a debut on Polytrack is inconclusive when the next start comes on a different surface, there were some aspects of Daaher's past performances that portended quick improvement: He had been purchased for $375,000, and being by Breeders' Cup Classic winner Awesome Again, the added distance figured to help; trainer Kiaran McLaughlin, who was off to a 3-for-7 start at the meet, had won with 36 percent of his second-time starters in 2006–07, and with 35 percent of starters ridden by Alan Garcia during the same period; and he had worked nicely before and after his first try, in which he swerved in and steadied at the break at a well-bet 5–1.

FOURTH RACE
Belmont
MAY 12, 2007

1¹⁄₁₆ MILES. (1.39²) MAIDEN SPECIAL WEIGHT . Purse $44,000 (UP TO $8,360 NYSBFOA) FOR MAIDENS, THREE YEAR OLDS AND UPWARD. Three Year Olds, 118 lbs.; Older, 123 lbs.

Value of Race: $44,000 Winner $26,400; second $8,800; third $4,400; fourth $2,200; fifth $1,320; sixth $294; seventh $294; eighth $292. Mutuel Pool $523,991.00 Exacta Pool $427,201.00 Quinella Pool $36,955.00 Trifecta Pool $355,311.00

Last Raced	Horse	M/Eqt.	A.	Wt	PP	St	¼	½	¾	Str	Fin	Jockey	Odds $1
19Apr07 ⁴Kee⁸	Daaher	L	3	118	7	2	4ʰᵈ	5¹	5¹¹⁄₂	4¹	1³¹⁄₄	Garcia Alan	12.50
6Apr07 ¹⁰Kee⁶	Uncle Indy	L	3	118	8	1	3¹⁄₂	3ʰᵈ	3¹	1ʰᵈ	2²¹⁄₂	Velasquez C	2.15
31Mar07 ²Aqu²	Buddy's Humor		3	118	6	3	2¹⁄₂	2¹⁄₂	2¹⁄₂	2ʰᵈ	3ʰᵈ	Coa E M	6.50
13Apr07 ⁶Kee²	Leap Day	L	3	118	5	5	5¹	4¹⁄₂	4¹⁄₂	5²¹⁄₂	4¹	Velazquez J R	5.70
7Apr07 ³Aqu²	Hedge Fund	L	4	123	3	4	1¹⁄₂	1¹⁄₂	1ʰᵈ	3ʰᵈ	5¹¹⁄₂	Prado E S	1.45
11Apr07 ²Aqu²	Herald Square	L b	3	118	2	7	7¹⁄₂	7³	6²¹⁄₂	6¹⁰	6¹³¹⁄₄	Martin E M Jr	28.25
11Apr07 ²Aqu⁴	Then and Now	L b	4	123	1	8	6ʰᵈ	6ʰᵈ	8	8	7¹¹⁄₂	Luzzi M J	18.40
14Apr07 ⁸GP³	Sculling	L	3	118	4	6	8	8	7³¹⁄₂	7²	8	Castellano J J	45.00

OFF AT 2:39 Start Good. Won driving. Track fast.

TIME :22⁴, :45³, 1:10¹, 1:35², 1:41⁴ (:22.86, :45.72, 1:10.36, 1:35.55, 1:41.90)

$2 Mutuel Prices:

7 – DAAHER	....	27.00	9.20	7.50
8 – UNCLE INDY	....		3.70	3.10
6 – BUDDY'S HUMOR	....			4.10

$2 EXACTA 7–8 PAID $113.50 $2 QUINELLA 7–8 PAID $52.00
$2 TRIFECTA 7–8–6 PAID $679.00

B. c, (Feb), by Awesome Again – Irish Cherry , by Irish Open . Trainer McLaughlin Kiaran P. Bred by Yvonne Schwabe & Dagmar Schwabe (Ont–C).

DAAHER raced close up early while between rivals, rallied wide into the stretch and drew away late, driving. UNCLE INDY chased the pace while three wide and stayed on gamely to the finish. BUDDY'S HUMOR contested the pace while between rivals and tired in the final furlong. LEAP DAY raced close up inside while in hand, was steadied in traffic in the stretch, altered course and finished well. HEDGE FUND contested the pace along the inside and tired in the final furlong. HERALD SQUARE raced inside, altered course in the stretch and was steadied. THEN AND NOW raced wide throughout and tired. SCULLING was outrun along the inside. Following a Stewards' inquiry and the dismissal of a claim of foul against the third place finisher by the rider of the fourth place finisher, alleging interference in the stretch, the result was declared official.

Owners– 1, Shadwell Stable; 2, Lazy F Ranch; 3, Kingfield Stables (Levine); 4, Schwartz Barry K; 5, Phipps Stable; 6, Kinsman Stable; 7, Clifton William L Jr; 8, Dogwood Stable

Trainers– 1, McLaughlin Kiaran P; 2, Penna Angel Jr; 3, Levine Bruce N; 4, Hushion Michael E; 5, McGaughey III Claude R; 6, Domino Carl J; 7, Bond Harold James; 8, Alexander Frank A

$2 Pick Three (11–3–7) Paid $1,441.00 ; Pick Three Pool $106,846 .

Hedge Fund dueled for the lead, but came undone in the stretch of his first route attempt. Uncle Indy reached a short lead in midstretch and appeared en route to victory, but Daaher, who broke much more alertly second time out, relished the added distance and unleashed a strong late run to win going away.

Considering his breeding, and his trainer's exceptional proficiency with second-time starters, Daaher offered enough incentive at 12–1 to merit a win bet on the come. In retrospect, that was a terrific price on a colt who returned to Belmont in the fall and won the Grade 2 Jerome Handicap; a wolf in sheep's clothing no more, he paid $8.30.

For multirace exotic purposes, this is the type of situation where a horse like Hedge Fund is a risky stand-alone at 7–5. Not only is he unproven at the distance, which is a basic handicapping factor, but you've only seen the proverbial tip of the iceberg as far as the other lightly raced horses are concerned. Daaher's Beyer figure improved from a 48 to a 90.

Two races later, horseplayers were presented with a similar scenario, this time on turf:

1 Eff Jaa Gee
Own: Castletop Stable
Red — White, Black Circle And 'Cs,' Black
GOMEZ G K (8 0 2 3 .00) 2007: (453 100 .22)
Dk. b or br g. 3 (Mar) FTKJUL05 $110,000
Sire: Orientate (Mt. Livermore) $20,000
Dam: Countless Affairs (Storm Cat)
Br: Gainesway Thoroughbreds Ltd (Ky)
Tr: Violette Richard A Jr(6 2 0 0 .33) 2007:(159 37 .23)
L 118

Life	2	M	0	2	$6,720	70	D.Fst	1	0	0	1	$3,300	70
2007	2	M	0	2	$6,720	70	Wet(375)	0	0	0	0	$0	-
2006	0	M	0	0	$0	-	Synth	0	0	0	0	$0	-
Bel (T)	0	0	0	0	$0	-	Turf(307)	1	0	0	1	$3,420	59
							Dst(T)(396)	0	0	0	0	$0	-

21Apr07–7GP fm 5f (T) :22^2 :44^4 :56^3 Md Sp Wt 38k **59** 9 8 75½ 75 6^3 3½ Leyva J C L122 5.50 84– 15 DeadlyAim122^{nk} Heavyweight122^{nk} EffJGee122^{nk} Bumped, steadied start 11
14Mar07–1GP fst 6f :21^4 :44^1 :56^{4}1:10^1 Md c-(80-75) **70** 4 5 3^2 32½ 34½ 33¾ Aguilar M L122 3.80 87– 09 Groundskeeper1152¼ Media City1221½ Eff JaaGee122^1 Couldn't keep pace 6
Claimed from Galiardo, Sr. Fred for $80,000, Rogers J Michael Trainer 2006: (113 17 13 14 0.15)
WORKS: May7 Aqu 4f fst :49^1 B *8/21* ●Apr14 PmM 4f fst :48 H *1/6* Mar31 PmM 4f fst :48^1 H *3/19* Mar9 GP 5f fst :59^2 Hg *2/9* Feb24 GP 4f fst :50^1 B *29/31* Feb17 GP 6f fst 1:15^1 Bg *2/2*
TRAINER: Turf(93 .14 $1.72) Sprint(254 .19 $1.38) MdnSpWt(141 .17 $1.32) J/T 2006-07 BEL(15 .27 $1.67) J/T 2006-07(42 .24 $1.54)

2 Bright Illusion
Own: Spruce Pond Stable
White — Fluorescent Orange, Black Diamond Hoop
ROJAS R I (15 4 2 0 .27) 2007: (89 12 .13)
Gr/ro. g. 3 (Feb) KEEJAN05 $20,000
Sire: Silver Ghost (Mr. Prospector) $7,500
Dam: Top Corsage (Topsider)
Br: Chris Nolan (Ky)
Tr: Jerkens H Allen(8 2 1 1 .25) 2007:(82 18 .22)
L 118

Life	4	M	0	0	$650	54	D.Fst	1	0	0	0	$200	27
2007	1	M	0	0	$130	39	Wet(356)	2	0	0	0	$310	39
2006	3	M	0	0	$520	54	Synth	0	0	0	0	$0	-
Bel (T)	1	0	0	0	$140	54	Turf(300)	1	0	0	0	$140	54
							Dst(T)(355)	0	0	0	0	$0	-

2May07–2Bel gd 7f :23 :46^2 1:11^{4}1:24^2 3↑ Md 50000(50-40) **39** 7 3 3^2 3^3 59½ 718½ Rojas R I L118 b 24.50 60– 17 TrumnsGold1239½ DoesntLie118^{no} FivDmonBg1181¼ Bumped start, inside 9
Previously trained by Turner William H Jr 2006(as of 11/10): (122 6 18 12 0.05)
10Nov06–4Aqu gd 1 :23^2 :47^1 1:13^{1}1:41 Md 50000(50-40) **10** 6 3½ 42¾ 5^{10} 6^{25} 7^{28} Martin E M Jr L120 b 32.00 34– 33 *Believeinmnow*120^6 WickdRtort1201¼ ShortTrip1201½ Finished after a half 8
6Oct06–4Bel gd 1 (T) :23^2 :47^3 1:12^{2}1:38^1 Md 75000 **54** 6 5^5 6^5 7^{10} 7^6 77½ Hill C L120 b 47.25 62– 28 T Harry120^{no} Star Studded120^2 Maven120^1 Tired after a half 10
17Sep06–2Bel fst 6f :22^2 :46 :58^{2}1:11^2 Md 65000 **27** 6 6 5^4 55¼ 8^{11} 713¼ Rodriguez A^5 L115 b 23.70 68– 14 Pacific Sun120^4 Dynamic Dino1201¾ *Lost Copy*120½ Greenly inside, tired 8
WORKS: May9 Bel tr.t 5f fst 1:01^3 B *4/6* Apr29 Bel tr.t 5f fst 1:01^4 B *4/14* Apr26 Bel 5f fst 1:02 B *6/8* Apr21 Bel 4f fst :49 Bg *18/37* Apr11 Bel 4f fst :50 B *14/20* Apr7 Bel 4f fst :48 B *3/33*
TRAINER: 2Off45-180(38 .18 $1.31) Dirt/Turf(26 .12 $0.83) Turf(64 .19 $1.62) Sprint(253 .15 $1.29) MdnSpWt(68 .13 $1.26) J/T 2006-07 BEL(12 .17 $1.93) J/T 2006-07(22 .18 $2.25)

4 Houbara
Own: Darley Stable
Yellow — Maroon, White Sleeves, Maroon Cap, White
GARCIA ALAN (42 6 10 1 .14) 2007: (466 86 .18)
Dk. b or br c. 3 (Mar)
Sire: Mt. Livermore (Blushing Groom*Fr) $25,000
Dam: Tethkar*GB (Machiavellian)
Br: Gainsborough Farm LLC (Ky)
Tr: McLaughlin Kiaran P(7 3 1 0 .43) 2007:(202 52 .26)
(L) 118

Life	0	M	0	0	$0	-	D.Fst	0	0	0	0	$0	-
2007	0	M	0	0	$0	-	Wet(398)	0	0	0	0	$0	-
2006	0	M	0	0	$0	-	Synth	0	0	0	0	$0	-
Bel (T)	0	0	0	0	$0	-	Turf(314)	0	0	0	0	$0	-
							Dst(T)(382)	0	0	0	0	$0	-

WORKS: May5 Bel 3f fst :36^2 Bg *5/18* Apr17 Kee ◇5f fst 1:04^1 B *25/26* Apr11 Kee ◇3f fst :37^2 Bg *9/17* Mar28 Kee ◇5f fst 1:03^4 B *12/12* Mar17 Kee ◇5f fst 1:04 B *15/17* Mar7 Kee ◇4f fst :49^2 B *7/11*
TRAINER: 1stStart(70 .17 $2.50) 1stTurf(32 .12 $5.15) Turf(142 .15 $2.73) Sprint(299 .24 $2.55) MdnSpWt(209 .26 $3.32) J/T 2006-07 BEL(7 .29 $8.49) J/T 2006-07(60 .35 $3.94)

5 Justy
Own: Zayat Stables LLC
Green — Turquoise, Gold Ball Sash And 'Z,' Gold
COA E M (45 10 4 6 .22) 2007: (531 102 .19)
B. c. 3 (Apr)
Sire: Danehill (Danzig) $39,277
Dam: Saintly Speech (Southern Halo)
Br: Swettenham Stud (Ky)
Tr: Mott William I(4 1 2 0 .25) 2007:(229 42 .18)
L 118

Life	3	M	1	1	$11,184	76	D.Fst	0	0	0	0	$0	-
2007	2	M	1	1	$10,640	76	Wet(395)	0	0	0	0	$0	-
2006	1	M	0	0	$544	-	Synth	0	0	0	0	$0	-
Bel (T)	0	0	0	0	$0	-	Turf(364)	3	0	1	1	$11,184	76
							Dst(T)(353)	1	0	0	0	$544	-

18Apr07–7GP fm 1$\frac{1}{16}$ (T) :23^4 :48 1:11^{2}1:40^4 Md Sp Wt 38k **76** 2 31½ 2^1 2^1 21½ 3¾ Castro E L122 *1.30 85– 20 Whata Ya Mean122½ Holiday Trip122^{nk} Justy122¾ Not enough late 12
8Mar07–3GP fm 1$\frac{1}{16}$ (T) :23 :47^1 1:11^{3}1:41 Md Sp Wt 38k **75** 10 43½ 4^4 41½ 41½ 2^{nk} Prado E S L122 2.60 85– 12 Spy in the Sky122^{nk} Justy122^{no} Broad River1221¼ 3 wide, missed 12
Previously trained by Michael Bell
31May06 Yarmouth (GB) gd 6f (T) Str 1:14^4 Totecoursetocourse EBF Novice Stks Alw 11300 43¾ Spencer J P 124 4.50 Danebury Hill124^{hd} Captain Marvelous1313½ Malaaq119^{hd} 6
Timeform rating: 79+ *Tracked in 3rd, weakened final furlong*
WORKS: May8 Bel 4f fst :48^4 B *5/30* May1 Bel 4f fst :49^3 B *17/25* Apr14 Pay 4f fst :50^2 B *12/27* Apr7 Pay 4f fst :49^4 B *4/29* Mar30 Pay 4f fst :50^4 B *16/26* Mar20 Pay 4f fst :50 B *3/17*
TRAINER: Route/Sprint(45 .18 $1.06) Turf(557 .18 $1.42) Sprint(208 .22 $1.81) MdnSpWt(319 .16 $1.42) J/T 2006-07 BEL(3 .67 $5.40) J/T 2006-07(8 .38 $2.40)

6 General Ryan
Own: G R and S Stable
Black — Yellow, Blue Triangular Panel, Yellow
CASTELLANO J J (21 2 5 4 .10) 2007: (371 58 .16)
Ch. c. 3 (Apr) KEESEP05 $180,000
Sire: Five Star Day (Carson City) $20,000
Dam: Strawberry's Charm (Strawberry Road*Aus)
Br: North Wales LLC (Ky)
Tr: Hennig Mark(8 1 0 3 .12) 2007:(154 21 .14)
L 118

Life	1	M	0	0	$380	54	D.Fst	1	0	0	0	$380	54
2007	1	M	0	0	$380	54	Wet(450)	0	0	0	0	$0	-
2006	0	M	0	0	$0	-	Synth	0	0	0	0	$0	-
Bel (T)	0	0	0	0	$0	-	Turf(249)	0	0	0	0	$0	-
							Dst(T)(442)	0	0	0	0	$0	-

7Apr07–3GP fst 6f :22^1 :45^1 :57^{2}1:10^1 Md Sp Wt 44k **54** 1 10 85½ 6^8 5^{10} 614¼ Velez J A Jr L122 20.90 77– 11 Minister'sAppeal1224¾ **BrazenlyBold**1225¼ InChargeAgain1222¼ Slow start 12
WORKS: May4 Bel 4f fst :48^3 B *9/28* Apr26 Pay 5f fst 1:03^4 B *4/4* Apr19 Pay 4f fst :51^1 B *8/9* Mar29 Pay 4f fst :49^1 Bg *2/19* Mar22 Pay 4f fst :49^1 Bg *2/24* ●Mar15 Pay 5f fst 1:02^4 B *1/6*
TRAINER: 2ndStart(41 .10 $0.94) 1stTurf(35 .06 $1.17) Dirt/Turf(36 .11 $1.23) 31-60Days(211 .16 $1.29) Turf(171 .18 $1.91) Sprint(149 .12 $1.33) J/T 2006-07 BEL(10 .00 $0.00) J/T 2006-07(44 .18 $2.50)

7 Letthesunshinein
Own: Gianca Stable
Orange — Red, Green Sash, Green Sleeves, White
DESORMEAUX K J (5 1 0 1 .20) 2007: (303 52 .17)
B. c. 3 (Mar)
Sire: Jade Hunter (Mr. Prospector) $5,000
Dam: I'm a Fighter (Fit to Fight)
Br: Tony Evangelista (Ky)
Tr: Streicher Kenneth(1 0 0 0 .00) 2007:(10 1 .10)
Blinkers ON
L 118

Life	3	M	1	0	$12,900	63	D.Fst	3	0	1	0	$12,900	63
2007	3	M	1	0	$12,900	63	Wet(355)	0	0	0	0	$0	-
2006	0	M	0	0	$0	-	Synth	0	0	0	0	$0	-
Bel (T)	0	0	0	0	$0	-	Turf(251)	0	0	0	0	$0	-
							Dst(T)(310)	0	0	0	0	$0	-

5May07–2Bel fst 7f :22^2 :46 1:10^{4}1:23^4 3↑ Md Sp Wt 43k **58** 3 3 11½ 3½ 58¼ 410¼ Fragoso P L118 5.80 72– 15 Pick Six1182¼ Charlie Caliente118^{no} Impossible118^8 Set pace, tired 7
14Apr07–2Aqu fst 6f :22 :45^1 :57^{3}1:10^3 Md Sp Wt 43k **62** 1 5 1½ 3½ 4^3 48¼ Martin E M Jr L120 f 3.90 81– 12 Da Gaffney120^1 Philomatt1202¾ **Bishop's Back**1204½ Vied inside, tired 7
25Mar07–6Aqu fst 6f ⊡ :22^4 :46^1 :58^{2}1:11^2 3↑ Md Sp Wt 43k **63** 4 6 64¼ 55½ 4^9 26½ Sutherland C L116 f 4.30 80– 14 McMagic1236½ Letthesunshinein1161¾ Aflarendpryer116^2 Rallied outside 7
WORKS: Apr26 Bel tr.t 4f fst :49^1 B *8/20* Apr7 Bel tr.t 4f fst :48 B *4/94* ●Mar21 Bel tr.t 4f fst :47 Hg *1/97* Mar12 Bel tr.t 5f fst 1:02^4 B *12/16* Mar5 Bel tr.t 5f fst 1:02^4 B *7/16* Feb25 Bel tr.t 4f fst :48 B *2/68*
TRAINER: 1-7Days(1 .00 $0.00) 1stTurf(1 .00 $0.00) 1stBlink(2 .00 $0.00) BlinkOn(2 .00 $0.00) Turf(3 .00 $0.00) Sprint(13 .08 $2.29)

8 Al Sheetahn
Own: Lucky Seven Stable
Pink Hot Pink, Royal Blue Ball, Pink 'T,'
PONCE J (22 0 2 1 .00) 2007: (274 25 .09)

B. c. 4 (Mar)
Sire: Lost Soldier (Danzig) $7,500
Dam: Betty's Nobility (Mark of Nobility)
Br: Raising Dust Stables (Fla)
Tr: Johnson Cleveland(1 0 0 0 .00) 2007:(4 0 .00)

L 118⁵

Life	6	M	0	0	$3,154	67	D.Fst	3	0	0	0	$1,827	56
2006	6	M	0	0	$3,154	67	Wet(302)	0	0	0	0	$0	–
2005	0	M	0	0	$0	–	Synth	0	0	0	0	$0	–
Bel(T)	1	0	0	0	$67	60	Turf(285)	3	0	0	0	$1,327	67
							Dst(T)(298)	0	0	0	0	$0	–

Previously trained by Terracciano Neal 2006(as of 8/18): (40 1 2 3 0.03)
18Aug06-6Sar fm 1 [T] :24 :481 1:122 1:363 3↑ Md 45000(45-40) 67 4 2 1½ 2hd 2½ 2hd 55 Rojas R I L119 b 31.25 79-07 Skatin Jake1171 Harlanquin117½ *Stratonic*1192½ Vied inside, tired 10
31Jly06-7Sar fm 1 1/16 (T) :231 :471 1:114 1:421 3↑ Md 45000(45-40) 65 6 11½ 1½ 1½ 3½ 54¾ Bridgmohan S X L118 b 16.40 80-14 Erdiston121hd Harlanquin1162½ Really Reilly1231½ Set pace, tired 10
4Jly06-10Bel fm 1 (T) :223 :452 1:10 1:343 3↑ Md 45000(45-40) 60 2 1hd 1½ 2½ 44½ 610 Rojas R I L118 b 45.50 77-14 Dodger Town1233½ Really Reilly123no Stratonic1182¾ Vied inside, tired 11
29Jun06-2Bel fst 6f :22 :45 :572 1:11 3↑ Md 75000 –0 2 1 68¾ 817 822 828¾ Rojas R I L118 fb 4.70 54-16 SugrExchng118½ GloryAtS118½ BrodwyProducr1182¾ Bumped start, tired 8
25Mar06-6Aqu fst 1 [•] :243 :49 1:141 1:392 Md Sp Wt 44k 56 2 67 67½ 58¾ 512 513½ Rivera J L Jr L120 34.00 72-17 [D]*Dirty Devil*120hd Mr. Hamlen1203½ *Tasteyville*1206½ Outrun inside 6
4Mar06-4Aqu fst 5½f [•] :223 :47 1:00 1:062 Md Sp Wt 43k 36 3 6 810 816 712 612 Espinoza J L L120 b 23.10 75-19 LittleCherokee120hd TrippdUp1203¾ UnclFstor120hd Bumped start, inside 8
WORKS: ●May5 Aqu 3f fst :353 H *1/6* Apr29 Bel 4f fst :52 Bg *56/56* Apr20 Bel 4f fst :481 H *12/23* Apr2 Bel tr.t 3f fst :38 B *8/9* Mar24 Bel tr.t 3f fst :38 B *20/30*
TRAINER: 1stW/Tm(2 .00 $0.00) Route/Sprint(1 .00 $0.00) Turf(1 .00 $0.00) Sprint(3 .00 $0.00)

9 Snowstalker
Own: Shortleaf Stable
Turqse Yellow And Chocolate Brown Diagonal
VELASQUEZ C (26 5 3 7 .19) 2007: (595 92 .15)

Dk. b or br g. 3 (Feb) KEESEP05 $50,000
Sire: Dynaformer (Roberto) $150,000
Dam: Snowy Range (Seattle Slew)
Br: Green Hills Farm (Ky)
Tr: Bohannan Thomas(1 0 1 0 .00) 2007:(16 3 .19)

118

Life	0	M	0	0	$0	–	D.Fst	0	0	0	0	$0	–
2007	0	M	0	0	$0	–	Wet(350)	0	0	0	0	$0	–
2006	0	M	0	0	$0	–	Synth	0	0	0	0	$0	–
Bel(T)	0	0	0	0	$0	–	Turf(333)	0	0	0	0	$0	–
							Dst(T)(300)	0	0	0	0	$0	–

WORKS: May6 Bel 4f fst :493 Bg *40/80* Apr30 Bel 4f fst :492 B *26/52* Apr14 OP 5f fst 1:02 B *8/11* Apr7 OP 5f fst 1:024 Hg *13/43* Mar30 OP 4f fst :502 B *22/37* Mar24 OP 3f fst :383 B *13/15*
●Mar16 OP 3f fst :352 B *1/12* Mar8 OP 4f fst :522 B *26/29* Mar3 OP 3f fst :373 B *6/10* Feb26 OP 3f fst :384 B *17/23*
TRAINER: 1stStart(5 .20 $3.52) 1stTurf(4 .25 $6.20) Turf(10 .10 $2.48) Sprint(13 .23 $2.26) MdnSpWt(17 .18 $2.35)

10 Brazenly Bold **SCRATCHED**

11 Tacticianor
Own: Mary Grant Kelly Thomas J Grant Josep
Gray Royal Blue, Yellow Chevrons, Yellow
ESPINOZA J L (25 1 0 3 .04) 2007: (190 13 .07)

Gr/ro. g. 3 (May)
Sire: Tactical Cat (Storm Cat) $5,000
Dam: Concolour (Our Native)
Br: Thomas J Kelly & Joseph M Grant (Ky)
Tr: Kelly Patrick J(6 1 0 1 .17) 2007:(74 5 .07)

L 118

Life	5	M	0	0	$1,011	26	D.Fst	5	0	0	0	$1,011	26
2007	1	M	0	0	$286	22	Wet(342)	0	0	0	0	$0	–
2006	4	M	0	0	$725	26	Synth	0	0	0	0	$0	–
Bel(T)	0	0	0	0	$0	–	Turf(313)	0	0	0	0	$0	–
							Dst(T)(338)	0	0	0	0	$0	–

10Feb07-4Aqu fst 6f [•] :224 :461 :582 1:112 Md Sp Wt 43k 22 6 8 77¼ 710 815 819¼ Ponce J7 L113 b 70.75 68-13 *Divine Park*1201¼ Jimmy G120½ Buddy's Humor120hd Steadied after start 8
16Dec06-6Aqu fst 6f [•] :223 :46 :583 1:114 Md Sp Wt 43k –0 6 6 76¼ 1015 1024 1132¾ Rodriguez R R L120 b 99.25 47-22 Happy Humor120½ *Pass the Punch*120½ Mariano120nk Off rail, no response 11
25Nov06-4Aqu fst 6f :22 :452 :57 1:091 Md Sp Wt 43k 24 1 11 87¾ 911 1120 1223 Cunningham T5 L115 b 93.00 69-11 *Sports Town*1204¾ Ten Forty1154¾ Piggott120½ Awkward start, inside 12
14Oct06-2Bel fst 1 :233 :471 1:12 1:373 Md Sp Wt 44k –0 7 3½ 86½ 1025 1039 1054½ Coa E M 119 b 77.00 18-30 SummerDoldrums1191½ PleasantStrike1195 Jagermn1191¼ Eased stretch 10
23Sep06-2Bel fst 7f :224 :463 1:121 1:251 Md Sp Wt 43k 26 3 8 814 815 821 724¾ Smith M E 119 57.75 50-19 RIEstt119hd MostDistinguishd1194½ NoRply1199½ Green, wide throughout 8
WORKS: May6 Bel 4f fst :502 B *59/80* Apr30 Bel 4f fst :49 B *20/52* ●Apr23 Bel 3f fst :354 H *1/4* Apr14 Bel tr.t 3f fst :37 B *15/38* Apr7 Bel tr.t 4f fst :494 B *40/94* Mar29 Bel tr.t 4f fst :51 B *33/37*
TRAINER: 61-180Days(16 .06 $1.18) 1stTurf(12 .00 $0.00) Dirt/Turf(26 .08 $0.71) Turf(73 .11 $2.55) Sprint(146 .10 $1.52) MdnSpWt(124 .08 $1.26) J/T 2006-07 BEL(15 .13 $4.71) J/T 2006-07(40 .10 $2.98)

12 Masterofthehouse
Own: Picarello Margaret
Lime White, Black Cross Sashes, Black
ARROYO N JR (22 5 2 3 .23) 2007: (259 43 .17)

B. g. 3 (May)
Sire: Chester House (Mr. Prospector) $20,000
Dam: Miss Cover Girl (Oh Say)
Br: Margaret J Picarello (Ky)
Tr: Tesher Howard M(2 0 0 0 .00) 2007:(38 4 .11)

L 118

Life	5	M	0	0	$2,903	70	D.Fst	1	0	0	0	$1,548	45
2007	3	M	0	0	$1,140	70	Wet(373)	0	0	0	0	$0	–
2006	2	M	0	0	$1,763	47	Synth	0	0	0	0	$0	–
Bel(T)	1	0	0	0	$215	47	Turf(367)	4	0	0	0	$1,355	70
							Dst(T)(360)	1	0	0	0	$215	47

18Apr07-7GP fm 1 1/16 (T) :234 :48 1:112 1:404 Md Sp Wt 38k 61 6 86½ 77 77½ 78 87¾ Lezcano J L122 14.20 78-20 Whata Ya Mean122½ Holiday Trip122nk **Justy**122¾ Ducked in, bmpd start 12
8Mar07-3GP fm 1 1/16 (T) :23 :471 1:113 1:41 Md Sp Wt 38k 70 2 76½ 67½ 53 73½ 62½ Maragh R L122 16.90 82-12 Spy in the Sky122nk **Justy**122no Broad River1221¼ Steadied 1st trn & str 12
3Jan07-7GP gd 1 1/16 (T) :25 :50 1:142 1:434 Md Sp Wt 44k 68 12 51¾ 32 3½ 22½ 73 Velasquez C L122 48.80 68-28 Vanquisher122nk *Duveen*122½ Storming Marine122½ Off slowly, bid, tired 12
13Oct06-4Bel fst 6f ⊗ :222 :454 :574 1:102 Md Sp Wt 51k 45 1 3 67¼ 45½ 412 516 Lezcano J L119 30.00 70-17 FirstDfnc1198¼ *Johnnsburgffir*1195¾ VimNVigor119½ Close up inside, tired 12
8Sep06-6Bel gd 6f (T) :223 :462 :584 1:121 Md Sp Wt 43k 47 4 1 53½ 66 69 78½ Migliore R 118 5.60 64-27 LedingOn1181 Chihulykee118½ PushedforTim1181½ Between foes, no rally 9
WORKS: May3 Bel 4f fst :482 B *8/22* Apr14 GP 4f fst :493 B *12/27* Apr4 GP 4f fst :503 B *6/6*
TRAINER: Route/Sprint(16 .06 $0.61) Turf(50 .06 $0.54) Sprint(68 .07 $1.23) MdnSpWt(40 .02 $0.15) J/T 2006-07(2 .50 $4.25)

3 Three Lions
Own: Peachtree Stable
Blue Purple, Tan Braces, Two Tan Hoops On
VELAZQUEZ J R (14 1 3 2 .07) 2007: (363 83 .23)

Ch. r. 3 (Feb) KEESEP05 $270,000
Sire: Hennessy (Storm Cat) $60,000
Dam: Beefeater Baby (Thunder Gulch)
Br: La Jolla Thoroughbred Stables (Ky)
Tr: Pletcher Todd A(7 1 2 4 .14) 2007:(343 89 .26)

L 118

Life	3	M	0	0	$2,847	73	D.Fst	1	0	0	0	$282	–
2006	3	M	0	0	$2,847	73	Wet(349)	0	0	0	0	$0	–
2005	0	M	0	0	$0	–	Synth	0	0	0	0	$0	–
Bel(T)	1	0	0	0	$215	73	Turf(293)	2	0	0	0	$2,565	73
							Dst(T)(319)	1	0	0	0	$215	73

28Sep06-6Bel fm 6f (T) :223 :452 :57 1:091 Md Sp Wt 43k 73 7 4 21 2hd 2½ 61½ Rodriguez R R L118 b 5.20 86-14 *QuietlyMine*118nk CherokeFlr118nk **RglOfficr**118nk Chased outside, weaken 9
21Aug06-4Sar fst 5½f ⊗ :22 :452 :573 1:041 Md Sp Wt 56k –0 7 8 913 919 922 938½ Velazquez J R L118 *1.70 59-12 Longley1184½ Mucho Gusto1183¼ Westwon1184 Bolted turn 9
7Aug06-2Sar fm 5½f (T) :213 :444 :564 1:03 Md Sp Wt 47k 58 5 3 53½ 33½ 22 43¼ Velazquez J R L118 *2.35 89-05 MrGoodkat1181½ YnkeeBy118½ CherokeeFlre1181¼ Ducked out, lost irons 7
WORKS: May8 Mth 4f fst :49 B *10/29* ●Apr13 PmM 5f fst 1:011 H *1/8* ●Apr6 PmM 4f fst :48 H *1/6* ●Mar30 PBD 4f gd :481 B *1/6* Mar23 PBD 3f gd :381 B *3/5* Mar16 PBD 3f gd :381 B *2/4*
TRAINER: +180Days(82 .23 $1.72) Turf(512 .22 $1.71) Sprint(516 .23 $1.51) MdnSpWt(455 .22 $1.47) J/T 2006-07 BEL(79 .25 $1.36) J/T 2006-07(544 .29 $1.81)

Also Eligible:

3x Copy That
Own: Scaturorchio James T Pletcher Jake J P
Blue Peacock Blue And Beige Diamonds, Blue
LUZZI M J (29 6 4 3 .21) 2007: (396 66 .17)

B. c. 3 (Mar) KEESEP05 $550,000
Sire: Thunder Gulch (Gulch) $30,000
Dam: Drina (Regal and Royal)
Br: ClassicStar (Ky)
Tr: Pletcher Todd A(7 1 2 4 .14) 2007:(343 89 .26)

(L) 118

Life	0	M	0	0	$0	–	D.Fst	0	0	0	0	$0	–
2007	0	M	0	0	$0	–	Wet(336)	0	0	0	0	$0	–
2006	0	M	0	0	$0	–	Synth	0	0	0	0	$0	–
Bel(T)	0	0	0	0	$0	–	Turf(294)	0	0	0	0	$0	–
							Dst(T)(311)	0	0	0	0	$0	–

WORKS: May8 Mth 4f fst :504 B *27/29* Apr15 PmM 4f fst :492 B *15/30* Apr9 PmM (T) 5f fm 1:032 B(d) *1/3* ●Mar25 PBD 5f gd 1:00 B *1/4* Mar17 PBD 5f gd 1:021 B *8/12* Mar10 PBD 5f gd 1:03 B *4/5*
Mar3 PBD 5f gd 1:024 B *5/7* Feb24 PBD 4f gd :492 B *3/8* Feb10 PBD 3f gd :372 B *1/2* Feb3 PBD 3f gd :39 B *5/6* Dec12 PBD 3f gd :38 B *3/3*
TRAINER: 1stStart(196 .18 $1.45) 1stTurf(100 .18 $1.66) Turf(512 .22 $1.71) Sprint(516 .23 $1.51) MdnSpWt(455 .22 $1.47) J/T 2006-07 BEL(36 .17 $1.34) J/T 2006-07(153 .22 $1.72)

The six-furlong turf sprint drew a full field of 12 maidens. Justy looked best among the six that had already run on the grass, but half the horses in the race were trying turf for the first time, including the first-time starters Copy That, Houbara, and Snowstalker.

The Tomlinson Ratings for the six horses making their grass debuts, along with their odds, looked like this:

HORSE	TURF TOMLINSON	ODDS
Copy That	292	3–1 (entry)
General Ryan	249	13–1
Houbara	314	18–1
Letthesunshinein	251	16–1
Snowstalker	333	25–1
Tacticianor	313	94–1

Copy That was a full brother to Spain, a $3.5 million earner who upset the 2000 Breeders' Cup Distaff, and who never raced on turf, but full sister Path of Thunder was a stakes winner on the grass. Copy That had decent turf breeding, but he was coupled with the returning Three Lions, who had been outfinished in three sprint races as a 2-year-old, and the Todd Pletcher-trained entry was being solidly bet at 3–1.

General Ryan and Letthesunshinein were poorly rated for turf. Tacticianor had not shown any ability whatsoever in five starts on dirt, and had never started any lower than 57–1.

That left Houbara for the red-hot Kiaran McLaughlin, and Snowstalker for Tom Bohannan, who had recently returned to racing after eight years away from the game.

The race was the first leg of a pick four. My published analysis contained the following advice:

"Justy ran two races of virtually identical quality off a layoff to begin U.S. career, but neither was anything truly exceptional, so one might get the feeling there's someone lurking in this field—either a first-time starter or a first-time turfer—that might jump up in this spot . . . Snowstalker and Houbara have been readied by capable first-out connections, and either could prove the key in a possible 'spread' race for multirace exotics."

Turf races for maidens are ideal spread races for pick-four purposes. When the top-rated horses trying grass for the first time are 25–1, their inclusion should be virtually automatic.

SIXTH RACE
Belmont
MAY 12, 2007

6 FURLONGS. (Inner Turf) (1.07) MAIDEN SPECIAL WEIGHT . Purse $43,000 INNER TURF (UP TO $8,170 NYSBFOA) FOR MAIDENS, THREE YEAR OLDS AND UPWARD. Three Year Olds, 118 lbs.; Older, 123 lbs.

Value of Race: $43,000 Winner $25,800; second $8,600; third $4,300; fourth $2,150; fifth $1,290; sixth $123; seventh $123; eighth $123; ninth $123; tenth $123; eleventh $123; twelfth $122. Mutuel Pool $624,218.00 Exacta Pool $516,211.00 Trifecta Pool $387,631.00

Last Raced	Horse	M/Eqt. A. Wt	PP	St	$\frac{1}{4}$	$\frac{1}{2}$	Str	Fin	Jockey	Odds $1
	Snowstalker	3 118	8	10	$9\frac{1}{2}$	5^{hd}	4^6	$1\frac{1}{4}$	Velasquez C	25.25
18Apr07 7GP3	Justy	L 3 118	4	4	5^2	$3\frac{1}{2}$	1^{hd}	$2^2\frac{1}{4}$	Coa E M	1.90
28Sep06 6Bel6	Three Lions	L b 3 118	11	2	$4\frac{1}{2}$	2^2	2^{hd}	$3^{1}\frac{3}{4}$	Velazquez J R	c- 3.00
	Copy That	L 3 118	12	3	$7\frac{1}{2}$	7^{hd}	$5\frac{1}{2}$	4^{hd}	Luzzi M J	c- 3.00
7Apr07 3GP6	General Ryan	L b 3 118	5	5	$1\frac{1}{2}$	1^{hd}	$3\frac{1}{2}$	$5^{3}\frac{1}{4}$	Castellano J J	13.80
5May07 2Bel4	Letthesunshinein	L b 3 118	6	9	$6\frac{1}{2}$	$6^{1}\frac{1}{2}$	$6\frac{1}{2}$	$6^{1}\frac{1}{2}$	Desormeaux K J	16.00
10Feb07 4Aqu8	Tacticianor	L b 3 118	9	12	$10\frac{1}{2}$	8^{hd}	$7^3\frac{1}{2}$	$7^{1}\frac{1}{2}$	Espinoza J L	94.00
21Apr07 7GP3	Eff Jaa Gee	L 3 118	1	11	12	$10\frac{1}{2}$	$8\frac{1}{2}$	$8^4\frac{3}{4}$	Gomez G K	2.60
18Aug06 6Sar5	Al Sheetahn	L bf 4 118	7	6	2^{hd}	$9^3\frac{1}{2}$	$10^3\frac{1}{2}$	$9^1\frac{1}{2}$	Ponce J5	36.50
18Apr07 7GP8	Masterofthehouse	L 3 118	10	1	3^{hd}	$4\frac{1}{2}$	$9\frac{1}{2}$	$10^1\frac{1}{2}$	Arroyo N Jr	25.25
2May07 2Bel7	Bright Illusion	L b 3 118	2	8	8^{hd}	11^{10}	11^{12}	$11^{13}\frac{1}{4}$	Rojas R I	57.25
	Houbara	3 118	3	7	11^{hd}	12	12	12	Garcia Alan	18.40

c–Coupled: Three Lions and Copy That.

OFF AT 3:46 Start Good. Won driving. Course firm.
TIME :21³, :44⁴, :57, 1:09¹ (:21.66, :44.83, :57.19, 1:09.22)

$2 Mutuel Prices:				
	9 – SNOWSTALKER	52.50	17.80	8.80
	5 – JUSTY		3.40	2.70
	3 – THREE LIONS(c–entry)			3.40

$2 EXACTA 9–5 PAID $203.00 $2 TRIFECTA 9–5–3 PAID $753.00

Dk. b or br. g, (Feb), by Dynaformer – Snowy Range , by Seattle Slew . Trainer Bohannan Thomas. Bred by Green Hills Farm (Ky).

SNOWSTALKER was outrun early, advanced inside on the turn, angled out in upper stretch, responded when set down, finished strongly outside and was clear at the finish. JUSTY raced close up early, rallied three wide into the stretch and stayed on to earn the place. THREE LIONS contested the pace while three wide and tired in the final furlong. COPY THAT was outrun early, raced four wide and lacked a rally. GENERAL RYAN contested the pace along the inside and tired in the stretch. LETTHESUNSHINEIN raced close up early, advanced four wide on the turn and tired in the stretch. TACTICIANOR had no rally. EFF JAA GEE was steadied on the backstretch and had no rally. AL SHEETAHN stumbled after the start, chased the pace along the inside and tired. MASTEROFTHEHOUSE tired after a half mile. BRIGHT ILLUSION had no response when roused. HOUBARA raced inside and tired.

Owners– 1, Shortleaf Stable Inc; 2, Zayat Stables LLC; 3, Peachtree Stable; 4, Scatuorchio J T and Pletcher J and T; 5, G R and S Stable; 6, Gianca Stable; 7, Grant Mary and Joseph and Kelly Thomas J; 8, Castletop Stable; 9, Lucky Seven Stable; 10, Picarello Margaret; 11, Spruce Pond Stable; 12, Darley Stable

Trainers– 1, Bohannan Thomas; 2, Mott William I; 3, Pletcher Todd A; 4, Pletcher Todd A; 5, Hennig Mark; 6, Streicher Kenneth; 7, Kelly Patrick J; 8, Violette Richard A Jr; 9, Johnson Cleveland; 10, Tesher Howard M; 11, Jerkens H Allen; 12, McLaughlin Kiaran P

Scratched– Kal El (15Apr07 4GP 7) , Bishop's Back (28Apr07 3Aqu4) , Brazenly Bold (07Apr07 3GP 2) , Regal Officer (05May07 9Bel10)

$2 Pick Three (7–6–9) Paid $3,460.00 ; Pick Three Pool $94,605 .

Justy ran well again, but Snowstalker kicked in suddenly after being angled to the outside in upper stretch and blew by late. Houbara, the other turf-bred overlay, trailed throughout. You can't be sure of what you're getting with these types of horses, but the odds compensate for the inherent risk involved. For pick-four purposes, you don't have to be a genius and somehow come up with the right longshot among a handful with similar credentials; you just have to recognize that spreading is probably the way to go and construct a play accordingly.

BETTING STRATEGIES

Most of us fancy ourselves as insightful handicappers who know a live-looking longshot when we see one. It's far more important, however, to successfully trade in that good opinion for cash at the betting windows, and there are a number of ways to go about it; moreover, the kind of longshots you consider for win bets are often quite different from those you consider for inclusion in multirace exotics.

Single-Race Betting

Protection against long losing streaks is essential for bettors who are constantly speculating on high-risk/high-reward horses. The way to do this is to bet a very small percentage of bankroll. A conservative player who focuses on low-priced overlays and wins 30 percent of his bets might regularly bet 5 percent of bankroll on a given race, but a longshot player who wins 15 percent of the time shouldn't be risking more than 2 percent, because run-outs of 15 to 20 races are fairly common. My personal style of play for win betting is as follows:

Under 2–1: pass

2–1 to 6–1: win bet only

6–1 to 10–1: win bet; possible exacta saver(s)

12–1 and higher: win bet; possible exacta and/or trifecta saver(s)

For the most part, win bettors who think they've spotted an overlay in the range of 2–1 to 6–1 should simply bet the good thing on the nose. There may be times, however, when you also think the favorite has an exceptionally good chance to finish off the board, in which case a place bet makes sense. Vulnerable favorites include: suspicious drop-downs; those facing a potentially ruinous pace scenario; those trying a new surface; and those compromised by a poor post-position draw, such as Sweetnorthernsaint in the Sunshine Millions Classic.

Hedging on medium-odds overlays to place won't make you rich, but it can do wonders for maintaining your equilibrium—and your bankroll—during the inevitable stretches of second-place finishes that are a part of racetrack life.

Hedging with exactas and trifectas on high-odds selections is not only an effective way to curtail losing streaks, but sometimes these "saver" bets turn out to be every bit as lucrative as cashing the win ticket would've been.

And let's face it, in the real world there are going to be many situations where the favorite looks absolutely legitimate, but there's also a sleeper in the field at a silly price.

2 Oh My Stars
Own: Calabrese Anthony
White Fuchsia, Chartreuse Chevrons, Chartreuse
ROJAS R I (15 4 2 0 .27) 2007: (89 12 .13)

B. c. 4 (Feb) EASSEP04 $210,000
Sire: Not For Love (Mr. Prospector) $20,000
Dam: Vicki's Vixen (Wolf Power*SAf)
Br: Peter R Bradley III (Md)
Tr: Persaud Atreo(3 1 0 0 .33) 2007:(47 6 .13)

L 122

Life	16	4	3	2	$92,655	84	D.Fst	15	3	3	2	$77,835	84
2007	5	0	1	1	$13,120	80	Wet(407)	1	1	0	0	$14,820	62
2006	7	3	2	0	$60,795	84	Synth	0	0	0	0	$0	–
							Turf(306)	0	0	0	0	$0	–
Bel	2	2	0	0	$25,200	77	Dst(374)	12	2	2	2	$57,995	84

14Apr07–3Aqu fst 6f :222 :46 :574 1:10 4↑Alw 45000N1x 57 2 5 67 73¾ 65¼ 610¾ Hill C L118 11.90 81–12 SilverFerrri1181¼ ToughShipmte123½ OcnForst1231¼ Steadied after start 7
24Mar07–6Aqu fst 6f ⊡ :224 :46 :574 1:10 4↑OC 75k/N1x 67 1 7 72¼ 74¼ 76¾ 610¼ Lopez C C L118 7.90 84–09 Suave Jazz1231 Trailing Twelve123¾ Rocky Blue118 Off slowly, inside 7
10Mar07–3Aqu fst 6f ⊡ :23 :46 :574 1:10 4↑OC 75k/N1x 80 3 2 1½ 2hd 2½ 35 Hill C L118 24.00 89–11 Hrcomshllywd123nk MstrSprm1184¾ OhMyStrs1181¾ Bumped start, inside 6
18Feb07–3Aqu fst 6f ⊡ :231 :47 :59 1:113 4↑Hcp 16000s 77 5 2 12 11½ 11½ 2nk Hill C L114 5.00 86–18 ItsaMonster117nk OhMyStars114nk Bookmster1241¼ Dug in gamely on rail 6
13Jan07–3Aqu fst 6f ⊡ :222 :451 :572 1:10 Clm 50000(50-40) 70 5 2 1hd 3½ 42½ 58 Lopez E10 L111 12.80 86–10 CrftyTricker119nk LptopComputer1191 TrilingTwelv1205 Vied inside, tired 6
30Dec06–1Aqu fst 6f ⊡ :221 :45 :571 1:102 3↑OC 75k/N1x 81 7 1 2½ 2hd 2hd 62 Hill C L119 13.00 85–16 SuvJzz119½ LordSnowdon1191 CopprtonKid119hd Dueled outside, weaken 7
15Dec06–2Aqu fst 6f ⊡ :222 :451 :571 1:101 Clm 35000(35-25) 84 3 2 11½ 11½ 13½ 12½ Hill C L120 6.80 88–13 OhMyStars1202½ SlickCityNites1193 CucinNick120hd Set pace, drew away 6
10Dec06–1Aqu fst 6f ⊡ :221 :451 :574 1:113 Clm c-20000 75 8 1 1½ 1hd 1½ 21¼ Hill C L120 13.30 80–18 SlickCityNites1201¼ OhMyStars1201¼ ItstheRitz120nk Drifted deep stretch 8
Claimed from Poston, Bill and Vicki for $20,000, Hushion Michael E Trainer 2006(as of 12/10): (242 50 52 34 0.21)
22Nov06–5Aqu fst 6½f :232 :462 1:114 1:184 Clm 25000 67 6 1 11 15 13½ 21 Hill C L120 8.30 82–16 Quahada1221 Oh My Stars1207 De Roode1201¼ Pace, clear, caught 8
4Oct06–7Bel fst 6½f :223 :46 1:112 1:181 Clm 14000 77 5 3 12 15 16 14½ Hill C L120 *1.95 81–20 OhMyStrs1204½ DesrtQust1132½ LuckyStright1183¼ Stumbled start, clear 8
13Sep06–7Bel fst 6f :222 :461 :584 1:121 Clm 14000 65 1 3 13 12 13½ 1nk Hill C L118 17.50 77–27 OhMyStars118nk Dontlevemrc1111¾ DesertQuest1202½ Pace, clear, held on 9
9Aug06–6Sar fst 6f :222 :46 :582 1:111 Clm 20000 49 2 5 31½ 73¾ 910 815¾ Migliore R L118 16.70 68–16 Marco'sTale1184¾ DrDoright1182½ UnbridledVow1181 Bumped start, tired 9
WORKS: Apr22 Aqu 4f fst :49 B *5/11* Mar4 Aqu⊡ 5f fst 1:014 H *7/11*
TRAINER: Dirt(131 .08 $1.42) Sprint(92 .08 $1.34) Alw(26 .00 $0.00)
J/T 2006-07 BEL(11 .18 $6.15) J/T 2006-07(24 .25 $5.91)

1 Unrequited SCRATCHED

3 Holy Canyon
Own: Streicher Judson L
Blue Tan, Red Hoop, Red Cap
SAMYN J L (14 1 2 2 .07) 2007: (123 4 .03)

B. c. 3 (May) KEEAPR06 $250,000
Sire: Holy Bull (Great Above) $15,000
Dam: Cherokee Canyon (Cherokee Run)
Br: Ramona Thomson & Larry Cannon (Ky)
Tr: Jerkens H Allen(8 2 1 1 .25) 2007:(82 18 .22)

118

Life	1	1	0	0	$25,800	94	D.Fst	1	1	0	0	$25,800	94
2007	1	1	0	0	$25,800	94	Wet(402)	0	0	0	0	$0	–
2006	0	M	0	0	$0	–	Synth	0	0	0	0	$0	–
							Turf(243)	0	0	0	0	$0	–
Bel	0	0	0	0	$0	–	Dst(359)	1	1	0	0	$25,800	94

21Apr07–2Aqu fst 6f :22 :454 :573 1:094 3↑Md Sp Wt 43k 94 2 3 32 22½ 11½ 16¼ Samyn J L 118 2.85 93–12 HolyCnyon1186¼ TheDukeofStnco1183¾ Vlidtion1185 Quick outside move 7
WORKS: ●May8 Bel 5f fst 1:004 B *1/8* ●Apr18 Bel tr.t 5f fst :592 Hg *1/17* Apr10 Bel tr.t 5f fst 1:021 B *8/27* Mar30 GP 3f fst :353 Hg *3/10* Mar24 GP 4f fst :483 Bg *18/55* Mar17 GP 3f fst :383 B *13/14*
TRAINER: 2ndStart(21 .10 $1.03) WonLastStart(61 .13 $1.02) Dirt(332 .15 $1.35) Sprint(253 .15 $1.29) Alw(101 .20 $1.16)
J/T 2006-07 BEL(10 .20 $1.71) J/T 2006-07(20 .15 $1.24)

1a Saratoga Jet
Own: Triple Diamond Stables White Owl Stab
Red Purple, White Diamond Hoop, White
VELASQUEZ C (26 5 3 7 .19) 2007: (595 92 .15)

B. c. 4 (Mar) SARAUG04 $25,000
Sire: A. P Jet (Fappiano) $5,000
Dam: Pierpont Account (Private Account)
Br: Bill Terrill (NY)
Tr: Dutrow Richard E Jr(12 3 3 2 .25) 2007:(194 53 .27)

L 122

Life	9	3	0	1	$93,222	83	D.Fst	7	3	0	1	$84,155	83
2007	2	0	0	0	$2,430	79	Wet(363)	2	0	0	0	$9,067	73
2006	7	3	0	1	$90,792	83	Synth	0	0	0	0	$0	–
							Turf(224)	0	0	0	0	$0	–
Bel	3	1	0	0	$32,740	79	Dst(335)	6	2	0	1	$58,355	79

14Apr07–3Aqu fst 6f :222 :46 :574 1:10 4↑Alw 45000N1x 77 7 2 41½ 4¾ 41¼ 43 Dominguez R A L118 *.55e 89–12 Silver Ferrari1181¼ Tough Shipmate123½ Ocean Forest1231¼ Outfinished 7
27Jan07–7Aqu fst 6f ⊡ :22 :443 :57 1:10 4↑OC 75k/N1x-N 79 2 6 68 77½ 86¼ 64½ Fragoso P L118 10.80e 90–06 Suave Jazz1231¼ Bold Mon118½ Coppertone Kid118no 3 wide trip, no rally 10
15Jly06–8FL gd 1 1/16 :232 :47 1:12 1:444 ⓈNYDerby177k 64 3 1½ 1hd 31½ 511 515½ Flores Jeremias L119 f 7.40 74–19 FrocousWon1191¾ ShfflngMddns1175¼ FrOnUp1187 Btwn pace, weakened 8
25Jun06–8Bel myS 7f :222 :451 1:11 1:244 ⓈMikeLee110k 73 7 5 73¾ 54¾ 43½ 44¾ Gomez G K L121 11.10 72–18 Ferocious Won117nk Classic Pack119½ Fire One Up1174 4 wide trip, no rally 8
10Jun06–5Bel fst 6f :214 :44 :554 1:081 3↑OC 75k/N1x-N 70 1 6 67 78¼ 613 614¼ Prado E S L119 4.60 83–08 Afrashad1214¾ CoolSpringsSaint121¾ MyoPost1216¾ Stumbled after start 9
7May06–2Bel fst 6f :221 :453 :58 1:11 3↑ⓈOC 25k/N2x-N 79 1 2 52½ 43 31 1nk Prado E S L118 3.05 83–20 Saratoga Jet118nk Just in Fun122¾ It's theRitz1181¾ Wide move, prevailed 8
1Apr06–3Aqu fst 7f :224 :453 1:103 1:233 ⓈAlw 43000N1x 83 5 5 1½ 1½ 1hd 11 Desormeaux K J L122 3.80 83–16 Saratoga Jet1221 Precise Action1221½ Fire One Up118½ Determinedly inside 7
16Feb06–4Aqu fst 6f ⊡ :223 :461 :584 1:113 ⓈMd Sp Wt 41k 78 2 6 21 31 1hd 11½ Coa E M L120 f *1.45 81–16 SaratogaJet1201½ PreciseAction1205½ BckDoorDel113¾ Found room on rail 10
16Jan06–4Aqu fst 6f ⊡ :223 :464 :59 1:113 ⓈMd Sp Wt 41k 67 1 8 62¾ 64½ 46½ 34 Fragoso P L120 f *.40e 77–17 Ferocious Won1203¾ PreciseAction120nk SaratogaJet1206¼ Going well late 9
WORKS: May7 Aqu 5f fst 1:014 B *11/16* Apr29 Aqu 5f fst 1:02 B *7/13* Apr6 Bel tr.t 4f fst :492 B *12/23* Mar21 Bel tr.t 4f fst :50 B *56/97* Feb13 Bel tr.t 5f fst 1:034 B *15/17*
TRAINER: 2Off45-180(130 .25 $1.88) Dirt(718 .25 $1.90) Sprint(485 .27 $2.05) Alw(249 .28 $1.83)
J/T 2006-07 BEL(18 .44 $3.82) J/T 2006-07(41 .29 $2.08)

4 Pulpiteer SCRATCHED

5 Trippi Appeal
Own: E Paul Robsham Stables LLC
Green Maroon, Gold Ball, Maroon 'R,' Gold
CASTELLANO J J (21 2 5 4 .10) 2007: (371 58 .16)

B. g. 4 (Mar) OBSMAR05 $265,000
Sire: Trippi (End Sweep) $10,000
Dam: Sennen Cove (Cox's Ridge)
Br: Ocala Stud Farm (Fla)
Tr: Hough Stanley M(8 0 2 0 .00) 2007:(78 10 .13)

L 122

Life	7	2	2	0	$61,190	89	D.Fst	3	1	2	0	$44,600	89
2007	1	1	0	0	$13,200	69	Wet(367)	3	1	0	0	$15,090	71
2006	3	0	0	0	$3,390	71	Synth	0	0	0	0	$0	–
							Turf(269)	1	0	0	0	$1,500	69
Bel	2	1	0	0	$26,190	89	Dst(402)	3	0	1	0	$11,290	82

11Apr07–4GP gd 5½f :214 :451 :58 1:044 3↑Clm 30000(30-25)N2L 69 7 3 41 3½ 3½ 1½ Centeno D E L124 f 3.50 91–15 Trippi Appeal124½ Snow Trick1172¾ Ultimate1241 4 wide, prevailed 7
16Sep06–1Bel gd 6f :223 :46 :583 1:114 Clm 50000(50-40) 46 1 3 2½ 41 75¼ 710¾ Coa E M L120 f 2.60 68–17 LemonsofLove1203 OcenForst1151¾ CountOnPl120¾ Finished after a half 7
3Sep06–4Sar gd 6f :221 :451 :571 1:093 3↑Alw 50000N2L 71 5 3 2hd 2½ 55¾ 511 Castellano J J L118 f 3.15 81–16 HitherLane1203½ MinersLamp1182½ DdeCounty1203¾ Between rivals, tired 7
9Aug06–8Sar fm 5½f Ⓣ :214 :443 :56 1:014 3↑Alw 50000N1x 69 3 4 2hd 2½ 53¼ 57 Castellano J J L117 4.00 91–05 SilverTimber1192½ ApolloJons121¾ WddingSingr117no Pressed pace, tired 7
29Aug05–7Sar fst 7f :222 :451 1:10 1:234 Alw 42300N1x 81 2 1 21½ 2½ 24½ 25½ Velazquez J R L120 f *.80 79–18 PrivateVow1205½ TrippiAppel12019¾ ShortCircuit120 Chased outside, tired 3
7Aug05–3Sar fst 6f :223 :452 :572 1:101 Alw 46060N1x 82 1 1 1½ 1hd 21½ 26 Velazquez J R L120 f 4.80 83–15 FirstSamurai1206 TrippiAppel1203 MoonsHlo1204¼ Steady, altered course 5
16Jly05–2Bel fst 5f :223 :46 :582 Md Sp Wt 43k 89 7 4 1½ 1hd 1½ 13 Coa E M L118 f *1.30 92–15 TrippiAppeal1183 PoliticlForce1183¾ DiscosSon1184¾ Vigorous hand ride 8
WORKS: May7 Bel tr.t 4f fst :483 B *4/15* Apr8 PmM 4f fst :50 B *13/21* Apr1 PmM 3f fst :372 B *3/10* Mar20 PmM 5f fst 1:012 H *5/22* Mar11 PmM 4f fst :483 H *13/41* Feb21 PmM 5f fst 1:01 H *12/19*
TRAINER: 2OffOver180(9 .11 $0.51) 31-60Days(72 .17 $1.63) WonLastStart(39 .13 $0.82) Dirt(168 .14 $1.13) Sprint(126 .14 $1.10) Alw(104 .12 $0.85)
J/T 2006-07 BEL(15 .07 $0.93) J/T 2006-07(69 .12 $1.19)

6 Greater Fool
Own: Klaravich Stables
Black White, Red Braces And 'Ks,' White And
GOMEZ G K (8 0 2 3 .00) 2007: (453 100 .22)

Dk. b or br c. 4 (Mar) OBSFEB05 $250,000
Sire: Exploit (Storm Cat)
Dam: Lanai City (Carson City)
Br: Kenneth C Roberts (Ky)
Tr: Violette Richard A Jr(6 2 0 0 .33) 2007:(159 37 .23)

L 122

Life	3	1	0	0	$27,225	79	D.Fst	2	1	0	0	$25,800	79
2007	1	0	0	0	$1,425	77	Wet(362)	0	0	0	0	$0	–
2005	2	1	0	0	$25,800	79	Synth	1	0	0	0	$1,425	77
							Turf(271)	0	0	0	0	$0	–
Bel	1	1	0	0	$25,800	79	Dst(368)	2	1	0	0	$27,225	79

12Apr07–6Kee fst 6f ◈ :222 :444 :562 1:081 4↑Alw 49450N1x 77 4 4 1hd 1hd 2hd 55¼ Gomez G K L118 4.50 97–05 He Loves MeNot1181 DeltaStorm1182¼ Markum118¾ Bmp start,weakened 11
8Oct05–8Kee fst 1 1/16 :234 :482 1:143 1:483 BrdrsFut-G1 52 3 65 54½ 44 714 721¼ Bridgmohan S X L121 8.40 48–39 DawnofWar1213½ Catcominatch1213¼ StremCt121nk Collapsed,vanned off 12
Previously trained by Cohen Melissa 2005(as of 9/14): (3 1 1 0 0.33)
14Sep05–6Bel fst 6f :22 :453 :574 1:11 Md Sp Wt 43k 79 6 6 43 3½ 12½ 17¾ Coa E M L118 6.70 84–17 GreterFool1187¾ TheRedPrinc118nk OdnsTl118hd Drew away when roused 8
WORKS: ●May7 Aqu 5f fst 1:002 H *1/16* May1 Kee ◈4f fst :472 H *6/32* Apr24 Kee ◈4f fst :481 B *3/35* ●Apr8 Kee ◈3f fst :341 H *1/8* Apr1 PmM 5f fst 1:01 H *2/18* Mar26 PmM 5f fst 1:004 H *2/13*
TRAINER: 2OffOver180(11 .18 $0.92) Dirt(403 .21 $1.66) Sprint+254 .19 $1.38) Alw(154 .25 $2.26)
J/T 2006-07 BEL(15 .27 $1.67) J/T 2006-07(42 .24 $1.54)

7 Executive Search
Own: Lake Star Stable McMahon Michael J Ve
Orange Black, Red Star, White Sleeves, Red
HILL C (28 0 4 2 .00) 2007: (400 33 .08)

B. c. 4 (Apr)
Sire: Regal Classic (Vice Regent) $10,000
Dam: Light for Regal (Majestic Light)
Br: Mr & Mrs Harry Stanyon (NY)
Tr: Ubillo Rodrigo A(2 0 1 0 .00) 2007:(46 4 .09)

L 124

Life	26	3	4	5	$150,798	86	D.Fst	17	3	3	4	$131,412	86
2007	9	2	1	2	$77,490	86	Wet(292)	5	0	1	1	$16,860	64
							Synth	0	0	0	0	$0	-
2006	16	1	3	3	$73,188	78	Turf(265)	4	0	0	0	$2,526	68
Bel	5	1	0	1	$31,582	72	Dst(311)	13	2	3	5	$105,090	84

28Apr07-6Aqu	fst	7f		:22 :44 1:083 1:213	4↑ Alw 45000N1x	86	2	7	67	77¼	53¾	53	Espinoza J L	L123 b	19.30	90-08 HesaPioneer118no **Pulpiteer**1131¼ GrndChmpion1231¼	Inside trip, no rally 9
14Apr07-7Aqu	fst	6f		:213 :443 :571 1:10	3↑ Ⓢ OC 30k/N2x-N	84	3	10	913	811	62¾	12	Smith M E	L123 b	5.90	92-12 Executive Search1232 Wild Vicar111no Heathrow1211¼	4 wide move, clear 10
31Mar07-5Aqu	fst	6f	⊡	:232 :461 :58 1:103	4↑ Ⓢ OC 50k/N2x-N	80	6	3	64½	65¾	64	41¼	Smith M E	L123 b	16.60	90-12 MrComponent123nk Stonewood123¾ SeekingthGlory118nk	Going well late 6
22Mar07-9Aqu	fst	6f	⊡	:224 :454 :574 1:103	4↑ Ⓢ OC 30k/N2x-N	78	6	8	84¼	88¼	58	32¾	Sutherland C	L123 b	8.90	88-12 ToughShipmt118nk RobsBoyMt1132½ ExcutvSrch1232½	Good finish inside 9
9Mar07-7Aqu	fst	6f	⊡	:232 :461 :581 1:10	4↑ Ⓢ OC 50k/N2x-N	77	2	5	43	43	45½	37¼	Sutherland C	L123 b	31.25	87-15 Stonewood1183 Heathrow1184¼ ExecutiveSerch1231½	Came wide, no rally 8
24Feb07-5Aqu	fst	6f	⊡	:234 :472 :593 1:122	4↑ Ⓢ Alw 43000N1x	73	1	4	42	22½	22	11¾	Sutherland C	L118 b	3.60e	82-15 ExecutiveSearch1181¾ CatsLd1182 *OneDySoon*1181½	Came wide, clear late 7
17Feb07-9Aqu	fst	6f	⊡	:223 :46 :583 1:111	4↑ Ⓢ Alw 43000N1x	71	3	8	76½	52	32½	23¼	Sutherland C	L118 b	9.20	85-14 PrecisAlloy1183¼ *ExcutivSrch*1181¼ KrkorumThundr118½	Rallied for place 9
25Jan07-7Aqu	fst	6f	⊡	:23 :47 :592 1:123	4↑ Ⓢ Alw 43000N1x	69	9	1	89¼	84¼	84¼	51	Sutherland C	L118 b	8.20	80-20 Unconcerned118no RawCat118nk HotLiketheSnd118½	Good finish outside 9
13Jan07-5Aqu	fst	170	⊡	:24 :474 1:124 1:422	4↑ Ⓢ Alw 44000N1x	71	6	86¼	55½	42¾	39	48¾	Sutherland C	L118 b	5.30	76-16 NotOnMyTurf1186 BoldJewllr118nk ChildrnsAnnx1182½	Wide throughout 9
30Dec06-5Aqu	fst	6f	⊡	:23 :461 :582 1:11	3↑ Ⓢ Alw 43000N1x	71	1	7	76	83½	3½	32½	Sutherland C	L120 b	4.90	81-16 BrveSirRobin114¾ *Unconcernd*1201¾ ExcutivSrch1202¾	Bumped after start 9
16Dec06-7Aqu	fst	6f	⊡	:224 :46 :581 1:111	3↑ Ⓢ Alw 43000N1x	78	10	3	75¼	56½	37½	34½	Sutherland C	L120 b	13.20	78-22 Daza1223½ Precise Alloy1211 Executive Search1203¼	4 wide, mild rally 11
3Dec06-9Aqu	fst	6f	⊡	:224 :454 :574 1:104	3↑ Ⓢ Alw 43000N1x	76	5	11	1012	89¼	58	23¼	Sutherland C	L120 b	15.90	82-13 MrBourbonStrt1203¼ ExcutvSrch120¾ Strkpthbls1221	Good finish outside 11

WORKS: May8 Bel 3f fst :362 B *3/10* ●Apr24 Bel tr.t 3f fst :354 H *1/5* Apr11 Bel 3f fst :37 B *4/10* Feb11 Bel tr.t 4f fst :50 B *29/73*
TRAINER: Dirt(93 .08 $1.28) Sprint(47 .06 $0.62) Alw(35 .06 $0.66) J/T 2006-07 BEL(1 .00 $0.00) J/T 2006-07(4 .00 $0.00)

8 King Alliance
Own: Kinsman Stable
Pink Royal Blue, Brown Sash, Brown Hoop On
LUZZI M J (29 6 4 3 .21) 2007: (396 66 .17)

Ch. c. 3 (Feb)
Sire: Awesome Again (Deputy Minister) $125,000
Dam: Valid Carnauba (Valid Appeal)
Br: Kinsman Farm (Ky)
Tr: Mott William I(4 1 2 0 .25) 2007:(229 42 .18)

Blinkers OFF

L 116

Life	4	1	0	1	$16,800	76	D.Fst	4	1	0	1	$16,800	76
2007	3	0	0	1	$4,800	76	Wet(400)	0	0	0	0	$0	-
							Synth	0	0	0	0	$0	-
2006	1	1	0	0	$12,000	66	Turf(281)	0	0	0	0	$0	-
Bel	0	0	0	0	$0	-	Dst(361)	0	0	0	0	$0	-

Previously trained by Zito Nicholas P 2006: (422 71 66 58 0.17)

12Mar07-8GP	fst	1	:231 :454 1:101 1:362	Alw 40000N1x	30	5	52½	78	713	723	729½	Cruz M R	L118 b	18.00	58-22 DontFluffWithm1182¼ BriscoNLogn1181 Vritsrum1181½	Done early, eased 7
11Feb07-7GP	fst	1	:23 :453 1:10 1:363	Alw 46000N1x	10	9	106¼	1110	1112	1118	1141½	Castellano J J	L118	18.00	46-17 Delightful Kiss1181½ Sightseeing118no *Chelokee*118hd	Showed little 11
13Jan07-5GP	fst	1	:233 :462 1:111 1:37	Alw 40000N1x	76	4	2hd	2½	2hd	3½	34¼	Bejarano R	L118	7.50	81-15 Our Sacred Honor1182½ Arcata1181¾ KingAlliance118¾	Pressed, weakened 9
18Dec06-6Crc	fst	7f	:222 :461 1:122 1:26	Md Sp Wt 20k	66	5	5	43½	3½	11½	12	Bridgmohan J V5	L113	*1.70	83-14 KingAlliance1132 SwornTestmony1183½ MtOrient118nk	4 wide, drew clear 7

WORKS: May8 Bel 4f fst :511 B *24/30* Apr30 Bel 4f fst :49 B *18/52* Apr21 Pay 4f fst :512 B *15/21* Apr14 Pay 4f fst :50 B *5/27* Apr7 Pay 4f fst :494 B *4/29* Mar31 Pay 3f fst :404 B *3/3*
TRAINER: 1stW/Trn(36 .14 $0.91) 61-180Days(103 .19 $1.23) BlinkOff(17 .12 $0.54) Route/Sprint(45 .18 $1.06) Dirt(281 .20 $1.79) Sprint(208 .22 $1.81) J/T 2006-07 BEL(5 .40 $1.88) J/T 2006-07(13 .23 $0.93)

When Unrequited and Pulpiteer scratched from Belmont's opener on May 12, 2007, it left Holy Canyon as a stick-out. Holy Canyon had worked a bullet five furlongs from the gate on April 18, and three days later had won his debut in exceptional time and manner; another solid five-furlong drill had taken place four days ago, and the colt looked rock solid at 3–5—exactly the kind of horse that is most preferred in first-level allowance races.

Despite that, Oh My Stars beckoned seductively at 20–1. He looked a little on the cheap side, but even so, he was interesting for several reasons:

1. Oh My Stars was a need-to-lead speed horse that had darkened form, after trouble at the break in two consecutive starts. In seven straight starts prior to that, he had been alert enough and quick enough to break first or second, so this was not a case of a habitually sluggish starter, just a case of bad racing luck. He was much better with the early lead, and several of his races at Aqueduct pointed him out as the main speed.
2. He had won both previous starts at Belmont.
3. There was a strong short-term trainer pattern for Atreo Persaud, an under-the-radar guy who had won four races across town on Aqueduct's main track in the month of April, each time with horses who were getting off the inner track and ridden by Raul Rojas, another guy who doesn't attract any attention.

4. Oh My Stars had started in the midst of Persaud's hot streak in mid-April, but had been compromised by a second straight slow start. Now, he was getting a switch to Raul Rojas.

In a sprint race on a conventional dirt track, a horse that figures to have the early lead is always a threat; when that horse is also 2 for 2 over the track, and being sent out by a hot trainer, he becomes an irresistible play in a short field at 20–1, no matter how good the favorite looks. Everything would have to break right for Oh My Stars to beat Holy Canyon, and even then, the favorite would probably win unless something went exceptionally wrong. In a case like this, where a prohibitive favorite is very likely to finish first or second, a win bet on the longshot can be protected with an exacta underneath the chalk.

FIRST RACE
Belmont
MAY 12, 2007

6 FURLONGS. (1.07³) ALLOWANCE . Purse $45,000 (UP TO $8,550 NYSBFOA) FOR THREE YEAR OLDS AND UPWARD WHICH HAVE NEVER WON A RACE OTHER THAN MAIDEN, CLAIMING, STARTER, OR RESTRICTED OR WHICH HAVE NEVER WON TWO RACES. Three Year Olds, 118 lbs.; Older, 124 lbs. Non-winners of $24,000 since March 12 Allowed 2 lbs. (Races where entered for $35,000 or less not considered in allowances). (Cloudy. 72.)

Value of Race: $45,000 Winner $27,000; second $9,000; third $4,500; fourth $2,250; fifth $1,350; sixth $450; seventh $450. Mutuel Pool $309,134.00 Exacta Pool $337,313.00 Trifecta Pool $246,021.00

Last Raced	Horse	M/Eqt. A. Wt	PP	St	¼	½	Str	Fin	Jockey	Odds $1
21Apr07 2Aqu¹	Holy Canyon	3 118	2	4	2½	23½	1hd	1½	Samyn J L	0.60
14Apr07 3Aqu⁶	Oh My Stars	L 4 122	1	1	12½	11½	25	22¼	Rojas R I	20.90
28Apr07 6Aqu⁵	Executive Search	L b 4 124	6	6	55	43	32½	34¼	Hill C	13.00
11Apr07 4GP¹	Trippi Appeal	L f 4 122	4	2	41	55	54½	4nk	Castellano J J	19.90
14Apr07 3Aqu⁴	Saratoga Jet	L f 4 122	3	3	33	32	42	5¾	Velasquez C	9.00
12Apr07 6Kee⁵	Greater Fool	L 4 122	5	5	7	7	6hd	65½	Gomez G K	2.55
12Mar07 8GP⁷	King Alliance	L 3 116	7	7	64½	61½	7	7	Luzzi M J	42.25

OFF AT 1:00 Start Good For All But GREATER FOOL. Won driving. Track fast.
TIME :22, :44², :56², 1:09¹ (:22.10, :44.54, :56.54, 1:09.36)

$2 Mutuel Prices:

3 – HOLY CANYON	3.20	2.40	2.10
2 – OH MY STARS		11.40	6.70
7 – EXECUTIVE SEARCH			3.70

$2 EXACTA 3–2 PAID $46.20 $2 TRIFECTA 3–2–7 PAID $149.00

B. c, (May), by Holy Bull – Cherokee Canyon , by Cherokee Run . Trainer Jerkens H Allen. Bred by Ramona Thomson & Larry Cannon (Ky).

HOLY CANYON raced with the pace from the outside while in hand, responded when roused in upper stretch, dug in determinedly outside and got the job done. OH MY STARS was hustled out to a clear lead, set the pace and dug in gamely along the inside in the stretch. EXECUTIVE SEARCH was outrun early, advanced inside on the turn, came wide for the drive and offered a mild rally outside. TRIPPI APPEAL chased the pace while three wide and tired in the stretch. SARATOGA JET tired after a half mile. GREATER FOOL stumbled badly at the start, raced inside and had no rally. KING ALLIANCE raced inside and had no response when roused.

Owners– 1, Streicher Judson L; 2, Calabrese Anthony; 3, Lake Star Stable Cosgrove Peter K McMahon Michael J and Veitch John G; 4, E Paul Robsham Stables LLC; 5, Triple Diamond Stables and White Owl Stable; 6, Klaravich Stables Inc; 7, Kinsman Stable

Trainers– 1, Jerkens H Allen; 2, Persaud Atreo; 3, Ubillo Rodrigo A; 4, Hough Stanley M; 5, Dutrow Richard E Jr; 6, Violette Richard A Jr; 7, Mott William I

Scratched– Unrequited (18Mar07 8SA 4) , Pulpiteer (28Apr07 6Aqu2)

Oh My Stars broke alertly this time and quickly went clear, and battled back gamely when collared by the favorite to drop a close decision. The exacta of $46.20 was more than Oh My Stars would have paid had he won.

One of the worst bets in racing is playing longshots across the board. On Belmont Stakes Day a few weeks later, Meribel was a perfectly legitimate favorite in the Foresta Stakes. She had recorded Beyers of 90 or better in her last six starts on turf, and had returned as a 4-year-old with two solid performances, including a strong closing kick to win under similar conditions.

But if Meribel was the one to beat at 8–5, Calla Lily had to have at least some kind of chance to make her presence felt.

Calla Lily had been good enough to run second to Meribel at Saratoga as a 3-year-old; both of her victories had come on Belmont's Widener turf course; and she was on an encouraging figure pattern, with two Beyers as a 4-year-old that were a slight improvement on her best races as a 3-year-old.

Calla Lily wasn't that far off Meribel on her best day, and might deserve the benefit of the doubt for her recent fourth-place finish as the favorite, considering that the early pace had been exceptionally slow.

FIFTH RACE
Belmont
JUNE 9, 2007

1$\frac{1}{16}$ MILES. (Turf) (1.38²) THE FLY EMIRATES FORESTA. Purse $80,000 FOR FILLIES AND MARES FOUR YEARS OLD AND UPWARD WHICH HAVE NOT WON A OPEN SWEEPSTAKES ON THE TURF. No nomination fee. A supplemental nomination fee of $200 may be made at time of entry. $1,000 to enter, starters to receive a $750 rebate. The added money and all fees to be divided 60% to the owner of the winner, 20% to second, 10% to third, 5% to fourth, 3% to fifth and 2% divided equally among the remaining finishers. Weight 123 lbs. Non-winners of $45,000 on the turf, allowed 3 lbs. Four Races, 5 lbs. Three Races, 7 lbs. (Maiden, claiming, starter and restricted allowance races not considered in allowances). A presentation will be made to the winning owner. Closed Saturday, June 2, 2007 with 30 nominations. (If the Stewards consider it inadvisable to runthis race on the turf course, this race will be run at One Mile and One Sixteenth on the main track.).

Value of Race: $83,500 Winner $50,100; second $16,700; third $8,350; fourth $4,175; fifth $2,505; sixth $334; seventh $334; eighth $334; ninth $334; tenth $334. Mutuel Pool $1,351,840.00 Exacta Pool $1,147,330.00 Trifecta Pool $950,755.00

Last Raced	Horse	M/Eqt.	A.	Wt	PP	St	¼	½	¾	Str	Fin	Jockey	Odds $1
17May07 8Bel¹	Meribel	L	4	120	7	8	9½	9½	82½	5hd	11¼	Gomez G K	1.75
13Apr07 8Kee²	I'm in Love	L f	4	116	3	9	4½	4½	4hd	3hd	2nk	Coa E M	15.80
11May07 1Bel⁴	Calla Lily	L	4	117	6	10	10	10	9hd	73	3½	Albarado R J	23.10
17May07 8Bel²	Fantastic Shirl	L	4	116	10	3	3½	3hd	32	4½	4hd	Velazquez J R	5.70
25May07 9CD¹	Flow Chart-UAE	L	4	118	1	2	1½	15	15	13½	5nk	Leparoux J R	5.20
27Apr07 6Kee¹	Criminologist	L	4	116	8	5	71	7½	52	61½	6¾	Prado E S	6.90
19May07 7Pim²	A True Pussycat	L f	4	120	4	1	2½	21	22	2hd	74	Garcia Alan	4.90
14May07 8Del²	Daytime Promise	L	4	116	2	6	82½	81½	10	96	81¼	Hill C	38.75
5May07 12CD²	Beautiful Daniele	L	4	116	5	4	6hd	5½	6½	8hd	910¼	Desormeaux K J	11.90
20May07 7Crc¹	Emma's Candy	L b	4	116	9	7	5hd	6hd	7½	10	10	Velasquez C	74.50

OFF AT 2:30 Start Good. Won driving. Course firm.

TIME :25¹, :48⁴, 1:11⁴, 1:35³, 1:41⁴ (:25.20, :48.90, 1:11.83, 1:35.75, 1:41.97)

$2 Mutuel Prices:

7 – MERIBEL	5.50	3.70	2.90
3 – I'M IN LOVE		12.20	7.90
6 – CALLA LILY			10.00

$2 EXACTA 7–3 PAID $80.00 $2 TRIFECTA 7–3–6 PAID $928.00

Dk. b or br. f, (Apr), by Peaks and Valleys – Count to Six , by Saratoga Six . Trainer Clement Christophe. Bred by Arthur B Hancock III & Catesby W Clay (Ky).

MERIBEL was outrun early, came wide for the drive, responded when shaken up, finished with a rush outside and was clear at the finish. I'M IN LOVE raced close up early, rallied inside into the stretch and finished gamely on the rail. CALLA LILY was outrun early, came wide into the stretch and finished well outside. FANTASTIC SHIRL chased the pace from the outside and tired in the stretch. FLOW CHART (UAE) quickly showed in front, set the pace, took a clear lead into deep stretch and faltered along the inside. CRIMINOLOGIST was rated along outside, raced four wide and lacked a rally. A TRUE PUSSYCAT chased the pace along the inside and tired in the stretch. DAYTIME PROMISE was outrun early, raced inside and had no response when roused. BEAUTIFUL DANIELE raced wide throughout and tired. EMMA'S CANDY raced five wide and tired.

Owners– 1, Hancock III Arthur B and Clay Catesby W; 2, Namcook Stables LLC; 3, Darley Stable; 4, Dell Ridge Farm; 5, Dream With Me Stable Inc; 6, Janney III Stuart S and Phipps Stable; 7, Bradley III Peter R; 8, Bilinski Darlene and Patten Harry; 9, Circle E Racing; 10, Eigner Michael and Pell Lewis

Trainers– 1, Clement Christophe; 2, McLaughlin Kiaran P; 3, Albertrani Thomas; 4, McLaughlin Kiaran P; 5, Biancone Patrick L; 6, McGaughey III Claude R; 7, Bush Thomas M; 8, Contessa Gary C; 9, Mott William I; 10, Kaplan William A

Scratched– Dean's List (11May07 1Bel¹)

$2 Pick Three (3–3–7) Paid $71.50 ; Pick Three Pool $254,432 .
$2 Pick Four (9–3–3–7) Paid $259.00 ; Pick Four Pool $475,301 .

In this case, a $30 outlay ($10 to win, place, and show) would have yielded only the $10 show price, for a return of $50 and a net win of $20 on the race.

Where 20–1 shots are concerned, the same $30 offers more profit potential if it is divided up as $10 to win, $10 in exactas, and $10 in trifectas—perhaps something as simple as a $1 part-wheel of Meribel-all-Calla Lilly for $8, and two additional $1 combinations with two other contenders. With that kind of a trifecta saver, Calla Lily's third-place finish would have generated a $464 return for each winning $1 combination.

Multiple-Race Betting

Longshots are viewed in an entirely different context when it comes to multiple-race bets, particularly the pick four and pick six. To catch big payoffs with these bets doesn't necessarily require bettors to be geniuses and to single $35 winners; the only requirement is to survive and advance—that is, get through one leg and move on to the next one.

The keys to successful multiple-race betting are (a) differentiating between straightforward races and those that are competitive and/or confusing, and (b) being sufficiently financed to cover *all* the possibilities in the races where you are spreading. Longshots that aren't appetizing win bets should be covered in these spread situations whenever their records contain even the most esoteric of redeeming qualities; they usually wind up being the catalyst for a score, because small tickets focusing on the most logical contenders in each leg will usually bypass them.

The seventh race at Belmont Park on May 10, 2007, was the second leg of the late pick four, and a mess in general—what author Mark Cramer has referred to as a "lesser of evils" race where nobody looks good.

Let's assume you're playing the pick four and have designated this restricted claiming sprint on the turf as a spread race. Without peeking at the result chart, which ones are you using, at least in some capacity?

1 The River Mon SCRATCHED

2 General Congress
Own: Lostritto Joseph A
White — Red, White Yoke And 'JI,' White Sleeves — $35,000
ROJAS R I (9 2 1 0 .22) 2007: (83 10 .12)

B. g. 6 (Apr)
Sire: Victory Speech (Deputy Minister)
Dam: Bounding Boldly (Bounding Basque)
Br: Joseph Lostritto (NY)
Tr: Lostritto Joseph A(4 0 0 0 .00) 2007:(55 7 .13)

L 121

Life	29	1	1	3	$36,148	70	D.Fst	16	1	1	1	$20,978	57
2007	7	0	0	1	$2,794	57	Wet(321)	5	0	0	0	$1,427	33
							Synth	0	0	0	0	$0	-
2006	12	1	0	1	$17,218	70	Turf(230)	8	0	0	2	$13,743	70
Bel(T)	5	0	0	1	$7,005	70	Dst(T)(301)	1	0	0	0	$1,230	54

21Apr07-1Aqu fst 1 :23 :462 1:122 1:383 3↑Clm 15000N2L 33 8 67¼ 66½ 79½ 716 619¾ Samyn J L L120 f 31.50 49-24 *Story Line*120hd On the Margin1232 Paving the Way1207¼ No response 9
6Apr07-7Aqu fst 7f :224 :46 1:11 1:231 3↑Clm 10000N2L 47 5 3 68 66½ 55¼ 69¾ Hill C L121 f 11.10 75-08 MaxCm1213¾ LuckyStright1161¼ TotheRepublic121nk 3 wide, no response 8
25Mar07-5Aqu fst 170 ⊡ :243 :491 1:143 1:452 3↑Clm 15000N2L 57 2 63 53½ 57 46½ 35¼ Sutherland C L120 fb 39.00 65-21 DH InthSrvc115 DH DoublAgnt1235¼ GnrlCongrss120hd Inside trip, no rally 7
1Mar07-6Aqu fst 6f ⊡ :23 :463 :59 1:12 4↑Clm 10000N2L 41 6 9 1012 811 89¼ 69¼ Samyn J L L120 fb 18.20 75-17 *Just Jack n' Water*120hd *Teakwood*1204¼ To the Republic120no Had no rally 10
19Feb07-5Aqu fst 170 ⊡ :241 :481 1:133 1:441 3↑Clm 15000N2L 43 3 810 813 613 716 718¾ Espinoza J L L120 fb 27.25 57-24 Bonus Size1203¾ *In by Two*1162 *Story Line*1202 No response 8
9Feb07-7Aqu fst 170 ⊡ :24 :474 1:13 1:434 4↑Clm 15000N2L 56 4 811 811 77 76 66 Ponce J7 L113 fb 39.75 72-15 Mister Zee1201 Teakwood1202 *Northern Storm*1201½ Had no rally 8
20Jan07-9Aqu fst 6f ⊡ :231 :481 1:004 1:141 4↑Clm 15000N2L 40 9 9 1114 89¾ 711 47¾ Messina R L120 fb 83.75 65-21 Ernie's Choice120no Afleet Force1233 Sultry City1204¾ Mild rally inside 11
Previously trained by Iorio Sal Jr 2006(as of 11/28): (198 21 30 23 0.11)
28Nov06-1FL fst 6f :231 :472 1:001 1:131 3↑Md 7500 49 5 1 11 11 12½ 15¼ Osorio J D L124 fb *.90e 76-20 GenerlCongrss1245¼ RundownRocky121½ PolicEscort1216¼ 3 path, driving 8
14Nov06-2FL slyS 5½f :224 :47 1:001 1:07 3↑Md 7500 33 2 2 21 21½ 32½ 47 Osorio J D L124 fb 2.65e 74-21 Teddy Hull121nk Rundown Rocky1245½ Police Escort1211¼ Weakened 9
31Oct06-6FL fst 170 :232 :474 1:122 1:45 3↑Md Sp Wt 17k 37 3 79½ 65½ 59 76¼ 67¼ Osorio J D L124 fb 7.10 73-18 KrisNHtch1203 Cpstonclrnc120no *Wtrlrgngcowboy*120hd 5w 5/16, weakened 8
Previously trained by Lostritto Joseph A 2006(as of 10/19): (118 6 16 14 0.05)
19Oct06-5Bel yl 1⅛ T :502 1:16 1:41 1:532 3↑S Md Sp Wt 42k 52 3 33½ 34 41½ 1010 109 Espinoza J L L122 fb 43.50 49-34 AcdemyRoyle120no Dubliner120no ElderSktsmn1201¼ Chased inside, tired 11
1Oct06-10Bel gd 1⅛ ⊗ :491 1:153 1:42 1:553 3↑S Md Sp Wt 50k –0 3 2½ 3nk 52¾ 825 838¼ Espinoza J L L122 fb 11.70 15-34 IWontDnc1201½ SrSlmdnc1224½ Bchlornumbron120¾ Finished after a half 10

WORKS: May7 Bel tr.t 3f fst :371 B *7/10* Apr30 Bel tr.t 4f fst :482 B *2/28* Apr14 Bel tr.t 4f fst :492 B *38/118* Apr1 Bel tr.t 3f fst :354 B *3/25* Mar21 Bel tr.t 3f fst :362 B *3/27*
TRAINER: Dirt/Turf(18 .11 $2.49) Route/Sprint(15 .13 $2.85) Turf(50 .08 $1.24) Sprint(107 .08 $1.70) Claim(41 .07 $1.56)
J/T 2006-07 BEL(1 .00 $0.00) J/T 2006-07(2 .00 $0.00)

3 Ballston
Own: Aquilino Joseph
Blue — White And Blue Stripes, White Sleeves — $35,000
MARTIN E M JR (20 2 1 4 .10) 2007: (329 38 .12)

Dk. b or br g. 4 (Mar)
Sire: A. P Jet (Fappiano) $5,000
Dam: Doublicious (Double Negative)
Br: Joseph Aquilino (NY)
Tr: Aquilino Joseph(4 0 0 1 .00) 2007:(49 2 .04)

L 121

Life	22	1	2	0	$55,670	77	D.Fst	14	0	1	0	$8,579	54
2007	3	0	0	0	$1,652	52	Wet(330)	3	1	0	0	$35,175	62
							Synth	0	0	0	0	$0	-
2006	16	1	2	0	$53,481	77	Turf(188)	5	0	1	0	$11,916	77
Bel(T)	3	0	1	0	$11,580	77	Dst(T)(322)	0	0	0	0	$0	-

26Apr07-1Aqu fst 6f :22 :451 :572 1:103 3↑Clm 15000N2L 44 8 6 64¼ 98½ 99¼ 911¼ Rivera J L Jr L121 b 34.00 78-15 DncingRobbins1183 CocknyGmblr121hd SlyDimondJm1211 Finished early 9
21Apr07-5Aqu fst 6f :222 :454 :581 1:103 4↑S Alw 43000N1x 52 2 7 713 710 79¾ 712 Rivera J L Jr L118 b 73.00 77-12 P. J. Indy1183½ Cat's Lad113nk Woodmere118hd Outrun inside 8
4Apr07-7Aqu slyS 6f :231 :462 :581 1:101 3↑S Alw 43000N1x 49 6 4 41½ 53¾ 59 512½ Ponce J5 L116 b 42.50 78-12 *Grand Refer*1181½ Woodmere1216¼ Trust Nobody111½ 3 wide trip, no rally 6
15Dec06-5Aqu fst 170 ⊡ :233 :464 1:11 1:424 3↑Clm 25000N2L 49 6 67½ 611 611 715 715 Lopez C C L119 b 25.00 71-15 Habsburg1193¾ Bold Love1201¼ Story Line1191¾ Inside, no factor 9
3Dec06-9Aqu fst 6f ⊡ :224 :454 :574 1:104 3↑S Alw 43000N1x 45 8 7 98¾ 1015 1017 1015½ Samyn J L L120 b 66.50 69-13 MrBourbonStrt1203¼ ExcutivSrch120¾ Strkupthblus1221 3 wide trip, tired 11
18Nov06-7Aqu fst 5½f ⊡ :222 :46 :58 1:043 3↑S Alw 43000N1x 54 6 9 810 810 912 77¼ Samyn J L L120 b 19.90 89-10 Speedjama121nk Strikeuptheblues1221¾ Phillip X.120hd No response 9
4Oct06-8Bel fm 6f T :221 :45 :563 1:083 3↑S Alw 43000N1x 71 6 7 85¼ 87½ 711 46 Samyn J L L119 b 17.00 95-02 Sigh You1194¼ *S. S. Crafty*119no Speaking Out1211¾ Going well late 10
16Sep06-10Bel fst 7f ⊗ :224 :461 1:111 1:242 3↑S Alw 51600N1x 46 7 3 72¼ 74¼ 813 815¼ Rodriguez A5 L112 b 16.80 64-17 Boysik1173¼ Back Door Deal1173 Minority Leader117½ 3 wide trip, tired 8
30Aug06-1Sar my 5½f ⊗ :223 :471 1:00 1:063 3↑S Md Sp Wt 56k 62 12 8 88½ 810 42 1¾ Leparoux J R5 L115 b 10.70 86-11 Ballston115¾ *Defrizz*120nk Pure Pro120hd 6wide, along in time 12
13Jly06-9Bel fst 6f ⊗ :224 :462 :59 1:123 3↑S Md Sp Wt 49k 51 3 4 45 46 45½ 43½ Samyn J L L118 b 4.40 71-15 StormProspector1181 PurePro1182 LiberationDy118½ Came wide, no rally 8
29Jun06-6Bel gd 6f T :232 :472 :593 1:112 3↑S Md Sp Wt 41k 77 8 2 21 21½ 22½ 23¾ Samyn J L L118 b 10.90 83-17 Yankee Thunder1183¾ Ballston1185½ Path ofPerfection118nk Second best 9
16Jun06-4Bel fm 6f T :223 :452 :57 1:084 3↑S Md Sp Wt 41k 57 6 6 31½ 33 47½ 59 Rojas R I L118 b 52.25 91 - Bgvond1186¾ RoscommonExpress1231½ Heights118½ Chased inside, tired 8

WORKS: ●Mar31 Aqu ⊡ 3f fst :35 H *1/8* Mar26 Aqu ⊡ 4f fst :504 B *4/4* Mar20 Aqu ⊡ 4f fst :501 B *3/6*
TRAINER: Dirt/Turf(18 .06 $0.70) Turf(39 .08 $0.81) Sprint(130 .08 $1.87) Claim(44 .09 $1.02)
J/T 2006-07 BEL(1 .00 $0.00) J/T 2006-07(3 .00 $0.00)

4 Indian Prayer
Yellow — Own: Candlin John
Yellow, Black Diamond Hoop, Black — $35,000
LAKEMAN A (1 0 0 0 .00) 2007: (28 0 .00)

Ch. g. 4 (Feb)
Sire: Regal Classic (Vice Regent) $10,000
Dam: Silver Jam (Silver Ghost)
Br: Dr Jerry Bilinski & Martin Zaretsky (NY)
Tr: Candlin John(2 0 0 0 .00) 2007:(48 1 .02)

L 121

Life	12	1	1	1	$15,806	47	D.Fst	9	0	1	1	$5,596 39
2007	5	0	0	0	$972	25	Wet(326)	2	1	0	0	$9,750 47
2006	1	0	0	0	$146	16	Synth	0	0	0	0	$0 -
							Turf(265)	1	0	0	0	$460 -
Bel (T)	1	0	0	0	$460	-	Dst(T)(326)	0	0	0	0	$0 -

2May07-1Bel -gd 1 (T) :243 :50 1:15 1:39 3↑ Alw 46000N1x −0 6 2hd 32 710 718 741¼ Lakeman A L122 b 74.50 23- 35 OpertionRedDwn1221¼ RedGint1185½ KrisAngel122nk Finished after a half 7
29Mar07-7Aqu fst 5½f [•] :23 :473 1:001 1:063 3↑ [S]Alw 43000N1x 15 5 6 88¾ 814 813 819½ Lakeman A L121 b 102.25 66- 20 KrkormThndr116½ BrdofPly1211¾ ThndrMnstr1161½ Bumped backstretch 8
1Mar07-6Aqu fst 6f [•] :23 :463 :59 1:12 4↑ Clm 10000N2L 5 10 4 41½ 1013 1017 923¾ Lakeman A L120 b 73.00 60- 17 *Just Jack n' Water*120hd *Teakwood*1204¼ TotheRepublic120no Finished early 10
15Feb07-5Aqu fst 6f [•] :222 :451 :574 1:113 4↑ Clm 10000N2L −0 7 5 69¼ 918 928 833¾ Rodriguez R R L120 b 71.25 52- 13 *More Impact*1201½ *Sultry City*1202¾ Notable Tiger1208 Finished early 9
10Feb07-5Aqu fst 6f [•] :224 :462 :59 1:12 4↑ Clm 15000N2L 25 2 6 66½ 813 817 817¾ Chang T10 L110 b 31.00 66- 13 SilthMystc1206¾ SouthrnProspct120nk InthSrvc113¾ Stumbled after start 8
Previously trained by Acquilano James 2006(as of 4/17): (6 0 2 1 0.00)
17Apr06-8FL fst 4½f :223 :46 :521 3↑ Alw 14600N2L 16 4 3 710 716 718 Messina R L119 b 5.70e 76- 12 *AVeryYoungJet*1207 LittleManPaputso117½ PhillyFrenzy114nk Rail, outrun 8
3Dec05-7FL fst 6f :214 :45 :581 1:112 Alw 14600N2L 22 7 3 51¾ 53½ 66¾ 610¼ Grabowski J A L122 b 10.90 78- 10 Connecticat122hd GoldEnd1163¼ *ZippyShnnon*1152½ 6 wide turn, weakened 8
3Nov05-3FL fst 6f :221 :452 :582 1:114 Alw 14600N2L 39 1 6 1hd 1hd 2½ 56 Davila M A Jr L122 b 2.40e 80- 11 Macon's Million1183¼ Mighty Good120nk Gold End118nk Weakened 9
10Oct05-3FL myS 5f :222 :462 :593 Md Sp Wt 15k 47 6 1 12 11 1hd 1½ Davila M A Jr 120 b 2.55 91- 10 Indian Prayer120½ Cash Bonanza115nk Page Six120½ Held on stubbornly 9
19Sep05-5FL fst 5½f :222 :463 :594 1:063 Md Sp Wt 15k 34 1 4 1½ 1hd 1hd 32 Gutierrez J A 124 b 3.50 81- 12 Gold End1201¾ Mixed Numbers120nk *Indian Prayer*124½ Missed place 8
9Sep05-7FL fst 5f :223 :47 :594 Md Sp Wt 15k 24 1 4 12 12½ 2hd 23 Gutierrez J A 122 b 3.55 87- 15 Connectict1203 IndinPryer1221¾ *ClrysContndr*120¾ No match, second best 9
28Aug05-7FL myS 5f :224 :47 1:00 Md Sp Wt 15k 19 2 7 53¾ 57 47½ 47¾ Gutierrez J A 120 b 3.95 81- 13 L'Es Marq1202¼ *Gold End*1194½ Darn Sweet1201 Dckd in sharply start 8
WORKS: Apr21 Bel tr.t 4f fst :51 B *42/57* Mar26 Bel tr.t 4f fst :524 B *29/29*
TRAINER: Route/Sprint(38 .03 $0.36) Turf(50 .00 $0.00) Sprint(131 .04 $0.76) Claim(58 .02 $0.40) J/T 2006-07 BEL(9 .00 $0.00) J/T 2006-07(23 .00 $0.00)

---

5 Red Stag
Green — Own: Dubb Michael Goldfarb Sanford J Cast
Yellow, Pink Circle And Rose, Pink Cuffs — $35,000
PRADO E S (10 2 1 1 .20) 2007: (467 95 .20)

Ch. c. 3 (Mar) OBSAUG05 $15,000
Sire: Running Stag (Cozzene) $7,500
Dam: Away to Fame (Local Talent)
Br: Lucy Edwards & Randell Edwards (Fla)
Tr: Dutrow Anthony W(2 0 0 1 .00) 2007:(196 56 .29)

L 117

Life	7	1	2	1	$14,540	68	D.Fst	2	1	0	0	$4,670 35
2007	3	0	1	1	$5,630	68	Wet(302)	1	0	0	0	$140 4
2006	4	1	1	0	$8,910	68	Synth	0	0	0	0	$0 -
							Turf(303)	4	0	2	1	$9,730 68
Bel (T)	0	0	0	0	$0	-	Dst(T)(301)	0	0	0	0	$0 -

Entered 10May07- 5 PIM
Previously trained by Pino Michael V 2007(as of 4/25): (117 17 19 17 0.15)
25Apr07-1Atl fm 1 (T) :244 :484 1:133 1:392 3↑ Alw 12500s 53 5 65 54½ 42½ 35 37 Carmouche K L116 b *.80 79- 16 Calagaitor1185¼ CrmeloStrbuckle1041¾ RedStg116½ Belated rally outside 8
10Feb07-10GP fm 1 (T) :233 :482 1:123 1:354 Clm c-(50-40) 51 9 44 31 3½ 108¾ 109½ Trujillo E L120 b 8.10 68- 17 Ballet Fever1201 Patriotic American1202¾ Zenfully120½ 3 wide, faded 10
Claimed from Frazee, Joyce and E. G. for $50,000, Braddy J David Trainer 2006: (201 33 25 25 0.16)
14Jan07-1GP fm 1 1/16 (T) :233 :48 1:121 1:423 Clm 30000(30-25)N2L 68 5 31½ 42½ 33 21½ 2nk Aguilar M L122 b *2.10 77- 16 *Ballet Fever*122nk Red Stag1222 Untuttable Affair1221½ Gaining 8
22Oct06-4Crc fm 7½f (T) :233 :472 1:114 1:294 Alw 24500N2L 68 2 2 31½ 21½ 23 23¼ Aguilar M L118 b 20.70 82- 11 Blue Sailor1183¼ Red Stag118½ Proclamation118½ Chased winner 11
30Sep06-5Crc fst 1 :241 :50 1:171 1:462 Md 12500 35 6 54 33½ 31½ 12 12¾ Trujillo E L118 b 11.60 59- 37 Red Stag1182¾ *Hajeen*1184 *El Pirata*1185½ Drew clear 7
2Sep06-13Crc slyS 6f :223 :474 1:013 1:152 Md 25000 4 12 1 114½ 127½ 98¼ 819 Trujillo E L118 b 19.30 50- 21 Three Miracles118½ Somes Sound1182½ Zion Train1185 Failed to menace 12
11Aug06-3Crc fst 4½f :23 :473 :541 Md 25000 15 6 6 911 910 712¼ Centeno D E L118 18.10 78- 17 Noted Appeal118½ *First Regent*108½ Booder's Brother1184½ Checked start 9
WORKS: Mar28 PmM 5f fst 1:02 B *12/16* Mar10 PmM 5f fst 1:02 B *12/23* Mar2 PmM 4f fst :492 B *8/17* Feb21 PmM 4f fst :49 B *12/32*
TRAINER: 1stW/Trn(132 .30 $1.85) 2Off45-180(89 .31 $1.60) Route/Sprint(49 .35 $1.97) Turf(59 .31 $1.93) Sprint(455 .32 $2.14) Claim(260 .27 $1.68) J/T 2006-07 BEL(25 .32 $1.91) J/T 2006-07(46 .26 $1.42)

---

6 Tsuris SCRATCHED

---

7 Growing Wild
Orange — Own: Peace Agnes
Yellow And Orange Blocks, Yellow — $35,000
VELASQUEZ C (22 4 3 6 .18) 2007: (591 91 .15)

Dk. b or br g. 5 (Jun)
Sire: Wild Again (Icecapade) $50,000
Dam: Ottomwa (Strawberry Road*Aus)
Br: Nordic Thoroughbreds & Wild Again Partners (Ky)
Tr: Weaver George(2 0 0 0 .00) 2007:(91 12 .13)

L 121

Life	5	1	0	0	$9,412	73	D.Fst	2	0	0	0	$512 52
2007	3	1	0	0	$8,900	73	Wet(379)	0	0	0	0	$0 -
2004	2	M	0	0	$512	52	Synth	0	0	0	0	$0 -
							Turf(310)	3	1	0	0	$8,900 73
Bel (T)	0	0	0	0	$0	-	Dst(T)(352)	0	0	0	0	$0 -

14Apr07-7GP fm 1 1/16 (T) :241 :471 1:11 1:403 4↑ Alw 46000N1x 68 3 45½ 57 96¼ 910 88¾ Fuentes R D L120 57.90 78- 22 TrippisStorm1202¼ SweetBrush1242¾ CapoDeiCapi120no Steadied far turn 10
19Mar07-7GP fm 1½ (T) :484 1:152 2:041 2:274 4↑ Alw 40000N1x 71 7 23½ 3½ 31½ 44 67 Bejarano R L120 13.30 69- 20 Tempt Fortune1201 Hard Deck1201¾ Blue Mon1281 Tired 8
8Feb07-4Tam fm 1 1/16 (T) :24 :493 1:151 1:461 4↑ Md 45000(50-45) 73 2 31½ 33½ 2hd 1½ 11¾ Lezcano J L116 8.40 69- 29 GrowingWild1161¾ Americnism120nk KrissMOnc120nk Swung out 1/4pole 7
25Nov04-11Crc fst 1 1/16 ⊗ :232 :482 1:142 1:484 Md Sp Wt 24k 52 1 75 86½ 89¼ 811 69¼ Alvarado R Jr L118 13.40 59- 24 Hurricane Mia1183¾ Padua'sGift118nk HonorGulch118nk Failed to menace 12
17Oct04-5Bel fst 1 1/16 ⊗ :24 :482 1:143 1:481 Md Sp Wt 46k −0 5 21½ 85¾ 820 731 745¼ Samyn J L L119 10.70 14- 38 *Stormy Jim*1191¾ Piety1192¼ *Pavo*1192¾ Brief speed, tired 8
WORKS: Feb25 PBD 4f gd :511 B *4/5*
TRAINER: Route/Sprint(18 .06 $0.47) Turf(180 .11 $1.21) Sprint(134 .09 $1.35) Claim(56 .20 $1.78) J/T 2006-07 BEL(4 .00 $0.00) J/T 2006-07(12 .00 $0.00)

---

8 Tuffy Gold
Pink — Own: Mary Grant Kelly Thomas J Grant Josep
Royal Blue, Yellow Chevrons, Yellow — $35,000
ESPINOZA J L (22 1 0 2 .05) 2007: (187 13 .07)

Dk. b or br c. 4 (May)
Sire: Formal Gold (Black Tie Affair*Ire) $5,000
Dam: Concolour (Our Native)
Br: Thomas J Kelly & Joseph M Grant (Ky)
Tr: Kelly Patrick J(5 0 0 1 .00) 2007:(73 4 .05)

L 121

Life	16	1	0	0	$17,039	70	D.Fst	11	1	0	0	$16,206 68
2007	4	0	0	0	$3,180	61	Wet(383)	1	0	0	0	$176 49
2006	11	1	0	0	$13,687	70	Synth	0	0	0	0	$0 -
							Turf(265)	4	0	0	0	$657 70
Bel (T)	3	0	0	0	$525	70	Dst(T)(343)	0	0	0	0	$0 -

22Apr07-1Aqu fst 6f :221 :461 :581 1:102 3↑ Clm 25000(30-25)N2L 61 3 6 86½ 73¼ 54 55¾ Fragoso P L119 b 30.00 84- 11 Specchio1193 Raw Cat121nk Win for Gold1211 Came wide, no rally 8
23Feb07-3Aqu fst 6f [•] :23 :47 :592 1:112 4↑ Alw 50000s 56 1 6 610 66¾ 67 611¾ Garcia Alan L118 b 30.25 75- 21 Ocean Forest118hd Lord Snowdon1186¼ Specchio1202¼ Had no rally 6
11Feb07-1Aqu fst 1 [•] :243 :481 1:132 1:382 4↑ Clm 30000(30-25)N2L 42 6 2½ 31 68 616 621¼ Ponce J7 L113 b 16.70 67- 21 Dividend Yield1235¾ Bronxdale1231¾ Max Cam1203½ Chased 3 wide, tired 6
1Feb07-3Aqu fst 6f [•] :222 :451 :572 1:103 4↑ Alw 45000N2L 49 2 4 46½ 512 514 513¾ Garcia Alan L118 b 30.00 77- 15 [D]Book Bishop118nk *Herecomeshollywood*1183 *Heretic*1185½ Outrun inside 6
14Dec06-7Aqu fst 6f [•] :223 :453 :58 1:11 3↑ Clm 30000(30-25)N2L 62 7 76¾ Rodriguez A5 L117 b 31.00 77- 18 *SilverFerrri*120½ *BrveSirRobin*1141¼ LivlyUpYourslf1213 Saved ground, fog 11
30Nov06-5Aqu fst 6f [•] :221 :452 :581 1:11 3↑ Clm 30000(30-25)N2L 68 5 8 711 77½ 74¼ 45½ Cunningham T5 L115 b 24.25 78- 16 One Day Soon1203¾ Unconcerned120nk Billy's Way1201½ Had no rally 8
10Nov06-7Aqu fst 6f :23 :463 :591 1:121 3↑ Clm 30000(30-25)N2L 64 4 8 86¾ 89 76¾ 54¼ Branch K5 L115 b 14.70 73- 26 ArchieBoy118½ Unconcerned1132 KillerSpeed1201¼ Very wide throughout 9
25Oct06-3Aqu fst 6f :232 :48 1:002 1:132 3↑ Md 35000(35-25) 61 1 7 32½ 4nk 2hd 12 Rodriguez A5 L115 b 9.30 71- 24 Tuffy Gold1152 Dodgem115no Suffolk County1206½ Found room on rail 7
27Sep06-9Bel fm 1 1/16 (T) :224 :46 1:101 1:404 3↑ Md 45000(45-40) 60 4 2½ 2½ 3½ 69½ 810½ Espinoza J L L120 b 35.25 78- 12 Ivanovsky120nk Watchtower1222¼ Silver Cliff1204¼ Pressed pace, tired 10
12Aug06-10Sar fm 1 3/16 (T) :463 1:103 1:354 1:543 3↑ Md Sp Wt 48k 53 3 32 52½ 52¼ 1110 1215 Fragoso P L118 b 74.00 77- 12 DncngForvr118½ *LgofNtons*1231¼ SwrlngSlmn1181¼ Steadied second turn 12
1Jly06-5Bel fm 1 (T) :23 :461 1:103 1:343 3↑ Md Sp Wt 44k 70 2 74¾ 74¾ 86 88¼ 68 Rodriguez R R L117 b 69.00 79- 16 Under Thunder1172 Exton1172¾ Benedict1171¾ Inside trip, no rally 11
6May06-5Bel fm 1 (T) :23 :454 1:093 1:333 3↑ Md Sp Wt 44k 64 8 811 76 76½ 710 710 Fragoso P L118 b 74.75 82- 11 Half Mask118¾ Carson's Band124hd *Under Thunder*1182¼ Had no rally 8
WORKS: May6 Bel tr.t 3f fst :374 B *8/12* Apr7 Bel tr.t 4f fst :51 B *77/94* Mar24 Bel tr.t 3f fst :361 B *5/30* Mar12 Bel tr.t 3f fst :364 B *5/29*
TRAINER: 2Off45-180(28 .11 $1.41) Dirt/Turf(26 .08 $0.71) Turf(73 .11 $2.55) Sprint(145 .09 $1.34) Claim(27 .15 $4.40) J/T 2006-07 BEL(15 .13 $4.71) J/T 2006-07(40 .10 $2.98)

9 Grancentral Pkwy.
Own: Peter Callahan
Turqse Blue And Red Vertical Halves, Red And — $35,000
MORALES P (10 0 0 2 .00) 2007: (160 16 .10)

Gr/ro. h. 6 (Feb)
Sire: Robyn Dancer (Crafty Prospector) $2,500
Dam: Unusual Color (Da' White Judge)
Br: Mr & Mrs A Francis Vanlangendonck (Fla)
Tr: Everett Scott(4 1 0 0 .25) 2007:(26 3 .12)

Blinkers OFF — L 121

Life	10	1	2	2	$55,246	96	D.Fst	9	0	2	2	$30,646	96
2007	4	0	0	1	$7,816	75	Wet(341)	1	1	0	0	$24,600	83
							Synth	0	0	0	0	$0	-
2005	1	0	0	0	$430	78	Turf(207)	0	0	0	0	$0	-
BelⓉ	0	0	0	0	$0	-	DstⓉ(320)	0	0	0	0	$0	-

18Apr07-5Aqu	fst	1	⊗	:232 :47 1:113 1:372	3↑	Clm 35000n2L	64	5	2hd	1hd	2½	25	49	Morales P	L121 fb	5.00	66-24	Pulpiteer1218 Wooden1211 Wally World121no	Vied inside, tired	9
11Apr07-8Aqu	fst	1		:223 :451 1:091 1:351	3↑	Alw 46000n1x	56	8	31	31	611	818	824	Martin E M Jr	L120 f	25.00	62-18	Vitruvius1173¾ Bond Fire1205¾ In the Woods1151¾	Tired after a half	8
9Mar07-5Aqu	fst	170	⊡	:241 :483 1:14 1:423	4↑	OC 50k/n2L-N	75	4	79½	77	74¾	36½	36¼	Martin E M Jr	L118 f	17.50	78-24	RunningDog1181½ CseysJoy1234¾ GrncentrlPkwy118hd	Mild rally outside	8
22Feb07-3Aqu	fst	6f	⊡	:232 :47 :593 1:122	3↑	Alw 44100n2L	39	3	1	53¾	510	511	516½	Lopez C C	L121 f	8.30	65-20	Heretic121½ Book Bishop1211½ Lemon Drop King1212	Finished early	5
16Mar05-7Aqu	fst	6f	⊡	:223 :454 :581 1:104	4↑	Alw 43000n1x	78	5	4	42¼	43½	74¾	66¼	Luzzi M J	L118 f	3.25	79-20	IronRogue113½ GiveFaith118no KarakorumPatriot1181½	Wide throughout	7
15Sep04-3Bel	fst	1 1/16		:231 :454 1:094 1:423	3↑	Alw 48000n1x	93	1	2½	2½	1hd	11	3½	Prado E S	L116	*2.20	86-15	InfiniteGlory116nk *GoNow*116nk GrncntrlPkwy1161¼	Dug in gamely on rail	7
28Aug04-2Sar	fst	7f		:22 :441 1:084 1:212	3↑	Alw 47000n1x	96	4	1	1hd	32½	22½	21¾	Bejarano R	L116	0.30	94-04	LckyGmbl1161¾ GrncntrlPkwy1161¾ JcobsArch1101½	Came again outside	0
14Aug04-8Pha	fst	170		:221 :452 1:103 1:414		PresdntsCp100k	64	5	76½	67½	87¼	78¾	617¼	Chavez L D	L117	4.80	77-17	Separato1175 Gadace's Khamseh117½ *Prince Joseph*1192	Failed to menace	10
17Mar04-4Aqu	my	6f		:223 :461 :581 1:11		Md Sp Wt 41k	83	2	4	1½	1hd	1½	1½	Luzzi M J	L121 f	*.80	83-18	GrncentrlPkwy121½ CherokeRp1163 JohnsIntrviw121nk	Resolutely on rail	7
29Feb04-4Aqu	fst	6f	⊡	:223 :453 :573 1:103		Md Sp Wt 41k	84	3	6	1hd	1hd	12½	2nk	Espinoza J L	L121	*2.40	86-16	LuckyGamble116nk *GrncentrlPkwy*1212¼ JckofClubs1212½	Greenly, gamely	9

WORKS: May6 Bel 4f fst :48 B *7/79* ●Apr8 Bel tr.t 3f fst :36 B *1/18* Mar31 Bel tr.t 5f fst 1:002 H *10/35* Mar23 Bel tr.t 5f fst 1:01 B *2/10* Mar4 Bel tr.t 5f fst 1:03 H *18/36* ●Feb20 Bel tr.t 3f fst :361 B *1/27*
TRAINER: 1stTurf(4 .00 $0.00) Dirt/Turf(8 .00 $0.00) BlinkOff(1 .00 $0.00) Route/Sprint(15 .40 $3.39) Turf(17 .06 $7.88) Sprint(64 .20 $2.49) J/T 2006-07 BEL(1 .00 $0.00) J/T 2006-07(2 .00 $0.00)

10 Karakorum Tornado
Own: Karakorum Farm
Purple Red And Black Vertical Halves, Red — $35,000
PONCE J (19 0 2 0 .00) 2007: (271 25 .09)

Dk. b or br g. 3 (Jan)
Sire: Thunder Rumble (Thunder Puddles) $1,500
Dam: Cheryl's Way (Go and Go*Ire)
Br: Bill DiScala (NY)
Tr: Odintz Jeff(2 0 0 0 .00) 2007:(66 8 .12)

L 112[5]

Life	9	1	0	0	$12,310	58	D.Fst	8	1	0	0	$12,223	58
2007	8	1	0	0	$12,223	58	Wet(267)	1	0	0	0	$87	21
							Synth	0	0	0	0	$0	-
2006	1	M	0	0	$87	21	Turf(214)	0	0	0	0	$0	-
BelⓉ	0	0	0	0	$0	-	DstⓉ(192)	0	0	0	0	$0	-

3May07-1Bel	fst	6f		:23 :454 :572 1:093		Clm 14000	58	6	5	74½	79	68½	56¼	Ponce J5	L113 b	28.00	84-11	Irish Brian118no In by Two1202¼ Devilish Tom1202¼	Had no rally	7
26Apr07-1Aqu	fst	6f		:22 :451 :572 1:103	3↑	Clm 15000n2L	55	6	3	54¼	64	74¼	77	Rodriguez R R	L116 b	22.90	82-15	DncngRobbns1183 CocknyGmblr121hd SlyDmondJm1211	Inside trip, tired	9
6Apr07-7Aqu	fst	7f		:224 :46 1:11 1:231	3↑	Clm 10000n2L	55	4	8	814	812	77¼	56¼	Espinoza J L	L118 b	17.20	79-08	MaxCam1213¾ LuckyStright1161¼ TotheRepublic121nk	Off slowly, rallied	8
15Mar07-4Aqu	fst	1	⊡	:253 :511 1:164 1:432	3↑	Clm 15000n2L	34	1	1½	1hd	21½	48	515¾	Rodriguez R R	L115 b	8.90	47-31	Officer One1204 Res Ipsa120hd Paving the Way1231	Set pace, tired	6
7Mar07-1Aqu	fst	6f	⊡	:232 :472 1:00 1:131		Clm 20000(20-18)	27	2	5	2hd	3½	54¼	511¼	Rodriguez R R	L120 b	17.60	67-19	DevilishTom1202 *SonnyPjms*120½ RestlessMind1201½	Between rivals, tired	5
8Feb07-4Aqu	fst	6f	⊡	:224 :471 1:003 1:144		[S]Md 25000	37	4	5	23½	21	2hd	1½	Rodriguez R R	L120 b	20.60	70-18	KrkorumTorndo120½ LkeButler1206½ CutButTough1201½	Along for score	11
19Jan07-6Aqu	fst	170	⊡	:224 :47 1:142 1:463		[S]Md 35000	25	6	23	21½	2hd	411	721	Hill C	120 b	43.00	43-29	TimPic1204½ RichbournCourt12010 ChstnutRidg120nk	Bumped after start	9
11Jan07-4Aqu	fst	6f	⊡	:221 :454 :59 1:123		[S]Md 25000	27	6	4	37	612	613	913¾	Rodriguez R R	120	15.90	67-14	BruceTickets1205 SaratogCowboy120½ SongSenor1202¼	Tired after a half	11
13Dec06-4Aqu	gdS	6f	⊡	:224 :47 :593 1:131		[S]Md 50000	21	2	9	54¾	810	916	921¾	Rodriguez R R	120	37.00	51-22	PrssngIss1207¾ Nvrbttrcty1204¾ Dnthmffnmn1201¾	Stalked inside, faded	11

WORKS: Mar31 Aqu⊡ 3f fst :393 B *7/8* Feb28 Aqu⊡ 3f fst :364 B *2/4*
TRAINER: 1-7Days(12 .08 $1.95) 1stTurf(7 .00 $0.00) Dirt/Turf(8 .00 $0.00) Turf(9 .00 $0.00) Sprint(181 .09 $2.34) Claim(47 .02 $0.50) J/T 2006-07 BEL(2 .00 $0.00) J/T 2006-07(10 .20 $5.44)

11 Maurice Ave.
Own: R Nortons Farms
Gray Orange, Pink Sash, Sleeves And Cap — $35,000
GOMEZ G K (5 0 2 1 .00) 2007: (450 100 .22)

Dk. b or br c. 3 (Feb) OBSMAR06 $45,000
Sire: Include (Broad Brush) $25,000
Dam: Gin Rummy Judy (Impressive)
Br: Equus Farm (Ky)
Tr: Violette Richard A Jr(6 2 0 0 .33) 2007:(159 37 .23)

L 117

Life	5	1	1	0	$15,406	71	D.Fst	5	1	1	0	$15,406	71
2007	4	1	1	0	$15,146	71	Wet(352)	0	0	0	0	$0	-
							Synth	0	0	0	0	$0	-
2006	1	M	0	0	$260	20	Turf(307)	0	0	0	0	$0	-
BelⓉ	0	0	0	0	$0	-	DstⓉ(283)	0	0	0	0	$0	-

18Apr07-2Aqu	fst	1	⊗	:232 :472 1:131 1:382	Clm 40000(40-30)	21	5	1hd	1½	99	911	1027¼	Rodriguez R R	L121 b	9.00	43-24	Stopbluffing1211½ Rich Mountain121no HeretoPlease1211¾	Set pace, tired	10
23Mar07-2Aqu	fst	170	⊡	:234 :482 1:141 1:45	Md 25000	71	4	1½	1½	2hd	1½	11	Luzzi M J	L120 b	*2.70e	72-25	MauriceAve1201 PhoenixHeat1208¼ FourSrtog1209	Dug in on rail stretch	9
11Feb07-6Aqu	fst	170	⊡	:232 :471 1:131 1:442	Md 50000(50-40)	41	3	55¾	53¾	42	46½	413¾	Luzzi M J	L120 b	6.10	61-21	RichMountin1201½ *JBThree*120no Westsidptitud12012¼	Inside trip, no rally	8
10Jan07-9Aqu	fst	1	⊡	:233 :473 1:141 1:422	Md 25000	57	2	2½	1hd	2hd	2hd	22	Luzzi M J	L120 b	8.40	66-29	Free of Secrets1202 Maurice Ave.1205 Na'lu1135¾	Vied inside, weakened	10
27Dec06-7Aqu	fst	6f	⊡	:222 :463 :584 1:12	Md 50000(50-40)	20	5	7	76½	77	714	615¾	Morales P	L120 b	21.10	63-17	Secretfairways120¾ *What a Boot*1206 War Tale1201¼	Outrun	7

WORKS: May6 Aqu 4f fst :484 B *4/8* Apr14 Aqu 4f fst :51 B *15/16* Apr7 Aqu 5f fst 1:011 H *9/36* Mar15 Aqu⊡ 4f fst :501 B *5/5* Mar9 Aqu⊡ 4f fst :514 B *5/7*
TRAINER: 1stTurf(30 .10 $1.75) Dirt/Turf(29 .14 $2.05) Route/Sprint(40 .25 $1.50) Turf(93 .14 $1.72) Sprint(254 .19 $1.38) Claim(69 .23 $1.77) J/T 2006-07 BEL(15 .27 $1.67) J/T 2006-07(42 .24 $1.54)

Unless you gave up in exasperation and hit the "all" button, it's relatively safe to whittle away 45–1 shot General Congress, who is 1 for 29 at age 6, and 78–1 Indian Prayer, who has beaten a grand total of two horses in five starts this year.

But if you're serious about getting through this leg, that's about as far as your eliminations should go.

Of the seven remaining entrants, Grancentral Pkwy., Karakorum Tornado, and Maurice Ave. are trying turf for the first time, and though the first two score low on Tomlinsons, turf breeding isn't as much of a predictive factor in turf sprints as it is in routes. None among the trio would need to be the second coming of Manila to prevail.

Below are the four with any semblance of turf form, along with their best applicable grass Beyers. The odds are not shown, because had we actually been playing this pick four, we wouldn't have been able to see them before wagering.

BEYER TURF FIGURES

Ballston	71, 77
Red Stag	68, 68
Growing Wild	68, 71, 73
Tuffy Gold	64, 70

Betting any among this quartet to win would be a stretch. Ballston has two good back figures on grass, but those were at six furlongs, and it's been a long time since he's been remotely competitive. Red Stag is virtually co-favored with Growing Wild, presumably because the shipper is getting a fashionable trainer change. Growing Wild is another new face, and looks logical off a class drop and a positive rider switch, but has raced exclusively in routes so far and is no bargain at 2–1.

Tuffy Gold doesn't get the pulse racing, but he is the key point of this example for exactly that reason. It's hard to "love" a horse whose maiden win is also his only in-the-money finish from 16 starts, but in multiple-race bets we don't have to love Tuffy Gold—we just don't want to let him beat us.

Despite his general futility to this point, Tuffy Gold was not a hopeless case: He ran his competitive figure on this turf course, beating half the field in a maiden special weight mile at 69–1; and he was repeating a form pattern—second race back from a layoff—that produced his maiden victory at 9–1.

SEVENTH RACE
Belmont
MAY 10, 2007

7 FURLONGS. (Turf) (1.19⁴) CLAIMING . Purse $25,000 (UP TO $4,750 NYSBFOA) FOR THREE YEAR OLDS AND UPWARD WHICH HAVE NEVER WON TWO RACES. Three Year Olds, 119 lbs.; Older, 123 lbs. Non-winners of a race since March 9 Allowed 2 lbs. Claiming Price $35,000 (Races Where Entered For $25,000 Or Less Not Considered) (Winners Preferred). (If the Stewards consider it inadvisable to run this race on the turf course, this race will be run at Seven Furlongs on the main track.).

Value of Race: $25,000 Winner $15,000; second $5,000; third $2,500; fourth $1,250; fifth $750; sixth $125; seventh $125; eighth $125; ninth $125. Mutuel Pool $280,055.00 Exacta Pool $197,756.00 Trifecta Pool $103,793.00 Superfecta Pool $24,434.00

Last Raced	Horse	M/Eqt. A. Wt	PP	St	¼	½	Str	Fin	Jockey	Cl'g Pr	Odds $1
22Apr07 ¹Aqu⁵	Tuffy Gold	L b 4 121	6	9	9	8ʰᵈ	3ʰᵈ	1²	Espinoza J L	35000	17.70
18Apr07 ⁵Aqu⁴	Grancentral Pkwy.	L 6 121	7	3	8½	5½	2½	2ⁿᵏ	Morales P	35000	3.50
3May07 ¹Bel⁵	Karakorum Tornado	L b 3 112	8	2	1ʰᵈ	2½	1½	3ⁿᵒ	Ponce J⁵	35000	34.75
14Apr07 ⁷GP⁸	Growing Wild	L 5 121	5	5	7ʰᵈ	6ʰᵈ	4ʰᵈ	4³½	Velasquez C	35000	2.30
26Apr07 ¹Aqu⁹	Ballston	L b 4 121	2	8	4ʰᵈ	4¹½	6³½	5ʰᵈ	Martin E M Jr	35000	15.40
25Apr07 ¹Atl³	Red Stag	L b 3 117	4	6	5½	3¹	5½	6⁵¾	Prado E S	35000	2.20
18Apr07 ²Aqu¹⁰	Maurice Ave.	L b 3 117	9	1	2½	1ʰᵈ	7⁵	7ⁿᵏ	Gomez G K	35000	5.00
2May07 ¹Bel⁷	Indian Prayer	L b 4 121	3	4	6¹½	9	8¹	8⁶¾	Lakeman A	35000	78.50
21Apr07 ¹Aqu⁶	General Congress	L f 6 121	1	7	3¹½	7¹½	9	9	Rojas R I	35000	45.00

OFF AT 4:10 Start Good. Won driving. Course firm.
TIME :22⁴, :46¹, 1:10³, 1:22⁴ (:22.89, :46.30, 1:10.76, 1:22.82)

$2 Mutuel Prices:

8 – TUFFY GOLD	37.40	13.40	9.10
9 – GRANCENTRAL PKWY.		6.30	4.40
10 – KARAKORUM TORNADO			10.00

$2 EXACTA 8–9 PAID $194.50 $2 TRIFECTA 8–9–10 PAID $2,037.00
$2 SUPERFECTA 8–9–10–7 PAID $9,231.00

Tuffy Gold came from last to win going away, and combined with two favorites (one in a four-horse field) and a second choice for a $2 pick four worth $1,263.

When all-stakes pick fours on big-event days are available, they are a consistent source of exceptional value. The pools are swelled with what the poker pros refer to as "dead money" from bettors who may be underinformed, underfinanced, or both. The result can be a terrific payoff whenever a good-priced winner or two land somewhere in the sequence.

For example, the National Thoroughbred Racing Association began offering the "Premier Pick 4" in 2005, a bet that linked the Blue Grass Stakes and the Commonwealth Breeders' Cup from Keeneland with the Arkansas Derby and the Instant Racing Breeders' Cup from Oaklawn Park.

In 2005, the winning combination was anchored by Afleet Alex ($6.80), and the $2 payoff of $2,532 was more than twice the win parlay that linked the Arkansas Derby winner with Diboll Dolly ($11.60), Clock Stopper ($11.60), and Bandini ($8).

In 2006, Lawyer Ron ($3) was a universal single in the Arkansas Derby, but the pick four still paid $3,062—nearly three times the win parlay—because the other three winners paid $10, $16.40, and $19.40.

The 2007 edition of the Premier Pick 4 also concluded with an odds-on winner in the Arkansas Derby. But even with Curlin ($3.60) winning easily as a universal single, the payoff was still $3,132 because of upsets by Dominican ($18) in the Blue Grass, Silent Name ($14.40) in the Commonwealth Breeders' Cup, and Cream Only ($63.20) in the Instant Racing Breeders' Cup.

Cream Only
Own: Padua Stables

Gr/ro. f. 3 (Mar)
Sire: Exchange Rate (Danzig) $10,000
Dam: Raspberry Eggcream (Time for a Change)
Br: Padua Stables (Fla)
Tr: Asmussen Steven M(0 0 0 0 .00) 2007:(1359 297 .22)

Life	10	2	3	3	$109,865	85	D.Fst	8	2	3	2	$102,750	85
2007	4	1	1	1	$76,415	85	Wet(394)	1	0	0	0	$2,000	49
							Synth	0	0	0	0	$0	–
2006	6	1	2	2	$33,450	80	Turf(265)	1	0	0	1	$5,115	64
Op	1	1	0	0	$60,000	85	Dst(385)	3	1	2	0	$74,300	85

14Apr07–10OP	fst	1	:231 :473 1:13 1:384	ⒻInstRcgBC95k	85	8	2½	2½	2hd	1hd	11½	Doocy T T	L115	30.60	89–17	Cream Only1151½ Nice Inheritance119½ Chatham1191	Edged away late	9
12Mar07–6FG	fst	140	:244 :484 1:14 1:422	ⒻAlw 47000N1x	71	5	32½	32½	32	2½	2¾	Meche D J	L118	5.00	79–22	Acrosstheborder118¾ *CrmOnly*118nk PrfckConnct1185½	3-wide both turns	7
15Feb07–7FG	fm	*5½f Ⓣ	:224 :471 :584 1:044	ⒻAlw 47000N1x	64	3	5	53¾	64¾	56½	35¼	Albarado R J	L118	6.60	85–10	Mount Glitter1171¼ Peaks Diamond1184 Cream Only118nk	Up for show	7
28Jan07–10Sun	gd	6½f	:214 :45 1:112 1:182	ⒻElPasoTmsH50k	49	4	9	96¼	910	610	412	Tohill K S	L117	3.70	67–16	StelthCt1204¾ Berriestoheven1226¼ TopSolitire1181	5wd 3/16,luggd in late	10
Previously trained by Blasi Scott 2006(as of 11/21): (783 156 134 118 0.20)																		
21Nov06–8RP	fst	6f	:214 :444 :571 1:10	ⒻMd Sp Wt 23k	80	3	3	83	42	2½	1½	Shepherd J	L119	2.90	94–10	CreamOnly119½ *EverythingsRosie*1191¾ *SusanJane*119hd	Off rail, up in time	11
10Oct06–3RP	fst	1	:234 :483 1:144 1:422	ⒻMd Sp Wt 25k	40	7	43	52¼	43	21	22¼	Shepherd J	L120	*.90	63–29	ABeutifulDrem1202¼ *CrmOnly*1204¼ *PointMthWy*1201¾	4-wide, best of rest	8
25Sep06–6RP	fst	6f	:221 :454 :581 1:104	ⒻMd Sp Wt 25k	49	8	1	4nk	2½	32½	35½	Shepherd J	L119	*.90	84–06	*East Hampton*1192½ Deputy Jet1193 Cream Only1192	Dueled, btwn, wknd	10
25Aug06–4AP	fst	6f	:23 :461 :58 1:103	ⒻMd Sp Wt 27k	67	4	2	31	32	33	21¼	Emigh C A	L118	*1.50	88–10	CozysPromise1181¼ CreamOnly1181½ MissBrook1185½	Inside, second best	8

WORKS: Apr11 **OP** 4f fst :50 B *3/12* Apr4 **OP** 5f fst 1:02 B *2/16* Mar21 **FG** 4f fst :512 B *12/16* Feb26 **FG** 4f fst :533 B *82/83* Feb8 **Hou** 4f fst :503 B *10/24* ● Jan21 **Hou** 4f sly :491 B *1/22*

TRAINER: 61-180Days(166 .22 $1.78) Dirt(2061 .23 $1.67) Routes(936 .22 $1.70) Stakes(425 .19 $1.92)

This winning trio underscores the point that longshots don't necessarily win because of sudden and unpredictable form reversals: Dominican, Silent Name, and Cream Only all were coming off good races.

Dominican had already won twice on Polytrack, and was a viable threat in the Blue Grass, which, despite its Grade 1 status and $750,000 purse, is nothing more than a glorified prep race for the Kentucky Derby. On grounds of intent, 2006 juvenile champion Street Sense was vulnerable as the 11–10 favorite, because the race was only a final conditioner for the main objective three weeks later at Churchill Downs. Dominican merely confirmed the good form he had shown winning the Rushaway in his first start of the year.

Silent Name embodied the "turf-to-synthetic" angle that has been quite productive on Polytrack and Cushion Track, and he certainly classed up based on a near-miss in the Grade 1 Kilroe Mile; a workout at the Commonwealth's seven-furlong distance on Cushion Track confirmed he was seriously meant in his first non-turf start. Lewis Michael (15–1) and Steel Light (5–1) were also coming off turf races, and completed the exacta ($224) and trifecta ($1,242) behind the winner.

Cream Only was one of four fillies in the Instant Racing to have recorded a Beyer of 80 or better. She had compiled a nice line of forward-moving figures since returning from a freshening in late January, while getting progressively closer at each point of call, and her first workout over the Oaklawn surface on April 4 was ranked second-fastest of 16 at the distance that morning. Cream Only had to improve a few lengths to win, but had already run a figure of 80 as a 2-year-old, and an 80 fit very well in this race.

Cream Only's breakthrough performance to upset the Instant Racing at 30–1 might not have been the most probable result, but neither was it entirely implausible.

At that kind of price, handicappers can afford to be optimistic about lightly raced and improving horses such as Cream Only, and view the glass as half full.

QUINN
ON CLASS ANGLES
By James Quinn

WHEN THE LEADING HANDICAP horse in the world won the Breeders' Cup Classic of 2006 at 6.70–1, class analysts who supported him had every right to conclude that they had benefited from perhaps the year's ripest longshot. On the cold dope of class evaluation, Invasor might have been regarded as at least slightly superior to the 3-year-old division leader Bernardini, and in any event, should have been respected at 5–2 or such against the brilliant sophomore.

No doubt the $15.40 mutuel and corresponding key horse to the surrounding exotics converted a number of losing cards into winners on that day, including mine. The outcome also reflected a traditional principle of class evaluation, long forsaken by too many handicappers in the current malaise of declining quality throughout the sport in the United States. Unless the 3-year-old division leader is clearly supreme, or the handicap division thin, the leading older handicap horses should be expected to win the classic stakes of the fall for 3-year-olds and up. Bernardini was top-shelf, but the colt was no 11–10 favorite against Invasor, who was no 6.70–1 shot against the 2006 Classic field.

While handicappers may not associate the class of the field with an expectation of finding a longshot, class standouts that win at 8–1, at double-digit odds, and occasionally at 20–1 and longer can be found with more than occasional repetition. Invasor's $15.40 mutuel reminds all of us that longshots can emerge on class evaluation as surely as any other facet of the art.

Longshots on class normally arrive from any of three directions:

- The best horse has been seriously underrated, a la Invasor.
- In a deeply competitive field, one of the top contenders will be severely underbet.
- The favorite is false, or vulnerable, such that the best horse or second-best has been overlooked to a fault.

The first of these provides the shortest supply. Nonetheless, two familiar situations suggest longshots may be available, and one of the two can be especially generous. Certain horses are what I call power sprinters. The power sprinters will have won Grade 1/Grade 2 stakes going long. When they sprint, if they can exhibit tactical speed, the power sprinters usually will possess too strong a combination of speed and stamina in the stretch drive vis-à-vis the one-dimensional sprint types.

Precisionist provided the indelible mark of the type more than two decades ago, when he won the Breeders' Cup Sprint following a four-month layoff. The horse had won Grade 1 events at a mile and a quarter, numerous stakes at middle distances, and when sprinting, his combination of speed and stamina was too great for the one-dimensional sprinters to resist.

The first great horse I experienced was Ack Ack, a Charlie Whittingham-trained 5-year-old and Horse of the Year of 1971 that could beat any horse in training from 5½ furlongs to 1¼ miles, the latter while toting more than 130 pounds. Ack Ack took them wire to wire, as he did in the Santa Anita Handicap (130 pounds) and the

Hollywood Gold Cup (134 pounds) of that season. Under the 134 pounds, Ack Ack completed Hollywood Park's signature race in less than two minutes.

At Del Mar the previous year, Whittingham entered Ack Ack in a minor feature at 5½ furlongs. The memory lingers, as has the lesson. Ack Ack not only won, but also now, 37 years later, retains the track record for the distance, at 1:02⅕ seconds. The classic-distance winner was also a sensational sprinter.

Ack Ack rarely ran as a nonfavorite and Precisionist was hardly a longshot to win the Breeders' Cup Sprint of 1985. He paid an unremarkable $8.80. But two years later in the same race, the filly Very Subtle performed the same trick. Very Subtle not only sprinted against the best, but also possessed the desirable Grade 1 credentials going long, and she paid $34.80. The very next year the miler Gulch won, and paid $13.60, not exactly a longshot, but nice enough. In 1991, Sheikh Albadou won as a longshot, paying $54.60, and the English import qualified as a main contender.

Other power sprinters have finished second in the Breeders' Cup Sprint at long odds, notably the Bobby Frankel-trained filly Honest Lady, a rallying half-length loser at 31–1 in 2000 to the champion Kona Gold. Ten-wide into the lane, Honest Lady finished in a remarkable 22⅗, but lost. The $2 exacta with the 8–5 favorite paid $138.80 and provided more than adequate compensation. Anyone who had coupled Honest Lady and Kona Gold over the others in the $2 trifecta that day spent an additional $48 and received a splendid $2,076.60.

The power sprinters will be dangerous in any Grade 1/Grade 2 sprint at six to seven furlongs and a number of them will be longshots. If they have won Grade 1/Grade 2 stakes going long, shape up as best on class, and the odds are long enough, back them with confidence. Less reliably, classy routers with tactical speed and high pace figures going long will be dangerous in sprints at long odds, notably if the speed figure for the same race matches par or approaches par. If the outcome will be contested throughout the stretch, the stronger combination of speed and stamina route-to-sprint usually prevails. I relish the presence of the power sprinters, and you will too.

A second source of longshots that win with more than occasional frequency can be found in routes on the turf. It's no longer the first-time starter with a potent grass pedigree, because nowadays the breeding information is readily available and widely distributed. At low odds, bets on first- and second-time starters on the turf tend to be poor plays. The bets ignore the red flag hoisted years ago by Bill Quirin, who pointed out that pedigree as a factor in handicapping is generally a poor predictor. Quirin argued that first and second starters on the grass should be backed only as longshots. It was sound advice.

The variation that gets longshots involves second starts in turf routes, provided the first start has resulted in a loss, but has been impressive enough to beget improvement.

The play does not fasten on maidens, but rather on experienced horses with insignificant records and dull dirt form that suddenly have shifted to the grass and have run surprisingly well. Either a late runner has finished faster than 12 seconds a furlong, or—and this is the horse to prefer that gets the juicy odds—the horse had impressed with a middle move under 12 seconds a furlong, before tiring.

The hidden move occurs between four furlongs and six furlongs at middle distances. The interval might go as fast as 23 flat. The public notices only that an inconsistent horse has lost again. But the singular grass finish has been better than it looks, and the data is clear that horses that have run well on the first turf try normally will run even better on the second try.

The more resourceful hunt for longshots on class depends upon competitive fields and false favorites. The latter appear far more frequently than the former and will be easier to exploit. The search can begin, as good horses do, at the preliminary steps of the eligibility conditions, the maidens and the nonwinners allowances.

MAIDEN RACES AND MAIDEN TO MAIDEN-CLAIMING

Before professional speed figures wedged their way into the past performances, second-time starters in maiden special weight races provided a steady flow of longshots. All that was required was that the second starters had run three to five lengths slower than more experienced maidens. The bettors almost certainly would favor the faster, more experienced maidens, but the second starters warranted the bet.

That's because second starters with talent typically would improve the three to five lengths defined as normal improvement, and often more dramatically. The odds would be inviting and if the trainer and jockey combinations for the second starters remained conveniently below the handicapping radar, the odds could be double-digit splendid. The positive cash flow never ceased, or so it seemed.

Those days have ended. Not only have professional speed figures been part of past performances for 16 years, but also the expanding supply of information resources repeatedly have touted the charms of second starters in maiden races. To hammer the point, in seminars I conduct weekly on Sundays at Santa Anita, I like to remind the participants that Secretariat lost the first time he ran. If second starters project to par and above, they have little to fear from the first starters, at least typically. The bad news is that promising second starters no longer will be underbet to a fault.

In one situation second starters can pay boxcars, with the result somewhat predictable, or not altogether unpredictable. First, the experienced maidens remain below par—so handicappers must be aware of the track's maiden par—and none of the second starters projects to par with normal improvement. In maiden races for 3-year-olds and up, following the first five months of the year, first starters become notoriously unreliable.

When these conditions coalesce, handicappers should pay attention to second starters that have one dull line. The horses may have been beaten badly at every call, the speed figures dismal. But the preponderance of the surrounding data is positive. Maybe the trip line looks slightly troubled, the workouts okay-to-fine, the trainer and jockey serviceable, if not among the leaders. Best of all, the odds in the debut should have been engaging, maybe 6–1 or below, or below 10–1. If the odds today beckon at double digits, the play makes sense, and these intriguing prospects should not be eliminated from the undersides of trifectas and superfectas, or from the win holes of the serial bets.

None of this applies to maiden races for juveniles, where the first-timers are dangerous at any time and normal improvement for second starters with talent is five to seven lengths.

Maidens exhibiting talent in their workouts and making their debut in sprints do not often masquerade as longshots, but very recent developments in the modern sport have altered even this basic equation.

In Southern California in 2007, perhaps as a tactic to trigger pick-six carryovers, many more races for maidens were carded at routes and on the turf. Pedigrees enter the handicapping window as never before, and it bears repeating that pedigree plays are best pursued at attractive odds, say 8–1 and higher. Favorites and low-priced contenders do not matter, because they do not win enough.

The most optimistic outcomes should be anticipated where the Tomlinson Ratings available in *Daily Racing Form* are 330 or higher for the routes, and correspondingly, where the trainer's $2 return on investment (ROI) for the maneuver with a relatively small sample exceeds $3. The trainer's rate of profit carries the cause, even though the trainer's win percentage with firsters may be suspiciously low. The lowly win percentages will repel many bettors, but the trainers win with these types frequently enough.

All handicappers appreciate the class drop from maiden special weight to maiden-claiming conditions, and those conventional drop-downs can still pay surprisingly well, although few will be longshots. A second textbook drop-down in maiden-claiming races remains less familiar and less accessible, but pays better. Any drop in claiming price accompanied by one of the two top pace figures in the field qualifies as a potential play. The reasoning is simple. It's advantageous to control the front into the stretch with slow horses running behind.

As pace figures have become more widely distributed—and the 2007 Moss Pace Figures of *Daily Racing Form* surely will accelerate the trend—the prices on these drop-downs have begun to plunge. Nonetheless, handicappers in possession of pace figures will find occasional longshots that qualify for support at double-digit odds. They need not hesitate to make the plays. At double-digit odds the horses will win frequently enough.

Until now I have resisted the pleas of fellow handicappers to favor second-time starters in maiden-claiming races, where the first start resulted in a loss under maiden-claiming conditions comparable to today's. The rationale for backing second starters in maiden-special circumstances does not transfer well to the maiden-claiming ranks. That is, the horses possess talent, fail to exhibit the talent in their debut, and learn a lot. Next time they explode. The translation problem is real. Maiden-claiming horses usually possess no talent.

It's probably time to change my mind. First, the number of maiden-claiming races on major cards has increased terrifically. Second, a number of these races are being won by second-time starters that have lost at the level. They may not improve dramatically, but they do improve sufficiently. First starters in maiden-claiming processions remain hard to swallow, but the second starters in decent form deserve a longer look.

Having conceded as much, the best opportunity of all for a genuine longshot among the cheaper maidens involves a pair of second starters, one that finished well in a maiden-claiming race similar to today's, the other a drop-down from the nonclaiming maiden ranks with one dull line.

The preceding discussion should alert handicappers to the horse to be preferred in the illustration below, which will be at fantastic variance with the horse the Hollywood Park crowd preferred on May 23, 2007.

The race was a five-furlong dash for 2-year-old fillies carrying a maiden-claiming tag of $40,000. Examine the past performances for the four fillies below. Jockey Corey Nakatani replaced named rider Aaron Gryder on Warren's Devonlane, and Martin Garcia replaced named rider Alex Bisono on Unlimited Gold. The odds apart for now, which filly might handicappers best prefer?

5 Skipper Mike — Green — Own: Meadowbrook Farms Inc — Pink, Turquoise Cross, Turquoise — $40,000
BAZE M C (139 29 15 20 .21) 2007: (429 73 .17)
B. f. 2 (Jan)
Sire: Lexicon (Conquistador Cielo) $3,500
Dam: Darn Kristin (Darn That Alarm)
Br: Meadowbrook Farms Inc (Fla)
Tr: La Croix David(10 2 2 2 .20) 2007:(27 3 .11)
Blinkers ON — L 120

Life	1 M 1 0	$4,000	34	D.Fst	0	0	0	0	$0	-
2007	1 M 1 0	$4,000	34	Wet(335)	0	0	0	0	$0	-
2006	0 M 0 0	$0	-	Synth	1	0	1	0	$4,000	34
Hol	1 0 1 0	$4,000	34	Turf(231*)	0	0	0	0	$0	-
				Dst(302)	0	0	0	0	$0	-

1May07-3Hol fst 4½f ◈ :224 :472 :541 ⒻMd 40000 34 4 4 33 44½ 23 Baze M C LB120 3.60 - RedHotRene1203 SkipprMik120½ ProudGrrison120¾ Came out str,late 2nd 9
WORKS: Apr27 Hol ◈3f fst :373 H 16/21 Apr21 Hol ◈4f fst :493 H 44/69 Apr14 Hol ◈3f fst :352 Hg 2/37 Apr7 Hol ◈3f fst :361 Hg 5/32 Mar31 Hol ◈3f fst :364 H 20/34 Mar24 Hol ◈3f fst :371 H 12/30
TRAINER: 2ndStart(10 .10 $0.62) 1stBlink(4 .00 $0.00) 2YO(58 .12 $1.02) Synth(19 .16 $1.03) BlinkOn(6 .00 $0.00) Sprint(86 .10 $1.25) J/T 2006-07 HOL(2 .50 $4.30) J/T 2006-07(2 .50 $4.30)

6 Warren's Devonlane — Black — Own: Benjamin C Warren — White, Black 'W' On Back, Black Bars On — $40,000
GRYDER A T (20 3 3 4 .15) 2007: (356 47 .13)
Dk. b or br f. 2 (Jan)
Sire: Devon Lane (Storm Cat) $3,500
Dam: Excessively Wild (In Excess*Ire)
Br: Benjamin C Warren (Cal)
Tr: Gutierrez Jorge(26 1 4 5 .04) 2007:(83 6 .07)
L 120

Life	1 M 0 0	$400	-	D.Fst	1	0	0	0	$400	-
2007	1 M 0 0	$400	-	Wet(357)	0	0	0	0	$0	-
2006	0 M 0 0	$0	-	Synth	0	0	0	0	$0	-
Hol	0 0 0 0	$0	-	Turf(410)	0	0	0	0	$0	-
				Dst(370)	0	0	0	0	$0	-

4Apr07-1SA fst 2f :112 :214 ⒻⓈMd Sp Wt 37k - 5 8 95½ 87¼ Cohen D B119 6.90e 89- 11 StarofMuqtrib118hd ToBDevon1181¼ CleverLdy120hd Off bit slow,steadied 9
WORKS: May15 Hol ◈5f fst 1:02 H 26/52 May8 Hol ◈4f fst :482 H 13/41 Mar28 Hol ◈2f fst :242 Hg 4/11 ●Feb28 Hol ◈2f fst :232 H 1/4
TRAINER: 2ndStart(30 .10 $1.57) MSWtoMCL(9 .22 $3.29) 1stLasix(3 .00 $0.00) 2YO(39 .10 $1.36) Synth(38 .08 $0.83) 31-60Days(69 .12 $1.73) J/T 2006-07 HOL(1 .00 $0.00) J/T 2006-07(1 .00 $0.00)

8 Unlimited Gold — Pink — Own: Broguiere or Gramer or Jones Et Al — Red, White M On Black Diamond, Black — $40,000
BISONO A (14 0 2 3 .00) 2007: (116 5 .04)
Dk. b or br f. 2 (Jan) BAROCT06 $14,000
Sire: Golden Gear (Gulch) $3,000
Dam: Unlimited High (High Brite)
Br: Harris Farms Inc Jeanne Bowers-LePore & Michael LePo (Cal)
Tr: Solis Walther(18 1 1 1 .06) 2007:(54 4 .07)
L 120

Life	1 M 0 0	$400	24	D.Fst	0	0	0	0	$0	-
2007	1 M 0 0	$400	24	Wet(352)	0	0	0	0	$0	-
2006	0 M 0 0	$0	-	Synth	1	0	0	0	$400	24
Hol	1 0 0 0	$400	24	Turf(242)	0	0	0	0	$0	-
				Dst(361)	0	0	0	0	$0	-

10May07-3Hol fst 4½f ◈ :22 :454 :521 ⒻⓈMd Sp Wt 47k 24 2 4 44½ 47 714¾ Enriquez I D LB120 b 78.40 - - Billie Bob1204½ Lauren C1201 Hi Lily Hi Lo1204¾ Off rail, weakened 8
WORKS: May4 Hol ◈4f fst :49 Hg 14/37 Apr28 Hol ◈4f fst :484 H 21/76 Apr21 Hol ◈3f fst :372 Hg 13/19 Apr14 Hol ◈4f fst :493 H 30/62 Apr7 Hol ◈3f fst :363 H 10/32 Apr1 Hol ◈3f fst :372 H 19/26
TRAINER: 2ndStart(25 .12 $3.37) MSWtoMCL(7 .14 $4.20) 2YO(32 .09 $5.28) Synth(27 .04 $0.60) Sprint(137 .07 $2.06) MdnClm(109 .06 $2.44) J/T 2006-07 HOL(5 .00 $0.00) J/T 2006-07(15 .07 $0.85)

9 Clever Lady — Turqse — Own: Costello or London or Lovingier — Maroon, White Hoops, White Cuffs On — $40,000
TALAMO J (101 20 20 12 .20) 2007: (651 124 .19)
Dk. b or br f. 2 (Feb)
Sire: Cactus Ridge (Hennessy) $6,500
Dam: Lady Regency (Vice Regent)
Br: Terry C Lovingier (Cal)
Tr: Dominguez Caesar F(7 1 0 1 .14) 2007:(26 1 .04)
Blinkers ON — L 115 5

Life	4 M 1 1	$14,800	28	D.Fst	3	0	1	1	$14,400	-
2007	4 M 1 1	$14,800	28	Wet(328)	0	0	0	0	$0	-
2006	0 M 0 0	$0	-	Synth	1	0	0	0	$400	28
Hol	1 0 0 0	$400	28	Turf(278)	0	0	0	0	$0	-
				Dst(329*)	0	0	0	0	$0	-

10May07-3Hol fst 4½f ◈ :22 :454 :521 ⒻⓈMd Sp Wt 47k 28 4 3 610 713 613¾ Baze M C LB120 7.90 - - Billie Bob1204½ Lauren C1201 Hi Lily Hi Lo1204¾ Angled in turn,no bid 8
19Apr07-2SA fst 2f :111 :214 ⒻMd Sp Wt 47k - 4 2 2hd 2no Baze M C LB118 *1.10e 96- 07 Alonewiththestorm116no CleverLady1181 CarlasGl118hd Dueled, willingly 8
4Apr07-1SA fst 2f :112 :214 ⒻⓈMd Sp Wt 37k - 1 4 5½ 3¼ Bautista C A LB120 11.90 95- 11 StrofMuqtrib118hd ToBDevon1181¼ CleverLdy120hd Inside, edged foe 3rd 9
21Mar07-1SA fst 2f :111 :214 ⒻⓈMd Sp Wt 38k - 3 4 42½ 53½ Delgadillo A B118 9.90 92- 12 ExcssivHt1181¼ ToBDvon1181 Alonwththstorm122½ Sent btwn,no late bid 10
WORKS: May18 SA 3f fst :36 Hg 3/21 May2 SA 4f fst :482 H 5/21 Apr15 SA 1f fst :121 H 2/2 ●Mar15 SA 2f fst :234 Hg 1/6 Mar8 SA 2f fst :233 Hg 4/13 Mar1 SA 2f fst :242 Hg 10/11
TRAINER: MSWtoMCL(5 .20 $0.92) 1stBlink(6 .00 $0.00) 2YO(55 .04 $1.09) Synth(10 .10 $1.52) BlinkOn(7 .00 $0.00) Sprint(93 .08 $1.00) J/T 2006-07 HOL(1 1.00 $15.20) J/T 2006-07(1 1.00 $15.20)

I hope handicappers agree that Warren's Devonlane should be preferred to Skipper Mike, not to mention a less convincing preference over Skipper Mike for Unlimited Gold and Clever Lady. It's perfectly proper to detest horses like Skipper Mike when they go off at low odds. The filly's second by three in a $40,000 maiden-claiming dash similar to today's has no redeeming value, including the pitiful speed figure of 34. In this common context figure analysts might remind themselves that the sucker bet in speed handicapping is the high-figure horse when all the figures are below par, let alone awful.

Warren's Devonlane is a second starter with one dull line, dropping from maiden state-bred to $40,000 maiden claiming, a dropper virtually out of the textbook. Consider the circumstances surrounding the drop-down:

- The filly broke badly and later steadied, in her debut.
- The odds for the debut are a respectable 6.90–1.
- The filly is a second starter getting first-time Lasix.
- A leading rider has replaced a minor journeyman for a minor barn.
- The works for the second start are longer and better. And finally:

- Trainer Jorge Gutierrez may be low percentage, but of his six wins of 2007, two have come on a maiden to maiden-claiming drop, and the trainer's ROI for the maneuver has been a robust $3.29 for every $2 wager.

The circumstantial case looks powerful enough, always a plus with second starters on the drop from maiden to maiden-claiming races. The other second starter on the drop-down, Unlimited Gold, offers no supporting data to encourage the handicapper's trust. She experienced a good trip at 78–1 for a minor-league barn. Still, Unlimited Gold is a second starter on the plunge, and serious improvement will be no surprise.

Now check the odds at post time:

Skipper Mike	8–5
Warren's Devonlane	11–1
Unlimited Gold	22–1
Clever Lady	9–2

The crucial capitulation: Skipper Mike at 8–5 must be dismissed. Horses such as Skipper Mike can easily disappoint and frequently will finish out of the money. Warren's Devonlane deserves first call, but has been ranked as low as sixth best on the board. The operative question becomes a common concern. If Warren's Devonlane improves enough to win, and Skipper Mike bows out, how should the race be bet?

At 11–1, Warren's Devonlane warrants a bet to win. In addition, the filly should be coupled in exactas with the other two maiden drop-downs and here's the kicker: The odds demand the trio of maiden drop-downs be covered for a petty $6 in a $1 trifecta box. Disciples of second starters on this type of drop likely would divide the win wager between Warren's Devonlane and Unlimited Gold, maybe in a 60–40 percentage split.

The result chart flatters the approach in every pool.

FOURTH RACE
Hollywood
MAY 23, 2007

5 FURLONGS. (.574) MAIDEN CLAIMING . Purse $20,000 (plus $2,000 Other Sources) FOR MAIDENS, FILLIES TWO YEARS OLD. Weight, 120 lbs. Claiming Price $40,000.

Value of Race: $22,000 Winner $12,000; second $4,000; third $2,400; fourth $1,200; fifth $400; sixth $400; seventh $400; eighth $400; ninth $400; tenth $400. Mutuel Pool $280,967.00 Exacta Pool $221,323.00 Quinella Pool $12,740.00 Trifecta Pool $196,503.00 Superfecta Pool $148,287.00

Last Raced	Horse	M/Eqt.	A.	Wt	PP	St	$\frac{3}{16}$	$\frac{3}{8}$	Str	Fin	Jockey	Cl'g Pr	Odds $1
4Apr07 1SA8	Warren's Devonlane	LB	2	120	6	7	6hd	61½	2½	11¾	Nakatani C S	40000	11.70
10May07 3Hol7	Unlimited Gold	LB b	2	120	8	3	1½	11	11	2no	Garcia M	40000	22.10
10May07 3Hol6	Clever Lady	LB b	2	115	9	2	5½	2hd	32	3nk	Talamo J5	40000	4.90
	King City Kitty	LB b	2	120	4	9	10	71	42½	46½	Antongrgi III W	40000	4.60
1May07 3Hol4	Kooky Kelly	LB	2	120	2	4	4hd	8½	81½	51	Landeros C	40000	8.40
	Harriette Topper	LB	2	120	10	5	71	3hd	61	61	Enriquez I D	40000	8.20
12May07 10Hol5	Stitchit	LB	2	120	7	1	31	4hd	5hd	71¾	Pedroza M A	40000	16.10
1May07 3Hol2	Skipper Mike	LB b	2	120	5	6	2hd	51	7hd	8¾	Baze M C	40000	1.70
1May07 3Hol8	Devons Tigress	LB b	2	120	1	8	81	92	93½	96½	Cohen D	40000	46.70
	Steel Kitten	LB	2	120	3	10	9½	10	10	10	Arias S	40000	15.90

OFF AT 2:59 Start Good. Won driving. Track fast.

TIME :22³, :46³, :59² (:22.63, :46.78, :59.40)

$2 Mutuel Prices:

6 – WARREN'S DEVONLANE	25.40	11.60	7.00
8 – UNLIMITED GOLD		21.80	11.80
9 – CLEVER LADY			4.20

$1 EXACTA 6–8 PAID $202.90 $2 QUINELLA 6–8 PAID $189.00
$1 TRIFECTA 6–8–9 PAID $1,228.10 $1 SUPERFECTA 6–8–9–4 PAID $8,785.40

Dk. b or br. f, (Jan), by Devon Lane – Excessively Wild , by In Excess–Ire . Trainer Gutierrez Jorge. Bred by Benjamin C Warren (Cal).

WARREN'S DEVONLANE broke in and a bit awkwardly, chased between horses then a bit off the rail leaving the turn, came out into the stretch, split rivals in midstretch, angled in and gained the lead past midstretch then proved best under urging. UNLIMITED GOLD had good early speed off the inside then dueled three deep, inched away off the fence on the turn, fought back between horses past midstretch and just held second. CLEVER LADY stalked between horses then three deep on the turn and four wide into the stretch and just held the show. KING CITY KITTY broke a bit slowly, settled off the rail then outside on the turn, came five wide into the stretch and finished willingly. KOOKY KELLY stalked the pace inside, was shuffled back a bit into the turn, came a bit off the rail in the stretch and lacked a further response. HARRIETTE TOPPER stalked outside then four wide on the turn and into the stretch and did not rally. STITCHIT prompted the pace between horses then stalked between foes on the turn and weakened. SKIPPER MIKE forced the pace between rivals then stalked inside on the turn and also weakened. DEVONS TIGRESS stalked inside, steadied in tight off heels into the turn, split rivals on the bend and had no response in the stretch. STEEL KITTEN broke a bit slowly, settled just off the rail, went three deep on the turn and failed to menace.

Owners– 1, Warren Benjamin C; 2, Broguiere Gramer Jones Et Al; 3, Costello John London Richard and Lovinger Terry C; 4, Tom Grether Farms Inc; 5, Said Thomas J; 6, Tommy Town Thoroughbreds LLC; 7, Feeley Bill; 8, Meadowbrook Farms Inc; 9, Archa Racing Inc; 10, Charles Cono LLC

Trainers– 1, Gutierrez Jorge; 2, Solis Walther; 3, Dominguez Caesar F; 4, Sherlock Gary; 5, Metz Jeff; 6, O'Neill Doug; 7, Van Berg Jack C; 8, La Croix David; 9, Stute Melvin F; 10, Paasch Christopher S

King City Kitty was claimed by Hess Jr, Robert B and Swanson, Ken; trainer, Hess R B Jr.

Scratched– Treadmill

$2 Daily Double (8–6) Paid $87.20 ; Daily Double Pool $32,305 .
$1 Pick Three (2–8–6) Paid $158.10 ; Pick Three Pool $60,140 .
$1 Pick Four (1–2–8–6) Paid $853.70 ; Pick Four Pool $171,787 .

It's instructive to consider why Skipper Mike went at 8–5, as well as Clever Lady at the respectable 9–2. Jockey M. C. Baze had emerged from journeyman ranks to be a leader at the 2007 Hollywood Park spring-summer meeting; he was the hot jock. And season upon season low-profile trainer David La Croix has played a shrewd hand with the juveniles. Skipper Mike added blinkers and was a second starter who had been backed to 7–2 in her debut. The field was unappealing. No works for the 2-year-old in the 22 days since the debut might have raised a warning sign, but did not.

As to Clever Lady, the filly would gain the services of the hot apprentice at Hollywood Park 2007, Joe Talamo, riding near 20 percent. The addition of blinkers and Talamo suggested the filly would revert to her speed tactics.

The presence of leading jockeys and trainers is never required—or even recommended—under maiden-claiming conditions. Handicappers should resolve to remember that low-percentage jockeys and trainers win low-level races all the time. It's a basic guidepost to beating these races and it helps boost the odds, as it certainly did on May 23, 2007, at Hollywood Park.

ALLOWANCE, NONWINNERS ONCE AND TWICE OTHER THAN MAIDEN OR CLAIMING

In the mid-1980s at Howard Sartin's invitation I fashioned a relationship with the leading members of the Sartin Methodology that would change my handicapping approach in one fundamental way, and for the better. Until then I had relied upon a primitive procedure for estimating pace ratings, based upon unadjusted fractional times and final times. The Sartin group instead emphasized energy expenditure at the various calls and intervals, and they related the several pace ratings they had developed to the running styles the local tracks had favored at the various distances.

A crucial component of the software estimated the percentage of energy expended from the start to the second call. Later on I recognized the same ability could be represented by carefully calculated pace figures. It took no longer than weeks to internalize one of the method's basic precepts. For the great majority of horses, energy expended early would not be available later; that is, in the stretch. In more common parlance, when the pace figure would go up, the speed figure would go down. It happened all the time, or so it seemed in the beginning.

The phenomenon led to the identification of one of the game's best, most repetitive opportunities for finding overlays and juicier longshots. The situation presents itself under nonwinners-once allowance conditions and features a recent maiden winner with a marvelous speed figure, preferably from a barn that attracts lots of money. But the impressive maiden graduate suffers a pace weakness. The speed figure may be strong, but the pace figure is weak, more than two lengths below par. When the allowance runners force the maiden graduate to run faster early, the lofty speed figure normally dips and dives, and the horse routinely loses.

Not the second, but absolutely the first time I used the Sartin software to play a nonwinners-once allowance sprint, I tabbed a 13–1 shot that won going away. The favorite that disappointed—out of the money—went off at even money with a standout speed figure. But his early energy output had been suspiciously low, and now he would be forced to run much faster early. The colt could not do that and still finish fast.

I called Tom Brohamer, a leading Sartin practitioner, to boast. Before I could relay the vital information, Brohamer anticipated which longshot and beaten favorite I had in mind. The lesson endures as vital. Pace figures will be critical to distinguish which maiden winners with fancy speed figures can move into the nonwinners-once allowances and repeat. When those favorites disappoint, the eventual winners should pay much more than they ought to, and several may be as attractive as 13–1.

A caution sign must be posted here, at least for certain tracks. Enthusiasm for the nonwinners-once pace weakness must be tempered in the current change to synthetic surfaces at a handful of major tracks. In Southern California the preferred balance between speed and pace figures on the synthetic surface has changed to a considerable degree. In reporting on the Hollywood Park races for the week of June 4, 2007, where the synthetic Cushion Track had been in service for a couple of months only, pace analyst Brohamer wrote the following to his figure-handicapping subscribers:

"One clue to this Cushion Track: The typical balance of high pace and speed figures has been supplanted by turf-type combinations of figures in sprints and routes. A 99–103 has been superior to the 105–103 pattern we normally search for. If you are having troubles with this meeting, give a look to the lower pace to speed figure pattern."

While maiden winners who have earned high pace figures and are now moving to the nonwinners allowances may no longer be preferred on synthetic surfaces, pace figures that remain too low are still anathema.

In Brohamer's example the Quirin-style 99–103 balance represents a pace figure approximately two lengths slower than the speed figure, a preferred pattern on Hollywood Park's Cushion Track. But an imbalance of 95–103 (the Beyer Speed Figure would be 91) among front-runners and pressers would not be similarly preferred, and would suggest the maiden grad with that kind of imbalance might be destined to lose. The logical alternatives at times will be longshots.

A more familiar source of overlays in the nonwinners allowance races will be the imports from Europe and to a lesser degree from elsewhere. Here too prices to win have dropped, notably so among imports from the familiar countries of France, England, and Ireland. The new imports from Germany and Dubai should continue to offer added value. South America presents an inviting situation that arises occasionally and in the advanced nonwinners allowances (nonwinners of two other and three other) and open and Grade 3 stakes it has emerged as an unfamiliar source of double-digit contenders.

As most handicappers now appreciate, European grass racing is far superior to the modern brand in the United States. A wrinkle embedded in the U.S. eligibility conditions intensifies the advantage these imports regularly enjoy. European imports often will have broken maiden ranks in handicaps or stakes races, but are nevertheless permitted to run back for nonwinners of one or two. The conditions specify those who are "nonwinners once (or twice) other than maiden or claiming, or *have never won two (or three) races.*" Many of the European imports ostensibly eligible to restrictive nonwinners allowances already have beaten better horses at comparable levels in their native lands.

Not many of this type from France or England will be longshots, but some from Italy and Germany will be and they may outclass the U.S. conditions just as handily. A seriously misapprehended matter is germane here. Several of the European imports may be competing at less than ideal distances, or returning from lengthy layoffs. Do not be repelled. The horses outclass the eligibility conditions, as well as the great majority of American horses still eligible. An exception to avoid will be the European marathoners. These plodding imports should not be expected to impress at shorter distances.

European imports from the minor ovals of France, England, and Ireland often will be eligible to the nonwinners-once and -twice allowance levels in the U.S. and these horses often will possess a greater measure of class than the home product. Their successes in American allowances will be less predictable, but the odds will be higher, often roaming into double digits. Prefer these foreigners at higher odds—but not so much in the more advanced nonwinners allowances, for nonwinners three or four times other than maiden and claiming, and not in classified allowances, or in the stakes having purses of $100,000-added and higher. Imports from minor tracks do not belong there.

Since the circumstance can apply at the nonwinners-twice allowance level in the U.S., it's convenient to conclude this section with the best-guarded secret of all. It embraces the leading horses of South America. The pattern delivers longshots that will win, including, once more, the 2006 Horse of the Year, the remarkable Invasor.

Any South American import that has won *two or more* Group 1 races in his native country can be accepted at any nonclaiming level in U.S. racing. The majority of these hidden class gems will be underestimated and often grossly underbet. Profits can run high for the season.

One Group 1 title is not sufficient. Multiple Group 2 titles are not sufficient. One Group 1 win with close finishes in other Group 1 events is not sufficient. But two Group 1 victories reflect an authentically leading horse. An index of this type's superiority is reflected in the purse structure of South American racing. The Group 1 purses generally will be far richer than those in Group 2.

To be fair, one Group 1 title and close finishes in another Group 1 stakes will be sufficient credentials for South American imports to take a number of nonwinners-twice allowance races in the U.S., but the pattern tends not to succeed beyond those preliminary nonclaiming levels.

Invasor can be invoked to illustrate the pattern exceptionally well. As a 3-year-old Invasor had won the triple crown of Uruguay, and who among the U.S. handicapping clubs ever had heard of an accomplishment like that, let alone would be prone to respect the graded stakes of Uruguay? How to classify such a horse?

Because the Uruguayan hero satisfied the multiple Group 1 guideline, I hold the distinction of having wagered on Invasor the only time he lost. Invasor lined up against Discreet Cat in the 2006 UAE Derby on the Dubai World Cup card in late March. He was sent away at 12–1 or thereabouts in the U.S. pools.

Invasor finished a nondescript fourth that night, never looking like a winner. Yet the colt quickly shipped to the U.S. and in the Pimlico Special the day before the Preakness the low-profile South American lined up against an American brand of Grade 1 company at 6.70–1. He won in smashing style. Many other South American imports bringing two or more Group 1 victories will arrive in the U.S. and win at double-digit odds in nonclaiming races. The heavily guarded secret is out of the bag.

STAKES AND TURF RACES

In the first edition of this book I concluded a wider discourse on class evaluation with the merits of superior final fractions on the turf. The operative guideline to finding winners recommended any horse able to complete the final fraction faster than 12 seconds a furlong, provided the fast finish had occurred at today's class level or higher. The chapter's sample race was a Grade 3 stakes at Hollywood Park won by a 6-year-old named Montemiro, who had previously finished at nine furlongs in 34⅕ seconds, to be second by a neck in a Grade 2 event. Montemiro won the Grade 3 stakes by completing the final five-sixteenths in a furious 28⅗, and he won drawing away.

The key to the victory would be the odds, as four horses in the Grade 3 stakes had finished faster than 12 seconds a furlong in classier races and the four looked closely matched. The odds on the horses separated the four as fundamental handicapping did not. Horse A was 3–1, Horse B was 5–2, Montemiro was 27–1, and Horse D was 2–1. In closely matched circumstances the imperative was to favor the overlays and longshots. It bears repeating here.

Despite the contemporary drift to short fields in stakes, a number of stakes and turf routes with large fields will be deeply competitive. Class handicappers may identify the contenders fairly well but will be hard pressed to isolate the likeliest winner. Instead of laboring over the past performances, attempting to discern fine distinctions which may not prove decisive, handicappers best proceed by constructing a fair-value odds line and settling on the horses, second and third choices in particular, that will go as longshots.

Situations such as those illustrated by Montemiro's victory, where three of four contenders will be similarly rated and the fourth absurdly ignored, will happen rarely. A more common circumstance finds one (or two) legitimate contenders at double-digit odds, when they should be proposed at 5–1 or 6–1. Whenever a leading contender in a competitive field goes as a 100 percent overlay, the situation entails a longshot that figures. The win percentage may drop to one of four or one of five, but the horses will win enough to throw profits.

A plush variation of this situation arises a few times during a racing meeting. The circumstance offers handicappers the chance, not only to back a longshot that figures, but also to complete the score of the season. The conditions bring together a large field of 10 to 12 runners, with half the field consisting of authentic contenders and the other half consisting of throwouts. Among the legitimate contenders handicappers prefer one horse strongly as the class of the field, a fundamental variation of "the speed of the speed." Because the several contenders in a large field appear closely matched, the class horse is likely to be underbet. Often enough the horse should go as a longshot.

A perfectly agreeable way to proceed sets the fair-value odds line equal to the number of contenders, say 6–1 for each of six contenders in a 12-horse field. If the handicapper's top choice does go at twice the fair-value line, that's a highly desirable longshot, but the prospects may be considerably richer than that. Because the race looks deeply competitive, encompassing as many as six horses that will be fighting for the wire, the inferior half of the field is unlikely to finish near the wire. That means none of the throwouts will be likely to sneak among the trifectas and superfectas.

If the key horse triumphs, a combination of the other contenders very likely will complete the trifectas and supers. If the key horse has run as a longshot, consider the possibilities. The bet to win is supplemented by singling the key horse to win in the exactas, trifectas, and superfectas, with all the other legitimate others to finish second, third, and fourth. Instead of chasing the pick six, where half the races in the sequence may be indecipherable, class analysts can prosper by pursuing this direction.

In the 2006–07 winter-spring meeting at Santa Anita (86 days), the circumstance presented itself three times. In one situation the key horse was surprisingly overbet, ruining the opportunity. In a second the key horse lost. Despite the contentious field, the key horse must win.

That's what happened in the third circumstance. It was a turf route for nonwinners twice other than maiden or claiming, and the key horse was a Bob Baffert-trained 5-year-old named Hockey the General. Review the gelding's record of 11 races.

```
7 Hockey the General                 B. g. 5 (Feb)                                      Life 11 3 2 0 $162,720 99   D.Fst      4 2 0 0 $89,740 99
  Own: Natalie J Baffert             Sire: General Meeting (Seattle Slew) $10,000       2007  1 0 1 0 $15,340  89   Wet(362)   0 0 0 0      $0  -
Orange Red, Navy Blue Chevrons On White Panel  Dam: Tiara Glow (Chief's Crown)  L 119   2006  4 1 0 0 $70,120  99   Turf(293)  7 1 2 0 $72,980 89
ESPINOZA V (255 43 41 32 .17) 2006: (1285 259 .20)  Br: Mrs John C Mabee (Cal)          SA(T) 6 1 2 0 $72,580  89   Dst(T)(363) 5 1 2 0 $72,180 89
                                     Tr: Baffert Bob(86 16 17 13 .19) 2006:(392 91 .23)
2Feb07-7SA fm 1 (T) :234 :471 1:103 1:343 4↑OC 62k/N2x-N   89 5 63½ 74¾ 65 42½ 2nk Migliore R  LB119 b 7.90 91-09 OldThunder119nk HockeythGnrl119nk StormMt119hd 3wd into lane,rallied 9
8Apr06-1SA fst 1 :231 :463 1:104 1:354 4↑OC 40k/N1x-N   99 2 43 32½ 31½ 1hd 11¾ Bejarano R  LB119 b *1.00 89-10 HockeytheGeneral1191¾ LeCopin119nk Courtnll1194 3wd bid,stdy handling 6
19Mar06-8SA fm 1 (T) :23 :464 1:104 1:35 4↑[S]CrystlWtrH113k   88 4 62¼ 52¼ 51½ 52½ 42 Espinoza V  LB114 b 5.00 86-12 SuperStrut119no Mr.Wolverine116no UncleDenny1182 Angled out, willingly 11
4Mar06-2SA gd 1⅛ (T) :484 1:132 1:37 1:492 4↑OC 40k/N1x-N   73 12 84¼ 86 73¾ 106½ 1010¼ Espinoza V  LB119 b 2.80 72-18 Cheroot1192¼ Pao Com Ovo119¾ Urban King1191½ 4-5wd,steadied 1/8 12
4Feb06-7SA fst 1⅛ :471 1:112 1:362 1:49 Strub-G2   94 6 118¼ 83¾ 73¼ 55½ 510¼ Espinoza V  LB117 b 10.70 81-09 High Limit1214½ Top This and That117½ Giacomo1234¼ Off bit slow,4-wide 11
26Dec05-2SA fm 1 (T) :231 :473 1:111 1:35 SirBeufort84k   89 2 54 52½ 52¼ 43 2no Espinoza V  LB118 b 6.80 88-10 ChineseDrgon118no HockeytheGnrl1181 Bcrux118½ Split foes,just missed 8
  Run in divisions
11Nov05-7Hol fst 1 1/16 :224 :461 1:103 1:43 3↑[S]Alw 45200N1x   89 2 87 76¼ 74¼ 31 12¼ Gomez G K  LB121 b 3.20 86-14 HockeythGnrl1212¼ LikNwMony1192 QuitnBoy122no 4wd into lane,rallied 8
30Oct05-6OSA fm 1 (T) :223 :46 1:10 1:341 3↑Md Sp Wt 52k   89 5 76½ 64¾ 63¼ 41½ 13 Espinoza V  LB120 b *2.30 92-13 HockeytheGener1203 Precis1242 Prchintothchoir120hd Tight 3/8,waited 1/4 8
13Oct05-3OSA fm 1 (T) :231 :471 1:111 1:351 3↑[S]Md Sp Wt 42k   85 5 73¾ 63¼ 66 43 3nk Espinoza V  LB120 b 2.20 87-16 TmtoHnr120nk Prchntthchr120no [D]HckythGnr1203½ Shifted out into lane 7
  Disqualified and placed 6th
30Jun05-6Hol fm 1 1/16 (T) :24 :501 1:151 1:444 3↑[S]Md Sp Wt 46k   67 1 66½ 54 53 65 65½ Baze T C  LB117 b 3.60 62-32 Der Ali124hd Cabo's Dawn117½ Bartok ofSiam117nk Pulled,tight 1/8,wkend 7
  Previously trained by Gomez Jaime H 2005(as of 5/30): (7 4 0 0 0.57)
30May05-5Hol fst 6f :22 :45 :572 1:103 3↑[S]Md 40000(40-35)   59 5 11 1314 1216 1112 79¼ Baze T C  LB118 b 5.40 75-15 Ranch Hand1241½ Colombini1241 Blind Harry118hd Off bit slow,no bid 13
WORKS: Feb15 SA 4f fst :474 H 7/35 Jan27 SA 5f fst 1:004 H 10/32 Jan21 SA 5f fst :591 H 3/56 Jan10 SA 6f fst 1:121 Hg 2/13 ●Jan4 SA 5f fst :583 H 1/52 Dec29 SA 6f fst 1:122 H 4/29
TRAINER: 2OffOver180(15 .53 $3.09) Turf(39 .08 $3.77) Routes(187 .21 $2.43) Alw(114 .23 $1.98)   J/T 2006-07 SA(78 .24 $1.27) J/T 2006-07(136 .29 $1.71)
```

A reliable approach to evaluating 3-year-olds and lightly raced older horses—those having fewer than 13 races—is to review the last running line for current form and class and then return to the beginning and move upward in the past performances. Hockey the General had begun cheaply for Jaime Gomez, but had broken maiden ranks three starts later at a mile on the turf with a sizzling 23⅘ final quarter. After beating Cal-breds easily next time out Hockey the General lost a minor turf stakes by a nose, despite running a final quarter in 23⅖.

Baffert attempted the Grade 2 level, but the horse was not ready, and soon veered off form. After beating open N1X allowances on the dirt with a sparkling Beyer of 99 (par was 93), Hockey the General went to the sidelines for 10 months. He returned at today's level to be second by a neck with a best-ever 23-flat final quarter. A repeat of that comeback would find Hockey the General best by a clear margin on speed and class, and grass runners from behind the pace do not bounce nearly as often as front-runners and pressers on the dirt.

I had determined the Baffert 5-year-old to be a stickout at the level, the kind that should not disappoint. In a field of 11, five of the other horses shaped up as closely matched, but clearly superior to the remaining five. If Hockey the General could win, the trifectas and supers should fall sweetly into line. Best of all, Hockey the General, 7.90–1 in the comeback loss, should be an attractive price, and he might run as a longshot.

As the wagering proceeded, Hockey the General was no longshot, but a fair price to win at 5–1. Minus Baffert, the odds might have slipped to twice as high, or so I imagined. All the intended bets were placed, which included exactas to any of the other five at 6–1 and higher, all the other five in a trifecta part-wheel to place and show, and all the other five in a superfecta part-wheel to finish second, third, and fourth. The $1 trifecta part-wheel (1 x 5 x 4) cost $20, and the $1 superfecta part-wheel (1 x 5 x 4 x 3) cost $60.

At the sixteenth pole Hockey the General, on the far outside, had drawn within a few lengths of the leaders and appeared to be going best. Even as I had shifted focus to the other contenders inside the sixteenth pole, anticipating the windfall, suddenly Hockey the General was no longer gaining a length per stride. He had flattened and was gaining still, but only incrementally. When a wall of horses hit the wire, Hockey the General looked to have prevailed, barely. The class standout was not as real as the handicapping had suggested.

Although he did finish again in 23 flat, Hockey the General won by only a nose. I had not analyzed the race as effectively as I had thought, survived a sliver of a photo, and did not collect a longshot's price to win ($12). On the other hand, the $1 exacta to a 15.60–1 shot, one of the positive five, paid $86.20; the $1 trifecta with a 4.80–1 shot third, another of the good-half five, paid $725.10; and the $1 superfecta with an 8.60–1 shot fourth, still another of the fabulous five, paid a sensational $3,437.10. The formula had worked.

Another intriguing and untapped supply of longshots can be found year after year in the stakes divisions. In the more obvious situations the popular favorites will be severely overbet. Second and third choices may be correspondingly underbet. The situation occurs annually among 4-year-olds and up in the first half of the calendar year, when the leading horses of the previous season have run back, but have recorded speed and pace combinations more than a couple of lengths below their previous best. The presumption must be the stars will not be shining as brightly. The sentimental public will be forgiving for a time. Now the second and third choices deserve the handicapper's added respect, notably at long odds, say 8–1 or better.

A precious subclass of the procedure attacks all Breeders' Cup winners of the previous fall, regardless of time away. Although Breeders' Cup Classic winners have returned as winners more often than the others, all winners of Breeders' Cup races should be expected to lose. Most of them will. Beyond being bet to a fault, they either will be past their peak or unintended today.

The other side of the equation, finding the upset candidates that will win at fancy prices, will prove more painstaking but handicappers must be determined to try. The pattern dates to 1993 for me, when a turf-to-dirt juvenile out of the Ron McAnally barn at 14–1 upset odds-on Breeders' Cup Juvenile winner Brocco in the Grade 1 Hollywood Futurity. Profits have run high. Do it.

Another subclass to beat will be older geldings that have been multiple stakes winners, notably those having a common background. As soon as the popular winners have run below their top form by a few lengths, even while winning, prepare to abandon them. The tactic cost me three attempts to upset the California-bred gelding Lava Man, an ex-claimer who retained top form longer than virtually all older geldings that have come before him.

On the other hand, when the popular Cal-bred gelding Best Pal was a 5-year-old, he was no longer the powerhouse and Horse of the Year candidate he had been at four. Best Pal left the gate as a short-priced favorite six times in 1993, disappointing on four of those occasions. On the rare days when they feel the part these jaded geldings may win again—Best Pal won the Hollywood Gold Cup convincingly that year—but in the interim they lose. When they do, unsentimental handicappers alert to the situations can prosper with long-priced alternatives that figure best.

Another caution sign must be posted here, for simulcast bettors especially. Certain trainers will be outstanding with the older geldings. It's local information, and local handicappers no doubt will know who's who. In Southern California Richard Mandella works with older geldings as well or better than any horseman in history, a compliment that can be tracked to the trainer's early years with aging claimers.

In 2006 Mandella won the prestigious Grade 1 Arlington Million with the 8-year-old The Tin Man, topping an amazing season of achievement with the old-timer. Following a layoff of many months Mandella next brought The Tin Man back in a Grade 1 turf route at Hollywood Park and he won that. The 9-year-old paid only 7–2.

In general, unless a trainer is particularly adept with older geldings, bet against them as favorites in stakes from the moment they have declined.

As a rule in the 3-year-old divisions, longshots become better bets when the favorites have impressive speed figures, but unimpressive pace figures. The point has been pressed before, but it bears repeating. It happens all the time, for example, en route to the Kentucky Derby. The vulnerable youngsters will be forced to run faster to the pace call and they lose. Not all of them lose, but most of them do. Go to the longshots.

The converse does not hold. Front-runners and pressers rising in class and having high pace figures but slightly suspect speed figures suddenly may put it all together and deliver a tremendous performance at a good price. A number of talented 3-year-olds require time to mature and seasoning. Once the developing colts and fillies have learned to relax, they can be rated kindly to the pace call and then explode late. If they have exhibited a high measure of speed for two-thirds of a sprint or three-fourths of a route before tiring but not stopping, support them when the situation and the odds beckon.

FIGURE PATTERNS AND FORM REVERSALS

A truly fascinating development in the contemporary game has been the study of figure patterns to anticipate improving and declining form. It's hardly an overstatement to assert that among clever figure analysts the traditional standards of recent races and workouts no longer count as much as recent speed figures and established cycles.

Two of the common patterns point handicappers toward longshots:

- Paired figures at the top of the form cycle, notably among 4-year-olds and up
- Lifetime tops among horses having 15 races or more, claiming horses especially

The paired-figure pattern is practically omnipresent. The recent pair of figures need not be identical, but should be separated only by a length, which translates to one, two, or occasionally three points on the Beyer scale.

First, paired-figure patterns can be positive and these do not contribute to longshot sightings. A developing 3-year-old or lightly raced 4-year-old pairs figures while moving through the nonwinner allowances or into the stakes. The pairing indicates the developing horses should move forward and the better colts and fillies typically will.

If the developing youngsters regress instead, it can be inferred that they probably already have demonstrated their best, the putative tops of their form cycles. When they deliver best efforts in the future, the speed figures will be at or near the previous paired-figure level.

Among experienced horses—4-year-olds and up—paired figures at the top of the form cycle are best interpreted to mean the horses should decline next time, often when favored or overbet. Lifetime tops among the experienced older horses presume the same decline at similarly low prices. Thus the possibility of spotting tenable longshots has improved.

The patterns can be illustrated by applying each to back-to-back Grade 1 events that were run at Hollywood Park on July 7, 2007, and a weekend of graded stakes elsewhere could supply similar examples. Let's first examine the newly prestigious American Oaks for 3-year-old fillies, a $750,000-added Grade 1 invitational across a mile and a quarter on the turf that Hollywood Park rightly can assert is the nation's definitive race of its kind.

Although the race occurs on grass, and speed handicapping therefore will be less decisive, the Beyer par is 99, and an acceptable performance within three lengths of par would require a Beyer 93. Previous figure patterns may not be decisive, but they can suggest whether the aspiring fillies should fit the class level, and how strongly.

The rail filly is Baroness Thatcher. Review her record. Look for the paired-figure patterns. What might they mean about the filly's chances in the American Oaks?

Four and five races back, Baronesss Thatcher paired Beyer figures of 91 and 92, while winning a Grade 3 by a half-length and gaining second by three-quarters in a Grade 1. Alas, Baroness Thatcher did not move forward following the paired figures, suggesting the filly's best efforts should cycle back to Beyers of 91–92. As the 8–5 favorite in her last, the Grade 2 Black-Eyed Susan at Pimlico on May 18, Baroness Thatcher enjoyed a clear lead, but lost. Her speed figure returned at—no surprise to figure analysts—Beyer 94. Unless the American Oaks will be a below-par affair, Baroness Thatcher would appear too long a stretch.

Next examine the race favorite, Valbenny, who annexed a Grade 2 last out with a late fraction of 34⅘, and two back won a Grade 3 with a late fraction of 23 flat. Three-year-olds need register just a single Grade 1 or Grade 2 title to be acceptable on class at the Grade 1 level limited to their age group. Valbenny satisfies the class level well enough. Examine her figure pattern.

3 Valbenny (Ire)
Own: LGL Racing DiPietro Lenner Et Al
Blue Black, White Sash, Green Polka Dots On
SOLIS A (152 22 20 25 .14) 2007: (328 45 .14)

B. f. 3 (Apr)
Sire: Val Royal*Fr (Royal Academy)
Dam: Dark Indian*Ire (Indian Ridge*Ire)
Br: Ken Lynch (Ire)
Tr: Gallagher Patrick(97 13 12 8 .13) 2007:(268 34 .13)

L 121

Life	8	5	1	0	$269,653	95	
2007	3	2	0	0	$149,610	95	
2006	5	3	1	0	$120,043	82	
Hol (T)	3	3	0	0	$209,610	95	
D.Fst	0	0	0	0	$0	-	
Wet(324)	0	0	0	0	$0	-	
Synth	0	0	0	0	$0	-	
Turf(359*)	8	5	1	0	$269,653	95	
Dst(T)(233*)	0	0	0	0	$0	-	

9Jun07-5Hol fm 1⅛ (T) :484 1:123 1:362 1:48 +HnymnBCH-G2 95 2 53 62¾ 62¾ 31½ 11¾ Solis A LB123 *1.00 81-09 Valbenny1231¾ Super Freaky120hd Mystic Soul1171¾ Came out str,rallied 7
12May07-7Hol fm 1 (T) :232 :471 1:104 1:342 Senorita-G3 95 7 77½ 53 52½ 41¾ 11¾ Solis A LB121 *2.20 92-16 *Valbenny*1211¾ Super Freaky1211¼ Passified121½ Came out str,rallied 8
7Apr07-7SA fm 1 (T) :231 :471 1:112 1:352 Prvdncia-G3 87 10 98½ 97¾ 98 105¼ 63¼ Valdivia J Jr LB121 *2.90 84-12 SuperFreaky117¾ Passified119¾ GottaHaveHer1151¼ Off bit slow,4wd lane 11
31Dec06-6SA fm 1 (T) :224 :472 1:12 1:36 BlueNorthr83k 82 1 84¾ 72¾ 42½ 2hd 11 Solis A LB122 *1.60 83-15 Vlbenny1221 *Courtwood*1183½ MissJosieyWls118nk 4wd into lane,led,game 11
25Nov06-9Hol fm 1 (T) :242 :491 1:131 1:362 Miesque-G3 76 2 108¼ 117¼ 107½ 73 1¾ Solis A LB117 9.30 82-14 *Valbenny*117¾ Mystic Soul115nk Spenditallbaby119½ 5wd into lane,up late 12
Previously trained by Alan Swinbank
25Jly06 Ayr (GB) fm 7f (T) LH 1:332 EBF Maiden Stakes (7f,50y) 1¾ McKeown D 124 9.00 *Valbenny*124¾ Al Raahi1291¼ Tartan Tie1292½ 5
Racing Post Rating: 67 Maiden 12900 *Rated in 5th,steadied when close up 2f out,led 100y out*
23Jun06 Ayr (GB) gd 5f (T) Str 1:003 Maiden Auction Stakes 25 McKeown D 119 10.00 Zanida1235 *Valbenny*119½ Spectacular Joy120¾ 7
Racing Post Rating: 56 Maiden 9100 *Slowly away,rated at rear,drifted left 2f out,2nd 100y out*
5Jun06 Carlisle (GB) gf 5f (T) RH 1:021 Median Auction Maiden Stakes 69¾ McKeown D 124 14.00 Russian Silk1242½ Bollin Franny129no Stepaside129¾ 10
Racing Post Rating: 35 Maiden 7500 *Slowly away,soon 5th,weakened over 1f out*
WORKS: ●**Jun30 Hol ◈6f fst 1:112 H** *1/12* **Jun23 Hol ◈4f fst :49 H** *16/64* **Jun2 Hol ◈6f fst 1:124 H** *4/22* **May26 Hol ◈4f fst :50 B** *35/49* **May3 Hol ◈6f fst 1:124 H** *4/18* **Apr26 Hol ◈5f fst 1:002 H** *2/41*
TRAINER: WonLastStart(97 .19 $1.53) Turf(349 .14 $1.22) Routes(404 .15 $1.23) GrdStk(43 .07 $0.72) J/T 2006-07 HOL(78 .19 $2.20) J/T 2006-07(168 .20 $1.81)

Valbenny paired figures in her most recent two races. Figure analysts had every expectation she would move forward. Valbenny did not. With dead aim at the winner in the lane, the filly finished an undistinguished second, the winner edging away again nearing the wire. The winner's Beyer 97 should have been well within the range of the favorite. Valbenny now looks very much like a good filly having an undistinguished future at the Grade 1 level.

The winner looked like this:

4 Panty Raid
Own: Glencrest Farm LLC
Yellow Yellow, Green Hoops And Bars On Sleeves
PRADO E S (—) 2007: (723 141 .20)

Dk. b or br f. 3 (Mar) KEEAPR06 $275,000
Sire: Include (Broad Brush) $25,000
Dam: Adventurous Di (Private Account)
Br: Heaven Trees Farm (Ky)
Tr: Pletcher Todd A(1 0 0 0 .00) 2007:(587 161 .27)

L 121

Life	5	3	1	0	$242,275	96	
2007	4	2	1	0	$214,075	96	
2006	1	1	0	0	$28,200	85	
Hol (T)	0	0	0	0	$0	-	
D.Fst	3	2	0	0	$178,600	96	
Wet(391)	0	0	0	0	$0	-	
Synth	2	1	1	0	$63,675	87	
Turf(233)	0	0	0	0	$0	-	
Dst(T)(343*)	0	0	0	0	$0	-	

18May07-12Pim fst 1⅛ :48 1:114 1:372 1:50 BlkEySsn-G2 96 2 42½ 42 33 21½ 11 Prado E S L116 2.40 91-14 PntyRid1161 WinningPoint116nk **BronessThtchr**1208 Rail,bid btw,drove clr 8
13Apr07-7Kee fst 1 1/16 ◈ :243 :501 1:153 1:442 Alw 53675N1x 79 11 42 73¼ 51½ 31½ 1nk Prado E S L115 *1.40 86-10 *Panty Raid*115nk Silence Dogood123no Bees1231½ Stiff drive,4-5w 11
24Mar07-8TP fst 1 ◈ :233 :47 1:121 1:372 BrbnttBC-G3 87 4 43 43½ 31½ 32½ 2hd Prado E S L115 7.00 91-07 Sealy Hill118hd *Panty Raid*1152¾ Aspiring1154¾ Brk thru gte, rallied 12
Previously trained by Sciametta Anthony Jr 2006: (24 4 7 1 0.17)
8Feb07-8GP fst 7f :221 :443 1:094 1:233 Alw 40000N1x 59 1 6 2½ 2hd 44 610½ Velazquez J R L117 *1.50 76-12 SilverKnockers1194 Awsugahnow1171¾ EarlyVintge117½ Pressed, faltered 8
Previously trained by Pletcher Todd A 2006(as of 8/10): (738 206 144 83 0.28)
10Aug06-2Sar fst 6f :223 :462 :584 1:114 Md Sp Wt 47k 85 3 5 1hd 1½ 16 17¾ Velazquez J R L118 4.00 81-13 PntyRd1187¾ AtobhnGrl1131 Mostbtflstrm1181¾ Drew away when roused 7
WORKS: **Jly1 Bel(T) 4f fm :493 B(d)** *9/24* **Jun24 Bel(T) 4f fm :49 B(d)** *8/21* **Jun17 Bel(T) 4f fm :504 B(d)** *9/11* **Jun10 Bel 5f fst 1:002 B** *5/22* **Jun3 Bel 4f fst :492 B** *24/58* **May12 Bel tr.t 5f fst 1:01 B** *3/13*
TRAINER: 1stTurf(117 .20 $1.72) Dirt/Turf(122 .21 $1.55) 31-60Days(712 .30 $1.96) WonLastStart(434 .29 $1.78) Turf(603 .23 $1.67) Routes(1156 .27 $1.76) J/T 2006-07(38 .26 $2.05)

Quite obviously, Panty Raid had never run on the turf. Did she fit the Grade 1 class level?

Absolutely, since the upset of Baroness Thatcher in the Grade 2 Black-Eyed Susan qualified her. The trainer was Todd Pletcher, and the Beyer Speed Figure of 96 satisfied par, the more important point. Unlike Baroness Thatcher, Panty Raid had every right to improve, provided she liked the grass, and handicappers might have recognized that. Panty Raid would not have been a longshot to win the American Oaks, but she would have paid better than $13 without the presence of Pletcher.

Two other participants in the 2007 American Oaks—one from Japan, the other from Australia—are worth a spot check. The Hollywood Park invitational affects an international scope and aura and imports from faraway places obtain much more than a cursory glare in the media.

5 Robe Decollete
Own: Koji Maeda
Green Turquoise, Red Cross Sashes, Turquoise
IWATA Y (—) (—)

Gr/ro. f. 3 (Apr) KEESEP05 $180,000
Sire: Cozzene (Caro*Ire) $35,000
Dam: Color of Gold (Seeking the Gold)
Br: Mr & Mrs Larry D Williams (Ky)
Tr: Matsumoto Shigeki(—) (—)

121

Life	8	3	2	0	$1,578,610	–	D.Fst	0	0	0	0	$0	–
2007	4	2	0	0	$1,361,264	–	Wet(357)	0	0	0	0	$0	–
							Synth	0	0	0	0	$0	–
2006	4	1	2	0	$217,346	–	Turf(323)	8	3	2	0	$1,578,610	–
Hol Ⓣ	0	0	0	0	$0	–	DstⓉ(308)	0	0	0	0	$0	–

20May07 Tokyo (Jpn)	fm *1½ Ⓣ LH 2:251	ⒻYushun Himba (Japanese Oaks)-G1 Stk 1525000	1no	Fukunaga Y	121	10.70	Robe Decollete121no Bella Rheia121¾ Love Caerna121nk *Rated in 7th,9th 2-1/2f out,dueled,led on line*	18
Racing Post Rating: 110								
8Apr07 Hanshin (Jpn)	fm *1 Ⓣ RH 1:333	ⒻOka Sho(Japanese 1000 Guineas)-G1 Stk 1415000	45	Fukunaga Y	121	75.80	Daiwa Scarlet121 1½ *Vodka*121 3½ Katamachi Botan121no *Rated in 14th,finished well,just missed 3rd*	18
Racing Post Rating: 106								
3Mar07 Hanshin (Jpn)	fm *1 Ⓣ RH 1:333	ⒻTulip Sho(Jpn 1000 Gns Trial)-G3 Stk 650000	56¾	Take Y	119	13.60	Vodka119nk *Daiwa Scarlet*1196 Rain Dance119no *Mid-pack,5th 2f out,one-paced late*	16
Racing Post Rating: 102								
14Jan07 Kyoto (Jpn)	fm *7f Ⓣ RH 1:222	ⒻKobai Stakes (Listed) Stk 300800	1½	Ando K	119	*1.30	Robe Decollete119½ Bakushin Heroine119nk Nishino Manamusume119nk *Rated in 12th,rallied to lead near line*	16
3Dec06 Hanshin (Jpn)	fm *1 Ⓣ RH 1:33	ⒻHanshin Juvenile Fillies-G1 Stk 987000	44	Fukunaga Y	119	21.80	*Vodka*119nk Aston Machan119 3½ *Luminous Harbor*119nk *Rated in 13th,finished fast*	18
Racing Post Rating: 106								
19Nov06 Kyoto (Jpn)	fm *1 Ⓣ RH 1:353	Conditions Race Alw 113000	2no	Ando K	119	1.90	Jungle Techno121no Robe Decollete119 1¾ T M Operetta119nk *Trailed to 1-1/2f out,late rush,just missed*	7
9Sep06 Sapporo (Jpn)	fm *1⅛ Ⓣ RH 1:482	Cosmos Sho Alw 260000	23½	Ando K	119	12.00	Namura Mars119 3½ Robe Decollete119¾ Imperfect1212 *Rated in 10th,wide turn,up for 2nd*	12
23Jly06 Hakodate (Jpn)	gd *1⅛ Ⓣ RH 1:562	Maiden Race Maiden 115000	11½	Ando K	119	5.50	Robe Decollete119 1½ Field Winner1196 Nozomi Hikaru119½ *Unhurried in 7th,rallied to lead 100y out*	9

WORKS: Jly4 Hol ◈5f fst 1:014 H *17/37* **Jly1 Hol ◈3f fst :362 H** *3/23*

6 Anamato (Aus)
Own: MBH Syndiate Ritchie & Ritchie
Black White, Green Sash, Black Sleeves And Cap
RODD M (—) (—)

Dk. b or br f. 4 (Aug)
Sire: Redoute's Choice*Aus (Danehill)
Dam: Voltage*Aus (Whiskey Road)
Br: J D Ritchie & Partners (Aus)
Tr: Hayes David A(—) (—)

125

Life	17	4	4	4	$638,672	–	D.Fst	0	0	0	0	$0	–
2007	7	3	0	1	$397,746	–	Wet(339)	0	0	0	0	$0	–
							Synth	0	0	0	0	$0	–
2006	10	1	4	3	$240,926	–	Turf(343)	17	4	4	4	$638,672	–
Hol Ⓣ	0	0	0	0	$0	–	DstⓉ(359)	2	1	0	1	$163,463	–

21Apr07 Morphetteville (Aus)	gd *1¼ Ⓣ LH 2:021	Australasian Oaks-G1 ⒻStk 209000	11½	Rodd M	123 b	*2.60	108	Anamato123 1½ Cancanelle123no Devil Moon123hd	*Trckd ldrs,led 150y out*	16
9Apr07 Randwick (Aus)	sf *1 Ⓣ RH 1:38 3↑	Doncaster Handicap-G1 Stk 1835000	126¼	Newitt C	114	20.00	94	Hrdsn117hd Mntlty121nk DvnMdonn118hd	*In tight,faded.Aqua d'Amore4th*	16
31Mar07 Rosehill (Aus)	gd *7½f Ⓣ RH 1:303 3↑	Queen of the Turf Stakes-G1 ⒻStk 323000	155	Rodd M	118 b	6.00	93	DivineMadonna1241 CheekyChoice118hd BeautyWtch1241	*Midpack,wknd*	15
10Mar07 Caulfield (Aus)	gd *1 Ⓣ LH 1:351	Kewney Stakes-G2 ⒻStk 234000	11	Newitt C	122	3.40		Anamato1221 Catechuchu1223 Flame Of Sydney122nk	*Trckd 4th,led late*	11
3Mar07 Caulfield (Aus)	gd *1 Ⓣ LH 1:353 2↑	Futurity Stakes-G1 Stk 547400	85	Williams C	118	14.00	97	Aqua D'Amore124 1¼ Seachange124 1¼ El Segundo130no	*Trckd 3rd,wknd*	8
17Feb07 Moonee Vly (Aus)	gd *7½f Ⓣ LH 1:31	Moonee Valley Oaks-G2 ⒻStk 137000	1¾	Rodd M	122	3.80		Anamato122¾ Deloraine1221 De Lago Mist1221	*Trcked 3rd,led 70y out*	10
26Jan07 Caulfield (Aus)	gd *6f Ⓣ LH 1:092	Kevin Hayes Stakes (Listed) ⒻStk 77400	3nk	Williams C	123	*1.90		Gina Lollawitcha121nk Mistake Creek119hd *Anamato*123hd	*Dueled,failed*	7
9Nov06 Flemington (Aus)	gd *1 3/16 Ⓣ LH 2:37	Crown Oaks-G1 ⒻStk 578000	33½	Dunn D	122	10.00	101	MissFinland122 2¼ *TuesdyJoy*122 1¼ Anmto122hd	*Close up,wkndJ'Adane8th*	15
4Nov06 Flemington (Aus)	yl *1¼ Ⓣ LH 2:023	Wakeful Stakes-G2 ⒻStk 231000	32¼	Dunn D	120	5.50		Tuesday Joy117 1¼ J'Adane1171 Anamato1201	*Trckd ldr,faded*	16
14Oct06 Caulfield (Aus)	gd *1 Ⓣ LH 1:354	Caulfield Guineas-G1 Stk 751000	73½	Dunn D	117 b	8.00	101	WonderfulWorld122 1¾ Excites122hd CourtCommnd122nk	*Trckd 3rd,faded*	13
23Sep06 Caulfield (Aus)	gd *7f Ⓣ LH 1:241	Tranquil Star Stakes-G3 ⒻStk 88200	2nk	Dunn D	122	9.00		Miss Finland124nk Anamato122 2¼ My Only Hope119hd	*2nd,led,headed*	14
9Sep06 Flemington (Aus)	sf *6f Ⓣ LH 1:102	Rory's Jester Stakes-G3 Stk 188600	2no	Dunn D	116	5.00		The One120no Anamato116¾ Sharkbite120hd	*Close up,dueled,game*	13

WORKS: Jly3 Hol ◈4f fst :533 B *33/34* **Jun24 Hol ◈1 fst 1:451 H** *1/1*

Neither of the imports fits the level well enough, at least by reasonable standards of class evaluation. To repeat, at the graded-stakes level, imports from South America, Australia, South Africa, Dubai, and Japan must have won two or more Group 1 events in their native land. Robe Decollete had won just one, and that at 10–1 by a nose across 1 ½ miles. The Racing Post Rating of 110 equates to Grade 3, well below Grade 1.

Although Anamato had been hyped to regrettable degree for the race, the Australian filly proved easier to dismiss. Anamato had been 4 for 17 lifetime, with a single Group 1 victory, her last, suggesting a backward slide might be likelier than a forward move. Not to be overlooked, the Grade 1 Australasian Oaks won by Anamato had been run at one of Australia's innumerable minor ovals, Morphetteville, not at Randwick in Sydney and not at Flemington in Melbourne. With the non-European imports it matters. Those countries' stakes have been graded by local jurisdictions, not by the international pattern committees.

The class standard that requires imports from the less familiar faraway countries to have won two or more Grade 1 events saves handicappers quite a measure of sweat and confusion. The standard serves well. Anyone who cares to dispute the assertion can examine the past performances of the Japanese Group 1 star Cesario, who won the American Oaks in a sparkling performance against a stronger lineup in 2005 and figured to do exactly that.

Cesario (Jpn)
Own: Carrot Farm

Dk. b or b. f. 3 (Mar)
Sire: Special Week*Jpn (Sunday Silence) $43,725
Dam: Kirov Premiere*GB (Sadler's Wells)
Br: Northern Farm (Jpn)
Tr: Sumii Katsuhiko(1 1 0 0 1.00) 2005:(0 0 .00)

Life	6	5	1	0	$2,578,568	106	D.Fst	0	0	0	0	$0	-
2005	5	4	1	0	$2,511,053	106	Wet(280)	0	0	0	0	$0	-
							Synth	0	0	0	0	$0	-
2004	1	1	0	0	$67,515	-	Turf(285*)	6	5	1	0	$2,578,568	106
Hol [T]	1	1	0	0	$450,000	106	Dst[T](269)	2	2	0	0	$549,186	106

3Jly05-8Hol	fm	1¼ [T]	:461 1:113 1:351 1:59	[F]AmrcnOks-G1	106	12	36½	32	12½	14	14	Fukunaga Y	B121 f	4.40	97-06	Cesario1214 Melhor Ainda1211½ *Singhalese*1211	Stalked,led,cleared 12
22May05 Tokyo (Jpn)	fm	*1½ [T]	LH 2:284	[F]Yushun Himba (Japanese Oaks)-G1 Stk 1708000							1nk	Fukunaga Y	121	*.50		*Cesario*121nk *Air Messiah*121nk Dia de la Novia121½	18 *Rated in 16th,12th 2f out,sharp run to lead late*
10Apr05 Hanshin (Jpn)	fm	*1 [T]	RH 1:332	[F]Oka Sho (Japanese 1000 Guineas)-G1 Stk 1559000							2hd	Yoshida M	121	*2.90		*Rhein Kraft*121hd *Cesario*121nk Daring Heart121¾	18 *Rated in 6th,10th 2f out,finished fast.AirMessiah4th*
19Mar05 Nakayama (Jpn)	fm	*1⅛ [T]	RH 1:49	[F]Flower Cup-G3 Stk 725000							12½	Fukunaga Y	119	*.40		Cesario1192½ Slew Rate1192½ Alphonsine119nk	14 *3rd early,2nd halfway,3rd 3f out,led 1f out*
9Jan05 Nakayama (Jpn)	fm	*1¼ [T]	RH 2:013	Kanchiku Sho Alw 181000							1nk	Fukunaga Y	119	9.30		*Cesario*119nk Admire Fuji1231¼ Cosmo Produce123nk	16 *Towards rear,rallied to lead late*

WORKS: Jun30 Hol[T] 4f fm :52 B(d) *7/8* Jun27 Hol 5f fst 1:013 H *28/35*
TRAINER: Turf(1 .00 $0.00) Routes(1 .00 $0.00) Stakes(1 .00 $0.00)

Now we turn our attention to the Grade 1 Triple Bend Handicap, a $300,000-added seven-furlong sprint for 3-year-olds and up. A longshot did not figure to win the American Oaks and none did. A long-priced upset was plausible in the Triple Bend Handicap and that was exactly what happened. Unfortunately, despite a personal disposition seeking a longshot, the winner eluded my methods and I doubt whether I ever have supported a similar winner in a Grade 1 event.

Consider a few of the participants. The Beyer figure standard now is a loftier 111 to 106, the smaller number within two lengths of par and the recommended window of tolerance in sprints. First up is a speed horse on the rail, Sailors Sunset.

1 Sailors Sunset
Red — Own: Everest Stables Inc
Black, Red Mountain Emblem On Back, Red
PEDROZA M A (169 19 17 25 .11) 2007: (396 51 .13)

Gr/ro. g. 4 (Mar)
Sire: Petionville (Seeking the Gold) $15,000
Dam: Cayman Sunset (Wolf Power†SAf)
Br: Everest Stables Inc (Ky)
Tr: Polanco Marcelo(31 4 4 4 .13) 2007:(85 8 .09)

L 116

Life	17	6	3	2	$308,090	106	D.Fst	12	4	3	2	$183,230	102
2007	3	1	1	1	$107,480	106	Wet(329)	0	0	0	0	$0	-
							Synth	3	2	0	0	$123,480	106
2006	12	4	2	1	$182,810	106	Turf(248)	2	0	0	0	$1,380	79
Hol	5	3	1	1	$156,560	106	Dst(327)	3	0	0	0	$0	99

12May07-4Hol	fst	6f ◈	:214 :441 :56 1:09	3↑LsAnglsH-G3	106	3	1	11	11	2hd	1½	Court J K	LB116 b	4.20	93-13	SilorsSunset116½ PeceChnt1161 NorthrnSoldir1161	Inside,headed,gamely	5
7Apr07-5SA	fst	6½f	:214 :441 1:081 1:144	4↑PtrGrBCH-G2	97	5	1	11	11	31½	36	Pedroza M A	LB117 b	4.40	90-09	SmokeyStover1224½ *GrgsGold*1181½ *SilorsSunst*1171¼	Speed,inside,held 3rd	5
24Feb07-9TuP	fst	6f	:211 :423 :543 1:073	4↑PhnxGldCpH100k	98	3	10	98¾	67½	44½	22¾	Stevens S A	L123 b	*.90	96-12	RelatoDelGto1162¾ SilorsSunset123½ FmilyGuy1201½	Poor start, stumbled	10
26Dec06-8SA	fst	7f	:221 :45 1:09 1:211	Malibu-G1	99	5	6	1hd	1hd	3½	65½	Court J K	LB119 b	18.50	89-13	*LatentHet*1152 SpringAtLst119hd MidnightLute1191	Inside duel,weakened	12
2Dec06-8Hol	fst	6f ◈	:214 :44 :553 1:073	3↑VOUndrwd-G3	106	1	4	11½	11½	12½	11¾	Court J K	LB118 b	13.40	- -	SailorsSunset1181¾ **SirenLure**1263 DeclansMoon1227	Speed,inside,gamely	5
4Nov06-7TuP	fst	6f	:214 :433 :552 1:073	Saguaro40k	98	8	3	1hd	1½	1½	1½	Stevens S A	L123 b	2.90	99-13	*Sailors Sunset*123½ *Smokey Stover*1195¼ *Trail This*1193	Vied lead, prevailed	10
13Oct06-9Kee	fst	*7f ◈	:224 :451 1:09 1:241	Perryvll-G3	76	7	3	3½	52	86¼	611¼	Castanon J L	L117 b	48.90	- -	MidnightLut1174¾ LwisMchl1173 CourtFolly123hd	Bobble,between,empty	11
8Sep06-12Fpx	fst	6½f	:22 :453 1:093 1:162	Foothill61k	102	4	1	2hd	1hd	14	111¼	Pedroza M A	LB122 b	*.60	93-17	SailorsSunset12211¼ KnightsLastStr120¾ HeySlick122½	Vied,clear,driving	5
28Jly06-7Dmr	fst	6f	:213 :442 :57 1:10	3↑Alw 61800N1x	90	4	10	31	3nk	1hd	1½	Court J K	LB118 b	13.20	89-17	*Sailors Sunset*118½ *Midnight Lute*120no Ramsgate120¾	Bid btwn,led,held	12
18Jun06-5Hol	fst	6f	:212 :451 :574 1:101	3↑Alw 49400N1x	86	4	2	4¾	21	31½	31¼	Garcia M5	LB112 b	*2.00	85-13	ThPhroh1121 ShkinNDncin119nk *SilorsSunst*1126½	Bid 4wd,btwn,missed 2d	6
27May06-7Hol	fst	6½f	:213 :434 1:092 1:161	3↑Alw 59020N1x	91	6	1	2hd	3nk	1hd	2½	Court J K	LB116 b	6.90	89-13	SwissAddress124½ SailorsSunset116¾ Chauncey1242¾	3wd duel,led,caught	8
5May06-4Hol	fm	5½f [T]	:211 :434 :551 1:011	3↑Alw 59820N1x	79	5	4	3½	31½	75¼	54½	Ochoa J5	LB111 b	12.30	92-03	ExcessTempttions1243¼ StormMte124nk Revenscnt119½	4wd,3wd,no rally	10

WORKS: Jun18 SA 3f fst :362 H *11/19* Jun11 SA tr.t 3f fst :391 H *1/1* Jun5 SA tr.t 3f fst :384 H *1/1* May29 SA tr.t 3f fst :382 H *1/1* May22 SA tr.t 3f fst :393 H *1/1* May4 SA tr.t 3f fst :361 H *1/2*
TRAINER: Synth(35 .17 $5.93) 31-60Days(52 .21 $2.85) WonLastStart(15 .13 $2.13) Sprint(161 .09 $2.04) GrdStk(12 .17 $3.27) J/T 2006-07 HOL(19 .00 $0.00) J/T 2006-07(49 .04 $0.71)

Sailors Sunset is a 4-year-old with 17 career starts and just equaled a lifetime top in his last, a narrow win in a Grade 3 stakes. The leap to Grade 1 company, which the horse has never managed, will be huge, and I trust handicappers can dismiss Sailors Sunset on speed and class without much of a strain.

3 Battle Won
Blue
Own: Jay & Gretchen Manoogian
Purple And Gold Halves, Gold Circle Rj
BAZE M C (337 64 37 48 .19) 2007: (627 108 .17)

Dk. b or br g. 7 (Mar)
Sire: Honour and Glory (Relaunch) $12,500
Dam: Call Her (Caller I. D.)
Br: Glencrest Farm LLC (Ky)
Tr: Mitchell Mike(70 16 15 11 .23) 2007:(130 26 .20)

L 116

Life	27	7	8	3	$708,356	108	D.Fst	19	4	8	3	$546,693	108
2007	1	0	1	0	$21,120	100	Wet(355)	2	1	0	0	$34,775	100
							Synth	0	0	0	0	$0	-
2006	5	0	2	1	$133,926	104	Turf(265)	6	2	0	0	$126,888	100
Hol	1	0	1	0	$60,000	104	Dst(348)	10	2	3	1	$328,658	107

21Apr07-9SA fst 6½f ⊗ :22² :45 1:08¹ 1:14² 4↑ SnSmeon-G3 **100** 4 2 1¹ 1¹ 2hd 2no Garcia M LB117 2.00 98-09 Bonfante117no Battle Won1173½ **Siren Lure**121nk Fought back,gamely 4
20Aug06-6Dmr fst 7f :21⁴ :44¹ 1:08³ 1:21⁴ 3↑ OBrinBCH-G2 **93** 6 4 3¹ 32½ 45½ 47¾ Gomez G K LB115 2.10 88-12 **SirenLure**1222¼ PuresGold1161¾ *Areyoutlkintom*1143¾ 3wd into lane,no bid 7
30Jly06-8Dmr fst 6f :21³ :44 :56 1:08³ 3↑ BCrosbyH-G1 **103** 4 6 42½ 41¾ 32½ 3½ Espinoza V LB114 3.20 95-13 Pure as Gold113½ *Bordonaro*120hd Battle Won1148¾ 3wd into lane,willing 6
2Jly06-9Hol fst 7f :21³ :43⁴ 1:08³ 1:21¹ 3↑ TrplBndH-G1 **104** 5 5 2¹ 2¹ 2hd 21½ Espinoza V LB115 4.20 95-09 ***Siren Lure***1211½ Battle Won115¹ Unfurl theFlag1162¼ Bid str,lost whip late 10
Previously trained by Simon Charles 2006(as of 5/6): (59 7 5 9 0.12)
6May06-5CD fst 7f :22² :45¹ 1:09¹ 1:21³ 4↑ CDH-G2 **95** 6 5 1hd 1hd 3³ 54¾ Bejarano R L116 *2.70 89-08 TrckyTrvor117³ WthDstncton116nk LvlPlyngfld113¾ Dueled,3w,weakened 10
12Apr06-7Kee fst 6½f :22¹ :45¹ 1:10 1:16⁴ 4↑ Alw 66495N$Y **86** 2 2 2¹ 2½ 2² 24¼ Bejarano R L118 *1.20 86-11 ChrgingIndin1184¼ BttleWon1185¼ RvingRocket118nk Chased,4w,2ndbest 7
29Oct05-6Bel fst 6f :22 :44² :56³ 1:08⁴ 3↑ BCSprint-G1 **66** 4 5 2½ 4² 118½ 1118¼ Dominguez R A L126 16.30 77-10 SilverTrain124hd TasteofPrdise126³ LionTmer126nk Between rivals, tired 11
9Oct05-4Kee fm 5½f Ⓣ :22 :45⁴ :57³ 1:04 3↑ Woodford112k **96** 3 10 5¾ 51¼ 41¾ 51½ Dominguez R A L120 *.60 86-12 Sgt. Bert118nk Atticus Kristy118nk Midwatch118nk 5w lane,no gain late 10
3Sep05-10Sar fst 7f :22¹ :44⁴ 1:09² 1:22² 3↑ Forego-G1 **106** 3 4 1½ 1½ 1hd 2½ Dominguez R A L121 4.30 91-16 Mass Media117½ BattleWon121¾ SilverWagon1171½ Stumbled start, inside 6
31Jly05-8Dmr fst 6f :21² :43³ :55³ 1:08 3↑ BCrosbyH-G1 **108** 4 6 2hd 1hd 1½ 21¼ Valenzuela P A LB117 4.20 98-06 *Greg's Gold*1151¼ Battle Won117² Taste of Paradise1151½ Dueled,held 2nd 9
25Jun05-9CD fst 6f :21 :43⁴ :55¹ 1:07² 3↑ AristBCH-G3 **107** 4 4 2² 2½ 21½ 21¾ Smith M E L117 *1.20 102-06 KellysLnding1161¾ BttleWon1171¼ JtProspctor116nk Pressed,second best 6
7May05-5CD fst 7f :22¹ :44 1:07⁴ 1:20² 4↑ CDH-G2 **107** 4 5 21½ 2hd 12½ 13½ Dominguez R A L115 16.90 104-02 BttleWon1153½ *LevelPlyingfield*112½ Pomeroy118nk Bmp start,forced,drvg 11
WORKS: Jun28 Hol ◈6f fst 1:13² H *7/24* ●Jun21 Hol ◈5f fst :58³ H *1/61* Jun14 Hol ◈5f fst 1:00² H *8/50* Jun7 Hol ◈3f fst :36³ H *4/21* May28 Hol ◈5f fst 1:00 H *3/57* May21 Hol ◈5f fst 1:03² H *50/59*
TRAINER: 61-180Days(28 .29 $2.97) Synth(80 .24 $2.93) Sprint(225 .17 $1.59) GrdStk(24 .17 $2.43) J/T 2006-07 HOL(26 .38 $3.24) J/T 2006-07(50 .28 $2.51)

Battle Won is a 7-year-old with a number of close finishes in Grade 1 company. He gets a switch to the leading man (M. C. Baze) for a reliable barn and normally would be the kind of longshot to entertain—except that Battle Won has just returned from an eight-month vacation and in an all-out battle on the front of a Grade 3 stakes had finished second by a nose with one of his stronger speed figures. He represents a textbook bounce candidate, so interested handicappers had best demand both a vulnerable favorite and double-digit odds on Battle Won.

5 Surf Cat
Green
Own: A Headley & Naify
Royal Blue And White Stripes, Blue Cuffs
SOLIS A (152 22 20 25 .14) 2007: (328 45 .14)

Dk. b or br h. 5 (Feb)
Sire: Sir Cat (Storm Cat)
Dam: Trust Greta (Centrust)
Br: William Taylor Nicholls & Gainsway Farm (Ky)
Tr: Headley Bruce(23 0 6 1 .00) 2007:(71 8 .11)

L 123

Life	11	7	3	0	$562,420	114	D.Fst	10	7	2	0	$550,620	114
2006	3	3	0	0	$240,000	110	Wet(355)	1	0	1	0	$11,800	89
							Synth	0	0	0	0	$0	-
2005	8	4	3	0	$322,420	114	Turf(264)	0	0	0	0	$0	-
Hol	4	3	1	0	$333,020	114	Dst(361)	1	1	0	0	$90,000	110

13May06-3Hol fst 1 1/16 :23² :46³ 1:09⁴ 1:40³ 3↑ MrvnLRyH-G2 **110** 1 5⁵ 5⁴ 4² 1² 13½ Solis A LB121 b *.20 98-13 Surf Cat12131½ Spellbinder1161½ *Dixie Meister*115¹ 3wd bid,drifted in 5
2Apr06-4SA fst 6½f :21³ :44¹ 1:08² 1:15 4↑ PtrGrBCH-G2 **105** 5 2 46¼ 45½ 41½ 12¼ Solis A LB119 b *.20 95-12 *Surf Cat*1192¼ Grinding It Out1161½ Oceanus114hd 4wd rally,handily 5
18Feb06-8SA fst 7f :22³ :45¹ 1:09⁴ 1:22 4↑ SnCrlosH-G2 **110** 7 3 65¼ 66¼ 31½ 12¼ Solis A LB117 b *1.70 90-16 *Surf Cat*1172¼ Major Success1183¼ Oceanus114no 4wd into lane,rallied 8
10Oct05-20SA fst 1 1/16 :23¹ :46⁴ 1:10³ 1:41³ 3↑ Alw 57240N3X **106** 5 44½ 46½ 44½ 3¹ 1³ Solis A LB118 b *.20 97-06 *Surf Cat*118³ Texcess116² Keep On Punching120¹ Bobbled start,4wd lane 5
21Aug05-8Dmr fst 1¼ :45⁴ 1:10¹ 1:35¹ 2:00³ 3↑ PacifcCl-G1 **104** 4 2hd 2hd 3¹ 22½ 66¼ Solis A LB117 b 5.00 86-07 *Borrego*124½ Perfect Drift124nk Lava Man124hd Dueled,btwn,weakened 11
9Jly05-7Hol fst 1⅛ :47¹ 1:11¹ 1:35¹ 1:48 SwapsBC-G2 **105** 4 2½ 2¹ 1hd 13½ 1⁵ Solis A LB115 b 1.70 95 - Surf Cat115⁵ Dover Dere117¹ Indian Ocean1183½ Vied,clear,ridden out 6
18Jun05-9Hol fst 1 1/16 :23¹ :46² 1:10² 1:42² AffirmdH-G3 **104** 3 32½ 3² 4nk 2hd 2nk Solis A LB116 b *1.00 89-11 Indian Ocean115nk *Surf Cat*116² Dover Dere118⁵ 4wd bid,willingly 4
15May05-7Hol fst 6½f :21⁴ :44¹ 1:08² 1:14² 3↑ Alw 53622N1X **114** 6 4 3nk 3¹ 1½ 14½ Solis A LB119 b 2.30 99-14 Surf Cat1194½ *Greg's Gold*124½ Rojo Blanco124⁶ Vied 3wd,clear,driving 7
9Apr05-4SA fst 6½f :21 :44 1:09² 1:16 Md Sp Wt 45k **93** 3 8 5⁸ 64¼ 2½ 13½ Solis A LB121 b *1.10 92-12 *Surf Cat*12131½ *Jack's Kid*121⁵ *Indian Ocean*1217½ Stdied early,riddn out 9
5Mar05-1SA wf 6½f :21⁴ :44¹ 1:08⁴ 1:15² Md Sp Wt 59k **89** 5 1 1hd 11½ 1½ 2½ Stevens G L LB121 b *.50 94-07 Blue Prince121½ *Surf Cat*121no Plunkit1214½ Held well,caught late 6
29Jan05-8SA fst 6f :21¹ :44 :56¹ 1:09 Md Sp Wt 45k **88** 8 3 86¼ 8⁸ 6⁶ 2nk Stevens G L LB121 b 5.60 93-06 Big Top Cat121nk Surf Cat121² Freeholder121² 5wd into lane,surged 9
WORKS: ●Jly2 SA 4f fst :45³ H *1/31* ●Jun24 SA 6f fst 1:12¹ H *1/7* ●Jun17 SA 6f fst 1:12¹ H *1/7* Jun10 SA 7f fst 1:26³ H *1/3* Jun3 SA 6f fst 1:11³ H *3/12* ●May27 SA 6f fst 1:11² H *1/11*
TRAINER: +180Days(18 .06 $0.50) Synth(24 .00 $0.00) Route/Sprint(14 .36 $2.41) WonLastStart(30 .27 $1.37) Sprint(160 .18 $1.27) GrdStk(21 .29 $1.39) J/T 2006-07 HOL(34 .09 $0.44) J/T 2006-07(135 .21 $1.32)

Surf Cat is the favorite, and he may be one of the nation's top sprinters. He fires fresh but has been absent for 14 months and had to be removed from training for a comeback earlier in the Santa Anita season. Trainer Bruce Headley knows his 5-year-old exceptionally well and he has targeted this Grade 1 plum for a couple of months. Surf Cat can win and he has been a terror at seven furlongs, but the favorite remains vulnerable off the lengthy layoff, provided a genuine upset candidate can be found.

Notice that Surf Cat did not regress off the paired-figure pattern of June (104) and July (105) of 2005, but instead moved forward and forward again. He has the glow of an authentically top horse by any standard of class evaluation and speed.

6 Black **Siren Lure**
Own: Kesselman Melkonian & Melkonian
Black, Red Tomato Emblem On Back, Red
MIGLIORE R (191 27 25 21 .14) 2007: (521 75 .14)

B. g. 6 (Feb)
Sire: Joyeux Danseur (Nureyev)
Dam: Cantamar (Gulch)
Br: Desperado Stables (Ky)
Tr: Sherman Art(64 10 8 5 .16) 2007:(446 104 .23)

L 120

Life	25	12	2	4	$824,521	110	D.Fst	11	5	0	2	$484,112	110
2007	3	0	1	1	$34,612	103	Wet(317)	2	1	0	0	$50,620	99
2006	8	5	1	1	$551,138	110	Synth	2	0	2	0	$41,940	103
							Turf(298)	10	6	0	2	$247,849	105
Hol	5	3	2	0	$304,140	107	Dst(326)	3	2	0	0	$360,000	110

9Jun07-9Hol	fst	7½f	◈	:222 :45 1:093 1:282	3↑AckAckH-G3	**103**	5	2	48	48	33½	22	Solis A	LB121	2.60	93-14	**El Roblar**1172 Siren Lure121nk Publication1161¾	Came out str,game 2nd 8
21Apr07-9SA	fst	6½f	⊗	:222 :45 1:081 1:142	4↑SnSmeon-G3	**91**	3	4	42½	42	31½	33½	Migliore R	LB121	*1.60	94-09	Bonfante117no **Battle Won**1173½ Siren Lure121nk	4wd 1/4,3wd into lane 4
17Feb07-9SA	fst	7f		:222 :442 1:08 1:21	4↑SnCrlosH-G2	**90**	7	8	87¾	88¼	77¾	77½	Migliore R	LB121	3.80	87-10	LatentHet118nk ProudTowerToo1201¾ Rmsgte1141½	Came out str,no rally 10
2Dec06-8Hol	fst	6f	◈	:214 :44 :553 1:073	3↑VOUndrwd-G3	**101**	5	3	56¼	55½	33½	21¾	Solis A	LB126	*1.10	- -	**SailorsSunset**1181¾ SirenLure1263 DeclnsMoon1227	3wd into lane,2nd best 5
4Nov06-6CD	fst	6f		:212 :442 :561 1:084	3↑BCSprint-G1	**92**	11	14	145½	116½	1110	89¼	Solis A	L126	6.20	84-09	*Thor's Echo*1264 *Friendly Island*126½ Nightmare Affair126hd	Wide trip 14
20Aug06-6Dmr	fst	7f		:214 :441 1:083 1:214	3↑OBrinBCH-G2	**110**	1	7	75¼	64½	22	12¼	Solis A	LB122	2.80	96-12	SirenLure1222¼ PursGold1161¾ *Aryoutlkintom*1143¾	4wd move,rallied,clear 7
2Jly06-9Hol	fst	7f		:213 :434 1:083 1:211	3↑TrplBndH-G1	**107**	6	4	75	54½	3½	11½	Solis A	LB121	3.30	97-09	*Siren Lure*1211½ **Battle Won**1151 Unfurl theFlag1162¼	3wd into str,bid,clear 10
13May06-9Hol	fst	6f		:214 :441 :561 1:082	3↑LsAnglsH-G3	**103**	4	8	76¾	64¾	41¾	11	Solis A	LB120	5.20	95-09	*SirenLure*1201 Areyoutlkintome118nk Prorunnr114½	Squeezed start,rallied 8
22Apr06-7SA	fm	*6½f	Ⓣ	:214 :44 1:062 1:122	4↑SnSmeonH-G3	**94**	3	5	65½	65½	64¼	32	Solis A	LB122	*1.10	91-07	Pure asGold1181¾ SaintBuddy114nk *SirenLure*122¾	Came out str,missed 2d 8
19Feb06-2SA	wf	6½f	⊗	:212 :441 1:091 1:161	4↑DaytonaH85k	**99**	4	3	42½	32	11½	11½	Solis A	LB122	1.70	89-11	Siren Lure1221½ *Railroad*114½ *Jungle Prince*1152½	4wd into lane,clear 5
25Jan06-7SA	fm	*6½f	Ⓣ	:204 :42 1:052 1:12	4↑ImprLckIIH86k	**100**	3	6	75¾	77	52¼	1no	Solis A	LB121	*1.60	95-05	*SirenLure*121no *ShadowofIllinois*1181½ BrandNme114no	4wd into lane,rallied 12
10Oct05-3OSA	fm	*6½f	Ⓣ	:211 :431 1:054 1:114	3↑ⓇBlueJayWay71k	**105**	10	3	22½	31	1hd	1hd	Douglas R R	LB124	3.70	96-04	*Siren Lure*124hd *Geronimo*118¾ Crystal Castle1181	Stalked,bid,led,game 10

WORKS: Jly1 Hol ◈4f fst :483 H *10/50* Jun24 Hol ◈4f fst :482 H *10/54* Jun2 Hol ◈6f fst 1:132 H *8/22* May26 Hol ◈6f fst 1:13 H *2/24* ●May19 Hol ◈5f fst :583 H *1/66* May12 Hol ◈4f fst :491 H *35/75*
TRAINER: 2Off45-180(121 .30 $1.91) Synth(90 .17 $4.51) Sprint(821 .25 $1.95) GrdStk(16 .25 $2.05) J/T 2006-07 HOL(6 .00 $0.00) J/T 2006-07(16 .13 $1.46)

Siren Lure is an upset candidate. The 6-year-old gelding is a multiple Grade 1/Grade 2 winner, both in sprints of seven furlongs, and his most recent speed figure, while strong, remains three lengths shy of his lifetime top. As an added attraction the Beyer 103 had been recorded on Hollywood's Cushion Track, which Surf Cat has not yet experienced. Halfway through the wagering Siren Lure stood firm at 10–1. The odds began to drift down late, however. At post time, Siren Lure stood less firm at 6–1—a slight overlay perhaps, but not a genuine longshot.

8 Pink **Silent Name (Jpn)**
Own: Stronach Stables & Wertheimer & Frere
Royal Blue, White Pinstripes On Back
NAKATANI C S (127 20 21 9 .16) 2007: (392 58 .15)

B. h. 5 (Feb)
Sire: Sunday Silence (Halo) $218,625
Dam: Danzigaway (Danehill)
Br: Wertheimer et Frere (Jpn)
Tr: Mandella Gary(28 2 6 6 .07) 2007:(93 9 .10)

L 119

Life	20	6	2	4	$639,431	109	D.Fst	1	0	0	0	$3,000	64
2007	3	1	0	1	$287,000	109	Wet(304*)	0	0	0	0	$0	-
2006	7	2	0	2	$219,720	105	Synth	1	1	0	0	$248,000	109
							Turf(358)	18	5	2	4	$388,431	105
Hol	0	0	0	0	$0	-	Dst(289)	1	1	0	0	$248,000	109

28May07-8Bel	fst	1		:231 :453 1:101 1:343	3↑MtropltH-G1	**64**	9	84½	74¼	810	816	823	Nakatani C S	L119	6.40	70-09	Corinthian117¾ *Political Force*116½ Lawyer Ron1193	Stumbled badly start 9
14Apr07-8Kee	fst	7f	◈	:232 :462 1:092 1:211	3↑CmwlthBC-G2	**109**	7	4	2½	2hd	12½	14	Nakatani C S	L118	6.20	101-09	SilentName1184 LewisMichael118½ SteelLight118½	Widened,under urging 11
3Mar07-7SA	fm	1	Ⓣ	:234 :48 1:11 1:334	4↑FKilroeH-G1	**100**	2	21	21½	1hd	11	3nk	Nakatani C S	LB119	4.50	95-10	*Kip Deville*115nk Bayeux114no *Silent Name*1191¼	Bid,led,willingly 12
24Nov06-9Hol	fm	1$\frac{1}{16}$	Ⓣ	:232 :462 1:093 1:393	3↑CitatonH-G1	**98**	4	52½	1½	11½	2hd	64½	Espinoza V	LB116	8.10	90-13	*Ashkal Way*1191 Hendrix116no Three Valleys1171¾	Pulled,lost whip 1/8 12
4Nov06-7CD	fm	1	Ⓣ	:231 :463 1:104 1:343	3↑BCMile-G1	**99**	2	11½	12	1½	1hd	64¾	Espinoza V	L126	31.80	91 -	MisqusApprovl1264 Argorn126hd BdgofSlvr126nk	Bobble start,2w,weaken 14
7Oct06-9Kee	fm	1	Ⓣ	:234 :474 1:112 1:341	3↑ShdwlTfM-G1	**102**	1	99¼	97¾	98¼	87¼	72¾	Espinoza V	L126	*2.60	93-11	AussieRules1231¾ *RemarkbleNews*126no OldDodge126hd	10w stretch,no bid 9
23Jly06-8Dmr	fm	1⅛	Ⓣ	:453 1:092 1:332 1:443	3↑EdReadH-G1	**103**	4	21	21	21	31	34½	Espinoza V	LB118	4.80	101-07	*Aragorn*1214 Sweet Return117½ Silent Name118no	Lost whip chute 7
29May06-8Hol	fm	1	Ⓣ	:243 :474 1:103 1:324	3↑ShoeBCM-G1	**102**	3	32½	31½	31½	21	32	Espinoza V	LB124	*1.90	98-01	*Aragorn*1241¾ Charmo124nk Silent Name1241½	3wd into str,lost 2nd 6
8Apr06-9SA	fm	1	Ⓣ	:223 :46 1:092 1:33	4↑ArcadiaH-G2	**105**	6	44	31½	1hd	12	11½	Bejarano R	LB116	6.20	98-08	Silent Name1161½ *Chinese Dragon*119¾ Milk ItMick117nk	Rail bid,clear,held 10
12Mar06-8SA	fm	1	Ⓣ	:224 :463 1:111 1:354	4↑Alw 70000N$MY	**95**	1	914	914	75	4nk	1¾	Espinoza V	LB119	4.10	84-15	*SilentName*119¾ RunawayDancer119hd HelmBnk119hd	6wd into lane,rallied 10

WORKS: Jly1 Hol ◈5f fst 1:00 H *4/72* Jun24 Hol ◈7f fst 1:264 H *1/2* Jun17 Hol ◈5f fst 1:004 B *10/61* Jun11 Hol ◈3f fst :393 B *26/28* May21 Hol ◈5f fst 1:03 B *45/59* May14 Hol ◈7f fst 1:263 H *1/3*
TRAINER: Synth(44 .14 $1.70) Route/Sprint(23 .09 $1.19) 31-60Days(80 .06 $0.95) Sprint(123 .13 $2.49) GrdStk(14 .14 $2.06) J/T 2006-07 HOL(3 .67 $6.00) J/T 2006-07(10 .30 $3.24)

Silent Name is a power sprinter. He had delivered a tremendous Beyer 109, a lifetime top, ostensibly against the closer's bias on Keeneland's Polytrack, doing so in a Grade 2 sprint at today's distance as recently as April 14 and won going away.

This power sprinter did not escape the favor of the bettors, who were disposed to excuse the bad stumble at the start of the Grade 1 Met Mile at Belmont. Silent Name may not possess the Grade 1 credential so valuable in these definitive races, but he is a multiple Grade 2 winner with close finishes on the turf against Grade 1 company. The bonus is a smashing win on the Cushion Track. Silent Name might have been attractive as a longshot, or even an overlay at 9–2 or such, but he left the gate as a co-favorite with Surf Cat; no play.

Now examine the longshot that did win and which I missed.

9 Bilo		Dk. b or br g. 7 (Apr)		Life 13 5 2 2 $254,036 114	D.Fst 9 4 2 1 $172,256 114

9 Bilo
Own: King Edward
Red And Black Checks, Red Cap
TALAMO J (309 55 55 41 .18) 2007: (860 159 .18)

Dk. b or br g. 7 (Apr)
Sire: Bertrando (Skywalker) $12,500
Dam: Raffle's Bag (Devil's Bag)
Br: Ed Nahem (Cal)
Tr: Jones Martin F (41 11 6 10 .27) 2007:(94 17 .18)

L 114

Life	13	5	2	2	$254,036	114	D.Fst	9 4 2 1	$172,256	114
2007	2	1	0	1	$57,780	97	Wet(408)	2 0 0 0	$24,000	88
2005	5	1	0	0	$85,620	114	Synth	2 1 0 1	$57,780	97
							Turf(323)	0 0 0 0	$0	–
Hol	5	3	1	1	$128,840	97	Dst(356)	3 2 1 0	$82,640	97

10Jun07–6Hol fst 7f :222 :452 1:092 1:22 3↑OC 62k/n2x 97 1 4 1hd 1½ 11½ 13½ Chavez J F LB120 3.20 96– 12 Bilo120³½ Grand Point124¹ Dilemma115½ Inside, ridden out 9
29Apr07–4Hol fst 7½f :223 :443 1:091 1:284 4↑ⓈTiznow150k 88 7 2 1hd 3nk 32½ 36½ Chavez J F LB120 20.40 87– 11 Greg's Gold120½ He's the Rage120⁵½ Bilo120¹ 3wd,drifted in lane 8
0Nov05–7OSA fst 6f :211 :430 :561 1:080 3↑ⓈCalCup3prH130k 82 7 4 3nk 3½ 7½ 8½ Valenzuela P A LB118 3.50 87– 03 Jet West116no Areyoutalkintome119½ Thor'sEcho117½ 4wd,5wd,weakened 11
8Oct05–6OSA fst 6f :21 :431 :554 1:084 3↑AncTtlBC-G1 93 7 2 3nk 3½ 41½ 63½ Espinoza V LB124 2.90 90– 10 Captain Squire124½ Zanzibar124no IndianCountry124¹ 3wd duel,weakened 7
21Aug05–2Dmr fst 6f :213 :434 :554 1:081 3↑OC 62k/n2x –N 114 6 3 2½ 1hd 11 14½ Valenzuela P A LB120 5.60 98– 07 Bilo120⁴½ Lifestyle120½ Bonus Pack120½ Dueled,clear,driving 8
20Feb05–8SA wf 6½f ⊗ :211 :432 1:074 1:142 4↑ⓈSensatStrH137k 88 9 2 43 42½ 63½ 74½ Nakatani C S LB117 *2.40 95– 05 GrndAppontmnt117¹½ RdWrror119½ Excssvplsr119½ 3wd into lane,wkened 9
29Jan05–4SA wf 6f :204 :433 :561 1:084 4↑ⓇSunMilSpnt300k 87 11 1 62½ 41½ 1hd 43½ Espinoza V LB122 12.00 90– 06 RdWrror122¹ FllMoonMdnss122hd Aryot1kntom1212½ 4wd,led,steadied late 11
19Dec04–6Hol fst 6f :22 :442 1:081 1:21 3↑Alw 45926n1x 94 5 4 1hd 1hd 11 13 Nakatani C S LB123 *1.90 97– 10 Bilo123³ Diamond Fury119½ Melanyhasthepapers119² Inside duel,clear 9
13Jun04–6BM fst 6f :222 :451 :572 1:10 4↑Alw 41573n1x 90 3 5 41½ 21½ 2hd 3hd Carr D LB119 *.80 89– 17 At a Boy Luther119hd Geardown119no Bilo119⁷ Bid 2w, outdueled 7
15May04–1Hol fst 6f :211 :434 :561 1:092 3↑ⓈAlw 47000n1x 92 6 3 3½ 2hd 12½ 11 Nakatani C S LB121 *1.10 90– 11 Bilo121¹¹ Fairly Crafty121² Timely Jeff121³ 3wd bid,driftd in,held 7
24Apr04–7Hol fst 7f :213 :44 1:084 1:214 3↑ⓈGldnEglFrm70k 91 5 8 2hd 2hd 11 2no Nakatani C S LB121 *1.90 93– 06 Throw Me a Curve119no Bilo121¹½ Fairly Crafty121² Inched away,caught 13
1Apr04–2SA fst 6f :212 :441 :564 1:092 4↑ⓈMd Sp Wt 44k 93 2 4 21 31 11 12 Nakatani C S LB122 1.90 91– 16 Bilo122² Flaming Moe122⁴ Jones Tale122⁵ Broke in bit,inside 7

WORKS: Jun29 Hol ◇5f fst 1:01¹ H 15/47 Jun23 Hol ◇4f fst :48¹ H 7/64 May31 Hol ◇5f fst 1:00⁴ H 12/59 May22 Hol ◇5f fst 1:01¹ H 25/51 May16 Hol ◇4f fst :53⁴ H 59/60 May9 Hol ◇3f fst :36 H 6/24
TRAINER: Synth(73 .19 $2.76) WonLastStart(36 .14 $0.97) Sprint(194 .15 $1.96) GrdStk(5 .00 $0.00) J/T 2006-07 HOL (1 .00 $0.00) J/T 2006–07(1 .00 $0.00)

Although price can alter all preconceptions, as a rule I do not back 4-year-old-and-up winners of nonwinners-twice allowance races on the leap to Grade 1 and Grade 2 competition. The maneuver does not often succeed. As matters proceeded Bilo exited the gate swiftly to a lonesome lead. Sailors Sunset did not challenge for the front and neither did any other horse.

The positives here were several. Bilo likes the long sprint and he looked to be cycling back to a lifetime top. That figure, the Beyer 114, could not be accepted at face value. It had occurred in 2005 at Del Mar under the same N2X allowances as Bilo's last race, and it reflected the unmistakable shine of the "giraffe" figure—a speed figure so superior to any other in the record that it sticks out like a giraffe's neck.

Bilo gets a positive jockey switch to the hot apprentice Joe Talamo. And perhaps most important on this day, the balance between Bilo's speed and pace combination was precisely the kind that had been winning on the front on Hollywood's virgin Cushion Track. So bettors that grabbed the 9.80–1 odds no doubt could easily explain why they liked the proposition.

As often happens in lone-speed scenarios where the front-runners should be outgunned, Bilo barely lasted and would have been overhauled by Surf Cat in another stride. The resulting Beyer Speed Figure of 102 represented a two-length improvement, the horse's second-best ever, but remained stalled below the conventional Grade 1 margins of 111 to 106 by another two lengths.

CLAIMING RACES

One of the most rewarding handicapping lessons of my time occurred as long ago as 1986, when new acquaintance Tom Brohamer delivered a seminar on a Hollywood Park Saturday card to 150 visitors from Canada. Professional speed figures did not yet appear publicly in the past performances.

Brohamer announced that a recent winner in a $10,000 claiming race now rising in class to $32,000 was the best bet of the day. Members of the audience snickered. When the horse later won by six and paid $38.60, no doubt the Canadians had learned a valuable lesson they could not forget. I certainly did.

A dedicated figure analyst, Brohamer merely had noted that the class jumper's speed figure in the $10,000 win had exceeded the Hollywood par for the $32,000 level. The observation coincided with the view expressed earlier in print by Andy Beyer that the best way to predict whether a claiming horse rising multiple levels in class can succeed is to examine its speed figure. If the figure matches par at the higher level, accept the horse. No better example has since been invoked to clarify the nexus between speed and claiming class.

Now that professional speed figures are abundantly present in the past performances and elsewhere, all handicappers have gained access to similar longshots, provided they have compiled par times and par figures for the local tracks, or have acquired them from a speed service—for a fee. Beyer Speed Pars at several class levels for all operating tracks can be found in the regular editions of *DRF Simulcast Weekly*, along with the Beyer figures for every winner of the previous week.

Like other opportunities for generously priced but legitimate contenders that have been impacted by the information age, the claiming horses rising multiple levels in class with acceptable speed figures no longer pay as much. The Canadians would not receive $38.60 on Brohamer's longshot today and few of them would snicker at the thought that the $10,000 horse might actually prevail.

Nonetheless, the play still can be expected to identify horses that figure at 8–1 and higher, at least occasionally, notably when the barn and rider fly below the handicapping radar, or perhaps when the horse up in class qualifies as a trip playback and the high-figure win occurred two back. It's one of three generous plays among the claiming horses that repeat themselves often enough to matter:

- A multiple rise in claiming class, accompanied by a par figure or better.
- In claiming races limited to 3-year-olds, any drop from a nonwinners allowance race, provided the allowance drop-down exhibited a mere spark of

ability, such as brief early speed, a midrace move, an even effort that has beaten half the field, or a finish within six lengths of the winner.

- Any claiming horse that delivers a new pace top, or one of the two strongest combinations of speed and pace in the field, provided the horse has exhibited back class within the past two seasons.

For too many years beginning in the 1990s when the older claiming game began to be phased out at major tracks in favor of races for younger horses, the notebooks showed I was taking a beating in the claiming races limited to 3-year-olds. The cheap young things were consistently inconsistent, rarely repeating best efforts, and when up in class they would be beaten by a faster pace. The races could not be avoided altogether, because they typically would be part of the serial bets.

A breakthrough occurred when I realized that not only could handicappers make profits by limiting action in these poor races to allowance drop-downs, but also the allowance drop-downs regularly returned more than they should. A fair number of winners would be 8–1 and better. That circumstance prevailed when the allowance performance would be less than convincing, revealing merely that spark of ability. A personal favorite was brief early speed in the allowance race, followed by a successive loss of ground at the other points of call. The margin of beaten lengths at the wire did not matter.

The play is particularly ripe in the first four months of the calendar year, when the 3-year-old claiming races will be bulging with early washouts running with seriously inflated claiming tags, such as the $80,000 at Santa Anita. The claiming 3-year-olds will be worth less than half that amount by fall, and many may have descended to the bottom of the claiming ranks before they turn 4. As the season progresses the play is less ripe for allowance drop-downs, but throughout summer and fall handicappers should stay on alert for longshots that fit the profile.

Catching the opportunities that follow any claiming horse that has delivered a new pace top came my way via New York handicapper Cary Fotias, a pro player who favors any horse next time as a result of the new high pace figure. My variation links the new top pace figure to claiming horses having back class. If current form has been bleak, the speed figures will be unattractive and several of the recent running lines may be dull. So the odds will be higher than they should be, maybe double-digit.

Suddenly the jaded horses run extra fast to the pace call before tiring. If those horses have beaten better in the past two seasons, they probably are cycling back to top form. The play is especially attractive if a respectable barn rises a level or two in class following the fast pace. These horses win enough and several of them will win again.

It's important to raise another caution sign. On synthetic surfaces generally the high-pace-figure horses have not been nearly as successful as on conventional dirt tracks. As mentioned earlier, the traditional balance between the pace figure and speed figure has been altered, such that more of the races have been won by horses having slightly lower pace figures and higher speed figures, not vice versa. Claiming front-runners and pressers will be particularly vulnerable. If the alteration continues and emerges as the status quo on synthetic surfaces, it represents a monumental change for figure analysts who rely routinely upon pace figures.

To stretch the previous point, no discussion of class and longshots in 2007—and presumably the years beyond—can conclude without a brief treatment of the impact now underway due to the increasing presence at major tracks of synthetic surfaces.

SYNTHETIC SURFACES

When Arlington Park opened with its brand-new Polytrack in May 2007, handicappers at the Midwest oval could have had scarcely a warning of the adjustments they soon would be pressed to undertake in their handicapping methods. From May 4 through May 20, the first two weeks and 91 races, the track reported the following statistics:

WINNERS' RUNNING STYLES ON ARLINGTON POLYTRACK (MAY 4–20)

Closers:	36–91 =	39%
Stalkers:	30–91 =	33%
Pressers:	8–91 =	9%
Wired:	17–91 =	19%

The closers on Arlington's Polytrack were winning more races than the front-runners and pressers combined. Is that an anomaly, or a new reality?

Handicappers familiar with similar outcomes on Keeneland's Polytrack and Hollywood Park's Cushion Track did not have to be advised of the obvious. No longer should horses that run first, second, and third at the first call in sprints be expected to win twice as many races as they should at six furlongs. Or win 1 ½ as many as they should at seven furlongs. Or win almost 1 ½ as many races as they should in the routes.

And horses that run in the rear halves of the fields no longer should be expected to win less than 40 percent of their rightful share of the races. They should be expected instead to win roughly as many races as the front-runners and pressers. This has much to do with the expectation of catching longshots.

The alteration of running styles that win most frequently on synthetic surfaces has a bright side that handicappers should not neglect. Arlington Park also reported the average payoffs in the exotic pools for the first 91 races on Polytrack:

AVERAGE EXOTIC PAYOFFS, ARLINGTON POLYTRACK, MAY 4–20, 2007 ($2 WAGER)

Daily Double:	$136.08
Exacta:	$114.83
Trifecta:	$1,002.76
Superfecta:	$12,613.78
Pick Three:	$2,621.90
Pick Four:	$11,058.80

The average payoff to win was $17.09.

When closers upset, no handicapper can deny that the mutuels will be bigger. What has irritated so many handicappers about synthetic surfaces is not that the number of upsets has increased terrifically, but rather that the past performances of the winners have reflected a torrent of unpredictable form reversals. How to anticipate the upsets?

Regardless, class analysts may find themselves on a faster track to longshots that rally from behind. Two procedures make sense. First, analytically, when closers predominate, handicappers having an aptitude for identifying the best horses should prepare to prefer horses with a class advantage and a strong closing style, often on the outside.

If current form looks dull, pay attention to the horses having back class. If they relish the synthetic surfaces, enough of them may rally to win at fancy prices to carry the cause. At double-digit odds the horses having back class are best covered on the undersides of exactas, trifectas, and supers, and included in the serial bets to win.

Beyond capitulation to closers with back class, the early returns on synthetic surfaces have resurrected the importance of the final fraction. The preeminent owner, breeder, Kentucky Derby winner (four times), and racetrack operator (Fair Grounds) Colonel E. R. Bradley was also an inveterate and successful gambler. He became revered among punters for his observation that any horse capable of completing the final fraction in 24 seconds or better should be bet the next time.

In the good colonel's time, the 1920s to the 1940s, the observation proved correct. The final fraction separated the horses on class amazingly well. Then the speed horses began to dominate, and turf routes apart, final fractions were no longer as salient. Synthetic tracks may have initiated a kind of recycling process, such that the final fractions on Polytrack, Cushion Track, Tapeta, and the rest will be decisive, at least much of the time.

Extrapolating from Colonel Bradley's standard of 24 seconds or better, applicable only to races at six furlongs and one mile, handicappers can invoke these final fractions as telltale:

- At 6½ furlongs and 1¹⁄₁₆ miles, 31 seconds or better
- At 7 furlongs and 1⅛ miles, 37 seconds or better

In the majority of races on synthetic tracks the desirable final fractions might not be eclipsed. Polytrack surfaces in particular may be unusually slow. Handicappers must be prepared not only to calculate the final fractions, but also to prefer horses that can rally by two lengths or faster than the others, regardless of the actual times.

The calculation is elementary, and occurs from the pace call to the wire in sprints and routes. The pace call in sprints occurs after four furlongs and is the second call in the points of call. The pace call in routes occurs after six furlongs and is the third call in the points of call (at a mile and a quarter the pace call occurs after a mile and is also the third call in the points of call).

Subtract the fractional time of the race from the final time of the race. The difference (in fifths) equals the final fraction of the race. One length equals one-fifth of a second. Modify the final fraction of the race by the lengths gained (or lost) by the horse. This is the final fraction of the horse. Handicappers should determine to calculate the final fractions for the good races in the previous two form cycles (six to eight races), with a higher regard for recent races.

If a $25,000 claiming sprint has been run in 45⅖ to the pace call and 1:11⅕ to the wire, the final fraction of the race has been 25⅘. If a rallying closer has gained seven lengths from the pace call to the wire, that horse's final fraction is estimated as 25⅘ minus seven-fifths, or 24⅖. Such a final fraction can be considered good, but unexceptional.

Needless to say, front-runners and pressers that can complete the final fractions on synthetic surfaces in 24 seconds or better will be hard for the latecomers to overtake. The final fractions of front-runners and pressers on conventional dirt surfaces, however, do not apply.

CLASS STANDOUTS

In 2002 the nation's leading miler by a handsome margin was the 4-year-old Congaree, and late in the season trainer Bob Baffert entered the colt in New York's Grade 1 Cigar Mile, annually run on the Saturday following Thanksgiving. On the overnight line of *Daily Racing Form* Congaree was listed at 5–1. The putative favorite was Red Bullet, winner of the Preakness Stakes in 2000. Congaree could be expected to slaughter Red Bullet on class alone. Class analysts might have been provoked to make their largest wager of the season.

The New York handicappers did not correct the unbalanced line. Congaree left at 9–2. He won waltzing by 5½ lengths. A rallying Aldebaran finished second, predictably. Red Bullet did not get a call and never looked like a contender.

Was Congaree a longshot? In my judgment Congaree qualified as a relative longshot, meaning only that the odds had veered seriously out of line on the field's best horse. If the two horses had met at the mile 100 times, Congaree would defeat Red Bullet rather easily 80 times or more.

The unbalanced line, however, had a tenable explanation, and customarily does. An occasional atypical situation in Thoroughbred racing finds much the best horse going off at a flagrantly inflated price. The reason is usually a last running line that looks worse than it is and can be explained logically. No decline in current form has occurred.

In the Congaree situation trainer Baffert understood all too well he had the nation's top miler, and he had flirted with starting Congaree at the mile on grass in the Breeders' Cup. That October Baffert had run Congaree during Oak Tree at Santa Anita in a stakes on the turf, Congaree's only grass experience. Congaree had run the first six furlongs of the Oak Tree turf route in 1:09⅕ before tiring to a nondescript seventh, beaten only three lengths, but beaten in a way that intimated declining form. Handicappers who understood the experiment Baffert had conducted would have excused the turf performance.

Baffert subsequently announced Congaree would not start in the Breeders' Cup, but instead would be aimed at New York's Cigar Mile, his best game. Too many New York handicappers were unaware of the experiment on grass, and not as forgiving, thus the 9–2 odds on much the best horse.

Years ago, when the Grade 1 title defined its stakeholder as authentically top of the line, my habit was to back any Grade 1 winner that had lost its most recent race. The reason for the recent flop was not as significant as the abiding class of the horse. None of the Grade 1 horses would go as longshots, but rather as low-priced overlays. The bottom line was consistently black. The situation no longer warrants the class handicapper's respect, as the contemporary Grade 1 title is not nearly as definitive.

But class standouts sometimes still will be disregarded to a fault. To repeat, it's often because the last running line has been better than looks or will be excusable for a logical reason that too many bettors choose to disrespect, as with Congaree. So the class standouts run as relative longshots. Handicappers should not hesitate to double the bet, or at least up the ante.

After all, if the best bet of the day can be defined as a horse having a good chance at a good price, it's particularly advantageous to be riding the best horse at a relatively inflated price. To come full circle in the chapter, it's the same reason the Horse of the Year and marvelous champion Invasor at 6.70–1 in the Breeders' Cup Classic can be saluted as one of the most engaging longshots of the 2006 season.

SHUBACK
ON BETTING FOREIGN IMPORTS

By Alan Shuback

FINDING WINNING LONGSHOTS first time out after having arrived from foreign climes these days is a bit easier than passing a camel through the eye of a needle and not quite as difficult as getting a rich man into heaven. More foreign imports are winning in their North American debuts than ever before, but only rarely do they return anything better than 5–1. In most cases their prices are considerably shorter than that.

So finding a winning foreign import at long odds may well be a hopeless task. There are a number of factors behind this phenomenon. An examination of them will clarify why that is so, as well as lay the groundwork for finding first-time imports that are capable of rewarding their backers at prices a bit better than 3–1, or at least provide them with a return that can fulfill dreams of overlay value.

THE STATE OF THE ART

It has become evident since the turn of the century that the quality of racing in Europe—which for the purposes of this exercise means Britain, Ireland, France, Germany, and Italy, but especially Britain, Ireland, and France—has outstripped its American counterpart in ways that would have been unfathomable to the owners and trainers of horses such as Secretariat, Seattle Slew, Affirmed, and Alydar. The diaspora of first-class American bloodstock into the bloodlines of Europe, Japan, and South America has thinned American Thoroughbred blood to the point where Kentucky-breds have become a virtual minority in New York and Southern California, where state-breds take up an increasing number of barns. Factor in raceday medications that are allowed in all North American jurisdictions, and the quality of the American Thoroughbred often pales when compared to his European cousin. Fortified by decades of input from the best Kentucky blood, as well as running drug free and being the product of stallions and mares who themselves raced drug free, the contemporary European racehorse is a better model of what a Thoroughbred should be.

Bloodstock agents around the world and bettors in America have taken notice. The price of a European-trained horse in recent years has rocketed. In the 1990s, a Group 3 winner in England and France might be had for $250,000. Nowadays, that kind of money will barely get you an allowance winner who has been unplaced in listed-race company. The weakness of the dollar has compounded the problems of American buyers in Europe. In 1995, a horse being offered in England for a 100,000-pound tag was worth the equivalent of $165,000. At today's exchange rate, the same horse would cost $206,000. But on top of that, the 100,000-pound British racehorse of 1995 cannot be had these days for less than 200,000 pounds, thanks not only to inflation, but also to the perceived difference in quality between American and British bloodstock, as well as an increasing desire on the part of European owners to keep as many of their better horses, especially fillies, in the European chain of command.

Indeed, since 2003, the European racing industry has been employing a continent-wide scheme to keep their best fillies and mares at home. During that time at least two dozen new distaff listed races have been inaugurated, while many listed races have been upgraded to Group 3 status by the European Pattern Race Committee. Meanwhile, two new races, Royal Ascot's Group 2 Windsor Forest Stakes and Chantilly's Group 3 Prix Allez France, have been introduced into the European program at those exalted levels. The idea behind the strategy has never been a secret. It is to provide more opportunities for good fillies and mares who in the past would have been sold to American interests before the end of their 3-year-old campaigns, and it has been successful.

The result of these machinations, coupled with the rise in prices and the weak dollar, has led to a decline in the quality of European imports to America in the last five years. The more precipitous concommitant decline in the overall quality of American racing, however, has meant that first-time imports from Europe continue to go off at relatively short prices, especially if they are properly spotted.

SOUTH AMERICAN MONEY

While the number of European imports has decreased, the number of South American imports during the same period has risen significantly.

The startling decline in the value of the Argentine peso and the Brazilian real in 2001 and 2002 did not go unrecognized by American bloodstock agents. In the autumn of 2001, the Argentine peso was trading at a ratio of 1:1 with the United States dollar. By June 2002, the peso was worth just 25 cents. Thus, an Argentine horse that was worth 100,000 pesos in October 2001 would have cost an American buyer $100,000. Eight months later, a 100,000-peso horse would have cost his American buyer just $25,000. The situation in Brazil was only slightly better from the South American point of view.

By the end of 2002, the number of South American imports to the U.S. had doubled from a year earlier. Since 2006, as the Brazilian and Argentine economies have begun to steady themselves, South American imports have declined slightly. The difficulty in dealing with South American imports is always separating the few bits of wheat from the considerable chaff. For every Invasor or Asiatic Boy emerging from South America, there are a dozen Group 1 stakes winners who prove barely capable of winning an allowance race up north.

BETTING THE IMPORTS

Finding 6–5 favorites from England who can win a division of Del Mar's Oceanside Stakes, as did Ten A Penny on the seaside track's opening day in 2007, is no difficult task. Ten A Penny had won his first four races in England before finishing a solid fourth in a good Newmarket handicap. Among the horses he had beaten was the subsequent Group 3 runner-up Mr Napper Tandy, so, in reality, his $4.40 win price, coming at the expense of a bunch of allowance types and ex-dirt horses, was something of value, worth a five-time increase in your normal $10 or $20 bet.

At heart, that is really the way to salvage value from the short-priced imports we get from abroad, especially those from Europe. It is almost impossible to find a longshot from Europe that is going to win first time out, most of them being just too good to be left alone at such inflated prices. So it is wise to try and make your own financial value by increasing your wagers on horses like Ten A Penny—a nice son of Gulch previously trained by the astute young former jump jockey Jamie Osborne—who was running against horses in the Oceanside that were worth little more than ten a penny.

KEY FOREIGN RACES

It would be nice if there were a magic formula for determining key foreign races but, sadly, there is not. Obviously, group races weigh in more heavily than listed races, top-class handicaps are better than most allowances, open allowances are better than restricted allowances (auction races or races in France restricted to horses bred or foaled in France), while most maidens at Ascot, Newmarket, Longchamp, Chantilly, the Curragh, and Leopardstown are superior to most other maidens in England, France, and Ireland.

But determining the inherent value of any given race, be it a Group 1, a listed race, a handicap, or a maiden for first-time starters, requires homework. Merely accepting the Racing Post Rating of the winner, or any other rating, for that matter, will not reveal the full story of any race.

In this day and age, it is essential that any serious player familiarize himself with racing in the three major European racing nations: Britain, France, and Ireland. If your home betting locale is Southern California, New York, Kentucky, Gulfstream Park, or Arlington Park in August, you are hurting yourself by not paying close attention to all group- and listed-race results in those three countries.

With the data available on the Internet these days, and with more and more races—especially those in Britain and Ireland—being televised on networks like Horse Racing Television (HRTV) and Television Games Network (TVG), following European racing is no longer the logistical problem it once was.

Moreover, *Daily Racing Form* provides previews and reports on all of the major

Group 1 and 2 races throughout Europe, Dubai, Japan, and Hong Kong. Detailed results with analyses of these races, as well as European Group 3 events, are available on the *Form*'s website, drf.com, and in *DRF Simulcast Weekly*. Assessments of the chances of first-time imports are a regular feature on *Daily Racing Form* handicapping pages.

The wealth of foreign information available should enable the curious and the wise (they are, in reality, the same thing) to make hay at the expense of the lazy handicapper who relies solely on figures and the face value of foreign form. By combining frequent use of the foreign-racing websites listed at the end of this chapter with daily study of *DRF*, serious players should be able to distinguish the value plays where first- and second-time North American starters are concerned.

The trick to determining the genuine value of any foreign race is knowing which horses in a race have previously run well in top-class company, or which of them have subsequently run well in top-class company. If you have done your homework, value plays like the ones described forthwith will begin to make themselves evident.

Keep in mind, however, that foreign first-timers winning at long prices are practically nonexistent. Longshot scores posted by ex-foreigners in their second North American starts are even less frequent.

THE WHATSTHESCRIPT METHOD

Perhaps the most perfect recent example of a value play on a first-time import was the victory of Whatsthescript in Santa Anita's restricted Pinjara Stakes on October 26, 2006. In his previous start at Leopardstown three months earlier, Whatsthescript had finished third, beaten just 2¾ lengths by Teofilo, the subsequent winner of two Group 1 races, the National Stakes at the Curragh and Newmarket's Dewhurst Stakes, the race generally regarded as the definitive 2-year-old event on the European calendar.

Both the National and the Dewhurst were run prior to the Pinjara, yet Whatsthescript was allowed to go off at a tasty 4.90–1. None of his seven rivals had faced anything remotely as classy as Teofilo, who by that time was widely regarded as the best 2-year-old in Europe, if not the world.

Moreover, Whatsthescript had beaten Dimenticata, who would next out finish second by a head in the Group 2 Debutante Stakes.

It was evident that very few American racegoers had ever heard of Teofilo or Dimenticata. Their ignorance cost them dearly as Whatsthescript got up to win by half a length.

Whatsthescript (Ire)
Own: Tommy Town Thoroughbreds LLC

B. c. 2 (Mar)
Sire: Royal Applause*GB (Waajib*Ire) $34,410
Dam: Grizel*GB (Lion Cavern)
Br: C. Mac Hale and J. Hyland (Ire)
Tr: O'Neill Doug F(0 0 0 0 .00) 2006:(968 163 .17)

Life	4	2	0	2	$58,041	79	D.Fst	0	0	0	0	$0	-
2006	4	2	0	2	$58,041	79	Wet(273*)	0	0	0	0	$0	-
							Synth	0	0	0	0	$0	-
2005	0	M	0	0	$0	-	Turf(309)	4	2	0	2	$58,041	79
SaⓉ	1	1	0	0	$37,500	79	DstⓉ(265)	1	1	0	0	$37,500	79

26Oct06–7OSA fm 1 Ⓣ :24 :48⁴ 1:12³ 1:35⁴ ⓇPinjara65k 79 5 7 7½ 7 3¼ 7 3¼ 5 2¼ 1½ Enriquez I D B118 4.90 84–15 *Whtsthescript*118½ *WrningZon*119hd ⒹEdwrdin1181½ Waited 1/8,got out,up 8
Previously trained by David Wachman
29Jly06 Leopardstwn (Ire) gf 7f Ⓣ LH 1:30 Tyros Stakes (Listed) Stk 63700 3 2¾ Lordan W M 127 6.00 *Teofilo*1271¾ Middleham1271 *Whatsthescript*1271¼ 11
Racing Post Rating: 97 — Tracked in 5th,3rd 2f out,hit by foe's whip,stayed on
10Jly06 Roscommon (Ire) yl 7f Ⓣ RH 1:34¹ Irish Stallion Farms EBF Maiden Maiden 17900 1hd Lordan W M 129 1.75 Whatsthescript129hd Dimenticata1243½ Spanish Parade1292½ 13
Racing Post Rating: 78 — Tracked in 4th,led 1-1/2f out,dueled,drifted left,led on line

Such value plays occur with a certain frequency, but they are only noticed by those who are acquainted with the intricacies of European black-type form. The rare recent example of a genuine European longshot scoring in America at first asking was Wilko, whose 28.30–1 upset of the 2004 Breeders' Cup Juvenile could not have been predicted by what we shall call the Whatsthescript method. Wilko had not been running in the very top European company before his arrival at Lone Star Park, nor had he been winning the Group 2 races in which he had been competing.

True, he had a dirt pedigree on his sire's side in Awesome Again, but all his American-trained opponents sported similar dirt bloodlines. Winless in 18 starts since his Breeders' Cup, Wilko appears to have gotten very lucky on the day of his greatest victory.

Numerous other examples of first-time value plays determined by the Whatsthescript method abound. The following are some of the most obvious. All are horses who have arrived in North America from Europe since January 1, 2005.

ASHKAL WAY: A close second in a Goodwood handicap to subsequent Group 3 Darley Stakes winner Enforcer indicated that he had a touch of class. That, coupled with a six-length rout of Enforcer two starts later, suggested that this Godolphin son of Ashkalani was overpriced at 4.60–1 in his U.S. debut, a modest Belmont allowance on May 25, 2006. He duly slammed his eight rivals by three lengths and has since gone on to win a Grade 1 and two Grade 2 races at lower prices.

Ashkal Way (Ire)
Own: Godolphin Racing LLC

Ch. g. 4 (Jan)
Sire: Ashkalani*Ire (Soviet Star)
Dam: Golden Way*Ire (Cadeaux Genereux*GB)
Br: Gainsborough Stud Management Ltd (Ire)
Tr: bin Suroor Saeed(9 4 1 1 .44) 2006:(39 17 .44)

Life	10	3	2	2	$147,349	102	D.Fst	0	0	0	0	$0	-
2006	2	1	0	1	$39,800	102	Wet(280*)	0	0	0	0	$0	-
							Synth	0	0	0	0	$0	-
2005	7	2	2	1	$107,549	-	Turf(324)	10	3	2	2	$147,349	102
BelⓉ	1	1	0	0	$28,800	102	DstⓉ(263)	2	2	0	0	$38,695	102

25May06–8Bel fm 1 1/16 Ⓣ :23¹ :45³ 1:09³ 1:40 3↑ Alw 48000N2x 102 7 6 12 6 7¾ 6 3¾ 1 1½ 1³ Gomez G K L122 4.60 93–12 *Ashkal Way*122³ All Trumps1221¾ Defer122nk 4 wide move, clear 9
Previously trained by Ismail Mohammed
24Feb06 Nad Al Sheba (UAE) gs *1¼ Ⓣ LH 2:08 3↑ Etisalat Cup Hcp 110000 3 2½ McEvoy K 127 - Anani1191¼ Realism1221¼ *Ashkal Way*1271¼ 12
Racing Post Rating: 99 — Handily placed,angled out 3f out,finished well.Morshdi(126)5th
Previously trained by Brian Ellison
10Oct05 Newmarket (GB) sf 1⅛ Ⓣ Str 1:51² 3↑ Cambridgeshire Handicap Hcp 229000 15 15 Fallon K 125 8.00 Blue Monday1292½ Evaluator1272½ My Paris1301 30
Racing Post Rating: 83 — Mid-pack,prgrss 3-1/2f out,wknd 1-1/2f out.Crosspiece(129)4th
17Sep05 Newbury (GB) gf 1¼ Ⓣ LH 2:03² 3↑ John Smiths Handicap Hcp 181000 7 1¾ Hayes C5 124 6.00 Star of Light125no *Blue Monday*135hd Crosspeace132nk 19
Racing Post Rating: 107 — Bunped,dropped to rear,fnsh well w/o threatening.Eccentric(134)8t
20Aug05 Beverley (GB) gd 1¼ Ⓣ RH 2:03¹ Totescoop6 Handicap Hcp 89800 1³ Hayes C5 115 *2.00 Ashkal Way115³ Tarraman117³ Enforcer133¹ 14
Racing Post Rating: 106 — Mid-pack,4th halfway,2nd 2f out,led 1f out,soon clear
28Jly05 Goodwood (GB) sf 1¼ Ⓣ RH 2:09¹ Ladbrokes.com Handicap Hcp 174000 2½ McCarthy A 110 10.00 Enforcer121½ *Ashkal Way*110³ Best Prospect108² 11
Racing Post Rating: 97 — Mid-pack,led 2f out,headed 75y out. Viva Pataca (133) 4th

SOL MI FA: Beaten just one-half length as a 2-year-old by subsequent Group 1 Poule d'Essai des Pouliches (French 1000 Guineas) winner Tie Black in a competitive Toulouse allowance with listed-race cache, she won at first asking in the U.S. for Tattersalls Sales sharpie James Cassidy at 5–1 when dropped into a Bay Meadows turf allowance on May 29, 2006. Tie Black had been awarded the French Guineas via the disqualification of Price Tag just 15 days earlier, so astute *DRF* readers and *Racing Post* and France Galop website surfers were in the know. (Also see "Good Relations," later in this chapter.)

Sol Mi Fa (Ire)
Own: Don Van Racing Inc

Dk. b or b. f. 3 (Mar)
Sire: Distant Music (Distant View)
Dam: Sil Sila*Ire (Marju*Ire)
Br: L. A. C. International (Ire)
Tr: Cassidy James M(6 2 1 2 .33) 2006:(163 23 .14)

Life	8	3	3	1	$85,415	84	D.Fst	0	0	0	0	$0 -
2006	3	2	1	0	$62,702	84	Wet(305)	0	0	0	0	$0 -
							Synth	0	0	0	0	$0 -
2005	5	1	2	1	$22,713	-	Turf(298)	8	3	3	1	$85,415 84
Bm[T]	1	1	0	0	$41,250	84	Dst[T](221)	1	1	0	0	$41,250 84

29May06–8BM fm 1 1/16 [T] :241 :483 1:1241:441 [F]BMBCOaks81k 84 4 5 4½ 54 3 1½ 1 1½ 1¾ Lopez D G LB117 5.00 86–17 Sol Mi Fa117¾ Soothsay1223½ Make a Pass1172½ Bid 4w 1/4p, driving 6
Previously trained by Jean-Claude Rouget
5Apr06 Marseille-Borely (Fr) gd *1⅛ [T] RH 1:52 [F]Prix Blanche Alw 27000 1hd Mendizabal I 128 *.60 *Sol Mi Fa*128hd Colca1281 Tizina1282½ 6
Tracked in 4th,rallied in hand to lead near line
16Mar06 Saint-Cloud (Fr) hy *1 [T] LH 1:492 [F]Prix Dorina Alw 39800 21½ Mendizabal I 126 2.00 Folle Biche1151½ *Sol Mi Fa*1261½ Private Dancer126nk 5
Racing Post Rating: 89
Tracked in 4th,bid 2f out,no chance with winner
16Nov05 Toulouse (Fr) sf *1 [T] RH 1:44 [F]Coupe des Pouliches de 2 Ans Alw 24600 2½ Mendizabal I 128 - Tie Black121½ Sol Mi Fa1282 *Miss Sissy*1282½ 7
Tracked in 4th,bid 1-1/2f out,held by winner

PRICE TAG: Odds of 2.20–1 might not sound like value, but that was the case with this Dansili filly when she made a winning U.S. debut in Hollywood Park's Grade 1 Matriarch Stakes on November 26, 2006. Most people felt she had been unjustly denied the French 1000 Guineas in the stewards' room. Unlucky when eighth in the Group 1 Coronation Stakes, she ran into unsuitably soft ground and European champion 3-year-old filly Mandesha in the Group 1 Prix d'Astarte, then showed American-style speed when beating the boys in the seven-furlong Group 3 Prix du Pin. Lasix and Butazolidin and her own considerable talent enabled her to overcome a 5¾-length deficit through the Matriarch stretch.

Price Tag (GB)
Own: Juddmonte Farms Inc

B. f. 3 (Feb)
Sire: Dansili*GB (Danehill)
Dam: Tarocchi (Affirmed)
Br: Juddmonte Farms Ltd (GB)
Tr: Frankel Robert J(42 11 2 9 .26) 2006:(585 139 .24)

Life	10	3	0	2	$457,177	99	D.Fst	0	0	0	0	$0 -
2006	7	2	0	2	$434,279	99	Wet(277)	0	0	0	0	$0 -
							Synth	0	0	0	0	$0 -
2005	3	1	0	0	$22,898	-	Turf(365)	10	3	0	2	$457,177 99
Hol[T]	1	1	0	0	$300,000	99	Dst[T](324)	6	1	0	2	$387,702 99

26Nov06–8Hol fm 1 [T] :232 :462 1:1031:343 3↑[F]Matriarc-G1 99 8 1214 1212 127 95¾ 1½ Prado E S LB120 *2.20e 91–08 *PriceTg*120½ ThreeDegrees123hd PommesFrites123hd 4wd into lane,rallied 14
Previously trained by Pascal Bary
30Sep06 Longchamp (Fr) gd *7f [T] RH 1:204 3↑ Prix de la Foret-G1 Stk 317000 124¼ Lemaire C-P 122 10.00 Caradak129nk [DH]Welsh Emperor129 [DH]Linngari129¾ 14
Racing Post Rating: 103
Never a factor.Impressionnante8th,Sleeping Indian11th
7Sep06 Longchamp (Fr) gd *7f [T] RH 1:223 3↑ Prix du Pin-G3 Stk 102000 11 Thulliez T 120 *2.20 Price Tag1201 Gwenseb120nk *Helios Quercus*127nk 10
Racing Post Rating: 108
Rated in 6th,close 8th 3f out,led 1f out
30Jly06 Deauville (Fr) sf *1 [T] Str 1:362 3↑ [F]Prix d'Astarte-G1 Stk 318000 52½ Thulliez T 119 3.50 *Mandesha*119½ Impressionnante1191½ Tie Black119hd 10
Racing Post Rating: 110
Tracked in 3rd,dueled briefly for 2nd,faded
23Jun06 Ascot (GB) gf 1 [T] RH 1:39 [F]Coronation Stakes-G1 Stk 490000 85½ Thulliez T 126 *6.00 Nannina1262 Flashy Wings126¾ Nasheej126no 15
Racing Post Rating: 103
Missed break,13th 2f out,lacked room,no threat.Silca'sSister6th
14May06 Longchamp (Fr) gs *1 [T] RH 1:363 [F]Poule d'Essai des Pouliches-G1 Stk 517000 11½ Thulliez T 126 28.00 [D]Price Tag1261½ Tie Black126nk *Impressionnante*126½ 13
Racing Post Rating: 114
Rated rear,wide bid,dueled 1f out,drftd right,led.NewGirlfriend6t
Disqualified and placed third

SWEET TRAVEL: Trained in France by Andre Fabre, this Danzig filly traveled to Newmarket in April 2006 for her first start at 3 in the Group 3 Nell Gwyn Stakes, in which she finished fourth by two lengths to Speciosa, the subsequent winner of the classic 1000 Guineas. The Nell Gwyn form laid all over that of Sweet Travel's nine rivals in a 6 ½-furlong Santa Anita maiden race on February 14, 2007. With the aid of first-time Lasix and Butazolidin (never to be underestimated where European debutants are concerned), she rewarded her devoted Valentine's Day supporters to the tune of 4–1.

Sweet Travel (Ire)
Own: Wertheimer and Frere

Dk. b or b. f. 4 (Feb)
Sire: Danzig (Northern Dancer) $200,000
Dam: Raise a Beauty (Alydar)
Br: Wertheimer et Frere (Ire)
Tr: Mandella Gary(56 5 6 10 .09) 2006:(165 22 .13)

Life 8 1 3 2 $89,510 83 | D.Fst 0 0 0 0 $0 –
2007 1 1 0 0 $27,600 83 | Wet(434) 0 0 0 0 $0 –
Synth 0 0 0 0 $0 –
2006 4 M 0 2 $20,685 – | Turf(391) 8 1 3 2 $89,510 83
Sa(T) 1 1 0 0 $27,600 83 | Dst(T)(440) 2 1 1 0 $32,046 83

14Feb07–3SA fm *6½f (T) :213 :442 1:0711:131 4↑(F)Md Sp Wt 48k **83** 3 9 75¼ 73½ 2½ 11 Valdivia J Jr LB122 4.00 89–11 SweetTrvel1221 TheverythoughtofU1221¾ *NoLullby*1221½ Led past 1/8,held 10
Previously trained by Andre Fabre
10Sep06 Longchamp (Fr) gd *5f (T) Str :56 3↑ Prix du Petit Couvert-G3 Stk 101000 1011½ Peslier O 120 3.90 Majestic Missile1241 *Peace Offering*124¾ Biniou1231½ 10
Racing Post Rating: 72 *Rated in mid-pack,weakened over 2f out*
1Aug06 Deauville (Fr) gs *6f (T) Str 1:113 Prix de Vire Alw 42100 33¼ Peslier O 120 *2.00 Mednaya12321½ Mister Chocolate122¾ Sweet Travel1201½ 7
Racing Post Rating: 91 *Chased in 6th,mild late gain*
8Jly06 Deauville (Fr) sf *7f (T) Str 1:253 (F)Prix Amandine (Listed) Stk 64000 3¾ Peslier O 123 *2.20 Sabasha123hd Grand Vadla123¾ Sweet Travel123no 9
Racing Post Rating: 101 *Tracked in 4th,bid 1f out,not good enough.Gwenseb6th*
18Apr06 Newmarket (GB) gd 7f (T) Str 1:232 (F)Nell Gwyn Stakes-G3 Stk 88400 42 Peslier O 124 *3.30 *Speciosa*1271 Spinning Queen124¾ Salut d'Amour124nk 9
Racing Post Rating: 98 *Tracked leaders,outfinished*
30Sep05 Maisons-Laffitte (Fr) gd *6f (T) Str 1:103 Prix Eclipse-G3 Stk 90300 2¾ Peslier O 120 *.70e Damoiselle120¾ Sweet Travel120no Alyzea1201 9
Racing Post Rating: 101 *Tracked in 4th,strong bid 100y out,held by winner.Gwenseb6th*
7Sep05 Chantilly (Fr) gd *5½f (T) Str 1:032 Prix d'Arenberg-G3 Stk 93500 2½ Peslier O 120 *1.50 Headache123½ Sweet Travel1202 Lady Angele1201 7
Racing Post Rating: 101 *Trailed to over 1f out,late rush,just failed*
9Aug05 Deauville (Fr) gd *6½f (T) Str 1:20 (F)Prix de la Potiniere-EBF Maiden (FT) 22200 2no Peslier O 126 *.30e Twinspot126no Sweet Travel126½ Mednaya126¾ 9
Racing Post Rating: 88 *Pressed pace,dueled over 1f out,lost bob.Impressionnante4th*

TWINSPOT: Her French career was intertwined with those of both Price Tag and Sweet Travel. She had beaten Sweet Travel to the line by a nose in their mutual debut at Deauville in August 2005, then finished just a neck behind Price Tag when sixth in the Group 3 Prix d'Aumale before finishing fourth in the Group 1 Prix Marcel Boussac behind European juvenile filly champ Rumplestiltskin. She was meeting much, much cheaper at Sam Houston in her U.S. debut on March 9, 2007, when winning a $16,000 allowance at 8–5. Two months later, disbelieving Texans let her get away at 4.10–1 when she won a Lone Star allowance.

Twinspot
Own: Wertheimer and Frere

Dk. b or b. f. 4 (Jan)
Sire: Bahri (Riverman)
Dam: Stormy Gold (Storm Cat)
Br: Wertheimer & Frere (Ky)
Tr: Stidham Michael(31 6 5 6 .19) 2007:(265 39 .15)

Life 8 3 0 0 $64,779 73 | D.Fst 0 0 0 0 $0 –
2007 2 2 0 0 $25,800 73 | Wet(301) 0 0 0 0 $0 –
Synth 1 0 0 0 $0 –
2006 2 0 0 0 $1,655 – | Turf(355) 7 3 0 0 $64,779 73
Ls(T) 1 1 0 0 $16,200 73 | Dst(T)(294) 4 2 0 0 $46,392 73

19May07–8LS fm 7½f (T) :233 :47 1:1141:29 3↑(F)Alw 27000N3L **73** 4 2 53½ 54½ 41¼ 1nk Murphy B G L122 4.10 94–04 Twinspot122nk Barbette122¾ Not in My House116nk Bit rank,closed well 9
9Mar07–7Hou fm 1 (T) :242 :484 1:1331:394 4↑(F)Alw 16000N1X **68** 4 65½ 74¼ 41¾ 1hd 12½ Nolan P M L118 1.60 87–11 *Twinspot*1182½ EnchntedLnding1181 *MyGryAngel*1131½ Settled, 3w, driving 8
Previously trained by Freddy Head
31Oct06 Maisons-Laffitte (Fr) sf *6f (T) Str 1:12 Prix Taboun Alw 33100 57½ Peslier O 120 8.00 Kenkaye1304 Fontaine Riant1201 Alyzea1212 10
Racing Post Rating: 77 *Rated in 9th,some late progress*
16Oct06 Deauville (Fr) ft *1 3/16 RH 2:00 (F)Prix de la Seulles (polytrack) Alw 26200 810¼ Lemaitre A 111 6.50 Kiriki118¾ Keladora122nk Dancing Eclipse1172 8
Racing Post Rating: 60 *Tracked in 4th,weakened over 1f out*
Previously trained by Christiane Head-Maarek
23Oct05 Longchamp (Fr) sf *7f (T) RH 1:273 Prix Herod (Listed) Stk 56100 45¾ Peslier O 124 *1.50 Grand Vadla1241½ *Salsalava*128nk Light of Joy1284 7
Racing Post Rating: 84 *Tracked in 3rd,outpaced 1-1/2f out*
2Oct05 Longchamp (Fr) gs *1 (T) RH 1:371 (F)Prix Marcel Boussac-G1 Stk 360000 44½ Thomas R 123 100.00 Rumplestiltskin1231 *Quiet Royal*1231½ Deveron1232 15
Racing Post Rating: 100 *Twrds rear,fnshd well.ConfidentialLady10th,Attima11th*
12Sep05 Chantilly (Fr) gs *1 (T) RH 1:39 (F)Prix d'Aumale-G3 Stk 93100 64½ Peslier O 121 13.00 Sirene Doloise121¾ Blue Blue Sky121nk Queensalsa1213 11
Racing Post Rating: 94 *Unruly & ran off pre-start,trckd ldr,wknd over 1f out.PriceTag5th*
9Aug05 Deauville (Fr) gd *6½f (T) Str 1:20 (F)Prix de la Potiniere-EBF Maiden (FT) 22200 1no Thomas R 126 *.30e Twinspot126no Sweet Travel126½ Mednaya126¾ 9
Racing Post Rating: 88 *Close up in 3rd,bid 1f out,dueled,led on line.Impressionnante4th*

AUSSIE RULES: Let us use this Aidan O'Brien-trained son of Danehill to distinguish between the terms "foreign invader" and "foreign import." Aussie Rules was a foreign invader; that is, he was sent to the United States from Ireland to run in a single race—in this case, Keeneland's Shadwell Turf Mile. A foreign import is a horse who is entering the United States, or any country other than the one in which he was previously trained, to stay. Aussie Rules duly landed odds of 4.90–1 in the Grade 1 Shadwell, pleasing those bettors who understood that winning the Poule d'Essai des Poulains, or French 1000 Guineas, and finishing close up behind the likes of Librettist and David Junior made him an overlay at the price. Add first-time Lasix and first-time blinkers and Ballydoyle had pulled off yet another successful foreign raid.

Aussie Rules
Own: Magnier Mrs. John, Tabor, Michael and

Gr/ro. c. 3 (Feb)
Sire: Danehill (Danzig) $39,277
Dam: Last Second*Ire (Alzao)
Br: Belgrave Bloodstock Ltd. (Ky)
Tr: O'Brien Aidan P(1 1 0 0 1.00) 2006:(11 1 .09)

Life	11	4	1	0	$874,570	108	D.Fst	0	0	0	0	$0	–
2006	7	2	0	0	$772,044	108	Wet(374)	0	0	0	0	$0	–
							Synth	0	0	0	0	$0	–
2005	4	2	1	0	$102,526	–	Turf(397)	11	4	1	0	$874,570	108
Kee Ⓣ	1	1	0	0	$372,000	108	DstⓉ(330)	5	2	0	0	$726,401	108

7Oct06–9Kee fm 1 Ⓣ :23^4 :47^4 1:11^2 1:34^1 3↑	ShdwlTfM-G1	**108** 3 7$6\frac{1}{4}$ 7$4\frac{1}{4}$ 7$4\frac{3}{4}$ 4$2\frac{3}{4}$	1$1\frac{3}{4}$	Gomez G K	L123 b	4.90	96– 11	AussieRules123$1\frac{3}{4}$ *RemrkbleNews*126no OldDodge126^{hd}	Off slow,split,4w,dr	9
3Sep06 Longchamp (Fr) gs *1 Ⓣ RH 1:38 3↑	Prix du Moulin de Longchamp-G1 Stk 385000	Racing Post Rating: 117	4^3	Fallon K	123	7.90		Librettist128½ Stormy River123½ Manduro128^2	*5th on rail,3rd 1f out,faded final 16th.Irridescence5th*	8
2Aug06 Goodwood (GB) gf 1 Ⓣ RH 1:36 3↑	Sussex Stakes-G1 Stk 595000	Racing Post Rating: 116	4^3	Kinane M J	126	8.00		Court Masterpiece133^2 Soviet Song130½ Rob Roy133½	*Rated 6th,bid 2-1/2f out,drftd rght late.Araafa5th,EchoOfLight6th*	7
8Jly06 Sandown Park (GB) gf 1¼ Ⓣ RH 2:07^1 3↑	Eclipse Stakes-G1 Stk 850000	Racing Post Rating: 116	4$1\frac{3}{4}$	Munro A	122	5.50		David Junior133$1\frac{1}{2}$ *Notnowcato*133^{nk} Blue Monday133^{no}	*Rated in 5th,bid 2f out,drifted right,faded late.OuijaBoard5th*	9
4Jun06 Chantilly (Fr) gd *$1\frac{5}{16}$ Ⓣ RH 2:05^4	Prix du Jockey-Club(French Derby)-G1 Stk 1938000	Racing Post Rating: 111	7^3	Fallon K	128	*3.60		Darsi128¾ Best Name128^{nk} Arras128^{no}	*Rated in 9th,hard ridden 1-1/2f out,one-paced*	15
14May06 Longchamp (Fr) gs *1 Ⓣ RH 1:37	Poule d'Essai des Poulains-G1 Stk 517000	Racing Post Rating: 117	1½	Fallon K	128	2.70		Aussie Rules128½ Marcus Andronicus128^{hd} Stormy River128^1	*6th on rail,rallied to lead 100y out,driving*	11

SILCA'S SISTER: Sometimes the Whatsthescript scenario deviates a bit from the expected plot. That was the case with this Inchinor filly who had beaten colts in the Group 1 Prix Morny at 2, been fourth in Speciosa's 1000 Guineas, and then an unlucky but close sixth in Royal Ascot's always highly competitive Grade 1 Coronation Stakes. Dropped into Churchill Downs's Grade 3 Cardinal Handicap off a 4 ½-month layoff with a relatively light weight on the eve of the Breeders' Cup, she ran a super race on the front end, narrowly missing out to Sabellina at a generous 4.70–1 that surely satisfied everyone who used her in the exacta.

BEE CHARMER: By Anabaa out of a Slew o' Gold mare, Bee Charmer had finished fourth by 3 ½ lengths to subsequent Irish Derby, Prix de l'Arc de Triomphe, and King George VI and Queen Elizabeth Diamond Stakes winner Hurricane Run in their mutual April 15, 2005, debut going 1$\frac{5}{16}$ miles at Longchamp. In his last start prior to arriving in America he finished fourth in a 1$\frac{9}{16}$-mile Chantilly allowance, eight lengths behind runner-up Freedonia, the subsequent winner of the 1$\frac{9}{16}$-mile, Group 2 Prix de Malleret, and runner-up to English Channel in the Grade 1 Joe Hirsch Turf Classic. Five months later in his American debut, he was in his element going 1½ miles on a yielding Keeneland turf course, getting up late for the win. A line through Hurricane Run and Freedonia, plus his stamina-laden pedigree, made him an overlay at 3.40–1.

KENDARGENT: By the underrated French sire Kendor out of a mare by the outstanding French stallion Linamix, Kendargent looked very much in need of Lasix and Butazolidin when he arrived in America in spring 2007, as he had weakened badly in his previous two outings in France. Prior to that he had chased Group 1 type Stormy River, finished ahead of subsequent Group 2 Prix de Muguet winner Racinger, bested subsequent Group 3 Prix Perth winner and Group 1 Lockinge Stakes third-place finisher Passager in a Maisons-Laffitte allowance, and finished just a length behind subsequent Group 2 Prix d'Harcourt winner Boris de Deauville. His 8–5 favorite's price in his American debut in a Hollywood allowance on July 7 only looks pinched if you don't understand the worth of horses like Stormy River, Racinger, Passager, and Boris de Deauville.

FANLIGHT FANNY: She finished second in the listed five-furlong Roses Stakes at York's prestigious mid-August Ebor Meeting, and a line through the winner of that race, Not For Me, suggests she ran just as well when ninth by five lengths in the five-furlong, Group 2 Flying Childers Stakes two weeks later, when Not For Me was seventh. Her identical Racing Post Ratings of 90 confirmed that judgment in a pair of races in which she had been pitched in against colts. By Lear Fan out of a mare by Nureyev, she was just screaming for longer than five furlongs and she got it in her American debut at Gulfstream Park on January 28, 2007. Coming off a 4½-month layoff, she was dropped into a 1¹⁄₁₆-mile turf allowance against fillies and led throughout to score at a juicy 7–2.

MAKDERAH: A filly who needs no introduction to American racegoers at this stage, Makderah had finished close up to Red Evie twice prior to her arrival at Keeneland, first in a listed race at Royal Ascot, then in Goodwood's Group 3 Oak Tree Stakes. As Red Evie would go on to next win the Group 1 Matron Stakes, there was reason to belief that Makderah, who next won a listed race at Ascot on September 24, had been progressing as well. Bettors at Keeneland seemed to understand much of this when they banged Makderah down to 6–5 favoritism in her U.S. debut, and while she failed that day, she obliged at Belmont five weeks later at 13–10. Hardly a great price, but value nonetheless, considering who she had been facing in England.

SHAMDINAN: This Dr Fong colt, bred by the Aga Khan, arrived at Arlington Park for the 2007 Secretariat Stakes having split two decisions with the redoubtable Zambezi Sun. Shamdinan had finished a neck in front of "Zambezi" when third in the French Derby and could be excused his unplaced effort next time in the Irish Derby on unmanageably heavy ground. Zambezi Sun had followed his French Derby fourth with a smashing five-length victory in the 1 ½-mile Group 1 Grand Prix de Paris, a performance that saw him installed second favorite for the Prix de l'Arc de Triomphe. There was nothing in the Secretariat that had faced anything remotely as good as Zambezi Sun, and Shamdinan proved it with his half-length victory at 4.80–1.

MOUDEZ, LADDIES POKER, and ITSAWONDERFULLIFE: These three imports—Moudez and Laddies Poker from England, Itsawonderfullife from Ireland—have intertwining form lines in Europe, and all three of them won in their first or second starts in America. Moudez was the first to score stateside. Swamped in his U.S. debut in the Laurel Futurity, he won at 5.70–1 in a Gulfstream allowance on March 7, 2007. The horse he had beaten in his Newmarket maiden debut was Strobilus, subsequently the runner-up in the Group 1 Gran Criterium at San Siro in Milan. Laddies Poker had only been 10th in Moudez's Newmarket maiden, but he improved to finish fifth by just 2¼ lengths in the $2 million Goffs Million two starts later. The winner of the Goffs, Miss Beatrix, would later win the Group 1 Moyglare Stud Stakes, so when Laddies Poker dropped into a maiden for his U.S. debut at Santa Anita on April 7, 2007, those who understood the value of that European form couldn't complain about his winning 2.40–1 price. Itsawonderfullife had finished third behind Miss Beatrix in her Leopardstown maiden debut, so an awareness of what Miss Beatrix had accomplished afterward, and what Laddies Poker had done in his first American start, saw her banged down to 8–5 in her own U.S. debut in which she lost all chance when breaking in the air. She made amends next time when scoring at 3–5 and while that can hardly be deemed value for a filly who hadn't yet learned how to get out of the gate, all the signs pointing to victory were there in her form, if only players knew who Miss Beatrix and Strobilus were. (Also see "Good Relations.")

Moudez (Ire)
Own: Zayat Stables LLC

Dk. b or b. c. 3 (Feb)
Sire: Xaar*GB (Zafonic)
Dam: Summer Dreams*Ire (Sadler's Wells)
Br: Sean Murphy (Ire)
Tr: Mott William I(0 0 0 0 .00) 2007:(429 84 .20)

Life	5	3	0	1	$110,117	86	D.Fst	0	0	0	0	$0	–
2007	2	2	0	0	$93,502	86	Wet(277*)	0	0	0	0	$0	–
							Synth	0	0	0	0	$0	–
2006	3	1	0	1	$16,615	47	Turf(298*)	5	3	0	1	$110,117	86
Kee Ⓣ	1	1	0	0	$69,502	86	DstⓉ(247)	2	2	0	0	$93,502	86

19Apr07–8Kee fm 1⅛ Ⓣ :49³ 1:14² 1:38¹ 1:50	Forerunner112k	**86** 2 3²½ 3½ 2hd 1½ 1¾	Velasquez C	L117	*2.00	85– 14	Moudez117¾ Bullara1171¼ Trimaran1171¼	Inside trip,driving	8
7Mar07–4GP fm 1⅛ Ⓣ :46² 1:10³ 1:34³ 1:46	Alw 40000N1x	**86** 12 108¼ 94¼ 83¾ 2½ 1³	Velasquez C	L118	5.70	93– 10	*Moudez*118³ Rahystrada118½ Brooklyn's Smart1201¾	Off slowly, 4 wide	12
25Nov06–7Lrl yl 1$\frac{1}{16}$ Ⓣ :24¹ :50¹ 1:15³ 1:45⁴	LrlFuturty100k	**47** 1 14¹⁵ 14¹¹ 14¹² 12²² 11¹⁸	Guidry M	122	*1.30e	53– 29	*Strike a Deal*1221¼ Rutledge Cat1227¾ Brainy Benny122no	Outrun	14
Previously trained by David Simcock									
7Oct06 Ascot (GB) sf 1 Ⓣ RH 1:43²	Autumn Stakes-G3	3⁸	Spencer J P	126	4.00		Caldra126⁵ Kid Mambo126³ Moudez126⁷		8
Racing Post Rating: 93	Stk 74800							*Unhurried in last,angled left 2-1/2f out,gained 3rd 1f out*	
25Aug06 Newmarket (GB) sf 7f Ⓣ Str 1:28⁴	Renault Master EBF Maiden Stks	1²	Spencer J P	126	12.00		Moudez126² *Strobilus*1261¾ Lion Sands1261¾		13
Racing Post Rating: 84	Maiden 13200							*Never far away,led 170y out,drifted right late.LaddiesPoker10th*	

Laddies Poker
Own: Meadow Creek Farm LLC

Gr/ro. c. 3 (May)
Sire: Stravinsky (Nureyev)
Dam: Lady in Waiting (Woodman)
Br: Crescent Hill Farm & Dr. W. A. Rood (Ky)
Tr: Cerin Vladimir(0 0 0 0 .00) 2007:(159 33 .21)

	Life	4	1	0	0	$68,820	91	D.Fst	0 0 0 0	$0	–
	2007	1	1	0	0	$28,800	91	Wet(374)	0 0 0 0	$0	–
	2006	3	M	0	0	$40,020	–	Synth	1 0 0 0	$638	–
	Sa ⊕	1	1	0	0	$28,800	91	Turf(312)	3 1 0 0	$68,182	91
								Dst⊕(331)	1 1 0 0	$28,800	91

8Apr07–5SA fm 1 ⊕ :224 :462 1:10 1:351   Md Sp Wt 50k   91 9 43 42½ 31½ 11½ 13   Cohen D   LB 123 b *2.40 88– 16 LaddiesPoker123³ BerkeleyCstle123¹½ Repetoire123¾   Off bit slow,3wd bid 11
   Previously trained by Jeremy Noseda
19Sep06 Curragh (Ire)   sf 7f ⊕ Str 1:292   Goffs Million (Restricted)   52¼ Quealy T P   126   100.00   Miss Beatrix121¹½ Regime126¾ Drumfire126ʰᵈ   28
   Racing Post Rating: 97   Never far away,stayed on without threatening.Finsceal Beo6th
6Sep06 Kempton (GB)   ft 7f ◆ RH 1:254   EBF Median Auction Mdn Stks(polytrack) 47 Quealy T P   129   12.00   Benfleet Boy129¼ Malyana124½ Keidas124⁶   13
   Racing Post Rating: 65   Maiden 13200   Slowly away,well behind,up for distant 4th
25Aug06 Newmarket (GB)   sf 7f ⊕ Str 1:284   Renault Master EBF Maiden Stks   10¹4½ Quealy T P   126   16.00   Moudez126² Strobilus126¹½ Lion Sands126¹½   13
   Racing Post Rating: 45   Maiden 13200   Rated in mid-pack,weakened 2f out

Itsawonderfullife (Ire)
Own: Fab Oak Stable and Lakin Lewis G

B. f. 3 (Apr)
Sire: Danehill Dancer*Ire (Danehill)
Dam: Cahermee Queen (King of Kings*Ire)
Br: Lynn Lodge Stud (Ire)
Tr: Biancone Patrick L(0 0 0 0 .00) 2007:(218 43 .20)

	Life	3	1	1	1	$34,591	81	D.Fst	0 0 0 0	$0	–
	2007	2	1	1	0	$32,308	81	Wet(269*)	0 0 0 0	$0	–
	2006	1	M	0	1	$2,283	–	Synth	0 0 0 0	$0	–
	Cd ⊕	2	1	1	0	$32,308	81	Turf(346)	3 1 1 1	$34,591	81
								Dst⊕(248)	2 1 1 0	$32,308	81

28Jun07–4CD fm 1 ⊕ :234 :473 1:12 1:372 3+ⒻMd Sp Wt 42k   81 7 64½ 73½ 52½ 13 15½ Leparoux J R   L117 *.60 83– 17 Itswondrfullif117⁵½ QuitAlc117²¼ BrdgtOFlynn117ⁿᵏ Awk start,ridden out 9
2Jun07–4CD   fm 1 ⊕ :233 :473 1:121 1:363 3+ⒻMd Sp Wt 45k   75 1 10¹¹107½ 106¾ 56 23 Leparoux J R   L118   1.60 84– 11 LdyAttck118³ Itsawonderfullife118¹½ FlyingDggers118³½ Broke slowly in air 12
   Previously trained by David Wachman
14Jun06 Leopardstwn (Ire)   gf 7f ⊕ LH 1:304   ⒻIrish Stallion Farms EBF Maiden   34½ Lordan W M   126   6.50   Miss Beatrix126³½ Evening Rushour126¾ Itsawonderfullife126¼   10
   Racing Post Rating: 64   Maiden 25100   Rated in 5th,3rd 170y out,stayed on

The Whatsthescript method is hardly foolproof. Any number of imports who have finished close up to, or beaten, subsequent big-race winners fail in their American debuts and continue to fail afterward. But their hit rate is so frequent that an understanding of the true nature of their form, which is frequently hidden from view to those who take foreign form at face value, can become a profitable path for hardworking, knowledgeable players.

GOOD RELATIONS

Being related to stakes winners, by which is meant being a full or half-sibling through the dam, or having a dam who was a major stakes winner herself, is not necessarily a valid handicapping tool. It can, however, and indeed should be used as reinforcement for notions arrived at through conventional tools such as key races, class, and time.

If in doubt about a foreign import's ability, his breeding (especially through the female line) might help you make a decision on whether to bet him or not, or how much to bet. Breeding is also a useful tool in handicapping juvenile races, where precocious families on both the sire's and dam's sides can help point out winners. The same holds true for races at 1¼ miles or longer, especially those on turf.

Moreover, breeding as a handicapping tool works better the farther up the class scale one goes. Down in the claiming ranks, its efficacy is not to be trusted.

The following horses, all imported to North America since January 2005, had bloodlines that could have been used to reinforce an already strongly held opinion based on form. In some cases, the horses' bloodlines were so superior to those of their American opponents that their breeding itself might have been enough to warrant a bet, as long as the recent form was at least satisfactory.

Whereas the nature of European racing is still largely based on breeding—that is, on the improvement of the breed—the game in the United States has devolved to the point where it is little different from a stock-market investment—get in quick, get out quick, and hope for decent profit during the interim. Consequently, well-bred European horses, especially those from families that raced drug free, are generally superior to horses racing on medication who hail from two or three generations of families that raced on drugs.

DANCE IN THE MOOD: By the great Sunday Silence, this mare is a full sister to both Dance Partner, winner of the 1½-mile, Group 1 Japanese Oaks and the 1¼-mile, Group 1 Queen Elizabeth II Commemorative Cup, and to 1½-mile Japanese Derby runner-up and two-time Grade 2 winner Dance in the Dark. When she arrived at Hollywood Park for the 2006 CashCall Mile, Dance in the Mood was coming off a nice fifth against colts in the one-mile, Group 1 Yasuda Kinen; prior to that, she had won the Victoria Mile, beating fillies at least as good as those she would be meeting in the CashCall. While her siblings were middle-distance performers and she was a miler, the class in her female family was worth more than a few extra dollars, even as the 2.60–1 favorite. In the race itself, Dance in the Mood hardly gave her backers an anxious moment as she swept wide for a 1¾-length victory.

FLOW CHART: This Jade Robbery UAE-bred was entered at Keeneland on April 22, 2007, for a 1⅛-mile Polytrack allowance after a series of so-so efforts going longer on turf in the French provinces. She had evinced talent through the Whatsthescript method by finishing a neck second to subsequent three-time Group 1 winner Mandesha four back in the listed 1⅞6-mile Prix Urban Sea. Her breeding may have been a factor in seeing her go off at 2.60–1 as her dam, Kartajana, had won the 1¼-mile, Group 1 Nassau Stakes at Goodwood as well as the 1¼-mile, Group 1 Bayerisches Zuchtrennen versus colts in Munich. Her victory in that Keeneland heat was also an example of how much easier it is for horses to switch from turf to Polytrack than from turf to dirt.

FOLK: Godolphin correctly gauged her talent when buying her after a 10½-length victory in an Aqueduct maiden on November 26, 2006. Sent to Dubai, this Quiet American filly proved to be the best 3-year-old distaffer in the Maktoum desert kingdom, airing from the front end in both the UAE 1000 Guineas and the UAE Oaks. While she didn't win in her return to New York in Belmont's Coaching Club American

Oaks on July 21, 2007, her 3.65–1 price should have been a little lower, considering that she is a half-sister to UAE Oaks winner Danuta.

EMIRATES TO DUBAI: What was there to recommend this Godolphin runner in his U.S. debut at Belmont Park on June 21, 2007, especially as he had failed as the favorite in a modest Newbury maiden in his only previous start 20 months earlier? It was his breeding. Not only is he a son of Storm Cat, he is out of Morn of Song, a two-time allowance winner on dirt. More importantly, he is a half-brother to Mezzo Soprano, winner of Nad Al Sheba's one-mile UAE 1000 Guineas on dirt and the 1½-mile, Group 1 Prix Vermeille on turf at Longchamp. Morn of Song herself is a full sister to the top sire Rahy and to multiple Group 1 winner Singspiel. With relatives like that, there would be no denying Emirates to Dubai against Belmont turf maidens. He duly obliged at a rather healthy 2.90–1.

SAALB: Trained by Saeed bin Suroor to finish third in a seven-furlong Nad Al Sheba dirt maiden in his racecourse debut in February 2005, this Unbridled colt made his American debut for Steve Asmussen at Aqueduct in a six-furlong maiden claimer on March 6, 2006, a winning one. Not only had he chased home subsequent $150,000 Al Bastikiya winner Parole Board in Nad Al Sheba, his dam, Majestic Legend, is a half-sister to the outstanding sprinter and sire Mr. Greeley. Saalb made short work of his claiming rivals, leading throughout at 2.35–1.

LOUVE DES REVES: From a most prominent French family, this daughter of Sadler's Wells made her first start in America in a Churchill Downs optional claimer on Kentucky Derby Day, 2007. Sent off at 3.90–1, Louve des Reves dispatched seven foes going 1¹⁄₁₆ miles on turf despite a six-wide trip. Her international owner, Joseph Allen, had entrusted her to Patrick-Louis Biancone, a man who knows a thing or two about French fillies. Louve des Reves's dam, Louve, had won the 1⁵⁄₁₆-mile, Group 3 Prix de Flore. Louve des Reves herself is a half-sister to Louve Royale, the winner of two listed races on turf in Kentucky, while Louve is a half-sister to Group 1 winners Loup Sauvage and Loup Solitaire.

ROSINKA: This daughter of Soviet Star, a Group 1 winner at a mile in France and at six furlongs in England, had failed to handle the step up to stakes competition after breaking her maiden by seven lengths going six furlongs at Goodwood. Dropped into a 1¹⁄₁₆-mile allowance that came off the turf at Keeneland on October 28, 2006, she was allowed to go off at 13.20–1.

Apparently Keeneland regulars failed to make note of her bloodlines. Rosinka is a half-sister to Self Feeder, the winner of Hollywood Park's ungraded Steinlen Handicap on turf as well as a dirt maiden at Churchill and a dirt allowance at the Fair Grounds. Moreover, Rosinka is a half to 1½-mile Sword Dancer winner King's Drama, who also won two Grade 2 turf stakes in America and a Group 3 race in France at Chantilly. Her class told at Keeneland that day as she came late for the win.

JAPENGO: The class-in-the-dam theory paid off handsomely in the case of this Theatrical filly who had failed miserably in her lowly Roscommon debut when she finished 14th of 16 going 1½ miles on turf. Sent to Ken McPeek, she was entered in a $25,000 maiden claimer going a mile on dirt at Gulfstream Park on February 24, 2007, and came home the 8.90–1 winner.

Students of breeding could have told you so, for Japengo is out of the Strawberry Road mare Fowda, whose three big stakes scores, the Grade 1 Hollywood Oaks, the Grade 1 Spinster, and the Grade 2 Monmouth Oaks, came on dirt.

Speed handicappers continued to disdain the value of Japengo's breeding in subsequent starts on dirt, dismissing her at 4.60–1 when she won a one-mile Gulfstream allowance, and again at 8.40–1 when she landed a one-mile Churchill Downs allowance.

MILAGO: The case of this Danzig filly is similar to that of Japengo. Although she was 1 for 6 in France on turf when trained by Criquette Head-Maarek, Milago handled the switch to Turfway Park's Polytrack with aplomb, and why shouldn't she? Against the inferior competition she was facing after being sent to Andrew McKeever, her breeding told the tale. Milago's dam is Hidden Lake, the winner of three Grade 1 races, the Go For Wand, the Beldame, and the Hempstead.

PUNTA ROSA: Most players seemed to be on to the international good thing that was Punta Rosa in her American debut at Laurel on September 26, 2006. After five decent but unsuccessful efforts on the high-class Parisian circuit in maidens, allowances, and handicaps, this War Chant filly was sent to Michael Matz. A half-sister to West by West, winner of three graded races on dirt (the Grade 3 Widener Handicap, the Grade 2 Jamaica Handicap, and the Grade 1 Nassau County Handicap), she wasn't facing much in that Laurel maiden and handled the switch to dirt to score at 2.40–1. Considering how infrequently a Laurel maiden includes a half-sister or half-brother to a multiple graded stakes winner, that price looks fat.

SOL MI FA: While her close-up second to subsequent French 1000 Guineas winner Tie Black qualified her for a confident wager in her American debut at Bay Meadows on May 29, 2006, the fact that she was out of 1996 French Oaks winner Sil Sila made her 5–1 price that day look even better.

CANTABRIA: Like Sol Mi Fa, this Dansili filly qualified for backing on both the Whatsthescript and "Good Relations" theories. A close third behind subsequent Group 1 winner Red Evie in the Group 3 Oak Tree Stakes, she is also a half-sister to Deportivo, winner of the five-furlong, Group 3 Flying Five. A combination of the two makes her winning 1.90–1 price in a Hollywood allowance look pretty good, considering the mediocrity of her competition that day. (See "Synthetic Surfaces," below.)

TIMIAS: There were a number of things to like about this Seeking the Gold's American debut in a one-mile Santa Anita turf allowance on April 21, 2006. A decent fifth to subsequent two-time listed winner Bellamy Cay qualified him through the Whatsthescript method. Winning a nice Chantilly allowance two back was another reason to like the ex-Pascal Bary trainee. If that was enough to make Timias your play, then realizing that his dam is a full sister to Grade 2 Bay Meadows Handicap winner Caesour should have convinced you that his 8.10–1 price couldn't be passed up.

MOUDEZ and LADDIES POKER: These two both qualified via the Whatsthescript method, but also came from very good female families. Moudez, a winner second time out in the U.S. at 5.70–1, is out of a Sadler's Wells mare who is a half-sister to German Derby winner All My Dreams. Laddies Poker is a half-brother to Kid Grindstone, the winner of a Grade 3 at Arlington and ungraded stakes at Arlington, the Fair Grounds, and Canterbury. He popped first time out in America in a Santa Anita maiden at 2.40–1.

SYNTHETIC SURFACES

Where racing on synthetic surfaces is concerned, we are Johnny-come-latelys on this side of the Atlantic. The first synthetic track was installed in England at Lingfield Park in 1989. It was an Equitrack surface that gave rise to a decided track bias in favor of horses drawing near the rail in sprint races. In 2001, the Equitrack was replaced by a Polytrack surface, and the bias disappeared.

Equitrack, Polytrack, Fibresand, and Cushion Track are all British inventions.

Kempton Park and Wolverhampton also have Polytrack surfaces, while Southwell has a Fibresand track, which is widely recognized as being slower than Polytrack.

In France, Cagnes-sur-Mer, where they race on the flat in late January and February, and Pau, where a few flat races add flavor to the jump-racing schedule, have Polytrack surfaces in addition to their turf courses. Great Leighs, a new track struggling to open near London, will also race on Polytrack.

Much has been written about the differences between traditional dirt and Polytrack, between Polytrack and turf, and between dirt and turf. Early returns from British imports who have run on Polytrack surfaces in England very strongly suggest that synthetic surfaces resemble turf courses much more than they do traditional dirt tracks.

In developing their synthetic surfaces, the British sought to replicate the turf experience with a dirtlike surface that could be used as often as traditional American dirt tracks, i.e., daily throughout the winter, spring, summer, and fall. They made the mistake of labeling their new products all-weather tracks, a misnomer if ever there was one.

The British soon learned that artificial surfaces were susceptible to freezing and flooding, but by and large their new surfaces were a success. Flat racing, albeit on a level much inferior to turf racing, could be conducted on a year-round basis on the new synthetic tracks, thus providing the British betting industry with increased opportunities to generate income.

Races run on the Polytrack surfaces at Lingfield and Kempton are now much better than was the general synthetic-surface product in Britain five years ago. The same can be said of Polytrack racing at Deauville, where at least 20 percent of the races at that track's prestigious August meeting are run on that surface. Deauville also runs 10 days of all-Polytrack racing in December and January. American horsemen have not yet begun to import French horses with Polytrack form in any but the meagerest of numbers, but the number of Polytrack performers from Britain is ever increasing. In fact, at least half of the horses imported from Britain in 2007 had run at least once on an artificial surface before their arrival in North America.

This raises the question, where do they fit in? This brings us back to the reason the British invented artificial surfaces to begin with. Polytrack, Fibresand, and Cushion Track, like the Tapeta surface Michael Dickinson has installed at his Maryland training base and at Golden Gate Fields, Presque Isle Downs, and Godolphin's Al Quoz training center in Dubai, are softer than traditional dirt tracks and so are more forgiving. That makes them, like turf courses, safer than traditional dirt tracks. But bettors have concerns other than safety—concerns such as track bias, which on synthetic surfaces seems to bear little resemblance to what is experienced on dirt tracks.

One of the major reasons for that discrepancy is the lack of kickback on synthetic surfaces. The only reason that American racing has been conducted since time immemorial in a so-called front-to-back style is to avoid the kickback. It took American jockeys nearly three decades of turf racing to realize that there was no need to cut out fractions like 22 and change or 45 and change. Such shenanigans had only become the norm to avoid the kickback generated on dirt. By going slower early in turf races, in which the kickback is minimal, riders discovered that they could conserve their mounts' energy for a big finish. And they are in the process of discovering much the same thing with some of the synthetic surfaces, such as Polytrack. Closers appear to be winning more frequently on that surface than they did on traditional dirt tracks.

The questions as far as this section is concerned are: Are foreign imports sharing in the spoils, and at what prices? And, do horses coming from European turf races easily make the switch to synthetics?

A horse running in a typical maiden or allowance at Lingfield and Kempton, the two best synthetic tracks in England, is probably running in the equivalent of a similar race at Arlington or Woodbine, whereas maiden races on the synthetic tracks at Hollywood Park and Del Mar are generally superior to those at Lingfield and Kempton.

As for the quality of competition at Wolverhampton, it is a notch lower than Lingfield and Kempton. Southwell, with its slower Fibresand course, is another half notch below Wolverhampton.

The Polytrack horse at the top end of the synthetic scale who alerted Americans to what could be accomplished here by British imports is Eccentric. Bought by Gary Tanaka in February 2005 after having won three of his four previous starts on the Lingfield Polytrack, Eccentric continued to do well on that surface in England, giving Tanaka and trainer Andrew Reid the idea that he might be successful in more lucrative races elsewhere on traditional dirt.

Eccentric was duly tried on dirt at Jagersro in Sweden, where he finished fifth in a $137,000 listed race. He later finished 16th and last in the 2005 Japan Cup Dirt and third, tenth, and sixth in races on the Nad Al Sheba dirt course.

Yet in between Jagersro in May 2005 and Tokyo in November 2005, Eccentric had reproduced his best Polytrack form by winning the Group 3 Winter Hill Stakes in England on Windsor's turf course.

Tanaka got wise to the nature of Polytrack when he sent Eccentric to Canada to be trained by Roger Attfield. After a promising third in a valuable turf allowance, he was shipped to Keeneland for a try on the new Polytrack surface there. He responded with a victory in the Grade 3 Fayette Stakes at 8.10–1 and has since won a Grade 3 and a Grade 2 on Woodbine's turf course.

In other words, Eccentric has reproduced both his best British turf and Polytrack form on turf and Polytrack in North America, after five dull efforts on traditional dirt tracks in Sweden, Japan, and Dubai.

Eccentric (GB)
Own: Tanaka Gary A

Ch. g. 6 (Mar)
Sire: Most Welcome*GB (Be My Guest)
Dam: Sure Care*GB (Caerleon)
Br: A. S. Reid (GB)
Tr: Attfield Roger L(99 17 5 11 .17) 2007:(131 19 .15)

Life	36	12	5	3	$754,499	101	D.Fst	4	0	0	1	$20,000	-
2007	3	2	0	0	$210,000	101	Wet(273*)	1	0	0	0	$5,548	-
2006	6	1	0	3	$139,169	96	Synth	19	8	4	1	$343,320	96
							Turf(330)	12	4	1	1	$383,522	101
Wo Ⓣ	3	2	0	1	$219,669	101	DstⓉ(279)	2	1	0	0	$120,000	101

2Jly07–9WO fm 1⅛ Ⓣ :47 1:111 1:344 1:464 3↑ KngEdBC-G2	101 4 6 5½ 6 3½ 5 2½ 1hd 1no	Clark D	L119 f	4.80	99–03	Eccentric119no *SkyConqueror*126nk Jambalaya1262¼	Bid 4w top str,driving	7
27May07–8WO yl 1 1/16 Ⓣ :24 :48 1:131 1:45 4↑ ConghtCp-G3	100 6 6 3½ 6 3¾ 6 3½ 2½ 1 2¼	Clark D	L119 f	3.25	71–29	*Eccentric*1192¼ *As Expected*1171¾ Shoal Water1171¼	Rallied 4w,driving	7
26Apr07–8Kee fst 1⅛ ◈ :494 1:134 1:373 1:494 4↑ BenAli-G3	85 2 2hd 1½ 1½ 9 5¼ 9 8¾	Prado E S	L119	13.00	86–11	JdesRevenge117no MinistrsJoy117no Mustnfr117nk	Vied,inside,weakened	11
18Nov06–6WO fst 1 1/16 ◈ :24 :47 1:114 1:444 3↑ WoSltCp-G3	87 4 6 9¾ 5 10 5 4¾ 3 3½ 3 5	Clark D	L121 f	3.15	- -	True Metropolitan1214 Edenwold1181 Eccentric1212½	Evened out	6
28Oct06–9Kee fst 1⅛ ◈ :491 1:133 1:372 1:49 3↑ Fayette-G3	96 1 8 2½ 9 3½ 9 4½ 3nk 1¾	Castro E	L121	8.10	- -	Eccentric121¾ Ball Four1231½ Good Reward1191½	Steadied 1/4p,drv,rail	12
8Oct06–8WO gd 1 Ⓣ :233 :473 1:114 1:361 3↑ Alw 89900NC	96 3 6 5½ 7 5¾ 7 3½ 3 1 3 1¼	Clark D	L118 f	11.60	77–28	Sky Conqueror1221 French Beret116nk *Eccentric*1183	All out,best of rest	10
Previously trained by Satish Seemar								
9Mar06 Nad Al Sheba (UAE) ft *1¼ LH 2:041 3↑ Azal Cup Hcp 175000 / Racing Post Rating: 101	6 8¼	Moore R L	132	-		Remaadd1211¼ Dubai Honor1223¾ Parasol1252¼	Tracked leaders,weakened final furlong	8
2Mar06 Nad Al Sheba (UAE) ft *1¼ LH 2:01 3↑ Maktoum Challenge-Round 3-G2 Stk 300000 / Racing Post Rating: 70	10 28¾	Murtagh J P	126	-		*Electrocutionist*1267 Chiquitin1262¼ Elmustanser1263¾	Tracked in 3rd,dueled briefly 3f out,weakened	14
9Feb06 Nad Al Sheba (UAE) ft *1⅛ LH 1:501 3↑ Maktoum Challenge-Round 2-G3 Stk 200000 / Racing Post Rating: 115	3 1	Murtagh J P	126	-		Jack Sullivan1261 Blatant126no Eccentric1262	5th on rail,finished well.Chiquitin4th,Lundy'sLiability6th	9
Previously trained by Andrew Reid								
26Nov05 Tokyo (Jpn) ft *1 5/16 LH 2:08 3↑ Japan Cup Dirt-G1 Stk 2073000	16 34	Tani K	126	122.60		*Kane Hekili*121no Seeking the Dia126nk Star King Man1261¼	Ridden into wide 8th early,weakened 3f out.Lava Man 11th	16
15Oct05 Newmarket (GB) gs 1⅛ Ⓣ Str 1:531 3↑ Darley Stakes-G3 Stk 88500 / Racing Post Rating: 109	8 3¼	Egan J F	130	20.00		Enforcer122hd Mullins Bay1301 *St Andrews*126¾	Tracked in 3rd,weakened 1f out	12
17Sep05 Newbury (GB) gf 1¼ Ⓣ LH 2:032 3↑ John Smiths Handicap Hcp 181000 / Racing Post Rating: 104	8 2¾	Robinson P	134	8.00		Star of Light125no *Blue Monday*135hd Crosspeace132nk	Prompted pace,2nd to 5f out,,outpaced final furlong	19
27Aug05 Windsor (GB) gd 1¼ Ⓣ RH 2:05 3↑ Winter Hill Stakes-G3 Stk 90000 / Racing Post Rating: 111	1¾	Holland D	126	7.00		Eccentric126¾ Hattan122¾ *Fruhlingssturm*1261	Rated in 5th,2nd 2f out,led over 1f out,ridden out	9
6Aug05 Haydock (GB) gf 1 5/16 Ⓣ LH 2:121 3↑ Totesport Handicap Hcp 142000 / Racing Post Rating: 99	2¾	Guillambert J-P	121	14.00		Courageous Duke126¾ *Eccentric*1211¼ Rehearsal122½	Rank tracking leaders,led over 1f out,headed 100y out	17
26Jly05 Goodwood (GB) gs 1¼ Ⓣ RH 2:071 4↑ Summer Handicap Hcp 87400 / Racing Post Rating: 95	6 3¾	Egan J F	121	12.00		Evaluator123nk Ofaraby1221¼ Nero's Return1191½	Led for 1f,trckd ldr,led again 3f out,headed 1f out,faded	20
9Jly05 Lingfield (GB) gd 1 ◈ LH 1:362 4↑ Silver Trophy (dirt)-G3 Stk 86800 / Racing Post Rating: 102	9 5½	Egan J F	125	3.50		Autumn Glory128nk *Court Masterpiece*1252½ Vortex128hd	Prompted pace,ridden 3f out,bumped & weakened over 1f out	12
3Jun05 Epsom (GB) gd 1¼ Ⓣ LH 2:074 4↑ Rose Bowl (Listed) Stk 136000 / Racing Post Rating: 94	1¾	Egan J F	114	8.00		Eccentric114¾ Realism110no Chancellor128¾	Tracked leader,led ovr 1f out, gamely	17
12May05 Jagersro (Swe) gd *1 1/16 RH 1:464 4↑ Proverum Pramms Memorial Stk 138700 / Racing Post Rating: 90	5 6	Egan J F	132	*2.20		Billy Allen132no Santiago Matias1325 Honeysuckle Player132½	Tracked in 4th,lacked rally	11
19Mar05 Lingfield (GB) ft 1¼ ◈ LH 2:033 4↑ Winter Derby(Listed)(polytrack) Stk 192000 / Racing Post Rating: 114	1 1¼	Egan J F	124	3.50		Eccentric1241¼ Blythe Knight1241¼ Hurricane Alan1241¼	Led throughout on easy lead,handily	14
26Feb05 Lingfield (GB) ft 1¼ ◈ LH 2:051 4↑ Winter Derby Trial (polytrack) Alw 49200 / Racing Post Rating: 109	1 3	Egan J F	124	2.50		*Eccentric*1243 Gig Harbor1251½ Tahtheeb119nk	Tracked leader,led 2f out,ridden clear 1f out	8
12Feb05 Lingfield (GB) ft 1¼ ◈ LH 2:053 4↑ Footballpools.com Handicap(polytrack) Hcp 47900 / Racing Post Rating: 109	2 1¾	Egan J F	132	*2.75		Counsel's Opinion1301¾ *Eccentric*132no Caledonian116¾	Trckd ldrs,led 1-1/2f out,drftd badly right,headed late	10
1Feb05 Lingfield (GB) ft 1 ◈ LH 1:354 4↑ Littlewoods Handicap (polytrack) Hcp 38400 / Racing Post Rating: 111	1 6	Egan J F	126	4.50		Eccentric1266 Secret Place1281 Binanti1201	Led throughout,drew clear over 2f out	8
29Jan05 Lingfield (GB) ft 1¼ ◈ RH 2:081 4↑ Littlewoods Bet Direct Hcp (polytrack) Hcp 48400	1 2	Egan J F	115	16.00		*Eccentric*1152 Little Good Bay1251¼ Howle Hill135½	Set slow pace to 4f out,pressed new leader,led late	9

Eccentric is the best proof that synthetic is much more like turf than it is like traditional dirt. But have we seen anything else in the U.S. or Canada like Eccentric? Here are a couple of horses who can answer in the positive.

EAGER LOVER: This More Than Ready gelding arrived at Woodbine and promptly broke his maiden on Polytrack. He scored at 6.80–1 on September 23, 2006, after a pair of so-so maiden efforts in England followed by a good sixth in a key race, the Group 2 Vintage Stakes. Eager Lover was merely reproducing his Vintage form in the Woodbine maiden while providing another proof of the turf-equals-Polytrack theory. Also keep in mind that going from a Goodwood Group 2 to a Woodbine maiden is a major drop in class.

Eager Lover
Own: Harlequin Ranches

Ch. g. 2 (Feb) FTKJUL05 $20,000
Sire: More Than Ready (Southern Halo) $30,000
Dam: True Love (Affirmed)
Br: Robert Berger (Ky)
Tr: Gallagher Patrick(0 0 0 0 .00) 2006:(422 65 .15)

	Life	4	1	0	0	$38,235	70	D.Fst	0 0 0 0	$0	–
	2006	4	1	0	0	$38,235	70	Wet(352)	0 0 0 0	$0	–
								Synth	1 1 0 0	$32,213	70
	2005	0	M	0	0	$0	–	Turf(353)	3 0 0 0	$2,235	–
	Wo	1	1	0	0	$36,000	70	Dst(370)	1 1 0 0	$36,000	70

23Sep06–5WO fst 7f ◇ :221 :442 1:103 1:242 Md Sp Wt 62k 70 6 10 96¼ 88¼ 21½ 1no McAleney J S L120 6.80 - - EagerLover120no MoneyPlyer115½ CrolusMgnus115¹ Circled 4w,led,held 10
    Previously trained by Barry Hills
2Aug06 Goodwood (GB) gf 7f ⓣ RH 1:26 Vintage Stakes–G2 6⁶ Hills M 126 100.00 Strategic Prince129nk Duke of Marmalade126² Kirklees126½ 10
    Racing Post Rating: 95 Stk 131000 Steadied start,rank at rear,mild late gain.Jo'burg 8th

CANTABRIA: Close up behind the very good fillies Red Evie and Makderah in Goodwood's Group 3 Oak Tree Stakes four starts prior to her American debut, this Dansili filly handled the turf-to-Polytrack switch as easily as she might have had she still been in England, winning at 1.90–1. Her next two starts provided additional proof of the turf-equals-synthetic theory when she failed on the Santa Anita dirt in the El Encino, but then won an optional claimer on the Santa Anita turf. She has since finished second in the Hawthorne Handicap on the Hollywood Polytrack.

The sample of Polytrack Europeans succeeding on American synthetics is still too small to be significant. It will become more so as the early fractions in American synthetic races come to more closely resemble those of turf races, as European horses are unused to fast early paces, especially in races shorter than a mile. That time will come just as surely as it came to the world of American turf racing.

SOUTH AMERICAN GROUP-RACE WINNERS

Every importer of a South American group-race winner is hoping for another Invasor, Bayakoa, or Paseana, but those hopes are seldom fulfilled.

While many South American imports are sent off as longshots, very, very few of them ever win. It is wise to lay off Argentine, Chilean, or Brazilian allowance winners running in allowances at all but the cheapest North American tracks. But it is just as wise to lay off stakes winners from those countries running in American allowances or stakes races.

Three Chilean-bred winners of multiple group races have arrived in America since January 2005 and have been luckless. Porfido, winner of three Group 1 events on turf, including the Chilean Derby at Santiago's Club Hippico and its summertime equivalent, El Derby, at Valparaiso, lost his first seven starts in North America, six of them on turf, five of them graded races. He appears to be an allowance horse at best.

Marsilio Ficino closed out his Chilean career winning the Group 1 Gran Premio Club Hippico de Santiago in his first try on turf, yet was 0 for 5 on that surface in Southern California allowances before failing again on Hollywood's Polytrack.

Rio Mistico ran off four turf wins in a row in Chile, concluding with big victories in a Group 1 and a Group 3, yet finished last of nine in his U.S. debut at Keeneland in a turf allowance.

Stakes-winning Argentines generally fare no better. Carla Stripes, a Group 1 winner on dirt at Palermo who was third in the Group 1 Estrellas Distaff, the Argentine equivalent of the Breeders' Cup Distaff, arrived at Santa Anita to finish seventh in the ungraded Paseana Handicap on dirt, then seventh again in a dirt allowance.

Cursora won a pair of 1¼-mile Group 1 turf contests at San Isidro to close out her Argentine racing career, only to accumulate a 1-for-8 record in America, her lone win coming in a Churchill Downs optional claimer on turf. Honey Rose, a five-furlong Group 1 winner on turf in his San Isidro finale, is only 1 for 6 since settling in Kentucky, his lone score coming in a turf allowance.

And Masterpiece, a Southern Halo Argentine-bred who had won the one-mile Group 1 Gran Premio San Isidro and finished second in Group 1 races on dirt and turf in his last three starts in Argentina in 2004, is since 0 for 7 in allowances and optional claimers in Southern California.

On this evidence, it seems that—generally speaking—Group 1 South American form is no better than allowance form in the U.S.

The exception to this rule appears to originate in Brazil in the form of that country's most powerful breeding and racing operation, Stud TNT.

Owned by Goncalo Borges Torrealba, Stud TNT wins regularly in America with their homebred Brazilian imports. Sporting the famous red-and-blue colors of Calumet Farm, Stud TNT has raced outstanding horses like Leroidesanimaux, Cagney, and Lundy's Liability. All of them became graded-race winners in America after having begun their careers abroad—Leroidesanimaux and Cagney in Brazil, Lundy's Liability in South Africa and the UAE.

Torrealba has also bred and raced Breeders' Cup Juvenile Fillies runner-up Cara Rafaela and Grade 3 winner and Beverly D third Melhor Ainda here in the States. More recently he imported his Brazilian homebred Out of Control into California where he has won the Grade 2 American Invitational Handicap and finished second in the Grade 1 Eddie Read Handicap.

Suffice it to say that anything Stud TNT brings into the United States from Brazil must be paid the most careful attention.

THE GAME AS NOW constituted mitigates against there ever being more than two or three foreign imports per year winning first or second time out at long prices in North

America. And those few are such complete surprises, they can only be found through the hatpin or Little Miss Marker methods.

As women rarely wear hats to the races these days, and as Shirley Temple, at the age of 79, has long since faded into retirement, your best bet in finding winners upon their arrival in America is to buckle down and study foreign form with the due diligence it deserves. The time spent in researching foreign form more thoroughly in *DRF Simulcast Weekly* and in the foreign racing websites listed below will ultimately prove to have been well worth your trouble.

RACING POST: Britain's leading racing daily has a full-service website with entries and results of all races in Britain and Ireland, plus results of all French races run on the Parisian circuit (Longchamp, Chantilly, Saint-Cloud, Maisons-Laffitte, and Deauville). It also includes bloodline analyses for all horses in training in Britain as well as the most prominent horses trained in Ireland. Free to all, it can be found at *www.racingpost.co.uk*.

FRANCE-GALOP: The official site of the French Jockey Club, it contains entries and results for all races run in France. Log on for free at *www.france-galop.com*.

For similar services from the Hong Kong Jockey Club, log on to *www.hkjc.com*.

The Japan Racing Association website can be found at *www.japanracing.jp*.

STICH
ON HIDDEN-TURF ANGLES AND SIRES

By Lauren Stich

WHEN HORSEPLAYERS FIRST HEAR the term "pedigree handicapping," they naturally assume that it's simply a matter of knowing whether or not a horse comes from successful bloodlines. While that information is certainly useful, there is much more to pedigree handicapping. It's not enough merely to know who a horse's relatives are; the savvy handicapper has to understand how to put that information to good use. One could argue that pedigree handicapping is the most profitable of all handicapping tools, and this chapter will show many examples of how it can lead to some major paydays.

First and foremost, the key to pedigree handicapping is analyzing what horse is most likely to win at a particular distance and surface. As I wrote in *Bet with the Best,* the male parts of the pedigree (sire and damsire, in particular) are the keys to distance and surface, while the dam and her female family are the key to racing class. This is the essence of pedigree handicapping.

Nevertheless, the betting public—including many professional handicappers—continue to get it wrong. For example, they reason that if the dam of a runner was a stakes winner on turf, her foals will be better on turf. Well, they *might* be, but it really depends on who the sire is. And remember, if the dam was a winner on turf, it is most likely because she was by a stallion who was a turf influence.

It bears repeating: When it comes to surface and distance, it's all about the sire and damsire.

THE HIDDEN-TURF ANGLE

Of all the different angles to pedigree handicapping, the one that I call the hidden-turf (HT) factor has always been my favorite, due to the fact that it has historically yielded the biggest paydays for pedigree-savvy players.

As a refresher, a hidden-turf sire is a stallion who is known for his success on dirt but was well-bred for turf. Because the HT sire is not associated with turf, his offspring are usually value plays with inflated odds. Just a few examples of HT sires include the late Hennessy, Unbridled's Song, Holy Bull, Arch, and any son of Gone West (e.g., Mr. Greeley, Grand Slam, Elusive Quality, Proud Citizen, etc.). By now, most horseplayers are well aware that any stallions descending from either the Northern Dancer or Roberto sire lines are very strong grass influences, even if they themselves never raced on turf.

Hennessy was a top-class 2-year-old, the only year he raced, winning the Hopeful, Sapling, and Hollywood Juvenile Championship stakes, and he just missed by a neck to Unbridled's Song in the 1995 Breeders' Cup Juvenile. He never raced on turf, but had an explosive pedigree for turf, being by Storm Cat out of a mare by Hawaii. Storm Cat is by European champion Storm Bird, who was by Northern Dancer. Any stallion descending from the Northern Dancer line automatically has a license to run well on grass, while Hawaii was the U.S. grass champion in 1969. Characterized by high speed, Hennessy gets plenty of winners from five to 8 ½ furlongs on dirt, but many have excelled on turf, such as Johannesburg, Silver Tree, Grand Armee, Perigee Moon, and Orchard Park.

Since this sire line (Hennessy-Storm Cat-Storm Bird-Northern Dancer) is a predictor for speed and turf, it stands to reason that Hennessy's sons should also be turf influences. While runners from this line certainly win on dirt, they usually offer greater value on turf. Hennessy's best son, the versatile Johannesburg, gets winners on all surfaces. Johannesburg, better known to U.S. horseplayers as a Breeders' Cup Juvenile winner (his American debut and first start on dirt) and 2-year-old champion, was also a champion juvenile in England, Ireland, and France on grass, so while he is a turf influence, he cannot really be categorized as a hidden-turf sire. Following his sire and sire line, Johannesburg is getting winners on all surfaces, but his offspring have a decided preference for grass, such as stakes-winning miler Marcavelly.

On June 17, 2007, Ingrid the Gambler, a filly by Johannesburg who had shown good speed to finish second twice at six furlongs on dirt at Santa Anita and over Hollywood's Cushion Track surface, made her grass debut at six furlongs over the Hollywood turf.

Since she had already shown speed, I felt certain that Ingrid the Gambler would move up on what I believed was her preferred surface. In addition to Johannesburg, Ingrid the Gambler got more turf breeding from her damsire, Forest Wildcat (a hidden-turf sire by Storm Cat).

Ingrid the Gambler showed her customary speed stalking a 50–1 bomb and then took over to draw clear to win by 2¼ lengths at 4–1.

Teuflesberg, a stakes-winning sprinter on dirt, also looked good in his first effort on grass, finishing second, and all runners by Johannesburg should be played with confidence if they show up on grass.

Wiseman's Ferry, a son of Hennessy whose speed carried him to victories in the West Virginia and Lone Star Derbies, was a 2007 freshman sire who should certainly get precocious winners on dirt. But they will often be double-digit odds on turf since Wiseman's Ferry is not associated with that surface.

And this is the fundamental nature of the HT factor—creating overlays because the general public does not recognize a sire as being a grass influence. It is particularly effective when identifying a freshman sire that has the hidden-turf angle.

From the 2007 freshman sire crop, the following 20 stallions should be considered HT sires:

Aldebaran (Mr. Prospector)
Cactus Ridge (Hennessy)
Changeintheweather (Gone West)

D'wildcat (Forest Wildcat)

Essence of Dubai (Pulpit)

Express Tour (Tour d'Or)

Full Mandate (A.P. Indy)

Greatness (Mr. Prospector)

Harlan's Holiday (Harlan)

Hook and Ladder (Dixieland Band)

Kafwain (Cherokee Run)

Macho Uno (Holy Bull)

Milwaukee Brew (Wild Again)

Najran (Runaway Groom)

Proud Citizen (Gone West)

Repent (Louis Quatorze)

Sky Mesa (Pulpit)

Whywhywhy (Mr. Greeley)

Wiseman's Ferry (Hennessy)

Yankee Gentleman (Storm Cat)

The results of an 8 ½-furlong maiden race on the turf at Gulfstream Park on March 9, 2006, are proof that the HT factor is the most lucrative betting angle for pedigree players.

TENTH RACE
Gulfstream
MARCH 9, 2006

1¹⁄₁₆ MILES. (Turf) (1.38) MAIDEN SPECIAL WEIGHT . Purse $32,000 FOR MAIDENS, FILLIES THREE YEARS OLD. Weight, 121 lbs. (Horses That Have Raced For A Claiming Price Will Be Least Preferred). (If deemed inadvisable to run this race over the Turf course, it will be run on the main track at One Mile) (Rail at 36 feet).

Value of Race: $32,000 Winner $19,200; second $6,080; third $2,880; fourth $1,280; fifth $320; sixth $320; seventh $320; eighth $320; ninth $320; tenth $320; eleventh $320; twelfth $320. Mutuel Pool $340,923.00 Exacta Pool $286,088.00 Trifecta Pool $220,247.00 Superfecta Pool $87,003.00

Last Raced	Horse	M/Eqt.	A.	Wt	PP	St	¼	½	¾	Str	Fin	Jockey	Odds $1
	Pine Island		3	121	8	12	11¹¹⁄₂	11¹⁄₂	9hd	6hd	1nk	Castellano J J	28.90
11Nov05 ⁴Aqu³	Hostess	L	3	121	4	3	4¹	3hd	3¹	1¹¹⁄₂	2¹¹⁄₂	Prado E S	2.80
	Bobbin	L	3	121	5	7	6¹⁄₂	6¹⁄₂	5hd	2¹⁄₂	3¹³⁄₄	Decarlo C P	21.80
	Judith Basin		3	121	1	2	5¹⁄₂	5hd	6¹¹⁄₂	5hd	4¹³⁄₄	Velasquez C	3.20
5Feb06 ³GP⁴	The Niagara Queen	L b	3	121	2	1	3¹	4¹	4¹⁄₂	7²	5nk	King E L Jr	10.60
	Ocean Sound	L	3	121	3	8	10hd	12	11¹¹⁄₂	8hd	6¹⁄₂	Guidry M	17.00
12Jan06 ⁶GP⁷	Holy Sunset		3	121	12	9	8²	8¹⁄₂	7¹⁄₂	9¹¹⁄₂	7¹³⁄₄	Douglas R R	6.30
	In Seconds		3	121	11	10	12	10hd	10¹⁄₂	10hd	8nk	Trujillo E	73.40
19Feb06 ⁹GP⁸	Queendom	L b	3	121	10	11	9hd	9¹¹⁄₂	8¹¹⁄₂	11³	9hd	Cruz M R	108.50
	With Affirmation	L	3	121	7	5	2¹⁄₂	2¹	2¹	3¹⁄₂	10¹¹⁄₄	Smith M E	15.40
	Dream Child	L	3	121	9	6	7¹	7¹	12	12	11¹	Velazquez J R	4.30
26Jan06 ⁶GP⁶	Tuscan Star	L	3	121	6	4	1¹	1¹	1¹⁄₂	4¹⁄₂	12	Rose J	17.20

OFF AT 5:17 Start Good. Won driving. Course firm.

TIME :23², :47⁴, 1:11², 1:35¹, 1:41 (:23.41, :47.86, 1:11.41, 1:35.37, 1:41.18)

$2 Mutuel Prices:	1 – PINE ISLAND	59.80	22.60	14.40
	5 – HOSTESS		4.80	3.40
	6 – BOBBIN			12.40

$1 EXACTA 1–5 PAID $143.40 $1 TRIFECTA 1–5–6 PAID $1,815.20
$1 SUPERFECTA 1–5–6–2 PAID $5,932.00

Dk. b or br. f, (Apr), by Arch – Matlacha Pass , by Seeking the Gold . Trainer McGaughey III Claude R. Bred by Phipps Stable (Ky).

PINE ISLAND unhurried early, angled to the outside in the stretch and rallied to be just up at the wire. HOSTESS stalked the pace, raced three wide on the far turn, rallied to take over at the top of the stretch and opened a clear lead, then just failed to last. BOBBIN rated off the pace, advanced four wide around the far turn to reach the attending position in the stretch but couldn't late. JUDITH BASIN well placed in behind the leaders into the stretch, lacked a late response. THE NIAGARA QUEEN hit the gate at the start, stalked the pace along the rail into the stretch, then weakened. OCEAN SOUND outrun after being steadied at the start, saved ground into the stretch and improved her position. HOLY SUNSET reserved while saving ground, steadied to avoid running up on rivals in the stretch and never threatened. IN SECONDS was not a factor. QUEENDOM rank in the early going, failed to menace. WITH AFFIRMATION chased the pace, made a run at the leader on the far turn, then tired. DREAM CHILD raced four wide and was done early. TUSCAN STAR set the pace along the rail to the top of the stretch, then faltered.

Owners– 1, Phipps Stable; 2, Clifton William L Jr; 3, Blyar Stable; 4, Dinwiddie Farm; 5, Bridle Path Stable and Roberts Tommy; 6, Jones Frank L Jr; 7, Circle C Group Stables; 8, D J Stable LLC; 9, Jim Tafel LLC; 10, Briggs & Cromartie Bloodstock Agency; 11, Zuckerman Donald S and Roberta Mary; 12, Robinson J Mack

Trainers– 1, McGaughey III Claude R; 2, Bond Harold James; 3, Pletcher Todd A; 4, Mott William I; 5, Blengs Vincent L; 6, Romans Dale; 7, Clement Christophe; 8, Orseno Joseph; 9, Nafzger Carl A; 10, Kimmel John C; 11, Pletcher Todd A; 12, Alexander Frank A

Scratched– Real Expectations (11Dec05 2Aqu[7]) , Western Flair (26Jan06 8GP [6]) , Aristo (26Jan06 6GP [4])

$2 Daily Double (7–1) Paid $165.40 ; Daily Double Pool $127,300 .
$1 Pick Three (5–7–1) Paid $1,296.00 ; Pick Three Pool $84,246 .
$1 Pick Four (7–5–7–1) Paid $12,978.10 ; Pick Four Pool $113,559 .
$2 Pick Six (3–1–7–5–7–1) 4 Correct Paid $366.80 ; Pick Six Pool $95,384 ; Carryover Pool $109,993.

Gulfstream Park Attendance: 4,545 Mutuel Pool: $738,619.00 ITW Mutuel Pool: $368,514.00 ISW Mutuel Pool: $5,779,722.00

Hostess, a filly by the late superior turf sire Chester House, was the 5–2 favorite, but the field of 3-year-old fillies was loaded with strong grass pedigrees, led by first-time starters Pine Island and Bobbin. (Pine Island, a Phipps Stable homebred, developed into the leading filly of her generation on dirt after winning the Alabama and Gazelle Stakes, and also finished second in the Mother Goose Stakes and Coaching Club American Oaks.)

Pine Island was by Arch, who won the Super Derby and Fayette Stakes, both of which were on dirt. But Arch is by the versatile Kris S., a son of renowned stamina and grass influence Roberto. In his very first crop, Arch sired Overarching, a champion sprinter (on turf) in South Africa; Les Arcs, winner of the Group 1 July Cup and Group 1 Golden Jubilee Stakes in Europe; and Chilly Rooster, winner of the Fort Marcy Handicap. Arch sired other notable turf stakes winners in his next few crops, including Prince Arch and Montgomery's Arch.

Being by a sire (and from a sire line) known for turf and stamina, it was a natural for trainer Shug McGaughey to debut Pine Island on grass at 8 ½ furlongs. What made Pine Island so attractive were her odds relative to her sire's aptitude for siring grass winners. With 20 minutes to post time, Pine Island was 19–1. With every flash of the tote board, however, her odds escalated until she was 28–1 when the gates opened.

Just knowing her sire is a strong turf influence was enough of a reason to include

Pine Island in all exotics, but that was only part of the pedigree equation. Once again, the dam and her female family are the keys to racing class, and Pine Island had all the class in the world.

Her dam, Matlacha Pass, won two of three races, displaying more talent than her older full sister, Country Hideaway, before an injury forced her early retirement. By Seeking the Gold, Matlacha Pass is out of the unraced Our Country Place, a half-sister to champion Sky Beauty by Pleasant Colony out of the high-class racemare and producer Maplejinsky (Nijinsky II), winner of the Alabama Stakes and Monmouth Oaks.

And, just four months before Pine Island's career debut, her dam's full sister, Pleasant Home, romped to a 9 ¾-length victory in the Breeders' Cup Distaff.

McGaughey is known for giving his runners plenty of time to develop, so it was understandable that Pine Island was cold on the board, but being armed with all this pedigree information, her 28–1 odds seemed rather extreme—which made her a great HT play.

The other filly that was extremely well-bred for turf was Bobbin. By HT sire Pulpit, Bobbin was a full sister to Wend, winner of the New York Handicap, Jenny Wiley Stakes, and Honey Fox Handicap—all on grass. Like Pine Island, she looked like a hot overlay at 21–1. In addition to her sire and dam (who had already produced a stakes winner on grass), Bobbin's first three damsires—Topsider (Northern Dancer), Majestic Light (Majestic Prince), and Round Table (Princequillo)—are all exquisite sources of turf breeding. There was one more thing about Bobbin's pedigree that gave her extra appeal: She was inbred to the very influential broodmare Knight's Daughter.

Female-family inbreeding (FFI) is the most powerful and successful form of breeding racehorses, and it usually results in a Thoroughbred of high quality. (If the FFI occurs within five generations, it is known as the Rasmussen Factor.) Knight's Daughter's most famous foal was Round Table, and she also produced Round Table's full sister, Monarchy. Monarchy won the Arlington-Washington Lassie Stakes and notable runners descending from Monarchy include Pulpit, Johannesburg, Tale of the Cat, Minardi, Preach, Blade, Envoy, Title, Region, Announce, Narrate, Northcote Road, Double Feint, Haint, Play With Fire, and Teuflesberg. Obviously, duplicating an influential name in a pedigree, such as Knight's Daughter, magnifies the likelihood of creating a racehorse of higher class.

Hostess appeared on the way to victory but Pine Island closed with a furious rally to just get up at the wire by a neck. Pine Island returned $59.80, and the $2 exacta with favored Hostess paid $286.80. Bobbin finished third, and the $2 trifecta payoff was a memorable $3,630.40.

The hidden-turf factor also provided pedigree players with several golden opportunities on August 31, 2007.

The key to the big payday was Namaste's Wish, a 2-year-old filly who was making her career debut on turf in the sixth race at Saratoga, a maiden event at 8½ furlongs. Namaste's Wish had showed little in two dirt races, one at 5½ furlongs and the other at six furlongs, but had a good work on turf since her last effort. Despite her poor form, she had many pluses in her corner, not the least of which was the fact that Bill Mott, who had one of the most memorable meets of his career at the Spa in 2007, was her trainer.

More importantly, she was bred to love the green, even though it was not readily apparent by looking at her pedigree. Namaste's Wish is by Pulpit, who raced exclusively on dirt in his brief career, winning the Blue Grass Stakes and Fountain of Youth Stakes. Despite suffering a career-ending injury in the Kentucky Derby, he gamely finished fourth. As a sire, Pulpit has been quite versatile, getting winners on all surfaces. But with his first few crops, he established himself as a superior sire of turf runners, which included Stroll, Wend, Melhor Ainda, Lydgate, and Ecclesiastic.

Namaste's Wish had more going for her. In addition to getting a surface switch, which was a big plus for her sire, she had a ton of class from her female family. A full sister to multiple-stakes-winning miler Purge, whose biggest victory was in the Cigar Mile, Namaste's Wish was out of the Copelan mare Copelan's Bid Gal, a half-sister to stakes winner and sprint sire Valid Wager, as well as to Miss Bold Appeal, the dam of Jersey Girl, who won the Mother Goose, Test, and Acorn Stakes. In addition, Foolish Pleasure, the 1974 2-year-old champion and 1975 Kentucky Derby winner, comes from this female line.

After being 4–1 and 7–2 in her previous races, she was sent off at 8–1 in her third start, and the only reason she was under 10–1 was because of the tremendous success of her trainer, Mott, and her jockey, Kent Desormeaux.

Namaste's Wish won by 1 ¾ lengths and returned $19.60.

Getting 8–1 on a win bet is certainly satisfying, but using a good play such as this in exotics—especially pick threes, where possible—always maximizes the return. So, I had looked at the races surrounding Namaste's Wish to formulate pick threes, and while it was not impossible to come up with Intuition Magic at 8–1 in the first leg of the pick three encompassing races 4, 5, and 6, I didn't have him. Undeterred, I had turned my attention to the next pick three (starting on race 5). Among my plays in that race was Hurricane Annie, a 5-year-old mare who inexplicably was making her grass debut after 11 dirt races despite being by Stormy Atlantic (Storm Cat), a solid grass sire. Hurricane Annie loved the turf, sprinting to the lead and wiring her field at one mile on the inner turf at nearly 11–1. It was nice way to begin a pick three.

After Namaste's Wish won the second leg at nearly 9–1, I was alive with five runners in the third leg, which included the winner, Miss Blarney Stone, who also wired her field at 7–2 in an 8 ½-furlong allowance on the grass. In the money 7 of 11 times on the grass and a daughter of established turf influence Dynaformer, she was obviously one of the contenders, along with the fact that her trainer, Thomas Bush, was having one of his best Saratoga meetings ever.

The $1 pick three of Hurricane Annie-Namaste's Wish-Miss Blarney Stone returned $1,023.

Another example of the power of the HT factor occurred at Saratoga that same afternoon, in the With Anticipation Stakes for 2-year-olds. A case could have been made for many of the juvenile colts and fillies, among them Nownownow, a Patrick Biancone trainee who had run three times, finishing second twice and fourth last time out—all on dirt. In addition to getting first-time Lasix, Nownownow was from the first crop of Whywhywhy, whom Biancone also trained.

Whywhywhy was a good 2-year-old, winning the Futurity, Sanford, and Flash Stakes; he also finished third in the Swale Stakes at 3 (all on dirt), behind Midas Eyes and Posse. Because he is associated with quality victories on dirt and not grass, he would not necessarily be thought of as a grass influence. But the high success of this sire line on turf (Mr. Greeley-Gone West-Mr. Prospector) suggested Nownownow was a *very* legitimate play on grass, as most runners by Whywhywhy should relish the surface. Mr. Greeley has become a strong HT sire and is simply one of the best sons of Gone West at stud.

Mr. Greeley's prowess as a turf sire is exemplified by his high-class runners in Europe, topped by Finsceal Beo, the 2006 European 2-year-old filly champion who also won both the English and Irish 1000 Guineas in 2007. Mr. Greeley is also the sire of Saoirse Abu, a 2-year-old filly who captured the Group 1 Moyglare Stud Stakes at the Curragh in Ireland on September 2, 2007, following a victory in the Group 1 Phoenix Stakes at Leopardstown in Ireland. Great Barrier Reef, a 2-year-old colt by Mr. Greeley, was third in the Group 3 Round Tower Stakes, also at the Curragh on September 2, 2007.

Nownownow, making his first start since June 16 at Churchill Downs, was training sharply for the With Anticipation, showing a bullet half-mile work on the turf that was the fastest of 39 at the distance on August 13. Despite bobbling at the start, Nownownow was always in good position, split horses entering the stretch, and showed an explosive late run to win by three lengths, paying $14.60.

Greater things were still to come, however, as Nownownow would go on to win the inaugural running of the Breeders' Cup Juvenile Turf in October, launching a late rally to score a $27.20 upset. The $2 exacta with 5–2 favorite Achill Island returned $180.

MORE HIDDEN-TURF SIRES

Kingmambo has long been known as a solid grass influence. A multiple Group 1-winning miler in Europe, he is by the versatile Mr. Prospector, who sired quality stakes winners on all surfaces. Kingmambo is out of champion and two-time Breeders' Cup Mile winner Miesque (by superior grass influence Nureyev) and he has sired many champions on turf around the world, including El Condor Pasa, Divine Proportions, King Kamehameha, Rule of Law, and Russian Rhythm. In the U.S., his prominent grass winners include King Cugat, Parade Ground, Parade Leader, and Voodoo Dancer.

Lorelei Legend, a 3-year-old filly by Kingmambo who had run an even effort in her first grass try for Bobby Frankel but then ran poorly over a sloppy track in her most recent race, was back on grass and a strong pedigree play at 7–1 in a seven-furlong maiden race on July 15, 2007. In addition to her sire, she had a ton of pedigree from her female family as she is a half-sister to stakes winners Mongoose and Hesanoldsalt.

A filly with a hidden-turf pedigree making her grass debut for Bill Mott in the field after showing speed on the dirt was Fancy Fusaichi, a 3-year-old daughter of Fusaichi Pegasus who was 4–1. Fancy Fusaichi was out of a half-sister to Joyeux Danseur, a Grade 1 stakes winner on turf. Fusaichi Pegasus (Mr. Prospector), of course, is remembered for his victory in the Kentucky Derby (as well as his quirky temperament), so his offspring are usually ignored on grass. But Fusaichi Pegasus does get winners on all surfaces. In addition, Fancy Fusaichi got a good dose of turf breeding from her damsire, Rahy, the sire of champion Arazi, who incidentally also descends from Fancy Fusaichi's classy female family.

Lorelei Legend rallied to win by a neck over Fancy Fusaichi (4–1), and the exacta returned $83.50.

Grand Slam, who won the Champagne and Futurity Stakes at 2, was a stakes-winning miler who was able to stretch his speed to win the Peter Pan Stakes and who also finished second in the Swaps Stakes, both at nine furlongs. By Gone West, one of Mr. Prospector's most successful sons at stud, Grand Slam is as versatile as his sire line, getting winners on all surfaces. His runners, such as Breeders' Cup Sprint winner Cajun Beat, and stakes winners Limehouse and Strong Hope, usually have speed.

Luvandgo, a 2-year-old colt by Grand Slam making his career debut in a five-furlong maiden race at Churchill Downs on June 16, 2007, was totally ignored by bettors and was a juicy pedigree play at 41–1. While all runners by Grand Slam deserve respect sprinting, there were many reasons—pedigree-wise—to believe Luvandgo would be a major player in his first start.

His dam descended in tail-female line (dam, dam's dam, dam's granddam, etc.) from Best in Show, the foundation mare who was the 1982 Broodmare of the Year, the year her daughter Blush With Pride won the Kentucky Oaks. Blush With Pride is the second dam of Rags to Riches, Jazil, and Europe's top-rated 2007 3-year-old filly, Peeping Fawn.

As if this weren't enough, Luvandgo also has the Rasmussen Factor (RF). The RF is a specialized female-family inbreeding pattern that is created when a horse is inbred to a superior female within five generations through different individuals. (Other examples of how the RF is a rewarding betting angle are discussed later in this chapter.)

Luvandgo shot out of the gate and appeared on his way to victory but was overhauled in deep stretch by Sok Sok, a colt by precocious and win-early sire Trippi (End Sweep). Sok Sok was making his debut for Steve Asmussen, a trainer who is known for his success with juvenile first-time starters.

The Sok Sok-Luvandgo exacta paid $236.40. Luvandgo also returned $29.60 to place.

Luvandgo was not the only attractive pedigree play on June 16. On the same day at Arlington Park, Fall Classic, a first-time starter by freshman sire **Yankee Gentleman**, was dismissed at 32–1 in a maiden race for 2-year-old colts. Yankee Gentleman, a son of Storm Cat, had sizzling speed and I expected his babies would be quite precocious. In my annual review of freshman sires in *Daily Racing Form* I wrote:

> Yankee Gentleman (Storm Cat-Key Phrase, by Flying Paster); stands for $10,000 in Kentucky. Unraced at 2, Yankee Gentleman won his maiden debut by 11 lengths at Gulfstream Park at 3 but did not win a stakes until age 4, when he captured the six-furlong Pirate's Bounty Handicap . . . Bred for speed, Yankee Gentleman is a full brother to the dam of the promising Half Ours, winner of the Three Chimneys Juvenile Stakes. With so many high-profile first-crop stallions, he could be another sleeper, since his 2-year-olds should have abundant speed. Yankee Gentleman is also an HT2 (hidden-turf top and bottom), and his runners should light up the tote board on turf . . ."

Indeed, Fall Classic went right to the lead but succumbed late to Deputy Dance, who was making his third start for Asmussen. The $2 exacta returned $91 and Fall Classic paid $19.40 to place.

Cactus Ridge was undefeated at age 2 in 2003, the only year he raced. His four victories included three stakes—the Arlington-Washington Futurity, James C. Ellis Juvenile, and Canterbury Park Juvenile Stakes. By speed influence Hennessy (who was also a top-class juvenile who only raced at 2), Cactus Ridge was a 2007 freshman sire and I expected his babies to have his speed. Because Cactus Ridge was not a "name" stallion, I thought that his first crop of runners might fly under the radar and offer value, on dirt and turf.

On June 24, 2007, Mims Eppi, a 2-year-old filly by Cactus Ridge making her career debut in a maiden race at Churchill Downs, was such an example. In addition to her sire, Mims Eppi had a lot of pedigree power. Her second dam was champion Our Mims, a half-sister to Alydar. An overlay at 21–1, she crossed the finish line in third, but was interfered with in the stretch and, luckily for me, was placed second behind the 4–5 favorite, Possible, for a $77.80 exacta.

A few weeks later, I was immediately drawn to the 2-year-old colt Sebastian County, a full brother to Cactus Ridge who was making his first start for trainer Don Von Hemel in a five-furlong maiden race at Arlington on July 14, 2007. All young runners by Hennessy demand extra consideration on dirt or turf, and since Sebastian County was a full brother to a brilliant juvenile, I expected him to be a short price.

But players settled on Ready for May, another first-time starter from the high-profile barn of Todd Pletcher, as the tepid favorite at 7–2, while Sebastian County was 8–1. Needless to say, I jumped all over Sebastian County and only hoped he had a fraction of his brother's talent.

Sebastian County showed speed, and while he was more workmanlike over the Polytrack surface and not as flashy as Cactus Ridge was on dirt, he got the job done and paid a very satisfying $18.80. Not only did Pletcher's entry run out of the money, but so did juveniles from Steve Asmussen, Paul McGee, and Michael Stidham. (The following day, Creekmore, a 3-year-old half-brother to Sebastian County and Cactus Ridge by another HT sire, Holy Bull, won a one-mile maiden race on grass, paying $6.40 after many runner-up efforts on turf.)

Sebastian County won his second race as well, and his third-place finish in the Arlington-Washington Futurity in his third start on September 1, 2007, contributed to another pedigree score.

Gold Coyote, fourth in his career debut, but lopsided winner of his next three races, all at Lone Star Park, was installed as the even-money favorite despite the fact that he was meeting better-quality horses than what he had faced in Texas.

Four other juveniles had superior pedigrees, including Sebastian County (8–1), Riley Tucker (3–1), Blackberry Road (6–1), and Wicked Style (8–1).

After winning his 5 ½-furlong maiden debut at Belmont by six lengths for Bill Mott, Riley Tucker was third in the Saratoga Special Stakes behind Kodiak Kowboy and The Roundhouse after being bumped at the start. By first-crop sire Harlan's

Holiday, who was among the leading 2007 freshman stallions as this was written, Riley Tucker was from the female family that produced stakes winners Strategic Maneuver, Hey Hazel, Halory Hunter, Van Nistelrooy, Prory, Brushed Halory, and Key Lory.

Blackberry Road, a son of Gone West, was fourth to Kodiak Kowboy in the Bashford Manor Stakes in his previous start and was a half-brother to 2-year-old champion and very hot freshman sire Vindication.

Wicked Style won his maiden debut over the Arlington Polytrack surface and was getting first-time Lasix. By yet another 2007 freshman sire, Macho Uno (another 2-year-old champion), Wicked Style also was out of a female family of exceptional quality. His dam was by Prix de l'Arc de Triomphe winner Trempolino, and his third dam, Polonia (Danzig), was a champion sprinter in Europe.

Excluding the overbet favorite and using an exotics box of these four colts was rewarding, as Gold Coyote finished fifth of seven runners.

Wicked Style stalked the early pace of Gold Coyote and took over in the stretch to outgame Riley Tucker by a head, who once again hit the gate at the start. Sebastian County rallied for third after being bumped and going wide. The $2 exacta box returned $95.80 and the $2 trifecta box came back a hefty $556.20.

WINTER-MONTH HOTSPOTS

Santa Anita, Gulfstream Park, and Fair Grounds are the three main tracks for pedigree handicappers during the winter months, specifically because of, but not limited to, their ability to provide turf racing.

As expected, first-time starters hold special appeal for pedigree handicappers, because other than trainer patterns, there is nothing else to go on. At Santa Anita on March 4, 2006, a maiden race on the undercard of the Frank E. Kilroe Mile was especially attractive due to the pedigree power of some first-time starters.

THIRD RACE
Santa Anita

6½ FURLONGS. MAIDEN SPECIAL WEIGHT . Purse $61,000 (plus $18,300 CBOIF – California Bred Owner Fund) FOR MAIDENS, THREE YEAR OLDS. Weight, 121 lbs.

MARCH 4, 2006

Value of Race: $62,600 Winner $36,600; second $12,200; third $7,320; fourth $3,660; fifth $1,220; sixth $400; seventh $400; eighth $400; ninth $400. Mutuel Pool $626,191.00 Exacta Pool $376,094.00 Trifecta Pool $347,749.00 Superfecta Pool $178,823.00

Last Raced	Horse	M/Eqt.	A.	Wt	PP	St	¼	½	Str	Fin	Jockey	Odds $1
	Neko Bay	LB	3	121	2	7	6³	5¹¹	3²	1¹¹	Nakatani C S	21.30
	Fear No Darkness	LB bf	3	121	7	1	3ʰᵈ	3¹½	2¹½	2ⁿᵏ	Flores D R	5.50
11Feb06 3SA²	Evaluate-Ire	LB b	3	121	1	9	8¹	7¹	4½	3²¾	Espinoza V	0.80
4Feb06 9SA⁵	Town Thief	LB b	3	121	9	2	2¹½	2¹½	1¹	4²½	Valdivia J Jr	21.40
11Feb06 3SA³	Consigner	LB	3	121	8	3	9	8³½	7⁴	5¹	Santiago Javier	9.80
27Jan06 3SA⁶	Miracle Hill	LB	3	121	5	4	4²	4¹	5ʰᵈ	6⁷½	Valenzuela P A	6.70
4Feb06 9SA⁴	Miura Bull	LB b	3	121	3	6	1ʰᵈ	1ʰᵈ	6¹½	7ⁿᵏ	Solis A	5.50
	Root Beer City	LB	3	121	6	5	7ʰᵈ	9	9	8²½	Baze T C	43.20
14Jan06 5SA⁷	Cherokee J. D.	LB b	3	121	4	8	5ʰᵈ	6²	8¹	9	Court J K	63.80

OFF AT 1:08 Start Good. Won driving. Track fast.

TIME :22¹, :44⁴, 1:09¹, 1:15¹ (:22.28, :44.99, 1:09.31, 1:15.31)

$2 Mutuel Prices:

2 – NEKO BAY	44.60	16.60	6.60
7 – FEAR NO DARKNESS		7.00	3.60
1 – EVALUATE–IRE			2.60

$1 EXACTA 2–7 PAID $112.50 $1 TRIFECTA 2–7–1 PAID $380.90
$1 SUPERFECTA 2–7–1–9 PAID $6,167.00

Dk. b or br. c, (Apr), by Giant's Causeway – Brulay , by Rubiano . Trainer Shirreffs John. Bred by Mr & Mrs J S Moss (Ky).

NEKO BAY saved ground chasing the pace, swung out into the stretch and closed gamely under urging to prove best. FEAR NO DARKNESS stalked the pace outside on the backstretch and off the rail on the turn, came three deep into the stretch, bid outside a foe past the eighth pole, was between horses in deep stretch and just held second. EVALUATE (IRE) settled inside then a bit off the rail without early speed, moved up on the turn, swung out a bit wide into the stretch and finished well. TOWN THIEF angled in and dueled outside a rival, gained the lead leaving the turn, inched away inside in the stretch, fought back along the rail in deep stretch and weakened late. CONSIGNER allowed to settle outside a rival then off the rail, came out some in the stretch and lacked the needed rally. MIRACLE HILL stalked the pace off the rail, came out into the stretch and weakened. MIURA BULL had good early speed and dueled inside but weakened in the stretch. ROOT BEER CITY settled three deep then off the rail, dropped back on the turn and lacked a further response. CHEROKEE J. D. chased between horses then off the inside, was floated out some into the stretch and had little left.

Owners– 1, Moss Mr and Mrs Jerome S; 2, Sunset Stables; 3, Robert and Beverly Lewis Trust; 4, Mueller David and Paula; 5, Marquez Alfredo; 6, Gary and Mary West Stables Inc; 7, Lenner Tom Headley Bruce Molasky Irwin et al; 8, Hughes B Wayne; 9, Jim Ford Inc K M Stable and Stutts James

Trainers– 1, Shirreffs John; 2, Baffert Bob; 3, Baffert Bob; 4, Cecil B D A; 5, Marquez Alfredo; 6, Frankel Robert; 7, Headley Bruce; 8, Semkin Sam; 9, Dollase Wallace

$1 Pick Three (5–6–2) Paid $1,253.50 ; Pick Three Pool $134,328 .
$2 Daily Double (6–2) Paid $160.00 ; Daily Double Pool $40,088 .

Although Neko Bay was superbly bred for turf (by Giant's Causeway out of a half-sister to Lemon Drop Kid), he was training well on dirt for John Shirreffs, who was always known for having his horses ready to win first time out long before he achieved greater fame winning the Kentucky Derby with 50–1 shot Giacomo. Despite the pedigree and connections, Neko Bay was totally ignored by bettors and returned a tasty $44.60.

Also sporting top-class pedigrees were two colts from Bob Baffert who were uncoupled—Fear No Darkness and Evaluate. While Fear No Darkness, who was making his career debut, also had a powerful pedigree for grass (by Horse Chestnut), he had many blazing works on dirt, typical for Baffert's runners. Also appealing was Fear No Darkness's strong female family. His dam, Dr. Redoubtable, was by Storm Cat out of multiple stakes winner Irish Actress (Seattle Song), who was a popular fixture on the New York circuit for many years for trainer Leo O'Brien.

Evaluate, by Fusaichi Pegasus, had shown some ability running second in his debut, and his female family also had quality. His dam, Viva Zapata (Affirmed), was a Group 2 winner in France, and his second dam, Viva La Vivi, was a full sister to stakes winner Viva Sec. This line produced Florida Derby and Fountain of Youth Stakes winner Vicar.

The Neko Bay-Fear No Darkness $2 exacta returned $225 and the $2 trifecta returned $761.80.

February 4, 2006, was a particularly gratifying day for pedigree handicappers. Two first-time starters—one at Gulfstream and one at Oaklawn—were all you needed to have a big afternoon.

Gulfstream's maiden races for 3-year-olds have always been a good source of play for pedigree handicappers. Jacinth, a first-time starter by the proven speed influence Crafty Prospector, was a juicy overlay at 15–1. In addition to his venerable sire, Jacinth was out of a mare by Ogygian, another speed influence, giving Jacinth an "SP2" pedigree (speed top and bottom). Adding to his allure was his classy George D. Widener female family. His dam, Ligurian, was a half-sister to Victory Speech, and his third dam, Bendara, was a very quick 2-year-old filly who finished a close third behind champion Numbered Account in the 1971 Fashion Stakes. His fourth dam was 1965 3-year-old filly champion What a Treat. Having a pedigree of speed on top and bottom (sire and damsire), plus a high-class female family, Jacinth was definitely a pedigree handicapper's play—especially at 15–1. Jacinth paid $32.80.

Later that day at Oaklawn, Impeccable, a $550,000 yearling purchase at Saratoga, was inexplicably sent off at 14–1 despite a high-powered pedigree that was perfectly suited to win a maiden sprint.

By speed influence Grand Slam (Gone West), Impeccable was out of Light of the Moon (Cox's Ridge), a half-sister to Sailor's Warning, who finished third in the Tom Fool Handicap. This Phipps female family, which descends from the legendary broodmare Grey Flight (dam of nine stakes winners), has produced dozens of stakes winners as well as champions, including Kona Gold, Inside Information, Misty Morn, and Misty Morn's two champion sons, Bold Lad and Successor. Impeccable returned $30.80.

BABY RACES

Maiden races on any surface really are the bread and butter of pedigree handicappers. Aside from Keeneland in April, the more precocious 2-year-olds start to show up at Belmont Park in late May and early June. While there are usually the obvious win-early pedigrees to look for in these baby sprints, sometimes there is a sneaky breeding angle that merits attention.

Such a pedigree appeared in the second race at Belmont on June 13, 2007, a 5½-furlong maiden race for 2-year-olds.

The public pounced all over Fiumes, making the first-time starter from the barn of Wesley Ward the 3–5 favorite. Ward is famous for his high win percentage with young runners, and Fiumes showed a couple of bullet works and had a very good pedigree. From the first crop of 2-year-old champion Macho Uno, Fiumes was out of the stakes-winning Easy Goer mare Relaxing Rhythm. Also getting support at 4–1 was the Todd Pletcher entry of Big Wig (a three-quarter brother to stakes winner Rutherienne) and Greystone Warrior (by Monarchos out of stakes winner Halo Miss America).

Two colts making their debuts who had equally compelling pedigrees to win first out, but were not getting the same action, were Make the Point and Windication.

Windication was one of the first runners by 2002 2-year-old champion Vindication to get to the races, but he was ignored by bettors, which was surprising, since he was out of Critical Eye, a New York-bred who was a popular stakes winner at Belmont. Critical Eye won Grade 1 races such as the Gazelle Stakes and the Hempstead Handicap. (Vindication became one of the best 2007 freshman stallions, siring Adirondack Stakes winner More Happy, as well as Maimonides—third in the Hopeful Stakes—and many promising winners, including Sargent Seattle.)

But my top selection was Make the Point (7–1). While most horseplayers only saw that he was by Menifee out of a Capote mare, I was excited because I knew that this mare came from a female family of exceptional class. The Capote mare New Dice was out of the stakes winner Get Lucky, also the dam of stakes winners Accelerator and Daydreaming, and the unraced She's a Winner, the dam of Bluegrass Cat. Get Lucky was a full sister to 2-year-old champion Rhythm as well as top Maryland-based sprint sire Not for Love. Oscillate, a half-sister to Get Lucky, produced speed influence Mutakddim.

Make the Point wired the field, paying $16.80, and the exacta with Greystone Warrior returned $71. Finishing third at 14–1 was Windication, and the trifecta came back a nifty $514.

Longshots can be found in state-bred maiden races as well.

On June 17, 2007, at Belmont in a six-furlong event for 3-year-old New York-breds, trainer Gary Contessa's Too Much Zip, by successful sprint sire City Zip, was made the 2–1 favorite off three races.

1 Pretty Gal
Own: Golob Lewis Fallone Michael
Red Colors Unavailable
PRADO E S (166 30 37 22 .18) 2007: (634 125 .20)

Dk. b or br f. 3 (Apr) KEESEP05 $100,000
Sire: Outofthebox (Montbrook) $7,500
Dam: Bigger Half (Megaturn)
Br: Sez Who Thoroughbreds (NY)
Tr: Bond Harold James(22 2 5 1 .09) 2007:(85 19 .22)

[L] 118

Life	0	M	0	0	$0	-	D.Fst	0	0	0	0	$0	-
2007	0	M	0	0	$0	-	Wet(325)	0	0	0	0	$0	-
2006	0	M	0	0	$0	-	Synth	0	0	0	0	$0	-
Bel	0	0	0	0	$0	-	Turf(189)	0	0	0	0	$0	-
							Dst(237)	0	0	0	0	$0	-

WORKS: Jun9 Sar tr.t 6f fst 1:14^{2} B *1/1* ●Jun3 Sar tr.t 5f fst 1:00 H *1/13* May29 Sar tr.t 5f fst 1:02^{4} B *15/23* May22 Sar tr.t 4f fst :48^{4} B *8/43* May14 Sar tr.t 4f fst :50^{3} B *10/21* May8 Sar tr.t 4f fst :50^{4} B *26/35* Apr12 PmM 3f fst :38 B *1/1*
TRAINER: 1stStart(28 .04 $0.56) Dirt(202 .21 $1.84) Sprint(76 .18 $1.36) MdnSpWt(85 .12 $1.28) J/T 2006-07 BEL(2 .00 $0.00) J/T 2006-07(13 .00 $0.00)

2 Vilify
Own: Nerud John A
White White, Two Red Hoops, Red Cap
GARCIA ALAN (195 27 29 30 .14) 2007: (625 108 .17)

Gr/ro. f. 3 (Apr) SARAUG05 $50,000
Sire: Silver Charm (Silver Buck)
Dam: Hot Gossip (Java Gold)
Br: Sugar Maple Farm (NY)
Tr: Baker Charlton(10 2 1 1 .20) 2007:(134 24 .18)

118

Life	1	M	0	0	$235	37	D.Fst	1	0	0	0	$235	37
2006	1	M	0	0	$235	37	Wet(383)	0	0	0	0	$0	-
2005	0	M	0	0	$0	-	Synth	0	0	0	0	$0	-
Bel	0	0	0	0	$0	-	Turf(223)	0	0	0	0	$0	-
							Dst(355)	0	0	0	0	$0	-

Previously trained by Hushion Michael E 2006(as of 7/30): (161 29 36 22 0.18)
30Jly06–7Sar fst 5½f :22^{3} :46^{3} :59 1:05^{2} [F][S]Md Sp Wt 47k **37** 8 6 5^{5} 6$^{6\frac{1}{4}}$ 6^{10} 6$^{12\frac{3}{4}}$ Migliore R 118 3.90 79–13 GraemeCentrl118^{2} SecondMrrige118^{7} LedfootLizzie118^{3} Greenly, no rally 9
WORKS: Jun12 Bel tr.t 5f fst 1:00^{2} H *2/6* ●Jun5 Bel tr.t 5f fst 1:01 B *1/4* May29 Bel tr.t 5f fst 1:01 B *2/5* May23 Bel tr.t 5f fst 1:03 Bg *9/13* May18 Bel tr.t 5f fst 1:02^{1} Bg *6/13* May10 Bel 4f fst :52^{2} B *14/15*
TRAINER: 1stW/Trn(44 .25 $1.88) +180Days(32 .00 $0.00) Dirt(511 .21 $1.55) Sprint(373 .19 $1.65) MdnSpWt(83 .19 $1.50) J/T 2006-07 BEL(1 .00 $0.00) J/T 2006-07(8 .13 $0.85)

3 Cupids Gallop
Own: Lynch Kenneth
Blue Lavender, Purple Star, Purple Stars On
MARTIN E M JR (93 4 6 9 .04) 2007: (402 40 .10)

Dk. b or br f. 3 (Mar)
Sire: Victory Gallop (Cryptoclearance) $10,000
Dam: Cupids Day (Star Gallant)
Br: Whispering Creek Farm (NY)
Tr: Giglio D Jr(—) 2007:(5 0 .00)

[L] 118

Life	1	M	0	0	$280	-	D.Fst	1	0	0	0	$280	-
2007	1	M	0	0	$280	-	Wet(343)	0	0	0	0	$0	-
2006	0	M	0	0	$0	-	Synth	0	0	0	0	$0	-
Bel	0	0	0	0	$0	-	Turf(209)	0	0	0	0	$0	-
							Dst(335)	1	0	0	0	$280	-

Previously trained by Martinez Jose 2007(as of 4/21): (88 12 6 16 0.14)
21Apr07–7Pha fst 6f :22^{2} :46^{2} :59 1:11^{4} [F]Md Sp Wt 29k **–0** 5 9 9^{17} 9^{13} 9^{18} 9$^{25\frac{1}{4}}$ Sosa P Jr 121 12.10 55–18 CpeWicklow121$^{1\frac{1}{2}}$ Loveysister121^{5} *SuchDimond*121^{nk} Bobbled at the start 9
WORKS: Jun8 Bel 3f fst :36^{3} Bg *2/34* Jun2 Bel tr.t 5f fst 1:02^{3} B *10/12* May26 Bel 4f fst :49 H *12/17* May19 Bel 4f fst :49^{2} B *10/24* ●May3 Pen 3f fst :35^{4} H *1/15* ●Apr19 Pen 3f fst :35^{2} H *1/7*
TRAINER: 1stW/Trn(1 .00 $0.00) 31-60Days(6 .00 $0.00) Dirt(18 .00 $0.00) Sprint(13 .00 $0.00) MdnSpWt(8 .00 $0.00) J/T 2006-07(5 .00 $0.00)

4 Turning Leaves
Own: Seymour Sy Cohen
Yellow Black, Red Cross Sashes, Black And Red
JARA F (58 5 5 8 .09) 2007: (272 26 .10)

B. f. 3 (May) KEESEP05 $30,000
Sire: Mutakddim (Seeking the Gold) $12,500
Dam: Duralea (Mr. Leader)
Br: Machmer Hall Sunny Crest Farm & G Golden (NY)
Tr: Levine Bruce N(39 9 4 3 .23) 2007:(255 54 .21)

[L] 118

Life	0	M	0	0	$0	-	D.Fst	0	0	0	0	$0	-
2007	0	M	0	0	$0	-	Wet(370)	0	0	0	0	$0	-
2006	0	M	0	0	$0	-	Synth	0	0	0	0	$0	-
Bel	0	0	0	0	$0	-	Turf(280)	0	0	0	0	$0	-
							Dst(380)	0	0	0	0	$0	-

WORKS: Jun9 Bel 5f fst 1:01^{1} B *7/12* Jun2 Bel 5f fst 1:03^{1} B *13/16* May26 Bel 5f fst 1:01^{3} B *5/15* May19 Bel 4f fst :49 B *7/24* May12 Bel tr.t 4f fst :48 B *2/17* May5 Bel 4f fst :50 B *24/45* Apr29 Bel tr.t 3f fst :37 B *8/26*
TRAINER: 1stStart(38 .13 $1.93) Dirt(733 .25 $1.77) Sprint(490 .26 $1.84) MdnSpWt(107 .20 $1.84)

5 Duchess of Rokeby
Own: Whitbred Howard T Christine Brennan
Green Beige, Ivory Braces, Ivory Sleeves, Two
GOMEZ G K (94 21 11 15 .22) 2007: (554 125 .23)

Ch. f. 3 (May)
Sire: City Zip (Carson City) $20,000
Dam: Palace Lady (His Majesty)
Br: Christine Brennan & H T Whitbred (NY)
Tr: Jerkens H Allen(28 6 4 2 .21) 2007:(102 22 .22)

118

Life	2	M	0	0	$1,940	32	D.Fst	2	0	0	0	$1,940	32
2007	2	M	0	0	$1,940	32	Wet(363)	0	0	0	0	$0	-
2006	0	M	0	0	$0	-	Synth	0	0	0	0	$0	-
Bel	0	0	0	0	$0	-	Turf(334)	0	0	0	0	$0	-
							Dst(337)	0	0	0	0	$0	-

Previously trained by Gyarmati Leah 2007(as of 4/6): (49 6 6 5 0.12)
6Apr07–9Aqu fst 6½f :22^{3} :46 1:10^{2} 1:16^{4} 3↑[F][S]Md Sp Wt 51k **32** 7 3 6$^{3\frac{1}{4}}$ 5$^{5\frac{1}{4}}$ 5^{14} 5$^{14\frac{1}{2}}$ Carrero V 118 f 32.75 78–08 So Smashley118$^{5\frac{1}{4}}$ Dash of Luck118$^{1\frac{1}{2}}$ Prom Dance118$^{1\frac{1}{2}}$ No response 9
22Mar07–2Aqu fst 5½f [•] :22^{2} :46 :58^{3} 1:05^{1} [F][S]Md Sp Wt 41k **10** 7 7 7^{20} 7^{25} 7^{25} 7^{21} Smith M E 120 f 15.50 72–12 Ruth Drive120$^{3\frac{1}{2}}$ Golden Manna120^{6} Kall Me K120$^{2\frac{1}{4}}$ Ducked out start 7
WORKS: Jun10 Bel tr.t 5f fst 1:03^{2} B *6/6* Jun6 Bel tr.t 4f fst :51 B *30/34* May29 Bel tr.t 3f fst :36^{3} B *3/5* Apr25 Bel 1 fst 1:47 B *1/1* Apr18 Bel tr.t 3f fst :36^{1} B *4/28*
TRAINER: 1stW/Trn(11 .00 $0.00) 61-180Days(31 .19 $1.08) Dirt(345 .15 $1.40) Sprint(265 .15 $1.51) MdnSpWt(74 .14 $1.46) J/T 2006-07 BEL(2 .00 $0.00) J/T 2006-07(4 .25 $3.25)

6 Parachute Jump
Own: Karches Susan
Black Forest Green, White Dots, White Sleeves
CASTELLANO J J (146 22 27 23 .15) 2007: (498 78 .16)

Dk. b or br f. 3 (Feb)
Sire: Montbrook (Buckaroo) $15,000
Dam: Coney Island Girl (Polish Numbers)
Br: Berkshire Stud (NY)
Tr: Clement Christophe(31 10 7 4 .32) 2007:(130 31 .24)

[L] 118

Life	0	M	0	0	$0	-	D.Fst	0	0	0	0	$0	-
2007	0	M	0	0	$0	-	Wet(382)	0	0	0	0	$0	-
2006	0	M	0	0	$0	-	Synth	0	0	0	0	$0	-
Bel	0	0	0	0	$0	-	Turf(272)	0	0	0	0	$0	-
							Dst(381)	0	0	0	0	$0	-

WORKS: Jun9 Sar tr.t 4f fst :50^{2} B *22/30* May15 Sar tr.t 4f fst :50 B *14/35* May8 Sar tr.t 4f fst :50^{1} Bg *16/35* ●Apr25 Pay 4f fst :49^{4} B *1/7* Apr17 Pay 4f fst :50^{2} B *5/10* Apr9 Pay 4f fst :52 Bg *8/9* Mar31 Pay 4f fst :51^{2} B *25/39* ●Mar24 Pay 3f fst :38 B *1/8* Mar17 Pay 3f fst :38 B *2/8* Mar3 Pay 3f fst :39^{4} B *6/6*
TRAINER: 1stStart(68 .10 $1.39) Dirt(131 .20 $1.43) Sprint(156 .24 $1.72) MdnSpWt(145 .17 $1.24) J/T 2006-07 BEL(25 .24 $1.78) J/T 2006-07(57 .28 $2.24)

7 Abby Morgan
Own: Goldfarb Sanford J Dubb Michael
Orange Black, Metallic Gold Yoke And 'Cgs,'
VELASQUEZ C (190 25 24 32 .13) 2007: (759 112 .15)

Ch. f. 3 (Mar) NEWAUG05 $43,000
Sire: Well Noted (Notebook) $3,000
Dam: Creed's Lass (Cutlass)
Br: Sanford Goldfarb (NY)
Tr: Dutrow Anthony W(23 4 8 2 .17) 2007:(262 71 .27)

Blinkers ON L 118

Life	2	M	0	0	$2,214	34	D.Fst	2	0	0	0	$2,214	34
2007	2	M	0	0	$2,214	34	Wet(372*)	0	0	0	0	$0	-
2006	0	M	0	0	$0	-	Synth	0	0	0	0	$0	-
							Turf(231)	0	0	0	0	$0	-
Bel	2	0	0	0	$2,214	34	Dst(366)	2	0	0	0	$2,214	34

Previously trained by Houghton Dove P 2007(as of 6/3): (60 17 7 7 0.28)
3Jun07–6Bel fst 6f :22^1 :45^3 :58 1:11^3 3↑ⒻⓈMd Sp Wt 41k 34 2 5 5^{3¾} 4^{8½} 4^{14} 4^{14} Velasquez C L118 29.25 66– 18 SeventeenLove123^{4½} Normlize118^{1½} TlentdTrsur123^8 Inside, no response 8
Previously trained by Dutrow Anthony W 2007(as of 5/20): (228 62 40 36 0.27)
20May07–6Bel fst 6f :22^3 :46 :58^3 1:10^4 3↑ⒻⓈMd Sp Wt 41k 30 9 10 5^{3¼} 5^6 8^{11} 9^{17¼} Velasquez C L118 11.50 67– 13 MagicalMona118^{3¼} **TooMuchZip**118^½ GoldenManna118^{hd} Tired after a half 10
WORKS: Apr29 Aqu 5f fst 1:02 B *7/13* Apr21 Del 4f fst :48^2 B *6/58* Apr14 Del 3f fst :37 B *2/22*
TRAINER: 1stBlink(34 .18 $2.58) BlinkOn(35 .17 $2.51) Dirt(687 .28 $1.71) Sprint(500 .32 $2.08) MdnSpWt(122 .24 $1.53) J/T 2006-07 BEL(8 .25 $1.19) J/T 2006-07(15 .40 $2.53)

8 Agreatfable
Own: Waring Henry T
Pink Dubonnet, Gray Panel, Gray And Dubonnet
DESORMEAUX K J (105 19 19 12 .18) 2007: (412 72 .17)

B. f. 3 (Apr)
Sire: Abaginone (Devil's Bag) $289
Dam: Hakucho (Raise a Cup)
Br: Henry T Waring (NY)
Tr: Bush Thomas M(38 4 5 6 .11) 2007:(131 20 .15)

Ⓛ 118

Life	0	M	0	0	$0	-	D.Fst	0	0	0	0	$0	-
2007	0	M	0	0	$0	-	Wet(310)	0	0	0	0	$0	-
2006	0	M	0	0	$0	-	Synth	0	0	0	0	$0	-
							Turf(271)	0	0	0	0	$0	-
Bel	0	0	0	0	$0	-	Dst(325)	0	0	0	0	$0	-

WORKS: Jun8 Bel 5f fst 1:02 B *12/22* May25 Bel 5f fst 1:02^4 Hg *7/11* May12 Bel 4f gd :51^4 B *21/27* May6 Bel 4f fst :51 B *67/80* Apr24 Bel 3f fst :38 B *2/3* Apr19 Bel 3f fst :38 B *8/10*
TRAINER: 1stStart(38 .11 $0.73) Dirt(289 .17 $1.35) Sprint(174 .11 $1.07) MdnSpWt(121 .12 $0.80) J/T 2006-07 BEL(29 .14 $0.84) J/T 2006-07(38 .16 $1.16)

9 Too Much Zip
Own: Team Penney Racing
Turqse Gold, Royal Blue Yoke And 'Tpr,' Blue
COA E M (223 37 30 32 .17) 2007: (711 131 .18)

B. f. 3 (Mar) OBSAPR06 $50,000
Sire: City Zip (Carson City) $20,000
Dam: Juniors Fortune (Imperial Falcon)
Br: William Fuccillo (NY)
Tr: Contessa Gary C(161 21 27 26 .13) 2007:(571 85 .15)

L 118

Life	3	M	1	0	$10,387	66	D.Fst	3	0	1	0	$10,387	66
2007	3	M	1	0	$10,387	66	Wet(342)	0	0	0	0	$0	-
2006	0	M	0	0	$0	-	Synth	0	0	0	0	$0	-
							Turf(316)	0	0	0	0	$0	-
Bel	1	0	1	0	$8,200	66	Dst(338)	3	0	1	0	$10,387	66

20May07–6Bel fst 6f :22^3 :46 :58^3 1:10^4 3↑ⒻⓈMd Sp Wt 41k 66 1 2 6^{3¼} 4^{4½} 3^2 2^{3¼} Garcia Alan L118 7.80 81– 13 MagicalMona118^{3¼} TooMuchZip118^½ GoldenMnn118^{hd} Good finish on rail 10
11Mar07–4Aqu fst 6f ⊡ :23 :47^1 :59^1 1:11^4 ⒻⓈMd Sp Wt 41k 31 1 10 9^{6¾} 9^{13} 7^{19} 8^{20} Dominguez R A L120 *1.75e 65– 17 *Mighty Eros*120^{11¼} *Greg's Lassy*120^¾ *AutomaticAppeal*120^{1½} Inside trip, tired 11
25Feb07–4Aqu fst 6f ⊡ :22^4 :47^1 1:00 1:13^1 ⒻⓈMd Sp Wt 41k 47 6 5 8^{13} 5^8 5^{2½} 4^½ Garcia Alan L120 6.20 77– 16 CliJen120^{no} GoldenMnn115^{nk} LittleMissPopeye120^{nk} Steadied after start 9
WORKS: Jun8 Aqu 5f fst 1:03^2 B *14/15* ●Jun1 Aqu 5f fst 1:00^2 B *1/6* May12 Aqu 5f fst 1:03^2 B *11/11* Apr29 Aqu 6f fst 1:15 B *1/2*
TRAINER: 2Off45-180(114 .20 $1.75) Dirt(1262 .18 $1.63) Sprint(743 .15 $1.36) MdnSpWt(301 .15 $1.44) J/T 2006-07 BEL(89 .18 $1.94) J/T 2006-07(199 .16 $1.53)

Nickey-Luv Lunni

10 Luv That Game
Own: Big Lick Farm
Purple Yellow, Green Chevrons, Orange Sleeves
CLIFTON T (—) 2007: (303 60 .20)

Ch. f. 3 (Apr) SARAUG05 $67,000
Sire: Grand Slam (Gone West) $35,000
Dam: Promise to Love (Affirmed) — Elevated love,
Br: Eaton & Thorne Inc (NY)
Tr: Johnson Cleveland(5 0 0 0 .00) 2007:(8 0 .00)

L 118

Life	1	M	1	0	$5,000	41	D.Fst	1	0	1	0	$5,000	41
2007	1	M	1	0	$5,000	41	Wet(353)	0	0	0	0	$0	-
2006	0	M	0	0	$0	-	Synth	0	0	0	0	$0	-
							Turf(333)	0	0	0	0	$0	-
Bel	0	0	0	0	$0	-	Dst(357)	0	0	0	0	$0	-

Previously trained by Kline Homer R Jr 2007(as of 5/25): (41 7 12 6 0.17)
25May07–10CT fst 6½f :24 :48^3 1:15^4 1:23 ⒻMd Sp Wt 25k 41 1 1 1^1 1^1 1^1 2^{1½} Soodeen R L119 b 3.60 69– 22 Unbridled Love114^{1½} Luv That Game119^{4½} Lady Genie119^{2½} Led until 1/16 10
WORKS: May16 BTC 4f fst :51^2 B *1/1* Apr26 CT 4f fst :50^4 Bg *6/14* Apr21 BTC 3f fst :41 B *1/1*
TRAINER: 1stW/Tm(4 .00 $0.00) Dirt(4 .00 $0.00) Sprint(7 .00 $0.00) MdnSpWt(1 .00 $0.00)

Honky Tonk Tune

11 Heavenly Ballad
Own: William J Lageman
Gray Dark Brown, Cream Star, Cream Stars On
LUZZI M J (136 14 13 13 .10) 2007: (503 74 .15)

B. f. 3 (Feb) ½ Lord of the Thunder
Sire: Two Punch (Mr. Prospector)
Dam: Honky Tonk Ballad (Cure the Blues)
Br: Barbara Brewer (NY)
Tr: Albertrani Thomas(26 5 3 3 .19) 2007:(110 18 .16)

L 118

Life	1	M	0	0	$2,050	64	D.Fst	1	0	0	0	$2,050	64
2007	1	M	0	0	$2,050	64	Wet(391)	0	0	0	0	$0	-
2006	0	M	0	0	$0	-	Synth	0	0	0	0	$0	-
							Turf(215)	0	0	0	0	$0	-
Bel	1	0	0	0	$2,050	64	Dst(382)	1	0	0	0	$2,050	64

20May07–6Bel fst 6f :22^3 :46 :58^3 1:10^4 3↑ⒻⓈMd Sp Wt 41k 64 2 1 1^{1½} 1^{1½} 1^½ 4^{3¾} Coa E M L118 11.50 80– 13 Magical Mona118^{3¼} **Too Much Zip**118^½ Golden Manna118^{hd} Set pace, tired 10
WORKS: Jun8 Bel 4f fst :49^3 B *24/62* Jun1 Bel 4f fst :48^2 B *3/27* May14 Bel 4f fst :48^2 B *28/107* May6 Bel 4f fst :49 Bg *23/80* Apr30 Bel 4f fst :51^3 B *45/52* Apr23 Bel 4f fst :48^1 B *2/12*
TRAINER: 2ndStart(27 .22 $1.02) Dirt(222 .21 $2.00) Sprint(87 .22 $1.59) MdnSpWt(122 .17 $1.94) J/T 2006-07 BEL(2 .00 $0.00) J/T 2006-07(12 .17 $1.51)

TENTH RACE
Belmont
JUNE 17, 2007

6 FURLONGS. (1.07³) MAIDEN SPECIAL WEIGHT . Purse $41,000 FOR MAIDENS, FILLIES AND MARES THREE YEARS OLD AND UPWARD FOALED IN NEW YORK STATE AND APPROVED BY THE NEW YORK STATE–BRED REGISTRY. Three Year Olds, 118 lbs.; Older, 123 lbs.

Value of Race: $41,000 Winner $24,600; second $8,200; third $4,100; fourth $2,050; fifth $1,230; sixth $164; seventh $164; eighth $164; ninth $164; tenth $164. Mutuel Pool $432,245.00 Exacta Pool $355,798.00 Trifecta Pool $281,985.00 Superfecta Pool $122,145.00

Last Raced	Horse	M/Eqt.	A.	Wt	PP	St	¼	½	Str	Fin	Jockey	Odds $1
	Turning Leaves	L	3	118	4	6	6³	31½	3⁶	1ⁿᵏ	Jara F	14.50
20May07 ⁶Bel⁴	Heavenly Ballad	l	3	118	10	4	23½	26	13	22½	Luzzi M J	3.25
30Jly06 ⁷Sar⁶	Vilify		3	118	2	10	8¹	6²	4²	35¾	Garcia Alan	9.20
21Apr07 ⁷Pha⁹	Cupids Gallop	L	3	118	3	9	10	10	7ʰᵈ	41½	Martin E M Jr	43.00
25May07 ¹⁰CT²	Luv That Game	L b	3	118	9	3	1½	1ʰᵈ	2ʰᵈ	5½	Clifton T	27.25
20May07 ⁶Bel²	Too Much Zip	L	3	118	8	5	4½	5½	53½	61½	Coa E M	2.10
	Pretty Gal	L	3	118	1	2	5½	9½	93½	7ⁿᵒ	Prado E S	3.25
	Parachute Jump	L	3	118	6	7	9⁷	7½	61½	82¾	Castellano J J	14.50
6Apr07 ⁹Aqu⁵	Duchess of Rokeby		3	118	5	1	3ʰᵈ	41	81	95¾	Gomez G K	14.20
	Agreatfable	L	3	118	7	8	72½	82	10	10	Desormeaux K J	28.25

OFF AT 5:49 Start Good. Won driving. Track fast.

TIME :22³, :46³, :59¹, 1:12² (:22.75, :46.61, :59.32, 1:12.55)

$2 Mutuel Prices:				
	4 – TURNING LEAVES	31.00	12.20	8.40
	11 – HEAVENLY BALLAD		4.70	3.90
	2 – VILIFY			6.10

$2 EXACTA 4–11 PAID $161.50 $2 TRIFECTA 4–11–2 PAID $1,345.00
$2 SUPERFECTA 4–11–2–3 PAID $10,813.00

B. f, (May), by Mutakddim – Duralea , by Mr. Leader . Trainer Levine Bruce N. Bred by Machmer Hall Sunny Crest Farm & G Golden (NY).

TURNING LEAVES was outrun early, rallied three wide approaching the stretch, dug in resolutely outside and was along late. HEAVENLY BALLAD raced with the pace from the outside, drew clear in the stretch and dug in gamely but was caught nearing the finish. VILIFY was steadied after the start, came wide into the stretch and finished well outside. CUPIDS GALLOP was outrun early and showed some interest late. LUV THAT GAME was hustled to the front, set the pace and tired in the final furlong. TOO MUCH ZIP tired after a half mile. PRETTY GAL chased the pace along the inside and tired in the stretch. PARACHUTE JUMP was bumped at the start, stumbled and tired. DUCHESS OF ROKEBY raced between rivals and tired. AGREATFABLE broke in the air, was bumped then raced wide and tired.

Owners– 1, Cohen Sy; 2, Lageman William J; 3, Nerud John A; 4, Whispering Creek Farm; 5, Big Lick Farm; 6, Team Penney Racing; 7, Golub Lewis and Falcone Michael; 8, Karches Susan; 9, Whitbred Howard T and Brennan Christine; 10, Waring Henry T

Trainers– 1, Levine Bruce N; 2, Albertrani Thomas; 3, Baker Charlton; 4, Giglio Dominic Jr; 5, Johnson Cleveland; 6, Contessa Gary C; 7, Bond Harold James; 8, Clement Christophe; 9, Jerkens H Allen; 10, Bush Thomas M

Scratched– Abby Morgan (03Jun07 ⁶Bel⁴)

But Turning Leaves (14–1), a first-time starter from Bruce Levine (who was on a roll at the time), caught my eye, as did firsters Pretty Gal (3–1), Parachute Jump (14–1), and Heavenly Ballad (3–1).

I have always been drawn to first-time starters by Mutakddim, whose offspring usually show high speed, such as Lady Tak and Hattiesburg. For some reason, his runners are overlays, and Turning Leaves was also out of Duralea, making her a half-sister to stakes winner Lea Carter. Added appeal came from the fact that Turning Leaves's fourth dam was a half-sister to the influential speed influence Intentionally (the sire of In Reality, Tentam, and Ta Wee).

Pretty Gal (by Outofthebox and out of a half-sister to stakes winners Tate and Top Secret) and Parachute Jump (by Montbrook out of a Polish Numbers mare, and thus having an SP2 pedigree) both finished out of the money, but Turning Leaves just got up to win by a neck, paying $31, and the exacta with Heavenly Ballad paid $161.50.

THE RASMUSSEN FACTOR

The aforementioned Rasmussen Factor (RF) has proven to be a lucrative angle for pedigree handicappers, but because this pedigree pattern may not be obvious to the average player, it takes a bit more research to discover this handicapping gem. A little more work, however, can yield great rewards.

The best-known example of the RF may be Charismatic, who upset the 1999 Kentucky Derby, paying $64.60. Proving that victory was no fluke, Charismatic returned to win the Preakness at $18.80.

Charismatic
Chestnut Horse; March 13, 1996

Looking at just his sire and dam would not show that Charismatic has the RF. But a deeper examination of his five-generation pedigree clearly reveals that he is inbred 4 x 4 to the superior female Somethingroyal, through her most famous sons, Secretariat and Sir Gaylord. Inbreeding to Somethingroyal has proven highly successful, creating dozens of stakes winners, including Grand Lodge, Key of Luck, Cherokee Rose, Flying Squaw, Ampulla, Do It With Style, Mighty Forum, Provins, Rufina, Gone for Real, and Verglas.

Notable horses with the RF who contributed to some memorable paydays in Triple Crown races include Sea Hero (La Troienne 5 x 5), who returned $27.80 winning the 1993 Kentucky Derby; Unbridled (Aspidistra, 4 x 4), who paid $23.60 in the 1990 Derby; Gato del Sol (Mumtaz Begum, 5 x 5), who returned $44.40 in the 1982 Derby; Chateaugay (Selene, 4 x 5), who returned $20.80 in the 1963 Derby; Louis Quatorze (Grey Flight, 3 x 5), who returned $19 in the 1996 Preakness; and Pass Catcher (Sun Princess 4 x 3), who won the 1971 Belmont at $71.

Cash Run
Dark Bay or Brown Mare; May 1, 1997

There are many other examples where a runner with the RF won at double-digit odds, including Cash Run, who upset the heavily favored Chilukki in the 1999 Breeders' Cup Juvenile Fillies.

After a brilliant maiden victory, Cash Run had developed physical problems that compromised her form. She finished third in the Alcibiades Stakes, her final prep for the Breeders' Cup, and used the glib Gulfstream surface that day to her advantage.

Cash Run qualified as an RF horse because she was inbred 4 x 4 to the outstanding broodmare Sequence, the dam of stakes winner Gold Digger (the dam of Mr. Prospector), who is also the third dam of stakes winner Shared Interest, the dam of Cash Run and stakes winner Forestry.

Cash Run paid $67, and the exacta with 6–5 Chilukki returned $225.60. The trifecta using Surfside (the 5–2 second choice), the highly regarded filly by Seattle Slew out of 2-year-old filly champion Flanders, paid $563.60.

RISING TO THE SURFACE

In many cases, horses with good pedigrees just need a surface switch.

Some days there are simply no plays for pedigree handicappers, and then there are days like April 8, 2006, which turned out to be a bonanza.

Tongass, an RF who had disappointed in three starts, found a wet track at Aqueduct on the Wood Memorial undercard very much to his liking after floundering at Keeneland. By speed sire Forestry, Tongass was out of a Mr. Prospector mare, and whenever you see Forestry mated to a mare that has either Mr. Prospector or any of his sons in her pedigree, it creates the RF to Sequence. (This was the reverse of Cash Run, who had Mr. Prospector on top and Forestry's female line on the bottom.) Tongass returned $45.20.

In the Wood Memorial Stakes, runners by Seeking the Gold ran one-two. While Bob and John only paid $6.40 to win, Jazil, who had finished a lackluster seventh in the Fountain of Youth Stakes in his previous race, closed with a flourish at 15–1 to make the exacta worthwhile at $72. (Distance-loving Jazil went on to dead-heat for fourth in the Kentucky Derby and then won the Belmont Stakes at $14.40.)

At Gulfstream Park on the same day, another Seeking the Gold runner who was a slight overlay won on the turf. Seek to Soar was meeting an easier bunch of fillies, since most of the better outfits had left southern Florida at the end of that meeting. Out of champion turf mare Soaring Softly, Seek to Soar won and paid $14.20.

FIFTH RACE
Gulfstream
APRIL 8, 2006

1 MILE. (Turf) (1.31²) ALLOWANCE . Purse $33,000 FOR FILLIES AND MARES FOUR YEARS OLD AND UPWARD WHICH HAVE NEVER WON A RACE OTHER THAN MAIDEN, CLAIMING OR STARTER OR WHICH HAVE NEVER WON TWO RACES. Weight, 123 lbs. Non–winners of a race other than Claiming at a mile or over since March 9 Allowed 2 lbs. Such a race since February 7 Allowed 4 lbs. (Condition Eligibility). (If deemed inadvisable to run this race over the Turf course, it will be run on the main track at One Mile) (Rail at 84 feet).

Value of Race: $33,000 Winner $19,800; second $5,115; second $5,115; fourth $1,650; fifth $330; sixth $330; seventh $330; eighth $330. Mutuel Pool $333,966.00 Exacta Pool $254,220.00 Trifecta Pool $207,104.00 Superfecta Pool $60,191.00

Last Raced	Horse	M/Eqt.	A.	Wt	PP	St	¼	½	¾	Str	Fin	Jockey	Odds $1
4Mar06 ¹¹GP⁷	Seek to Soar	L bf	4	119	3	3	3¹	3ʰᵈ	4ʰᵈ	1ʰᵈ	1½	Sutherland C	6.10
23Oct05 LCH⁷ [DH]Resound–Ire		L	4	119	1	7	7²	5ʰᵈ	3ʰᵈ	2½	2	Cruz M R	2.50
27Mar06 ¹⁰GP¹ [DH]Fired Gold		L b	4	123	7	5	6½	4¹½	5¹	4ʰᵈ	2ⁿᵏ	Trujillo E	1.60
13Aug05 ¹¹ElP¹	Resolution	L	4	119	4	1	5½	7³	6³	3²	4²¾	King E L Jr	12.80
16Mar06 ⁹GP⁹	Stashed Away	L b	4	115	5	2	1½	1¹½	1¹	5³	5³¼	Arce J⁵	18.10
14Feb06 ⁷Tam¹	Sweet Melody	L b	5	121	8	4	2²½	2²	2ʰᵈ	6⁵	6⁶¼	Maragh R	17.40
27Mar06 ⁹GP⁵	Shesa Fast Lady	L b	4	119	6	6	4ʰᵈ	6ʰᵈ	7²	7³	7³¾	Leyva J C	24.30
22Feb06 ¹⁰GP¹	Pretty Possible	L b	5	119	2	8	8	8	8	8	8	Potts C L	5.20

[DH]–Dead Heat.

OFF AT 2:55 Start Good For All But RESOUND (IRE). Won driving. Course firm.
TIME :23¹, :45⁴, 1:09¹, 1:33³ (:23.33, :45.88, 1:09.31, 1:33.71)

$2 Mutuel Prices:

3 – SEEK TO SOAR	14.20	3.60	3.40
1 – [DH]RESOUND–IRE		2.40	2.60
7 – [DH]FIRED GOLD		2.20	2.40

$1 EXACTA 3–1 PAID $13.90 $1 EXACTA 3–7 PAID $11.70
$1 TRIFECTA 3–1–7 PAID $41.20 $1 TRIFECTA 3–7–1 PAID $31.20
$1 SUPERFECTA 3–1–7–4 PAID $223.30 $1 SUPERFECTA 3–7–1–4 PAID $173.70

Ch. f, (Feb), by Seeking the Gold – Soaring Softly , by Kris S. . Trainer Toner James J. Bred by Phillips Racing Partnership (Ky).

SEEK TO SOAR stalked the pace along the rail, slipped through inside STASHED AWAY to gain the lead at the top of the stretch while coming off the inside, then was fully extended to prevail. RESOUND (IRE) unhurried after bumping with PRETTY POSSIBLE and stumbling at the start, circled rivals four wide on the far turn to reach even terms for command with SEEK TO SOAR at the top of the stretch but was outgamed to the wire while dead heating with FIRED GOLD. The latter, rated off the pace, raced three wide on the far turn, then rallied along the outside to finish on even terms for the place. RESOLUTION allowed to settle, rallied along the rail to reach the leaders in midstretch and hung. STASHED AWAY set the pace along the inside, came off the rail entering the stretch and gave way. SWEET MELODY chased the pace, then was tiring when steadied in tight quarters leaving the turn. SHESA FAST LADY was through after six furlongs. PRETTY POSSIBLE trailed after bumping with RESOUND at the start.

Owners– 1, Phillips Racing Partnership; 2, All In Racing LLC; 3, Live Oak Plantation; 4, Humphrey G Watts Jr; 5, Keating Paul M Sr; 6, Anderson Paxton; 7, Grisham Lin and Hatchett James; 8, Ng Helen and Tam Ping W

Trainers– 1, Toner James J; 2, Clement Christophe; 3, Wolfson Martin D; 4, Arnold George R II; 5, Ritvo Timothy; 6, Ziadie Kirk; 7, Pilotti Larry; 8, Breen Kelly J

$1 Pick Three (6–8–3) Paid $101.00 ; Pick Three Pool $39,645 .

While the HT is a great handicapping tool, turf races in general usually provide golden opportunities for pedigree handicappers.

At Keeneland on April 8, 2006, pedigree handicapping unearthed a winner ($16.60); a $2 exacta ($76); a $1 trifecta ($138.60); and a $1 superfecta ($634.90).

The horses who took the first four spots all were bred to excel on grass, starting with the winner, Giant Basil (Giant's Causeway—Verbasle, by Slewpy), a half-brother to Florida Derby and Fountain of Youth Stakes winner High Fly. The runner-up, Galantas (Tale of the Cat—Colonial Debut, by Pleasant Colony) had an HT2 pedigree; third-place finisher Devil's Preacher (Pulpit—All the Crown, by Chief's Crown) was already proven on grass; and finishing fourth was Mercurius

(Lemon Drop Kid—Danara, by Danzig), who was by the very successful HT sire Lemon Drop Kid and out of a mare by Danzig, another well-known source of turf.

Because pedigree handicapping can provide tremendous value with first-time starters, it sometimes only takes one race to make a profit.

Such an opportunity presented itself at Del Mar on September 1, 2007, when Reflect Times unleashed a Silky Sullivan-type effort to win going away at 17–1.

SEVENTH RACE
Del Mar
SEPTEMBER 1, 2007

6 FURLONGS. (1.11) MAIDEN SPECIAL WEIGHT . Purse $53,000 (plus $15,900 CBOIF – California Bred Owner Fund) FOR MAIDENS, TWO YEAR OLDS. Weight, 120 lbs. (Non–Starters for a claiming price of $32,000 or less in the last 3 starts preferred).

Value of Race: $55,400 Winner $31,800; second $10,600; third $6,360; fourth $3,180; fifth $1,060; sixth $400; seventh $400; eighth $400; ninth $400; tenth $400; eleventh $400. Mutuel Pool $471,890.00 Exacta Pool $255,450.00 Quinella Pool $21,605.00 Trifecta Pool $202,959.00 Superfecta Pool $127,508.00

Last Raced	Horse	M/Eqt. A. Wt	PP	St	1/4	1/2	Str	Fin	Jockey	Odds $1
	Reflect Times–Jpn	LB 2 120	9	9	$10\frac{3}{4}$	10^4	7^{hd}	$1\frac{3}{4}$	Smith M E	17.40
	Southwest	LB 2 120	8	4	7^{hd}	8^4	$4\frac{1}{2}$	$2\frac{23}{4}$	Flores D R	28.60
11Aug07 6Dmr10	Chop House George	LB b 2 120	10	1	6^4	$2\frac{1}{2}$	$11\frac{1}{2}$	3^1	Talamo J	19.40
	Honourmongfriends	LB 2 120	11	2	8^5	7^{hd}	$5\frac{21}{2}$	4^1	Baze M C	2.20
4Aug07 2Dmr5	Huss the King	LB 2 120	4	8	5^{hd}	$5\frac{11}{2}$	3^{hd}	$5\frac{23}{4}$	Migliore R	4.30
	Arabian Cheetah	LB b 2 120	1	6	1^{hd}	$1\frac{21}{2}$	2^1	6^{hd}	Nakatani C S	4.50
	Quarter Moon	B 2 120	5	11	11	11	11	$7\frac{11}{4}$	Solis A	29.20
	Come in Almighty	LB b 2 120	7	10	9^4	9^3	$10\frac{21}{2}$	$8\frac{23}{4}$	Garcia M	34.40
	Cohen Thebarbarian	LB 2 120	3	5	4^2	6^2	6^2	9^{nk}	Potts C L	12.80
	Harlans Fortune	LB bf 2 120	2	7	2^{hd}	4^{hd}	$8\frac{1}{2}$	$10\frac{53}{4}$	Pedroza M A	10.10
4Aug07 2Dmr6	Volos	LB b 2 120	6	3	$3\frac{11}{2}$	3^1	9^2	11	Baze T C	5.90

OFF AT 5:10 Start Good. Won driving. Track fast.
TIME :22², :47, 1:00³, 1:14 (:22.57, :47.04, 1:00.70, 1:14.15)

$2 Mutuel Prices:

11 – REFLECT TIMES–JPN	36.80	16.20	9.20
10 – SOUTHWEST		19.20	12.80
13 – CHOP HOUSE GEORGE			10.60

$1 EXACTA 11-10 PAID $332.00 $2 QUINELLA 10-11 PAID $335.80
$1 TRIFECTA 11-10-13 PAID $4,156.10
$1 SUPERFECTA 11-10-13-14 PAID $7,536.30

Ch. c, (Apr), by French Deputy – Franca , by Seeking the Gold . Trainer Shirreffs John. Bred by North Hills Management (Jpn).

REFLECT TIMES (JPN) settled off the rail, angled in on the turn and rallied along the fence under urging in the stretch to prove best. SOUTHWEST angled in and saved ground off the pace, moved up on the turn, came out in upper stretch and finished well. CHOP HOUSE GEORGE chased off the rail, moved up on the turn and into the stretch, took the lead in upper stretch, inched away, drifted out late and could not match the top pair. HONOURAMONGFRIENDS settled off the inside, went outside on the turn and three deep into the stretch and the needed late kick but steadied nearing the wire. HUSS THE KING stalked the pace off the rail, came out in the stretch and could not summon the necessary response. ARABIAN CHEETAH had good early speed and dueled inside, inched clear into the turn, came off the rail and weakened in the stretch. QUARTER MOON broke slowly, saved ground off the pace and improved position in the stretch. COME IN ALMIGHTY also slow to begin, settled off the inside, came out into the stretch and did not rally. COHEN THEBARBARIAN had speed between horses then stalked off the rail or outside, came four wide into the stretch and weakened. HARLANS FORTUNE dueled between horses, dropped back leaving the turn and had little left for the stretch. VOLOS had speed between foes then dueled three deep, dropped back into the stretch and gave way. The stewards conducted an inquiry into the late stretch run of the third and fourth finishers but made no change when they ruled the incident did not alter the original order of finish.

Owners– 1, Maeda Koji; 2, Lazy Lane Farms Inc; 3, Magenta Racing Inc; 4, Fields Joe McClanahan Jerry and Unruh Gregory; 5, Zetcher Arnold; 6, Scott Phil; 7, Stute Annabelle and The Hat Ranch; 8, Lail Lynda G; 9, IEAH Stables Cohen Andrew and Zimmerman Earle; 10, Shepard Robert H; 11, Dapple Stable.

Trainers– 1, Shirreffs John; 2, Mandella Gary; 3, Rosales Richard; 4, Mullins Jeff; 5, McAnally Ronald; 6, Harty Eoin; 7, Stute Melvin F; 8, Puype Mike; 9, Chatlos Donald Jr; 10, Chew Matthew; 11, Koriner Brian.

Scratched– Meetingwithdestiny , Mr. Zarrow , Villa Park.

$2 Daily Double (8–11) Paid $1,397.00 ; Daily Double Pool $31,704 .
$1 Pick Three (13–8–11) Paid $4,645.00 ; Pick Three Pool $105,541 .

There were many things to like about Reflect Times. While he was listed as a Japanese-bred, his pedigree was pure Kentucky.

First, his sire, French Deputy (Deputy Minister) raced only six times for Neil Drysdale, and was a quality horse, winning four races, including the 1995 Jerome Handicap over Mr. Greeley and Top Account in a quick 1:33.53. Standing only briefly in this country, he was whisked away to Japan for stud duty just as his first few crops started showing talent. His early stakes performers included Bella Bellucci, Blue Burner, Boozin' Susan, Cogburn, First Blush, Freefourracing, French Assault, Flying Notes, House Party, Left Bank, Mayo On the Side, Queue, and True Direction.

Second was the high quality of his female family. His dam, Franca, was by Seeking the Gold, and his third dam, Secret Asset (Graustark), was a half-sister to Private Account, Dance Number, and Polish Numbers. Secret Asset had produced a Group 1 winner in Italy, and Reflect Times's fourth dam was the 1971 2-year-old filly champion, Numbered Account.

The combination of an underrated stallion, an impeccable female family, and the high appeal of his trainer, the previously mentioned John Shirreffs, made Reflect Times an irresistible longshot play.

Running 10th of 11 horses and about 17 lengths off the leader after the first quarter over a Polytrack that has favored this running style, Reflect Times steadily raced up the rail and was moving strongly late to win by three-quarters of a length, paying $36.80.

FRESHMAN STALLIONS

Freshman stallions often provide some terrific overlays simply because most horseplayers don't know what to expect from them. To help players in this regard, I write an annual alphabetical overview of the new freshman sires in December and January in *Daily Racing Form*.

For instance, in my early analysis of one of the 2007 freshman stallions, Proud Citizen, I wrote the following:

"Proud Citizen (Gone West—Drums of Freedom, by Green Forest); stands in Kentucky for a private fee. All attention is rightfully being focused on Empire Maker, Mineshaft, Vindication, Sky Mesa, and Aldebaran, but the freshman stallion whom I'm most attracted to is Lexington Stakes winner Proud Citizen. He is an exceptionally well-bred horse who was bred for high speed but was good enough to stretch that speed to finish second in the 2002 Kentucky Derby and third in that year's Preakness. Proud Citizen showed brilliance at 2, winning his 5½-furlong maiden debut at Belmont Park by 9¼ lengths. His third dam is a full sister to Northern Dancer, and his female family also produced champions Danehill, Machiavellian, and La Prevoyante. His 2-year-olds should have high speed on dirt, and he is a hidden-turf sire whose runners should be brilliant on turf."

In fact, Proud Citizen got off to a great start at stud. Two of his European runners—River Proud and Francesca d'Gorgio—were rated among the best juveniles overseas on grass late in 2007. At the time, he ranked fourth on the freshman sire list behind Posse, Harlan's Holiday, and Van Nistelrooy, and had 10 winners from 27 starters, including stakes winner Proud Spell.

On September 1, 2007, How Bout Tonight, a 2-year-old filly by Proud Citizen making her career debut for trainer Henry Carroll, scored a front-running 3 ½-length victory in a 5½-furlong maiden race on dirt at 13–1, defeating babies from the high-profile barns of Todd Pletcher and Shug McGaughey and paying $28.60.

How Bout Tonight had an SP2 pedigree, as she was out of a mare by brilliant influence Saint Ballado, and she descended from a female family that produced stakes winners Diablo, Roamin Rachel, Darling My Darling, and Plucky Roman.

As shown in the many varied examples in this chapter, pedigree handicapping can be utilized to uncover longshots in everyday handicapping, as well as for racing's biggest days.

WATCHMAKER
ON GRADE 1 RACES
By Mike Watchmaker

THIS IS THE LAST chapter of this book, which many of you might find to be entirely appropriate. And that is because a lot of horseplayers believe that Grade 1 stakes races are about the last place one would hunt for winning longshots, or even successful value horses.

After all, with the notable exception of the Kentucky Derby and the eight established Breeders' Cup events, aren't Grade 1 races characterized by small fields, talent mismatches, and short-priced winning favorites? Be honest now.

Instead of viewing Grade 1 races as places to look for longshot winners, aren't they often the first places many of us look for "singles" in our pick-four and pick-six plays?

As national handicapper for *Daily Racing Form*, I focus on major stakes races all acoss the country. But as a bettor who calls the three New York Racing Association tracks his home circuit, I have vivid recent memories of Bernardini crushing three opponents in the Jockey Club Gold Cup, Henny Hughes whipping four opponents in the Vosburgh, Fleet Indian wiring four opponents in the Personal Ensign, Saint Liam winning over only two coupled entries in the Woodward, and Ashado beating four opponents in the Go for Wand, just as she had earlier done in the Ogden Phipps. And the combined parimutuel return on all of them probably wouldn't cover two hot dogs and two beers at Shea Stadium. So when I was asked to write a chapter for this book on playable longshots in major stakes races, I thought, "I know how I feel. How in the world am I going to do this?"

It then occurred to me that perhaps the best way to tackle this subject was to find a means to prove whether attempting to make longshots win in Grade 1 races is really a worthwhile pursuit, or if our major stakes races are indeed the festivals of chalk so many of us sense they are. If, after applying a scientific approach to the topic, the latter proved to be the case, it might not dovetail with the overall theme of this book, but it would still be perfectly valid, and useful, information. If the former proved to be true, it would dispel a widely held myth, and alter the mindset many of us have when it comes to wagering on Grade 1 races. That is to say, we would be able to take the kid gloves off and treat Grade 1 races from a betting perspective like any other type of race.

I decided to take the composition of Grade 1 races and break them into five betting categories. The first category consisted of odds-on favorites, which meant all horses who started at odds of 95 cents to the dollar or less. The second category comprised horses I would consider to be strong favorites—horses who started at odds of even money (1.00) up through 1.95. The third category was all other favorites whose odds were 2–1 or higher. The fourth category comprised the second through fourth betting choices, and the fifth category was made up of all other starters.

The information I wanted from each category was the number of starters and the number of winners, so that I could get a win percentage from each category. I also wanted the parimutuel return for each winner in each category so that a $2 return on investment could be calculated. And I decided to focus the study on all Grade 1 races run on the flat in the United States in the five-year period from 2002 through 2006.

Now, I will admit that when it comes to mathematical minds, you don't have to look much farther than the lowest percentile to find me. But I thought these parameters would give me the answers I was looking for. So with the help of *Daily Racing Form's* Chuck Kuehhas and Duane Burke, the masters who developed the means to query *Daily Racing Form's* database, I got the stuff. And to steal a line from Steven Crist after he got a peek at them, the results were worth the price of admission.

There were many things in these results that jumped out at me, but for the sake of order, let's start with field size. In the five-year span from 2002 through 2006, there were 502 Grade 1 races run on the flat in the U.S., and these races attracted a total of 4,146 runners. This resulted in an average of 8.26 runners per Grade 1 race. This number is actually fractionally higher than the average field size of 8.23, as compiled by The Jockey Club for all races—that means every type of race run—during this period.

In the interest of full disclosure, the statistics compiled by The Jockey Club include all races run in the U.S. and Canada, while I restricted my Grade 1-stakes study to this type of race run only on the flat, and only in the U.S. On the other hand, my Grade 1 races included events like the eight established Breeders' Cup races, which always attract very big fields, and the Kentucky Derby, which makes news these days when it doesn't attract a field of 20. This latter point bothered me a bit, so I went back and manually calculated the average field sizes for our Grade 1 stakes excluding the three Triple Crown events and the eight established Breeders' Cup races in 2005 and 2006. The average field size I got for my 2005 Grade 1 stakes was 8.21, better than the 8.17 average field size The Jockey Club reported for all U.S. and Canadian races in 2005. And the average field size for my 2006 Grade 1 stakes was 8.15, again fractionally better than the 8.14 average field size The Jockey Club reported for all North American races in 2006.

The point here is clear: Our impressions about field size were wrong. While there are, and will be, occasional Grade 1 races that will be an intimate four- or five-horse gathering, Grade 1 races, in the main, offer fields just as large in size as any other type of race out there.

Let's move on to win percentage. The overall results of the *Daily Racing Form* database study reveal that in this arena, Grade 1 stakes once again, in general, act like other types of races. There is a gradual, completely logical decline in the success rate of horses as determined by the odds established by the betting public. Over our five-year period, odds-on favorites won 55.3 percent of the Grade 1 stakes they competed in. Strong favorites, those just under 2–1 to even money, won 33 percent of the time. All other favorites won 25.7 percent of their Grade 1 starts. Second through fourth betting choices had a win rate of 13.6 percent, while all other starters won only 5.1 percent of the time.

If there were any deviations from the norm here, it would appear to be in two areas. First, the fact that there were 152 odds-on favorites in the 502 Grade 1 races studied—a high rate of 30.3 percent—strongly suggests that Grade 1 races offer more perceived talent mismatches than other types of races. It is noteworthy that all favorites combined won 37.5 percent of their Grade 1 starts from 2002 through 2006, which is above the universal standard-success rate for betting favorites of 33 percent.

It is not a surprise that there were some dramatic, year-to-year swings within the five categories, and I will note them for the record. Odds-on favorites won only 44.1 percent and 47.8 percent of the time in 2004 and 2005, respectively, while in the other three years of the study, they scored at a rate between 60.7 percent and 61.5 percent.

Strong favorites succeeded 39.5 percent of the time in 2002, but then settled down to win at a clip between 28.6 percent and 34.1 percent the remaining four years.

All other favorites won at a steady rate of between 24.1 percent and 25.9 percent the first three years of the study, but jumped to a success rate of 37.1 percent in 2005, and then plummeted to a win rate of only 15.6 percent in 2006.

The remaining two categories posted fairly consistent success rates through the five-year period, with second through fourth betting choices winning at clips of between 11.9 percent and 15 percent, and all other starters connecting at rates of between 3.9 percent and 6.4 percent.

Now, let's get to the payoff—literally. The return on investment for a $2 win wager in each category over our five-year study yielded three results that most people could have anticipated, plus one substantial surprise, and one enormous shocker.

Let's first talk about the relatively mundane. For the odds-on favorites, the five-year return on investment was narrowly the second highest in our five categories at $1.77, edging out by a penny the category involving all other favorites. Strong favorites, those horses who went off at even money through 1.95–1, produced an ROI of only $1.58.

The surprising category was the dramatic parimutuel underperformance of the second through fourth betting choices. These horses, the horses afforded the best chance of beating the favorite by the betting public, produced a five-year ROI of only $1.47. That, in the most sophisticated financial parlance I know, stinks.

Now, grab on to something so you don't fall down, because the shocker in this study just might knock you over. The ROI in our final category, all other starters, was $2.10. Yes, $2.10. Yes, that is an actual flat-bet profit over five years' time.

In other words, you could have blindly bet on the 2,143 starters in U.S. Grade 1 races on the flat between 2002 and 2006 who were fifth choice in the betting or higher, and realized a 5 percent profit on your investment. It didn't matter what these horses' names were, or if there was one or seven of them in the race. It didn't matter how these horses were affected by pace or distance, or who rode them. The only thing that mattered was that they weren't fourth choice or lower in the betting. And for knowing only that, you could have turned a 5 percent profit. That might not sound like a lot to the average horseplayer, but there are big firms on Wall Street that have been household names for decades and have built their reputations on less.

Go ahead. Take a minute, or a month, to wrap your head around this.

There are several possible reasons why horses that were the fifth betting choice and higher in U.S. Grade 1 stakes from 2002 through 2006 were able to show a flat-bet profit. One explanation that might prove the most logical would be that Grade 1 races attract big-name horses, and as a result, the attention of casual and neophyte racing fans. The name horses in these races probably receive more betting support simply because of who they are, which would, in effect, inflate the odds of other horses in the race, especially those who were fifth choice or higher in the betting. A case could be made that the handful of horses who win Grade 1 races each year at odds of 30–1 or higher—horses who contribute significantly toward a positive ROI in this category—would be a fraction of that price under circumstances almost the same, with the notable exceptions that the race was unnamed, and run on a Thursday afternoon.

In any event, it's not as if the five-year flat-bet profit in this category was the result of a one- or two-year aberration. This category actually produced a flat-bet profit in four of the five years sampled, ranging from a high positive ROI of $2.29 in 2003 to a low positive ROI of $2.03 in 2006. The only year this group did not yield a positive ROI was 2002, the year that this category's win percentage was the lowest at 3.9 percent, when the ROI was $1.76.

Interestingly, 2002 was the year that odds-on favorites generated, by a hair, a positive ROI of $2.01. With ROIs of $1.89 in 2003 and $1.95 in 2006, this category did manage to beat the takeout, if not to show a flat-bet profit. But in 2004 and 2005, the years odds-on favorites had a poor win percentage, the ROI was correspondingly poor, at $1.42 and $1.56, respectively.

Strong favorites, which again were horses whose odds ranged from even money to 1.95–1, came closest to showing a flat-bet profit in 2002. That was the year this group's win percentage was decidedly the highest, and the ROI was $1.93. Otherwise, in the years from 2003 through 2006, this category's ROI ranged from only $1.38 to $1.59.

Win-percentage swings in the "all other favorites" group also resulted in corresponding ROI swings. In 2005, when this category had unusual success in terms of win percentage, it resulted in a stunning ROI of $2.53, which was the highest one-year ROI outcome in any category. But in 2006, when this group's win percentage was less than half what it was the year before, the ROI was only $1.07, which was the lowest single-year result in any category. Otherwise, the ROI in this category from 2002 through 2004 ranged from $1.63 to $1.74.

Finally, for the record, the second-through-fourth-betting-choices grouping under-performed consistently in each year of our five-year study, producing ROIs that ranged from a high of $1.62 in 2004 to a low of $1.27 the year before.

I know what some of you are thinking. You're thinking that while a study of U.S. Grade 1 races over, as of this writing, the five most recent complete years is worth-while, and certainly illustrative of today's game at its highest level, is five years enough of a sample to reach a larger conclusion? That's a fair question, and to address it, I contacted Adelphi University in Garden City, New York, and spoke with Robert Bradley, a professor of mathematics. I asked Bradley, who earned his Ph.D. at the University of Toronto in 1989, and who has been teaching at Adelphi since 1991, if a margin of error could be applied to this study as it is in various polls we read about in the newspaper or see on television newscasts.

"In polling, say with the next presidential election, for example, you can get a clear idea of what the margin of error is by the number of people polled, by knowing how many are in the sample," Bradley said. "When you see in the paper a plus or minus 3 percent margin of error, there is a standard formula that applies. This is very much like a polling question. By breaking down win percentages and applying an applicable for-mula, you can arrive at the margin of error."

And after selecting the appropriate formula and applying it to the win percentage that our study revealed, that's what Bradley graciously did. In the category of odds-on favorites, Bradley came up with a margin of error of plus or minus 4 percent. "That is a standard sampling error," he said.

In the grouping of strong favorites, those horses who went off at odds of even money to 1.95–1, the margin of error was plus or minus 3.4 percent, while in the all-other-favorites category, the margin of error was plus or minus 3.5 percent.

Regarding the second through fourth betting choices, the margin of error plum-meted to plus or minus .9 percent, while in the all-other-starters category—the one that produced the surprising overall flat-bet profit—the margin of error was only plus or minus .5 percent. "With these categories, there is so much more data," Bradley said. Indeed, in our 502-race five-year sample, there were 1,502 runners who were the sec-ond through fourth betting choices, and 2,143 runners who comprised the all-other-starters grouping. "Big samples mean more robust results," Bradley said.

"This appears to not be a biased sample, and it looks like a very complete sample," he added. "This is also standard stuff. The only thing to look out for here is if things change over time, like the ability of handicappers, or horses taking steroids, or something else very big changing in the future. But this seems like a very valid sample, and as long as the system remains relatively unchanged, you can go with it."

So now that it has been demonstrated that looking for longshot winners in Grade 1 stakes races is a perfectly legitimate betting approach, the questions become "Where do you look?" and "What do you look for?"

Certainly, a track-bias situation can compromise the chances of many a horse that looks like a solid favorite on paper in a Grade 1 stakes event, yielding big-priced winners to dialed-in bettors. The first such example that comes to mind is Keeneland, a track that was intensely speed-favoring when it had a conventional dirt surface. This factor certainly played a big role Sinister Minister's front-running $19.40 upset of the 2006 Blue Grass Stakes. And for evidence of just how much the Keeneland of old carried Sinister Minister, three weeks after he won the Blue Grass by almost 13 lengths, he was beaten 30 lengths in the Kentucky Derby, finishing 16th.

Of course, Keeneland no longer has a conventional dirt track. It installed Polytrack in time for its 2006 fall meeting, and horseplayers nationwide found it ironic, to say the least, that over this synthetic surface, a racetrack once renowned for being a speed horse's paradise turned completely in the opposite direction. Keeneland suddenly became a haven for closers, particularly those who had shown a prior affinity for a synthetic racing surface. And this no doubt helped make the stretch-running Dominican a highly playable $18 upsetter of the 2007 Blue Grass. Notably, when he ran back in the Kentucky Derby, Dominican finished almost 18 lengths behind the colt he beat in the Blue Grass, Street Sense.

The problem with track bias is that in the example of Keeneland, it is too specific for the purposes of our discussion. Besides, track bias in general is something that bettors throughout the country should be attuned to, as in most cases it can come and go quickly with, for example, a change of weather conditions or track-maintenance procedures.

There are, however, a few scenarios where I have had some success uncovering double-digit win payoffs in Grade 1 stakes, and these can be applied in the more general sense that we all are looking for, as they do occur with some frequency:

THE PHONY GRADE 1 RACE

We have all seen these types of races with increasing regularity over the years, races that carry Grade 1 status and big, fat purses even though the fields lack even a single legitimate Grade 1 performer. Instead, these races feature fields consisting of Grade 3 or marginal Grade 2 horses, running for three or four times the money they really should be competing for.

Perhaps this is a reflection of the growing lack of depth, if not quality, at the top of every division. And in a larger sense, this could be taken as evidence of what effect a few decades of breeding for speed, and race-day medication, has had on the Thoroughbred breed as a whole. That, however, is a discussion for another time and place.

While such phony Grade 1 races may be unsatisfying to the sport's purists, they often provide more appealing betting opportunities than the Grade 1 race that pits one, or even two, legitimate Grade 1 performers against a collection of animals who on their best days might be mistaken for Grade 3 horses. Phony Grade 1 races surely won't make you forget the 1973 Belmont Stakes, but because they lack that one standout Grade 1 performer, they also lack an overwhelming favorite who may be impossible to beat because he is just so much better than the rest of the field. So, in many instances, these phony Grade 1's are more competitive than some "real" Grade 1 races. And really, what else can a horseplayer ask for besides competitive races to bet on?

The 2005 Hollywood Gold Cup was exactly the kind of phony Grade 1 race I'm talking about. Now, the Gold Cup is one of America's truly great races for older horses. Its roll call of winners includes such legends as Seabiscuit, Citation, Swaps, Round Table, Gallant Man, Native Diver, Affirmed, and Cigar. But when it was run in 2005, the male handicap division was in a state of flux. Ghostzapper, the reigning Horse of the Year, had just been retired after injuring himself in his sensational comeback win in the Metropolitan Mile. Rock Hard Ten, winner of the Santa Anita Handicap and Strub early in the year, was sidelined all spring and summer, and Roses in May was never to be seen again after winning the Dubai World Cup in March. So even though the 2005 Hollywood Gold Cup boasted Grade 1 status and a hefty $750,000 purse, the field, at least going in, fell far short in terms of the quality one might hope to find in such an event.

One-third of the nine-horse field—Borrego, Deputy Lad, and Keep On Punching—had never before won a stakes race of any kind. Two others, Anziyan Royalty and Musique Toujours, had one state-bred and one restricted stakes win, respectively, to their credit. Pt's Grey Eagle was the field's lone Grade 1 stakes winner, but that particular victory the previous fall, a 29–1 upset of the Ancient Title Breeders' Cup Handicap, had "fluke" written all over it. He had failed to run back to that performance in three subsequent starts, and his Ancient Title was at six furlongs, a full half-mile shorter than what he would be asked to negotiate in the 1¼-mile Gold Cup.

It was now down to Limehouse, Congrats, and Lava Man. Limehouse was going to be the favorite off his recent victory in the Brooklyn Handicap, his second straight stakes win and the second Grade 2 victory of his career. But having been intimately familiar with the horses Limehouse defeated in the Brooklyn, I knew right away I would be looking elsewhere for the winner.

Congrats was also a Grade 2 winner, having won the San Pasqual in his first start of the year. But both that victory and his only previous career stakes win had been accomplished on sloppy tracks, and he was not going to catch slop on Gold Cup Day. That, combined with the fact that he appeared to be suffering from Dubai World Cup hangover, as evidenced by his recent loss as the favorite in the listed Ack Ack Handicap, made me eager to bet against him.

That left Lava Man, which was fine with me, because I already liked Lava Man. Lava Man had shown real ability when he ran Rock Hard Ten to a half-length in the Grade 1 Malibu in late 2004, and I became intrigued by him when he won with blinkers on at Hollywood in May. The addition of blinkers really helped Lava Man turn the corner—so much so that he won the Californian at nearly 9–1, earning a career-best Beyer Speed Figure of 112, which tied Limehouse for the highest Beyer in the Gold Cup field.

So Lava Man was a horse who had clearly come around with blinkers on, was in career form, was as fast as any horse in the Gold Cup field, and was coming off two straight wins over the track. If this edition of the Hollywood Gold Cup were a "real" Grade 1 event with one or two legitimate Grade 1 horses in it, even that combination of handicapping considerations might not have been enough for Lava Man. But with this Gold Cup being a phony Grade 1, these handicapping considerations took on added weight. And the combination of them in this case, for me, made Lava Man a standout. He won by nearly nine lengths, and paid $14.

The funny thing about this example is, while Lava Man was not a legitimate Grade 1 horse going into the 2005 Hollywood Gold Cup, he subsequently turned into one, at least in California. Included among his victories in 2006 were Grade 1 scores in the Santa Anita Handicap, the Charles Whittingham Handicap, a repeat in the Gold Cup, and the Pacific Classic, the last three as the heavy favorite. And in July of 2007, Lava Man won the Hollywood Gold Cup for a third straight year, again as the chalk, joining Native Diver, the only other horse to accomplish this feat.

And to think, I knew Lava Man back in the day when he would actually pay double digits to win.

THE GOOD HORSE PAST HIS OR HER PRIME

The career arcs of athletes who are fortunate to avoid major injury are easy to trace. The athlete begins his or her career, and with seasoning and maturity, soon reaches a peak of maximum performance. Then, with age and physical wear and tear acting as prominent factors, the athlete's efficiency begins to diminish, eventually to the point where the athlete's competitive career comes to its inevitable end.

Of course, not all career arcs are identical. Some athletes mature quickly, while others take longer to reach their peak. Some are able to maintain their peaks longer than others. And for some, the decline is graceful, where for others the drop in ability is precipitous. But the fundamental properties of the career arc—up, peak, down—apply to all.

We fans of Thoroughbred racing know better than anyone else that the horses we wager on are athletes, so they are just as governed by the career cycle as baseball and football players are. We all know of numerous examples of horses who showed promise at 2, fulfilling their potential as they became more mature at 3, only to eventually be overtaken by newer, younger guns as they aged. Ironically, this is often an unfortunate slap in the face to owners who are brave enough to resist the temptation of breeding dollars promised by early retirements, and are sporting enough to keep good horses in training for meaningful periods of time. But this is the way it is.

No one takes pleasure in seeing a horse in decline struggle in races he once could have won. But the cold, hard fact of the matter is, these situations exist. And if you can spot past-peak horses before it becomes obvious to the rest of the world what is going on, it can present prime opportunities to cash on longshot winners in major stakes races.

Flower Alley is a good case study of this topic. He showed considerable potential early in his 3-year-old season, winning the 2005 Lane's End in just his third career start. He then finished second in the Arkansas Derby behind Afleet Alex, who would go on to dominate the last two legs of the Triple Crown, the Preakness and Belmont Stakes, races Flower Alley did not compete in. Even Flower Alley's ninth in the Kentucky Derby was a respectable effort, as he was beaten only 7½ lengths after being close to a wickedly fast early pace.

It was in the summer of his 3-year-old season that Flower Alley really blossomed. He won the Jim Dandy Stakes impressively, earning a strong Beyer Speed Figure of 112, and followed with a decisive victory in the prestigious Grade 1 Travers Stakes over the talented pair of Bellamy Road and Roman Ruler. As a result of those big stakes wins, Flower Alley was by far the strongest half of the favored entry in the Grade 1 Jockey Club Gold Cup. That race was, for him, an unfortunate time to turn in what was up to that point perhaps the worst performance of his career, a distant fourth-place finish. But Flower Alley rebounded in a big way in the Grade 1 Breeders' Cup Classic, finishing a sharp second ahead of 11 opponents, and beaten only a length by Saint Liam, who went on to be voted Horse of the Year of 2005.

With Saint Liam having been retired after his Breeders' Cup Classic score, and Afleet Alex unable to race again after his Belmont Stakes win due to physical ailments, Flower Alley entered 2006 in prime position to be one of racing's biggest stars of the year. Don't forget, no one had yet heard of Invasor or Bernardini. It was not hard to envision Flower Alley ripping off one Grade 1 victory after another, returning anywhere in the unappetizing range of $3.20 to $3.60.

Flower Alley finally made his 4-year-old debut in late June in the Grade 3 Salvatore Mile at Monmouth Park against four outclassed opponents. It wasn't until the last furlong that Flower Alley finally asserted his superiority. But he did what he had to do, winning by just over three lengths, although his final time, which resulted in a modest Beyer Figure of 99, was nothing to get excited about.

For those who think optimistically, it was reasonable to accept Flower Alley's Salvatore Mile as a successful prep race designed to sharpen him for the major summer and fall stakes to come. In retrospect, however, the Salvatore was actually the first indication that Flower Alley might not be what he once was. First, it took more than half the year for Flower Alley to get back to the races, although his connections indicated that was by design so that he would be fresh for the fall. Then, when he did return, it was in an odd Grade 3 spot at Monmouth, in which he didn't run particularly fast, or dominate the way he could have, or should have.

After Flower Alley ran back against Invasor and Sun King in the Grade 1 Whitney at Saratoga, hindsight was no longer necessary. There were now warning signs all over the place that he really was nowhere close to the horse he had been the previous summer and fall. Flower Alley finished seventh in the Whitney as the 3–2 favorite, and an objective assessment of his effort would be that he tired after making a mild, wide middle move. But there was more to be read into Flower Alley's Whitney than just that.

One of the surefire, telltale signs of an important horse who has lost his mojo is that he has lost his speed. When Flower Alley ran so big winning the Jim Dandy and Travers the previous summer at Saratoga, a track he clearly liked, he was right with the pace in both races. And when Flower Alley ran so well in the Breeders' Cup Classic, he was prominent throughout with a show of good positional speed. But the pace in this Whitney was not fast. And despite that, Flower Alley was simply unable to secure close early striking position. That fact, which is not to be underestimated, combined with the way Flower Alley gave it up in the final furlong of the Whitney, made him a big-time bet-against from that point forward.

Flower Alley made his next start late in the Saratoga meeting in the Grade 1 Woodward Stakes, which had been moved from its customary slot at Belmont Park. Flower Alley's trainer, Todd Pletcher, made a point of noting that his colt had three workouts between the Whitney and the Woodward, suggesting he was ready for his best. And despite his poor showing in the Whitney, Flower Alley was the morning-line favorite for the Woodward, where he finished a badly beaten seventh.

THE BREEDERS' CUP

Whether you are a racing fan, a hard-core bettor, or a combination of the two, you have to agree that there really is nothing like the Breeders' Cup. Where else can you find Grade 1 race after Grade 1 race where it's news when the starting field doesn't reach double digits in size? Where else can you routinely get double-digit odds on multiple Grade 1 winners whose earnings have surpassed the seven-figure mark? Where else can you find fields so deeply competitive that you might actually be able to turn a year's worth of betting profit in one afternoon?

The latter was actually the topic of one of the panel discussions at *Daily Racing Form*'s 2007 Horseplayers Expo in Las Vegas. The title was "Attacking Racing's Biggest Days: Making a Year's Profit in a Day," but it is no surprise that the majority of the discussion revolved around the Breeders' Cup. There is no bigger racing day. The outcome of the Breeders' Cup events determine the vast majority of the sport's championships, and with amazing frequency present the opportunity to hit three-figure daily doubles, four-figure pick threes, and five-figure pick fours.

I went back and reviewed the results of the seven most recent Breeders' Cups, those run from 2000 through 2006, and calculated an average exacta payoff. Of course, I needed something to compare those results to, and I settled on a recent seven-day run of results at Gulfstream Park, from February 18 through February 25, 2007. I picked Gulfstream because it offered field sizes as big as could be found anywhere in the U. S., because it offered turf and dirt racing, and because it offered a wide variety of class of races, from stakes to claimers to maidens.

It just so happened that the seven-day period I picked at Gulfstream featured some especially inscrutable racing, which made the results of my comparison all the more surprising. The average win payoff during this period at Gulfstream was $15.67, and the average exacta payoff was $121.42. I think we can agree those are some healthy numbers, but they pale in comparison to the results in the same categories of the seven Breeders' Cups I looked at. The average win payoff in the Breeders' Cups from 2000 through 2007 was $25.81, or 64.7 percent higher than the comparable Gulfstream average. The average exacta payoffs over these seven Breeders' Cups was $273.22, a whopping 125 percent increase over the comparable average exacta at Gulfstream.

I subsequently took a 10-year look at Breeders' Cup winners, from 1997 through 2006, and found that the seven-year average Breeders' Cup win payoff I noted at the Horseplayers Expo was in line with the 10-year average win payoff of $23.25. But in looking back in the expanded 10-year Breeders' Cup sample, I came across a couple of interesting points. One that really caught my eye was that there were 12 odds-on favorites during this period, but only four, or 33 percent, won. That number is well below the 55.3 percent success rate of odds-on favorites in all U.S. Grade 1 races on the flat run from 2002 through 2006, noted early in this chapter. For a more consistent comparison, odds-on favorites in the Breeders' Cups from 2002 through 2006 were successful three of seven times, or 42.9 percent, which is still well below the norm.

Another interesting outcome of this Breeders' Cup study is that although all favorites in U.S. Grade 1 races run from 2002 through 2006 had a success rate of 37.5 percent, as noted early in this chapter, they did not do as well in the Breeders' Cup, either over a 10-year span or over the comparable five-year period. Favorites won at a 30.8 percent clip in the 10 Breeders' Cups from 1997 through 2006, a rate that dipped to 30 percent over the comparable period from 2002 through 2006. And that 30 percent success rate owes its health almost entirely to the Breeders' Cup Juvenile Fillies, a race in which favorites won every year from 2002 through 2006, and the Breeders' Cup Filly and Mare Turf, in which favorites won in 2003, 2004, and 2006.

All of these numbers I just threw at you might be open to differing interpretations. But it is hard to look at them and not come away with the conclusion that the Breeders' Cup offers a unique betting opportunity to succeed with good-priced winners.

Of course, the trick is, how do you isolate these big-odds winners? One of my favorite angles is looking for horses who have pointed specifically to their Breeders' Cup race. This is not as simplistic as it sounds. There is, in fact, a huge distinction between horses who point to a certain Breeders' Cup race and horses who run in the Breeders' Cup as a natural course of their campaigns. Invariably, the latter horse will have accomplished more, making his form look better, which results in depressed odds. But that in itself doesn't make that horse better than the one whose form might not look as imposing because he has taken a well-timed break during the season, and has been shrewdly prepped for his Breeders' Cup goal.

The 2002 Breeders' Cup Mile featured Rock Of Gibraltar, who had won seven straight Group 1 races in Europe, and who had not lost in more than a year. In some circles, he was being touted as the best horse in the world. Rock Of Gibraltar was certain to be an odds-on favorite, and not one of the 13 who were entered against him was given much chance to beat him.

Jay Privman, national correspondent for *Daily Racing Form,* liked Domedriver. Now, Domedriver's form wasn't bad. He was a Group 2 and Group 3 winner at the distance on the year before coming to Arlington, but most didn't think he was in the same league as Rock Of Gibraltar.

"My experience over the years with European horses coming to the Breeders' Cup," said Privman, "is those who seem to do best are pointed to the Breeders' Cup by virtue of having a mid-to-late-season break, and then a prep for the Breeders' Cup. This horse had that kind of pattern."

Rock Of Gibraltar broke slowly from the 10 hole, and by the time the field hit the first turn, he was looking at the rear ends of all 13 of his opponents. He made a big move on the turn, but took up at the top of the stretch, halting his momentum. Somehow, Rock Of Gibraltar got back in gear, and he finished with an incredible burst of speed, but he couldn't quite get to the one who got a better trip and first run on him—26–1 Domedriver.

"I obviously got lucky," Privman admitted. "No question Rock Of Gibraltar would have won with a better post."

Or with a scintilla of better racing luck. But that's beside the point. As horseplayers, we suffer so many bad beats with horses who are obviously tons the best, that on the rare occasions when we're on the good side of such a situation, we shouldn't have to apologize. Especially when it involves a $54 winner like Domedriver.

Another approach that often leads to big-priced winners in the Breeders' Cup is putting emphasis on sharp recent form over sometimes stronger form established earlier in the season. As big and as critically important as it is, the Breeders' Cup still is, after all, horse racing. It can be easy to lose sight of this fact, and forget that just because Horse A could have crushed Horse B running backward in August, it doesn't guarantee the same will be true in late October or early November. Horse A might simply not be as good as he was three months earlier, while Horse B might suddenly be many lengths better than he was in the summer.

The 2003 Breeders' Cup Sprint at Oak Tree at Santa Anita is a case in point. Cajun Beat had won the Kentucky Cup Sprint earning a Beyer Speed Figure of 113. This was the third-highest last-out Beyer figure in this Breeders' Cup Sprint field, surpassed only by the 122 Aldebaran got for winning the Forego, and the 115 Shake You Down earned for winning an allowance race at Belmont.

The interesting thing about Aldebaran's and Shake You Down's last-out Beyers was that there were solid reasons to think they might not approach them on Breeders' Cup Day. Aldebaran's Forego Beyer stuck out like a sore thumb in that it didn't quite seem to fit with most of the other Beyers in the 101-to-111 range that appeared in his past performances. Moreover, Aldebaran would be making his first start off a more than two-month layoff. As for Shake You Down, his last-out Beyer was earned at the expense of an allowance field he completely outclassed.

As for Cajun Beat, his 113 was a career best, but as a still relatively lightly raced and improving 3-year-old, he had room to do better. And when you considered that the top last-out-Beyer horse, Aldebaran, was sent off the 2–1 favorite in this Breeders' Cup Sprint, and that Shake You Down, the second-highest last-out-Beyer horse, was sent off the second choice at 7–2, and that Cajun Beat, the third-highest last-out-Beyer horse, was let go at almost 23–1, well, there was an obvious betting opportunity there.

Cajun Beat won comfortably, paying $47.60.

We only wish the game always seemed that clear to us.

ABOUT THE AUTHORS

Andrew Beyer is the author of the all-time best-selling handicapping book, *Picking Winners,* and the popular *My $50,000 Year at the Races, The Winning Horseplayer,* and *Beyer on Speed.* A columnist for the *Washington Post,* Beyer is the creator of the Beyer Speed Figures, the industry standard for measuring racehorse performance, which appear exclusively in *Daily Racing Form.* He lives in Washington, D.C.

Tom Brohamer is the author of the classic *Modern Pace Handicapping* and is widely recognized as the leading pace analyst in this country. In addition to playing the races professionally, Brohamer lectures about racing throughout Southern California. He lives in Palm Desert, California.

Steven Crist is chairman and publisher of *Daily Racing Form.* Crist was formerly the turf writer for *The New York Times,* editor-in-chief of *The Racing Times,* and a vice president of the New York Racing Association. He is known in racetrack circles as the King of the Pick Six. Crist is also the author of *Exotic Betting, Betting on Myself, Offtrack,* and *The Horse Traders.* He lives in Hempstead, New York.

Steve Davidowitz is the author of the handicapping classic *Betting Thoroughbreds,* his signature text in 1977 and most recently *The Best and Worst of Thoroughbred Racing* (2006). Davidowitz writes a regular column for *The HorsePlayer Magazine, DRF Simulcast Weekly,* and an Internet feature for Track Master. Davidowitz was also the editor of *The American Racing Manual* from 2000 to 2003. He lives in Las Vegas, Nevada.

Brad Free is the author of the back-to-basics text *Handicapping 101* and is a longtime Southern California handicapper for *Daily Racing Form.* Prior to arriving at DRF, Free completed handicapping tours with the *Pasedena Star-News,* the daily sports newspaper *The National,* and *The Racing Times.* Free lives in Claremont, California.

Dave Litfin is the New York handicapper for *Daily Racing Form* and the author of *Expert Handicapping* (revised in 2007) as well as *Real-Life Handicapping*. Besides his daily analysis, Litfin writes a weekly column on handicapping. Before joining *Daily Racing Form,* Litfin was a handicapper for New York's *Daily News*. He lives in Wilton, New York.

James Quinn has been a leading author on playing the races since he wrote the paperback version of *The Handicapper's Condition Book* (1981), which remains in print through three later hardcover editions. His popular anthology *The Best of Thoroughbred Handicapping* was re-released by DRF Press after Quinn updated the 1987 original with 13 new essays. He is recognized as the leading authority on identifying the class of horses, and conducts handicapping seminars throughout Southern California. Quinn has also written the lead articles on the Kentucky Derby and the Breeders' Cup Classic for *The HorsePlayer Magazine*. He lives in Arcadia, California.

Alan Shuback is the European racing writer and editor for *Daily Racing Form* and is one of this country's foremost experts on European racing. At *The Racing Times,* Shuback developed the two-line format for past performances of imports that has become the industry standard and a great benefit to handicappers. Shuback has reported on major races throughout the world. He lives in New York City.

Lauren Stich is a regular contributor to *Daily Racing Form* and *DRF Simulcast Weekly* on pedigree analysis and breeding. Stich has worked for *The Morning Telegraph, The Racing Times,* and has freelanced on television and for *American Turf Monthly.* Stich also is a Thoroughbred breeder, bloodstock agent, and consultant at Thoroughbred auctions. She lives in Las Vegas, Nevada.

Mike Watchmaker is the national handicapper for *Daily Racing Form*. He helps shape handicapping policy for the paper and improve the data in the past performances. Watchmaker, a former handicapper at *The Racing Times* and New York Racing Association linemaker, also ranks the leaders in each racing division throughout the year and writes regular columns on major events of Thoroughbred racing. He lives in Hicksville, New York.